TWO JEWS, THREE OPINIONS

A Collection of Twentieth-Century American Jewish Quotations

Edited by
SANDEE BRAWARSKY AND DEBORAH MARK

A PERIGEE BOOK

A Perigee Book
Published by The Berkley Publishing Group
A member of Penguin Putnam Inc.
375 Hudson Street,
New York, New York 10014

Copyright © 1998 by Sandee Brawarsky and Deborah Mark
Book design by Lisa Stokes

First edition: December 1998

Published simultaneously in Canada.

The Penguin Putnam Inc. World Wide Web site address is
http://www.penguinputnam.com

Library of Congress Cataloging-in-Publication Data

Two Jews, three opinions : a collection of twentieth-century American
    Jewish quotations / edited by Sandee Brawarsky and Deborah Mark.
        p. cm.
    ISBN 0-399-52449-5
    1. Jews—Quotations.   2. Judaism—Quotations, maxims, etc.
I. Brawarsky, Sandee.   II. Mark, Deborah.
PN6095.J4T96   1998
081'.089924—dc21   98-35849
                                                 CIP

Printed in the United States of America

10 9 8 7 6 5 4 3 2

With love to
Erica DeVos, Sarah DeVos, Marnina Cherkin, Emily Cherkin, Sara Noa Mark,
Tamar Blanchard, Rebecca Mark, Elana Blanchard, Zev Mordechai Mark

And in loving memory of my father Dr. Mortimer L. Mark, my teacher
and kindred spirit and the inspiration for this effort

(D.M.)

CONTENTS

LIST OF TOPICS

ACKNOWLEDGMENTS

W E LEARNED FROM a southern Jewish friend that the way to express real grati- tude is to triple it. So thank you, thank you, thank you.

We're grateful to all the individuals we've quoted, whose words moved and inspired us, and to the many friends who shared quotes and sources, opinions and support, and helped us to fine-tune the manuscript. Special thanks to Deb- orah Brodie, Lisa Goldberg, Caroline Harris, Nancy Miller, Dail Stolow and Norbert Freuhauf; to Bill Wollheim for his computer expertise; to Carla Glasser, our agent and friend; to Sheila Curry, our editor who shares our love of history and words and does everything so well; to Pamela Mohan for her careful reading of the manuscript; to the staff of Perigee for helping us to be happily published.

We each are blessed with parents and grandparents and family who have told—and keep telling—stories of the times in which they grew up, the things they saw, how they experienced events that are now part of history. We both lament: If only we could continue some of those conversations; if only we had recorded them. This book is a tribute to our parents and grandparents and all those generations that came before us, whose words spoke and continue to speak to us. We hope that future generations will keep listening.

Special thanks to Elaine Mark, Jonathan Mark and Ruth Seligman, Tsvi Blanchard and Naomi Mark, Muriel and Jack Brawarsky, Phyllis Brawarsky and Noah Fasten, Diane Brawarsky and William Cherkin, for their immeasurable love, inspiration, and support, and in whose homes the ongoing exchange of ideas is celebrated.

෨෨ ෨෨ ෨෨

Thanks also to Allan Malz, Jonathan Wolf and Elli Wohlgelernter for borrowing privileges from their own extensive libraries and for each one's appreciation of the ironies inherent in the passage of time; to my colleagues at the Hebrew Immigrant Aid Society, past and present, for their encouragement, and especially Michael Gendel for providing me with the peace of mind to take the needed time to see this through; to Linda and David Machlis for providing the retreat, to Deena and Tali Blanchard for their keen and youthful curiosity that started me wondering how to begin to sum up a century of American Jewish life.
(DM)

INTRODUCTION

WE'RE TWO JEWS, and between us we seem to have even more than three opinions.

We're typical of many people—both Jews and non-Jews—who can't look at a statement without turning it inside out and flipping it around. With this approach to life, questions lead to questions as readily as to answers.

"Two Jews, Three Opinions" is frequently the punch line of jokes that suggest an ongoing debate—a lively conversation, punctuated with laughter, that, in spite of constant interruptions, never ends. Picture a noisy kitchen table, an auditorium packed with people who want a turn at the microphone, or just two people, talking, talking, talking.

Although throughout the book we do our best to place quotations in context and be specific in attributions, we can't do so with our title line. It's a line repeated so often—by rabbis, comedians, politicians—that it's in the public domain; it's proverbial. Who said it first? No doubt there are many opinions on that, too.

Whoever said it first, though, probably said it quite some time ago. The notion of "Two Jews, Three Opinions" goes back as least as far as the Talmud, the compilation of Jewish law that records discussions by generations of scholars from the year 200 to the year 500. Its pages preserve prevailing opinions of the time as well as dissenting views. These questions draw contemporary readers and scholars into the debate, studying the accumulation of opinions and adding their voices to the symphony.

In Talmudic tradition, opposing viewpoints are treated with respect, as sincere efforts toward reaching an understanding. Disagreement is not the same as disunity—which is a useful reminder when contemporary debate turns cacophonous. As Shimon Peres, former prime minister of Israel, is quoted: "When you have two views, you don't have to have two peoples." (See the section on reconciliation.)

❧ ❧ ❧

A quote is a moment remembered. It's a short sequence of words that manages to capture some essential truth. Some great quotes are one-liners, literary sound bites. They're jewels, remarkable in their turn of phrase. Several are wordier yet still succinct, cutting to the core of an important idea. Some people have a gift for recalling the great lines they hear; others need—and love—quote books.

Browsing through any bookstore will prove that there's no shortage of quote books. Since John Bartlett compiled *Bartlett's Familiar Quotations* in 1855, many wonderful treasuries of quotations have been published, ranging in format, focus, and approach. So why another? Both of us collect quotes and quote books, and we decided to put together the book we wished we had on our shelves. While several first-rate collections of Jewish quotes feature wisdom culled from biblical times to the present, none focused on twentieth-century Jewish life in America, in all its variety and contradictions. We searched for and then decided to create a book that conveyed not only the wit and wisdom of the times, but the immediacy and the drama, as well as a sense of life as it was experienced.

During these last one hundred years, Jews have made tremendous and profound impact in America—and America has had an equally great impact on the Jewish community. Not to compare the design of the atomic bomb to the flourish of Hollywood, or to equate the Holocaust with anything else, but in all major events of the era, American Jews participated and/or observed, sometimes at the center, other times as outsiders. Throughout this century like no other— with its waves of immigration; the Great Depression; communism, Zionism, and so many other isms; the two World Wars; the Holocaust; the creation of the state of Israel and its pull on American Jews; the women's, civil rights, and peace movements; advances in medicine and technology; shifts in Jewish-Christian and Jewish-Black relations as well as the relationship between Israel and the United States; assimilation and intermarriage; anti-Semitism; the ascent of the counterculture—Jews have reflected, commented, and analyzed. As events unfolded, Jews were there and in many cases not merely present but significantly involved.

Indeed, for Jews, the twentieth century has in many ways been the American century: The United States succeeded Europe as the center of the Jewish world outside the land of Israel. American Jews came into their own as a community, as part of the American mosaic, with influence on cultures far beyond their own. Twentieth-century American Jews have assimilated like never before, but they are still solidly, unmistakably Jewish, in their roots and sensibility. And, they are outspoken.

To view the century through words, written and spoken, is to eavesdrop on history. We tried to include the voices of those not usually recorded in quote books, and to track down previously unpublished material. Some of the quotes do not express opinions we admire, and there are many we dispute, even between ourselves. However, we felt it important to include them, to provide as complete a picture as possible. Interestingly, reading the selections prompted some surprises: When dealing with complex issues, it's not always easy to predict whom you're going to agree with — or disagree with.

The range of quotes makes possible discussion and dialogue across generations too. In 1901, Dr. Isadore Singer wrote: "Life is short; the problems before modern Judaism are great; and small, very small indeed is the number of those among us who are working unselfishly for the highest interests of our race and our faith." And nearly a century later, Singer's dilemma — and many others — remain. Other quotes, however, seem inconceivable or ironic in retrospect. We have been struck by how discussions about Jewish identity and assimilation seem fresh, whether the quotes are from 1930 or 1990, while many of the comments about women seem hopelessly dated.

In the Jewish community of the late 1990s, with all its divisiveness and infighting, the proverbial "Two Jews, Three Opinions" seems like an understatement. We've brought together people on the same page when, sadly, it is often impossible to get them in the same room. Perhaps juxtaposing conflicting views in the peaceful atmosphere of white space on the printed page can bring new light to the discussion.

ᗑ᎒ ᗑ᎒ ᗑ᎒

Some people will enjoy reading this book from cover to cover (and might find humor in the juxtapositions); others will browse and find their own path through its pages. Still others will use it as a reference tool, searching specific categories for quotable material, while discussion groups might focus on a section as the basis of a conversation. Our hope is that disseminating these quotes will give them and the issues they address renewed life and perspective, prompting others to cite them, whether in books or speeches or research. And since quotes represent only a flash of a person's point of view, we hope the book inspires readers to familiarize themselves with the speakers' work in full.

Putting this book together has been a wonderful exercise in self-education. Mostly, the selections come from wide reading and listening. At times, we felt like detectives, sometimes librarians, as we tracked down quotations. We asked people we knew who had written or said interesting things to send us material, we asked for unpublished papers, we scanned the Internet. Often one reference led to many others, whether in a footnote or a passing reference to related works.

The speakers range from the well-known to the obscure: The criterion for inclusion was that they had something significant to contribute to the conversation. Those quoted are judges, actors, writers, theologians, students, lawyers, politicians, rabbis, critics, scientists, and individuals from other walks of life; they are drawn from all the denominations as well as the unaffiliated, and range widely in age and geographical location. Our definition of Jewishness is inclusive. In quotations from fictional works, the character is named as well as the author. The attributions reflect the speaker's job or position at the time. We broke our own rule of including only people who spent the major part of their lives in America; a few Israelis and European voices are scattered throughout. How could we leave out Golda Meir?

After decades of collecting quotes, we had many more than we were able to include in this volume. For a quote to make the final cut, it had to stand out—and it had to stand alone. We looked for lines that rang with poetry, that conveyed ideas succinctly, a chain of words we knew we'd want to remember; we recognized the great ones as soon as we came across them. In some cases, we realized that a longer narrative—rather than one line—was essential to expressing an opinion, so we included quotes of varying lengths. We tried to avoid lines that were too familiar, and we hoped to steer clear of platitudes (although, admittedly, sometimes the distinction is fine—one person's wisdom can be another's cliché). And, even a cliché is new the first time you encounter it.

Some categories are descriptive, others tell stories. In most sections, the entries are arranged in alphabetical order by author. In cases where the dates enhance the meaning of the quotes, the entries are chronological. And when the sheer juxtaposition was intriguing and even lyrical, we allowed the statements to dictate the order: In those instances, determining the placement was like deciding who should sit next to whom at a dinner party full of interesting people.

No quote book can be complete, and we apologize in advance to the many articulate people whose words aren't included. By its very nature, the book has a random quality; ultimately it was impossible not to emphasize our own interests and biases. We tried to present all quotes in the context, place, and spirit in which they were expressed, hoping to preserve the speakers' integrity. To keep the dialogue going, we invite suggestions for future editions, which can be sent to us in care of Perigee Books.

Although Rabbi Abraham Isaac Kook (1865–1935), Palestine's first Ashkenazic Chief Rabbi, doesn't fit into our categories of inclusion, his words express the spirit behind this book: "For the building is constructed from various parts, and the truth of the light of the world will be built from various dimensions, from various approaches, for these and those are the words of the living God (Eruvin 13b). It is precisely the multiplicity of opinions, which derive from variegated souls and backgrounds which enriches wisdom, and brings about it enlargement. In the end, all matters will be properly understood and it will be recognized that it was impossible for the structure of peace to be built without those trends which appeared to be in conflict."

 familiarity familiarity familiarity

A note about attributions: The date in parentheses that follows the title of a book cited refers to the book's publication date; for newspapers and magazines, unpublished works, and plays, the dates are not in parentheses. Other dates cited (also not in parentheses) within the description refer to the time when the quote was actually said. When several quotes by an individual are included in a category, the individual is fully identified only in the first instance, unless his or her title or position is changed. Hebrew and Yiddish phrases can be spelled in many different ways in English. Here, the individual source's version has been retained.

❖ ABORTION ❖

And the doctor called me in and he said to me, "Mrs. W., if you go and have another child, it's a sure death. You cannot have any more children." I told him and started to cry, "Doctor, if that would be up to me, I will never want to see a man in my life and I would never want to have any more children. What should I do? I've got a young man and he's a brute, he's not a gentleman. I'm afraid he'll kill me . . ." My husband came and the doctor talked to him . . . as soon as the taxi started to go, he says, "What do you think, I should stay with a 'kranker' [sick, a misfit]?" Like a dead dog, a dead anything. "You think I'm going to stay with you?" What should I tell him? I didn't say nothing.

— "Frieda W.," a poor, illiterate, recent immigrant, early 1900s, quoted in *The World of Our Mothers* by Sydney Stahl Weinberg (1988)

Women who decide to terminate a pregnancy for medical reasons often feel as if they have suffered a death in the family and need to mourn the "child soul" that they have lost, just as one would mourn the death of a fully living human being.

— Rabbi Leila Gal Berner, congregational rabbi and composer of Jewish music, "Our Silent Seasons" in *Lifecycles 1*, edited by Rabbi Debra Orenstein (1994)

Yes or no? Back and forth like a tortured laboratory animal in an impossible maze: There are two exits, but both give the animal an electric shock.

— Aviva Cantor, author, "The Phantom Child" in *The Woman Who Lost Her Names: Selected Writings by American Jewish Women*, compiled and edited by Julia Wolf Mazow (1980)

The view of the majority of citizens will prevail because, unlike the issue of racial segregation, the right to life versus the right to choice cannot be decided on the basis of one correct principle that all sides will eventually accept. It will have to be decided on the basis of power.

> —Alan M. Dershowitz, law professor, appellate lawyer, activist, and author, *Contrary to Popular Opinion* (1992)

Those who oppose abortion are pro-life only up to the moment of birth.

> —Barney Frank, U.S. Congressman (D-Mass.), quoted in *The New Republic*, November 30, 1992

It has long seemed wrong to me for women, for feminists, to be pushed into a position where they are for abortion, and let the right wing preempt the position "for life" or "for family." I am for life and for family; those are basic values for me, and they should be for every feminist. I am not for abortion—I am for the choice to have children. At this stage of medical technological development, when birth-control devices . . . are not completely safe and can, in fact, pose terrible long-term threats to women's health and life, there has to be safe, legal medical access to abortion.

> —Betty Friedan, author and activist, *The Second Stage* (1981)

Do we really fight for abortion—or do we fight for a diversity of pluralistic means whereby women, according to their own consciences and values, can choose to have children? . . . Do we really mean ourselves to push abortion, except as a last resort—not as lightly used birth control? . . . We can respect the values and consciences—and agonies—of those who truly regard abortion as sin. They are not the real enemy.

> —Betty Friedan, *The Second Stage* (1981)

Being without theology isn't the slightest hindrance to being pro-life.

> —Nat Hentoff, journalist, quoted in *The New Republic*, November 30, 1992

Abortion is a mother's act. It is an act of sacrifice, love, power, and necessity.

> —Merle Hoffman, feminist activist, "Trojan Horses" in *On the Issues*, Winter 1995

"Pro-life feminism" is indeed not an oxymoron, but a radical vision for a community.

> —Ellen Judith Reich, attorney, author, and mother, *Tikkun*, January/February 1997

Friends who gladly debate other volatile issues—political philosophy, war, race—shy away from abortion. The problem is too private, too personal, too bound up with one's faith and spiritual identity. Give abortion five seconds of thought, and it quickly spirals down in the mind to the most basic questions about human life, to the mysteries of birth and our relationship with our souls.

> —Roger Rosenblatt, essayist and author, *Life Itself: Abortion in the American Mind* (1992)

I think we have to learn to live on "uncommon ground" in the matter of abortion; that we must not only accept but embrace a state of tension that requires a tolerance of ambivalent feelings, respect for different values and sensibilities, and no small amount of compassion.

> —Roger Rosenblatt, *Life Itself: Abortion in the American Mind* (1992)

Though I was raised passionately pro-choice in a pro-choice era, though my parents and partners would without question have supported me if I needed an abortion, though everyone I knew had one, the fact remains that I am mortally afraid of needing to have one, and desperate to get through my life without having to make that choice.

> —Naomi Wolf, author, *Fire With Fire: The New Female Power and How It Will Change the 21st Century* (1993)

One of the things I think is so corrupt about the pro-life movement is that they so often use legislation as a kind of shortcut to a clear conscience, rather than do the hard work in our communities of asking the question, have I taken in a child? Do I give money to the poor?

> —Naomi Wolf, author, *Tikkun*, January/February 1997

❖ ACTIVISM ❖

(see also Soviet Jewry)

Another Zionist Against Apartheid

> —Button worn by a Jewish student at UCLA, quoted in "Anti-Zionism: The Sophisticated Anti-Semitism" by Kenneth S. Stem, a publication of the American Jewish Committee, September 1990.

External compulsion can, to a certain extent, reduce but never cancel the responsibility of the individual.

— Albert Einstein, Nobel Prize–winning theoretical physicist and humanist, "The State and the Individual Conscience," an open letter published in *Science*, December 22, 1950

If you look at a half-empty glass and say it's half full, that doesn't make you an optimist. That makes you a fool. An optimist is somebody who looks at a half-empty glass and says "It's half-empty; what do we do now to fill it?"

— Jules Feiffer, cartoonist and writer, quoted in *On the Edge of Darkness: Conversations about Conquering Depression* by Kathy Cronkite (1994)

We cannot solve the Jewish problem until there is justice for all. In a world of injustice Jews will always suffer. For the past 25 years we carried on our work as a little nation with imperialistic strivings. We have been isolationists. We must be rid of all isolationists. We must turn attention to theological problems bringing cure to the entire world.

— Rabbi Louis Finkelstein, president of The Jewish Theological Seminary of America, unpublished papers, 1943, cited in "The Finkelstein Era" by Michael Greenbaum, in *Tradition Renewed: A History of The Jewish Theological Seminary of America*, edited by Jack Wertheimer (1997)

I want you men and women not to give all your enthusiasm for a man, no matter who he may be. I would prefer that you put all your enthusiasm into your union and your cause.

— Samuel Gompers, president of the AFL (American Federation of Labor), addressing the Cooper Union meeting in New York where the workers decided to go on strike against the Triangle Shirtwaist Company, quoted in *The Call*, November 23, 1909, cited in *Out of the Sweatshop*, edited by Leon Stein (1977) (Gompers had just received a standing ovation for several minutes after he was introduced.)

And so, in expiation of the sins of the fathers, whose quiet interventions in Washington did little good, this generation of American Jewish leaders is largely confrontationist with enemies and critics. Holocaust consciousness has created a sense of Jews as an embattled bastion in the very America of today which is free and open enough for Jews to enshrine their most painful memory in museums in very public places.

— Rabbi Arthur Hertzberg, author and professor, "A Lifetime Quarrel With God," *The New York Times Book Review*, May 6, 1989

You can always rally people against; It's very hard to rally people for.

> —Malcolm Hoenlein, executive director, President's Conference of Major Jewish Organizations, commenting on gaining support for the Oslo Peace Process, quoted in *Jewish Power* by J. J. Goldberg (1996)

I think you are faced with the same decisions. The decision to be blindly obedient to authority versus the decision to try and change things by fighting the powers that be is always, throughout history, the same decision.

> —Abbie Hoffman, activist, speaking about student activism at the First National Student Congress, Seattle, March 10, 1988

No one who came to Chicago because of our influence had any doubts that they were risking their life.

> —Abbie Hoffman, referring to the demonstrations at the 1968 Democratic National Convention in Chicago, *Revolution for the Hell of It* (1968)

In one afternoon the Jews of Russia had received more publicity than from all of the carefully prepared press releases of the Jewish Establishment.

> —Rabbi Meir Kahane, founder of the Jewish Defense League, recalling December 29, 1969 when JDL members simultaneously struck at Soviet offices of TASS (the Soviet press agency), Intourist (the tourist agency), and Aeroflot (the airline office) and leaped aboard a Soviet jetliner that had just landed at Kennedy Airport, *The Story of the Jewish Defense League* (1975)

It is not enough to say "Never again!" unless one refuses to create new victims and throws out a lifeline when boat people are sighted on the horizon.

> —Helen Fein, author, quoted in *The Challenge of Shalom*, edited by Murray Polner and Naomi Goodman (1994)

The electrifying slogan "Never Again" was never meant to declare that a Holocaust would never occur again . . . what "Never Again" always meant was quite another proposition. That as long as anyone attempted to repeat that Holocaust, never again would there be that same lack of reaction, that same indifference, that same fear. Never again would JDL allow the Jewish Establishment to repeat its obscenity of World War II.

> —Rabbi Meir Kahane, *The Story of the Jewish Defense League* (1975)

If we could start working together before we trust, understand, or like each other, we might learn to.

> —Melanie Kaye Kantrowitz, author and activist, "To Be a Radical Jew in the Late 20th Century" in *The Tribe of Dina: A Jewish Woman's Anthology*, edited by Melanie Kaye Kantrowitz and Irena Klepfisz (1989)

I'm very pessimistic at the moment, but it's a pessimism of the intellect and an optimism of the will. The more terrible things look, the more galvanized we should be, the more eager to jump into action.

> —Tony Kushner, playwright, interviewed in *Jerusalem Post Literary Supplement*, August 8, 1996

To speak idealistically is easier than to act idealistically. In Judaism, the proper action is the test of one's belief.

> —Rabbi Ezekiel Landau, rabbi of HIAS (Hebrew Immigrant Aid Society) and spiritual leader of the American Congregation of Jews from Austria, from his 1965 Kol Nidre sermon, quoted in *Bridging Two Worlds* by Sol Landau (1968)

The question is, how can Jews in Germany offer civil resistance? . . . It is usually in the dead of night that they are spirited away. No one, except their terrified families, is the wiser. It makes not even a ripple on the surface of German life. . . . Contrast this with a single hunger strike in an American or English prison, and the public commotion that this arouses. Contrast this with one of your fasts, or with your salt march to the sea, or a visit to the Viceroy, when the world is permitted to hang upon your words and be witness to your acts. Has this not been possible largely because, despite all the excesses of imperialism, England is after all a democracy with a Parliament and considerable measure of free speech? I wonder if even you would find the way to public opinion in totalitarian Germany, where life is snuffed out like a candle, and no one sees or knows that the light is out.

> —Rabbi Judah L. Magnes, communal leader and first president of the Hebrew University of Jerusalem, letter to Mahatma Gandhi, November 26, 1938, referring to an article by Gandhi in *Harijan*, reprinted in *Modern Jewish Thought*, edited by Nahum N. Glatzer (1977)

Is it sheer stupidity to bother yourself for another's well-being? Isn't it much wiser to not become involved in your neighbor's misery? Why should one take the trouble to listen to the groans and moans of others? For one very good reason. Because life without sensitivity and responsibility is an ode to narcissism, a cacophony of egocentrism, to say nothing of the fact that your silence is acquiescence, and in the ultimate analysis culpability.

> —Rabbi Marshall T. Meyer, human rights activist, founder of the Seminario Rabinico Latinoamericano, and spiritual leader of B'nai Jeshurun in New York City, Baccalaureate sermon at the Claremont Colleges, California, May 18, 1986

We must confront the cancers within our society. We must be bold enough not only to analyze the sins of our city but to take it upon ourselves to search out the ways to redeem our bleeding and beaten masses who desperately need health care, prenatal care, education, job opportunities, avenues of expression to recover lost dignity—no, not recover but uncover for the first time. It is time to state our priorities clearly. We who gather in churches and synagogues are not afraid to pray. And yet it behooves us to understand that prayer is not enough. We must accept the responsibility of translating our prayers into action.

> —Rabbi Marshall T. Meyer, speaking at Riverside Church, New York City, January 11, 1990

To those who complain that most of the money in Eastern Europe is going to the ultra-Orthodox, all I can say is this: they were the first ones out there taking care of the poor Jewish populations left behind. A few months ago I went to a place in the Ukraine, in the middle of nowhere, where there are a few thousand elderly Jews and a couple of little Jewish kids. Chabad had two rabbis and their wives and their children slogging through mud and sewage . . . Without wanting to point fingers, I ask, Where are all the others? Where are the Conservative and Reform movements?

> —Bernie Moscovitz, leader of the National United Jewish Appeal, quoted in *Lifestyles*, New Year 1998

The mandate is deceptively simple: Imitateo Deo. Imitate what God did for us and do it for others. How do we imitate God? By relieving suffering. By helping to free the oppressed. By undertaking the ritual of empathy and the search for justice as commitments of our own. Thus does the theology of hope inspire the politics of social change.

> —Letty Cottin Pogrebin, author and activist, *Deborah, Golda, and Me: Being Female and Jewish in America* (1991)

Convictions and ideals, no matter how exalted, are meaningless without the zeal to live for them and in them; the readiness to undergo privation, if need be, to endure suffering for their realization. Only the union of the ideal and the capacity for self-sacrifice bears lasting fruit and enriches mankind.

> —Dr. Bernard Revel, founder of Yeshiva College of Yeshiva University in New York City and leader in the modern orthodox community, delivering the Yeshiva College commencement address, June 17, 1937, quoted in *Bernard Revel: Builder of American Jewish Orthodoxy* by Aaron Rothkoff (1972)

There are certain moments in time when acts of zealotry become necessary. I expect acts of zealotry—but not acts of violence.

> —Rabbi Shlomo Riskin, founder of yeshiva in Efrat, Israel, and founding rabbi of Lincoln Square Synagogue in New York City, commenting on the dem-

onstrations over the disputed territories at a New York press conference, July 14, 1995, quoted in *The Jewish Week*, July 20, 1995

The so-called political or economic matters are religious in their essence — and in their solution. The dichotomy between the "secular" and the "religious," between "activism" and "commandment" is diminishing to the point of irrelevance in our world.

—Rabbi Alexander M. Schindler, president of the Union of American Hebrew Congregations, speaking at a Christian-Jewish dialogue, Chicago, November 1990, quoted in *The Jewish Condition: Essays on Contemporary Judaism Honoring Rabbi Alexander M. Schindler*, edited by Aron Hirt-Manheimer (1995)

Why judge my motivations? All you can judge are my actions, and they speak for themselves.

—Mitch Snyder, activist for the homeless in Washington, D.C., quoted in "Saint Mitch" by Gwenda Blair, *Esquire*, December 1986

I just was not and am not capable of being a traditional father and husband. Who I am does not allow me to do things that other people do. I wasn't able to provide for them, and they had to provide for themselves. It was not my responsibility to get a job for money, which I don't think anybody should ever do.

—Mitch Snyder, commenting on his failure to furnish any child support for his children, quoted in "Saint Mitch," *Esquire*, December 1986

In any one audience, there is enough energy, skill, anger, and humor for a revolution.

—Gloria Steinem, author and activist, "Life Between the Lines," *Outrageous Acts and Everyday Rebellions* (1983)

Do not forget to give at least ten percent of everything you earn to social change. It is the best investment you will ever make.

—Gloria Steinem, commencement speech at Tufts University, Medford, Mass., May 17, 1987, quoted in *Hold Fast Your Dreams: Twenty Commencement Addresses*, compiled by Carrie Boyko and Kimberly Colen (1996)

Activism is perceived as an activity in which you kill yourself and burn out . . . well, burnout is a way of telling you that your form of activism was perhaps not very full circle. If we want a world in which you can tell jokes and get massages and have sex and dress however you please, then we have to create a form of activism that reflects that, and have fun while we're doing it.

—Gloria Steinem, quoted in *Mother Jones*, November/December 1995

The New Left and even its moderate allies are still operating in a fog of misconceptions. The main one is that "the people" are against the war [Vietnam]. The people on the contrary are confused and divided. To say that the streets "belong to the people" . . . is to overlook those people who feel the streets belong to them too, for the ordinary business of their lives. The need is for dialogue, not monologue, to win them over.

> —I. F. Stone, journalist and author, "When a Two-Party System Becomes a One-Part Rubber Stamp," *I. F. Stone's Bi-Weekly*, September 9, 1968, *Polemics and Prophecies 1967–1970* (1989)

Because I must hold myself ready to meet a thousand claims from the outside, I have neglected my own little garden. I am not allowed to mature what is in me, because I must do all the time—morning, noon, and night—what others impose on me. Some years ago I resigned myself to my fate; I no longer kick against the traces. I accept the task life seems to have set me.

> —Henrietta Szold, founder of Hadassah, quoted in *Henrietta Szold: Record of a Life* by Rose Zeitlin (1952)

We commit ourselves to any wrong or degradation or injury when we do not protest against it.

> —Lillian Wald, social worker and founder of Henry Street Settlement House on New York's Lower East Side, speaking at a meeting under the auspices of the National Association for the Advancement of Colored People, 1914

Interests sometimes have to be defended, and sometimes fiercely. But if we defend only Jewish interests and not Jewish values, if we lose the sense of ourselves as a historic community, a community of shared values, then we have lost too much. We should protect the positions we have won in the secular world, but the collective pronoun *we* refers to a people, and not just a collection of persons, only if we protect something apart from our own group interests.

> —Michael Walzer, author and philosopher, "Liberalism and the Jews: Historical Affinities, Contemporary Necessities" in *Values, Interests and Identity: Jews and Politics in a Changing World*, edited by Peter Y. Medding (1995)

A basic principle of activism is that access should never lead to a compromise in integrity.

> —Rabbi Avi Weiss, senior rabbi of the Hebrew Institute of Riverdale, professor of Judaic Studies, and president of Coalition for Jewish Concerns, quoted in *The Jewish Week*, July 15, 1995

And the truth is, those on the inside often don't say it the way it is. And those who are on the outs, at the gates, are often able to speak more powerfully and honestly.

> —Rabbi Avi Weiss, quoted in *The Jewish Week*, July 15, 1995

Ideologues must not forget the human factor. As a longtime advocate on a whole variety of issues, I have often found activism to be impersonal, distant and harsh.

> —Rabbi Avi Weiss, speaking at the International Conference on Feminism and Orthodoxy in New York, February 17, 1997

When it comes to helping someone in need, do not rely on prayer alone. Let the person in need pray, not you, your task is to help.

> —Elie Wiesel, *Somewhere a Master* (1981)

It is not enough to talk like a preacher. You have to have something to preach.

> —Leon Wieseltier, author and literary editor, *The New Republic*, February 10, 1997

If I am to be silent on every great moral issue because I am a Jew, if my lips are to be sealed when truth and conscience bid me speak lest I hurt the Jewish name, then I wish to live in some place, small or large, near or remote, where a man can live without forfeiting his self-respect.

> —Rabbi Stephen S. Wise, Jewish leader and activist, 1919, quoted in *Rabbi and Minister: The Friendship of Stephen S. Wise and John Haynes Holmes* by Carl Hermann Voss (1964)

The Hebrew Bible is a radical book, and you don't have to look in the Prophets to see that.

> —Rabbi Eric H. Yoffie, president of Union of American Hebrew Congregations, from panel discussion, "God Does Not Belong to the Religious Right," *Tikkun*, July/August 1996

❖ AFFIRMATIVE ACTION ❖

(see also *Black-Jewish Relations, Civil Rights Movement*)

They had a quota here, a quota of Jewish students, just as they did in Russia. My great-uncle had been a physician, but he had been the one Jewish student in the whole province admitted to the college. My daughter, almost a whole century later, in the United States of America, came with a name of a Gentile father, and because her mother was a Jewess, she, too, was to be allowed in, or squeezed out—by a quota that decided how many "Jews" could receive an education.

> —Leah Morton (pseudonym of Elisabeth G. Stern), author, *I Am a Woman— And a Jew* (1926), reprinted in part in *Writing Our Lives: Autobiographies of American Jews, 1890–1990*, edited by Steven J. Rubin (1991)

You know, my parents tell me all about this black-Jewish alliance and about Schwerner, Chaney and Goodman. But the only way I know about blacks is through affirmative action. I know it is going to be harder for me to get into law school because I will be competing against someone black.

> —A Jewish senior at Yale University, quoted in *Broken Alliance* by Jonathan Kaufman (1988)

The honest argument against the [Clarence] Thomas appointment is that it is a race-specific affirmative action appointment made by a president who purports to be against such appointments. The president's assurance that he picked Thomas because he was "the best man" for the job will not pass the giggle test. . . . In that respect, the Thomas nomination—hypocritical as it is— was a political masterstroke. It is affirmative action with deniability, a quota appointment that will place the blame for quotas on the doorstep of those who oppose the nomination.

> —Alan M. Dershowitz, law professor, appellate lawyer, activist, and author, commenting in 1991 on the nomination of Judge Clarence Thomas to be a Supreme Court Justice, *Contrary to Popular Opinion* (1992)

Is the kid a legacy? That is, the child of an alumnus? If so, the kid is in. There are all kinds of good reasons for this. . . . But as it stands, it's an affirmative action program for one of the most privileged groups in the country: the sons and daughters of people like me.

> —Al Franken, comedian, *Rush Limbaugh Is a Big Fat Idiot and Other Observations* (1996)

All the time I was at Harvard, I never heard a Lowell or a Cabot remark, "I dare say, I despise this godawful legacy policy. It makes me so suspect in the eyes of my classmates."

> —Al Franken, *Rush Limbaugh Is a Big Fat Idiot and Other Observations* (1996)

The category "white" not only obscures tremendous ethnic diversity but also diversity of economic condition. Despite the clear fact that, all other things being equal, one is benefited by being white instead of black in the United States, white is far from a perfect proxy for privilege. What do successful urban bankers or lawyers, who may be devoutly religious Catholics or Jews or Muslims or Sikhs, have in common with white Protestants in Appalachia whose families have experienced four or five generations of poverty?

> —Lawrence H. Fuchs, professor of American civilization and author, "What We Should Count and Why," *Society*, September/October 1997

If the last Jewish liberals cannot get it through their brains that affirmative action is nothing less than the end of civilization as we know it, then maybe it's time for a collective lobotomy. With their luck, it would be performed by a quota-ordained neurosurgeon.

> —Hilly Gross, political activist, quoted in *The Jewish Week*, March 24, 1995

Most of us are not even aware of a tension between our desire for justice and our passion for education. In resisting Negro demands that we give a secondary place to objective standards, we really think we are on the side of justice. Negroes are more candid with themselves than Jews in recognizing privately and often publicly that their ideology is designed to serve their interest.

> —Milton Himmelfarb, social critic, *Commentary*, January 1965

Affirmative action is a Band-Aid on the cancer of black underdevelopment. It's poisoning racial attitudes—encouraging blacks to think they can't compete and fueling white resentment—and it isn't helping the people who need it.

> —Tamar Jacoby, journalist and author of *Someone Else's House: America's Unfinished Struggle for Integration* (1998)

There may be good reason for the state to deviate from equal racial treatment. But to do so in the name of "equal protection" is Orwellian.

— Charles Krauthammer, journalist, commenting on the California Civil Rights Initiative, Proposition 209, *Time*, December 9, 1996

Narrowly construed affirmative action programs, while better than the alternative, have generated justified resentment because they have come to be perceived by the American majority as little more than an attempt by yet another group to get their snouts in the public trough. . . . We at *Tikkun* continue to support affirmative action, but we believe that until it is reformulated to reclaim its original meaning as part of a struggle to build a just world for everyone, it will generate even greater opposition.

— Michael Lerner, author and editor, *Tikkun*, January/February 1997

It is the black devotion to affirmative action in its current form that renders meaningless all the talk of rebuilding a black-Jewish alliance.

— Joshua Muravchik, resident scholar at the American Enterprise Institute, *Commentary*, December 1995

Jews have flourished in America as nowhere else in the Diaspora because it is the most meritocratic society in which they have ever had the good fortune to dwell. The principle of equal treatment has liberated Jews from both the injury and the insult of disabilities that were imposed on them for centuries. In that sense, equal treatment constitutes an "interest" of theirs.

— Joshua Muravchik, *Commentary*, December 1995

What one deserves, and what is good for one, are not always the same answer.

— Dennis Prager, author and radio commentator, C-SPAN live broadcast, December 1994

❖ AGING ❖

(see also Generations)

When you're 23, in 20 years, you're going to be 43. That's a trillion years away. But when you're 63, in 20 years, you may not be. You get very selective about where you spend your time.

> —Emanuel Azenberg, Broadway producer, quoted in "Back on That Infuriating but Irresistible Broadway" by Sylviane Gold, *The New York Times*, November 2, 1997

We mock the things we are to be. Yes, yes, we make fun of the old; then we become them.

> —Mel Brooks, comedian, writer, performer, and director who teamed up with Carl Reiner to create "The Two Thousand Year Old Man," quoted in *The Jewish Comedy Catalog* by Darryl Lyman (1989)

An elderly and wise woman once gave me some excellent advice. "Aaron," she said, "it is very important, as you get older, to engage in an activity that you didn't engage in when you were very young, so that you are not continually in competition with yourself as a young man." The conductor's baton was my answer to that problem.

> —Aaron Copland, composer, *The New Music 1900–1960* (1969)

Can you imagine me with a woman old enough to be my wife? No, really, I'm serious. Can you imagine me walking into Spago with a 70-year-old woman? Forget that. I don't have the spirit. My girlfriend is 25 years old—perfect!

> —Tony Curtis, actor, quoted in *US*, May 1996

Most important to remember is that by providing care and hospitality for our aging parents, we mirror the act of making a place for the Creator of every living thing in our hearts and homes.

> —Rabbi Eliezer Diamond, professor of Talmud and rabbinics, "Do Not Cast Us Away in Our Old Age," *The Melton Journal*, Fall 1994

One of the few advantages to not being beautiful is that one usually gets better looking as one gets older.

> —Nora Ephron, author, screenwriter, and director, "On Never Having Been a Prom Queen," *Esquire*, August 1972

Originally, I wasn't interested in the subject of age. I had the same dreary view of age as anybody in America, the same absolute denial. It didn't apply to me. But once I began on that large path that led me to break through an even more pernicious, pervasive mystique—the mystique of age only as a decline from youth. I guess all the thirty years of writing *The Feminine Mystique* and the women's movement gave me a way to . . . be able to break through this other thing.

> —Betty Friedan, author and activist, *Booknotes* interview with Brian Lamb, C-SPAN, November 28, 1993

I have heard people wonder how much would change if they could live their lives backward, knowing at life's beginning the lessons gleaned at its end. I often ponder how greatly all of our lives would be enriched if we were able to take in not just Pirkei Avot [Wisdom of the Fathers] and other classic texts of our tradition, but Pirkei Savim, the wisdom of the bubbes and zaydes [grandmothers and grandfathers]. Their lessons for living are myriad.

> —Rabbi Dayle Friedman, former director of chaplaincy services at Philadelphia Geriatric Center, *Central Conference of American Rabbis Journal*, Summer 1997

In the old days, this neighborhood had plenty of room for everybody's opinions. Now . . . our neighbors die or go to Homes. Every day our world shrivels. It frightens people. And those who are left are all thrown together at the Center. Many of them have nothing in common, but they have to stay together. They remind each other of what they are reduced to.

> —"Shmuel" Goldman, member of the Aliyah Senior Citizens' Center in California, quoted in *Number Our Days* by Barbara Myerhoff (1978)

At the beginning of the journey, a baby has a loving mother thumbing through volumes of Dr. Spock for clues and cues. But in the seventh age of woman, there is no loving mother (long since dead), no designated caretaker, no books. We make this backward journey all alone.

> —Erica Jong, author, *Fear of Fifty* (1994)

The generational panic attack—it's our turn, and where am I?—is all the more severe because the moment has arrived with unexpected swiftness. Just a few months ago, it seemed almost certain that the president would be a man in his 70's for at least the next four years, with aides and cronies almost as, er, mature. It's shocking enough to find yourself in your 40's. The added shock of finding that suddenly the people running the country are also in their 40's is doubly cruel.

> —Michael Kinsley, columnist, from an article written in anticipation of the

inauguration of President Bill Clinton, the first president of the post–World War II generation, *The New Republic*, January 25, 1993

Do you know the worst of all vices? It is being over 55.

> —Jerzy Kosinski, novelist who died by suicide, *The Hermit of 69th Street: The Working Papers of Norbert Kosky* (1991)

Halfway between my fortieth and fiftieth birthdays, something happened. I calculate that for the first time in my life, the years behind almost certainly outnumbered the years ahead. I began to write books instead of giving sermons, perhaps out of an unconscious need to be assured that something of me would survive in a permanent state. I not only had to confront my own mortality, I had to confront (somewhat belatedly) the American notion that life peaks between age twenty-five and thirty and begins to decline after that.

> —Rabbi Harold S. Kushner, author and rabbi emeritus of Temple Israel in Natick, Mass., foreword to *A Heart of Wisdom*, edited by Susan Berrin (1997)

A midlife crisis is merely God's way of making us ask ourselves if we are living to our full potential, of making us take responsibilities for that within us which remains unlived.

> —Julius Lester, professor of English and Jewish studies, quoted in *Massachusetts*, Winter 1990

I've noticed that people who are blessed enough to die of old age die in stages, not all at once.

> —Deb Margolin, performance artist, *"Oh Wholly Night" and Other Jewish Solecisms*, 1996

You either rust with disuse, or grow musty with stagnation. Or, if you've got a feeling there's something you're endowed with the talent to accomplish, doing so (or even trying to do so) will make the inevitable remnant of life a little easier to bear.

> —Henry Roth, novelist, foreword to *Holding On: Dreamers, Visionaries, Eccentrics and Other American Heroes* by David Isay, photographs by Harvey Wang (1995)

If middle-aged Jews do not set the example for their own care by providing for their parents, who will be left to care for them?

> —Michael J. Salamon, founder and director of the Adult Development Center in Woodmere, N.Y., "Jewish Family: Mid-Life and Beyond" in *Crisis and Continuity: The Jewish Family in the 21st Century*, edited by Norman Linzer, Irving N. Levitz, and David Schnall (1995)

The joy of passing on wisdom to younger people not only seeds the future, but crowns an elder's life with worth and nobility.

> —Rabbi Zalman Schachter-Shalomi, leader of the Jewish renewal movement, *From Age-ing to Sage-ing* (1995)

If we compare our lives to dramas . . . then old age is the time when the meaning of the play becomes clear to us.

> —Rabbi Zalman Schachter-Shalomi, *From Age-ing to Sage-ing* (1995)

I do not believe that one necessarily becomes wise with age any more than one becomes patient, understanding, or kind. There is significant continuity to personality; kindness, patience, nastiness, and hostility are usually lifelong characteristics, and not likely to spring forth full-blown in old age.

> —Mildred Seltzer, gerontologist, "A Voice from the Older Generation" in *Lifecycles 1,* edited by Rabbi Debra Orenstein (1994)

Of course in my age there's more to look back than to look forward to. Still, I'm looking forward too, because tomorrow I intend to sit down and write another story. The story itself might look back. But I'm looking forward to the story.

> —Isaac Bashevis Singer, Nobel Prize–winning Yiddish writer, in his 80s, quoted in *Isaac in America: A Journey With Isaac Bashevis Singer,* documentary film directed by Amran Nowak, 1986

Fifty was the end of this long familiar plateau that you enter at 13—you know, the country of the female stereotype. And when I got to 50, which is the edge of this territory—indeed the edge used to be 35, 40, we've pushed it to 50—then it was like falling off a cliff. There was no map. Now it's true that I had been fighting with the map. But you're enmeshed in it either way, whether you're obeying it or fighting with it. It was very difficult. So I'm not saying it's all cheerful. I'm just saying that even though you realize the only country described to women is this 13-to-50-year-old country, there is another country after 50. It's so exciting and so interesting.

> —Gloria Steinem, author and activist, quoted in *Mother Jones,* November–December 19, 1995

They probably will introduce me as the heroine, because they won't believe that eulogies are distasteful to a person who has never considered herself (and never will consider herself) as a public character, and who knows her own shortcomings as a simple member of a community—whose eighty years have served primarily to teach her that years alone are not important.

—Henrietta Szold, founder of Hadassah, from her diary on her eightieth birthday, quoted in *Henrietta Szold: Life and Letters*, edited by Marvin Lowenthal (1940)

If I have an angel hovering over me, it is Sarah. The older I get, the more I identify with her, understand what she experienced, appreciate her as my ancestor and spiritual guide. Without Sarah, I could not have grown old laughing, as she did. She, too, had to learn that miracles are possible; that sexual pleasure does not evaporate with age, and that creativity is the essence of life, whether one creates a child of the body or of the intellect.

—Savina J. Teubal, scholar and author, referring to the biblical Sarah, "Have You Seen Sarah?" in *A Heart of Wisdom*, edited by Susan Berrin (1997)

I believe people fix on an age at which they see themselves . . . I see myself at 27. So, I'm still 27.

—Mortimer B. Zuckerman, real estate and publishing executive, age fifty-nine, *Newsweek*, June 24, 1996

❖ ALCOHOL ❖

(see also Prohibition)

This was exactly the price of hangovers . . . they reduced you to the meanest side of yourself where the old wound had not exactly healed.

—Norman Mailer, author, *The Armies of the Night* (1968)

We drank too much but we and our friends, especially those of us who were Jewish—and that was most of us—are not to be confused with characters in a Hemingway novel. No Jew I knew drank with the abandon and virtuosity of the people in Hemingway. . . . We were old enough to go to speakeasies and even to marry but there was an important sense in which we were still children, good Jewish children within quick and decisive call of our parents.

—Diana Trilling, essayist and critic, looking back at her life in the 1930s, *The Beginning of the Journey* (1993)

. . . and to Johnnie Walker, without whom none of this would have happened.

—Sidney Zion, journalist, dedication in *Trust Your Mother but Cut the Cards* (1993)

❖ Aliyah ❖
(Jewish Immigration
to Israel)

(see also Israel, Zionism)

Being here has enabled me to witness and occasionally participate in the romantic adventure of re-creating a Jewish state after two thousand years. Not bad for the price of an airline ticket from Michigan.

> —Ze'ev Chafets, Israeli journalist, "My Twenty-Fifth Anniversary," *Jerusalem Report*, August 13, 1992

Hearing the air raid siren go off on Yom Kippur, 1973, my first thought was, "The Israeli army will stop them." My second thought was, "I am the Israeli army." My third thought, needless to say, was "uh-oh."

> —Ze'ev Chafets, "My Twenty-Fifth Anniversary," *Jerusalem Report*, August 13, 1992

I do believe my husband and I have a lot to offer the Jewish nation, and I do hope it's above the ground, and not below. If we die for Israel, they'll name some bourgeois apartment house after us. What irony! Please spare us.

> —June Leavitt, resident, with her husband and five children, of Kiryat Arba, adjacent to Hebron, who moved to Israel from Long Island, quoted in *U.S. News & World Report*, April 18, 1994

After choosing between Nixon-McGovern, Ford-Carter, Reagan-Carter and Bush-Clinton, why has the thought of making such a choice here, between Labor's Shimon Peres and Likud's Binyamin "Bibi" Netanyahu, in the country I've been longing to live in for a decade, not filled me with excitement and pride? Is it a case of diminished expectations? Or self-inoculation against disappointment?

> —Winston Pickett, Israeli journalist, *Long Island Jewish World*, May 24, 1996

I am free to tear up my American roots and live in Israel. I would do well there—we would all flourish and grow. But for me, Israel is a spiritual thing: not a place to live but an inspiration on how to live.

> —Paul Schutzer, staff photographer for *Life* magazine, from a letter to his

daughter, April 1, 1965, quoted in *Israel: The Reality*, edited by Cornell Capa (1969) (Schutzer was killed in the Six-Day-War.)

From an ocean of hatred I find myself in an ocean of love. Having left a country where only the government knows what must be done, I arrive in a society where everybody but the government knows what must be done. . . . Having left a country in which criticizing the government can land you in prison, I now live in a society where the easiest thing in the world is to criticize the government, and the louder your criticisms the more popular you are.

—Natan Sharansky, former refusenik, *Fear No Evil* (1988)

For all their talk and influence, even though they can walk into the Prime Minister's office on their every trip to Jerusalem, I'm the one who'll choose who'll be in that office. Not even the most committed Diaspora "macher" ["big wheel"] can do that!

—Fiona Sharpe, Israeli journalist, *Long Island Jewish World*, May 24, 1996

In L.A. and Miami, the federations support aliyah but here where I sit there's no sense that it's important. The New England Holocaust Memorial is of far more concern to this community, which I think is a horrendously skewed allocation of Jewish priorities and money.

—Jay Shofet, Jewish Agency representative to Boston, "The End of Aliyah?" *Jerusalem Post*, July 24, 1997

❖ ANARCHISM ❖

Ultimate human justice for everybody. That's the ideal anarchism stands for.

—Irving Abrams, activist, interviewed in the film *Free Voice of Labor: The Jewish Anarchists*, 1980

I'm a man of peace. That's why I'm an anarchist. They might sound contradictory, but this is a fact: Anarchism is a peace movement.

—Ahrne Thorne, activist, interviewed in the film *Free Voice of Labor: The Jewish Anarchists*, 1980

❖ ANGELS ❖

The story of Isaac's dream of the ladder reaching to the heavens with angels ascending and descending is not a story of divine control. Rather, it is a statement that the divine is wherever man lets him in. Angels do not fashion the world. It is we who create or lay it waste.

> —Rabbi Samuel Z. Glaser, rabbi emeritus of the Elmont Jewish Center on Long Island and professor of psychology, excerpt from sermon, 1990

If we view angels as parts of our own beings, we affirm that God needs no angels—but we mortals do.

> —Rabbi Morris B. Margolies, congregational rabbi in Kansas City and professor of Jewish history, *A Gathering of Angels* (1994)

Angels are metaphors for the most basic human drives and emotions: love, hate, envy, lust, charity, malice, greed, generosity, sadism, delusion, vision, despair, fear, and hope. "The gathering of angels" set in heaven by John Milton is placed right here on earth by Jewish teaching. That gathering is within each one of us.

> —Rabbi Morris B. Margolies, *A Gathering of Angels* (1994)

❖ ANTI-SEMITISM ❖

(see also Leo Frank Case, Soviet Jewry)

The true emancipation of the Jews of Eastern Europe will come only with the emancipation of the non-Jews from the role of oppressor, from the psychology of the persecutor.

> —Annual Report of the Executive Committee of the American Jewish Committee at its 13th annual meeting, October 19, 1919, quoted in *American Jewish Year Book 1920–1921*

Oh, ho, ho, ho. Would you like to pay for all the noses I broke, and all the glasses I broke? I also have a violent temper. . . . People would say things that they would never say had they known I was Jewish. . . . I'd hit 'em! My mother and father were forever paying for glasses. Whack!

> —Lucy, a sixty-two-year-old in a large midwestern city who claims she doesn't

look Jewish, responding to whether she has experienced anti-Semitism, quoted in *Facing the Mirror* by Frida Kerner Furman (1997)

Hatred of outsiders is commonplace; anti-Semitism is unique. Unique because of its source, its intensity, its duration — indeed, its very nature — it is a major component of European, as well as of Jewish, history over the past 2000 years, and in the 20th century has had a decisive effect on the world.

— Joel Carmichael, author and editor, *The Satanizing of the Jews* (1992)

Indeed, it is no exaggeration to say that, in this century and at this moment, Jew hatred is the one common characteristic of otherwise unrelated totalitarian regimes, dictators, religious fanatics and international terrorists. If the Jews have been chosen for anything it is, tragically, to serve as the world's moral weather vane.

— Ze'ev Chafets, Israeli journalist, *Jerusalem Report*, April 2, 1992

Cogent lessons should be learned about antisemitism from recent experiences. It is not what happened that often matters, but what did not happen.

— Jerome A. Chanes, Jewish communal professional author, and professor, *Anti-Semitism in American Today* (1995)

Anti-Semitism is the longest-running, most widely adopted social pathology in history.

— Rabbi Irving Greenberg, author, scholar, and founder of CLAL, quoted in *The Jewish Week*, March 12, 1992

My parents and I used to listen to [Father Charles E.] Coughlin on the radio; now I watch Farrakhan on C-SPAN. The world doesn't turn that much.

— Nat Hentoff, journalist and author, *Speaking Freely* (1997)

Over the centuries it has fallen to the lot of my people to be the testing agent of human decency, the touchstone of civilization, the crucible in which enduring human values are to be tested. A nation's level of humanity could invariably be judged by its behavior toward its Jewish population. Persecution and oppression have often enough begun with the Jews, but it never ended with them.

— Chaim Herzog, Israeli president, speaking before the U.N. General Assembly, during the debate of the "Zionism Is Racism" resolution on November 10, 1975 (At the conclusion of his remarks he demonstratively tore up the text of the resolution before the General Assembly.)

If a man thinks Jews are terrible, I call him an anti-Semite, but not a Nazi. If he thinks the Versailles Treaty was too harsh against Germany, I don't call him a Nazi. If he thinks Germany really needs more Lebensraum as Hitler demands, I still don't call him a Nazi. But if he thinks all three things simultaneously, then I decide he's a Nazi.

> —Laura Z. Hobson, author, *Laura Z: A Life* (1986)

Anti-Semites have slim pickings during good times: a steak in the broiler and a new automobile in the garage dilute the appeal of a hater.

> —Rabbi Meir Kahane, founder of the Jewish Defense League, *Our Challenge* (1974)

Jews and what happens to them fascinate me more that Judaism does . . . the phenomenal history of anti-Semitism tantalizes me more than a faith I never knew.

> —R. B. Kitaj, artist, quoted in *R. B. Kitaj* by Marco Livingston (1985)

Modern man had harbored the illusion that humanity had reached a point in civilization where progress would take place automatically. However the events of "Crystal Night" shattered such illusions.

> —Rabbi Ezekiel Landau, sermon for commemoration of Kristallnacht, November 10, 1957, quoted in *Bridging Two Worlds* by Sol Landau (1968)

Are American Jews forfeiting all claim to moral seriousness by our anachronistic obsession with anti-Semitism to the exclusion of all other ills? We avert our gaze from every indicator of social decay. We ignore rap music's exhortation to torture women and murder policemen. But as soon as someone criticizes Israel or says something nasty about Jews, we explode in a mighty paroxysm of public indignation. Do we indeed have no stake in general society?

> —Rabbi Daniel Lapin, president of Toward Tradition, a national organization of Jewish conservatism, Op-Ed section, *The Washington Times*, July 12, 1995

Whether a boy or a man may join a particular fraternity or club is of no great importance. The important thing is to demonstrate that you are a good citizen, willing to bear your share of the responsibilities of citizenship as well as its blessings.

> —Herbert H. Lehman, banker, governor of New York State, and U.S. Senator (D-N.Y.), responding to a 1960 letter from Steven Schlussel, a pupil of the religious school of Temple Beth-El of Great Neck, Long Island, quoted in *This I Believe: Documents of American Jewish Life* by Jacob Rader Marcus (1990)

Anti-Semitism is not ignorance, it is insanity — human rage directed against a target deemed both allowed and unprotected. A woman cannot defend against the would-be rapist by quick access to Feminist reason. Rape is not caused by misapprehension. It is not caused by its victim. Neither is anti-Semitism.

> — David Mamet, Pulitzer prize–winning playwright, novelist, essayist, screen-writer, and director, "In Every Generation" in *Make Believe Town* (1996)

In the issues of May 22 and 29 of the *Dearborn Independent*... there have appeared two articles which are disseminating anti-Semitism in its most insidious and pernicious form.... They constitute a libel upon an entire people who had hoped that at least in America they might be spared the insult, the humiliation and the obliquy which these articles are scattering through the land and which are echoes from the dark middle ages.

> — Louis Marshall, president of the American Jewish Committee, from a letter to Henry Ford dated June 3, 1920, quoted in *American Jewish Year Book 1920–1921*

To what other people has the morally and politically diseased phrase "the right to exist" been applied?

> — Cynthia Ozick, novelist and essayist, "Writers and Editors Discuss Anti-Semitism," a symposium held on May 5 and 6, 1994, at the 92nd Street Y, reprinted as "Is There a Cure for Anti-Semitism?" *Partisan Review*, Summer 1994

On hearing that I had planned to write about anti-Semitism, one feminist asked, "Won't *Ms.* have to give equal time to the PLO?" Incredible. When did Palestine Liberation Organization interests become the other side of this issue? Wasn't it obvious that people who are against anti-Semitism are against Jew-hating? The opposite is not to be pro-PLO. The opposite is to be for Jew-hating.

> — Letty Cottin Pogrebin, author and activist, "Anti-Semitism in the Women's Movement," *Ms.*, June 1982

I wondered why Jewish women are applauded by the Women's Movement when we trudge through Judaic subculture ruffling beards with our feminist demands but not when we bring Jewish consciousness back the other way into feminism; or why we are cheered when we critique the Bible for its anti-woman bias but not when we criticize feminists for their anti-Jewish jokes.

> — Letty Cottin Pogrebin, "Anti-Semitism in the Women's Movement," *Ms.*, June 1982

The term anti-Semitism was coined in 1879 by Wilheim Marr, an anti-Jewish spokesman in Germany, as a euphemistic substitute for *judenhass*, Jew-hatred. The term is a misnomer, of course, since it has nothing to do with Semites.

> —Dennis Prager and Joseph Telushkin, authors, *Why the Jews? The Reason for the World's Greatest Hatred* (1983)

The phobia of anti-Semitism has ravaged our inner lives. It affects our morale, our morality and our statesmanship. Anti-Semitism has become our dybbuk, shaping our character, forming our judgment, planning our future. Anti-Semitism must be attended to.

> —Rabbi Harold Schulweis, "Anti-Semitism, Malignant Obsession," *Moment,* June 1985

I think that there continues to be a lot of anti-Semitism in America—not as much as there is racism, but still a fair amount. And I think being Jewish costs votes.

> —Arlen Specter, U.S. Senator (R-Pa.), asserting his plans to run for the office of president, quoted in *The New York Times,* October 29, 1995

One of the more charming benefits of being the editor of a Jewish newspaper is that you get the opportunity to be called an anti-Semite by crazies who call in and are angry about newspaper policies . . . it does bring into focus the sloppy way many people use language.

> —Jonathan S. Tobin, editor, *Stamford Jewish Ledger,* June 23, 1995

I noted it. I found it ugly. I didn't want to brood about it.

> —Diana Trilling, essayist and critic, "At Journey's End," interview with Joseph A. Concotti, *Jerusalem Report,* December 30, 1993

Though the anti-Zionists are fond of referring to the Western Jews as "Europeans," the Europeans themselves took a rather different view of the matter.

> —Ellen Willis, writer, *Beginning to See the Light: Pieces of a Decade* (1981)

The appeal of Jews as a political target so far exceeded any of their other functions that sooner or later their plunder or removal was worth more than their presence . . . anti-Semitism trumped communism and fascism as an organizing ideology.

> —Ruth R. Wisse, professor of Yiddish and comparative literature, "Zionism at 100: A Symposium," *The New Republic,* September 8 & 15, 1997

There have been lots of premature obituaries written about anti-Semitism.

> —Leonard Zakim, regional director of the Anti-Defamation League, quoted in *Boston Jewish Advocate*, November 14, 1997

❖ APATHY ❖

Did the public concern itself about the sanitary conditions under which garments were produced? About the grievously long hours which the toilers were compelled to labor? About the little children deprived of the right to play and grow, and even to live? Did this public busy itself in trying to right these wrongs and accord justice to those misused? On the contrary, this disinterested "just" public continued its search for bargains, cheap clothing, and gave little thought to the dangers incurred by themselves and others through unsanitary working conditions or the waste and loss of human life.

> —Samuel Gompers, president of the American Federation of Labor, "Struggles in the Garment Trade," *American Federationist*, March 1913, cited in *Out of the Sweatshop*, edited by Leon Stein (1977)

Somewhere within men and women of my generation remains the question I ask myself in my darkest thoughts about each of those friends who are not Jews: who among them would risk his life, if Hitler ever came again, to hide my grandchildren? But that fearful doubt is always accompanied by another: how would I behave inside Auschwitz if it were ever built in Scarsdale, or in Idaho, or near Camp David? I cannot answer either of these questions with certainty. I must hope—and work to increase the hope—that these questions will never be asked again.

> —Rabbi Arthur Hertzberg, author and professor, "A Lifetime Quarrel With God," *The New York Times Book Review*, May 6, 1989

Indifference can sometimes be as deadly as the assassin's bullet.

> —Gaynor I. Jacobson, Executive Vice President of United HIAS Service, New York, "Jews in Jeopardy," presented at the annual meeting of the National Conference of Jewish Communal Service, San Francisco, June 4, 1974

The opposite of love is not hate but indifference; the opposite of life is not death but insensitivity.

> —Elie Wiesel, author, *Somewhere a Master* (1981)

Neutrality and silence favor the killer; never the victim.

—Elie Wiesel, *Somewhere a Master* (1981)

1938 . . . the debate, insofar as it penetrated my inattention, seemed to me mere chatter in a vacuum. I classed the idea of a Jewish state, when I thought about it at all, with such futuristic imaginings as rockets to Mars . . . As for the menace of Hitler, I thought it must be greatly exaggerated, probably for the purpose of Jewish fund-raising. . . . God help me, how I want to strike out those lines! But they are the truth . . . As to my skepticism about the Nazis, I will die regretting it. So will every Jew of my generation who disbelieved until it was too late; and that is ninety percent of us.

—Herman Wouk, writer, *Inside, Outside* (voice of I. David Goodkind) (1985)

❖ ARTS ❖

(see also Literature, Music, Poetry, Writing)

If you're working in an office job, it's likely that you can have a period of years without being tested all the time. While a writer or a painter or a playwright is tested every time out. The notion that this is not a statement on your worth as a human being, as opposed to your last work, doesn't carry very far.

—Jules Feiffer, cartoonist and writer, quoted in *On the Edge of Darkness* by Kathy Cronkite (1994)

The teacher said the one who draws the bird exactly the way it is will get a gold star. I looked at the bird and thought it should fly. So I made the bird fly and I didn't get the gold star. Since that time, I have been opposed to gold stars, prizes, bribes . . . I'm all for developing the depth and richness of every human being.

—Temima Gezari, director of art education at the Board of Jewish Education of Greater New York since 1940, age 90, explaining her opposition to contests and competition between students in *The Jewish Week*, December 15, 1995

In times of violence, personal predilections for niceties of color and form seem irrelevant. All primitive expression reveals the constant awareness of powerful forces, the immediate presence of terror and fear, a recognition . . . of the brutality of the natural world as well as the eternal insecurity of life. That these feelings are being experienced by many people throughout the world today is an unfortunate fact, and to us, an art that glosses over or evades these feelings is superficial or meaningless.

> —Adolph Gottlieb, artist, from radio interview with Mark Rothko, "The Portrait and the Modern Artist," WNYC, October 13, 1943

The role of the artist . . . has always been that of image-maker. Different times require different images. Today, when our aspirations have been reduced to a desperate attempt to escape from evil, and times are out of joint, our obsessive, subterranean and pictographic images are the expression of the neurosis which is our reality.

> —Adolph Gottlieb, artist, "The Ides of Art," *Tiger's Eye*, December 1947

The purpose of ritual art objects in Judaism is not to inspire love of God but to enhance our love of doing a mitzvah; to add pleasure to obedience, delight to fulfillment. Thus the purpose is achieved not in direct contemplation but in combining it with a ritual act; the art objects have a religious function but no religious substance.

> —Rabbi Abraham Joshua Heschel, author, activist, and theologian, *Man's Quest for God* (1954)

In a snowstorm, you see someone with their back to you, and you can't see their nose or face, and you recognize them. It has nothing to do with anatomy. It's more to do with alchemy, I think. . . . My talent is to reduce that recognition to line so they see what I saw. And sometimes the reaction is humorous, because I think all humor is really based on recognition.

> —Al Hirschfeld, illustrator whose line drawings of Broadway entertainers have been in *The New York Times* for seventy years, quoted in *Washington Jewish Week*, June 12, 1997

Although Judaism has emphasized words, language, interpretation, and commentary, I have found the visual in our tradition equally illuminating. For me, the life of the soul is integrally bound up with the beauty of the created world, with the rituals and symbols that are our people's medium. Like language, what we see can be a benediction.

> —Tobi Kahn, painter, wall text for exhibition on sacred space, 1994

Art forms such as poetry, drama, music, dance, sculpture, and the graphic arts are no longer viewed as extra-curricular in the life of a people. . . . If Judaism is to have a humanizing and spiritualizing influence it must accord to the arts no less significant a position than that which they occupy in all modern civilizations.

—Rabbi Mordechai M. Kaplan, founder of Reconstructionism, "The Recon-structionist Foundation," 1940, in *Critical Documents of Jewish History*, edited by Ronald H. Isaacs and Kerry M. Olitzky (1995)

Art is that chalice into which we pour the wine of transcendence.

—Stanley Kunitz, poet, introductory essay to *Passing Through: The Later Poems* (1995)

Sometimes I think that great art—music, painting, poetry—is only born out of great pain, the sort of pain that shatters your old self, your old world-view, and compels you to give birth to a new one.

—Rabbi Harold S. Kushner, author and rabbi emeritus of Temple Israel in Natick, Mass., *Who Needs God* (1989)

I come of people who do not even acknowledge Jesus Christ. Why am I supposed to acknowledge Abstract Expressionism?

—Jack Levine, painter, quoted in "A Child of Daumier Confronts the 1990s" by Robin Cembalist, *Forward*, August 22, 1997

The Jew has this in common with the artist: he means nothing to be lost on him, he brings all his mind and senses to bear on noticing the Ordinary, he is equally alert to Image and Experience, nothing that passes before him is taken for granted, everything is exalted.

—Cynthia Ozick, novelist and essayist, "The Riddle of the Ordinary," *Moment*, July/August 1975

The greatness of the American audience is connected to the fact that we don't have snob value attached to art the way some societies do. There's not an elite, not a singular folk tradition. We're too diverse and multiple for that.

—Robert Pinsky, U.S. poet laureate, interviewed in "Bard's Eye View," *The Jewish Week*, April 25, 1997

Perhaps the artist was a prophet and many decades ago discovered the un-predictability which lay under man's seemingly ascending reason, or saw the potentiality for carnage we know too well today.

—Mark Rothko, artist, quoted in *About Mark Rothko* by Dore Ashton (1983)

I think that artists are the antennae of a community. Not everybody can express this; only the people who have the language and the sensibility can express what everybody feels, which is why we hunt for artists. But the consciousness has to be universal.

—George Segal, painter and sculptor, interview with Stephen Lewis, *Art Out of Agony* (1984)

The religious and artistic impulse are not that different. Both begin with questions; both are concerned with myths and rituals in life. You question the values and times you live in.

—Susan Seidelman, filmmaker, quoted in *The Invisible Thread: A Portrait of Jewish American Women* by Diana Bletter (1989)

After I've got a relationship of the forms working, then I go back to the details. They've got to be right too. There's a difference in the way a twelve-dollar coat wrinkles from the way a seventy-five-dollar coat wrinkles, and that has to be right. It's just as important esthetically as the difference in the light of the Ile de France and the Brittany coast. Maybe it's more important. If I look at an ordinary overcoat as I never saw it before, then it becomes as fit a subject for painting as one of Titian's purple cloaks.

—Ben Shahn, painter, printmaker, muralist, and activist, 1944, quoted in *Ben Shahn*, edited by John Morse (1972)

I believe that there is, at this point in history, a desperate need for a resurgence of humanism, a reawakening of values. I believe that art—art of any kind—can play a significant part in the reaffirming of man.

—Ben Shahn, 1949, quoted in exhibition catalog, *Ben Shahn: A Retrospective* at The Jewish Museum, 1976

Like Rabbi Abulafia [13th-century mystic], I had learned first of all the Hebrew alphabet. Like him, I learned to draw and to contemplate the big flowing letters; I was most at home with them and could make them long before I could do anything else with my hands. It was such a pleasure to copy them from the prayer book, because in each letter there was some subtle part of the others, and as one learned to make the new ones he discovered those familiar parts that he already knew.

—Ben Shahn, "Love and Joy About Letters," 1963, in *Ben Shahn*, edited by John Morse (1972)

The way to painting is a lonely road, a one-man path. It holds no security; it is not cozy. Every moment of painting is a moment of doubting. The only criterion is the criterion of self, of what one wants, what one thinks he believes, his own shaky philosophy. There are no guideposts, no maps, no geography to tell him that he is on the right path. . . . The only vindication of his course of action is a realized image, a work of art.

—Ben Shahn, afterword to his illustrated edition of Rilke's *For the Sake of a Single Verse* (1968)

Art is the signature of a civilization. It is through the arts—beginning with paintings left on the walls of caves—that we have always known who we were and who we are.
—Beverly Sills, opera singer, *Beverly: An Autobiography*, written with Lawrence Linderman (1987)

I knocked down a lot of barriers people had put between themselves and opera. Before I came on the scene, the public regarded opera stars as exotic hothouse plants. I think I changed that. I was a home-grown product the public could identify with. I looked and talked the way they did.
—Beverly Sills, *Beverly: An Autobiography*, written with Lawrence Linderman (1987)

When I make a picture, I make love.
—Alfred Steiglitz, photographer, quoted in *Alfred Steiglitz, A Biography* by Richard Whelan (1995)

Photography is not an art. Neither is painting or sculpture, literature or music. They are only different media for the individual to express his aesthetic feelings; the tools he uses in his creative work . . . You do not have to be a painter or sculptor to be an artist. You may be a shoemaker. You may be creative as such. And if so, you are a greater artist than a majority of the painters whose work is shown in the art galleries of today.
—Alfred Steiglitz, "Is Photography a Failure?" *New York Sun*, March 14, 1922, quoted in *Alfred Steiglitz, A Biography* by Richard Whelan (1995)

Art used to be definable as what men created. Crafts were made by women and natives. Only recently have we discovered they are the same, thus bringing craft techniques into art and art into everyday life.
—Gloria Steinem, author and activist, "Words and Change," 1979, *Outrageous Acts and Everyday Rebellions* (1983)

I realized in Dachau that the arts in general have the power to keep you not just alive, but to make your life meaningful, even under the most dreadful circumstances.
—Herbert Zipper, composer and conductor who is an Austrian-born Holocaust survivor, recalling his formation of a clandestine orchestra with makeshift instruments in Dachau, quoted in the *Los Angeles Times*, April 9, 1997

❖ ASSASSINATIONS ❖

When George Moscone, the Mayor of San Francisco, was killed, I was asked for my reaction . . . I happen to believe in the doctrine of beshert, which means "God ordains"—your life is laid out, predestined. Obviously, you're not supposed to make it easy for those who want to dispose of you—you don't throw yourself in front of a train—but nevertheless, when it's all said and done, I'm a child of God, as we all are, and whatever He wants to do with me, He will do with me.

> —Edward I. Koch, mayor of the City of New York, interview with Peter Manso in *Playboy*, April 1982

ASSASSINATION OF PRESIDENT JOHN F. KENNEDY

No bugler sounded taps, no drum beat its ruffle, no band pealed "Hail to the Chief" as John F. Kennedy, 35th President of the United States, returned for the last time to Washington, the city where he practiced the magic art of leadership.

> —Theodore White, journalist, *Life*, November 29, 1963

Power changes very quickly and very brutally in Washington. I'll never forget the exchange of those two pieces of furniture within a twenty-minute period.

> —Sander Vanocur, NBC News correspondent who was standing outside the White House west wing when he saw Kennedy's rocking chair being brought out and LBJ's mounted saddle brought in hours after the assassination, from "JFK: A Time Remembered" shown on PBS, November 21, 1988, cited in *Covering the Body: The Kennedy Assassination, the Media, and the Shaping of Collective Memory* by Barbie Zelizer (1992)

That next Monday, I had one of my first on-the-air assignments, reporting on the funeral of President John F. Kennedy, and still being a novice, I wondered how I could possibly manage to keep the tears out of my voice.

> —Barbara Walters, television journalist, recalling that she was a writer on the "Today Show" when she heard the news of the assassination, quoted in "Ten Years Later: Where Were You?" *Esquire*, November 1973, cited in *Covering the Body: The Kennedy Assassination, the Media, and the Shaping of Collective Memory* by Barbie Zelizer (1992)

I wanted to be a hero. It looks like I fouled things up.

> —Jack Ruby, speaking to James Leavelle, the homicide detective who trans-
> ferred Ruby to the Dallas County Jail the day after he shot and killed alleged
> assassin Lee Harvey Oswald, November 25, 1963, quoted in *Newsweek*, No-
> vember 22, 1993

What I saw, you have on film.

> —Abraham Zapruder, a Texas businessman who, by chance, filmed the pres-
> idential motorcade including the twenty-six seconds depicting the assassi-
> nation; from his 1964 testimony to the Warren Commission investigating
> the assassination, quoted in *Video*, October 1966

Why Ruby did it. Ruby came from Texas. . . . and a Jew in Texas is a tailor.
So what went on in Ruby's mind, I'm sure, is that "Well, if I kill the guy that
killed the President, the Christians'll go: 'Whew! What balls he had, hey? We
always thought the Jews were chickenshit, but look at that! See, a Jew at the
end, saved everybody!' " And the Christians'll kiss him and hug him and they'll
lift him on high.

> —Lenny Bruce, satirist, quoted in *The Essential Lenny Bruce*, edited by John
> Cohen (1967)

His Jewishness was obviously a red herring to his actions. I don't think the
ultimate analysis of what happened on November 22, 1963, will ever turn up a
Jewish card. Ruby's Jewishness was merely one thin thread in the tapestry.

> —Stephen Davis, screenwriter responsible for *Ruby*, a film about the life of
> Jack Ruby, quoted in *Jerusalem Report*, April 2, 1992

After the Kennedy assassination, I did a cartoon where it ended with "you're
no longer paranoid to feel paranoid."

> —Jules Feiffer, cartoonist and writer, quoted in *On the Edge of Darkness* by
> Kathy Cronkite (1994)

The assassination of a President would be seismographic in its effect. For
Americans, the aftershocks would not cease for the rest of the century or more.

> —Norman Mailer, author, *Oswald's Tale* (1995)

The conclusion I reached is that he probably did it . . . but I hedge it with
a great many qualifications, the first of which was that . . . any good lawyer could
have gotten him off because there is so much confusion of the evidence. . . .There's an awful lot of evidence that would have him doing it but
there's an awful lot that wouldn't. I felt finally that he did it because it was the
logic of his life.

—Norman Mailer, about Lee Harvey Oswald, *Booknotes* interview with Brian Lamb, C-SPAN, June 25, 1995

Looking back, it all seemed to start at 12:29, Dallas time, November 22, 1963, and it would take years, decades to rebuild American confidence. Nor is the work complete. Our generation of Americans may never be quite so sure—of anything—again. It was a harrowing way to come of age.

—Paul Greenberg, editorial page editor, *Pine Bluff Commercial* and syndicated columnist, "A Certain Slant of Light" in *Entirely Personal* (1992)

ASSASSINATION OF DR. MARTIN LUTHER KING, JR.

The assassination of Dr. Martin Luther King, Jr., was the occasion for one of those massive outpourings of hypocrisy characteristic of the human race. He stood in that line of saints which goes back from Gandhi to Jesus; his violent end, like theirs, reflects the hostility of mankind to those who annoy it by trying hard to pull it one more painful step further up the ladder from ape to angel . . . Nothing could be more deceptive than the nationwide mourning. Beneath the surface nothing has changed, except perhaps for the worst.

—I. F Stone, journalist and author, "The Fire Has Only Just Begun," *I. F. Stone Bi-Weekly*, April 15, 1968, *Polemics and Prophecies 1967–1970 (1989)*

We come here with a great deal of sorrow and frankly with a great deal of anger. What has happened in this city is a result of oppression and injustice, the inhumanity of man to man, and we have come to appeal to you for leadership. . . . There are laws greater than the laws of Memphis and Tennessee and these are the laws of God.

—Rabbi James A. Wax, senior rabbi of Temple Israel, the oldest Jewish congregation in Memphis, remarks to Memphis mayor Henry Loeb following a memorial service two days after King's death in Memphis, quoted in *The Quiet Voices: Southern Rabbis and Black Civil Rights, 1880s to 1990s*, edited by Mark K. Bauman and Berkley Kalin (1997)

ASSASSINATION OF SENATOR ROBERT F. KENNEDY

In the enduring battle between the noble and the base, between the graceful and the tawdry, this has been a cruel year for the children of light. Last June, our night was lit by roaring jets and massive artillery; this June, our day was darkened by a lonely pistol.

—Leonard Fein, political scientist, noting that the assassination of Senator Robert Kennedy occurred on the anniversary of the Six-Day War in Israel, speaking at the Annual Meeting of the National Conference of Jewish Communal Service, Detroit, June 8, 1968

During my half century on this earth, I have seen touching sights beyond forgetting. I have seen a million people stand in massed silent tribute to Mahatma Gandhi. I have listened to Korean refugees singing to each other at night to keep up their spirits. I have seen maimed and disfigured victims of the Hiroshima bombing pray for an end to all war. I have seen compassionate respect and love on the faces of people looking at Jacqueline Kennedy. These are all vivid pictures in the mind, and now there is another, of a slow-moving mass of human beings in the heart of Manhattan paying individual respect to a man who had touched them and who had been touched by them.

> —Norman Cousins, editor of *The Saturday Review,* author and educator, remembering the late Robert Kennedy lying in state at St. Patrick's Cathedral in New York, "A Tribute to Robert Kennedy," *The Saturday Review,* June 22, 1968

The sixties came to an end in a Los Angeles hospital on June 6, 1968. . . . I felt helpless, sad, angry. I cried a little, then, denying grief, hurled silent, defiant curses at fate, at God Himself. Then when it seemed I was too tired to feel anything, I sensed the dampness of unanticipated tears.

> —Richard Goodwin, advisor and speechwriter for Presidents Kennedy and Johnson and advisor to Robert Kennedy in his presidential campaign in 1968, *Remembering America* (1989)

He had, so far as I know, the deepest concern for the underdog of anyone I had ever met. . . . He was not only the only man in public life to have this feeling in his heart; but, in my judgment, it burned in him more brightly than in any other man I have ever known.

> —Jacob K. Javits, U.S. Senator (R-N.Y.), in his eulogy of Senator Kennedy on July 30, 1968, quoted in *An Honorable Profession: A Tribute to Robert F. Kennedy* (1993)

ASSASSINATION OF ISRAELI PRIME MINISTER YITZHAK RABIN

(see also Israel)

For 27 years I was a military man. I fought all the time. There was no chance for peace. I believe now there is a chance for peace and we must take advantage of it. . . . This rally must broadcast to the Israeli public, to the world

Jewish public and to many in the Western and outside world that the people of Israel want peace, support peace. Thank you.

> —Yitzhak Rabin, addressing a peace rally in Tel Aviv moments before he was shot, quoted in the *Washington Post*, November 5, 1995

We know how to make peace. We don't know how to sing. But in the making of peace we won't be off-key.

> —Shimon Peres, Israeli foreign minister, at a peace rally in Tel Aviv, when microphone was passed to Rabin and Peres to join in the singing of a popular peace song, moments before the assassination, quoted in the *Washington Post*, November 5, 1995

The government of Israel announces with astonishment and deep sorrow the death of Prime Minister Yitzhak Rabin, who was murdered by an assassin tonight in Tel Aviv.

> —Eitan Haber, senior Rabin aide, quoted in the *New York Daily News*, November 5, 1995

What will happen to our country, to the people of Israel, if he will die here on my operating table?

> —Dr. Yoram Kluger, head of Ichilov Hospital's Trauma Unit, reaction when he saw Rabin lying on the operating table, quoted in *Boston Jewish Advocate*, November 10–16, 1995

I acted alone on God's orders and I have no regrets.

> —Yigal Amir, assassin, in his comments to police as reported on Israeli radio, quoted in the *New York Daily News*, November 5, 1995

Yitzhak Rabin was my partner and my friend. I admired him, and I loved him very much. Because words cannot express my true feelings, let me just say "shalom chaver." Goodbye, friend.

> —President Bill Clinton, excerpt from his statement on the death of Yitzhak Rabin, White House news conference, November 4, 1995

The mind cannot take it and the heart weeps.

> —Benjamin Netanyahu, leader of the opposition Likud party, quoted in the *New York Daily News*, November 5, 1995

Only in the Arab world do leaders who want peace endanger their lives. Last night we realized we lived a mistake. We are not immune.

—Nachum Barnea, Israeli political commentator, quoted in the *Chicago Tribune*, November 6, 1995

This is an event whose reverberations are so large that it is hard to assess it at this moment.

—Yaron Ezrachi, Israeli political scientist, quoted in the *Washington Post*, November 5, 1995

No man—Israeli, Palestinian or American—was more essential to the Middle East peace process than Yitzhak Rabin, the Israeli Prime Minister who was gunned down by an assassin in Tel Aviv last night.

—Glenn Frankel, former Jerusalem bureau chief of the *Washington Post*, "The Quintessential Israeli: A Soldier Who Longed for Peace," the *Washington Post*, November 5, 1995

One man did it, but there were many more inciters.

—Yossi Sarid, Israeli Environment Minister, quoted in the *Washington Post*, November 5, 1995

I think some people are going to be happy and some people are not going to be upset that Rabin is dead, but worried about what the future will bring . . . I guess for the short run, it's going to be difficult for people on the right wing because Peres will probably come down and try to arrest everyone who breathes the wrong way.

—Robert Davidsky, New York member of Kahana Chai (Kahana lives), quoted in the *New York Daily News*, November 5, 1995

There will not be a situation where the bullet of a murderer will determine who will be in power in Israel. The government of Israel is decided through elections.

—Benjamin Netanyahu, leader of the opposition Likud party, quoted in the *Chicago Tribune*, November 6, 1995

By splitting the Jews, Mr. Rabin dug his own grave.

—Yitzhak Ben Dayan of Miami, Fla., letter to the editor, *Miami Herald*, November 7, 1995

They killed him; he is an idiot. I am not interested in him or his parents.

—Leah Rabin, interview on Israel's Army Radio before Yitzhak Rabin's funeral, when asked if she had anything to say to the parents of the confessed killer, Yigal Amir, *Jerusalem Post*, November 7, 1995

Others greater than I have eulogized you. But none of them ever had the pleasure I had to feel the caresses of your warm, soft hands, to merit your warm embrace that was reserved only for us, to see your half-smile that always told me so much, that same smile which is no longer, frozen in the grave with you.

> —Noa Ben-Artzi Philosof, eighteen-year-old granddaughter of Yitzhak Rabin, speaking at his funeral, November 6, 1995

Israel is not a superpower whose favors and protection are sought by the nations of the world, but not since John F. Kennedy's funeral in 1963 has there been an assembly of world leaders like yesterday's gathering in Jerusalem in tribute to Yitzhak Rabin. It was almost as if Zion had really been a light into the nations, as if the love of peace had replaced the awe of power.

> —Editorial, *Jerusalem Post*, November 7, 1995

How many people who said "traitor" have been in the battlefield even one percent of the time that Rabin was there? How many have faced the need to send soldiers to battle?

> —Eric Mizrachi, student at the Yeshiva of Flatbush, at the ceremony in tribute to Rabin at Carnegie Hall, quoted in the *Jerusalem Post*, November 8, 1995

These attempts now to make political hay out of this, to try to say it's the responsibility of the Likud, are like asking whether Lee Harvey Oswald was a Republican or a Democrat and then blaming the party.

> —Benjamin Netanyahu, Likud leader, quoted in the *Chicago Tribune*, November 8, 1995

This is not Lee Harvey Oswald, a disturbed assassin whose motives we still cannot fathom. This is John Wilkes Booth, a man with a plan. This is assassination in the long tradition of self-styled tyrannicide stretching back to Brutus. Understanding such assassins falls not in the realm of abnormal psychology . . . but in the realm of politics.

> —Charles Krauthammer, columnist, *Washington Post*, November 10, 1995

We had been told, pompously, that all Jews are family, while our leaders — and ourselves — we dare not absolve ourselves — ignored or papered over the many ways in which we are a dysfunctional family.

> —Editorial, "A Death in the Family," *Long Island Jewish World*, November 10, 1995

In deference to the memory of Prime Minister Yitzhak Rabin, who was assassinated last Saturday night, we are refraining from any direct, personal comments about his policies. It is not fitting for us to appear to be judging him when he comes to the mighty Judge of all the world, before Whom there is no deceit, concealment or forgetfulness.

> —"Julius Liebb"(pseudonym), "What's Wrong With Us? An Enquiry and an Answer," *The Jewish Press*, November 10, 1995

That Saturday night I felt bound to caution my children to distrust anyone who tells them they know what God wants.

> —Harold S. Steinberg, columnist, *Long Island Jewish World*, November 10, 1995

A man who spoke in biblical cadences, he lived a life of biblical dimensions and met a death of almost biblical purpose.

> —Charles Krauthammer, columnist, *Washington Post*, November 10, 1995

When you elevate a terrorist like Yassir Arafat to the level of a statesman, you help create a world in which morality is turned upside down and murder can be seen to have positive results.

> —Beth Gilinsky, founder and president of the Jewish Action Alliance, quoted in *Long Island Jewish World*, November 10, 1995

The truth is that you can't shamelessly exploit the electorate's fears, appeal to its basic instincts, expecting to make it all right in the end (because the end will justify the means), any more than you can fire a bullet and draw it back into the barrel.

> —Harold S. Steinberg, columnist, *Long Island Jewish World*, November 10, 1995

The bullet came from a gun whose trigger was pulled by the same hand that wrapped tefillin around an arm every morning. Had we looked at this man on the Saturday morning before the assassination we would have considered him our pride and joy. He turned out to be our worst nightmare.

> —Rabbi Haskel Lookstein, rabbi of Congregation Kehilath Jeshurun and principal of the Ramaz School in New York City, quoted in the *Jerusalem Post*, November 17, 1995

Jews in New York live a ten-hour flight away from Tel Aviv, and yet these images and their implications absorbed their conversation utterly, as if the blood were fresh not only on the cobblestones of Tel Aviv but on West End Avenue and Eastern Parkway.

> —David Remnick, journalist and author, *The New Yorker*, November 20, 1995

Would most of us who strongly opposed the war in Vietnam in the 1960s have sanctioned the assassination of Lyndon Johnson? No. But would we feel guilty to go on opposing the war after LBJ's assassination? Absolutely not.

—Rabbi Meir Fund of the Flatbush (Brooklyn) minyan, quoted in *Long Island Jewish World*, November 24, 1995

Yigal Amir had good reason to murder, but no right to do so.

—Rabbi Moshe Tendler, Rosh Yeshiva (dean), quoted in *Long Island Jewish World*, November 24, 1995

What Rabin was trying to tell [President] Carter prior to his 1977 defeat was that peace was not simply declared or given. It has to emerge from real facts, from certain possibilities open and other alternatives closed. This is, I think, what Henry Kissinger, tear-streaked and choked, meant when he characterized Rabin as a master of circumstances with which he was faced, a master in war and a master at trying for peace. . . . Kissinger's tears show the depth of his own Jewish feelings, and it is a mark of how deeply pluralist America is that it hardly thinks strange the Jewish passions of even its most powerful citizens.

—Martin Peretz, editor-in-chief, *The New Republic*, November 27, 1995

Personal feelings and political disagreements aside, my judgment is that his [Yitzhak Rabin's] assassination was a crime so horrible that it will be remembered as one of the great infamies of Jewish history.

—Norman Podhoretz, senior fellow at the Hudson Institute and former editor of *Commentary*, "Israel with Grandchildren," *Commentary*, December 1995

The assassin has a wide stage to not only glorify his outlook, but the murder itself. Somewhere out there in the dark, watching him with admiration and envy, is the next "ideological" killer, just as this killer certainly envied the horrid holy ritual that sprouted around the Cave of the Patriarchs from which he drew inspiration.

—Amos Oz, Israeli author, *Yediot Aharonot* [Israeli newspaper], December 4, 1995, comparing Yigal Amir and Baruch Goldstein, quoted in the *Chicago Tribune*, December 7, 1995

If we've learned anything from the Rabin assassination, it is that we each have a responsibility to distinguish between unity and uniformity, between dissent and delegitimization.

—Gary Rosenblatt, editor and publisher, "One People?" *The Jewish Week*, December 15, 1995

This year, when you finish lighting the candles, hold the shamash [candle used to light the others] gently for a moment and think of Rabin and the other good people who paid for the future with their last full measure of devotion. Say a silent blessing over his memory and name. Perhaps the martyred Hebrew poet Hannah Senesh wrote our prayer for us: Blessed is the match, consumed in kindling the flame. Blessed is the flame, burning in the heart in secret places. Blessed is the heart with the strength to stop its beating for honor's (peace's) sake.

— Rabbi Irving Greenberg, author, scholar, and founder of National Jewish Center for Learning and Leadership (CLAL), speaking at Chanukah, several weeks after the assassination, quoted in *The Jewish Week*, December 15, 1995

❖ ASSIMILATION ❖

(see also Jewish Identity)

The byword of past generations of Jewish Americans has been shanda — fear of embarrassment in front of our hosts. The byword of the next generation should be chutzpah — assertive insistence on the first-class status among our peers.

— Alan M. Dershowitz, law professor, appellate lawyer, activist, and author, quoted in *Insight*, July 8, 1991

I want now to be of today. It is painful to be conscious of two worlds. The Wandering Jew in me seeks forgetfulness.

— Mary Antin, writer, *The Promised Land* (1927)

One may be surprised that the apparent uselessness of all our odd disguises has not yet been able to discourage us. . . . But before you cast the first stone at us, remember that being a Jew does not give any legal status in this world. If we should start telling the truth that we are nothing but Jews, it would mean that we expose ourselves to the fate of human beings who, unprotected by any specific law . . . are nothing but human beings. I can hardly imagine an attitude more dangerous, since we actually live in a world in which human beings as such have ceased to exist for quite a while; since society has discovered discrimination as the great social weapon by which one may kill men without any bloodshed.

— Hannah Arendt, German-born American philosopher and social critic who was forced to flee Germany in 1933 (she moved to Paris and in 1941 to the

United States), "We Refugees," 1943, in *The Jew as Pariah: Jewish Identity and Politics in the Modern Age*, edited by Ron H. Feldman (1978)

I don't seem to be able to get accustomed to my luxurious life. I am always more or less conscious of my good clothes, of the high quality of my office furniture, of the power I wield over the men in my pay. As I have said in other connections, I still have a lurking fear of restaurant waiters.

I can never forget the days of my misery. I cannot escape from my old self. My past and my present do not comport well. David, the poor lad swinging over a Talmud volume at the Preacher's synagogue, seems to have more in common with my inner identity than David Levinsky, the well-known cloak manufacturer.

> —Abraham Cahan, author and editor, *The Rise of David Levinsky* (1917)

If you are a Jew of the type to which I belonged when I came to New York and you attempt to bend your religion to the spirit of your new surroundings, it breaks. It falls to pieces. The very clothes I wore and the very food I ate had a fatal effect on my religious habits.

> —Abraham Cahan, *The Rise of David Levinsky* (1917)

To an unrecognized extent, we're a nation of professional, religious, ethnic, and racial tribes—the Tribes of America—who maintain a fragile truce, easily and often broken. We had to conquer this continent—and its original tribes—in order to exploit its resources. But we were never able to conquer our atavistic hatreds, to accept our widely diverse pasts, to transcend them, to live together as a single people.

> —Paul Cowan, journalist, *The Tribes of America* (1979)

If we insist, as I believe we should, upon the moral basis and universal validity of democracy, we should at the same time emphasize less and less the particularism in our Jewish heritage, those particularisms that separate us from others, and stress the universal concepts and outlooks more and more.

> —Rabbi Samuel Goldenson, rabbi of Temple Emanu-El in New York City, quoted in the *Central Conference of American Rabbis Yearbook*, 1939

I will no longer be confined in the narrow, grimy margins, where my father and mother were born.

> —Rebecca Goldstein, novelist, *Mazel* (voice of the character Sasha), talking about the "possibilities and promises of the new world" (1995)

Neither my father nor any of our family ever took part in the Jewish community. . . . I never got used to being singled out in that way. . . . I'm proud of my ancestors and heritage. I've never practiced the Jewish faith or seen myself or our family as primarily of the Jewish culture. In the jargon of today's sociologists, we've been assimilated. We're Americans.

— Barry Goldwater, former U.S. Senator (R-Ariz.) and Republican nominee
for president of the United States in 1964, whose paternal grandparents were
Polish Jews who immigrated to the United States during the gold rush,
quoted in "The Alrightnik of Arizona" by John B. Judis, *The New Republic,*
November 28, 1988

It has become commonplace to equate a Jew who converts, assimilates, or marries out with one who has been killed. The equation may resonate emotionally, but it's time to remove it from Jewish rhetoric. . . . It's time to stop using death to promote Judaism. We need a different message, one that begins with life as a sacred gift, and then speaks of how to live.

— Gershom Gorenberg, Israeli journalist, *Jerusalem Report,* June 15, 1995

A supreme value of this [American] culture is the right to personal choice. Any discussion of the future of the American Jewish community must include the ramifications of this ethos, for as sociologists repeatedly remind us, all Jews are now Jews by choice. No one has to be Jewish anymore.

— Joshua Halberstam, philosopher and author, *Schmoozing: The Private Conversations of American Jews* (1997)

But how does one bend toward another culture without falling over, how does one strike an elastic balance between rigidity and self-effacement? How does one stop reading the exterior signs of a foreign tribe and step into the inwardness, the viscera of their meanings? Every anthropologist understands the difficulty of such a feat; and so does every immigrant.

— Eva Hoffman, author, *Lost in Translation* (1989)

I think Jews have assimilated amazingly well. But if you're so anxious to give it away, it's hard for the next generation to find it. You change your nose, change your name, lose your accent. You learn to talk with your hands folded together in your lap. And what have you got left?

— Susan Isaacs, author, quoted in *Forward,* July 26, 1996

The Judaism of his temple and his UJA [United Jewish Appeal] and his Bar Mitzvah and his lox and his Miami Beach and his B'nai Brith also went the way of old as his child nonchalantly cast off all vestiges of the Judaism that his parents had so carefully diluted and "modernized." That which his father had bankrupted the son cheerfully jettisoned.

— Rabbi Meir Kahane, founder of the Jewish Defense League, *Our Challenge* (1974)

[Policy should] seek to provide conditions under which each group might attain the cultural perfection that is proper to its kind.

> —Horace Kallen, sociologist who was critical of the "melting-pot" metaphor and maintained that it was unrealistic and cruel to force new immigrants to shed their familiar cultural attributes as the price of admission to American society; he called for "cultural pluralism," quoted in *Assimilation: American Style* by Peter D. Salins (1997)

Anyone who has heard—as I have—Jew-hating remarks said to her face because to the speaker she didn't look Jewish knows both the survival value and the knife twist of passing.

> —Melanie Kaye Kantrowitz, "To Be a Radical Jew in the Late 20th Century" in *The Tribe of Dina: A Jewish Woman's Anthology*, edited by Melanie Kaye Kantrowitz and Irena Klepfisz (1989)

Being Jewish in a Catholic country, gay in an Orthodox Jewish school, an artist in a business school, and coming to the United States and becoming a Latino has given me an outsider's perspective.

> —Moises Kaufman, playwright of *Gross Indecency: The Three Trials of Oscar Wilde*, who emigrated to the United States from Venezuela, quoted in *The New York Times*, May 25, 1997

It is one of the remarkable properties of Judaism that, phoenix-like, it seems to die and to be reborn. Our "lost" generation, when the final accounting came, did not lose itself in assimilation. It groped its way through a period of defiance and irresolution. It woke to the meaning of the Hitlerist phenomenon, came to grips with its eternal challenge, and encouraged a new Jewish life-form that was at home in the freedom, mobility, and variety of American life.

> —Philip M. Klutznick, lawyer, public official, and national president of B'nai Brith, *No Easy Answers* (1961)

No number of Jewish Nobel laureates, no impressive statistics about the high number of Jews in the learned professions, can have any positive bearing on the ability of this people to survive the test of freedom. Without Torah, there can be no Judaism, and without Judaism, there can be no Jews.

> —Rabbi Norman Lamm, president of Yeshiva University, *Torah Umadda: The Encounter of Religious Learning and Worldly Learning in the Jewish Tradition* (1990)

What chance do our young people have in co-ed dorms with co-ed bathrooms? Torah does not preach a segregated ghetto, but participation in civic affairs. But we must not forget the importance of boundaries, of separation.

—Rabbi Bernard Lander, president of Touro College in New York City, speaking at the 98th annual convention of the Union of Orthodox Jewish Congregations of America, November 1996, quoted in *Jewish Telegraphic Agency,* December 4, 1996

So long as there is discrimination, there is exile.

—Ludwig Lewisohn, author, *Upstream: An American Chronicle* (1922)

For the Jewish assimilationist, the issue is not freedom of religion, but freedom from religion.

—Kenneth Libo, author and editor, essay, "John and Frances Loeb and the Legacy of 'Our Crowd,' " 1997

Assimilation is a two-way street. Some people move further away but some people move closer [to Judaism].

—Rabbi Mordechai Liebling, executive director of the Jewish Reconstructionist Federation, quoted in *Jewish Telegraphic Agency,* November 28, 1996

The great social adventure of America is no longer the conquest of the wilderness but the absorption of fifty different peoples.

—Walter Lippmann, journalist, "Some Necessary Iconoclasm" in *A Preface to Politics* (1914)

We American Jews have prided ourselves on being the people who went from Poland to polo in three generations.

—Egon Mayer, author and director of the Jewish Outreach Institute, speaking at Hadassah National Convention, July 1992

Multiculturalism is intellectual deceit. Indifferent to the singularity of genius, it prides itself on rescuing groups from the margin (with the exception of Jews) and ends by marginalizing nearly everyone.

—Cynthia Ozick, novelist and essayist, quoted in "Making Our Way Back to the Mother Ship," *Forward,* November 17, 1995

If one leaves the tight world of one's ancestors, if one abandons the synagogue, the High Holy Days, the Sabbath Queen, the Torah, the Talmud, the Midrash, what replacements are made in the building of the soul? How are the crises of life marked: birth, marriage, death? How are festivals managed? Men and women need ways of living within ethical frameworks, ways of passing on to their children their morality and their lifestyles. What do we do—we who once thought only of abandoning the ways of our parents and parents' parents and gave no heed to the necessary replacements, substitutes we would need to make—what do we in our empty apartments, do to make furniture and fabric for ourselves?

> —Anne Roiphe, essayist and novelist, *Generation Without Memory: A Jewish Journey in Christian America* (1981)

To be raised as a post-immigrant Jew in America was to be given a ticket out of the ghetto into a wholly unconstrained world of thought. Without an old-country link and a strangling church like the Italians, or the Irish, or the Poles, without generations of American forebears to bind you to American life, or blind you by your loyalty to its deformities, you could read whatever you wanted and write however and whatever you pleased. Alienated? Just another way to say "set free!" A Jew set free even from Jews—yet only by steadily maintaining self-consciousness as a Jew. That was the thrilling paradoxical kicker.

> —Philip Roth, novelist, *The Anatomy Lesson* (voice of the character Nathan Zuckerman) (1983)

It doesn't take much, after all, for the people of any society to find others alien.

> —Peter D. Salins, professor of urban affairs and author, whose parents immigrated to the United States from Germany in 1938, *Assimilation: American Style* (1997)

It is no great revelation to point out that there are differences in Jewish group life and in Jewish philosophical premises. This is not new. But what is especially novel is the decreasing competence of the discussants from the point of view of their knowledge of Jewish group life, its history, literature, beliefs and practices.

> —Judah J. Shapiro, "The Jewish Community and the Synagogue in Perspective," presented at the annual meeting of the National Conference of Jewish Communal Service held in St. Louis, May 28, 1956, *Journal of Jewish Communal Service*, Fall 1956

. . . like inviting the arsonist to help put out the fire.

> —Rabbi Moshe Sherer, head of Agudath Israel, in response to a 1990 proposal by the North American Commission on Jewish Continuity to enlist the Reform movement in a campaign to stop assimilation, quoted in *Jewish Power* by J. J. Goldberg (1996)

The crucial thing about the melting pot was that it did not happen: American politics and American social life are still dominated by the existence of sharply defined ethnic groups.

> —Charles Silberman, sociologist, *Crisis in Black and White* (1964)

The future of American Judaism will ultimately depend on the ability of my fellow Jews to discern what manner of land it is in which we dwell. The choice is clear: whether, through fear of strangers, we live like weaklings behind cells of our own construction or whether we have the courage to live like mighty warriors in this great open place we call the United States.

> —Charles Silberman, *A Certain People: American Jews and Their Lives Today* (1985)

For the overwhelming majority of Jews, separatism in any form is a nonstarter; Jews may approve of multiculturalism for others, but not for themselves.

> —David Singer, director of research and publications of the American Jewish Committee, *Commentary*, April 1995

The way you see things, Borukh, if one doesn't follow every petty decree by every two-bit rebbe, one is automatically an assimilationist. Believe me, if Moses were to rise from the dead and take a good look at those primitive Williamsburg loudmouths in their black coats, always waving their arms about, he would curse them. Remember, Moses was a prince of Egypt, not a shmegege with sidelocks. According to Freud, he was as Egyptian as they come.

> —Isaac Bashevis Singer, Nobel Prize–winning Yiddish writer (voice of the character Dr. Margolin), *Shadows on the Hudson*, serialized in Yiddish in 1957, published in English in 1998

Everyone thinks Jews are all the same, but we didn't think so in the South. People were uncomfortable with being Jewish there. The way I was brought up, the best thing to be was Episcopalian. In our temple the music was Christmas hymns. I was brought up with Christmas trees, Easter egg hunts—and my Jewish face.

> —Alfred Uhry, playwright, quoted in "Remembering Prejudice, of a Different Sort," *The New York Times*, February 23, 1997

A Judaism which has only organizations, socializing, and fund-raising cannot speak to souls in crisis. Parents whose Judaism is just talk or just for their children cannot expect their children to buy it. A Judaism without prayer or study or guts will not hold the sensitive or the unhappy or the brilliant. They will seek out alternatives and many will find the Church. We should not be surprised at this outcome. Our bland and thoughtless Judaism will not forever win the new generation. They will demand something serious and deep. If we do not offer them Maimonides and Buber, they will find Tillich and St. Thomas.

> —Rabbi Arnold Jacob Wolf, rabbi of Congregation Solel in Chicago, "Pathfinder," November 29, 1960

Assimilation, like frostbite, begins at the extremities of Jewry.

> —Herman Wouk, *This Is My God* (1959)

There she lies, the great Melting-Pot—Listen! Can't you hear the roaring and the bubbling? There gapes her mouth—the harbour where a thousand mammoth feeders come from the end of the world to pour in their human freight.... How the great Alchemist melts and fuses them with his purifying flame! Here they shall all unite to build the Republic of man and the Kingdom of God.

> —Israel Zangwill, from "The Melting Pot," a 1908 play by Israel Zangwill, whose title became the popular metaphor for the assimilation idea, quoted in *Assimilation: American Style* by Peter D. Salins (1997)

❖ AUTOBIOGRAPHY ❖

I took life as it was presented to me and then did my best to improve it.

> —Rachel Calof, reflecting on her life as a homesteader on the Western plains after immigrating from a Russian shtetl at the turn of the century, *Rachel Calof's Story* (1936)

My life—I had lived in its heights and its depths, in bitter sorrow and ecstatic joy, in black despair and fervent hope. I had drunk the cup to the last drop. I had lived my life. Would I had the gift to paint the life I had lived!

> —Emma Goldman, anarchist and a founder of the women's rights movement, final words of her autobiography, *Living My Life* (1931)

I don't think anybody should write his autobiography until after he's dead.

> —Samuel Goldwyn, film producer, quoted in *Goldwyn: The Man Behind the Myth* by Arthur Marx (1976)

Every time I go back to Brownsville it is as if I had never been away. From the moment I step off the train at Rockaway Avenue and smell the leak out of the men's room, then the pickles from the stand just below the subway steps, an instant rage comes over me, mixed with dread and some unexpected tenderness. It is over 10 years since I left to live in "the city"—everything just out of Brownsville was always the "the city." Actually I did not go very far; it was enough that I could leave Brownsville, yet as I walk those familiarly choked streets at dusk and see the old women sitting in front of the tenements, past and present become each other's faces; I am back where I began.

— Alfred Kazin, author and literary critic, *A Walker in the City* (1951)

The trouble with writing a book about yourself is that you can't fool around. If you write about someone else, you can stretch the truth from here to Finland. If you write about yourself the slightest deviation makes you realize instantly that there may be honor among thieves, but you are just a dirty liar.

— Groucho Marx, quoted in *Groucho and Me* (1959)

Book reviews are kind of autobiographies, diaries of our tastes and predilections, judgments of the activity that you, yourself, are also engaged with.

— Laurie Stone, critic, accepting the 1995 Nona Balakian Award for book reviewing given by the National Book Critics Circle, March 21, 1996

"Memoirs?" people ask. "What's the hurry? Why don't you wait a while?" It puzzles me. Wait for what? And for how long? I fail to see what age has to do with memory.

— Elie Wiesel, Nobel laureate and author, *All Rivers Run to the Sea* (1995)

❖ Bar Mitzvah/Bat Mitzvah ❖

It was vulgar, crass, thoroughly unspiritual, and my parents spent far too much money for all the wrong reasons. And yet—something happened in spite of that. Through the long process of preparing for my bar mitzvah, I learned that I was Jewish and received the barest taste of what that might mean. Years later, I would come to know more, much more.

> —Howard Berkowitz, psychiatrist, whose Bar Mitzvah was in 1961, quoted in *Bar Mitzvah: A Jewish Boy's Coming of Age* by Eric A. Kimmel (1995)

This little packet of plush velvet [containing tefillin and prayer book] became the symbol of my rebellion: If I knew my parents were having their friends over, I would slip it onto the ledge in the entryway so it could not be missed when the front door opened.

> —Carl Bernstein, journalist, recalling his insistence on having a Bar Mitzvah over the objections of his parents, *Loyalties: A Son's Memoir* (1989)

The resolution . . . deplored "social pressures, excesses of wasteful consumption, expression of wealth and status and glitzy 'theme' events."

> —The Reform movement's call for the end of Bar and Bat Mitzvah receptions that have reached a point of "absurdity," quoted in *Broward Jewish World*, June 12, 1992

I was signaled to step forward to a place below the bimah [synagogue platform] at a very respectable distance from the scroll of the Torah, which had already been rolled up and garbed in its mantle. I pronounced the first blessing, and from my own humash [Five Books of Moses] read the selection which

Father had chosen for me, continued with the reading of the English translation, and concluded with the closing brachah [blessing]. That was it. The scroll
was returned to the ark with song and procession, and the service was resumed.
No thunder sounded, no lightning struck. The institution of Bat Mitzvah had
been born without incident and the rest of the day was all rejoicing.

> —Judith Kaplan Eisenstein, the first woman to have a Bat Mitzvah, who was
> the daughter of Mordechai M. Kaplan, founder of the Reconstructionist
> movement, recalling the May 1922 event, quoted in *Judaism: An Anthology
> of the Key Spiritual Writings of the Jewish Tradition, Third Edition*, edited
> by Arthur Hertzberg (1991)

If Spielberg had your parsha [weekly Torah portion] what would he do with
it?

> —Rabbi Henry Glazer, rabbi of a New Jersey synagogue, posing a question to
> Avi Yosef Klein, who was looking for inspiration to write his D'var Torah
> [interpretive public talk] for his Bar Mitzvah portion on the binding of Isaac,
> quoted in *The Jewish Week*, December 27, 1996

Why do American Jews make big bar mitzvahs? To celebrate the end of
the religious life of the child. But in orthodoxy it's the beginning of the religious
life. It's like the first day of school.

> —Shalom Goldman, author and professor of Jewish studies, quoted in *Grow-
> ing Up Jewish in America: An Oral History* by Myrna Katz Frommer and
> Harvey Frommer (1995)

My most challenging teaching assignment, however, was preparing my own
son for his Bar Mitzvah. . . . Even as we struggled together every night, I sensed
that this was a very special opportunity I'd have to be so close to him. And, I
wasn't unaware that someday he might be saying to his grandchildren, "When
my mother taught me to lehn." [chant from the Torah]

> —Ruth Berger Goldston of the Jewish Center of Princeton, New Jersey,
> "Chanting Torah, Lehning Life," *Sh'ma*, May 12, 1995

They decided to rent a loft downtown and bring lots of folksingers and call
it a bar mitzvah. That was the big compromise that everybody made. . . . Everyone avoided me. I was just walking around with other kids, saying, "When do
we do something?"

> —Arlo Guthrie, folksinger and songwriter, interview with Linda Ellerbee on
> *Later With Bob Costas*, 1991

Once the day and date are set, it is time to decide on the kind of celebration
to be arranged. And here we must enter a plea for simplicity. What was initially

a minor ceremonial recognition by the community of the individual's informed acceptance of his religious duties has, in our day, mushroomed into a series of formal social occasions whose festive aspects rival elaborate weddings.

> —Helen Latner, advice columnist, *The Book of Modern Jewish Etiquette* (1981)

On the night before my bar mitzvah, I was so nervous that the cantor had to give me a glass of schnapps to keep me going. On the day of my bar mitzvah, Mr. Rosenbaum sang with me to keep me on tune. I was exhausted when it was over. My parents had no money, but I was adamant about having a party. So we had a little lunch in the shul [synagogue]. I remember I had a new suit.

> —Yochanan Muffs, biblical scholar whose Bar Mitzvah was in 1945, quoted in *Bar Mitzvah: A Jewish Boy's Coming of Age* by Eric A. Kimmel (1995)

Weeping silently at the sight of my grandson becoming a full-fledged Jew, I pray to God that I am wildly mistaken in fearing what I fear for him and for all Israel. As I have done over and over again in the last three years, I find myself, here in this shul [synagogue] in Jerusalem, praying that those who seek peace and harmony and prosperity ahead for this country will for once in their political lives turn out to be right, and that those of us cursed with visions of disaster and war will be granted the blessing of an outcome that proves us utterly wrong.

> —Norman Podhoretz, senior fellow at the Hudson Institute and former editor of Commentary, "Israel with Grandchildren," *Commentary*, December 1995 (Written before the assassination of Rabin but gone to press at time of the shooting.)

More than when I learned to drive, more than my first sexual experience, more than going away to college, my Bat Mitzvah was my most intoxicating rite of passage. It was a conscious farewell address to childhood and I was wearing a black velvet dress—the first time my superstitious mother had let me wear black. How clearly I can recall the ecstasy of standing before the whole congregation and reciting my haftarah, a portion from the Prophets, then delivering the speech I had written describing my continuing commitment to Jewish life and my gratitude for my parents' love.

> —Letty Cottin Pogrebin, author and activist, *Deborah, Golda, and Me: Being Female and Jewish in America* (1991)

Before I knew it, we were checking out temples, religious schools, and car pools to Hebrew school: on the road, actually, by fourth grade, to Scott's Bar Mitzvah.

> —Randi Reisfeld, author, *The Bar/Bat Mitzvah Survival Guide* (1992)

Grandma Estelle/Estelle You are so much fun,/Please come and light/ Candle number one. . . . No one quite knows just how the candle-lighting ceremony, so crucial to Bar and Bat Mitzvahs as we know them, originated. . . . It probably started a few decades back in the U.S.A.

> —Randi Reisfeld, *The Bar/Bat Mitzvah Survival Guide* (1992)

It seems . . . that the loudest and most vociferous voices against a big party are from those who a) haven't made a Bar Mitzvah yet and aren't about to any time soon, b) don't have children, and c) aren't Jewish.

> —Randi Reisfeld, *The Bar/Bat Mitzvah Survival Guide* (1992)

It was a very special moment. I knew that there was no turning back. I knew I wasn't just practicing anymore. This was real. Wearing the tallit reminded me that God was there.

> —Allison Rodin, student whose Bat Mitzvah was in 1994, describing putting on her tallit (prayer shawl) on the day of her Bat Mitzvah ceremony, quoted in *Bat Mitzvah: A Jewish Girl's Coming of Age* by Barbara Diamond Goldin (1995)

The reasons to celebrate do not appear to be very strong, but in fact, there seem to be reasons not to celebrate a Bas Mitzvah: . . . When we celebrate such practices, we appear to be endorsing the Reform's and Conservative's actions, confirming them as acceptable to us. . . . We are mimicking the non-Jews. We are introducing our daughters to society, as they do in their debutante balls. . . . A precious and valuable jewel is kept hidden away, not out in the open where harm may befall it. The Jewish woman is held in such a lofty position that she is kept hidden and not put out on display. The whole nature of the Bas Mitzvah celebration is exposing, displaying the girl.

> —9th grade student, from her winning entry in the 1987 Asher Essay Contest in Chicago, "The Bas Mitzvah Celebration—Yes or No?" *The Jewish Press,* June 26, 1987

Much of what happens in connection with bar and bat mitzvah is spiritual sleepwalking.

> —Rabbi Jeffrey Salkin, author, professor, and spiritual leader of a synagogue on Long Island, *Putting God on the Guest List* (1996)

I found out I could sing, be in front of a group, and perform. I got a lot of pats on the back and later went on to get a B.A. in drama. My bat mitzvah was my first realization that I could be a performer, that I had talent.

> —Sherry Ellowitz Silver, religious school director at Temple Israel of Holly-

wood, whose Bat Mitzvah was in 1965, quoted in *Bat Mitzvah: A Jewish Girl's Coming of Age* by Barbara Diamond Goldin (1995)

I don't need their gala extravaganza: the bad band with the accordion player; bowls of punch for the kids; the lopsided tables under a slouching tent; chairs sinking into the mud. I am tired, cranky, and worn to the bone. Did I ask for a spiritual coming-out party? Do I look like a debutante? My parents can't pronounce the words, but they expect me to grace the entire family with religion. Why should I enroll in their efforts to regain their lost spiritual footing? They threw it overboard: let them swim after it. I want to be left alone to ride my new bicycle up and down the block every afternoon. To chew bubble gum and collect the trading cards like any normal American kid.

> —Cameron Stracher, novelist and lawyer, *The Laws of Return* (voice of the character Colin Stone) (1996)

It has not escaped my attention that there are those among the pious who [always] forbid and who insist on stringencies, who in matters of religious practice pay no attention to logical considerations or even to halakhic [Jewish legal] clarifications; they reach their conclusions solely on the basis of feelings, and the Jewish heart, which clings to the tradition of parents and teachers, and is taken aback at every change in religious practice. . . . Those who side with the permission for this new practice of celebrating bat mitzvah also have hearts beating with concern for the support of the religious education of Jewish girls. Events of life in our time have created a special need for spiritual strengthening and moral encouragement of girls when they reach the age of obligation to fulfill the commandments.

> —Rabbi Yehiel Yaakov Weinberg, leading Orthodox rabbinical authority, 1966, quoted in *Judaism: An Anthology of the Key Spiritual Writings of the Jewish Tradition*, edited by Arthur Hertzberg (1991)

The Dickensian Christmas is the nearest thing in literature I know to an American bar mitzvah. It has in much the same degree the fantastic preparations, the incredible eating, the enormous wassailing, the swirl of emotions and of family mix-ups, all superimposed with only partial relevance on the religious solemnity. . . . In the freedom of the United States, where for the first time in centuries we have known equality of opportunity, we have made of the bar mitzvah a blazing costly jubilee. I do not see that there is anything wrong with that.

> —Herman Wouk, *This Is My God* (1959)

❖ BIBLE ❖

The Biblical characters are so captivating because they are so real. Moses is devoted to a people he helped create; but he has no time to circumcise his sons. Abraham is the symbol of religious constancy who is prepared to sacrifice another, his son, to prove his faith. Sarah is the symbol of hospitality who drives out Hagar and Ishmael. Spiritual identity does not necessarily lead to good deeds. Just because one wears the trappings of faith he is not free to function as if the law does not apply to him.

> —Samuel Z. Glaser, rabbi emeritus of the Elmont Jewish Center on Long Island and professor of psychology, excerpt from sermon, 1990

Why does the Almighty spend the first five books of the Bible writing such morally problematic, bewildering stories? We've always had the answer to that one, because the Torah is not clarification, but the world itself. It is the world's goad towards perplexity, interpretation, toward midrash and Talmud.

> —Tony Kushner, playwright, interviewed in the film *Jewish Soul, American Beat,* produced, directed, and written by Barbara Pfeffer (1997)

Our sages read the Torah as genealogy, family history, and Abraham is "our father Abraham," Sarah "our mother, Sarah." That way of reading Scripture as Torah, our Torah, God's personal letter to us, Israel, about us and our family is so profound that at every turning in life we reread that letter and find in it sentences written as though this morning.

> —Rabbi Jacob Neusner, author and professor, explaining how Jews and Catholics read Scriptures differently, *The Bible and Us: A Priest and a Rabbi Read Scripture Together* by Andrew W. Greeley and Jacob Neusner (1990)

Genesis remains a fundamentally optimistic story because it always offers the possibility of a new beginning. Every generation represents a new start in life, each new child is ripe with potential. Regardless of the obstacles set in their paths, the characters in Genesis find within themselves the strength to begin again, to rebuild and renew their lives.

> —Naomi Rosenblatt, psychotherapist and teacher, *Wrestling with Angels* (1995)

A literature that all the time praises its people cannot exist. The Old Testament does not flatter us; it says the worst things about the Jews. I know one man who, reading the Bible for the first time, said, "I thought I was reading Mein Kampf." The Bible calls us thieves, murderers, lechers, on every page, almost. And yet the ancient Jews made it their holy book. The modern Jew wants to be flattered.

> —Isaac Bashevis Singer, Yiddish writer, quoted in *Moment*, September 1976

While Genesis ends with a promise of redemption and reunification, it stops short of portraying the reality of brothers living together in the land. So, too, does the Pentateuch as a whole, ending as it does with a glimpse of the promised land, but not with the reality of nationhood in the land. Brothers dwelling together in the land — or nation living as one in the land — is not an impossibility but neither is it a reality. Both Genesis and Deuteronomy end one step before that; family and nationhood at last are achieved, but the sharing of the patriarchal heritage in its fullness has yet to be realized. The promise of two brothers living together in the land remains always a promise.

> —Devora Steinmetz, professor and educator, *From Father to Son: Kinship, Conflict, and Continuity in Genesis* (1991)

The important texts in Jewish tradition such as the Bible and the Talmud are kept alive by being endlessly studied and interpreted rather than by being slavishly followed. It is this commitment, if not commandment, to interpret that makes the one Torah given to all Jews at Sinai a personal Torah for each and every one.

> —Michael Strassfeld, director of programming at Ansche Chesid in New York City and author (who later became a rabbi), *The Jewish Holidays: A Guide and Commentary* (1985)

We bring our insights to illuminate the Bible and the more we do so, the more the text of Scripture illuminates our lives.

> —Rabbi Burton Visotzky, author and professor of midrash, *Reading the Book: Making the Bible a Timeless Text* (1991)

Read simply, Genesis is an ugly little soap opera about a dysfunctional family. That is what causes us to have such a strong identification with it in the first place.

> —Rabbi Burton Visotzky, quoted in *Time*, October 28, 1996

The Bible is a radical book, but radicalism of that sort, a literary sort, can always be repressed through interpretation, overwhelmed by erudition, constrained by legal enactment.

—Michael Walzer, author and philosopher, "Liberalism and the Jews: Historical Affinities, Contemporary Necessities" in *Values, Interests and Identities: Jews and Politics in a Changing World*, edited by Peter Y. Medding (1995)

A good Bible class is very confusing—it will be filled with controversy . . . because we honor Scripture best by taking it seriously enough to argue about it.

—Rabbi Arnold Jacob Wolf, activist and rabbi of Kam Isaiah Israel Congregation in Chicago, "Teaching the Bible Today" in *Unfinished Rabbi: Selected Writings of Arnold Jacob Wolf*, edited by Jonathan Wolf (1998)

❖ BIRTHDAY ❖

Because time itself is like a spiral, something special happens on your birthday each year: The same energy that God invested in you at birth is present once again.

—Rabbi Menachem Mendel Schneerson, the Lubavitcher Rebbe, quoted in *Toward a Meaningful Life*, adapted by Simon Jacobson (1995)

I bless you that through your acts of good deeds, on each birthday you should be able to reflect on all the good you have done to make this world a better place to live in, and a more peaceful one, so that we may all merit the great coming of the Messianic days when all the world will be one.

—Rabbi Shlomo Carlebach, quoted in *Connections*, Passover 1987

May I say to you that I am deeply touched by your beautiful, if to some extent at least, unmerited appreciation of my life upon my attainment this day of the Biblical Age. God has blessed me so lavishly that had I done less in the years that are now behind me than it was my privilege to do I should feel no respect for myself, but that I have gained the respect and good will of men like you is certainly the highest reward I can wish for. I care very much for the good opinion and good will of my friends.

—Jacob Henry Schiff, banker and philanthropist, responding to friends' tributes to him in honor of his 70th birthday, January 10, 1917, quoted in *American Jewish Year Book 1921–1922*

❖ BLACK-JEWISH RELATIONS ❖

(see also Affirmative Action, Civil Rights Movement)

Jew-baiting and Negro lynching are two blunders well worth being freed from; Kisheneffing outside of the land of Kisheneff is a greater blot upon civilization than in that "hell's kitchen," Russia.

> — Rose Pastor Stokes, radical, from her editorial "Kishineffing It," written after the 1903 pogrom in Kishinev, quoted in *The Journey Home: Jewish Women and the American Century* by Joyce Antler (1997)

Jews cannot ensure equality for themselves unless it is assured for all.

> — American Jewish Committee Founding statement, 1906

The tragic fact is that love is not the answer to hate — not in the world of politics at any rate. Color is indeed a political rather than a human or a personal reality and if politics (which is to say power) has made it into a human and a personal reality, then only politics . . . can unmake it once again. But the way of politics is slow and bitter, and as impatience on the one side is matched by a setting of the jaw on the other, we move closer and closer to an explosion and blood may yet run in the streets.

> — Norman Podhoretz, editor, "My Negro Problem — And Ours," *Commentary*, February 1963

In New York today, the educational self-interest of Jews clashes with the educational self-interest of Negroes. It is a serious clash because education is a serious matter, determining how much your children will earn, what kind of life will they live. . . . It is also a matter in which Jews have a big investment of tradition and emotion; and Negroes, of aspiration and resentment. Wherever justice lies in that clash of self-interests, there is going to be a fight.

> — Milton Himmelfarb, critic, "How We Are," *Commentary* , January 1965

[SNCC] disqualified itself from any claim to be taken seriously in the struggle for human decency. There is no room for racists in the fight against racism.

> — Will Maslow of the American Jewish Congress, responding in 1967 to a statement made by leaders of SNCC (Student Non-Violent Coordinating Committee) that Jews were "imitating their Nazi oppressors," quoted in *American Jewish Year Book* 1968 (These anti-Semitic remarks were denounced by significant leaders of the civil rights movement including Dr.

Martin Luther King, Jr., A. Philip Randolph, Bayard Rustin, and Whitney Young, Sr.)

In this whole area of racial injustice . . . our goal is to take the initiative though it be unpopular. Here we Jews must fulfill our destiny as gadfly to the conscience of mankind.

> —Irving Fain, chairman of the Union of American Hebrew Congregations Commission on Social Action, speaking at the 1967 Biennial Assembly of the UAHC, quoted in *American Jewish Year Book,* 1968

While anti-Negroism is more pervasive than Negro anti-Semitism, and while both are dangerous, both are irrelevant to the desperate problems of saving the American city from decay, violence and even insurrection.

> —Albert Vorspan, director of the Union of American Hebrew Congregations' Commission on Social Action, speaking at the 1967 Biennial Assembly of the UAHC, quoted in *American Jewish Year Book,* 1968

Where in America today do we hear a voice like the voice of the prophets of Israel? Martin Luther King is a sign that God has not forsaken the United States of America. His presence is the hope of America. I call upon every Jew to hearken to his voice.

> —Rabbi Abraham Joshua Heschel, author, activist, and theologian, introducing Dr. Martin Luther King as keynote speaker at the 68th Annual Convention of the Rabbinical Assembly (Conservative), March 25, 1968—ten days before the assassination of Dr. King

There are those in the metropolis who found a variety of defenses for these atrocious statements; the museum carried on in its sublime way; the radio station garnered a bit of needed publicity; and the teacher and student who spoke their Jew-hatred in public went on teaching and studying at the public expense—as if it were the most normal thing to say and do in New York City in 1969.

> —Max Geltman, journalist and author, recalling the exhibit "Harlem On My Mind" at the Metropolitan Museum of Art and the introduction to the museum's catalogue that stated that "Our contempt for the Jew makes us feel more completely American in sharing a national prejudice," and the broadcast of an anti-Semitic poem on New York radio station WBAI, read by Leslie Campbell, a teacher at Junior High School 271 in Ocean Hill-Brownsville, *The Confrontation: Black Power, Anti-Semitism, and the Myth of Integration* (1970)

From what I had heard and read about you up to that time, you were the most relevant, most together radical organization in this country. . . . Let it suffice to say that the Panthers have declared themselves to be the enemies of my

people's national aspirations, and supporters of those who want to commit genocide against us. Whatever justice there is in the Panthers' own struggle, I must
view them from now on as my enemies. . . . Though you are my enemy, I am
not yours. . . . I would rather it not be this way, but it was you who disowned
us, not we who betrayed you.

> —Itzhak Epstein, member of various Zionist youth movements, an SDS (Stu-
> dents for a Democratic Society) organizer, cofounder of the Jewish Liber-
> ation Project and secretary-general of the North American Jewish Student
> Network, reacting to a *New York Times* article on July 23, 1969, that re-
> ported on Eldridge Cleaver's appearance in Algiers with Al Fatah dignitaries,
> "Open Letter to the Black Panther Party" in *Jewish Radicalism: A Selected
> Anthology,* edited by Jack Nusan Porter and Peter Dreier (1973)

Therefore it is as a Jew that I must accept black nationalism. The black
nationalists may or may not be the equivalents of the militants of the early
Zionist organizations, and Malcolm X may or may not be a black Vladimir
(Zev) Jabotinsky, but surely the parallel is there.

> —M. J. Rosenberg, journalist, "To Uncle Tom and Other Jews," *Village
> Voice,* February 13, 1969

The parallel experiences of persecution and exile, of being reduced to pariahs, have cast both Blacks and Jews in a prophetic circumstance. Both their
histories and their biblical theologies require of Blacks and Jews . . . to cast critical questions before every American ideologue, or any other ideologue, who
wishes to proclaim his system of values as ultimates that demand total
obedience.

> —Rabbi Marc Tanenbaum, activist on behalf of human rights and interreli-
> gious understanding, "Introduction: The Black Experience and Perspective"
> in *American Religious Values and the Future of America,* edited by R. Van
> Allen (1978)

The votes cast by black members of Congress on issues related to Soviet
Jewry and Israel are almost perfect. They have a much better aggregate voting
record on these so-called Jewish issues than do white members of Congress.

> —Hyman Bookbinder, Washington representative of the American Jewish
> Committee, quoted in *Moment,* May 1981

I'm not unaware of basic trends and developments—but I do reject the
notion that our agendas are that far apart, that our interests are so far apart, that
our antagonisms are so great that we have to operate on the premise that black-
Jewish cooperation is not possible anymore. I reject that premise.

> —Hyman Bookbinder, quoted in *Moment,* May 1981

The main impetus of black resentment of Jews as Jews seems to be that black people do not perceive Jews as vulnerable.

> —Ellen Willis, author, *Beginning to See the Light: Pieces of a Decade* (1981)

The black leader who opened my eyes the most was probably Malcolm X. He gave me a great understanding of the black movement. . . ." Do you think, Mr. King," he said to me, "that if you were my color, you'd have your job? In your wildest dreams?" That put things in perspective for me. Malcolm was the first to say to me, "I never see my people in a commercial. Did you ever think about that, Larry?"

> —Larry King, radio and television talk show host, *Tell It to the King* (1988)

Yiddish epithets have a way of seeming harmless even when they are not. . . . Jackie Mason cannot have it both ways and neither can we. Either we forgive Jesse Jackson for using an epithet like Hymietown—since Jews have equally raunchy terms for blacks—or we hold Jesse and our own to the same standard of humanism in discourse. We cannot undo the trauma that led us to construct the shvartzer [Yiddish for black]. But we can take the first step toward experiencing ourselves—and black people—as we really are by retiring the word.

> —Richard Goldstein, journalist, discussing Jackie Mason calling David Dinkins a "fancy shvartzer," *Village Voice*, October 17, 1989

As a feminist and a Jew, I am asking women of color not to abandon us as we assert our Jewishness, not to hear this assertion as a lowered vigilance against racism.

> —Melanie Kaye Kantrowitz, author and activist, "To Be a Radical Jew in the Late 20th Century" in *The Tribe of Dina: A Jewish Woman's Anthology*, edited by Melanie Kaye Kantrowitz and Irena Klepfisz (1989)

Dialogue has taught me that each group inaccurately perceives the negative power of the other. Blacks are not really in a position to hurt Jews, but because of their superior numbers and a few high-profile anti-Semites, Jews fear them. Jews are not really in a position to hurt blacks, but blacks believe we are determined to keep them down.

> —Letty Cottin Pogrebin, author and activist, "Ain't We Both Women?" in *Deborah, Golda, and Me: Being Female and Jewish in America* (1991)

A dreamer came into our midst who stood on this pulpit, who ignited the hopes and aspirations of his brothers and sisters. His nation. He paid for those dreams with his life. Twenty-three years later, how can we recapture that capacity to dream and to strive, to quest and to love? Surrounded by grinding poverty, tragic hopelessness and cynicism, how can we pray today? What has happened to the dream?

> —Rabbi Marshall T. Meyer, human rights activist, founder of the Seminario Rabinico Latinoamericano, and rabbi of B'nai Jeshurun in New York City, speaking at Ebenezer Baptist Church in Atlanta on Martin Luther King's birthday, 1991

To be Black and to be Jewish are not mutually exclusive. . . . What we want from each side is respect.

> —Robin Washington, managing editor of *The Bay State Banner* whose father was black and mother was white and Jewish and who considers himself "100 percent of both" of his heritages, "Black, Jewish . . . and Proud," *The Jewish Advocate*, January 5, 1996.

Not every fight is the result of misunderstanding. There are fights that are the results of understanding.

> —Leon Wieseltier, literary editor of *The New Republic*, "The Rift Between Blacks and Jews," *Time*, February 28, 1994

The overriding question is does America care about black life? When the nation is able to respond with a resounding YES, Farrakhan and his ilk will find themselves speaking to near empty audiences.

> —Julius Lester, professor of Judaic Studies, history, and English, quoted in *Reform Judaism*, Fall 1994

Demagogues understand that Jews are white folks whose skin you can get under. Baiting them gets a rise out of at least a part of the white establishment, no small thing for aggrieved blacks to whom no one listens. Out of their peculiar mix of insecurity and idealism, Jews do listen. . . . Others show far less concern, and, truth to tell, some of them don't care much for Jews, either.

> —James Sleeper, urban affairs columnist and author, "Writers and Editors Discuss Anti-Semitism," a symposium held on May 5 and 6, 1994, at the 92nd Street Y in New York City, reprinted as "Is There a Cure for Anti-Semitism?" *Partisan Review*, Summer 1994

Farrakhan has won. He is not just at the table. It is his table.

> —Charles Krauthammer, columnist, after the Million Man March in Washington, D.C., *The Washington Post*, October 20, 1995

On this stage, Jesse Jackson illuminated the sad trajectory of his career and, perhaps symbolically, of the traditional civil rights leadership. It was a scene of "Blue Angel"-style pathos: a man who had once marched with [Dr. Martin Luther] King and run for president, reduced to warm-up act for the strutting popinjay that Jackson himself had once, long ago, brought to the national scene.

> —Charles Krauthammer columnist, about the validation of Louis Farrakhan at the Million Man March in Washington D.C., *The Washington Post*, October 20, 1995

The reactions I have read, heard and seen by some Jews to the [O. J.] Simpson verdict demonstrate painfully to me that we Jews still have much work to do on Jewish-black relations and not all of it is external

> —Alan M. Dershowitz, law professor, appellate lawyer, activist, and author, quoted in *Jerusalem Report*, November 16, 1995

As the controversy surrounding the role of Louis Farrakhan in the Million Man March underscored once again, the greatest story of unrequited love in American political life may be the relationship between blacks and Jews.

> —Joshua Muravchik, resident scholar at the American Enterprise Institute, "Facing Up to Black Anti-Semitism," *Commentary*, December 1995

Did not many Jewish participants in the civil rights movement love the blacks as a first child loves the second, basking in their role of benefactor and protector, and unwittingly inviting the resentment that is ever directed at the self-conscious doer of good deeds?

> —Joshua Muravchik, "Facing Up to Black Anti-Semitism," *Commentary*, December 1995

The redistribution of wealth and privilege helps explain the friction between blacks and Jews. For all the historic talk about commonality in persecution, our statuses are today sharply different. Jews still vote liberal and talk about social justice; meanwhile, we do just fine. I think blacks understand this about us better than we do.

> —Philip Weiss, journalist, "Letting Go: A Personal Inquiry," *New York*, January 29, 1996

Today a black church, tomorrow a synagogue. Casual Jews become Jewish casualties.

> —Rabbi Marc Schneier, president of the Foundation for Ethnic Understanding, responding to the series of arsons destroying thirty black churches in the South, quoted in *Newsday*, June 19, 1996 (The Foundation created the "From the Ashes" Fund to help rebuild the churches.)

To be Jewish and Black and interracial — is to occupy a three-tier standpoint position that is inherently political but neither an essentialist idea nor a constructionist social category; it is a standpoint position from which to challenge racialist nationalism and misguided prejudice.

> —Katya Gibel Azoulay, professor of anthropology, *Black, Jewish and Interracial* (1998)

CROWN HEIGHTS

The Crown Heights pogrom is the most disgusting example of anti-Semitism ever to confront us. Remember that what is occurring here is occurring notwithstanding the so-called lessons of Adolf Hitler, and is occurring with the condoning of the so-called representatives of your people.

> —Norman Rosenbaum, activist brother of the Jewish victim who was slain by rioters in Crown Heights, speaking to Yeshiva University students after the 1992 verdict (of acquittal) for Lemrick Nelson, the sole suspect in the Rosenbaum murder, quoted in *Jewish Power* by J. J. Goldberg (1996)

I will not play the game of "there are two sides to every story." Sometimes there is only one side to a story and in the case of Crown Heights it is very simple. Thugs rioted, Jews were injured, one was murdered, the police and the mayor stood idly by and Yankel Rosenbaum's blood is on all their hands.

> —Joseph R. Rackman, attorney and columnist, *Broward Jewish World*, August 6–12, 1993

I have known him [David Dinkins] for 15 years and to call him an anti-Semite is just unacceptable . . . if he's not good for the Jewish community, I'm not sure who is.

> —Herbert Block, assistant to New York City Mayor David Dinkins and his liaison to the Jewish community, quoted in *Jerusalem Report*, January 14, 1993

There is nothing fundamental in Black or Jewish identity that requires antagonism between the two communities. The tensions that do exist are driven by competition for turf, for power. Economic disparity, lack of jobs, inadequate housing and health care — these are the real enemy, not David Dinkins and not each other.

> —Rabbi Balfour Brickner, rabbi emeritus of the Stephen Wise Free Synagogue in New York City, *Tikkun* Roundtable: "Beyond Crown Heights," *Tikkun*, January/February 1993

We look at Crown Heights and we say it was an aberration in black-Jewish relations. It was a tribal conflict, a turf battle between two groups. That's not Kristallnacht.

> —David Luchins, senior aide to Senator Daniel Patrick Moynihan (D-N.Y.), quoted in *Jewish Power* by J. J. Goldberg (1996)

Ironically, each group [blacks and Jews] thinks that the other group is more powerful than it really is.

> —Betty Ehrenberg, executive director of the Institute for Public Affairs of the Union of Orthodox Jewish Congregations, *Tikkun* Roundtable: "Beyond Crown Heights," *Tikkun*, January/February 1993

The great leaders of the great Jewish organizations did nothing and said next to nothing. For the first time in history, a Jew was lynched on the streets of New York, and the great Jewish leaders didn't even come to his funeral.

> —Sidney Zion, journalist, "Pogrom in Brooklyn" in *Trust Your Mother but Cut the Cards* (1993)

You wouldn't have perceived it as a local issue if it had happened at Temple Emanu-El [historic reform synagogue on Fifth Avenue].

> —Sidney Zion, speaking to Abraham Foxman of the Anti-Defamation League, "Pogrom in Brooklyn" in *Trust Your Mother but Cut the Cards* (1993)

Without our reopening the debate over how quickly we might have intervened, one thing is certain: At no time during ADL's discussions and decisions on Crown Heights did the social status or religious practices of the riot victims play any part.

> —Abraham H. Foxman, national director, Anti-Defamation League, responding to a *New York* magazine article characterizing the ADL's actions during the 1991 riot, letter to the editor, *New York*, August 11, 1997

I am sure that during the Anti-Defamation League's policy discussions regarding the Crown Heights riots, Abe Foxman never articulated any negative feeling about the social status or the religious practices of the Lubavitch Hasidim. I'm equally sure that no other executive of a major Jewish organization did, either. However, the fact remains that the overall response to the riots by the organized Jewish community was curiously slow and muted. Without "reopening the debate" . . . I must say that I have done dozens of interviews with Hasidic residents of Crown Heights since the riots, and to a person, they believe that when it really counted, they were abandoned.

> —Craig Horowitz, journalist, reply to Abe Foxman's letter to the editor, *New York*, August 11, 1997

People will attack people, and that is the way it is. But the police are supposed to be there to protect you, and they weren't.

> —Isaac Bitton, young Hasidic man attacked during the 1991 Crown Heights riots, settling a lawsuit against New York City for negligence and violation of civil rights, quoted in *The Jewish Week*, January 23, 1998

We've come a long way. We have many lines of communication open.

> —Rabbi Shea Hecht, Lubavitch community leader, speaking at a August 16, 1997, news conference on the sixth anniversary of the Crown Heights riots, with boxing promoter Don King announcing $100,000 to be distributed to several educational organizations to buy computers and other educational aids for the Jewish and black communities, quoted in *The Jewish Week*, August 22, 1997

❖ BOOKS ❖

(see also Literature, Poetry, Writing)

Wherever I may die, let me be buried not among the rich and famous but among plain Jewish people, the workers, the common folk, so that my tombstone may honor the simple graves around me, and the simple graves honor mine, even as the plain people honored their folk writer in his lifetime. . . . The best monument for me will be if my books are read.

> —Sholem Aleichem, Yiddish writer, from his Ethical Will to his family, quoted in *Ethical Wills: A Modern Jewish Treasury*, edited by Jack Riemer and Nathaniel Stampfer (1986)

In my view, books should be brought to the doorstep like electricity, or like milk in England: They should be considered utilities, and their cost should be appropriately minimal.

> —Joseph Brodsky, Russian-born poet exiled to the United States in 1972 who won the Nobel Prize in 1987 and was appointed poet laureate of the United States in 1991, quoted in "Remembering Joseph Brodsky," *Newsday*, April 21, 1996

For Soviet Jewish activists, *Exodus* was probably more meaningful than even the Bible. . . . They didn't treat it as a literary experience, it was history—the only knowledge they had of the Jewish experience.

> —Jerry Goodman, former executive director of the National Conference on Soviet Jewry, recalling the impact of Leon Uris's novel *Exodus*, which was banned in the Soviet Union, quoted in *Challenging the Kremlin: The So-*

viet Jewish Movement for Freedom 1967–1990 by Edward R. Drachman (1991)

The first priority of our nation . . . is the right to read. Educators are inundating our schools with massive surveys, innovative techniques and expensive gimmicks to combat illiteracy and improve the reading skills of our children — at the same time that our public libraries are gradually closing their doors. . . . It seems to me that especially now, when there are so many people in our city whose language is not English, whose homes are barren of books, who are daily seduced by clamorous offers of instant diversion, especially now we must hold on to something that will endure when the movie is over, the television set broken, the class dismissed for the last time.

—Bel Kaufman, author, "The Liberry," *The New York Times*, July 26, 1976

Whenever I was free to read, the great Library seemed free to receive me.

—Alfred Kazin, author and literary critic, *New York Jew* (1978)

In the way of books, I don't know about kinds; I know there are good books and bad books, it can be fiction, non-fiction . . . when it comes to books, it is its value and depth. You make an acquaintance with a book as you do with a person. After ten or fifteen pages you know with whom you have to deal. And when you have a good book, you really have something of importance. Books are as important as friends and maybe more so, because all of us are living in very limited circles; books enable us to run away from them.

—Shimon Peres, former prime minister of Israel, interviewed at Independence Hall in Philadelphia, asked about his plans to visit bookstores in New York, C-SPAN, July 4, 1996

Because of the U.N. condemnation of Israeli "aggression" and anti-Semitic rage flaring up in the Black community, many American Jews must surely be feeling more alienated than they have been in a long time; consequently, I don't think it's a moment when I can expect a book as unrestrained as this one to be indulged or even tolerated, especially in those quarters where I was not exactly hailed as the Messiah to begin with. I'm afraid that the temptation to quote single lines out of the entire fictional context will be just about overwhelming on upcoming Saturday mornings. The rabbis have got their indignation to stroke, just as I do. And there are sentences in that book upon which a man could construct a pretty indignant sermon.

—Philip Roth, novelist, interview by George Plimpton in *The New York Times Book Review* when *Portnoy's Complaint* was reviewed, 1969

A film must act, a book has time to think and wonder. There is the essential difference which keeps me, for all my love of movie-going and film-writing, still a confirmed novel writer and an enthusiastic novel reader. In the flush of TV spectaculars, wider and wider screeneramas, and all the rest of our frightful, fruitful mechanical advancements, the book is still the essential civilizing influence, able to penetrate the unknowns of human aspiration.

> —Budd Schulberg, novelist and screenwriter, "Why Write It if You Can't Sell It to Pictures?" *Saturday Review*, September 3, 1955

What kind of a society is this? People don't read books anymore. They open television or the Internet. What about the feeling of a book? You read a book with your fingers, not just your eyes.

> —Elie Wiesel, Nobel laureate and author, quoted in *The Christian Science Monitor*, December 10, 1996

We can glimpse God in other human beings, in the marvels of the world, and in the depths of one's own soul, but what shaped the history of Judaism was a book. Judaism is an astonishing testimony to the magical power of words, transmitted through generations, to alter lives and change history.

> —Rabbi David J. Wolpe, author, *Why Be Jewish?* (1995)

❖ BOSNIA-HERZEGOVINA ❖

Fifty years ago, we watched with anguish . . . as the world stood by and did nothing to stop atrocities . . . Today as we watch the carnage in the former Yugoslavia, we cannot remain silent.

> —Miles Lerman, Chairman of the U.S. Holocaust Memorial Museum, quoted in *Jewish Telegraphic Agency Daily News Bulletin*, August 4, 1995

Tell your prime minister to acknowledge Bosnia's past, or else I'll do it myself and it will be much stronger. . . . We have done more for your country, more than anyone else in the world. . . . Unless your present government is prepared to acknowledge that some Bosnians were collaborators with Nazi Germany and wore the uniforms of the SS, this support cannot last forever.

> —Miles Lerman, speaking to Ambassador Alkalaj, Bosnia-Herzegovina's ambassador to the United States, after an ecumenical prayer service designed to call attention to ethnic cleansing in the former Yugoslavia, quoted in *Jewish Telegraphic Agency Daily News Bulletin*, August 4, 1995

To the best of my knowledge, the Jewish religion does not prescribe loving your enemy. Yet proportionately many more Jews than Christians act on this principle. Our enemies never have. The Serbs helped us in World War II, and have every reason to be our friends. [Croatia's] Tudjman and [Bosnia's] Izatbegovic will hate us no matter what we do. Let us shed no tears for them.

—Yohanan Ramati, head of Jerusalem Institute for Western Defense, *Jerusalem Post*, September 1993

We in the United States represent a certain moral aspect of history. A great nation owes its greatness not only to its military power, but also to its moral consciousness, awareness. What would future generations say about us, all of us here in this land, if we do nothing?

—Elie Wiesel, Nobel laureate and author, speaking in an Oval Office meeting with President Bill Clinton about the dispatch of a U.S. peacekeeping mission to Bosnia, quoted in *The New York Times*, December 14, 1995

❖ BUSINESS ❖

(see also Careers, Economics)

A speculator is one who thinks and plans for a future event — and acts before it occurs

—Bernard Baruch, financier, statesman, and self-described speculator, quoted in *A Nation in Torment: The Great American Depression, 1929–1939* by Edward Robb Ellis (1970)

Wrestling and arbitrage are both solitary sports in which you live or die by your deeds, and you do it very visibly.

—Ivan Boesky, arbitrageur (later convicted of insider trading), quoted in a 1984 interview with Connie Brock in *Atlantic Monthly*, cited in *Den of Thieves* by James B. Stewart (1992)

Greed is all right, by the way. I want you to know that. I think greed is healthy. You can be greedy and still feel good about yourself.

—Ivan Boesky, remarks as the 1986 commencement speaker at the University of California Business School (the students responded with laughs and applause), quoted in *Den of Thieves* by James B. Stewart (1992)

The goose that lays the golden egg has been considered a most valuable possession. But even more profitable is the privilege of taking the golden eggs laid by somebody else's goose. The investment banker and their associates now enjoy that privilege. They control the people through the people's own money.

—Louis D. Brandeis, attorney and judge, "The Use of Other People's Money," *Harper's Weekly*, 1914

These guys would hand out samples at nursery school if they were allowed.

—Richard Cohen, columnist, discussing the tobacco industry, *Washington Post*, October 20, 1995

Nor do I believe that the vast private corporations of the United States are suitable to the needs of these times. If a visitor should come to this country from another planet, would he not find it strange that in this country so much is permitted to private corporations without their having commensurate responsibility?

—Albert Einstein, Nobel Prize–winning theoretical physicist and humanist, quoted in *Atlantic Monthly*, November 1945

This my father told me as a little boy. In a situation which is devoid of morality, try to be a man and do something worthwhile.

—Aaron Feuerstein, president and owner of Malden Mills Industries Inc. in Massachusetts, quoting the sage Hillel as he explained his decision to pay salaries of workers in his factory after it was destroyed by fire, quoted in "Plume of Hope Rises from Factory Ashes" by David Herszehorn, *The New York Times*, December 16, 1995

I think what's happened today is you have some of your modern-day CEOs who consider what I did, which I thought was right and normal, they consider it abnormal. And there's a big reaction going around the country against the excesses of some of the CEOs and it's for that reason I'm receiving the publicity and celebrity status that I'm enjoying. It's not that I deserve it because that's the way I've always been. It's a poor reflection, unfortunately, on our times.

—Aaron Feuerstein, accepting the Emma Lazarus Award from the American Jewish Historical Society, May 1996, quoted in *Boston Jewish Advocate*, May 10, 1996

It is economic treason to shop carelessly.

—Edward A. Filene, one of the Filene Brothers who owned Filene's Automatic Bargain Basement in the 1920s in Boston, quoted in *Merchant Princes* by Leon Harris (1979)

The consumer is protected from being exploited by one seller by the existence of another seller from whom he can buy and who is eager to sell to him.

Alternative sources of supply protect the consumer far more effectively than all the Ralph Naders of the world.

> —Milton and Rose Friedman, economists and authors, *Free to Choose: A Personal Statement* (1980)

Can you name any of those additions to our well-being that have come from government? It wasn't government that produced the microwave. It wasn't government that produced the improved automobiles. It wasn't government that produced computers that led to the information age. On the other hand, consider our problems. Our major problems are not economic. Our major problems are social.

> —Milton Friedman, *Booknotes* interview with Brian Lamb, C-SPAN, November 20, 1994

Lack of profits is the hallowed American excuse for abolishing anything.

> —Harry Golden, journalist *Ess, Ess, Mein Kindt* (1966)

Some people for ethnic reasons may get through this period easier than others. For example, I have never felt better or slept sounder, but I do have an advantage over some of my peers at other firms—I am the beneficiary of 5,000 years of persecution. This market will not get me down. It is just a minor challenge.

> —Alan C. Greenberg, chairman of Bear Stearns, from an October 17, 1990, memo acknowledging a "tough period," in *Memos From The Chairman* (1996)

Government regulation is not an alternative means of protecting the customer. It does not build quality into goods, or accuracy into information. Its sole "contribution" is to substitute force and fear for incentive as the "protector" of the consumer. The euphemisms of government press releases to the contrary notwithstanding, the basis of regulation is armed force. At the bottom of the endless pile of paperwork which characterizes all regulation lies a gun.

> —Alan Greenspan, economist, "The Assault on Integrity" in *Capitalism: The Unknown Ideal* by Ayn Rand (1967)

Slowly and steadily we are creating a new class system, starting at birth, through early education, and finally through colleges and professional and graduate schools. The people on Wall Street who today make such horrendous decisions to close down plants in small towns do it more readily because they have never known the people they are damaging.

> —David Halberstam, journalist, "Coming in From the Cold War," *The Washington Monthly*, January/February 1991

When I conceived Barbie, I believed it was important to a little girl's self-esteem to play with a doll that has breasts. Now I find it even more important to return that self-esteem to women who have lost theirs.

> —Ruth Mosko Handler, inventor of the Barbie doll, cofounder with her husband of Mattel, Inc. and manufacturer of breast prostheses, 1980s press interview, cited in *Jewish Women in America: An Historical Encyclopedia*, edited by Paula E. Hyman and Deborah Dash Moore (1997)

Thirteen million children are born in China every year. Imagine if each of them will someday purchase a diamond.

> —Eli Izhakoff, president of the New York Diamond Dealers Club and the World Federation of Diamond Bourses, commenting on his industry's outreach to China for its potential as a consumer market, quoted in *Lifestyles*, pre-Spring 1996

We're bigger than U.S. Steel.

> —Meyer Lansky, Jewish gangster who led organized crime syndicates that flourished between the two world wars, quoted in *But—He Was Good to His Mother* by Robert A. Rockaway (1993)

Being interested in other people's ideas for the purpose of saying, "We can do it better," is not copying. Innovation doesn't always mean inventing the wheel each time; innovation can mean a whole new way of looking at old things.

> —Estee Lauder, founder of Estee Lauder Cosmetics, "What I Didn't Learn From Business School or Books" in *The Book of Business Wisdom*, edited by Peter Krass (1997)

There is always only one person on top who must be the final authority . . . at the office, the name of the game is Lauder, imperial as that may sound. Running a business is rarely a matter of group vote.

> —Estee Lauder, "What I Didn't Learn From Business School or Books" in *The Book of Business Wisdom*, edited by Peter Krass (1997)

"Millionaire"

> —Ralph Lauren, fashion designer and executive, aspiration listed under the name of Ralph Lifshitz (Lauren) in the 1957 De Witt Clinton High School Yearbook, quoted in *Ralph Lauren: The Man Behind the Mystique* by Jeffrey A. Trachtenberg (1988)

Today, still, the American businessman is an unheroic character in the literature of television . . . some of it deservedly. But there are true American heroes in business.

> —Norman Lear, television producer, interview on *Straight Talk With Roger Ailes*, America's Talking Cable Network, October 9, 1995

The emphasis has been on enhancing what you have and acquiring what you need.

> —Gerald Levin, CEO of Time-Warner, discussing the acquisition of Ted Turner's $7.5 billion empire, quoted in "The New Establishment," *Vanity Fair*, October 1997

While I resisted the temptation for a while, somewhere between Queens and Wall Street I was losing track of [those] values. Throughout my college and graduate studies, I believe, I did not even hear the word ethics. In the big business environment of the late seventies, morality was not an issue.

> —Dennis Levine, Drexel Burnham Lambert employee who was convicted for insider trading, quoted in *New York*, September 16, 1991

The [insider trading] game is fun, Bob, it's easy. . . . The government is stupid. Nobody with any brains is in that operation. They make only 30 grand, if that.

> —Dennis Levine, conversation with a friend who became an eventual accomplice at Lazard Freres, quoted in *Den of Thieves* by James B. Stewart (1992)

In the process of deal making, the prime question is getting the deal done; the focus is not so much on the continuing relationship of the parties . . . as it is on the transaction itself. The "deal" syndrome — the atomized transaction for which the law firm's fee will be greatly enlarged as part of the package if the deal is accomplished — tends to give lawyers an unprecedented stake in getting the deal done even if in their professional judgment there may be a doubt as to whether the deal should be done.

> —Sol M. Linowitz, lawyer, diplomat, and businessman, *The Betrayed Profession: Lawyering at the End of the Twentieth Century*, written with Martin Mayer (1994)

You cannot ruin a country by conserving its life. You can ruin a country only by stupidity, waste and greed.

> —Walter Lippmann, journalist, writing in support of minimum-wage legislation, *The New Republic*, March 27, 1915

I got a little sidetracked in the '80s with other things that were taking my time.

> —Michael Milken, former Drexel Burnham Lambert executive, referring to the lengthy SEC investigations that led to his 1990 guilty plea to six felonies, quoted in *The Wall Street Journal*, June 30, 1995

Death of a Salesman questioned the ethos of the business civilization, which the play intimates has no real respect for individual human beings, whereas the going mythology was quite the opposite: in that nobody of any competence ever fails and that everything was pretty sound and terrific for everybody. So to put a play on where somebody who believes in the system as Willy Loman does to his dying minute, ends up a suicide, it was rather a shock.

> —Arthur Miller, Pulitzer Prize–winning playwright, quoted in *Red Scare: An Oral History* by Griffen Fariello (1995)

Customers learned that the business hours were governed by orthodox law, and some were aware of the anomaly that one of the largest television retailers in the United States did not watch television or own a television set.

> —Jerome Mintz, author, discussing the 47th Street Photo enterprise in *Hasidic People* (1992)

Modern accountants who paint an overly optimistic picture of the financial health of the company, or who ignore the societal costs of polluting the environment, are much like the merchants of the Talmudic period who painted their old utensils to fool customers into thinking that they were new. Avoiding gnevat da'at [literally, the "stealing of knowledge," that is, stealing trust, deception] is, of course, not only good ethics, but in the long run good business. Just as a new coat of paint will quickly peel, financial window-dressing is almost always a self-defeating strategy.

> —Moses Pava, author and professor of accounting and business, "The Bottom Line," *Jerusalem Report*, October 18, 1997

Does she . . . or doesn't she?

> —Shirley Polykoff, advertising copywriter who created this line for Clairol in the first advertising campaign to try to sell hair dye to a mass audience, 1955 (She also wrote the line "Is it true blondes have more fun?")

We have two religions in this country, fundamentalism and money, and I don't know which is worse. I don't see the death of greed. I see people worried that they may have come along a couple of years too late.

> —Felix G. Rohatyn, senior partner at Lazard Freres and chairman of New York's Municipal Assistance Corporation, quoted in *Esquire*, June 1988

It is better to sit in the back row and be discovered than to sit in the front row and be found out.

> —Irwin Rosen, Harvard Square bookshop owner [Mandrake Books] who shunned most of the technological and marketing conventions of recent years, quoted in his obituary, *The New York Times*, June 30, 1997

The most wonderful thing about a bull market is that it creates its own hopes. If people buy because they think stocks will rise, their act of buying sends up the price of stocks. This causes them to buy still further, and sends the dizzy dance off on another round. And unlike a game of cards or dice, no one loses what the winners gain. Everybody gets a prize! Of course, the prizes are all on paper and would disappear if everyone tried to cash them in. . . . Learn the first rule of propery values: "A thing is worth what people think it is worth." Unfortunately, to be successful this has to be applied in connection with the second rule, which is as hard to follow in practice as belling the cat or catching birds by putting salt on their tails: "Don't be the sucker left holding the bag."

> —Paul A. Samuelson, economist, *Economics* (1948)

My dear Eddie, this is a company of men, not of charts.

> —David Sarnoff, businessman and pioneer in the broadcasting industry responding to a 1939 request from Edward L. Bernays, a pioneer in public relations, to see an organization chart of NBC, quoted in *Sarnoff: An American Success* by Carl Dreher (1977)

In my investing, I have often done the right thing for the wrong reason.

> —George Soros, international investor, quoted in *The New Republic*, January 10 & 17, 1994

Over the years, people often told me that I ran the business by the seat of my pants. If it were only true that I ran my business purely by instinct, how much easier my life would have been. While it's true that instinct played a part, I tempered my natural talents with hard work, training, and experience. Instinct will get you started, but it won't sustain you: after all, your competitors have instincts, too.

> —Lillian Vernon, founder, chairman, and CEO of the specialty catalog company that bears her name, *An Eye for Winners* (1996)

The only way you find out what is going on is to talk to your customers. That's true in banking; it's true in advertising; it's true in development.

> —James Wolfensohn, president of the World Bank, quoted in *Singular Voices: Conversations With Americans Who Make a Difference* by Barbaralee Diamonstein (1997)

❖ CAPITAL PUNISHMENT ❖

*W*hen I requested in Washington that these executions be put off so that they would not occur on the Jewish Sabbath, the request was granted by a barbarian who instead of postponing the hour of death, pushed it up so they could be done away with before the beginning of the Sabbath.

> —Emanuel Bloch, attorney for Julius and Ethel Rosenberg, commenting after their execution in 1951, *Ethel Rosenberg: Behind the Myth* by Ilene Philips (1988)

If John Paul Penry is "put to sleep," as one friend of Penry's put it, it will not be because of his crimes alone—only eleven people were executed in the United States in all of 1988. It will be because he picked the wrong person to kill, he was born to the wrong parents, and the wrong lawyer represented him.

> —Alan M. Dershowitz, law professor, appellate lawyer, activist, and author, discussing the 1989 U.S. Supreme Court case about whether it would be cruel and unusual punishment for the state of Texas to execute a mentally retarded man convicted of rape and murder, *Contrary to Popular Opinion* (1992)

I shall struggle against capital punishment in even the most extreme and dastardly of cases until I have demonstrated to me the infallibility of mortal men.

> —Rabbi Maurice Eisendrath, president of the Union of American Hebrew Congregations, "Thou Shalt Not Kill—Period," 1964, in *The Challenge of Shalom*, edited by Murray Polner and Naomi Goodman (1994)

It's a terrible commentary on society, but I'm afraid we have reached a point where some people, by their acts, do give up the right to survive.

> —Diane Feinstein, mayor of San Francisco, quoted in the *Los Angeles Times*, February 17, 1990

In light of the circumstances, I feel that I must pass such sentence upon the principals in this diabolical conspiracy to destroy a God-fearing nation, which will demonstrate with finality that this nation's security must remain inviolate; that traffic in military secrets, whether promoted by slavish devotion to a foreign ideology or by a desire for monetary gains must cease.

> —Judge Irving R. Kaufman, presiding judge in United States vs. Rosenbergs and Sobell, speaking at the sentencing of Julius and Ethel Rosenberg to death in 1951, quoted in *Invitation to an Inquest* by Walter and Miriam Schneir (1965)

O. J.'s real guarantee against capital punishment is his celebrity, not his wealth. . . . Because O. J. Simpson's celebrity means that for most Americans he is a flesh-and-blood human being. . . . Even if convicted of murder, he'll never be an abstract symbol of evil like the typical death penalty customer with three names—Robert Alton Harris, Rickey Ray Rector, John Wayne Gacy et al. For once, in the competition of humanization between the murderer and his victims, the murderer would have an unbeatable edge.

> —Michael Kinsley, journalist, "What Americans Won't Do," *Time*, June 27, 1994

Mr. Darrow was pleading not so much for Dick and me as he was pleading for the human race. For love, for charity, for understanding. Especially for understanding.

> —Nathan F. Leopold, Jr., sentenced, with Richard Loeb, to life imprisonment for the kidnap and murder of young Bobby Frank on May 21, 1924, *Life Plus 99 Years* (1957) (They were represented by Clarence Darrow, whose efforts helped them to avoid the death penalty.)

I'm for capital punishment. You've got to execute people. How else are they going to learn?

> —Mort Sahl, satirist, attributed

❖ CAREERS ❖

I always told myself that I was talking to my friends. I thought that was a pretty good deal, sitting at the ballpark and watching a game and telling friends of yours who weren't there what they were missing.

> —Mel Allen, former longtime broadcaster for the New York Yankees, opening day at Yankee Stadium, April 1995, quoted in "How About that Mel?" by Mike Lupica, *New York Daily News*, June 1, 1996

I didn't want to play Bogart, I didn't want to play John Wayne. I wanted to be the schnook. The guy with the glasses who doesn't get the girl but who's amusing.

> —Woody Allen, actor, writer, and director, quoted in "The Imperfectionist" by John Lahr, *The New Yorker*, December 9, 1996

It's fabulous. You talk to beautiful girls. They make you happy. It's the best business you can be in.

> —Jean Paul Amsellem, "the father of hairdressing in Washington" who was Jacqueline Kennedy's hairdresser when she was First Lady, quoted in *Forward*, January 19, 1996

What else can I do? It's too late to become a doctor.

> —Emanuel Azenberg, Broadway producer, reflecting on his return to Broadway at age 63, quoted in *The New York Times*, November 2, 1997

I have a lot of regrets about things I did and said, for the way I pushed and shoved and bullied during those hysterical years. My only defense, which is no defense, is the pressure.

> —Milton Berle, comedian and actor, remembering the prime of his career, quoted in *The Jewish Comedy Catalog* by Darryl Lyman (1989)

You know who I used to be. Max Bialystock. King of Broadway. Six plays running at once. Lunch at Delmonico's. Two-hundred-dollar suits. . . . Look at me now. I'm wearing a cardboard belt. Used to have thousands of investors begging, pleading to put their money in a Max Bialystock production. Look at my investors now. Hundreds of little old ladies. Stopping off at Max Bialystock's office to grab a last thrill on their way to the cemetery.

> —Max Bialystock (played by Zero Mostel) in *The Producers* by Mel Brooks (1968)

The kind of comedy I do isn't, like, going to change the world; but certain areas of society make me unhappy, and satirizing them—aside from being lucrative—provides a release for me.

> —Lenny Bruce, satirist, quoted in *The Essential Lenny Bruce*, edited by John Cohen (1967)

Now see, in a Jewish family, when an only son goes wrong, it's a terrible thing—a tragedy. I mean, if you have four sons, if two go to jail and one goes to the electric chair, well, one guy can still go on to be a lawyer or a doctor. But here I was the only son, with four sisters—and I was going to be a songwriter? Terrible. I was going bad. But I was determined . . . I was going to make it.

> —Sammy Cahn, lyricist, 1971 interview with Max Wilk, "Bei Mir Bist Du Schon" in *They're Playing Our Song* (1997)

And so I began to sing my songs, and in between one song and another I realized I could talk to people about Judaism, because when they sing their hearts are open. I made a living singing.

> —Rabbi Shlomo Carlebach, 1993 interview with Michael Lerner, *Tikkun*, September–October 1997

I earn everything I make. I'm not getting nothing for nothing. . . . I put in an eight-hour day in two hours on stage.

> —Bob Dylan, singer and songwriter, 1978, quoted in *No Direction Home: The Life and Music of Bob Dylan* by Robert Shelton (1986)

I don't even know what I did that was so wrong, I was nothing more than an agent. I brought people together who wanted consensual sex. What's wrong with that?

> —Heidi Fleiss, "the Beverly Hills madam," before her sentencing in which she faced a minimum of seven years behind bars, quoted in *New York*, December 4, 1995

I was a Jewish child in the Midwest, and Father Coughlin used to frighten the life out of me! . . . In later life, I read endlessly about the rise of the Nazis, and the thing that stuck in my mind is that Joseph Goebbels came to prominence through radio, spewing the same kind of racial nonsense as Bob Grant, except that it was aimed at Jews. So I could not remain on a station that went out and recruited a racist ideologue like Grant.

> —Arthur Frommer, author of travel books, speaking about quitting his weekly radio show on WOR radio in New York, in protest against the station's

decision to hire talk-radio host Bob Grant, quoted in the *New York Daily News*, May 13, 1996

I wanted to live in a big tragedy-comedy Dostoevskian universe; that was my ideal. A universe where the characters would all rush up and confront each other. A universe where everybody was involved in seeking God and all the heroes were holy idiots. Everybody else at Columbia was like very practical and going to business school.

—Allen Ginsberg, poet, quoted in *Allen Ginsberg in America* by Jane Kramer (1968)

I pray that I may be all that she would have been had she lived in an age when women could aspire and achieve.

—Ruth Bader Ginsburg, speaking at the White House when President Clinton nominated her to the U.S. Supreme Court, quoted in *People*, June 28, 1993 (She was seventeen when her mother Celia Bader died of cancer.)

It is not the way of a Jew to make his work like there was no human being to suffer when it's done badly. A coat is not a piece of cloth only. The tailor is connected to the one who wears it and he should not forget it.

—"Shmuel" Goldman, member of the Aliyah Senior Citizens' Center in California, commenting on his work as a tailor, quoted in *Number Our Days* by Barbara Myerhoff (1978)

You know, I'm still a licensed New York City taxi driver. I renew my taxi license because I expect one day to be poor again.

—Al Goldstein, publisher of *Screw* magazine, quoted in *New York*, February 10, 1997

What I might have become if I didn't play an instrument—never stopped to think about that. Judging from the neighborhood where I lived, if it hadn't been for the clarinet, I might just as easily have been a gangster.

—Benny Goodman, clarinetist and bandleader, quoted in *Swing, Swing, Swing: The Life and Times of Benny Goodman* by Ross Firestone (1993)

Our first desire is to promote from within. If somebody with an MBA degree applies for a job, we will certainly not hold it against them, but we are really looking for people with PSD degrees. They built this firm and there are plenty around because our competition seems to be restricting themselves to MBA's. [PSD stands for poor, smart and a deep desire to become rich.]

—Alan C. Greenberg, chairman of Bear Stearns, from a 1981 memo circulated to all general and limited partners, in *Memos from the Chairman* (1996)

Friends and relatives sympathized with my mother because she was the parent of a big gawk who cared more for baseball. . . . I was Mrs. Greenberg's disgrace.

> —Hank Greenberg, baseball player, quoted in *Detroit Jewish Chronicle*, April 12, 1935

Bob Dylan proved to me that you didn't have to be an opera singer to make a living . . . you didn't even have to be coherent.

> —Arlo Guthrie, folksinger and songwriter, interview with Linda Ellerbee on *Later With Bob Costas*, 1991

I never thought of doing anything else, which is one of my limitations.

> —Al Hirschfeld, illustrator, responding to the question of why he is an artist, quoted in *Washington Jewish Week*, June 12, 1997

Don't allow yourself to "go stale" on your act. Keep up your enthusiasm! There is nothing more contagious than exuberant enthusiasm, and it is sure to "get" an audience.

> —Harry Houdini, performer, quoted in *Houdini on Magic*, edited by Walter B. Gibson and Morris N. Young (1953)

I'd just been tutoring Aimee Rubin for an exam—for nothing. I felt like a kid suddenly asked if he wanted to play for money! . . . And that's how I started my career.

> —Stanley H. Kaplan, founder of the worldwide network of test-preparatory centers, recalling the day he was called to the principal's office and asked if he would be willing to tutor students for twenty-five cents an hour, quoted in *Newsday*, November 23, 1995

I can't believe all the recognition I get. . . . I was in Israel at the Wailing Wall, and this old rabbi was there praying. He looked at me and says, "So what's with Perot?" I have a nice franchise and I totally enjoy it. I feel like I'm part of history.

> —Larry King, radio and television talk show host, quoted in the *New York Daily News*, July 2, 1995

I'm trying to retire a little, to come in at eight instead of six. But I wake up at five anyway. I'm too impatient to read or watch TV. I'm thinking of all the disasters that could be happening. I have no hobbies. I need Zabar's more than Zabar's needs me.

> —Murray Klein, reflecting on running Zabar's for forty-five years, quoted in *New York*, April 18, 1988 (Zabar's evolved from a small Jewish deli into a

giant grocery and housewares store—a New York landmark—on the Upper West Side of Manhattan.)

My father was listening to some of these [Edward R.] Murrow broadcasts which were being rebroadcast on the BBC. And one of my earliest childhood memories is that I thought, boy, that sounds good, I like the idea of doing that. I never went through the fireman stage, the stage of wanting to be a doctor. I always wanted to be a foreign correspondent.

> —Ted Koppel, journalist, recalling his family living in England as refugees from Germany during WWII, *The Charlie Rose Show*, February 2, 1996

Even women who stay home, particularly if they have children, are working.

> —Mathilde Krim, chair and cofounder of American Foundation for AIDS Research, quoted in "A New Agenda," *Working Woman*, November 1992

The ultimate takeover by a woman of a man's space.

> —Madeleine M. Kunin, three-term governor of Vermont, recalling her first day of being governor when she went into the executive bathroom for the very first time and put the toilet seat down, National Public Radio interview with Susan Stamberg, April 16, 1994

I love the religious tradition out of which I come and I love the several hundred members of the congregation I serve. The enduring frustration of my rabbinic career has been my inability to get my two loves to find and love each other.

> —Rabbi Harold S. Kushner, author and rabbi emeritus of Temple Israel in Natick, Mass., *Who Needs God* (1989)

[I'm] Just a square Jewish housewife from Sioux City, Iowa.

> —Eppie Lederer, advice columnist also known as Ann Landers, *U.S. News & World Report*, October 23, 1995

What my son is doing is more important than what I have ever done.

> —Gerald Levin, CEO of Time-Warner, speaking of his son Jonathan, a beloved teacher at William Howard Taft High School in the Bronx, who was murdered in June 1997, quoted in *Newsday*, June 4, 1997

Ambition eclipsed rationality. I was unable to find fulfillment in realistic limits. One deal was piled upon the next. The hours grew longer; the numbers grew bigger; the stakes grew more critical; the fire grew even hotter. By the time I became a managing director of Drexel, I was out of control. So was Boesky. So was Milken. So was Drexel.

—Dennis Levine, reflecting after he was freed from prison on September 8, 1988, after serving seventeen months of his sentence, quoted in *New York*, September 16, 1991

Today in America no one has to choose between religious observance and personal ambition. I really do believe that our children can pursue whatever dreams they have for success and not feel that they have to dilute their loyalty to Torah Judaism one millionth.

> —Joseph I. Lieberman, U.S. Senator (D-Conn), the first Sabbath-observant member of the Senate, speaking at Agudath Israel of America's 75th annual dinner, quoted in *The Jewish Week*, June 6, 1997

. . . the life of a working mother who lives without the constant presence and support of the father of her children is three times harder than that of any man I ever met.

> —Golda Meir, prime minister of Israel from 1969–1974, *My Life* (1975)

In this long post-eden stretch, the punishment has become the prize. . . . Stalked by technology, snared by our own creations, we have become our own worst taskmasters. We work late and work our weekends, honing our bodies, dulling our souls. Overtime is the norm. "I'm still at the office!" boasts a friend one Friday night at 10, in a tone she might have used in the past to announce she was in Paris or Hawaii. We worship a new idol: The God of Work.

> —Martha Mendelsohn, journalist, "Observing the Sabbath," *Tikkun*, May/June 1996

I have opened hundreds of courtroom doors in many states, but the excitement has never been diminished. Indeed it has grown. The challenge is ever new. The contest is ever intense. Surprise is ever present. The satisfactions of a noble calling are unique and bright.

> —Louis Nizer, trial lawyer, *My Life In Court* (1961)

Ed Sullivan came to Israel to audition the acts over there. He auditioned dancers and singers, acrobats and folk dancers—even classical musicians. I was not a wonder child but I was, age appropriate, pretty talented. Certainly not ready to star with the Philharmonic. Sullivan was a very, very nice man. But did he take me because I was cute or because I could play?

> —Itzhak Perlman, violinist, recalling the first time he came to America at age thirteen to perform on the *Ed Sullivan Show*, quoted in *Parade*, interview with James Brady, November 26, 1995

... having married a beautiful woman, fathered three beautiful children, and written some good books.

> —Chaim Potok, novelist, from his 1987 entry in "Who's Who in World Jewry" in response to the question of what made him most proud, quoted in *The God I Believe In* by Joshua O. Haberman (1994)

There aren't too many Jewish cops out there; you can go out and find a precinct that happens to have more Jewish cops than any other in town assigned there, and you still wouldn't have enough to make a minyan [quorum of ten].

> —Stefanie Rich, New York Police Department detective in the 112th precinct in Forest Hills, N.Y., quoted in *Forward*, June 21, 1996

Next to cancer, work has been the most interesting thing in my life.

> —Betty Rollin, journalist, *Am I Getting Paid for This?* (1982)

Frankly, I don't believe people think of their office as a workplace anyway. I think they think of it as a stationery store with Danish. You want to get your pastry, your envelopes, your supplies, your toilet paper, six cups of coffee, and you go home.

> —Jerry Seinfeld, actor and comedian, *SeinLanguage* (1993)

From the point of view of our history, this is a very significant thing. That a Jew can be a cop is an extraordinary American tale. That a Jew can be a cop who can then not worry about being killed tomorrow for coming forward, that's extremely significant.

> —Henry Sheinkopf, Democratic political consultant, discussing Eric Turetzky, the NYPD officer who first stepped forward to name the officers at the 70th precinct who were allegedly involved in the torture of a Haitian immigrant, thereby breaking the police department's notorious "blue wall of silence," quoted in "Rudy, the Cops and the Election" by J. J. Goldberg, *The Jewish Week*, August 22, 1997

I really love what I'm doing, but at the same time, I'd rather be married and have beautiful babies and millions of animals and eat delicious food and get as fat as I want. . . . Live! You know?

> —Alicia Silverstone, actress, quoted in *Vanity Fair*, September 1996

I think that anyone who works for money is stark raving mad, because prostitution is bad, and it doesn't matter whether you're standing on Fourteenth Street or in a boardroom for AT&T.

> —Mitch Snyder, activist on behalf of the homeless in Washington, D.C., quoted in "Saint Mitch" by Gwenda Blair, *Esquire*, December 1986

One dealer told me in 1932 that the only three things he could sell were milk, bread and greeting cards.

> —Irving Stone, founder and chairman of American Greetings, the world's largest publicly held greeting card company, quoted in *Cleveland Jewish News*, January 12, 1996

I hated singing—I wanted to be an actress. But I don't think I would have made it any other way.

> —Barbra Streisand, singer, actress, producer, and director, interview with Lawrence Grobel in *Playboy*, October 1977

Singing is easier. A song is only three minutes long. If you have a good voice, a good instrument, you're halfway home. Three quarters of the way home. Acting is undefinable. It's different. It's also less impressive, unless you have a crying scene or a very dramatic moment. When you sing a song, the sheer musicality of the experience can move people; they don't even have to hear the lyric.

> —Barbra Streisand, interview with Lawrence Grobel in *Playboy*, October 1977

I have had a full and rich life, not a happy one.

> —Henrietta Szold, founder of Hadassah, from a 1917 letter to her friend and coworker Jessie Sampter, quoted in *Henrietta Szold: Record of a Life* by Rose Zeitlin (1952)

I suppose I am a musical rabbi, which is what most good conductors are. We use our own knowledge and experience to help others.

> —Michael Tilson Thomas, music director of the San Francisco Symphony, principal guest conductor of the London Symphony Orchestra and grandson of Boris and Bessie Thomashefsky, founding members of the Yiddish Theater in America, quoted in *92nd St. Y Bulletin*, 1995

What did I accomplish? I'm said to have had a good career. What does it mean? A few people may have felt—at best, maybe a few people—felt a little enlightened.

> —Diana Trilling, essayist and critic, quoted in "At Journey's End," interview with Joseph A. Concotti, *Jerusalem Report*, December 30, 1993

Suppose you could earn a living by singing and making people laugh, wouldn't that be better than spending your life drudging in a kitchen?

> —Sophie Tucker, singer and comedian known as "Last of the Red Hot Mamas," 1945, quoted in *The Journey Home: Jewish Women and the American Century* by Joyce Antler (1997)

You can be the nice girl reporter who doesn't offend, or you do what you have to do.
> —Barbara Walters, journalist who was the first network anchorwoman and the first to land a million-dollar contract, quoted in *Life*, February 1996

My father said, "You can't be a movie star. They're beautiful." And I said, "Okay then, I'll be an actress."
> —Debra Winger, actress, quoted in "Debra Winger Making It" by Nancy Collins, *Esquire*, December 1986

The only profession I know that does not bar Jews is the rabbinical profession.
> —Rabbi Stephen S. Wise, Jewish leader and activist, 1920s, quoted in *Merchant Princes* by Leon Harris (1979)

❖ CATSKILLS ❖

Of course you heard that joke before. You wore that dress before.
> —Phil Allen (played by Freddie Roman), comedian, addressing a woman in a Catskills theater audience in the film *Sweet Lorraine* (1987)

"Don't dance with her so much. Dance with one of the ugly girls." All employees of the hotel, from busboy to social director, had to obey this rule of the Catskill resorts. The ugly girls had to be danced with; otherwise, God forbid, they might not come back next season.
> —Sid Caesar, comedian, recalling summer work in 1942 at the Avon Lodge in the Catskills quoted in *Where Have I Been?* written with Bill Davidson (1982)

Mom Grossinger, sheitel-wearing [wig required by orthodox women] founder of the famous Catskills resort, loved to walk to a hilltop on the golf course overlooking Grossinger Lake and enjoy the magnificent view. A guest, seeing the radiant look on her face, remarked that it must be wonderful to own 1000 such beautiful acres. "Oh, no," said Mom. "We don't own this land. It belongs to God. We're only his caretakers."
> —Howard Eisenberg, author, Catskills alumnus and former press agent to Eddie Fisher, conversation in 1998

After Adam and Eve were evicted from Gan Eden [the Garden of Eden], the Lord heard the cry of the Jews of the sweatshops, and gave them the Catskills.

> —Howard Eisenberg, 1998

It was the Catskills, not early socialist teachings at my father's knee, that made me a Marxist.

> —Vivian Gornick, essayist and author, recalling working as a waitress at Catskills hotels in the 1950s, *Approaching Eye Level* (1996)

She required my dismissal for the appeasement of her lousy life—her lined face, her hated husband, her disappointed New Year's Eve—and he, the headwaiter, was required to deliver it up to her. For the first time I understood something about power. I stared into the degraded face of the headwaiter and saw that he was as trapped as I, caught up in a working life that required someone's humiliation at all times.

> —Vivian Gornick, recalling her role as a waitress in a hotel on New Year's Eve when an dissatisfied guest demanded that she be fired, not merely reprimanded, *Approaching Eye Level* (1996)

People would go up there for the season with boxes and ropes and mattresses on top of their cars. They trekked and they schlepped and anything they were not sure about, they took with them anyway. "I don't know . . . I'm only going up for two days . . . better pack the large unabbreviated version of the World Atlas. Just in case. . . . Also, the little box refrigerator filled with food." Because Jews must play safe. Why take a chance on all the stores being closed once they got up there?

> —Bill Graham, rock music impresario who owned the Fillmore East and Fillmore West theaters, *Bill Graham Presents*, written with Robert Greenfield (1992)

We must never let anyone go away from Grossinger's hungry.

> —Malke Grossinger, mother of Jennie Grossinger, founder of the Grossinger's resort hotel in the Catskills, quoted in *The Art of Jewish Cooking* by Jennie Grossinger (1958)

Grossinger's was parasols and cabanas, distinctive house buses and paintbox rowboats, the taste of frost and coffee nut, photo galleries of celebrities on vacation winding down corridors around posts to exotic dead ends at underground passages lit from ancient portals, cologned air blowers in washrooms, tables filled with prune and poppyseed Danish, coffeecakes and cheesecakes, hard rolls, onion rolls, fat doughy saltsticks, and sweet buns (replaced regularly with new platters), malted-milk machines whirring, the canteen musk of comics and magazines, glass passageways between buildings (steaming in winter to give misty vistas of snow on evergreens).

> —Richard Grossinger, anthropologist, author, publisher, and grandson of Jennie Grossinger, *The Story of Grossinger's* (1997)

With the attraction of a modern theater and upscale audience, actors, singers, and comedians arrived in droves. . . . They ad-libbed mercilessly until they became Red Buttons and Danny Kaye (once Aaron Chwatt and David Daniel Kominsky). Joseph Gottlieb turned into Joey Bishop. Baritone Moishe Miller starred in the Grossinger Terrace Room and then sang for the Metropolitan Opera as Robert Merrill. Young staff members Moss Hart, Harold Rome, and Don Hartman directed shows. Jerry Lewis grew up Joseph Levitch, the son of a Grossinger's athletic-staff actor. George Jessel arrived unexpectedly to perform with Al Jolson. Jennie ordered a young Jackie Gleason off the grounds because she thought his humor too crude.

> —Richard Grossinger, *The Story of Grossinger's* (1997)

How can you expect to have a solemn religious service in a converted nightclub, where the whole congregation was dancing the Watusi just the night before?

> —Israel Margolies, New York City rabbi, commenting about the increasing number of Jews who were spending the High Holidays in the Catskills in the 1960s, quoted in "Dusk in the Catskills" in *A Summer World* by Stefan Kanfer (1989)

I have to be very honest with you; I have never tasted borscht in my entire life.

> —Sharon Parker, director of guest relations of the Concord Hotel, interview with Zev Brenner, *Talkline*, October 22, 1995

Perhaps the least appealing aspect of being an arts-and-crafts counselor was that, after seeing that your work area had been straightened up, you had to finish off the projects that the kids didn't complete so that they had the requisite artifacts to take home. I still shudder at the thought of all the misshapen baskets I helped to bring into the world.

> —Irwin Richman, professor of American studies and history who grew up in the bungalow colony business, *Borscht Belt Bungalows: Memories of Catskill Summers* (1998)

It's a sad, sad time. What can you say? It's the passing of what used to be. The third generation wanted out.

> —Mac Robbins, Catskills comedian, commenting as he gathered with others to witness the 1986 destruction of an old building at Grossinger's as the resort passed to new management, quoted in *A Summer World* by Stefan Kanfer (1989)

❖ CHANGE ❖

We do not know the extent of our own power to change and to effect change. But we must act; that is in our power. We have to do our part and we have to hope that God is indeed attentive.

> —Rabbi Baruch M. Bokser, author and professor, D'var Torah (sermon), Rosh Hashanah, 1989

The ultimate disinterest in new possibilities is death. Life is an openness to stimulation. We prefer to eat the foods of our past and have lost an appetite to fashion new ideas.

> —Rabbi Samuel Z. Glaser, rabbi emeritus of the Elmont Jewish Center on Long Island and professor of psychology, excerpt from sermon, 1992

There is more to Judaism than tranquility and peace of mind. It is a challenge to change, to repair and grow; not to return to the past.

> —Rabbi Samuel Z. Glaser, excerpt from sermon, 1993

Every man who changes is often a traitor in the eyes of those who can never change.

> —Amos Oz, Israeli author, "An Unsentimental Dove," Op Ed piece in *The New York Times*, November 6, 1995

The status quo proves the most illusory of goals.

> —David Riesman, sociologist, *The Lonely Crowd* (1961)

I realize that, unless women organize, support each other, and force change, nothing basic is going to happen. Not even with the best of men. And I wonder: Are women—including me—willing to face that?

> —Gloria Steinem, author and activist, "Campaigning," 1969, *Outrageous Acts and Everyday Rebellions* (1983)

We draw on ancient wisdom to create new wisdom. What went before we turn and turn like a kaleidoscope; with every turn, there appears new beauty, new patterns, new complexity, new simplicity.

> —Rabbi Arthur Waskow, author and activist, *Godwrestling Round 2: Ancient Wisdom, Future Paths* (1995)

Uncanny are the social explosions that suddenly uproot the values, ethics and morals that we have come to believe exist independently ourselves. The Holocaust, mob violence, the Jonestown mass suicide, the chaos of war, all of these strike horror in us because they are evil, but they also stun us because they inform us that nothing is as we have always thought it to be, that contingency reigns, that everything could be otherwise than it is; that everything that we consider fixed, precious, good can suddenly vanish; that there is no solid ground; that we are "not-at-home" here or there or anywhere in the world.

> —Irvin D. Yalom, author and professor of psychiatry, *Existential Psychotherapy* (1980)

❖ CHARACTER ❖

One of the most significant things that can be said about the Jewish concept of menschlichkeit [the chracteristic of being a good person, one whose behavior reflects a high standard of values] is that it never propounds a behavior which is not clearly within the realm of reasonable expectation for performance. Our tradition never sets up as a virtue the doing of an act which is alien to the general abilities of people.

> —Ronald A. Brauner, president of The Foundation for Jewish Studies and visiting professor of Judaic Studies, "Be a Mensch—Dynamic Torah" in *Being Jewish in a Gentile World* (1995)

We must seek perfection, but never lay claim to it.

> —Rabbi Samuel Z. Glaser, rabbi emeritus of the Elmont Jewish Center on Long Island and professor of psychology, excerpt from sermon, 1993

Every man has an image of himself which fails in one way or another to correspond with reality. It's the size of the discrepancy between illusion and reality that matters. The closer a man gets to knowing himself, the less likely he is to trip up on his own illusions.

> —Arthur Miller, playwright, quoted in "Arthur Miller Grew in Brooklyn" by Murray Schumach, *The New York Times*, February 6, 1949, reprinted in *Conversations with Arthur Miller*, edited by Matthew C. Roudane (1987)

You can really learn something about a person when he's put into circumstances in which civilized values places his own identity, even his very being, in jeopardy. . . . I often think: How would a friend with whom you've drunk a lot of vodka and had a lot of fun respond when one morning you plant yourself on his doorstep and say, "Hide me. I'm being chased by the Nazis."

> —Roman Polanski, film director, interview with Larry Dubois, *Playboy*, December 1971

If you have to choose character or intelligence—in a friend or in a candidate—choose character. Intelligence without character is dangerous, but character without intelligence only slows down a good result.

> —Gloria Steinem, author and activist, commencement speech at Tufts University, Medford, Mass., May 17, 1987, in *Hold Fast Your Dreams: Twenty Commencement Addresses,* compiled by Carrie Boyko and Kimberly Colen (1996)

Everyone stumbles. Everyone falls. It's really how you pick yourself up that's the measure of a person.

> —Lillian Vernon, founder, chairman, and CEO of the specialty catalog company that bears her name, quoted by her friend Beverly Sills, awards luncheon, January 20, 1998

Deep in the Jewish tradition, deep in the psyche of the Bible, is a human being who can experience guilt. And it is true, whether one seeks to praise the fact or bury it very deep, that the culture of the Jews is a culture rooted in that conception of a human being. More than guilt's a problem, it is second nature to Jews.

> —Rabbi Harlan Wechsler, author and spiritual leader of Congregation Or Zarua in New York City, *What's So Bad About Guilt?* (1990)

❖ CHRISTIANS AND JEWS ❖

I remember mouthing a lot of words, then chiming in on those I figured would be OK. ("Born is the King of I-I-srael.") It was a compromise between the demands of faith and sociability.

> —Paul Greenberg, editorial page editor, *Pine Bluff Commercial* and syndicated columnist, remembering public school in the South during Christmas season, "Growing Up in Shreveport" in *Entirely Personal* (1992)

I would consider it almost a sin to say one word against the Christmas festival; it opens so many hearts and tears them out of their self-absorption; friends are tied closer to the bonds of friendship; enemies are forgetful of hatred and animosity and join with zest in the pleasure of the season; the poor are remembered and amply provided for . . . Christmas truly fulfills its mission of bringing peace and good will to men.

> —Henrietta Szold, founder of Hadassah, quoted in *Henrietta Szold: Record of a Life* by Rose Zeitlin (1952)

The [Vatican's] statement fails to recall the fact that it is the Church itself which is chiefly responsible for the spread of Jew-hatred down through the ages.

> —Editorial, *The Reconstructionist,* October 29, 1965, commenting on the controversial conclusion of Vatican Council II, in which the Roman Catholic Church attempted to address its historical attitude toward Jews

What a glorious day! We are no longer rejected by God nor accursed.

> —Editorial, *Detroit Jewish News,* November 5, 1965, commenting on the conclusion of Vatican Council II

"Christ-killer" is a phrase that evokes much emotion, for it stirs among Jews their deepest fears and it reminds Christians of their most shameful guilts. Even the Pope cannot, today, utter the phrase, regardless of what he may mean by it in context, without provoking open criticism even among his own flock. Nonetheless, at their very root, Judaism and Christianity do not divide over the question of who killed Jesus. . . . The ultimate issue is . . . not the past. It is the present. It is not who killed Jesus nineteen centuries ago but who accepted him and who does not today.

> —Rabbi Arthur Hertzberg, professor, and author, commenting on the struggles taking place at the Vatican Council II in the fourth and concluding session, regarding the Church and the Jews, quoted in *National Catholic Reporter,* May 5, 1965

Not to condemn the demonic canard of deicide . . . would mean condoning Auschwitz, defiance of the God of Abraham, and an act of paying homage to Satan.

> —Rabbi Abraham Joshua Heschel, theologian, activist, and author, commenting on the conclusion of Vatican Council II in 1965, quoted in *American Jewish Year Book 1966*

[I have] never suggested the revision of scripture which Christians hold sacred. Nor has any responsible Jewish leader to the best of my knowledge . . . What we have asked for and what we consider necessary and justifiable in the light of centuries of persecution and vilification of Jews, is an appropriate interpretation of those passages of Christian scripture which are most easily open to distortion.

> —Rabbi Marc Tanenbaum of the American Jewish Committee, commenting on the conclusion of Vatican Council II, letter to the editor, *Camden Star Herald*, June 18, 1965

My plan is to call a Jewish Ecumenical Council in Jerusalem some time in 1967, for the purpose of issuing a Jewish Schema on the Christians. The Catholics and many of the Protestant brotherhoods have recently issued the Christian Schema on the Jews. We have been absolved from personal responsibility in the Crucifixion of Jesus. Now it is our turn. I propose that we forgive the Christians for the Inquisition, the Crusades, the ghettos, and the expulsions. I think we can also include forgiveness for the usurpation of property which continued unabated for one thousand, six hundred years, the worldwide discrimination; and we may also waive our annoyances at the barriers that guard country, city, and fraternal clubs.

> —Harry Golden, journalist, regarding a Jewish response to the conclusions of Vatican Council II, *Let Jews Forgive Christians, Too* (1966)

[In light of] moral failure, the much-touted Christian-Jewish dialogue is revealed as fragile and superficial.

> —Malcolm L. Diamond, professor of religion, commenting on the lack of response by most of the Christian community to the dangers facing Israel in the Six-Day War, "Christian Silence on Israel: An End to Dialogue?" *Judaism*, Fall 1967

Our support has been solicited by these same people in other issues, such as Vietnam, race relations, and the like which are no less political. . . . The middle ground of religious and theological conversation has . . . been closed by the massive indifference and, I think, craven silence of those from whom some of us hoped for better things.

> —Rabbi Jacob Neusner, author and professor of Jewish studies, regarding churches' general reluctance to involve themselves in the events leading up to the 1967 Six-Day War because it was a "political" issue, "Communication," *Judaism*, Summer 1967

In the contemporary world, Christianity has joined Judaism in the role of a minority. Faced with the growth of other faiths in Asia and Africa and of Marxism, atheism, and nonbelief in the Western world, Christianity now is fighting an uphill battle. Compared with each other, the differences between Christianity and Judaism are obvious, but in world perspective, the two are on the same side of the fence. Those committed to dialogue point to the many positive entries in the ledger—and recall that not so long ago there was not even a ledger.

> —Geoffrey Wigoder, editor-in-chief of the *Encyclopedia of Zionism*, "Ecumenism" in *Contemporary Jewish Religious Thought*, edited by Arthur A. Cohen and Paul Mendes-Flohr (1987)

The first time I saw Jimmy Swaggart was on TV in my kitchen at 8 o'clock Sunday morning. I was making porridge when this voice boomed out, "You are a sinner and you are damned to burn in hell until you beg forgiveness and cleanse your soul"—or words to that effect. I was so amazed at how much Swaggart knew about me that I sent him a check for $50.

> —Art Buchwald, columnist, *New York Newsday*, March 1, 1988

The same utterances that had been pronounced by Hitler and Goebbels could be heard again . . . emanating from Cairo to Damascus. Once again, the Christian world was silent. I came to the conclusion that, if the Christian world was silent, it was not because they were indifferent to the poisonous words and threats . . . it was because they didn't hear them. They failed to recognize the danger of a second Holocaust because they had yet to recognize the fact of the first one.

> —Emil L. Fackenheim, philosopher, interview with Micha Odenheimer, *Jewish Spectator*, Fall 1989

The two covenants—Judaism and Christianity—are like two parallel lines which will meet in eternity. Until that time we remain separate, but respectful and loving of each other.

> —Rabbi Seymour Siegel, professor of theology, quoted in *Jewish Spectator*, Spring/Summer 1989

Since there has been no change with respect to the evacuation of the nuns from the Auschwitz convent, the prospect of demonstrations as a result of this deplorable behavior will cause immense harm to the cause of mutual understanding, to which we are both dedicated. May I therefore ask that you invoke your personal influence so that this issue can be resolved before it becomes a malignant tumor in our mutual relationship.

> —Edgar M. Bronfman, chairman of The Seagram Company Ltd. and president of the World Jewish Congress, from a letter to Pope John Paul II, March 30, 1993, referring to the continued existence of the Carmelit convent at Auschwitz, as the commemoration of the 50th anniversary of the Warsaw Ghetto Uprising was approaching the following month in Warsaw, *The Making of a Jew* (1996)

I cannot understand why Pope John Paul II could have done such a thing. It's like giving a rotten structure a fresh coat of paint. The structure still rots, and will still collapse. Giving such a man such an honor demeans the honor, and does nothing for the man. . . . Anything you could do to enlighten me would be very much appreciated.

> —Edgar M. Bronfman, from his 1994 letter to Cardinal Cassidy, President of the Vatican Council, who was involved with interfaith relations regarding Kurt Waldheim's invitation to the Vatican from Pope John Paul II, *The Making of a Jew* (1996)

We're both Jewish, neither of us ever held a job, neither of us ever married, and we both traveled around the country irritating people.

> —Kinky Friedman, country singer and author, observing the parallels of his life to the life of Jesus, quoted in *Newsweek*, September 6, 1993

I didn't have any Jewish friends growing up in Phoenix. I felt like I was the only Jewish kid in my high school. [I remember feeling] ashamed because I was living on a street where at Christmas, we were the only house with nothing but a porch light on.

> —Steven Spielberg, film director, discussing his family's move to Phoenix from New Jersey when he was seven years old, quoted in *Newsweek*, December 20, 1993

One question we prepare them for is "Why did the Jews kill Christ?" We teach our volunteers to explain we didn't do it. Beyond that, everyone has their own experience and approach to their Jewishness. We're not trying to be missionaries. We just want to let people know who the Jews are and that they care.

> —Andrew Griffel, executive director of the American Jewish World Service, a private relief organization, describing the orientation to prepare volunteers for encounters with rural people in developing countries, quoted in *Jerusalem Report*, July 28, 1994

It is a measure of the insecurity of Jews that they should be so pleased that the Pope has at least conceded the nationhood, as if his assent were needed to validate the proposition. In this, however, he is very late, coming just after Yasir Arafat.

> —Martin Peretz, editor-in-chief, discussing the Vatican's recognition of the State of Israel, *The New Republic*, January 10 & 17, 1994

I believe that Jews who are afraid of a call to morality in the name of Christianity also fear calls to morality expressed by rabbis.

—Joseph R. Rackman, columnist "In the Name of God: The Value of the Christian Right," *Miami Jewish Sentinel*, August 13, 1994

As a Jew, I do not like to hear that I am living in a Christian nation. On the other hand, it is true that I live in a Christian nation.

—Joseph R. Rackman, "In the Name of God: The Value of the Christian Right," *Miami Jewish Sentinel*, August 13, 1994

When I saw him in Rome, I felt that I was in the presence of a special human being. He was a nice guy.

—Rabbi Gary Bretton-Granatoor, spiritual leader of the Stephen Wise Free Synagogue in New York City, describing his meeting with Pope John Paul II, quoted in *The New York Times*, October 4, 1995

[Anti-Semitism] made me distrust anyone who wants to come along and impose a kind of uniform orthodoxy on America. I say to my friends, who like the idea of school prayer in principle, that they should understand it ain't going to be Sh'ma Yisrael.

—Barney Frank, U.S. Congressman (D-Mass.), quoted in *Jerusalem Report*, April 6, 1995

There is nothing inherently wrong with people who profess a strong religious core to their political convictions getting involved in the political process. As long as we're not in the area where people are saying "God wants you to vote for the Balanced Budget amendment," I am more sanguine about this than many others might be.

—Jeff Greenfield, television journalist and syndicated columnist, quoted in the *92nd St. Y Review*, Fall 1995

The big news about Catholics and Jews these days is that there is not much news at all.

—Clyde Haberman, journalist, *The New York Times*, October 4, 1995

For Jews to get upset that evangelicals do exactly what their faith demands of them is ridiculous. In the free market of ideas, what inferiority complex suffuses the Jews to think that we can't compete? Let the evangelicals do what they like. To whatever extent they succeed, the indictment is not on them, but on us.

—Rabbi Daniel Lapin, founder of Toward Tradition, a national activist group in support of politically conservative causes, commenting about missionary activities aimed at Jews, quoted in *Jewish Telegraphic Agency*, April 3, 1995

The things Robertson says that are anti-Semitic have to be apologized for . . . they have to be condemned and addressed; it's very unusual in the Jewish experience that someone's actions toward Jews are so much better than his ideas.

> —Norman Podhoretz, author and former editor of *Commentary*, regarding Reverend Pat Robertson, central figure in the religious right, and his pro-Israel positions, quoted in *Jerusalem Report*, June 15, 1995

I'm not violently against it [school prayer] and I'm not violently for it. It doesn't seem to me as important an issue as it is to others. I grew up in Brooklyn, in a Yiddish-speaking world, and sang the hymn at school starting at age six. At 30, I realized it had been a Christian hymn. It had no effect on me.

> —Norman Podhoretz, quoted in *Jerusalem Report*, June 15, 1995

Anyone who lived so close to that place [Auschwitz], who lived under Nazi persecution and then the repression of Communism, has a heightened sensitivity to religious freedom.

> —Rabbi Arthur Schneier, senior rabbi of the Park East Synagogue in New York City, speaking about Pope John Paul II, quoted in *The New York Times*, October 4, 1995

You have a fringe here and I think America is at risk. I don't see how anybody can look at a guy like Pat Robertson, who says there shouldn't be a separation between church and state, and say it's not a hell of a risk.

> —Senator Arlen Specter, U.S. Senator (R-Pa.), commenting on Rev. Pat Robertson and the religious right, quoted in *Jerusalem Report*, June 15, 1995

Jews are not put on earth just to give employment to missionaries.

> —Statement from the American Jewish Congress regarding a Southern Baptist Convention resolution to convert Jews, quoted in *Baltimore Jewish Times*, July 19, 1996

I have no fear of conversion efforts by any church—so long as they do not have the power of the state behind them. . . . So what do Jews have to fear? We can just say no. If a Baptist can persuade a Jew that his salvation is in Jesus, so be it. If a Jew can persuade a Baptist to convert to Judaism, so be it. That is the American way. . . . Jews today do have a problem but it does not come from other religions trying to convert us. . . . Our enemies are not Christians seeking to convert us, but rather our own lethargy.

> —Alan M. Dershowitz, attorney, law professor, and author, responding to the resolution adopted by the Southern Baptist convention calling for a major campaign to convert the Jews, quoted in *Detroit Jewish News*, July 26, 1996

I wish them a notable lack of success.

> —Rabbi Jordan Ofseyer, spiritual leader of Congregation Shearith Israel in Dallas, responding to the Southern Baptist Convention's resolution to work harder at converting Jews to Christianity, quoted in *The Dallas Morning News*, June 14, 1996

It is this seemingly intractable human tendency toward aggression and deceit that daunts those who desire a more humane world. We must respect the other while keeping our own guard up. Sadly, it's the first part of this equation — the granting of humanity to the Gentile either as an individual or as a people — that is often lacking in Orthodox circles. Suffering from a kind of moral blindness, we find it difficult to see the non-Jew as anything more than a bit player in our own drama.

> —Rabbi Mayer Schiller, author and teacher of Talmud, "We Are Not Alone in the World," *Tikkun*, March/April 1996

The religious right understands that America is the most religious of the world's democracies. . . . It knows that pleas for civic action have always been laced with theological insights. It knows that the greatest protest movements in American history—abolition, disarmament, civil rights—all have been religiously motivated and led. Why was Martin Luther King Jr. such a towering voice? Because he was religiously powerful and authentic. White Christians had to listen to King because he was speaking their language.

> —Rabbi Eric H. Yoffie, president of the Union of American Hebrew Congregations, from panel discussion "God Does Not Belong to the Religious Right," *Tikkun*, July/August 1996

❖ CIRCUMCISION ❖

The Bris Milah [covenant of circumcision] has made me kin to . . . every other Jew, living and dead. One apprehends this awesome belonging while yet a child, indeed, it spills over one at birth like a secondary trauma.

> —Leonard Baskin, artist, 1961, quoted in *Depiction & Interpretation: The Influence of the Holocaust on the Visual Arts* by Ziva Amishai-Maisels (1993)

Circumcision's ancient roots and its tenacious hold upon Jewish identity may be responsible for the ritual's surviving not only the persecution of Jews throughout the ages but also the various assimilations of Jews in every society in which they have sojourned.

—Dale Lieberman, photographer and lawyer, *Witness to the Covenant of Circumcision* (1997)

I believe using anesthesia will help us see brit milah for what it is—elective surgery on sentient beings. Only with this perspective can we enter into a fresh discussion not only of how, but whether we should continue with this ancient ritual.

—Lisa Braver Moss, "A Painful Case," *Tikkun*, September/October 1990

Circumcision makes it clear as can be that you are here and not there, that you are out and not in—also that you're mine and not theirs. . . . Circumcision confirms that there is an us.

—Philip Roth, novelist, *The Counterlife* (1987)

A humanistic morality that defends female equality would have a hard time justifying a birth ritual that excludes women. . . . The brit is, by its very nature, inconsistent with a humanistic value system.

—Rabbi Sherwin Wine, founder of Humanistic Judaism, *Judaism Beyond God* (1985)

The levellers like to say that when you strip off men's clothes, nobody can tell the beggar from the king. But naked or dead, the Jew is recognizable for what he is.

—Herman Wouk, author, *This Is My God* (1959)

❖ CIVIL RIGHTS MOVEMENT ❖

(see also Affirmative Action, Black-Jewish Relations)

The moment that there is a differentiation in our courts between white and black, Catholic and Protestant, Jew and non-Jew, hatreds and passions will inevitably be aroused and that which has been most noble and exalted and humane in American life will have been shattered.

—Louis Marshall, lawyer and civil rights activist, speaking in one of his first appearances in the 1920s on behalf of the NAACP, arguing a restrictive covenant case in the U.S. Supreme Court, quoted in *What Went Wrong? The Creation and Collapse of the Black-Jewish Alliance* by Murray Friedman (1995)

You will be a sadder but wiser man when you are finished. We have been down there and we know what we are talking about.

> —Joseph Brodsky, chief attorney of the International Labor Defense, speaking to attorney Samuel Leibowitz, who was confident of his ability to get beyond the prejudices in Alabama while defending his clients, the "Scottsboro Boys," in 1933, quoted in *Stories of Scottsboro* by James Goodman (1994) (In 1931, nine young blacks were tried and convicted in state court in Scottsboro, Alabama, on charges that they raped two white women in a freight car. In fact, no rape had occurred. The ensuing series of trials focused international attention on the legal inequality of blacks and whites in the South.)

We have fought the good fight. We have kept the faith and will carry on. The nine innocent Scottsboro Boys will not die so long as decent men and women survive and there exists in Washington the Supreme Court of our land. . . . It'll be a merry-go-round, and if some Ku Kluxer doesn't put a bullet through my head I'll go right along until they let the passengers off.

> —Samuel Leibowitz, attorney who represented the "Scottsboro Boys," speaking at a 1933 rally, quoted in *Stories of Scottsboro* by James Goodman (1994)

Tired of these poor negroes, tired of punishing them, trying to reason with them. Such a shame for people with education to let such ignorance exist. . . . What goes on in a man's mind who can't tell a seven from a two? Men who can hardly understand English—how can they be good soldiers? And citizens? Is it fair that we treat them as our equal when we go inducting them into the army and treat them as a domestic animal when it comes to education?

> —Captain Hyman Samuelson, Jewish officer in charge of African-American troops in New Guinea during World War II, diary entry October 6, 1941, Fort Bragg, North Carolina, cited in *Love, War, and the 96th Engineers (Colored)*, edited by Samuelson and Gwendolyn Midlo Hall (1995)

As a Jew, I have no room in my mind or heart for racial prejudice. But . . . I have come to know that if we sell one house to a Negro family, then 90 or 95 percent of our white customers will not buy into the community. This is their attitude, not ours. . . . As a company our position is simply this: We can solve a housing problem, or we can try to solve a racial problem but we cannot combine the two.

> —William Levitt, builder who revolutionized the process of home building via mass production to provide single-unit housing for middle-class citizens in "Levittown" in the 1950s, quoted in *The Fifties* by David Halberstam (1993) (For two decades Levittown housing was not made available to blacks who were willing and able to buy.)

If you are going to take sides and agitate, you accomplish nothing, except the hostility of the people.

> —Rabbi Moses Landau, spiritual leader of the Jews in Cleveland, Mississippi, expressing a common fear of retribution from both the white community and Jewish congregants, quoted in *The Quiet Voices: Southern Rabbis and Black Civil Rights, 1880s to 1990s*, edited by Mark K. Bauman and Berkley Kalin (1997)

Why are we here? Are we here because the law is being obeyed, because the law is being carried out, because there is no discrimination, because there is no violence, because everyone is receiving equal protection under our law; or are we here to correct a situation which we on our side of the argument consider to be a national shame, and that the federal government, therefore, must do something about it, because the local agency will not? . . . Somebody has to defend rights which are not being defended. We are asking the United States to do it. That is what it comes down to.

> —Jacob K. Javits, U.S. Senator (R-N.Y.), speaking during Senate debate over passage of a 1957 civil rights bill, *Javits: The Autobiography of a Public Man*, written with Rafael Steinberg (1981)

Please demand of religious leaders personal involvement not just solemn declaration. We forfeit the right to worship God as long as we continue to humiliate Negroes. . . . A Marshall Plan for aid to Negroes is becoming a necessity. The hour calls for moral grandeur and spiritual audacity.

> —Rabbi Abraham Joshua Heschel, author, activist, and theologian, from a letter to President John F. Kennedy, June 16, 1963, accepting an invitation to the White House, in *Moral Grandeur and Spiritual Audacity: Essays by Abraham Joshua Heschel*, edited by Susannah Heschel (1996)

The Negro now demands entry into a world, a society, that does not exist, except in ideology. In that world there is only one American community, and in that world, heritage, ethnicity, religion, race are only incidental and accidental personal characteristics. There may be many reasons for such a world to come into existence—among them the fact that it may be necessary in order to provide full equality for the Negroes. But if we do move in this direction, we will have to create communities very different from the kinds in which most of us who have already arrived—Protestants, Catholics, Jews—now live.

> —Nathan Glazer, sociologist, "Negroes and Jews: The New Challenge to Pluralism," *Commentary*, 1964

If we're not back by four-thirty, start phoning. But we'll be back by four.

> —Mickey Schwerner, civil rights worker, speaking to one of his coworkers, June 20, 1964, quoted in *Broken Alliance* by Jonathan Kaufman (1988)

(Schwerner, Andrew Goodman, and James Chaney never returned; they were murdered in Mississippi.)

It never occurred to any of us or to Andy that he went down [to Mississippi] as a Jew; they went down because it was the most important thing to do at the moment.

> —Carolyn Goodman, mother of slain civil rights worker Andrew Goodman, quoted in *Broken Alliance* by Jonathan Kaufman (1988)

[I] admire men who practice what they preach; that they do so under difficulty makes it even more impressive. . . . I admire your courage more than I do that of my son and his friends who face only the loss of 39 days while you face the social pressures of your community and your service to it. . . . Believe me, Rabbi, there are many Jewish hearts who are proud of these young men and women, and would even be more so of you, if I were free to tell them. . . .

> —Father of a jailed rabbinical student who had been arrested as one of the Freedom Riders, from an August 1961 letter he sent to Rabbi Perry Nussbaum of Temple Beth Israel of Jackson, Mississippi, who had quietly assumed responsibility for visiting those in jail, quoted in *The Quiet Voices: Southern Rabbis and Black Civil Rights, 1880s to 1990s*, edited by Mark K. Bauman and Berkley Kalin (1997)

I felt my feet were praying.

> —Rabbi Abraham Joshua Heschel, author, activist, and theologian, commenting after the 1965 civil rights march in Selma, quoted by Susannah Heschel in introduction to *Moral Grandeur and Spiritual Audacity* (1996)

I've been reading in the newspapers that the voter-registration tests in Mississippi are quite difficult. In fact, when I read that my friend the Reverend Theodore Hesburgh, president of the University of Notre Dame, said that he didn't think the dean of the Law School could pass the test—I got the distinct impression that it must be rather stiff. Sooner or later you are going to have to change those tests. I hope it's sooner rather than later.

> —Eppie Lederer, advice columnist also known as Ann Landers, from a private letter written in 1965 to Mississippi's governor, Paul Johnson, quoted in *Eppie: The Story of Ann Landers* by Margo Howard (1982)

The civil rights movement is not for the Negro, it's for America.

> —Harry Golden, journalist, *Ess, Ess, Mein Kindt* (1966)

It was easier for the children of Israel to cross the Red Sea than for the Civil Rights legislation to pass the floor of the United States Senate.

—Rabbi Abraham Joshua Heschel, author, activist, and theologian, *The Insecurity of Freedom* (1967)

The difference in color between races can not obliterate the intellectual and moral differences that may obtain between two individuals, irrespective of race. . . . Why we should regard scholarship or gentlemanliness in the negro as something that does not or can not make him the superior of any white man altogether passes my poor understanding.

—Rabbi Max Heller of New Orleans, 1904 letter to the *New Orleans Times-Democrat,* quoted in *The Quiet Voices: Southern Rabbis and Black Civil Rights, 1880s to 1990s,* edited by Mark K. Bauman and Berkley Kalin (1997)

Did America deserve Jackie Robinson? I think it didn't, and I know for sure that Jackie deserved better than us.

—Joel Oppenheimer, poet, columnist, and ardent fan of the New York Mets, *The Wrong Season* (1973)

These signs were the greatest shock to us. Even long before we were arrested and taken away to the camps, there had been these signs forbidding Jews to sit in the park, or to walk certain places. My husband and I were frightened of the regime in the South as soon as we saw this, and we decided, as soon as we could, to get out of there whatever we had to do. . . . There was no use trying, we could never be comfortable, because racial laws meant only one thing to us.

—A Holocaust survivor describing her experience arriving for the first time from Germany to New Orleans where signs posted everywhere designated "Colored" and "White" public facilities, *New Lives* by Dorothy Rabinowitz (1976)

Martin Luther King, who is now eulogized by people like George Bush as they sing "We Shall Overcome," was a very different man from the one they conjured up. . . . Martin Luther King was an outlaw. He went to jail again and again; he was beaten and reviled. The head of the FBI, J.Edgar Hoover, attacked him as a puppet of communism and called him "the most dangerous man in America." The Justice Department infiltrated his organization, illegally wiretapped his phones, systematically harassed and threatened him. That's how much they loved Martin Luther King. This is the real history.

—Abbie Hoffman, activist, speaking on student activism at the University of South Carolina, September 16, 1987

❖ COLD WAR ❖

(see also Communism)

It is so natural a thing for us to be close to each other. What is it that makes us alike in spite of the obvious differences? Perhaps music can tell us some surprising things we can't find out from books and newspapers. The first thing of all to be said is that Americans and Russians simply love each other's music.

— Leonard Bernstein, conductor and composer, speaking in a visit to Moscow in 1959 with the New York Philharmonic, interviewed in *The Gift of Music*, television documentary, broadcast on PBS, September 22, 1996

To assume that Soviet policymakers prefer being alive to being blown up or shriveled into nothingness does not seem to be an excessively generous tribute to their sense of human vulnerability. It is not necessary to be "soft on Communism" to believe that Soviet leaders prefer to be alive rather than dead.

— Abba Eban, former foreign minister and Israeli ambassador to the United Nations, *The New Diplomacy: International Affairs in the Modern Age* (1983)

Indeed this country has conducted its Russian policy as though it were convinced that fear is the greatest of all diplomatic instruments.

— Albert Einstein, Nobel Prize–winning theoretical physicist and humanist, *Atlantic Monthly*, November 1945, reprinted in *Ideas and Opinions: Albert Einstein* (1982)

Standing in Red Square in 1990, I could finally see Russia for what it was . . . a sluggish society with a great many missiles and not much else. Now we must look at our own shortcomings and judge ourselves not by the standard of competition with the Soviets but by our own norms of a harmonious and decent society. Finally, after all these years, the face in the mirror is our own.

— David Halberstam, journalist, "Coming in From the Cold War," *The Washington Monthly*, January/February 1991

I had an excellent education in Communism at City College and in my Trotskyist youth group, and I knew that if you took Marxist-Leninist doctrine as seriously as the Soviet leadership did, the broad outline of an appropriate American foreign policy almost designed itself. To be a "hard-liner" vis-à-vis the

Soviet Union or another Communist regime meant that you were likely to be right far more often than wrong.

> —Irving Kristol, social critic, editor, and publisher, *Neoconservatism: The Autobiography of an Idea* (1995)

While our history may leave us not well enough prepared to deal with tragedy, it can teach us that great achievement does not result from a quest for safety. Even so, our task will remain psychologically more complex than that of the Soviets. As the strongest and perhaps the most vital power of the free world, we face the challenge of demonstrating that democracy is able to find the moral certainty to act without the support of fanaticism and to run risks without a guarantee of success.

> —Henry Kissinger, scholar, "Reflections on American Diplomacy, Foreign Affairs October 1956," reprinted in *The American Encounter: The United States and the Making of the Modern World* edited by James F. Hoge, Jr., and Fareed Zakaria (1997)

❖ COMEDY ❖

(see also Entertainment)

There's no particular need [for obscenity in humor]. If the material is funny, that's what counts. I could watch nuns do an act if they were funny. However, if you're dirty and funny, you run a greater risk than being clean and funny. Dirty and funny—you're a comic. Dirty and unfunny—you're a child molester.

> —Woody Allen, interview with Sol Weinstein in *Playboy*, May 1967

Most above all, above anyone on earth, I adore Jackie Gleason. That's what I want my series to be—"The Honeymooners," only I'm Ralph.

> —Roseanne Barr, comedian and star of the TV sitcom *Roseanne*, quoted in *The Jewish Comedy Catalog* by Darryl Lyman (1989)

I'm a woman who's a comic, not a woman's comic.

> —Elayne Boosler, comedian, quoted in *The Jewish Comedy Catalog* by Darryl Lyman (1989)

In anything Jewish I ever did, I wasn't standing apart, making fun of the race. I was the race, and what happened to me on stage is what could happen to them. They identified with me, and then it was all right to get a laugh, because they were laughing at me as well as themselves.

—Fanny Brice, actress, quoted in *The Fabulous Fanny: The Story of Fanny Brice* by Norman Katlov (1953), cited in *The Journey Home: Jewish Women and the American Century* by Joyce Antler (1997)

You want to know where my comedy comes from? It comes from not being kissed by a girl until you're sixteen. It comes from the feeling that, as a Jew and as a person, you don't fit into the mainstream of American society. It comes from the realization that even though you're better and smarter, you'll never belong.

—Mel Brooks, comedian and actor, quoted in *Hollywood's Image of the Jew* by Lester D. Friedman (1982)

The only honest art form is laughter, comedy. You can't fake it, Jim. Try to fake three laughs in an hour — ha ha ha ha ha — they'll take you away, man. You can't.

—Lenny Bruce, quoted in *The Essential Lenny Bruce*, edited by John Cohen (1967)

A lot of our humor was a mixture of the sad and the funny. Charlie Chaplin knew that in 1910 and we knew it in 1950. A guy who's in trouble is a very funny guy. A man who's got enough money to pay the rent, there's nothing funny about him. You've got to be involved with and worried about the person you're going to laugh at, or cry at.

—Sid Caesar, comedian, *Where Have I Been?* written with Bill Davidson (1982)

It's a bad drug, jealousy. Eats people up. It's the crack of comics.

—Billy Crystal, comedian and actor, quoted in "Crystal Bawls" by Bruce Buschel, *Gentleman's Quarterly*, August 1989

After tonight, Jose Jimenez is dead.

—Bill Dana, comedian who regularly appeared as Hispanic character Jose Jimenez, at a gathering of the Congress of Mexican-American Unity, April 4, 1970, quoted in *The Jewish Comedy Catalog* by Darryl Lyman (1989) (Latinos considered the character to be an insulting representation of their people.)

Comedy is a camouflage for depression.

—Rodney Dangerfield, comedian and actor, quoted in *The Jewish Comedy Catalog* by Darryl Lyman (1989)

These days, everybody keeps telling me I should slow down and smell the roses. Believe me, I've smelled the roses, and it's nowhere near as pleasurable as getting laughs.

> —Alan King, comedian and actor, *Name-Dropping*, written with Chris Chase (1996)

Comedy is a rebellion against hypocrisy, against pretense, against falsehood and humbug and bunk and fraud; against false promises and base deceivers; against all evils masquerading as true and good and worthy of respect. It is, therefore, the role of comedy to put to the test whatever offers itself as piety.

> —Zero Mostel, actor, Theodore Spencer Memorial Lecture at Harvard University, May 20, 1962

Jewish humor . . . has in some ways come to replace the standard sacred tests as a touchstone for the enitre Jewish community. Not all Jews can read and understand a page of Talmud, but even the most assimilated tend to have a special affection for Jewish jokes.

> —William Novak and Moshe Waldoks, editors of *The Big Book of Jewish Humor* (1981)

Cancer is the most unfunny thing in the world, but I'm a comedienne, and even cancer couldn't stop me from seeing humor in what I went through.

> —Gilda Radner, comedian who died of cancer in 1989, *It's Always Something* (1989)

Comedy should always be on the brink of disaster. Otherwise it is pap, and who cares?

> —Joan Rivers, comedian, quoted in *McCall's*, September 1983

People are shocked that I prepare, but even if you do penis jokes, you've still got to know where you're going with it, or it can get real old.

> —Howard Stern, radio talk show host, quoted in *TV Guide*, March 8–14, 1997

It always disturbed me that people say, "He's a racist and a sexist and a homophobe." They really don't get it. They don't understand that I'm ridiculing all that stuff. . . . I would love people to get the joke, but maybe it's healthy that some people never get it and that it causes so much outrage, because I feed off that outrage.

> —Howard Stern, quoted in *Newsday*, March 2, 1997

You turn what you're usually defensive about into the offensive so people can't touch you.

> —Alan Zweibel, writer for NBC's *Saturday Night Live*, quoted in interview with cast of *Saturday Night Live* by John Blumenthal and Lindsay Maracotta in *Playboy*, May 1977

❖ COMMUNISM ❖

(see also Cold War, Red Scare, Soviet Union)

The fear of Communism has led to practices which have become incomprehensible to the rest of civilized mankind and exposed our country to ridicule.

> —Albert Einstein, Nobel Prize–winning theoretical physicist and humanist, address to the Chicago Decalogue Society, February 20, 1954

History will record that it was in your administration that resolute opposition and careful, discreet statesmanship began the process of eliminating communism as a threat to mankind.

> —Abe Fortas, Supreme Court justice, letter to President Johnson in 1967, quoted in *Abe Fortas: A Biography* by Laura Kalman (1990)

In this best of all possible worlds—though it did seem a bit fragile—only a specter called Communism stood between us Americans and the fulfillment of all our dreams.

> —Alfred Kazin, author and literary critic, *New York Jew* (1978)

Conservatives, having said the collapse of communism would never happen, now claim credit for it. . . . Communism obviously deserves more credit than it has gotten for being able to produce its own collapse.

> —Michael Kinsley, journalist, following the dismantling of the Berlin Wall, November 1989, *The New Republic*, December 4, 1989

There was nothing to fear—perhaps there never had been. For the more Communism expanded, the more monumental would become its problems, the more flaccid its preoccupations with world conquest. In the expansion of Communism was its own containment. The only force that could ever defeat Communism, was Communism itself.

> —Norman Mailer, author, *The Armies of the Night* (1968)

Communism doesn't have anything to say about eternity, nothing to say about death, except to be shot by a firing squad. Such a system cannot satisfy people's yearnings for things we cannot grasp, things we don't know, and things we have reverence for, or feel a sense of mystery about.

> —Yehudi Menuhin, violinist, quoted in *Conversations with Menuhin* by David Dubal (1992)

It is a cruel and humourless sort of pun that so powerful a present form of modern tyranny should call itself by the very name of a belief in community. . . . But perhaps only a malignant end can follow the systematic belief that all communities are one community; that all truth is one truth; that all experience is compatible with all other; that total knowledge is possible; that all that is potential can exist as actual. This is not man's fate; this is not his path; to force him on it resembles not that divine image of the all-knowing and all-powerful but the helpless, iron-bound prisoner of a dying world.

> —J. Robert Oppenheimer, physicist, 1953, quoted in *J. Robert Oppenheimer: Shatterer of Worlds* by Peter Goodchild (1981)

Communists are people who fancied that they had an unhappy childhood.

> —Gertrude Stein, author, quoted in *Writers at Work*, edited by George Plimpton (1958)

❖ COMMUNITY ❖

Wednesday evening, 8 P.M. Few Jews on board and for this reason, it's dispiriting. Jews are peculiar in that way. If there are many, they are not easy to bear; if they are not there, you long for them.

> —Sholem Aleichem, Yiddish writer, from his diary "From London to New York" that he kept on board the ship *St. Louis*, October 1906, quoted in *My Father, Sholem Aleichem* by Marie Waife-Goldberg (1968)

Judaism doesn't tell me how to live my life, but it does keep me oriented in the direction I want to go. It reinforces the values that I want to stay true to but am constantly being seduced away from. Life is a narrow bridge. It's easy to fall. Being Jewish—living in a Jewish community—helps to keep me focused on the path.

> —Ellen Bernstein, author and founder of Shomrei Adamah, Keepers of the Earth, "How Community Forms a Jew" in *Ecology and the Jewish Spirit: Where Nature & the Sacred Meet* (1998)

Today, Jewish affiliation is the result of conscious choices and acts. In the old ethnic immigrant community, it took great effort to disaffiliate and break away; now a major effort is required to maintain affiliation. Many Jews no longer participate in organized Jewish communal life, and therefore even if it is appropriate to count them in a census of Jews, it would not be accurate to include them as part of the Jewish community.

—Sara Bershtel, editor and author, and Allen Graubard, teacher and author, *Saving Remnants: Feeling Jewish in America* (1992)

In the final analysis, it is community which enables us to have access not only to holiness, but to Godliness itself, and so to our own souls.

—Ronald A. Brauner, president of The Foundation for Jewish Studies, "Accessible Holiness: Working for the Jewish Community" in *Being Jewish in a Gentile World* (1995)

The greatest evil in the whole world is . . . to think I'm all by myself, nobody loves me, nobody is really connected to me and my actions don't affect anybody.

—Rabbi Shlomo Carlebach, quoted in the video *Good Purim*, 1992

The family today is asked to do things which it can't possibly do. It is called upon to replace community, to provide leisure, love, respect, satisfaction, fulfillment. But that's impossible, because we can't do these things in isolation. We can do them only as a community.

—Gerson D. Cohen, chancellor of the Jewish Theological Seminary, address at the Jewish Educators Assembly, 1979

A congregation of Jews that reads from the Torah every Saturday, that includes babies and grandparents, the memories of Holocaust survivors and the enthusiasm of converts, will show you that you need not live and die on your own island of time. You are part of an extended family whose memories stretch back past Mount Sinai.

—Paul Cowan, journalist and author, with Rachel Cowan, rabbinical student, *Mixed Blessings: Marriage Between Jews and Christians* (1987)

Instead of conceiving the American Jewish community as a series of concentric circles with a small core of real Jews at the center and surrounding rings of increasingly marginalized people, we must begin to see our community as a woven tapestry with many contemporary colors threaded across the long strands of tradition and history, creating vivid patches of activity.

—Rabbi Rachel Cowan, director, Jewish Life Program, The Nathan Cummings Foundation, "The New Spirituality in Jewish Life" in *The Nathan Cummings Foundation Annual Report 1994*

It is now more than ever necessary to preserve the Jewish community in a vital form.

—Albert Einstein, Nobel Prize–winning theoretical physicist and humanist, *Cosmic Religion* (1929)

As a Jew, I belong to an enormous, venerable, worldwide family, whose tragedies I mourn because they are my own, and whose triumphs I celebrate — often with shameless immodesty — as though they were those of a beloved sister or brother.

—Louise Kehoe, journalist, who learned at age forty that she was of Jewish descent and decided to covert formally, quoted in an ad sponsored by the American Jewish Committee in its "What Being Jewish Means To Me" series, 1995

We don't go to church or synagogue at a stipulated time because God keeps "office hours." We go because that is when we know there will be other people there, seeking the same kind of encounter we are seeking.

—Rabbi Harold S. Kushner, author and rabbi emeritus of Temple Israel in Natick, Mass., *Who Needs God* (1989)

[Finally] the members of the congregation must nurture one another because they need one another. They simply cannot do it alone. Hermits and monasteries are noticeably absent from Jewish history; we are a hopelessly communal people.

—Rabbi Lawrence Kushner, author and rabbi of Temple Beth El in Sudbury, Mass., "The Tent Peg Business: Some Truths About Synagogues," *New Traditions* 3, Summer 1986

The postwar children of havurot [informal prayer groups] recalculated what was to be remembered. . . . Its members wanted intense communal ties of a sort, and vibrant spirituality. They did not wish to become Hasidim, but they saw them as their inspiration. Their Judaism could find no model in contemporary American Jewish life. . . . They encountered the counterculture through their Judaism. The counterculture rejected American society. Judaism could be their alternative if it could be unharnessed from their parents. And it could, if those buried treasures of mysticism, radicalism, and community could be unearthed from a Jewish past hidden from them in America.

—Riv-Ellen Prell, professor of anthropology and author, "The Havurot in

American Judaism" in *Events and Movements in Modern Judaism*, edited
by Raphael Patai and Emanuel Goldsmith (1995)

The covenant between God and the Jews may lead to separation and stick-
iness. But the covenant binds the people together and the Jewish people are a
leaf of the tree of life, drenched in sun, rain and wind like the other. Each leaf
matters.

> —Anne Roiphe, novelist and essayist, "On Being Jewish: Beyond Bagels and
> Disasters," *The New York Observer*, January 12, 1996

It takes infinitely more effort for a whole community, or nation, to carry
out soul-searching than it does for a lone man or woman.

> —Rabbi Adin Steinsaltz, Talmudic scholar, *The Strife of the Spirit* (1988)

When the tradition is vital and active within the community, it carries on
almost without words. It is transmitted because the Jewish tradition is not only
a verbal deposit, it is a very inclusive message that relates to the whole of life
and not only to religion or to the historic past. Therefore it is passed on via
almost all the channels of daily life. The written past of the tradition lives within
the details of contemporary work and food and blessings.

> —Rabbi Adin Steinsaltz, interview in *Parabola*, Summer 1989

The Jewish social group on its middle and wealthy levels . . . is now one of
the most self-indulgent and self-admiring groups it is possible to imagine . . . as
the Jewish community now exists, it can give no sustenance to the American
artist or intellectual who is born a Jew.

> —Lionel Trilling, critic, *Contemporary Jewish Record* (precursor to *Com-
> mentary*), February 1944

Judaism is not a single solitary path and it is not a totally communal path.
It's a community made up of individuals. It's individuals in search of a community. There is always the idea of a minyan, of nine Jews who are looking for
the tenth, of one Jew who's looking for the other nine.

> —Rabbi Levi Weiman-Kelman, American-born rabbi in Jerusalem, inter-
> viewed in the film *A Jew Is Not One Thing*, produced for The Jewish
> Museum's core exhibition, 1993

The one constant in the family of Judaism is that it has been nourished by
the same sources. The Torah and tradition have been the single thread which

ties together all the strands of our people who have survived. Even at the Passover table, the wicked son is still part of the family—at least he asks a question about the tradition, however rebelliously that question is meant.

—Rabbi David J. Wolpe, author, *Miami Jewish Tribune*, August 27, 1993

❖ COMPUTERS ❖

The simple act of addition, subtraction, multiplication and division to calculate a trip to Venus would take one man eight hundred years. Yet now there were supercomputers to calculate the journey in thirty seconds. That plastic brainpower could turn over every straw in the haystack to find the needle.

—Norman Mailer, author, *Of a Fire on the Moon* (1969)

Even though today's technology provides us with mountains of data, it is useless without judgement.

—Felix G. Rohatyn, financier address to graduating class, Middlebury (Vt.) College, May 1982, quoted in *Lend Me Your Ears: Great Speeches in History*, edited by William Safire (1992)

And however ingenious its simulacra of reality, no computer, I guarantee you, is going to offer me the smell of the past, not in my lifetime, and I think, not in yours.

—Simon Schama, professor of the humanities at Columbia University, "The Fate of the Past in the Electronic Future," address at the Jerusalem International Book Fair, Aspen Institute Forum, March 14, 1995

I have no doubt about the indifference of the computer to good and evil. This technology, like all technology, will lend efficiency to our ends, but it will make the devising of those ends no easier.

—Leon Wieseltier, author and editor, "Washington Diarist," *The New Republic*, February 10, 1997

❖ CONVERSION ❖

(see also Intermarriage)

Today, in our free and open society, Judaism is in a sense a matter of choice for everyone—both those who have been born Jews as well as those individuals who have not been raised in the Jewish tradition.

> —David Belin, author, attorney, and president of the Jewish Outreach Institute, "Choosing Judaism," 1990s

If your son or daughter is married to someone who has converted to Judaism, then there is no intermarriage. An intermarriage means a marriage between someone born Jewish and someone born non-Jewish who has not converted.

> —Lawrence J. Epstein, "Conversion to Judaism: A Guide for Jewish Parents," 1990s

Ignorance about converts causes pain. The world we've left behind does not understand us. And as strangers in the Jewish community, we've often been misunderstood and mistreated, our contributions discounted.

> —Nan Fink, psychotherapist, teacher, and writer, *Stranger in the Midst* (1997)

All my life experience is connected to my conversion.

> —Nan Fink, *Stranger in the Midst* (1997)

Some people dislike the term "conversion," preferring to call those who enter the Jewish family other than by birth "Jews by choice." Well, I am a Jew by choice, and if I had to choose again I'd choose Jewishness with all my heart, and without a second's hesitation—only this time I'd choose it forty years sooner.

> —Louise Kehoe, journalist, who learned at age 40 that she was of Jewish descent and decided to covert formally, quoted in an ad sponsored by the American Jewish Committee in its "What Being Jewish Means to Me" series, 1995

The history of the Jews will now be your story, and you are just as much a part of the Jewish people as Moses was.

> —Rabbi Robert Levine of Congregation Rodeph Shalom in New York City, commenting on the conversion of a teenage girl from St. Petersburg, Russia,

who was adopted by a congregant, quoted in "Total Immersion" by Martha Mendelsohn, *The Jewish Week*, July 11, 1997

All vestiges of negative or quizzical attitudes toward converts must be totally eradicated. Not only are these attitudes counterproductive to the future of the Jewish community but, much more important, they are in opposition to Jewish law.

> —Deborah E. Lipstadt, author and professor of modern Jewish studies, speaking at Hadassah National Convention, July 1992

❖ COURAGE ❖

The president is selling hope when he should be selling courage, which is hope toughened, hope disabused.

> —Leon Wieseltier, author and editor, "Washington Diarist," *The New Republic*, February 10, 1997

❖ CREATIVITY ❖

(see also Arts)

In order for new ideas to be born, new actions to be forged in the smithy of our souls, we have to be prepared to rethink our positions with regard to many things, even some of our most cherished ideas. Genuine creativity is reserved for those brave souls who are capable of changing their minds and their feelings. Who is willing to risk changing hatred to love, inflexibility to patience and elasticity and understanding?

> —Rabbi Marshall T. Meyer, human rights activist, founder of the Seminario Rabinico Latinoamericano and spiritual leader of B'nai Jeshurun in New York City, interview on ABC radio, September 28, 1986

It seems to me that in my case, the return to creativity was not a question of doggedly holding on, so much as it was a process which doggedly wouldn't let go.

> —Henry Roth, novelist who published a novel following a sixty-year silence after the publication of *Call It Sleep*, foreword to *Holding On: Dreamers,*

Visionaries, Eccentrics and Other American Heroes by David Isay, photographs by Harvey Wang (1995)

I have in mind a plan of development which would make radio a "household utility" in the same sense as the piano or the phonograph. The idea is to bring music into the home by wireless.

> —David Sarnoff, broadcast executive at the time working at the Marconi Company (before it became RCA), from memo in November 1916 with the Subject: Radio Music Box, quoted in *Sarnoff: An American Success* by Carl Dreher (1977)

The pessimism of the creative person is not decadence, but a mighty passion for the redemption of man.

> —Isaac Bashevis Singer, Yiddish writer, Nobel Prize lecture in Stockholm, December 1978

❖ CRIME ❖

Being an uneducated person, what walk of life could I have gotten into that I could have become involved with such people? I'm talking about celebrities, politicians, people in the higher walks of life and education. Where could I have ever come to meet these kind of people if I had gone into some other line of work than I did?

> —Mickey Cohen, Jewish mobster, quoted in *But—He Was Good to His Mother* by Robert A. Rockaway (1993)

A criminal trial is not a game in which the state's function is to outwit and trap its quarry. The state's pursuit is justice, not a victim.

> —Abe Fortas, Supreme Court justice, trying to safeguard the rights of the accused from certain discovery procedures employed by the state, Giles v. Maryland, 386 U.S. 66 (1967), quoted in *Fortas: The Rise and Ruin of a Supreme Court Justice* by Bruce Allen Murphy (1988)

This is pricking us in a very deep place. This is a tragedy not just happening in my neighborhood. This is a tragedy happening in my heart and the soul of my people.

> —Rabbi Claire Magidovitch Green, coordinator of the Coalition Against Jewish Domestic Violence of Delaware Valley, commenting on the murder of a young Jewish woman and the arrest of her Jewish husband, quoted in *Jewish Telegraphic Agency*, May 30, 1997

It's universally wrong to steal from your neighbor, but once you get beyond this one-to-one level and pit the individual against the multinational conglomerate, the federal bureaucracy . . . or the utility company, it becomes strictly a value judgment to decide who exactly is stealing from whom. One person's crime is another person's profit.

> —Abbie Hoffman, activist, *Steal This Book* (1976)

Looking back from the vantage point of today, I cannot understand how my mind worked then. For I can recall no feeling then of remorse. Remorse did not come until later, much later. It did not begin to fully develop until I had been in prison for several years; it did not reach its full flood for perhaps ten years. Since then, for the past quarter century, remorse has been my constant companion.

> —Nathan F. Leopold, Jr. sentenced, with Richard Loeb, to life imprisonment for the kidnap and murder of young Bobby Frank on May 21, 1924, *Life Plus 99 Years* (1957) (They were represented by Clarence Darrow, whose efforts helped them avoid the death penalty.)

The only thing is that whatever you choose to do, I would say to him, you gotta, put on tefillin [phylacteries] every morning, you gotta eat kosher meat, you have to maintain certain principles. That means you have to keep your word. A word is a bond. After that, whatever a person chooses to do, that's his business. . . . As far as illegality is concerned, since that changes every day of the week, just like the weather, I'm not in a position to say what's illegal.

> —"Mervin" (hidden identity), whose father was in the mob during the 1930s and 1940s, describing his dreams for a son, quoted in *But—He Was Good to His Mother* by Robert A. Rockaway (1993)

❖ DATING ❖

(see also Relationships, Romance)

I come here because it's sort of like a department store sale. A lot of potential mates you find are a little shopworn or damaged, but there are lots of bargains, too. It all depends on lunch and getting to the counter first. I hate it, but what are you going to do?

> —A forty-year-old divorcee attending a Catskills singles weekend in the 1960s, quoted in "Dusk in the Catskills" in *A Summer World* by Stefan Kanfer (1989)

No one is going to present the kind of character that wakes up at six o'clock in the morning after having been up half the night with the baby, rocking the baby to sleep. I mean that's not the character that you meet. If you go out for a year's time, you still wouldn't see that person.

> —Satmar Hasid from Borough Park in Brooklyn, quoted in *Hasidic People, A Place in the New World* by Jerome Mintz (1992)

It's like a Chinese restaurant. There are too many choices.

> —An unnamed Upper West Side male, talking about the Orthodox Jewish singles scene with its large number of available women, quoted in "Single, Jewish and Frum [observant] on the Upper West Side" by Tova Stern, *Long Island Jewish World*, December 22, 1995

Conservative SJM, 39, teacher. Seeking Lady who is plain, simple, unsophisticated, unmaterialistic, undemanding, passive, deferential, catering, tolerant, open, gentle, soft, delicate, not fussy. No makeup, please.

Princess wanted. SJ professional 38. She should be 28–40, NS and athletic, she should enjoy travel, the beach and life's finer things.

Beautiful blonde model with California looks, highly educated, is looking for a Jewish (NR) successful, marriage-minded, slim, GQ looks, MD/DDS, 37–42.

Chutzpah, oomph and kosher too. Looking for NS, SJM, 6'3"+, who still believes in chivalry. For the record . . . I'm SJF, 34, 6'3", NS and lots of fun. Let's talk.

> —Love Lines (personal ads) appearing in *The Jewish Week*, August 4, 1995

I hated being a bachelor and I hated all my bachelor years, and I hated having to do what I had to do to have a sex life, which often was to become a different person than I was to get girls to go to bed with me. There wasn't a moment in those single years I look back on with any kind of pleasure.

> —Jules Feiffer, cartoonist and writer, quoted in *On the Edge of Darkness: Conversations About Conquering Depression* by Kathy Cronkite (1994)

I have men coming in here, "I want 'em this way, I want 'em that tall, I want a blonde, I want a this . . ." I say, "My friend, I'll put her in a mold, we'll take her out, and we'll give her to you." But you didn't ask the right question, my friend. You didn't say: "She should be a model inside. Outside people change, clothes you could always buy, neighborhoods you could always move, but you didn't say the inside." The inside you cannot change.

> —Dan Field, matchmaker, quoted in *Holding On: Dreamers, Visionaries, Eccentrics and Other American Heroes* by David Isay, photographs by Harvey Wang (1995)

I must say, first dates have changed a lot.

> —Ted Koppel, television journalist, responding to comments by panelists at a *Nightline* town meeting on AIDS about the urgency of recommending a condom for oral sex "especially on a first date with a partner that one doesn't know," June 1987, *Nightline: History in the Making and the Making of Television* by Ted Koppel and Kyle Gibson (1996)

Though the dress may range from casual to formal, underneath all Jewish singles events, much is the same. You will still find yourself trying to meet the eyes of that potentially special someone while avoiding at all costs the glance of Mr. or Ms. Wrong.

> —Leron Kornreich, journalism student, "A Guide to Surviving a Night in 'Utopia' " in *Forward*, November 24, 1995

Schoolteachers don't go as fast as stenographers, and career women generally are harder to pair off than the fluffy types.

> —Louis Rubin, proprietor of Rubin's Prominent Matrimonial Bureau, quoted in a profile by Meyer Berger in *The New Yorker*, 1938, quoted in *The Wonders of America: Reinventing Jewish Culture, 1880–1950* by Jenna Weissman Joselit (1994)

What is a date, really, but a job interview that lasts all night?

> —Jerry Seinfeld, comic, *SeinLanguage* (1994)

Standing in line waiting is a good way to start meeting people. Of course, if your name begins with B you'll only meet people with names A through F, in the beginning. But it's a start.

> —Morton Sunshine, general manager of Grossinger's, describing the first day of singles weekends, quoted in "Dusk in the Catskills" in *A Summer World* by Stefan Kanfer (1989)

Customs of courtship vary greatly in different times and places, but the way things happen to be done here and now always seems the only natural way to do it.

> —Herman Wouk, author, *Marjorie Morningstar* (1955)

❖ Death ❖

I had a theory about death in its various forms—for instance, drowning, being run over or buried alive, which were death by accident, or something like infantile paralysis, which was death by germ: It was simply that if I thought of it, if I had imagined it, it would not happen to me. I would be guarded against it, made immune merely by an act of thought, foiling this or that particular death with a natural inoculation against it.

> —E. L. Doctorow, novelist, *World's Fair* (voice of the young narrator) (1985)

Now we were cut off in midsentence. Now I would never be able to tell her how sorry I was for everything. I still grieve for the words unsaid. Something terrible happens when we stop the mouths of the dying before they are dead. A silence grows up between us, profounder than the grave. If we force the dying to go speechless, the stone dropped in the well will fall forever before the answering splash is heard.

—Faye Moskowitz, writer, reflecting on her mother's death, "A Leak in the Heart" in *Her Face in the Mirror: Jewish Women on Mothers and Daughters*, edited by Faye Moskowitz (1994)

Jewish attitudes concerning death may be summed up in the phrase "repent one day before your death." Since man does not know the time of his death, he ought to treat each day as if it were to be his last. This awareness of the imminence and inevitability of death, far from demoralizing Jews, brings them all the more into life and its divinely conceived moral dimension.

—Henry Abramovitch, psychologist and anthropologist, "Death" in *Contemporary Jewish Religious Thought*, edited by Arthur A. Cohen and Paul Mendes-Flohr (1987)

We are a society of orphans.

—Rabbi Marc D. Angel, author and rabbi of Congregation Shearith Israel New York City, *The Orphaned Adult* (1987)

As my mother was dying, becoming physically more and more helpless, she was also radiating a deep, silent wisdom; she was becoming more and more philosophical. She was in great pain and discomfort for most of the time. More than once she said that she was ready to die, that she wished it was all over. One time I responded to her: "I can't offer you any consolation on your suffering. You are going through it. I am on the outside. But I can say this: as long as you live, you give us added strength and wisdom. Your life means a lot to us." Even holding on to those last moments was important.

—Rabbi Marc D. Angel, *The Orphaned Adult* (1987)

Death after a long illness we can accept with resignation. Even accidental death we can ascribe to fate. But for a man to die of no apparent cause, for a man simply to die because he is a man brings us so close to the invisible boundary between life and death that we no longer know which side we are on. Life becomes death, and it is as if this death has owned this life all along.

—Paul Auster, author, *The Invention of Solitude* (1982)

The coining of the phrase "death with dignity" by advocates of passive euthanasia was a stroke of genius. Opponents of such practices are immediately disarmed. Everyone respects "rights" and no one decries "dignity." Yet, while repeated use of a glib phrase by the press and media may influence attitudes, the coining of a cliché is not the same as making a case.

—Rabbi J. David Bleich, professor of Talmud, "The Karen Quinlan Case: A Torah Perspective," *Jewish Life*, Winter 5736, 1976

The mitzvah of saving a life is neither enhanced nor diminished by virtue of the quality of life preserved.

> —Rabbi J. David Bleich, "The Karen Quinlan Case: A Torah Perspective," *Jewish Life*, Winter 5736, 1976

At times I cannot believe I ever was alive, that I ever was another self, and wrote—and loved or failed to love. I do not really understand this erasure. Oh, I can comprehend a shutting down, a great power replacing me with someone else (and with silence), but this inability to have an identity in the face of death—I don't believe I ever saw this written about in all the death scenes I have read or in all the descriptions of old age.

> —Harold Brodkey, novelist who died of AIDS in January 1996, "This Wild Darkness," *The New Yorker*, February 5, 1996

Memory, so complete and clear or so evasive, has to be ended, has to be put aside, as if one were leaving a chapel and bringing the prayer to an end in one's head.

> —Harold Brodkey, "This Wild Darkness," *The New Yorker*, February 5, 1996

There was always someone missing at the dinner table, at a wedding, a birthday. Always someone you couldn't tell [that] the kids were born. Always someone missing—twenty-five years and such a hold. I miss him. I think we could be good friends now. . . . Just as we were getting close, he was gone, suddenly. I was 15. When someone leaves you that way, there's forever a brown spot on your apple, that soft mushy place, no matter how perfect the rest of the apple is. You have to eat around it.

> —Billy Crystal, comedian, reflecting on his father's death, quoted in "Crystal Bawls" by Bruce Buschel, *Gentlemen's Quarterly*, August 1989

Though in tangible achievement I have not done what perhaps I dreamed of doing and what the world may rightly have expected me to achieve, the very living of my life has been supremely successful. There has been no day in which my heart has not leaped with gratitude to God for the joy of life and its fulfillment in the perfect love that has been given to me . . . and the day of death shall be but one more such day.

> —David de Sola Pool, Jewish leader and spiritual head of American Sephardic and Levantine Jewry, excerpted from "Affirmation of Life," 1970, written shortly before his death, quoted in *This I Believe: Documents of American Jewish Life* by Jacob Rader Marcus (1990)

Last one out, please close the gate.

> —Joe Erber, an auxiliary police officer who is acting rabbi of Ahavath Rayim
> Synagogue in Greenwood, Mississippi, recounting what he and a friend say
> whenever they go to a funeral of a member of their dwindling community,
> quoted in *Holding On: Dreamers, Visionaries, Eccentrics and Other American Heroes* by David Isay, photographs by Harvey Wang (1995)

These small monuments are more than symbolic. They are proof that a person lived and died.

> —Jerry Feldhamer, president of the Hebrew Free Burial Society (which has
> been burying poor Jews for more than a century), speaking at a ceremony
> to unveil 1,000 headstones at the unmarked graves at the burial grounds for
> indigent Jews, quoted in "Earning a Special Blessing" by Charles W. Bell,
> *New York Daily News*, September 20, 1997

No more than any other human being do I know what will happen to me after I die. But what I believe will happen to me after I die affects how I lead my life today.

> —Neil Gillman, professor of philosophy and rabbi, *The Death of Death* (1997)

The first thing the folks will think of, when death enters their lives on a Friday, is that their weekend has been completely smashed up.

> —Harry Golden, journalist, *Only in America* (1958)

On this table, all wear the same clothing and all are equal, rich and poor.

> —Betsy Kaplan, describing her experience as a member of the Chevra Kad-
> disha (burial society) formed in Atlanta, "The Rituals of Death," *Lilith*,
> Winter 1989

A funeral home deals with bodies; we were dealing with a person, and we felt the power of this mitzvah as we worked. . . . It has given me the ultimate awareness of the link between the human and the Divine. We are sending this daughter of God off on her journey, from earth to her heavenly home.

> —Betsy Kaplan, "The Rituals of Death," *Lilith*, Winter 1989

The way I see it, you get to do what you want to do and have a great life, then you have to die—that's the deal.

> —Irving "Swifty" Lazar, show business agent and dealmaker, *Swifty: My Life
> and Good Times*, written with Annette Tapert (1995)

Yizkor [memorial prayers] offers what each of us need most—a moment to say our loved ones meant something to us that we can never express in words. A moment to say that although we have gone on with our lives, we will remember them always, that their lives mattered.

> —Rabbi Steven Z. Leder, associate rabbi of Wilshire Boulevard Temple, in Los Angeles, quoted in *The Jewish Journal of Los Angeles*, May 24–30, 1996

I am sorry that President Clinton went from his mother's funeral to the summit meeting in Europe. . . . I am sorry he does not know that summit meetings come and go every five years, but the death of a mother is an event that happens only once, and it deserves to be honored and respected. I am sorry we do not live in a nation that would say to the President that we want him to take the time he needs to do the grieving he needs to do. . . . But we are unable to tell ourselves and each other that it is all right to take the time to grieve. We would be better men and women if we did.

> —Julius Lester, professor of Judaic Studies, history, and English, from essay first delivered on National Public Radio's "All Things Considered," included in the *Book of Eulogies*, edited by Phyllis Theroux (1997)

My father was head of the Chevra Kadisha, the group that prepares the dead for burial. I was only seven years old when he took me to watch them prepare a body, I was terrified and pale as a ghost. My father noticed my fear. "Mein kind, hob nitkein moro far de toyteh; hob more far de lebedikeh." [My child, don't fear the dead, fear the living.] How right he was.

> —Rabbi Haskel Lindenthal, scholar, recalling his childhood in Poland before the Holocaust, *Pages of My Life* (1997)

The last day the agony was perpetual. Time after time it lifted her almost off the bed. So they had to fight to hold her down. He could not endure and left the room; wept as if there never would be tears enough.

> —Tillie Olsen, author, *Tell Me a Riddle* (1960)

Officiating at weddings is my favorite duty as a rabbi, but I never feel more useful than at a funeral when I offer the hesped [eulogy]—a careful and truthful summing up of a life and its gifts. Somehow, at least in part, the cosmic order is restored by a story.

> —Rabbi Debra Orenstein, author, editor, and actress, *Lifecycles 1* (1994)

Today in this caring community, we are one heart to help those whose hearts are broken, one voice for those who cannot speak, and one hand for those who need a hand to hold.

—Rabbi Joseph Potasnik, vice president of the New York Board of Rabbis, delivering a eulogy along with Cardinal O'Connor at a private service for the families of those killed in the explosion of TWA Flight 800, quoted in *The Jewish Week*, July 26, 1996

It is not self-sacrifice to die protecting that which you value: If the value is great enough, you do not care to exist without it. This applies to any alleged sacrifice for those one loves.

—Ayn Rand, writer and philosopher, interview with Alvin Toffler in *Playboy*, March 1964

It's so different from any other bereavement, because of the guilt. . . . You get through the guilt by saying to yourself, which I truly believe, that you can't take a splinter out in a depression; a person has got to cure themselves. If a friend has cancer, you can't take the cancer out of them. It's the same thing. If they're lucky, they're going to come out of it.

—Joan Rivers, comedienne, reflecting on her husband's suicide, quoted in *On The Edge of Darkness* by Kathy Cronkite (1994)

My father died at seventy-seven, 1937—just before another war broke up the world . . . he had died, actually, years before 1937, over a pressing iron, in his unions, meeting halls.

—Harry Roskolenko, author "America the Thief" in *The Immigrant Experience: The Anguish of Becoming American*, edited by Thomas C. Wheeler (1971)

After he died I swam a lot, every day. You can weep in the water, and when you come out red-eyed, people attribute it to the swimming. The sea my father loved is a fine place for crying.

—Leo Rosten, author, reflecting on his father's death, *People I Have Known, Loved or Admired* (1970)

The Talmud cautions: Everything is in the hands of God except the fear of God. As even God cannot legislate trembling, I tremble that legalizing assisted suicide will ultimately corrode the sanctity of life and the integrity of the medical profession.

—Shira Ruskay, therapist involved in hospice care, "Death With Dignity: An Alternative Model," *Sh'ma*, September 1996

When a person with a terminal illness expresses suicidal ideation—and I believe almost all terminally ill people have suicidal thoughts—it is symbolic communication. It should be the beginning of intimate inquiry, not a trigger to phone the pharmacy.

—Shira Ruskay, "Death With Dignity: An Alternative Model," *Sh'ma*, September 1996

For the Jewish family, the death of a loved one is a time for gathering in community. . . . At no other juncture in Jewish life is there any greater sense of family, of a people bound together at a time of personal crisis to share in the loss and render solace.

—Dr. Jack Shechter, professor of Bible, "Saying Kaddish," *Direction*, Spring 1993

The message is to choose life in this moment, not to try and live forever. Someday, when you're tired and sore and want to leave your body, your death will be a healing—not a failure. You will have been an example of how to deal with adversity and leave a legacy of love.

—Bernie S. Siegel, surgeon, teacher, author, and president of the American Holisitic Medicine Association, *Love, Medicine and Miracles* (1990)

What the Living Will makes possible is the giving of the privilege to the patient himself to stop those things "that delay the soul's leaving the body." The developments of medical technology have caused problems which our ancestors could hardly have foreseen. We must not forget, in our loyalty to tradition, the welfare of the suffering patient who, when the Giver of Life has proclaimed the end of his earthly existence, should be allowed to die in spite of our machines.

—Rabbi Seymour Siegel, professor of theology, "Jewish Law Permits Natural Death," *Sh'ma*, April 15, 1977

I think it was more love of George.

—Beverly Sloan, sister-in-law of George DeLury, who helped his wife (who suffered from multiple sclerosis) die "out of love and devotion," quoted in the *New York Daily News*, October 19, 1995

Many religions view the phenomenon of death as a positive spectacle, inasmuch as it highlights and sensitizes the religious consciousness and "sensibility." They, therefore, sanctify death and the grave because it is here that we find ourselves at the threshold of transcendence, at the portal of the world to come. Death is seen as a window full of light, open to an exalted, supernal realm. Judaism, however, proclaims that coming into contact with the dead precipitates defilement. It bids one to choose life and sanctify it.

—Rabbi Joseph B. Soloveitchik, Talmudic scholar, professor, and author, *Halakhic Man* (1984)

The Jewish approach to death is that it is a problem to be solved by and for the living. Death, preparation for death, and mourning are all worked into the fabric of day-to-day life. The essence of mourning is not sorrow for the deceased, but rather compassion for the surviving relatives in their loneliness.

—Rabbi Adin Steinsaltz, Talmudic scholar, *The Strife of the Spirit* (1988)

Death is what distinguishes the mortal from the immortal, the divine from the human. In every place and at every moment, God is present. We are never alone, except at the moment of death.

—Rabbi Ira Stone, author and rabbi of Beth Zion/Beth Israel Synagogue in Philadelphia, *Seeking the Path to Life: Theological Meditations on God and the Nature of People, Love, Life and Death* (1992)

In modern America, you're not supposed to cry, you have to be strong. But in traditional Jewish culture, crying is accepted and valued. . . . Jews have learned not to be afraid of mourning, perhaps because Jewish history is a continuous cycle of grief and rebirth, death and renewal.

—Phyllis Toback, resident of Chicago, quoted in *The Invisible Thread: A Portrait of Jewish American Women* by Diana Bletter (1989)

Death is the condition that makes it possible for us to live life in an authentic fashion.

—Irvin D. Yalom, author and professor of psychiatry, *Existential Psychotherapy* (1980)

❖ DELI ❖

(see also Food)

KOSHER
Sausages, Bologna, Frankfurters and Wiener Wurst
Smoked and Corned Beef, Smoked and Cooked Tongue
Kosher Cooking Fat, 1,2,5, and 10 lb. Cans

—Advertisement for M. Zimmerman in New York City, *The American Hebrew*, June 7, 1901

Without fat a pastrami sandwich is a worthless commodity. Extra lean annoys me.

—Abe Lebewohl, Ukrainian-born deli owner and caterer who in 1954 founded the Second Avenue Deli in New York City, 1991, quoted in "New Deli" by Peter Beinart, *The New Republic*, Jan 8–15, 1996

The original Uncle Sam ad had an enormous impact on business. Here was Hebrew National claiming that since it was kosher, its product was superior because it answered to an authority higher than the USDA. And it worked.

> —Steven B. Silk, president of Hebrew National, quoted in *Lifestyles*, New Year 1998

When I gave a speech at a Jewish community center in the Chicago suburbs, I called it "Midwestern Jews: Making Chopped Liver with Miracle Whip." After the speech, someone came up to me and said that the title was an interesting metaphor. "It's not a metaphor," I said. "It's a recipe." That was how my mother made chopped liver. I believe she considered schmaltz declasse.

> —Calvin Trillin, columnist and author, *Messages from My Father* (1996)

❖ DENOMINATIONS ❖

(see also Jewish Observance, Pluralism)

There are tens of thousands of mixed marriages. In a vast majority of these cases the non-Jewish extended family is a functioning part of the child's world, and may be decisive in shaping the life of the child. It can no longer be assumed, a priori, therefore, that a child of a Jewish mother will be Jewish any more than that the child of a non-Jewish mother will not be. This leads us to the conclusion that the same requirements must be applied to establish the status of a child of a mixed marriage, regardless of whether the mother or the father is Jewish.

> —Report of the Committee on Patrilineal Descent on the Status of Children of Mixed Marriages as Adopted by the Central Conference of American Rabbis (Reform), 1983

Given our changing world, finality and certainty are illusory at best, destructive at worst. Rather than claiming to have found a goal at the end of the road, the ideal Conservative Jew is a traveler walking purposefully toward "God's holy mountain."

> —*Emet Ve-Emunah*, Statement of Principles of the Conservative Movement, 1988

Traditional Judaism is often pictured as a barren legalism, in which the observance of the external laws takes the place of a relation with a living

God. . . . This is nothing but a gross caricature. . . . Traditional Judaism was always a religion, not of law, but of commandment. . . . Obedience to a law does not necessarily create a relation to its giver. Obedience to a commandment . . . creates such a relation.

> —Emil L. Fackenheim, professor of philosophy, "The Dilemma of Liberal Judaism," *Commentary*, October 1960

The old conflict between Hasidism and normative Judaism is but another face of the mythical conflict between Dionysus, the god of ecstasy, and Apollo, the god of form and reason.

> —Rabbi Samuel Z. Glaser, rabbi emeritus of the Elmont Jewish Center on Long Island and professor of psychology, excerpt from sermon, 1991

To demand equal rights for Reform and Conservative Judaism in Israel today is like calling for Eskimo rights in Guatemala: in principle justified, but where's the constituency?

> —Gershom Gorenberg, Israeli journalist, *Jerusalem Report*, April 20, 1995

The decline of modern orthodoxy has been bad for the Jews. This is the group that is most needed to make the religious synthesis: this is the group that could be a natural bridge between Judaism and modernity. The collapse of the bridge leaves a dangerous and growing gap between classic Jewish religion and contemporary culture.

> —Rabbi Irving Greenberg, author, scholar, and founder of the National Jewish Center for Learning and Leadership (CLAL), quoted in *In the Service of God* by Shalom Freedman (1995)

The forces of modernity, being so ubiquitous and powerful, sometimes forced deniers to become so consumed by their resistances that these overshadowed the very Judaism they were trying to preserve. Ignoring modernity is harder to live with than ignorance of it.

> —Samuel C. Heilman, professor of sociology and Jewish studies, "The Many Faces of Orthodoxy," *Modern Judaism*, February 1982

Postmodern feminist rock'n'roll kabbalistic neo-hasidic quadruple worlds . . .

> —Rodger Kamenetz, author and professor of English, describing the Jewish renewal movement, *Stalking Elijah* (1997)

We are now entering a new stage in Judaism, a time of crisis but also of renewal. The old foundations, whether of Reform Judaism at one end or of Orthodoxy at the other, have been shaken. If I were to define myself denominationally, I'd say I'm an under-constructionist—and I wear a yellow hard-hat yarmulke.

> —Rodger Kamenetz, *Stalking Elijah* (1997)

Judaism has passed through three distinct stages . . . and is now on the threshold of a fourth stage. It was primarily national in character during the First Commonwealth era; ecclesiastical during the Second Commonwealth era, and rabbinical from then until the end of the eighteenth century. It is now developing into a democratic civilization.

> —Rabbi Mordechai M. Kaplan, founder of Reconstructionism, *The Principles of Reconstructionism and Questions Jews Ask*, 1956, reprinted in *Modern Jewish Thought*, edited by Nahum N. Glatzer (1977)

We are Orthodox Jews . . . who have, however, undergone the modern experience—and survived it; who refuse to accept modernity uncritically, but equally so refuse to reject it unthinkingly.

> —Rabbi Norman Lamm, president of Yeshiva University, 1985, quoted in *Critical Documents of Jewish History*, edited by Ronald H. Isaacs and Kerry M. Olitzky (1995)

Torah Umadda holds that modernity is neither to be uncritically embraced nor utterly shunned nor relentlessly fought, but is to be critically engaged from a mature and responsible Torah vantage. It does not assume that all that is new is good—or bad.

> —Rabbi Norman Lamm, *Torah Umadda: The Encounter of Religious Learning and Worldly Knowledge in the Jewish Tradition* (1990)

It is this Conservative Rabbi's opinion that whereas historical conditioning can explain the divisions between Conservative and Reform Judaism in the United States and Canada, if not justify them, there is neither compelling historical arguments nor justification for exporting this competition to other parts of the world, especially South America and Israel. For the initiated, differences can be pointed out, although a modus operandi could certainly be worked out; for the secular or orthodox Jew, there is but one distinction: you are either orthodox or non-orthodox, and it seems abundantly clear to me who we are, unless we want to be orthodox in our liberalism.

> —Rabbi Marshall T. Meyer, human rights activist, founder of the Seminario Rabinico Latinoamericano, and spiritual leader of B'nai Jeshurun in New York City, talk at Hebrew Union College, May 23, 1990

Modern Orthodox should make it clear that often we not only disagree with many who purport to speak for all who are Orthodox, but at times, we even are embarrassed by them.

> —Rabbi Emanuel Rackman, chancellor of Bar Ilan University, author, and columnist, *The Jewish Week,* January 3, 1997

I met real Chasidim, some of them the warmest and most genuine people I ever met—and I would aim for that kind of menschlichkeit—and I met others who were not so wonderful. But I did learn to respect Chasidim as individuals who know something we don't understand. Chasidim imbue a ceremony with a meaning that 90% of the Jewish people miss; they invest a holiness and a meaning in it that takes them to another plane.

> —Oren Rudavsky, filmmaker, codirector with Menachem Daum of *A Life Apart: Chasidism in America,* quoted in *Lifestyles,* New Year 1998

Orthodox Jews believe—as do all people not "committed" to a totally relativistic rendering of reality—that certain truths are absolute. To deny this and present the Torah as "one opinion" is to falsify our ancestral faith. The very nature of humankind's God-given dignity and the Creator's great love for all, however, demand that we rethink our evaluation of and response to the "other." By approaching all people with understanding, empathy, respect and perhaps even love, we can begin to realize the universal implications of God's descent upon Sinai millennia ago.

> —Rabbi Mayer Schiller, author and teacher of Talmud, "We Are Not Alone in This World," *Tikkun,* March/April 1996

We need to move away from the "neutral," non-proselytizing stance that has hitherto informed our outreach programs. Our desire to welcome converts should be made explicit. We need to affirm our Judaism frankly, freely, proudly, and without fear that it will offend non-Jewish spouses. If we lack missionary zeal, they are bound to surmise that we have no message.

> —Rabbi Alexander M. Schindler, president of the Union of American Hebrew Congregation, addressing four thousand delegates at their Baltimore 1991 convention, quoted in the *Jerusalem Post,* December 21, 1991

It is time to reassert with courage and conviction in word and by deed the wisdom of Conservative Judaism. Though but one movement in modern Judaism, we have the power to convey the greatest religious good to the largest number of Jews. It is to that historic challenge that I summon you today; the welfare of all Israel hangs in the balance.

> —Rabbi Ismar Schorsch, chancellor of the Jewish Theological Seminary, "Retrospect and Prospect," JTS website, 1998

For the whole community, it is time to think post-denominational. There is an urgent need to upgrade denominations and indeed move beyond them to create a universal language of Judaism with new vital centers.

> —Michael Steinhardt, philanthropist, "Stopping the Drift: An Entrepreneurial Vision for Jewish Renewal," speaking at a Hillel conference in Baltimore, reprinted in *Forward*, April 10, 1988

The old question for Reform Judaism was "How do you make changes in Judaism to adapt to the modern world?" The question today is "How do we take modern people and bring them to a loving encounter with Torah?"

> —Rabbi Sheldon Zimmerman, president of Hebrew Union College-Jewish Institute of Religion, New York, quoted in *The Jewish Week*, August 4, 1995

❖ DIASPORA ❖

(see also Aliyah, Israel)

Through a historical catastrophe—the destruction of Jerusalem by the Emperor of Rome . . . —I was born in one of the cities of the Diaspora. But I always deemed myself as one who was really born in Jerusalem.

> —S. Y. Agnon, Israeli author, Nobel Prize acceptance speech, 1966

The Jewish people need what I call a "global Jewish strategy." I don't believe that it is possible today to have a Jewish policy that will be run by American Jewry as they see fit and by Israeli Jewry as they see fit. There is a single Jewish world—intertwined, interconnected.

> —Ralph I. Goldman, executive vice-president of the American Jewish Joint Distribution Committee, statement, May 1979

I am not saying . . . that you cannot live, if you try hard enough, an authentically Jewish life in the Diaspora. I am saying that if the criterion is the future of our people, you are living in the wrong place.

> —Hillel Halkin, Israeli author, *Letters to an American Jewish Friend* (1977)

Zionism is supposed to make Jews realize how uncomfortable they are in the Diaspora and how such living has too little dignity. In the United States, Zionism has acted to the contrary—to make Jews more comfortable in the Diaspora and a greater force within the society at large. . . . Their involvement in Israel gives content and verve to lives they intend to continue to live in the American Diaspora.

—Rabbi Arthur Hertzberg, author, and professor, *Being Jewish in America: The Modern Experience* (1979)

It's time to say that America is a better place to be a Jew than Jerusalem. If there ever was a promised land, we Jewish Americans are living in it.

—Rabbi Jacob Neusner, professor of Jewish studies, "Is America the Promised Land for the Jews?" *The Washington Post*, May 8, 1987

Diaspora, with glass jars of cucumbers pickled in parsley and garlic on every windowsill, with pale flesh, stooped shoulders. Diaspora, in the liturgy, in the jokes, in the sermons, self-satisfied. Diaspora, with all of its symbols and refinements.

—Amos Oz, Israeli novelist and essayist, *In the Land of Israel* (1983)

Montana is the true Diaspora.

—Tammie Reiter, resident of Billings, Montana, location of the only synagogue in the state, quoted in *The Invisible Thread: A Portrait of American Jewish Women* by Diana Bletter (1989)

How will committed Jews in the diaspora deal with the fact that Israeli Arabs who identify as Palestinians will be voting in an election which basically will accept or reject the Oslo accords and may determine the future of the Golan Heights, while there will be no polling stations in Teaneck, Borough Park, Flatbush or Monsey?

—Efraim Zuroff, director of the Israeli office of the Simon Wiesenthal Center in Jerusalem, *The Jewish Week*, October 6, 1995

❖ DIVORCE ❖

(see also Marriage, Relationships)

One man who came to me for advice because he was contemplating a divorce told me mournfully why he thought the marriage went wrong. He said, "I know what my problem was. I was looking for a Ferrari and I got a Ford." I said, "I think the problem was you were looking for a car."

—Rabbi David Aaron, director of the Isralight Institute, *Endless Light* (1997)

Max! . . . You left us in such a terrible state. You had no compassion for us. For six years I loved you faithfully, took care of you like a loyal servant, never had a happy day with you. Yet I forgive you for everything. Have you ever asked yourself why you left us? . . . I was a young, educated, decent girl when you took me. You lived with me for six years, during which time I bore you four children. And then you left me.

> —Anonymous, quoted from letter printed in the advice column "A Bintel Brief" in *The Forward* in 1908 signed by "Your Deserted Wife and Chil-
> dren," quoted in *A Bintel Brief: Sixty Years of Letters from the Lower East Side to the Jewish Daily Forward*, compiled and edited by Isaac Metzker (1971)

The non-support "plague" is the worst plague of all. For the merest none-such, a man is caught and committed to the workhouse. He doesn't even get a chance to defend himself. Even during the worst of times of the Russian reaction people didn't suffer as the men suffer here in America because of their wives. For a Jewish wife it's as easy here to condemn her husband to impris-onment as it is for her to try on a pair of gloves. In all the world there isn't such legal injustice as here in the alimony courts.

> —Anonymous letter to the editor of the "Bintel Brief" advice column from thirty-seven men who were imprisoned in the workhouse of Blackwell Island Prison for nonsupport of their families, quoted in *A Bintel Brief: Sixty Years of Letters from the Lower East Side to the Jewish Daily Forward*, compiled and edited by Isaac Metzker (1971)

Studying this work [Shostakovich's Fourteenth Symphony] I came to realize that as death approaches [he was fifty-eight] an artist must cast off everything that may be restraining him and create in complete freedom. I decided that I had to do this for myself, to live the rest of my life as I want.

> —Leonard Bernstein, conductor, commenting about his decision to leave his wife, prefacing his performance with the New York Philharmonic in De-cember 1976, quoted in *Leonard Bernstein* by Humphrey Burton (1994) (Bernstein and his wife were later reconciled before her death in 1978.)

Frankly, I'm getting a little sick of cranky Republicans who can't keep their own families together telling everybody else about family values. Quick. What do Newt Gingrich, Bob Dole, Phil Gramm, and George Will have in common? They've all been married only one less time than Rush Limbaugh.

> —Al Franken, comedian, writer for *Saturday Night Live*, and author, *Rush Limbaugh Is a Big Fat Idiot and Other Observations* (1996)

To my mind, divorce is a deplorable breach of contract, and I say without humor that children should be allowed to sue. Consider the facts: Two people agree to create a human being and promise to give it love, a home, security and happiness. They take this step with the best of intentions, to be sure, but then something goes awry. They find they really hate each other or for some other reason cannot live together. But in separating, they put themselves first and forget about the contract they have with their child. I do not believe, as you often hear soon-to-be-divorced parents say, that the separation will be "best for the child." My experience has taught me better.

> —Ari L. Goldman, journalist and author, *The Search for God at Harvard* (1991)

Falling in love at first sight may be a myth, but annihilation in one moment is not. It was like . . . a bullet to the inner brain.

> —Laura Z. Hobson, author, *Laura Z. A Life: Years of Fulfillment* (1986)

When my marriage became unbearable, and I was losing any sense of myself inch by inch, and I knew I had to leave my husband or disappear completely, I was more worried about telling my parents than I was about telling my husband because here was their pride and joy disappointing them by leaving their son-in-law.

> —Penny Kaganoff, editor and journalist, "Other Uses for a Wedding Gown" in *Women on Divorce: A Bedside Companion*, edited by Kaganoff and Susan Spano (1993)

Divorce laws can be highly discretionary; to have faith in them, you have to have faith in judges. . . . It's possible to infer from this not just gender bias but vindictiveness on the part of judges applying the new divorce laws in what they may consider to be a postfeminist world. It's as if they were paying back feminists for demanding equality by thrusting it on women who were raised to be content with inequality and shaped their lives around it.

> —Wendy Kaminer, attorney and author, *A Fearful Freedom: Women's Flight From Equality* (1990)

That is not to say that I don't acknowledge the necessity of divorce as a way to end a bad marriage. I do. What I don't accept is the view of divorce as an alternative equal to the choice of staying married. I don't accept the idea that when conflict disrupts a marriage, or when change causes stress, equal weight should be given to trying to solve problems within the marriage and solving the problem by leaving the marriage.

> —Francine Klagsbrun, author, *Married People: Staying Together in the Age of Divorce* (1985)

Divorce didn't force me to abandon the idea that I would find a man who would take care of me—marriage had done that.

> —Rhoda Koenig, author, "Till Divorce Do Us Part," *Vogue*, October 1997

In my twenty years as Ann Landers this is the most difficult column I have ever tried to put together. . . . As I write these words, it is as if I am referring to a letter from a reader. It seems unreal that I am writing about my own marriage . . . I apologize to my editors for not giving you your money's worth today. I ask that you not fill this space with other letters. Please leave it blank—as a memorial to one of the world's best marriages that didn't make it to the finish line.

> —Eppie Lederer, advice columnist also known as Ann Landers, excerpt from her column in which she announced to her readers that she and her husband were getting divorced after thirty-five years of marriage, July 1, 1975, quoted in *Eppie: The Story of Ann Landers* by Margo Howard (1982)

I no longer believe that marriage means forever no matter how lousy it is—or "for the sake of the children."

> —Eppie Lederer, quoted in *U.S. News & World Report*, October 23, 1995

Unlike the elegant lifestyle liberals who seem to have endless opportunities for new relationships and hence have seemingly little fear of divorce, many Americans feel that their lives would be much worse off if their marriage were to collapse. The freedom of endless opportunities for new relationships that liberals seem to celebrate actually feels to many of the "less elegant" set as endless opportunities for rejection, loneliness and pain.

> —Michael Lerner, editor of *Tikkun*, "A Meaning-Oriented Contract With American Families," *Tikkun*, July/August 1995

The breakup of a marriage, American style—especially if there's a child involved—is more in the spirit of war than you'd believe possible of a negotiation involving two people who once slept side by side.

> —Daphne Merkin, novelist and essayist, "In the Country of Divorce: Confessions of a Soon-to-Be Divorcee" in *Women on Divorce: A Bedside Companion*, edited by Penny Kaganoff and Susan Spano (1995)

I think it's wonderful to stay home and take care of children, but it's deceptive. If this could happen to me, this could happen to you because I didn't have a clue.

> —Marilyn Nichols Kane, ex-wife of Jeffrey Nichols, who was arrested because he owed his family over $500,000 in child support, quoted in "Deadbeat Dads Beware," *Lifestyles*, Summer 1996

I was wrong. I should have, to the best of my ability, made some payments so that I could look my three older children in the face and say "I did the best I could."

> —Jeffrey Nichols, "King of the Deadbeat Dads," CBS-TV's *60 Minutes*, his

first interview after being nabbed for refusing to pay more than $500,000 in back child support, quoted in the *New York Daily News*, October 27, 1995

I leave the psychiatrists the explanation of the volatile transformation from love to hate. The chemical ingredients of rejection, jealousy and possessiveness certainly play a part in the explosive content. But there is something more, a mysterious element, which unbalances the mind, changes the personality, and distorts the character. It derives undoubtedly from the sexual ties which, if profound and ecstatic, can never be completely severed. The mutual enslavement of love will not tolerate unilateral freedom. Two people joined together in intimacy are often like Siamese twins, the separation of one causing the death of the other.

> —Louis Nizer, attorney, litigator, and author, *My Life in Court* (1961)

At 4 or 40, most children of divorce continue to resent the rupture in normalcy. As far as I'm concerned, it doesn't really matter if your stepmother pulls all-nighters for a week preparing for Passover (as my first stepmother did) or whether she dyes Easter eggs. In my evaluation of stepmothers, only one thing counts: They have to know when it's judicious to say, "Your father really does love you."

> —Vanessa Ochs, author and Dorot Fellow at CLAL, "When Parents Intermarry," *Sh'ma*, March 17, 1995

Every divorce is a story and while they can begin to sound the same—sad and cautionary—each one is as unique as a human face.

> —Anne Roiphe, author "A Tale of Two Divorces" in *Women on Divorce: A Bedside Companion*, edited by Penny Kaganoff and Susan Spano (1995)

I want to make my life different from what my mother chose. I guess the best thing about me moving out on my own is to prove to myself that if, God forbid, something happens when I do get married, I know that I can survive on my own and won't have to be stuck in a marriage that I'm afraid of leaving.

> —Cora Sands, twenty-four-year-old woman born and raised in Los Angeles, quoted in *Generations: A Century of Women Speak Out about Their Lives* by Myriam Miedzian and Alisa Malinovich (1997)

In none of my assiduous eavesdropping on the street did I ever hear any mentions of unhappy marriage or happy marriage. Marriage was married. Although a Jewish divorce was a singularly easy matter except for the disgrace it carried, the Jewish women were as firmly embedded in their marriages as the Catholic. A divorce was as unthinkable as adultery or lipstick. No matter what—beatings, infidelity, drunkenness, verbal abuse, outlandish demands—no woman could run the risk of making her children fatherless. Marriage and children were fate.

—Kate Simon, author, *Bronx Primitive: Portraits in a Childhood* (1982)

It's as though after a serious car crash, my wife remained inside to extricate herself and the kids from the wreckage, while I opened the only working door and went off to recuperate, promising to send money, phone the kids, and stop by on the weekend to take them off her hands.

—Ted Solotaroff, editor and author, "Getting the Point" in *Men on Divorce*, edited by Penny Kaganoff and Susan Spano (1997)

Sharing kids with a person you have come to despise must be a bit like getting caught in a messy car wreck and then being forced to spend the rest of your life paying visits to the paraplegic in the other vehicle. You are never allowed to forget your mistake.

—Elizabeth Wurtzel, author, *Prozac Nation* (1994)

Of all the odd demands that modern life makes on humanity, the most difficult may be not only its insistence that we comfortably spend our adult lives going from one situation of serial monogamy to another, but its expectation that we get along, maintain friendships, share parental duties, and in some cases even attend the second and third wedding of our exes. It asks that we pretend that heartbreak is a minor inconvenience that can be overcome with just the right amount of psycholanguage, with just a few repetitions of the mantra "for the sake of the children."

—Elizabeth Wurtzel, *Prozac Nation* (1994)

JEWISH DIVORCE

The sad truth is that many women are remarrying . . . without having received a Jewish divorce because of their first husband's intransigence. The sad truth is that many other women are being doomed to loneliness and isolation because they will not rebel against rabbinic authority. The sad truth is that the entire structure of Jewish law is being charged with rigidity and insensitivity because of its seeming inability to find an acceptable solution. . . . Indeed, whenever a solution has been offered, legal objections have caused it to be set aside. And yet, Amemer found a solution; Maimonides found a solution; the sages of our generation must dare do no less. The legal precedent exists; the courageous legalists must make their voices heard and their position accepted.

—Rabbi Shlomo Riskin, founder of yeshiva in Efrat, Israel, and founding rabbi of Lincoln Square Synagogue in New York City, *Women and Jewish Divorce* (1989)

Based on our experience, we believe that the solution of the agunah [an "anchored" woman whose husband has left her and refuses to give her a Jewish divorce; without this, she cannot remarry. A man in a similar position is in a more advantageous position] problem for those already married is strong communal sanction against those who abuse the get [Jewish divorce decree] process; and for those not yet married, the universal adoption of the prenuptial agreement . . . approved by world-renowned rabbinic authorities, which would prevent the problem from arising.

> —Rabbi Howard Jachter and Rabbi Eliyahu Teitz, of Elizabeth, New Jersey, letter to the editor, *The Jewish Week*, January 23, 1998

The fundamental flaw in Jewish divorce is its underlying principle: That it is a man's absolute right and therefore the get can be given only at his will. . . . Today, I no longer believe it is sufficient to address the symptom without addressing the root cause. No one should any longer try to defend or justify something which is unethical in principle and corrupt in practice. Clearly the original intent of the law was otherwise.

> —Blu Greenberg, writer and activist, "For the Love of Law," *Hadassah*, May 1993

It is not unthinkable that a daring, progressive rabbinate, basing itself on Talmudic precedent, will some day once and for all declare Biblical marriage at an end and usher in a well regulated marriage that is free from the encumbrances of the present Jewish marriage. But who can wait for that day? The agunot cannot afford to wait. And evidently they do not wait. They defy Jewish law and the purity of the Jewish family is being broken down. Needless to say that something must be done immediately, lest we lose the last thread of respect for Jewish law.

> —Rabbi Louis M. Epstein, Conservative rabbi with Orthodox ordination who served as president of the Rabbinical Assembly and chairman of its committee on Jewish law, suggesting a premarital agreement that would give protection to the agunah, quoted in *Proceedings of the Rabbinic Assembly 1930–1932*

Most of the agunah cases also blame rabbanim [rabbinic authorities]. Where are their fathers and mothers and brothers? What happened to Shimon and Levi, the brothers of Dina? The parents, in many cases, took the easy way out by not being appropriately diligent in arranging the shidduch [the matchmaking]. They abdicated their responsibility after the shidduch. Shidduch-phobia is so common, that the fear of not being able to marry off a child clouds people's judgment and they take the easy way out.

—Rabbi Mendel Epstein, columnist, *The Jewish Press*, February 28, 1997

Master of the Universe, ask the agunah to forgive me. Be my witness that I wanted to ease her lot so that a Jewish woman would not consider your Torah heartless.

—Chaim Grade, Yiddish writer, *The Agunah* (1974)

The more the agunah values the halakhic [Jewish legal] system, the more she is hurt by it.

—Netty C. Gross, Israeli journalist, "A Horror Story—Ours," *Jerusalem Report*, June 17, 1993

Until a rabbinic will is found on this issue, every Jewish woman is a potential agunah.

—Netty C. Gross, "A Horror Story—Ours," *Jerusalem Report*, June 17, 1993

Of course, we'd prefer a system, the way it was once, where the Jewish community is in control of its own. Then you take the stubborn fellow in and you lay him down on a table, give him a few slaps, tell him he has to free the woman, and that's it. But we don't have that control. So we try to get binding arbitration and that way, through the side door, receive some sort of support from the [local] government. In Eretz Yisrael, it's a mechayeh [a delight]. Divorce falls within the jurisdiction of a bes din [rabbinic court]. The bes din consists of reasonable people, they come up with a reasonable settlement, and if people don't live up to it, they go to jail.

—Rabbi Levi Horowitz, the Bostoner Rebbe, a member of the World Executive Committee of Agudat Israel, quoted in "A Moment Report: Who Is a Jew," *Moment*, September 1981

We must all understand that there is no justification for what is occurring today. The "logical" arguments to continue accepting this travesty of injustice is created by an atmosphere of "ad delo yada," [hebrew, "until he does not know"], where an individual cannot tell the difference between Haman and Mordechai—between right and wrong.

—Marilyn Mattie Klein, "To Whom It May Concern," *The Jewish Press*, March 21, 1997

How many of us could withstand the tremendous test for faith that these women endure daily, teaching their children to love Torah, when clearly the Torah law cannot protect them?

> —Marilyn Mattie Klein, "To Whom It May Concern," *The Jewish Press,* March 21, 1997

It's an abuse of Jewish law to put a price on a get [a Jewish divorce], but that's what's happening more and more. A get has become a commodity with a price on it like any other.

> —Dennis Rapps, attorney, quoted in "Playing Hard to Get: Orthodox Jews and the Women Who Have Trouble Divorcing Them," *New York,* January 25, 1993

I know that it was your intention to spare me the vilification of colleagues and the demeaning of my status in the eyes of those who heretofore respected me. But all my life I pained the agony of Agunot, and if, before I die, I can make a major contribution to the amelioration of their plight, I simply must do it and suffer whatever will happen to me and my image.

> —Rabbi Emanuel Rackman, chancellor of Bar-Ilan University, author, and columnist "An Open Letter to a Cherished Friend," *The Jewish Press,* February 13, 1998

✤ DRUGS ✤

Pot will be legal in ten years. Why? Because in this audience probably every other one of you knows a law student who smokes pot, who will become a senator, who will legalize it to protect himself. But then, no one will smoke it anymore. You'll see.

> —Lenny Bruce, satirist, quoted in *The Essential Lenny Bruce,* edited by John Cohen (1967)

[In politics] the general standard apparently seems to be, "I smoked marijuana once, I hated it, I'm genuinely sorry I did it." You're allowed, if you're a member of that generation—if you 'fess up—to say, yeah, I was a part of that.

> —Jeff Greenfield, television journalist, after the New Hampshire presidential primaries, discussing the emergence of Bill Clinton and a new generation in politics, appearance on *Later With Bob Costas,* NBC, February 1992

You be careful. Like, if you're going to take acid, make sure you have competent friends around. And lots of nature. A lot of familiar, reassuring images to focus on . . .

> —Allen Ginsberg, poet, quoted in *Allen Ginsberg in America* by Jane Kramer (1968)

I am a little frightened to present myself—the fear of your rejection of me, the fear of not being tranquil enough to reassure you that we can talk together, make sense, and perhaps even like each other, enough to want not to offend, or speak in a way which is abrupt or hard to understand.

> —Allen Ginsberg, introducing himself to Senators Quentin Burdick, Jacob Javits, and Edward Kennedy at a special Judiciary Subcommittee hearing on narcotics legislation, quoted in *Allen Ginsberg in America* by Jane Kramer (1968)

I always thought the thing about getting high was overdone. Even at its height, I think I conditioned myself not to do it for a simple reason. Somebody had to be in control of their senses. Somebody had to touch base with reality at all times.

> —Bill Graham, rock music impresario who owned the Fillmore East and Fillmore West theaters, 1991, *Bill Graham Presents*, written with Robert Greenfield (1992)

LSD confirmed everything I had been reading about in the mystical texts. It opened my mind to understand that there were infinite other levels of reality beyond ordinary consciousness and that the states these Hasidic texts were talking about, gadlut ha-mochin [higher consciousness] and so on, were forms of expanded consciousness.

> —Rabbi Arthur Green, professor of Jewish thought, interview with William Novak, *Kerem*, Spring 1995

Drugs have become a surrogate for all other problems. They're an enormously convenient and powerful scapegoat, a code word for attacking groups of people, whether they be hippies, blacks, or Hispanics.

> —Dr. Ethan Nadelman of the Lindesmith Center, a research institute on drug policy, quoted in "The Drug Peacenik," *New York*, January 23, 1995

When you grow up with the kind of Jewish identity I had, with a father who is a rabbi, you notice that whenever Jews lived in a place where the majority said, "You live your way; we'll live ours," the Jews were fine. Whenever Jews live where the majority said, "You have to live by our code because we know what's good for you," the Jews were fucked. And that's why I get worried when a society turns a group of people into bogeymen. The thing you learn from this is the basic need for tolerance of dissident or deviant groups. It's important to see drugs as a human rights issue.

> —Dr. Ethan Nadelman, quoted in "The Drug Peacenik," *New York*, January 23, 1995

The flat rules like "Just say no" are easy to pronounce but hard to enforce. It's so easy to make that kind of statement, and so hard to live it Saturday night by Saturday night.

> —Anne Roiphe, author and mother of three daughters, responding to the question "What do you tell your children about marijuana?" quoted in *Time*, December 9, 1996

Everybody has a mission, and part of mine has been dealing with unpopular subjects.

> —Rabbi Abraham J. Twerski, Hasidic rabbi, psychiatrist, writer, and founder and medical director of Gateway Rehabilitation Center, a nonprofit drug and alcohol treatment system near Pittsburgh, quoted in the *Baltimore Jewish Times*, November 13, 1997

❖ DUAL LOYALTIES ❖

(see also Disapora, Israel)

Let no American imagine that Zionism is incompatible with Patriotism. Multiple loyalties are objectionable only if they are inconsistent.

> —Louis D. Brandeis, lawyer named to the U.S. Supreme Court, 1916 speech, quoted in *Brandeis on Zionism* (1942)

I found no conflict in myself between my sentiments toward America and Israel. As a Jew I believe that peace is the central factor of my credo. I abhor the way some of my fellow Jews brandish the Bible in order to justify making war.

> —Leon H. Charney, New York lawyer who was instrumental in negotiating— through back-door channels—the 1979 Camp David peace treaty between Israel and Egypt, *Special Counsel* (1984)

The only loyalty of an American Jew is to the United States of America without any ifs, ands or buts. The State of Israel is the ancestral homeland of his forefathers, the birthplace of his faith. As a haven for over a million Jews after the agony of the past 20 years, it has special meaning for Jews all over the world. But spiritual bonds and emotional ties are quite different from political loyalty.

—Rabbi Morris Kertzer, from his 1952 articles in *Look* magazine and *Reader's Digest*, quoted by Samuel C. Heilman, *The Jewish Week*, July 7, 1995

America is a luxury hotel—five stars. But Israel is home. Look, they say a man can only truly love one woman, and it's true. I have a lot of respect and appreciating for America, I've expressed remorse for my deeds. I never did and never would do anything to harm the U.S. But for Israel, I am ready to lay down my life, here and now.

—Jonathan Pollard, U.S. federal employee imprisoned for spying on behalf of Israel, interviewed by Ben Caspit in the Federal Correctional Institute, Butner, North Carolina, quoted in *Long Island Jewish World*, June 6, 1997

❖ ECONOMICS ❖

(see also Business)

In a healthy society, every useful activity is compensated in a way to permit a decent living. The exercise of any socially valuable activity gives inner satisfaction; but it cannot be considered as part of the salary. The teacher cannot use his inner satisfaction to fill the stomachs of his children.

> —Albert Einstein, Nobel Prize-winning theoretical physicist and humanist, message for Canadian Education Week, March 1952, reprinted in *Ideas and Opinions: Albert Einstein* (1982)

Capitalism, at least, took women seriously as consumers; it had to concern itself in some ways with their needs, if only to manipulate them for profit.

> —Betty Friedan, author and activist, *The Second Stage* (1981)

When the alcoholic starts drinking, the good effects come first; the bad effects only come the next morning when he wakes up with a hangover—and often cannot resist easing the hangover by taking "the hair of the dog that bit him." The parallel with inflation is exact.

> —Milton and Rose Friedman, *Free to Choose: A Personal Statement* (1980)

Capitalism is based on self-interest and self-esteem; it holds integrity and trustworthiness as cardinal virtues and makes them pay off in the marketplace, thus demanding that men survive by means of virtues, not of vices. It is this superlatively moral system that the welfare statistics propose to improve upon by means of protective law, snooping bureaucrats, and the chronic goad of fear.

—Alan Greenspan, economist, "The Assault on Integrity" in *Capitalism: The Unknown Ideal* by Ayn Rand (1967)

Health isn't a good like other goods. If someone can't afford a car, we're willing to say, well, he doesn't have a car. But if a man who can't afford medical care is bleeding on the sidewalk, we are going to provide him with it one way or another, at public expense if necessary. . . . We can debate how to pay for those who can't afford care. But no respectable American politician would leave the man on the sidewalk.

—Mickey Kaus, journalist, *The End of Equality* (1992)

The most frightening transformation for me in recent years is the absolute triumph of the notion that the economy is a force of nature and that there's nothing we can do about the ravaging of our lives in the face of economic shortfall. There's virtual slave labor all around the world and grotesque disparities of income. We're told the money has sort of gone somewhere, just disappeared, and there simply isn't enough to go around.

—Tony Kushner, playwright, quoted in the *Jerusalem Post*, August 8, 1996

It is all very well to say of a woman that "she is working for her living," but suppose she is working and not making her living? What are you to say then? You can remark that you are indeed very sorry, and leave the matter there. Or you can say with more piety than wisdom that wages are determined by natural laws which man must let alone. Or, you can insist that she is being sweated; that a business which does not pay a living wage is not paying its labor costs; that such businesses are humanly insolvent, for in paying less than a minimum wage they are guilty of as bad business practice and far worse moral practice than if they were paying dividends out of assets.

—Walter Lippmann, journalist, *The New Republic*, March 27, 1915

Capitalism in Russia has produced far more Al Capones than Henry Fords, more Luca Grasis than Ward Cleavers.

—David Remnick, journalist and author, "Letter From Moscow," *The New Yorker*, November 22, 1993

The basic test of a functioning democracy is its ability to create new wealth and see to its fair distribution. When a democratic society does not meet the test of fairness, when, as in the present state, no attempt seems to be made at fairness, freedom is in jeopardy. Whether the attack comes from the left or from the right is irrelevant; both extremes are equally lethal.

> —Felix G. Rohatyn, financier, address to graduating class of Middlebury (Vt.) College, May 1982, quoted in *Lend Me Your Ears: Great Speeches in History*, edited by William Safire (1992)

❖ EDUCATION ❖

(see also Jewish Education)

There are few things that I respect more than a really good question.

> —Joseph Aaron, editor of the *Chicago Jewish News*, quoted in *The Jewish Advocate*, November 3–9, 1995

Education was free. That subject my father had written about repeatedly, as comprising his chief hope for us children, the essence of American opportunity, the treasure that no thief could touch, not even misfortune or poverty. It was the one thing he was able to promise us when he sent for us; surer, safer than bread or shelter.

> —Mary Antin, author, *The Promised Land* (1912)

Education that is essentially pareve—that's neutral and doesn't take a strong stand—has little chance of succeeding. . . . All effective education has at its foundation a distinct and well-considered vision.

> —Seymour Fox, professor of Jewish education, *Vision at the Heart* (1996)

Our job is not to make up anyone's mind, but to open minds—to make the agony of decision-making so intense that you can escape only by thinking.

> —Fred Friendly, journalist who began the Media and Society Seminars on PBS, introduction to 1984 broadcast, quoted by Nat Hentoff, *The Washington Post*, May 3, 1997

The line between those who will be winners and those who will be losers seems sharper than ever, and the line is the product of education.

> —David Halberstam, journalist, "Coming in From the Cold War," *The Washington Monthly*, January/February 1991

I was raised to believe that teachers were infallible and superhuman. A teacher was not like a relative, a neighbor, or even a friend. . . . She was above parents and just a little below God, and as such was held in the kind of awe that bordered on fear. . . . Educated people could do no wrong.

—Sam Levenson, humorist and author, *Everything but Money* (1966)

Education is something more than the acquisition of facts. Education is the power and love of thinking.

—Dr. Bernard Revel, founder of Yeshiva College of Yeshiva University, delivering the first Yeshiva College commencement address, June 16, 1932, quoted in *Bernard Revel: Builder of American Jewish Orthodoxy* by Aaron Rothkoff (1972)

Students are depicted as at their most alive when they have as little to do with school as possible. Huck and Holden light out for their respective territories; Ferris Bueller is the god of glorious truancy. Or make an Animal House, and trash the joint. School is anticreativity, antifreedom, anti-American—an attitude only logically contradicted by a society that insists on higher education for all and accreditations up to the eyeballs.

—Roger Rosenblatt, journalist, *Time,* May 12, 1997

Part of the job of education is to be able to tell what is baloney and what is not.

—Carl Sagan, author and professor of astronomy and space sciences, commencement address at Wheaton (Ill.) College, May 22, 1993, quoted in *Hold Fast Your Dreams: Twenty Commencement Speeches*, compiled by Carrie Boyko and Kimberly Colen (1996)

In the Talmud, it says a lesson taught with humor is a lesson retained. I'm not a comedian, but I can use humor to make a point and use it as a teachable moment.

—Dr. Ruth K. Westheimer, author and sex therapist, quoted in *Jewish Bulletin of Northern California*, July 19, 1996

To me it's very simple. If a person goes to the Washington museum and leaves saying, "Now I don't know—I have to learn about it," then it's a success. If the person leaves and says, "Now I know," then it's a failure.

—Elie Wiesel, Nobel laureate and author, *The New York Times,* March 5, 1997

What do you think your teachers or mine have tried to do when they taught you Shakespeare or Plato or mathematics or physics or health, especially? They tried to be sensitive to other people's pain and to other people's concern, and to other people's fear. Not to be sensitive to them would mean not only a tragedy to them but for yourselves.

> —Elie Wiesel, commencement address at Ithaca College, (N.Y.), quoted in *USA Today*, May 24, 1996

The business of the American teacher is to liberate American citizens to think apart and act together.

> —Rabbi Stephen S. Wise, Jewish leader and activist, quoted in *A Little Learning Is a Dangerous Thing*, edited by James Charlton (1994)

❖ EICHMANN TRIAL ❖

(see also Holocaust)

The Jerusalem trial thus brought out clearly once again the basic notions of right and wrong and drove them home with exemplary force, in the hope that if a man finds himself in the future entrusted with a task similar to Eichmann's he will stop in his tracks to reflect whether he may not share Eichmann's fate. In this alone the trial has performed a service to humanity.

> —Gideon Hausner, attorney general of Israel when Nazi war criminal Adolf Eichmann was found and brought to trial in Jerusalem in 1961 for his crimes against the Jews, *Justice in Jerusalem* (1966)

In rising to present the case against the accused, I am not alone. I am accompanied and surrounded by 6,000,000 prosecutors, who, alas, cannot stand and point their finger of accusation against the man in the dock, declaring "I accuse!" Their ashes are either at Auschwitz and Treblinka, or in graves scattered all over Europe. Their blood cries out but their voices are silent and unheard. It is in their name I present this awful indictment.

> —Gideon Hausner, from his opening statement of the prosecution's case against Eichmann, quoted in *Jewish Telegraphic Agency*, April 17, 1961

The dignity of the trial communicated its purpose at once. By the first of June there were few journalists and lawyers in the Western world who were not satisfied that this story not only had to be recorded for history, but that it was being told at the right time and in the right place and under the correct circumstances.

> —Harry Golden, journalist, *The Carolina Israelite*, May–June 1961

He [Eichmann] was in complete command of himself, nay, he was more: he was completely himself. Nothing could have demonstrated this more convincingly than the grotesque silliness of his last words. . . . It was as though in those last minutes he was summing up the lesson that this long course in human wickedness had taught us—the lesson of the fearsome, word-and-thought-defying banality of evil.

> —Hannah Arendt, philosopher, *Eichmann in Jerusalem: A Report on the Banality of Evil* (1963)

Once they cease to inspire fear, dictators and their servants are bound to become pathetic creatures and it is difficult to understand in retrospect how anyone could have been awed by them. Miss Arendt's appraisal of Eichmann, in brief, is too much influenced, I feel, by his performance in Jerusalem. Men tend to be banal in prison.

> —Walter Z. Laqueur, historian and author, from a book review written in November 1965 focusing on the Eichmann controversy, quoted in *The Jew as Pariah: Jewish Identity and Politics in the Modern Age*, edited by Ron H. Feldman (1978)

Far from lynching Eichmann or hanging him on the nearest tree, those who pursued him over fifteen years and finally seized him have handed him over to the process and judgment of the courts of law. The reference to mob passions and lawless justice in this context is unwarranted and provocative.

> —Golda Meir, foreign minister of Israel, United Nations Security Council Official Records, 866th meeting, June 22, 1961, quoted in *Justice in Jerusalem* by Gideon Hausner (1966)

Eichmann was an extraordinary not an ordinary man, whose record is hardly one of the "banality" of evil. For the author of that ineffable phrase—as applied to the murder of six million—to have been so taken in by Eichmann's version of himself is one of the puzzles of modern journalism. From a presumed historian it is inexplicable.

> —Barbara W. Tuchman, historian and author, criticizing Hannah Arendt's assessment of the trial and Eichmann, from the introduction to the paperback edition of *Justice in Jerusalem* by Gideon Hausner (1968)

Duvall met me, and I believe he understood well that Eichmann has to be a man who would say "excuse me" in the bathroom, but when you kill a child, there's no excuse me, it's an order.

—Peter Malkin, Mossad agent who captured Eichmann in Argentina in 1960, commenting on the casting of Robert Duvall to portray Eichmann in a movie adaptation of Malkin's 1990 memoir *Eichmann in My Hands,* quoted in "The Double Life of Peter Malkin," *Moment,* October 1995

❖ ENTERTAINMENT ❖

(see also Comedy)

I notified the rebbe every step of the way, sending him lyrics, checking with him on whether to perform in this or that place. The fact that he always took the time to answer me about my desire to sing is one of the reasons I was able to see it as a valuable and important thing. Even today, if I have to decide whether a particular lyric or piece of music is appropriate, I ask myself, what would the rebbe say?

—Avraham Fried, singer of Jewish spiritual music, commenting on his relationship with the Lubavitcher Rebbe, Menachem Mendel Schneerson, "Music With a Soul" by Calev Ben-David, *Jerusalem Report,* February 23, 1995

In my forty years in Hollywood, the moguls had such firm control of the business that the average executive kept his job for almost three decades. Starting in the 1970s, the average stay was around three years. It seemed as if being chosen to head a studio was like being appointed the president of a Central American democracy—each day, you wondered if this was the day you were going to be shot.

—Irving "Swifty" Lazar, show business agent and dealmaker, *Swifty: My Life and Good Times,* written with Annette Tapert (1995)

What ails today's films has nothing to do with the prowess or professionalism of the filmmakers. The true sickness is in the soul.

—Michael Medved, author and media commentator, *Hollywood vs. America* (1992)

The most significant difference between the Jews and non-Jews who participate in the entertainment industry is that the Jews are even more ill-informed concerning the fundamentals of their faith.

—Michael Medved, *Hollywood vs. America* (1992)

[Gene Roddenberry] was anti-Semitic, clearly. Roddenberry had Jewish associates; Bill [Shatner] and I were both Jewish. To be fair, Roddenberry was anti-religion, and apart from being a racial-cultural entity, Jews, to him, were a religious group. But he was certainly anti-Semitic. I saw examples not only of him practicing anti-Semitism, but of him being callous about other people's differences as well.

> —Leonard Nimoy, actor who portrayed Mr. Spock (the pointy-eared half-human, half-Vulcan first officer of the 24th-century starship *Enterprise*), recalling the notable absence of Jews from the multi-ethnic future universe envisioned by *Star Trek* creator Gene Roddenberry, quoted in "Der Yiddesher Vulcan" by Sheli Teitelbaum, *Jerusalem Report*, 1995

When I was a boy, there was a particular blessing used in our local shul. The four fingers of each hand were split to create the Hebrew letter shin, representing Shad-dai, the name of the Almighty. When we were creating the television program Star Trek, we needed a salute. I thought back to that hand symbol and proposed it. The rest, as they say, is history. Why did I think back to that hand gesture? Actors are always looking for something personal to bring to their professional lives. Maybe, then, it was the convergence of my spiritual and artistic lives. Maybe, in a way, I can call that salute my Vulcan shalom, my greeting of peace, my yearning for the blessing of peace—the age-old quest of the Jewish people, my people.

> —Leonard Nimoy, "What Being Jewish Means to Me," ad prepared by the American Jewish Committee, printed in *The New York Times*, December 22, 1996

I don't know if I am moving up or down the cultural ladder, or simply sideways, when I recall that there has been the song "Exodus," preceded by the movie *Exodus*, preceded by the novel *Exodus*. However you slice it, there does not seem to be any doubt that the image of Jew as patriot, warrior, and battle-scarred belligerent is rather satisfying to a larger segment of the American public.

> —Philip Roth, author, 1961 speech delivered at Loyola University for a symposium on "The Needs and Images of Man," reprinted in *Reading Myself and Others* (1975)

I've never put *Star Trek* down. On the contrary. It's a show biz phenomenon. I can only say good things about it.

> —William Shatner, actor, interview with Elliott Forrest, *A&E Monthly*, January 1996

The [radio] formats are boring. None of the formats on the radio apply to me, with the possible exception of public radio. Almost none of the mainstream interests me. So where do you go if they're not interested in what you're doing, and you're not interested in what they're doing?

> —Paul Simon, singer and composer, commenting two days after the preview of his score for the Broadway musical *Capeman*, quoted in *Entertainment Weekly*, October 3, 1997

Hollywood has a huge Jewish community and its share of political activists, especially on the liberal side, who are very concerned with Israel. But my overall impression is that most of the Jews in the entertainment industry prefer a shallow, glitzy "bagels and lox" Judaism. The high point of their Jewish life is a Seder at Spago's.

> —Sheli Teitelbaum, Los Angeles correspondent, *Jerusalem Report*, December 30, 1993

If a Jew appeared on a television drama in the 1950s, he was an Italian.

> —Edward Zwick, television director and cocreator of *Thirtysomething*, quoted in *The New York Times*, November 23, 1996

❖ ENVIRONMENT ❖

Every time you look out the window there is a constant reminder that our planet is not all that big, and the atmosphere is not all that high, and we've got to take care of what we have.

> —Ellen Baker, astronaut, quoted in *Singular Voices: Conversations With Americans Who Make a Difference* by Barbaralee Diamonstein (1997)

We can surely be good Jews and good people if we live out of nature, but we become lopsided. We tend to overdevelop our cerebral sense, or our cynicism, or our fashion sense, or our appetite for culture, or our musculature in an effort to compensate for what can only reach us through nature.

> —Shira Dicker, writer, "Nature, Spirit, Body" in *Ecology and the Jewish Spirit: Where Nature & the Sacred Meet*, edited by Ellen Bernstein (1998)

Public discussion of the environment issue is frequently characterized more by emotion than reason. Much of it proceeds as if the issue is pollution versus no pollution, as if it were desirable or possible to have a world without pollution. That is clearly nonsense.

—Milton and Rose Friedman, economists and authors, *Free to Choose: A Personal Statement* (1980)

The development of the automobile did add to one form of pollution—but it largely ended a far less attractive form.

—Milton and Rose Friedman, *Free to Choose: A Personal Statement* (1980)

Nature is the garb of God, the coat of many colors in which the One is ever both hidden and revealed.

—Rabbi Arthur Green, professor of Jewish thought, "Judaism for the Post-Modern Era," the Samuel H. Goldenson Lecture delivered December 12, 1994, at the Hebrew Union College-Jewish Institute of Religion, Cincinnati, Ohio

People talk about the silence of nature, but of course there is no such thing. What they mean is our voices are still, our noises absent.

—Sue Halpern, author, "Solo," *Migrations to Solitude* (1992)

There are three ways in which we may relate ourselves to the world—we may exploit it, we may enjoy it, we may accept it in awe.

—Rabbi Abraham Joshua Heschel, author, activist, and theologian, *God in Search of Man* (1955)

In a society that has made of extravagance a commonplace and of distraction a fiendish art, Judaism at its best holds out one model—often dismissed or abused in reality—for reining in the appetites of human consciousness—a strain of asceticism blended with a love of learning. To learn to live with less . . . will demand of all of us, each in his own way, a rapid expansion of our inner resources.

—Rabbi Ismar Schorsch, chancellor of the Jewish Theological Seminary, "Learning to Live with Less: A Jewish Perspective," presented at a 1990 symposium at Middlebury (Vt.) College, reprinted in *Spirit and Nature: Why the Environment Is a Religious Issue*, edited by Steven C. Rockefeller and John C. Elder (1992)

The environmental crisis is not only a crisis of technology, nor a crisis of human values, but most assuredly also a crisis of the human spirit. How we respond to the challenge has implications not only with how we deal with our world, but also with how we deal with ourselves, our fellow human beings, and our God.

—Eilon Schwartz, educator, "Judaism and Nature: Theological and Moral

Issues to Consider While Renegotiating a Jewish Relationship to the Natural World," *Judaism*, Fall 1995

Religion and science alike agree that there is a profound integrity to the fabric of life — and when we tear at that fabric, we, in the end, endanger ourselves, especially, all too often, the poor and disenfranchised of the world. There is no escaping it — factually and morally, we are a part of, not apart from, nature.

— Rabbi Daniel Swartz, associate director of the National Religious Partnership for the Environment and spiritual leader of Temple Beth Shalom in Chevy Chase, Md., quoted in *The Washington Post*, December 1, 1996

As an issue, the environment is about as distinctively Jewish as white bread.

— Julian L. Simon, professor of business and author, "The Environmental Crisis That Isn't," *Moment*, June 1992

Dr. Simon says the environment is not a uniquely Jewish issue. Does he mean that since Jews are not uniquely affected, Jews have no stake in averting these dangers? Does he mean there is no chance that Jewish wisdom and experience might have something unique to say about what to do about environmental dangers?

— Rabbi Arthur Waskow, activist, author, and member of the International Coordinating Committee on Religion and the Earth, "Waskow's Response to Simon," *Moment*, June 1992

Thousands of years of Jewish experience about these matters is embodied in the wisdom of Shabbat and the sabbatical year — a time to work and a time to rest, a time to build and time to heal — so our work does not destroy us.

— Rabbi Arthur Waskow, "Waskow's Response to Simon," *Moment*, June 1992

During the last three hundred years we have learned how to consume some of the fruits of Planet Earth, fruits of the Tree of the Knowledge of Opposites and Distinctions, which were hidden away throughout history: fossil fuels and nuclear energy. The result of this consumption has been both enormous wealth and a new kind of war with the earth. We have eaten so carelessly that we have poisoned the earth, and she is responding by punishing us.

— Rabbi Arthur Waskow, *Down to Earth Judaism: Food, Money, Sex, and the Rest of Life* (1995)

❖ ETHICS ❖

(see also Morality)

I have one rule in my life and I live by it, and that is that if you're not prepared to defend it in public, don't do it.

> —Alan M. Dershowitz, law professor, appellate lawyer, activist, and author, quoted in *Boston*, November 1995

A new necessity has arisen for the ethics of Judaism in our time. What has been broken must be mended. Even for a Jew who cannot believe in God, it is necessary to act as though man were made in His image.

> —Emil L. Fackenheim, philosopher and professor, "The Ethics of Judaism," *The Jewish Spectator*, Fall 1989

In a healthy and functioning society, law represents a lower rung of a ladder of which ethics is the highest.

> —Rabbi Robert Gordis, author, and scholar, *Love and Sex: A Modern Jewish Perspective* (1978)

A person who has no fundamental ethical intuition can't be part of the human community. We don't need a Jewish interpretation of music and we don't need a specifically Jewish insight to know that this is morally wrong. The act of ruling over a people who don't want to be ruled over is one such morally wrong act. There should be menschlichkeit [the qualities of a good person, one whose behavior reflects a high standard of ethics] that is independent of, though intertwined with, the discourse of Judaism.

> —Rabbi David Hartman, founder and director of the Shalom Hartman Institute for Advanced Jewish Studies in Jerusalem, quoted in "Reflections of Yishayahu Leibowitz: An Interview with David Hartman," *Tikkun*, November/December 1994

How does one teach children to live an ethical life? By walking hand in hand to the synagogue. That is when sons and daughters ask their questions.

> —Francesca Lunzer Kritz, journalist, 1998

It does not matter to Kellogg's Corn Flakes whether the purchaser is John Gotti or Cardinal O'Connor—but it should matter to a law firm whether or not what its client wants should be done for him.

—Sol M. Linowitz, attorney, diplomat, and author, *The Betrayed Profession: Lawyering at the End of the Twentieth Century*, written with Martin Mayer (1994)

Many children raised in observant homes observe Jewish laws not from an appreciation of the laws' moral basis, but out of fear of what parents and neighbors would say if they were "caught" violating a law.

> —Dennis Prager and Joseph Telushkin, authors, *Eight Questions People Ask About Judaism* (1975)

Ethics logically comes to us by virtue of reason, and as we become increasingly "virtuous" we hear the voice of inner conscience more and more from within ourselves. When that inner voice has grown identical with God's voice, then the law will no longer be chiseled on tablets of stone, but, as the prophet said, written as "the new covenant" on the tablets of the human heart, and the kingdom of God will have been established on earth.

> —Rabbi Steven S. Schwarzschild, professor of philosophy and Judaic studies, "Conscience" in *Contemporary Jewish Religious Thought*, edited by Arthur A. Cohen and Paul Mendes-Flohr (1987)

Improving one's ethical conduct, moreover, lies not in exercising greater strength in the act of choice but in activating or raising one's consciousness. The higher mankind's level of consciousness, the less possibility there is for sin.

> —Rabbi Adin Steinsaltz, Talmudic scholar, *The Strife of the Spirit* (1988)

I feel strongly that the code of Jewish ethics has protected me from some of the ethical difficulties encountered by members [of Congress] concerned only with federal law or formal congressional ethics rulings. For a politician, there are many sober lessons to be learned from the halachic stricture of mar'it ayin—the mere appearance of wrongdoing.

> —Henry Waxman, U.S. Congressman (D-Ca.), quoted in *Moment*, February 1993

The Talmud has a marvelous saying that no one should be named to a position of leadership unless he has something to be reproached for.... At the same time we ask from our leaders a certain degree of honesty, decency. If they made mistakes they should simply say, "Look, we are human . . . sorry, I made a mistake."

> —Elie Wiesel, author and Nobel laureate, quoted in *The Christian Science Monitor*, December 10, 1996

❖ EXILE ❖

(see also Diaspora)

I am from Jerusalem, but because Titus destroyed the Temple, I was born in Poland.

> —S. Y. Agnon, Israeli writer, responding to the question—when asked in Stockholm, upon winning the Nobel Prize for literature—where he was from, 1966

What is the whole question of being in exile—in need of help, as opposed to being free? Being in exile means I am not in the place where I am supposed to be. Being free means I am in the place where I am supposed to be. It doesn't have to be a different address.

> —Rabbi Shlomo Carlebach, c. 1972, quoted in *The Holy Beggars Banquet: Traditional Jewish Tales and Teachings of the Late, Great Shlomo Carlebach and Others*, edited by Kalman Serkez (1998)

For me, being a Jew is living in exile. I inherited the exile of my people beginning with the destruction of the first Temple. I still ask, "How can I sing the Lord's song in a strange land?" But I have come to understand that this sacred song I long to sing is temporal; each Jew must confront the exile of her own generation, for one person's exile is another person's home.

> —Jyl Lynn Felman, author and professor, "Why I Want to Be a Rabbi"— response on her rabbinical school application—in *The Tribe of Dina*, edited by Melanie Kaye Kantrowitz and Irena Klepfisz (1984)

What is exile? What is galut? Whenever I have a problem, I go to the original Hebrew idioms. After all, the world was created in that language. Let's go back to the relations of that word: gal, move, gil, joy: it means movement, continuous movement. It means that everything is moving, except me; or the other way—I am moving and everything else stands still; or a third way, we are not moving in the same direction. Then exile means to be displaced, I am here and I am not here. The content and form do not espouse one another. That means they are in exile. When a person is in exile, nothing fits.

> —Elie Wiesel, author, interview in *Parabola*, May 1985

❖ EXPERIENCE ❖

There is, in reality, only one school: the school of experience. I have been a student all my life.

> —Leon Edel, biographer, quoted in his obituary, *The New York Times*, September 8, 1997

Experience is what we choose to attend to.

> —Rebecca Goldstein, novelist, *The Dark Sister* (1991)

❖ FAITH ❖

(see also God)

*T*o you, I'm an atheist; to God, I'm the loyal opposition.

— Woody Allen, actor and director, from the film *Stardust Memories*, 1980; reprinted in *Four Films of Woody Allen* (1982)

On a rational level, I am not a believer in Pascal's wager: the notion that faith is a worthwhile gamble, since we lose nothing if we believe and God doesn't exist, but we risk spending eternity in hell if we don't believe and God turns out to be real. On an emotional level, maybe, just maybe . . .

— Alan M. Dershowitz, law professor, appellate lawyer, activist, and author, *The Vanishing American Jew* (1997)

Jewish faith after the Holocaust calls for more than faith in God; it also calls for faith in humankind. Post-Holocaust, the former may be much easier to have than the latter. But without faith in humanity, belief in God is empty.

— Rabbi Michael Goldberg, author, *Why Should Jews Survive? Looking Past the Holocaust Toward a Jewish Future* (1995)

The Jewish spiritual odyssey is not about blind faith. It celebrates the mind, the soul, and even the skeptic. But it also asks the skeptic to invest, to live fully, to participate in the richness that Jewish life has to offer.

— Rabbi Daniel Gordis, author and professor, *God Was Not in the Fire* (1995)

It's harder to lose irony than to lose innocence, as hard as going back to childhood. If sages suggested the Temple would be rebuilt only after the Messiah came, perhaps it was because they knew how hard it would be to take prophecy back from fools—how hard to make cracked faith perfect again.

> —Gershom Gorenberg, Israeli journalist, "The Birth of Irony," *Jerusalem Report*, August 13, 1992

The crisis of the Holocaust was that not in their wildest dreams did Jews imagine that this kind of pain and destruction was the price of the covenant. Nor did they realize that the covenant might unfold to the point where God would ask them to take full responsibility and unlimited risks for it. Yet, in the ultimate test of the Jews' faithfulness to the covenant, the Jewish people, regardless of ritual observance level, responded with a reacceptance of the covenant, out of free will and love. For some, it was love of God; for others, love of the covenant and the goal; for others, love of the people or of the memories of the covenantal way.

> —Rabbi Irving Greenberg, author, scholar, and founder of the National Jewish Center for Learning and Leadership (CLAL), *Voluntary Covenant* (1982)

Faith is a vision of a truth that will come into being, backed by a commitment to make it happen. Faith is trust in the Divine promise that this is not a quixotic mission but that the situation of redemption can be attained and realized in this world.

> —Rabbi Irving Greenberg, *The Jewish Way: Living the Holidays* (1988)

Hope in a renewed future is one of the most profound gifts of a life of faith.

> —Rabbi David Hartman, founder and director of the Shalom Hartman Institute for Advanced Jewish Studies in Jerusalem, quoted in *The Jewish Week*, November 3, 1995

Evaluating faith in terms of reason is like trying to understand love as a syllogism and beauty as an algebraic equation.

> —Rabbi Abraham Joshua Heschel, author, activist, and theologian, *Man Is Not Alone* (1951)

Our certainty is the result of wonder and radical amazement, of awe before the mystery and meaning of the totality of life beyond our rational discerning. Faith is the response to the mystery, shot through with meaning; the response to a challenge which no one can forever ignore. "The heaven" is a challenge. When you "lift up your eyes on high," you are faced with the question. Faith is an act of man who, transcending himself, responds to Him who transcends the world.

> —Rabbi Abraham Joshua Heschel, *Between God and Man* (1959)

A religious person doesn't "believe" in God, he has faith in God. One's relation to God is existential, not rationalist. . . . Pure reason will never get you beyond—pure reason. But the more you pray, the more likely you are to have faith. That is why children are taught to pray, rather than being instructed in "proofs" of God's "existence."

> —Irving Kristol, social critic, editor, and publisher, *Neoconservatism: The Autobiography of an Idea* (1995)

However you may choose to resolve the contradictions between patriarchal religion and the ethics of equality, belief in male supremacy must not be permitted to be the badge of the faithful.

> —Letty Cottin Pogrebin, author and activist, *Growing Up Free: Raising Your Child in the 80s* (1980)

After Auschwitz belief in God may be difficult, but belief in man is impossible.

> —Dennis Prager and Joseph Telushkin, authors, *Eight Questions People Ask About Judaism* (1975)

America, as an image, has changed the edifice, the manner, if not all the tokens of faith. . . .The dollar's green sign hangs seen and unseen from churches and synagogues. Faith is not enough today. The dollar and doubt are more inspirational at times. The "big giver" and the sociological lecturer have replaced the moral and spiritual leader who guided my father in his time.

> —Harry Roskolenko, author, quoted in *The Immigrant Experience: The Anguish of Becoming American*, edited by Thomas C. Wheeler (1971)

After Auschwitz, Jewish religious belief has been thrust on the horns of an exceedingly bitter dilemma: One can affirm either the abiding validity of Israel's covenant with God or the nonpunitive character of the Holocaust—but not both.

> —Richard L. Rubenstein, philosopher, "Evil" in *Contemporary Jewish Religious Thought*, edited by Arthur A. Cohen and Paul Mendes-Flohr (1987)

To find the world interesting lies at the heart of Judaism. To be a Jew of faith is to be anything but bored. To be a Jew is not to yawn away one's life, but to stand slack-jawed in amazement at the world of possibilities and to rise with excitement toward its realization.

> —Rabbi Harold Schulweis, author and rabbi of Congregation Valley Beth Shalom in Encino, Calif. "High Holiday Message," 1977, quoted by Dr. David Elcott in *A Sacred Journey* (1995)

Without a deep connection to our past and a belief in the special mission of the Jewish people, how can we, a new nation of Israelis, justify our position among people who have lived here for centuries? How can we survive at all, on either side of the Atlantic, without this belief?

> —Natan Sharansky, former refusenik, quoted in *The Jewish Week*, August 4, 1995

If modern times have shown us anything, it is that we must affirm some faith in order to live. The human being finds his anchor in a reality beyond himself. We are, in the words of T. S. Eliot, either consumed by fire or fire. We can serve the God of Israel or some other god.

> —Rabbi Seymour Siegel, professor of theology, "Theology for Today," *Conservative Judaism*, Summer 1974

Faith is experienced not . . . as something which has been brought into existence by man's creative cultural gesture, but rather something which was given to man when the latter was overpowered by God. Indeed, faith is born of the intrusion of eternity upon temporality.

> —Rabbi Joseph B. Soloveitchik, Talmudic scholar, professor, and author, "The Lonely Man of Faith," *Tradition*, Spring 1965

As we Jews now enter the High Holidays again, preparing ourselves to pray for a year of peace and happiness for our people and all people, let us make up, Master of the Universe. In spite of everything that happened? Yes, in spite. Let us make up: for the child in me, it is unbearable to be divorced from you so long.

> —Elie Wiesel, Nobel laureate and author, "A Prayer for the Days of Awe," *The New York Times*, October 2, 1997

❖ FAME AND CELEBRITY ❖

People discover you because of the most horrible day in your life.

> —Noa Ben-Artzi Pelossof, nineteen-year-old granddaughter of slain Israeli Prime Minister Yitzhak Rabin who delivered the family eulogy at his funeral

I was a survivor. I had surmounted my personal difficulties through acts that took considerable initiative and will. In the summer of 1994, I was not Marcia Kleks, the gambler's girlfriend. I was a lawyer—and an intelligent and accomplished one, at that. I was a damned good mother. And everything admirable that I'd accomplished seemed threatened by this disturbing and unsolicited celebrity.

> —Marcia Clark, prosecutor in the criminal trial of O. J. Simpson, quoted in *Time*, May 12, 1997

The rules are, I will speak on behalf of my clients when I have to defend them, that is the predominant reason I'm on television. Number two, I will speak on behalf of civil liberties or Jewish causes or other causes that I care deeply about. Number three, and here I am absolutely shameless—I will do anything permissible to sell my books.

> —Alan M. Dershowitz, law professor, appellate lawyer, activist and author, when asked whether he was overexposed, quoted in *Boston*, November 1995

I tried to get rid of the burden of the Bob Dylan myth for a long time, because it is a burden. Just ask anybody who is considered a star. There are certain advantages and rewards to it, but you're thinking: "Shit, man, I'm only me."

> —Bob Dylan, folksinger and songwriter, 1975, quoted in *No Direction Home: The Life and Music of Bob Dylan* by Robert Shelton (1986)

It strikes me as unfair, and even in bad taste, to select a few . . . for boundless admiration, attributing superhuman powers of mind and character to them. This has been my fate, and the contrast between the popular estimate of my powers and achievements and the reality is simply grotesque.

> —Albert Einstein, Nobel Prize-winning theoretical physicist and humanist, reflecting on America, *Berliner Tageblatt*, July 7, 1921, reprinted in *Ideas and Opinions: Albert Einstein* (1982)

Do not confuse notoriety and fame with greatness. . . . I have met great people in the most obscure roles in life. . . . And greatness can crown the head of a janitor just as readily as it can come to the President of our country or someone of great rank.

> —Annette and Judge Sherman G. Finesilver, Denver, from a statement on the occasion of the 1969 Bar Mitzvah of their son Steve, quoted in *This I Believe: Documents of American Jewish Life* by Jacob Rader Marcus (1990)

Hell, I'm a musician. And let me tell you something. I was just as good a musician ten years ago, when nobody knew me or made any noise or hullabaloo about me.

> —Benny Goodman, jazz musician, quoted in *Swing, Swing, Swing: The Life and Times of Benny Goodman* by Ross Firestone (1993)

That kind of thing has to drive a person crazy . . . Want to listen to my tape? Want to fuck me? Can I carry your bag? He [Jim Morrison] and Janis and Hendrix, they became involuntary leaders. And that was the pressure. They all became slaves to idolatry.

> —Bill Graham, rock music impresario who owned the Fillmore East and Fillmore West theaters, *Bill Graham Presents*, written with Robert Green-field (1992)

I was representing a couple of million Jews among a hundred million gen-tiles and I was always in the spotlight. . . . I felt a responsibility. I was there every day and if I had a bad day every son of a bitch was calling me names so that I had to make good. . . . As time went by I came to feel that if I, as a Jew, hit a home run I was hitting one against Hitler.

> —Hank Greenberg, baseball Hall of Famer, *The Story of My Life*

It says something about modern celebrity that only a few people in this popular but unbelievably noisy restaurant seemed aware that they had a Nobel laureate in their midst. Many more heads swiveled when a television weather forecaster walked in.

> —Clyde Haberman, journalist, interviewing Elie Wiesel over dinner at a res-taurant in New York City, *The New York Times*, March 5, 1997

You don't get to choose what you're famous for and you don't get to control which of your life's many struggles gets to stand for you.

> —Erica Jong, novelist and poet, *Fear of Fifty* (1994)

Looking back over my years as Mayor, I once made a statement that re-porters have never stopped trying to disprove. I said, "Every day, seven days a week, three hundred sixty-five days a year for eleven years, I have been men-tioned in at least one story in the newspapers, on the radio or on television."

> —Mayor Edward I. Koch of New York City, "The Press" in *His Eminence and Hizzoner: A Candid Exchange*, coauthored with John Cardinal O'Connor (1989)

We are creating a lot of false idols in this society. We are famous and admired because we're famous and admired.

> —Ted Koppel, television journalist, quoted in *Esquire*, June 1988

I sometimes have visions of these organizations sitting in meetings and say-ing, "Whom do we want to address our group? Do we want some deep thinker?" "No, let's get someone on television." "Well, what do you think Koppel's fee is?" And someone says "X thousand dollars." And then they say, "Well, how about if we gave him the Greatest Human Being in Universe Award? How much is a plaque, Charlie?" It troubles me about our society. . . . Look who the stars of our civilization are. God help us.

> —Ted Koppel, quoted in *Esquire*, June 1988

She stood up to the royals. They recruited her as a pliable ingenue, and she ended up besting them. She defied their rigidities and cruelties and in the end, transcended the very royalty that had tried to dispose of her. This isn't, mind you, Natan Sharansky standing up to the KGB. But it is something.

> —Charles Krauthammer, journalist, reflecting on the public reaction to the death of Diana, Princess of Wales, *The Dallas Morning News*, September 6, 1997

When I was on the cover of *Time* and everybody thought I was riding high and the king, I knew I had to go in for the operation. I was living through my worst moments. No one has it all.

> —Ralph Lauren, fashion executive, recalling his discovery of a brain tumor (benign) in 1986, quoted in *Ralph Lauren: The Man Behind the Mystique* by Jeffrey A. Trachtenberg (1988)

None of this matters. It doesn't matter as long as you're famous. . . . I hear I'm on the cover of *Newsweek*.

> —Dennis Levine, former trader, when the government charged him with insider trading activities, quoted in *Den of Thieves* by James B. Stewart (1992)

Celebrity has become our first national disease. It's the price we pay for having neither gods nor leaders nor a society we can respect.

> —Norman Mailer, author, "Black and White Justice," *New York*, October 16, 1995

If you didn't hear anything new from me for six months or a year, I don't think America is gonna say, "What the heck is going on? Where is he?" But it sure would make me feel good if they did.

> —Paul Reiser, comedian, reflecting on what he'll do when his hit television series *Mad About You* is over, quoted in *US*, September 1997

That the ballplayers are millionaires seems only to enhance their stature, since money is the way we pay respect in this country. If they had suddenly been granted fine minds as a result of labor negotiations no one would admire them more than they do already.

—Anne Roiphe, author and columnist, *The New York Observer*, August 28, 1995

Being a star is so peculiar and unnatural that it can make a person interesting even if the person is boring.
> —Betty Rollin, journalist, *Am I Getting Paid for This?* (1982)

My public reputation—as distinguished from the reputation of my work—is something I try to have as little to do with as I can.
> —Philip Roth, novelist, interviewed in 1974 by Joyce Carol Oates, reprinted in *Reading Myself and Others* by Philip Roth (1975)

When the rush abates, that's when you get back in touch with yourself and find the humility you lost.
> —George Segal, actor, quoted in *Lifestyles*, New Year 1996

So here I am at the top of the heap, and some heap it is—a heap of shit. I'm too talented for radio.
> —Howard Stern, radio talk show host, quoted in *Jerusalem Report*, May 19, 1994

My nightmare is that I'm driving alone and have to go to the hospital. I'd say, "Please, help me" and people say, "Hey, you look like . . ." And I'm dying while they wonder if I'm Barbra Streisand.
> —Barbra Streisand, singer, actress, producer, and director, interview with Lawrence Grobel in *Playboy*, October 1977

Even though I hope to go the rest of my life without ever having been exposed to one of his videos, it's more than likely that even an inept Michael Jackson slam on bigotry will influence a few hundred million more people than the most brilliant editorial in the *Jewish Ledger*.
> —Jonathan S. Tobin, editor, *Stamford Jewish Ledger*, June 23, 1995

Certainly it strains justice as well as imagination that the world's most glamorous woman should have been alone, with no date, on a Saturday night—for it was, in fact, a Saturday night when she killed herself. On other nights but Saturday, we are allowed our own company. Saturday night is when all American boys and girls must prove themselves sexually. This is when we must be "out" in the world where we can be seen among the sexually chosen. Yet the American girl who symbolized sexual success for all of us spent her last Saturday night in despair. Every man in the country would have wanted to date Marilyn Monroe, or so he would say, but no man who knew her did.

> —Diana Trilling, essayist and critic, reflecting on the death of Marilyn Monroe in 1962, quoted in *The Book of Eulogies*, edited by Phyllis Theroux (1997)

❖ FAMILIES ❖

(see also Generations, Marriage)

Older sisters are a reward from Heaven. With an older sister, I wouldn't be the one doing all the fighting. God must love those he gives older sisters.

> —Pearl Abraham, novelist, *The Romance Reader* (voice of the character Rachel Benjamin) (1995)

But one thing I do know, that any man who will testify against his own blood and flesh, his own sister, is repulsive, is revolting, who violates every code that any civilization has ever lived by. He is the lowest of the lowest animals that I have ever seen.

> —Emanuel Bloch, attorney for Julius and Ethel Rosenberg, speaking in summation to the jury at their 1951 trial for espionage, regarding prosecution star witness David Greenglass (Ethel Rosenberg's brother), quoted in *Ethel Rosenberg: Beyond the Myths* by Ilene Philipson (1988)

If you want to understand any woman you must first ask about her mother and then listen carefully. Stories about food show a strong connection. Wistful silences demonstrate unfinished business. The more a daughter knows the details of her mother's life—without flinching or whining—the stronger the daughter.

> —Anita Diamant, author, *The Red Tent* (voice of the biblical Dinah) (1997)

I was forty-two when my mother died and it felt as though I had been left in the world alone. Although I was myself a mother, although I had a husband, two sons, two brothers and many friends, with whom my relations were passionate and often complicated, my relation to my mother was the most passionate and complicated of all. So intense was our bond that I was never sure what belonged to whom, where I ended, and she began.

> —Helen Epstein, journalist and author, *Where She Came From* (1997)

If you are too busy to spend time with your children then you are busier than God intended you to be.

> —Rabbi Mendel Epstein, columnist, *The Jewish Press*, May 24, 1996

In ten years, the child under eighteen who spends Father's Day with his father will be one of the fortunate few.

> —Don Feder, columnist, "In Search of the Father Figure," *Boston Herald*, June 19, 1994

For me, as for others, now that that part [mother years] is nearly finished, there is relief, release, a lightening of shadow, as I see them make their own way into life at last, their own persons — my kids, so intensely, satisfyingly themselves, in work, in love, and now, beginning with kids of their own. As they enter this new cycle of generation, they even seem to come back home again, in a different way.

> —Betty Friedan, feminist author and activist, "Thoughts on Becoming a Grandmother," *Ladies' Home Journal*, 1983

This being a grandmother is not the same kind of experience, not at all. I marvel at this mysterious treasure, this grandbaby, suddenly with us, here, now, himself, a new person carrying on our life stream; I stare at him, I take him in with my eyes and heart, but I don't have to change his diapers, or get up in the middle of the night with him, or feel responsible for him all the time.

> —Betty Friedan, "Thoughts on Becoming a Grandmother," *Ladies' Home Journal*, 1983

A family's dream is making sure the children don't have to do what their parents did.

> —Lillian Garber (played by Maureen Stapleton) in the film *Sweet Lorraine*, 1987

During the last conversation I had with her, she was recovering nicely from a very serious stroke. She could still talk, and I asked her what she attributed her miraculous recovery to, and she said, "I recovered because I have no envy, no jealousy and no hate." For someone to have lived through a revolution [Russian], exile, the Depression and the slaughter of her entire family and still have no hate — well, that's a remarkable thing.

> —David Geffen, entertainment executive, speaking of his mother, quoted in "King David," *US*, April 1997

Today, if a couple adopts a baby, most of us react with joy for them. However, if a woman places a baby for adoption, we are shocked. I often hear, "How can she give up her baby?" Only when we present adoption as an act of courage and love, and often the wisest choice, will more Jewish babies become available for adoption. We must tell society that every adoption placement begins with two acts of love. It's an act of love when a birth mother places a baby and an act of love when strangers accept that baby into their home and hearts.

> —Rabbi Michael Gold, author, *And Hannah Wept: Infertility, Adoption, and the Jewish Couple* (1988)

I am very proud that my son, who went to Georgetown . . . 781 students— he finished first. He won a two year Oxford Scholarship. He's there now and he's accepted for Harvard. So there's a Jewish word, kvell—"to be proud." I am so haimish [informal] and so bourgeois, and so proud of my son . . . oftentimes, I say to him, "Jordan, you don't do drugs, you don't use vulgarity, you're the only person who hasn't seen *Midnight Blue* on the East Side or read *Screw*. . . . Where have I gone wrong?"

> —Al Goldstein, publisher of *Screw* magazine, quoted in *New York*, February 10, 1997

Only occasionally would parents let the war slip out, usually as a rebuke to their children for some offense: "For this I survived Hitler?"

> —Yossi Klein Halevi, Israeli journalist and author, *Memoirs of a Jewish Extremist* (1995)

It is the most challenging job. Business is a breeze. You learn one thing and you do it. The most difficult thing is to raise good kids which is what my wife did.

> —Syshe Heschel, son and brother of the Kapitshinitzser Rebbes, father-in-law of the present Boyaner Rebbe, speaking about raising children, quoted in *Hasidic People* by Jerome Mintz (1994)

Birth control, family planning—call it what you will—is a fad that has gripped Jewish women for too long. . . . Children, many children, are the greatest gift and blessing God can bestow upon us; do not let imagined obstacles stand in the way of enjoying these blessings.

> —From an essay based upon the words of the Lubavitcher Rebbe, "Family Planning," *Sichos (teachings) in English*, 1981

While it is an axiom of Judaism that man has free choice, do not confuse this with unlimited opportunity to choose. A child is not a faucet, to be turned on at will. No power on earth can guarantee the birth of a baby. That decision, that power, is God's, and God alone, the third Partner in every child. The possible blessing so disdained earlier may not be available later. Take His blessings when He offers them.

> —From an essay based upon the words of the Lubavitcher Rebbe, "Family Planning," *Sichos (teachings) in English*, 1981

The one thing that should never be denied any young person is the certainty that at home someone is looking, listening, and loving.

> —Rabbi Ben Kamin, senior rabbi at Temple-Tifereth Israel in Cleveland, *Raising a Thoughtful Teenager: A Book of Answers and Values for Parents* (1996)

Children are holy and are meant to be the products of human love. I dare say that holiness is fleeting in this culture of ours where students share hypodermic needles sometimes as often as they share ideas.

> —Rabbi Ben Kamin, *Raising a Thoughtful Teenager: A Book of Answers and Values for Parents* (1996)

They [children] are strong in their faith in God, they believe in the decency of others, and they are not yet soiled by the knowledge that their country doesn't like them.

> —Jonathan Kozol, author and champion of the plight of children in America, quoted in the *Los Angeles Times*, November 8, 1995

"May you have joy from your children" was the greatest blessing conceivable. They were the parting words on happy and sad occasions. Honor brought to parents by their children was the accepted standard of measuring success. It also became an incentive for us. Our personal success was to a great extent predicated upon the happiness we could bring to our parents. It would not be long before this idea would be completely reversed.

> —Sam Levenson, humorist and author, *Everything but Money* (1966)

Were they proud of me, then or later? I like to think so, of course, but I am not really sure that being proud of one's mother makes up for her frequent absences.

> —Golda Meir, prime minister of Israel, speaking of her children Sarah and Menachem, *My Life* (1975)

I would like to say something to all adoptive parents. Please give your child all the love you can. Please hold them and hug them all the time. Please listen to them. Most of all please let them know that their birth and their life has blessed your life.

—Denny Mosesman, national field promotion director for Warner Brothers Records in Nashville and an adopted child, "Letter from an Adopted Child" in *Ultimate Issues: A Quarterly Journal*, published by Dennis Prager, 1993

When Robert and I are together, whether in my home or on his ward, we're happy. Not always, and not without a pervasive sense of loss and sadness, but happy to be with each other, no matter the context, because it seems good, simply, in an often frightening and miserable life, to be known — and to be able to be near the person who knows you and is known by you.

—Jay Neugeboren, novelist and essayist, *Imagining Robert: My Brother, Madness, and Survival* (1997)

At this point in history, we cannot rear our children in a world free of sexism. But we can try our best to rear free children at the same time as we work to change the world.

—Letty Cottin Pogrebin, author and activist, *Growing Up Free: Raising Your Child in the 80s* (1980)

The mother role comes with a guaranteed midlife crisis. It has built-in obsolescence. For many women, the departure of grown children is experienced as abandonment, and the husband, if he is still living, cannot fill the gap because his salience has so long been eclipsed by the children. For such a woman, the "empty nest" is synonymous with an empty life.

—Letty Cottin Pogrebin, *Growing Up Free: Raising Your Child in the 80s* (1980)

The Jewish desire to have children well-educated and professionally successful is praiseworthy, but it often entails a price. . . . Perhaps we ought to redefine nachas [pride] as wanting to say: "My son? He's a highly accomplished electrician whose clients adore him, who spends lots of time with his wife and kids, and who is deeply committed to Judaism."

—Dennis Prager, author and radio commentator, *Moment*, February 1997

The term family is not generally applicable when the union does not have as its principal goal the birth, raising and education of offspring. When the principal goal is sexual gratification, or even companionship alone, then there is no social interest to be legally protected by rules for the creation and dissolution of the relationship. Society, as such, has no stake in it. And, of course, it is sacrilege to attribute to it an added dimension of holiness.

—Rabbi Emanuel Rackman, chancellor of Bar-Ilan University, author, and columnist, *The Jewish Week*, August 4, 1995

But Manny—it's foolish—but I'd still give anything in the world for one kind word from her.

> —Ethel Rosenberg, speaking to her attorney after being visited by her mother Tessie Greenglass on death row, 1953, quoted in *Ethel Rosenberg: Behind the Myth* by Ilene Philipson (1988)

Good Christ, a Jewish man with parents alive is a fifteen-year-old boy and will remain a fifteen-year-old boy till they die.

> —Philip Roth, novelist, *Portnoy's Complaint* (1970)

The exodus from the Warsaw Ghetto that brought us to America took three aunts to Buenos Aires, one uncle to Paris, another to London. I have made sporadic efforts to locate them, with no success. The only relative on my mother's side whom I actually ever met was a cousin, chic and multilingual . . . married to an Englishman. I've lost her, too, as I've lost a number of unknown relatives of two or three generations destroyed in the Warsaw Ghetto.

> —Kate Simon, author, *Bronx Primitive: Portraits in a Childhood* (1982)

My language is crude, but my behavior is proper.

> —Howard Stern, radio talk show host, reflecting on his successful marriage to his wife Alison and his decision to keep his kids out of the limelight, quoted in *George*, April/May 1996

Deep down in the bottom of my heart I have always held that I should have had children, many children. It is only in rearing children that minute service piled on minute service counts.

> —Henrietta Szold, founder of Hadassah, 1917 letter to Jessie Sampter, friend and coworker on the Central Committee of Hadassah, quoted in *Henrietta Szold: A Record of a Life* by Rose Zeitlin (1952)

True Torah observance is not conducive to any kind of abuse, physical, emotional or otherwise. . . . Abuse is based on destroying the other person's dignity. It is a violation of dignity to say: you're stupid, you don't know what you're talking about, you haven't got a brain in your head.

> —Rabbi Abraham J. Twerski, Hasidic rabbi and psychiatrist, author, founder, and medical director of Gateway Rehabilitation Center, a nonprofit drug and alcohol treatment system near Pittsburgh, speaking out against spouse abuse, quoted in the *Baltimore Jewish Times*, November 14, 1997

The whole situation was and is very strange for me, because I don't remember what it is to have a cousin.

> —Eddy Wynschenk, a 68-year-old resident of San Bruno, Calif., who was recently reunited with his long-lost first cousin after 51 years (both cousins were Holocaust survivors), *The Boston Jewish Advocate*, June 14, 1996

❖ FASHION ❖

Women have this thing in common, which is loving clothes. It doesn't matter your age or your size, we all go through the same thing. One of the things all women have control over is their closets. Every morning, every woman makes selections to create herself, re-create herself.

> —Ilene Beckerman, advertising executive and author, interviewed in "Wearing Her Life on Her Sleeve" by Alex Witchel, *The New York Times*, January 24, 1996

Excuse me, is green the only color these come in?

> —Judy Benjamin (played by Goldie Hawn), a Jewish woman who joins the U.S. Army after her husband's death, when handed her uniform, in the film *Private Benjamin*, 1980

I want the woman to enter the room first, not the clothes; the clothes should not be wearing the woman.

> —Donna Karan, fashion executive, quoted in *Jerusalem Report*, April 6, 1995

Although gloves are no longer absolutely required for a ladylike appearance, they add a finishing touch to any ensemble. A well-dressed woman still wears or carries harmonizing gloves for every costume.

> —Helen Latner, advice columnist, *The Book of Modern Jewish Etiquette: A Guide to All Occasions* (1981)

Women like to be noticed, of course, but regard for modesty of neckline and hemline, especially when bending over files and worktables, is sensible. Regardless of one's religious outlook, avoiding bareness, sheerness, and a provocative no-bra look is a good way to prevent annoying attentions and comments from the men with whom one associates, not to mention malicious gossip from the women.

> —Helen Latner, *The Book of Modern Jewish Etiquette: A Guide to All Occasions* (1981)

I was the baby brother. The clothes went from Lenny to Jerry to me.

> —Ralph Lauren, fashion executive, quoted in *Ralph Lauren: The Man Behind the Mystique* by Jeffrey A. Trachtenberg (1992)

A fur coat was an affirmation of femininity. It was always a male's decision whether a wife got a fur coat or not. It was almost never the woman's decision. I think it was obviously peer pressure.

> —Fred Schwartz, furrier known as "Fred the Furrier" in New York, quoted in *Jewish Times* by Howard Simons (1988)

❖ FEMINISM ❖

(see also Women and Judaism)

This has been the century of The Woman and I know myself fortunate to have been part of the revolution. In another generation, perhaps the next, equality will be taken for granted. Those who come after us may find it easier to assert independence, but will miss the grand adventure of having been born a woman in this century of change.

> —Vera Caspary, novelist and screenwriter, age eighty, *The Secrets of Grown-Ups* (1979)

Even after the revolution, we will be left with all the literature. After liberation, we will still have to reckon with Sleeping Beauty and Cinderella. . . . short of mass book burning, which no one wants, things may well go on as they are now: women pulled between the intellectual attraction of liberation and the emotional, psychological, and cultural mishmash it's hard to escape growing up with.

> —Nora Ephron, author, screenwriter, and director, "Fantasies" in *Wallflower at the Orgy* (1972)

With the granting of the vote [to women] the establishment coopted the woman's movement. . . . Though the antifeminist forces appeared to give in, they did so in name only. By the time the vote was granted the long channeling of feminist energies into the limited goal of suffrage had thoroughly depleted the Women's Rights Movement. The monster Ballot had swallowed everything else. . . . They never had time to develop a broader consciousness.

> —Shulamith Firestone, writer, *The Dialectic of Sex* (1970)

176 · *Feminism*

On election day, November 3, 1914, Montana's suffrage amendment was approved. . . . Even now I never go to the polls without a silent thank you to those many energetic, earnest women in Montana and supporters from other states who made it possible.

>—Belle Fligelman, author, suffragist, and aide to Jeannette Rankin (the first woman to serve in the United States Congress), 1917, quoted in *The American Jewish Woman: A Documentary History* by Jacob Rader Marcus (1981)

That bra-burning image and other phenomena of "sexual politics" in general distorted the main thrust of the women's movement for equality and gave its enemies a powerful weapon. For it played into the fears and violated the feelings and needs of a great many women, and men, who still look to the family for security, love, roots in life. And it may have led other women, especially younger women, who ardently embrace the new opportunities . . . to deny those other needs.

>—Betty Freidan, author and activist, *The Second Stage* (1981)

As long as women remain locked in reaction, they will continue to swing between extreme versions of one half-life or another—the feminine mystique or its feminist reversal—never transcending the terrible split that has tormented women for so long, never to embrace the fullness of life that is open to women now, in love and work, as it never was to women before.

>—Betty Friedan, *The Second Stage* (1981)

By the year 2000, I doubt there will be any need for the likes of Phyllis Schlafly, or, for that matter, Gloria Steinem or Betty Friedan. The arguments about equal rights for women will be nostalgic history.

>—Betty Friedan, *The Second Stage* (1981)

A woman needs a man. Without a man who desires her, a woman has no visa. Cleopatra and the Empress Josephine knew nothing about college education. They didn't even know they were sexually emancipated. If they were alive today, they probably wouldn't know how to drive a car. But they both knew they had to have a man. Two hundred years from today, some guy will be operating a computer the likes of which we can't imagine . . . and some little gal will say to him, "Never mind all beeping and booping in outer space. Get over here now. I miss you." And he will get over there now. And she will have proved her worth to herself.

>—Harry Golden, journalist, *Ess, Ess, Mein Kindt* (1966)

Early feminism remains, for me, the vital flash of clarifying insight. It redeems me from self-pity, bestows on me the incomparable gift of wanting to see things as they are.

>—Vivian Gornick, author, *Approaching Eye Level* (1996)

Well, I did what I did because I had to do it. And I learned that I could do whatever I wanted from my mother and father. I didn't use the word because we didn't have the same vocabulary then.

>—Laura Z. Hobson, author, responding to the question of whether she considered herself a feminist, quoted in "Remembering Laura Z. Hobson" by Julia Wolf Mazow, *Lilith*, Summer 1986

The models of motherhood we had did not serve us in the lives we led. . . . We were often the first female members of our families to stay in hotel rooms alone, to raise children alone, to face tax problems alone, to stare at the glass ceiling alone and wonder how to crash through.

>—Erica Jong, novelist and poet, *Fear of Fifty* (1994)

My sisters and I had always felt that while women's interests ought to begin at home and ought to end there, they need not necessarily confine themselves to it alone.

>—Rebekah Bettelheim Kohut, leader of the National Council of Jewish Women, *My Portion: An Autobiography* (1925)

Women can wield and accrue influence by having more respect for themselves, having a better idea of their own value. That's where it starts.

>—Mathilde Krim, chair and cofounder of American Foundation for AIDS Research, quoted in "A New Agenda," *Working Woman*, November 1992

Every woman does not want the vote.
Every woman does not need the vote.
Every woman will not use the vote.
Yet, if only one woman wanted, needed and would use the vote, every other woman should see to it that she gets it.

>—Sophie Irene Loeb, social and civic reformer and reporter for the *New York Evening World*, from a 1915 symposium on woman's suffrage, quoted in *The American Jewish Woman: A Documentary History* by Jacob Rader Marcus (1981)

Naturally women should be treated as the equal of men in all respects, but as is also true of the Jewish people, they shouldn't have to be better than everyone else in order to live like human beings or feel that they must accomplish wonders all the time to be accepted at all.

> —Golda Meir, prime minister of Israel, *My Life* (1975)

Women have qualities of mind peculiarly feminine, but they are not the intellectual equals of men. Their intuitive sense is the biggest thing they bring to politics. Combined with the thinking ability of men, this makes a splendid working team.

> —Belle Lindner Israels Moskowitz, social worker and political advisor to Governor Alfred E. Smith, quoted in her 1933 obituary in *The New York Times*, reprinted in The *American Jewish Woman: A Documentary History* by Jacob R. Marcus (1981)

Judaism has always been the keynote of liberty and I cannot conceive of one [Jewish] man voting against the amendment [granting women the right to vote].

> —Maud Nathan, social reformer and political activist, speech to an audience of over four thousand Jews at the Arch Street Theater in Philadelphia, November 1915, in support of women's suffrage, quoted in *The Journey Home: Jewish Women and American Century* by Joyce Antler (1997)

Cultivation precedes fruition. Perhaps we cannot have our great women architects, painters, playwrights, sailors, bridgebuilders, jurists, captains, composers, and so forth, until we have — until, in short, women enter into the central stream of mankind's activities, until woman-as-person becomes as flat and unremarked a tradition as man-as-person.

> —Cynthia Ozick, novelist and essayist, from the 1969 essay "Women and Creativity: The Demise of the Dancing Dog," quoted in *Women in Sexist Society*, edited by Vivian Gornick and Barbara K. Moran (1971)

If anything remains more or less unchanged, it will be the role of women.

> —David Riesman, sociologist, quoted in *Time*, July 21, 1967, reprinted in *The New York Times Magazine*, December 24, 1995

These days, a brokenhearted woman is as likely to be a woman who has lost her promotion as one who has lost her man.

> —Betty Rollin, journalist, *Am I Getting Paid for This?* (1982)

I always felt I was the equal of any man. I could think like a man. I could step on the sidewalk without help. I didn't have to have a man to hold my arm or open the door. We'd go to the theater. I'd pay my own way. I like the young feminists today.

—Dora Rosenzweig, born 1885, quoted in *American Dreams: Lost and Found* by Studs Terkel (1980)

The ideas of this great sea-change in women's view of ourselves are contagious and irresistible. They hit women like a revelation, as if we had left a dark room and walked into the sun.

> —Gloria Steinem, author and activist, "Sisterhood," 1972 *Outrageous Acts and Everyday Rebellions* (1983)

Perhaps well-to-do women and unemployed ghetto teenagers have something in common. Neither group has been allowed to develop the self-confidence that comes from knowing you can support yourself.

> —Gloria Steinem, "College Reunion," 1981, *Outrageous Acts and Everyday Rebellions* (1983)

We have terms like sexual harassment and battered women. A few years ago they were just called life. Now we are becoming the men we wanted to marry. Once women were trained to marry a doctor, not be one.

> —Gloria Steinem, "Words and Charge," 1979, *Outrageous Acts and Everyday Rebellions* (1983)

She [Golda Meir] did not make a cult of women's rights but took feminine equality for granted. From the outset she was a leader who was a woman rather than a woman leader.

> —Marie Syrkin, author, *Way of Valor: A Biography of Golda Meyerson* (1955)

Instead of acknowledging with humble gratitude the conditions that had allowed women to raise their families in relative peace and prosperity, the women's liberation movement encouraged a generation of Jewish daughters to feel contempt for their mothers.

> —Ruth R. Wisse, professor of Yiddish and comparative literature, reflecting on Betty Friedan's *The Feminist Mystique* in *Jerusalem Report*, January 9, 1992

To me, a strong woman is . . . a woman who isn't afraid of the power that comes from being a winner.

> —Naomi Wolf, author, interview in *Women Sports and Fitness* with editor Kathleen Gasperini, March 1994

❖ FOOD ❖

(see also Deli)

The Hebrew race has been waiting 4000 years for Crisco.

—Advertising campaign, introducing new kosher vegetable shortening, 1912

My mother taught me . . . no matter how poor, we would eat off clean white linen, and say the prayers before touching anything to the mouth. And so I do it still. Whenever I sit down, I eat with God, my mother, and all the Jews who are doing these same things even if I can't see them.

—"Basha," member of the Aliyah Senior Citizens' Center in California, preparing her dinner eaten alone in her tiny room, over an electric hot plate, quoted in *Number Our Days* by Barbara Myerhoff (1978)

We consider a meal to be a religious act, an act which calls to mind our relationship with the world around us and our dependence upon the benevolence of the Source of all nourishment.

—Ronald A. Brauner, president of The Foundation for Jewish Studies and professor of Judaic Studies, "Kosher Has Nothing to Do With Food" in *Being Jewish in a Gentile World* (1995)

My wife likes Chinese food and I eat it with docility.

—Abba Eban, former foreign minister and Israeli ambassador to the United Nations, quoted in "Abba Eban at Columbia" in *The Lonely Days Were Sundays: Reflections of a Jewish Southerner* by Eli N. Evans (1993)

The food pages of newspapers give equal space to the preparation of a ham with cloves and egg decoration as well as to chicken soup with matza balls. This is authentic multiculturalism. It does not need a multisyllabic description. It flourishes at its best with commonplace grace in our homes, at our tables and in our common understanding of universal truth underlying the religious rituals of everyday life.

—Suzanne Fields, columnist, *The Washington Times*, April 21, 1997

Jewish foods survive only in the tired humor of tired comedians; American Jews are more familiar with sushi than gefilte fish.

—Joshua Halberstam, philosopher and author, *Schmoozing: The Private Conversations of American Jews* (1997)

I said, "You don't know what they named it: Hershel!"

> —Mike Jacobs, Polish-born Texan, age seventy-one, recalls his reaction when
> a American soldier tossed him a chocolate bar at the time of the liberation
> of Mauthausen in 1945, quoted in *USA Today*, May 2, 1997

I am appalled by the number of chemicals that are added to our food, and long for the days when one did not need a degree in chemistry in order to understand what one was eating. From my perspective, I'm tempted to brand all food additives as treif [not kosher] and hail as glatt kosher only those fruits and vegetables that are organically grown.

> —Rabbi Bonnie Koppell, "Vegetarianism" in *Rabbis and Vegetarianism: An
> Evolving Tradition* (1995)

The first time I set foot in a restaurant was on my first date with the man who would later become my husband, and then only to drink a cup of coffee. I was young, eager to please, and defensive about the supposed lack of variety and undistinguished preparation of kosher food. I will never forget an incident which occurred a year after we were married. My husband invited a friend home for dinner. I served roast duck. Our guest, aware that he was eating in a kosher home, jokingly asked if the duck was circumcised. I was so taken aback by this question. . . . Perhaps it was then that I decided to prove that kosher food could be as varied, light, elegant, and exciting as one wished to make it.

> —Helen Nash, cookbook author, *Kosher Cuisine* (1984)

I still find myself lying, saying, "I'm allergic to pork," because if I were to say, "I'm kosher," no one would understand.

> —Tammie Reiter, resident of Billings, Montana, quoted in *The Invisible
> Thread: A Portrait of Jewish American Women* by Diana Bletter (1989)

Every cuisine tells a story. Jewish cuisine tells the story of an uprooted, migrating people and their vanished worlds. It lives in people's minds and has been kept alive because of what it evokes and represents.

> —Claudia Roden, food writer and cookbook author, *The Book of Jewish Food:
> An Odyssey from Samarkand to New York* (1996)

A Hasid goes into a Jewish restaurant and asks if it is super-kosher. The waiter shows him the portrait of a rabbi hanging on the wall and says, "You can trust us with him hanging there." And the Hasid replies, "I could trust you if he was standing in your place and you were hanging up there."

> —Claudia Roden, retold in *The Book of Jewish Food: An Odyssey from Sam-
> arkand to New York* (1996)

Perhaps at the beginning of the meal or even at each major course, one of the cooks might explicitly say that the food is intended to nourish the body, not to overfill it. That hungers of the mind, heart, and spirit must be met by the quality of conversation and of silence at the table, not by gobbling to fill this emptiness.

—Rabbi Arthur Waskow, author and activist, *Down to Earth Judaism: Food, Money, Sex, and the Rest of Life* (1995)

❖ FRANK CASE ❖

(see also Anti-Semitism)

[The lynching] had a real effect on all the Jews of Atlanta. . . . This was before I was born. I heard it so often as I grew up, I feel as if I remember it.

—Cecil A. Alexander, architect, age sixty-eight, in Atlanta, Georgia whose uncle had been one of Leo Frank's lawyers, quoted in *The Jewish Times* by Howard Simons (1988)

The lynching of Leo Frank was a kind of shorthand symbolism, enacting the nightmares that troubled the sleep of the white Southerner. In this action was caught the twisted myths of sexual perversity and sexual superiority of the alien and the blood paranoia of a thousand years of European anti-Semitism. It was transmogrified into that peculiar American tradition of lynching, the orgiastic sacrifice by the frustrated and politically impotent mob.

—Lenora E. Berson, author, *The Negroes and the Jews* (1971)

The story as to women coming into the factory with me for immoral purposes is a base lie and the occasion that he claims to have seen me in indecent positions with women is a lie so vile that I have no language with which to fitly denounce it.

—Leo Frank, statement under oath at his 1913 trial for the murder of Mary Phagan, quoted in *The Lonely Days Were Sundays: Reflections of a Jewish Southerner* by Eli N. Evans (1993)

I, Leo Frank, did not kill Mary Phagan.

—Leo Frank, written from a prison cell in Fulton County, Ga., 1914, in a point by point rebuttal of the prosecution's murder case against him,

"Frank's Last Protest Emerges—From Old Trunk," *Forward*, October 13, 1995

Every conceivable rumor has been put afloat that would do him and me harm, with the public. . . . I know my husband is innocent, he is utterly incapable of committing the crime that these detectives and this solicitor are seeking to fasten upon him.

—Lucille Selig Frank, wife of Leo Frank, June 5, 1913, quoted in *The Leo Frank Case* by Leonard Dinnerstein (1966)

It would be most unfortunate if anything were done . . . from the standpoint of the Jews. Whatever is done must be done as a matter of justice, and any action that is taken should emanate from non-Jewish sources.

—Louis Marshall, president of the American Jewish Committee, responding to requests from Atlanta Jews for assistance, 1913, quoted in *The Leo Frank Case* by Leonard Dinnerstein (1966)

There should be no suggestion that the Frank case involves any element of anti-Semitism.

—Louis Marshall, 1913, enlisting the help of Adolph Ochs, publisher of *The New York Times*, quoted in *The Leo Frank Case* by Leonard Dinnerstein (1966)

I fear that I shall never again be able to feel that reliance upon the courts in respect to the accomplishments of the ends of justice, than I had hitherto entertained.

—Louis Marshall, after the U.S. Supreme Court rejected a defense motion for a writ of habeas corpus, 1915, quoted in *The Leo Frank Case* by Leonard Dinnerstein (1966)

Lynchings were not unusual in Georgia. Lynchings of white people were.

—Dale M. Schwartz, attorney in Atlanta, member of the Board of Directors of the Anti-Defamation League, an organization that arose out of the Frank experience, quoted in *The Jewish Times* by Howard Simons (1988)

❖ FREEDOM ❖

Liberty is indeed universal and indivisible. The world today has become a small neighborhood. As long as slavery exists anywhere, liberty is everywhere endangered. There cannot be permanent liberty in one country if there be tyranny in another. The new space age, with the possibility of nations claiming control of the planets, makes it imperative for humanity to proclaim liberty everywhere.

> —*The Passover Haggadah*, newly revised edition, compiled by Morris Silverman, edited by Jonathan D. Levine (1959)

The sign of a free man is being able to keep your hands in your pockets.

> —Lee Berendt, survivor of Auschwitz and Dachau, quoted in *When They Came To Take My Father: Voices of the Holocaust*, photographs by Mark Seliger, edited by Leora Kahn and Rachel Hager (1996)

A society that puts equality—in the sense of equality of outcome—ahead of freedom will end up with neither equality nor freedom. The use of force to achieve equality will destroy freedom, and the force, introduced for good purposes, will end up in the hands of people who use it to promote their own interests.

> —Milton and Rose Friedman, economists and authors, *Free to Choose: A Personal Statement* (1980)

The moral leaders who capture the world's imagination today are by and large people who have spent time in prison—Natan Sharansky and Ida Nudel, Nelson Mandela and Vaclev Havel, to name a few. It is as if people appreciated freedom more because of the examples of those to whom it was denied.

> —Carmela Efros Kalmanson, president of Hadassah, "The Haggadah Idea," *Hadassah*, April 1990

They will say of us either that we used our new freedom—the freedom we sought but were never granted by Europe—to vanish as a people, or that we took advantage of the secret opportunity concealed within the persistent but hidden trauma we are now experiencing—a Jewry and Judaism decisively changed by its confrontation with modern paganism—to reeducate ourselves, rebuild our core from the treasures of our past, fuse it with the best in secularism, and create a new philosophy, a new literature, a new world of Jewish art, a new community, and take seriously the meaning of the word emancipation—a release from the authority of the father in order to become adults in our own right.

> —Chaim Potok, author, *Wanderings* (1978)

A free mind and a free economy are corollaries. One cannot exist without the other.

> —Ayn Rand, writer and philosopher, interview with Alvin Toffler in *Playboy*, March 1964

A man is free only when he has an errand to do on earth.

> —Rabbi Abba Hillel Silver, reform rabbi and Zionist leader for more than fifty years, until his death in 1963, attributed

❖ FREEDOM OF SPEECH ❖

I believe that what some deride as "political correctness" is really only a caricatured description of what I always defined as common decency; a variation on the Levitical precept that what is hateful to you, you should not do to others.

> —Rabbi Rebecca T. Alpert, author and codirector of Women's Studies Program at Temple University, "Coming Out of the Closet Is Politically Correct," *Tikkun*, March/April 1996

Free speech is being limited to the politically correct. This is a real danger in a democratic society, because when you have what we call free speech without debate, you have the beginning of demagogy, and we're experiencing that demagogy right now.

> —Saul Bellow, Nobel-Prize winning novelist, "Writers and Editors Discuss Anti-Semitism," a symposium held on May 5 and 6, 1994, at the 92nd Street Y in New York City, reprinted as "Is There a Cure for Anti-Semitism?" *Partisan Review*, Summer 1994

Those who won our independence . . . knew that order cannot be secured merely through fear of punishment for its infraction; that it is hazardous to discourage thought, hope and imagination; that fear breeds repression; that repression breeds hate; that hate menaces stable government; that the path of safety lies in the opportunity to discuss freely supposed grievances and proposed remedies; and that the fitting remedy for evil counsels is good ones.

> —Louis D. Brandeis, United States Supreme Court justice, concurring opinion in Whitney v. California; excerpted from *Law as Literature*, edited by Ephraim London (1960)

In our system, state-operated schools may not be enclaves of totalitarianism. School officials do not possess absolute authority over their students. Students in school as well as out of school are "persons" under our constitution. They are possessed of fundamental rights which the State must respect, just as they themselves must respect their obligations to the State. In our school system, students may not be regarded as closed-circuit recipients of only that which the State chooses to communicate. They may not be confined to the expression of those sentiments that are officially approved. In the absence of a specific showing of constitutionally valid reasons to regulate their speech, students are entitled to freedom of expression of their views.

> —Abe Fortas, United States Supreme Court justice, delivering the opinion of the court on the question of the authority of school officials to censor symbolic speech in classrooms, Tinker v. Des Moines (1969)

Rudeness is a deeply held constitutional value.

> —Barney Frank, Congressman (D-Mass.), defending a Mississippi preacher's right to call homosexuality "self-destructive," quoted in *Jerusalem Report*, April 6, 1995

Blasphemy may be a crime in Iran but it ought not be a crime in America.

> —Ira Glasser, executive director of the ACLU (American Civil Liberties Union), regarding flag-burning, quoted in *Newsweek*, July 10, 1989

In an academic institution, truth must be a primary value. In making free speech the central issue in these cases, truth becomes irrelevant.

> —Nathan Glazer, sociologist, quoted in *William and Mary Law Review*, January 1995

Serious offense does not always result in a breach of the peace.

> —William Kunstler, lawyer, from argument before the United States Supreme Court, in Texas v. Johnson (1989) on the question: Does the First Amendment protect the right to burn the flag? quoted in *May It Please the Court*, edited by Peter Irons and Stephanie Guitton (1993)

Ignorance in action is a frightening spectacle—as frightening as a small group deciding what subjects Americans may or may not discuss.

> —Paul Greenberg, editorial page editor, *Pine Bluff Commercial*, and syndicated columnist, "Family Feud" in *Entirely Personal* (1992)

To hear things and see things that we hate tests the First Amendment more than seeing or hearing things that we like.

> —William Kunstler, lawyer, from an argument before the United States Su-

preme Court, *Texas v. Johnson* (1989), regarding the question of whether
the First Amendment protects the right to burn the flag, quoted in *May It
Please the Court*, edited by Peter Irons and Stephanie Guitton (1993)

I wondered what we were all doing there, and how insane a people can get
in a democracy, to have the flower of their youth listening to plans for mass
murder, and treating him as if he represented some substantial body of rational
if wrong-headed opinion.

> — Max Lerner, columnist and social critic, commenting on the appearance of
> George Lincoln Rockwell, founder and leader of the American Nazi Party,
> before a Harvard Law School audience, "A Sick Envoy," *New York Post*,
> September 28, 1966

Censorship is the most popular of these quick-fix prescriptions—and it is
also the most dangerous.

> — Michael Medved, author and media commentator, *Hollywood vs. America*
> (1992)

Much of the debate focused not on whether the Nazis had a right to speak
but on whether the ACLU should be defending that right.

> — Aryeh Neier, former national executive director of the American Civil Lib-
> erties Union, regarding the right of Nazis to hold a demonstration in Skokie,
> Ill., home of many Holocaust survivors, *Defending My Enemy: American
> Nazis, the Skokie Case, and the Risks of Freedom* (1979)

While I defended (Frank) Collins' freedom to speak, I did not propose to
act as his press agent, and said so.

> — Aryeh Neier, defending the right of Frank Collins and other American Nazis
> to demonstrate in Skokie, Ill., *Defending My Enemy: American Nazis, the
> Skokie Case, and the Risks of Freedom* (1979)

It would be more pleasant for defenders of freedom to rally around the
causes of a better class of victims. But if we wait until nice people are victimized,
it may be too late. The first place to defend freedom is the first place it is
denied.

> — Aryeh Neier, *Defending My Enemy: American Nazis, the Skokie Case, and
> The Risks of Freedom* (1979)

There seemed something fundamentally unseemly about a group of Jewish
lawyers, financed by a membership which is heavily Jewish, defending the rights
of a few punks to go into a Jewish area and shout from the rooftops that it was
too bad that Hitler didn't finish the job.

—Rabbi Daniel Jeremy Silver, sermon in Cleveland on the Skokie case, quoted in *Defending My Enemy: American Nazis, the Skokie Case, and the Risks of Freedom* by Aryeh Neier (1979)

In desperate days, it seems, it always seems wise to throw something or someone overboard, preferably Jonah or Arion, the prophet and the poet.

—Lionel Trilling, critic, "Science, Literature and Culture," *Commentary*, June 1962

❖ FRIENDSHIP ❖

(see also Relationships)

She has women friends here who will neither let her starve nor weep.

—Esther M. Broner, novelist, *A Weave of Women* (1985)

Honor thy friends for thou art the accumulation of them.

—Esther M. Broner, *A Weave of Women* (1985)

It's not so bad to discover when you're still young just who your friends are not.

—Roy M. Cohn, attorney, quoted in *The Autobiography of Roy Cohn* by Sidney Zion (1988)

There are two categories of friendship: those in which people are enlivened by each other and those in which people must be enlivened to be with each other. In the first category one clears the decks to be together. In the second one looks for an empty space in the schedule.

—Vivian Gornick, essayist and author, *Approaching Eye Level* (1996)

Friendship is a long conversation. I suppose I could imagine a nonverbal friendship revolving around shared physical work or sport, but for me, good talk is the point of the thing.

—Philip Lopate, essayist and author, "Modern Friendships" in *Against Joie de Vivre: Personal Essays* (1989)

Friendship is a heart-flooding feeling that can happen to any two people who are caught up in the act of being themselves, together, and who like what they see. The feeling is deeper than companionship; one can hire a companion. It is more than affection; affection can be as false as a stage kiss. It is never one-sided. It elevates biology into full humanity.

> —Letty Cottin Pogrebin, author and activist, *Among Friends* (1987)

❖ FUTURE ❖

And so, after thousands of years, the Jews stand as they have so often stood, small, dispersed, vulnerable, but still inspired by a large and spacious ambition, still hoping to see great visions and to dream great dreams, the people with a voice whose echoes never die.

> —Abba Eban, former foreign minister and Israeli ambassador to the United Nations, *Heritage: Civilization and the Jews* (1984)

Our vision of the end of days has often been clearer than our vision of this day.

> —Leonard Fein, activist and author, *Where Are We? The Inner Life of America's Jews* (1988)

A vision is inspired by your belief about human possibility, while being influenced by your experience of human fallibility.

> —Seymour Fox, professor of Jewish education, *Vision at the Heart* (1997)

I believe that in the twenty-first century all religions will have to be drawn upon to create a somewhat shared religious language that will make for the great transformation of human consciousness needed for the very survival of our world.

> —Rabbi Arthur Green, professor of Jewish thought and former dean and president of Reconstructionist Rabbinical College, "Judaism for the Post-Modern Era," the Samuel H. Goldenson Lecture, delivered December 12, 1994, at the Hebrew Union College-Jewish Institute of Religion, Cincinnati

Let them remember that there is a meaning beyond absurdity. Let them be sure that every deed counts, that every word has power, and that we all can do our share to redeem the world in spite of all absurdities and all frustrations and all disappointments. Above all, let them remember to build a life as if it were a work of art.

> —Rabbi Abraham Joshua Heschel, author, activist, and theologian, television

interview with Carl Stern of NBC, offering a message for young people,
1972

The twentieth century has made a mockery of any ability to predict the
Jewish future, and anybody who presumes to do that at this late date in this
century has very little understanding of how Jewish history operates.

> —Egon Mayer, author and director of Jewish Outreach Institute, interviewed
> in the film *Jewish Soul, American Beat*, produced, directed, and written by
> Barbara Pfeffer, 1997

Life is a murmur between two eternities. I enjoin you to make of this
murmur a beautiful symphony with all the counterpoint and harmony of which
you are capable; a polychromatic canvas where you will find beauty and meaning—in your tears as well as in your joy, in your togetherness as well as in your
solitude, in your pain as well as in your moments of elation and nobility of
being.

> —Rabbi Marshall T. Meyer, human rights activist, founder of the Seminario
> Rabinico Latinoamericano and spiritual leader of B'nai Jeshurun (New
> York), Baccalaureate Sermon at the Claremont Colleges, California, May
> 18, 1986

I am one member of one people confronting these closing decades of the
twentieth century. Whether it knows it or not, my people is now engaged in an
attempt to create for itself a third civilization. I feel myself part of that venture.
I think of Sumer and its rushing rivers, Egypt and its rising Nile, Canaan and
its terraced hills and fertility cults, Greece and Rome, Islam and Christianity,
Jerusalem, Babylon, Cordova, Toledo, the Rhine valley, the Ukraine, Vilna,
Odessa, Kishinev. What will Jewry make of itself for the next thousand years?

> —Chaim Potok, author, *Wanderings* (1978)

We may not be prophets, but the struggle to be engaged with a living
Judaism can confer on us some of the attributes of prophecy—the gift of dreaming, of elaborating a vision toward which mankind can continue to set forth.
Behind the fascinating, sophisticated artificial intelligences we are constructing
daily lie the human mind and the human heart—the destinations toward which
all our miraculous advances, technological and medical, are oriented.

> —Nessa Rapoport, author, "Vitality" in *At the Crossroads: Shaping Our Jewish
> Future*, published by the Wilstein Institute of Jewish Policy Studies (1995)

The question now is whether the American Jewish community can do better, forging a new image of Israel that is at once credible enough to pass the
test of reality, inspiring enough to command a following, and powerful enough

to carry the relationship between the two communities into the 21st century and beyond.

—Jonathan D. Sarna, professor of American Jewish history, "The Israel of American Jews," *Sh'ma,* September 30, 1994

If anti-Semitism should continue at a low level or even decrease from here, I would say you would have a very diluted Jewish community 50 years from today, except for the right-wing Orthodox. It's unfortunate, but I think that's the direction we are headed in.

—Laurence Tisch, executive and philanthropist, interview with Jonathan Perlman in his documentary "Being Jewish," quoted in *The Boston Jewish Advocate,* January 12, 1996

❖ GAY AND LESBIAN JEWS ❖

(see also Homosexuality)

I have only one identity, one self. The feeling of two conflicting identities, one gay and one Jewish, was a false consciousness. I need to be part of a Jewish community.

> — Student at New York's Congregation Beth Simchat Torah, quoted in "Talmud Class in a Gay Synagogue," by Henry Rabinowitz, *Judaism*, Fall 1983

The yarmulke is the greatest cover on earth.

> — "Chaim," thirty-two-year old who is committed to observant Judaism and a member of the Gay and Lesbian Yeshiva Day School Alumni Association, quoted in *Jewish Telegraphic Agency*, April 6, 1995

We are raised in insular communities and our lives are mapped out for us. We're told, "if you follow the rules everything will be fine." But then we realize that we can't follow the rules and suddenly, we have no rules to follow. The community we grew up with threw us out and we don't know where else to turn.

> — "Moshe," a twenty-five-year-old member of a Young Israel synagogue in the New York area and one of the organizers of the Gay and Lesbian Yeshiva Day School Alumni Association, formed by Orthodox Jews, quoted in *Jewish Telegraphic Agency*, April 6, 1995

These people can't have it both ways. They are saying that their [sexual] orientation is something they can do nothing about and saying that they want to be observant to Torah and still engage in behavior which is abhorrent to Orthodoxy. They're banding together because they want to equate what they're doing with a legitimate movement, but what they're doing is illegitimate.

> —Rabbi Steven Dworkin, executive vice-president of the Rabbinical Council of America (Orthodox), quoted in *Jewish Telegraphic Agency*, April 6, 1995

In the long run, if you're a Jewish boy growing up gay, the best thing you can do is get out of there. That's the reality.

> —Sheldon Golub, a fifty-two-year-old man, recalling his childhood, "AIDS—How Can Judaism Help?" *Hadassah*, August–September 1992

We have to assume that the proportion of homosexuals born into the Orthodox communities is the same as in the rest of society. Where is that 5 to 10 percent? Everyone assumes we are all heterosexual, but it's not the case.

> —Israel Kestenbaum, Orthodox rabbi and chaplain of Manhattan's Beth Israel Medical Center-North Division, who also counsels a small group of secretly gay Orthodox men, in "Dying of Shame" by Vince Beiser, *Jerusalem Report*, February 23, 1995

I'm ordained as a rabbi, not as a lesbian.... Some of my dearest mentors have been gay and lesbian rabbis. But to me, they are just successful rabbis. Coming out of five years of training, contributing to the Jewish community is in the forefront of my mind.

> —Rabbi Sydney Mintz, the first openly lesbian rabbi at Congregation Emanuel in San Francisco, who, after graduation from Hebrew Union College, joined the synagogue's staff as its fourth rabbi, quoted in *Jewish Bulletin of Northern California*, May 23, 1997

A significant number of frum [Orthodox] Jews, including myself, have decided not to throw out the baby with the bathwater. Yes, there are problems, but a life of Torah and mitzvos is worth maintaining, even if one is negligent in one area of observance. Aren't there countless fine people in all committed Jewish circles who neglect one major mitzvah or another?

> —Student at New York's Congregation Beth Simchat Torah, quoted in "Talmud Class in a Gay Synagogue" by Henry Rabinowitz, *Judaism*, Fall 1983

If I said nothing about my sexuality, wouldn't I be guilty of deception?

> —Student at New York's Congregation Beth Simchat Torah, responding to advice from certain rabbis to marry regardless of how he felt, quoted in "Talmud Class in a Gay Synagogue" by Henry Rabinowitz, *Judaism*, Fall 1983

I wish that homosexual men would realize that there will never be a Jewish consensus that accords their lifestyle equal status and acceptance with the more historic male-female marriage.

> —Rabbi Emanuel Rackman, chancellor of Bar-Ilan University, author and columnist, *The Jewish Week,* August 4, 1995

Most of us do not want the isolation or punishment of homosexuals but will never accept recognition of unlimited choice in lifestyles. The nations which did no longer exist; the people committed to Torah still do.

> —Rabbi Emanuel Rackman, *The Jewish Week,* August 4, 1995

In our denial, in our failure to see one another as one family—indeed as one holy body—we forget Jewish history, we opt for amnesia. We who were beaten in the streets of Berlin cannot turn away from the plague of gay-bashing. We who were Marranos [Jews forced to renounce their Judaism and practice in secret] in Madrid, who clung to the closet of assimilation and conversion in order to live without molestation, we cannot deny the demand for gay and lesbian visibility. In all of this, I am working to make the Reform Jewish community a home: a place where loneliness and suffering and exile ends; a place that leaves it to God to validate relationships and demands of us only that these relationships be worthy in God's eyes; a place where we can search—together—through the written Torah and the Torah of life, to find those affirmations for which we yearn.

> —Rabbi Alexander M. Schindler, president of the Union of American Hebrew Congregations, presidential biennial address, 1989

Everybody knows who they are so why do they have to announce it with a banner? I would have no problem with a gay person marching next to me, but why do they have to flaunt their aberration?

> —Rabbi Fabian Schonfeld, spiritual leader of the Young Israel of Kew Garden Hills, New York, regarding the threat by Orthodox Jewish leaders to boycott the 1993 "Salute to Israel" parade if members of a gay synagogue were allowed to march with a banner bearing the name Congregation Beth Simchat Torah, quoted in the *New York Post,* April 1993

Minorities always confront the task of imagining a culture for themselves. Jews have always done this, but gay and lesbian Jews have to do it a second time.

> —Aaron Mack Schloff, theatre critic, "A Culture of Their Own," *The Jewish Week,* August 4, 1995

Your election creates considerable expectation in our community. It is a community out of the slavery of Egypt, sitting in a vast expanse of wilderness wondering, struggling, looking for leadership to bring us to some kind of a promised land. While we know that no one person can do it, it is clear that this country needs the leadership that you indicate a willingness to accept.

> —Sharon Kleinbaum, rabbi of Congregation Beth Simchat Torah in New York City, writing as Bill Clinton was about to assume the presidency, "Memo to Clinton: Gays and Lesbians," *Tikkun*, January/February 1993

❖ GENERATIONS ❖

(see also Families)

I find that learning about my family history draws me farther and farther into Jewish Tradition. The more I learn about my ancestors, the more I learn about Jewish history and therefore, Jewish learning. The more facts I have about the lives of my ancestors, the more I learn to respect them and feel grateful to them for their decisions. . . . I learn much about courage when I understand what it was like to make the decision to journey to America. I continue to learn about faith and belief as I discover the obstacles set before my ancestors in Jewish history.

> —Arthur Kurzweil, genealogist, author, editor, and publisher, *From Generation to Generation: How to Trace Your Jewish Genealogy and Family History* (1994)

Something in them, something about their background must have given them tremendous courage and independence. We don't know what that "something" really is. It would be good if you can find out. You don't have long, because they'll be gone soon. And when they go, there's nobody else. The sixty- and even seventy-year-olds who were born here, they're nothing like that. So if you really want to do this study, you had better get going.

> —Abe, director of the Aliyah Senior Citizens' Center, a group of elderly who were former migrants to the United States from Eastern Europe, quoted in *Number Our Days* by Barbara Myerhoff (1978)

They have grown up in a world where anti-Semitism is not something that affects their lives personally, where Israel is stronger than ever and is talking about peace not war, where the Holocaust is part of history, where the Jews of Russia and Ethiopia and Syria are no longer being held captive.

> —Joseph Aaron, editor of the *Chicago Jewish News*, reflecting on the per-

spective of those in "Generation X," quoted in *The Jewish Advocate*, November 3, 1995

We slip through our lives like water, says my aunt. What we know is a blur. But history does not repeat itself. Little by little, knowledge is passed on. Fish to fish, we press small morsels of the truth into each other's mouths as we swim past.

—Magda Bogen, novelist, *Natalya, God's Messenger* (1994)

Mine is the first generation that will be poorer than our parents. We can't find jobs. We look around us and understand that what we were taught was our birthright is now a myth.

—Andrea Gurwitt, journalist, "The Seduction of Certainty: Losing Feminist Daughters to Orthodoxy," *On the Issues*, Winter 1996

Sometimes I'd pair up for a few days with fellow backpackers, strangers sharing the trust of the road. . . . I was part of history's first youth internationale, the first generation for whom there were no borders. Europe had been sealed to my father, but it was entirely open to me. No experience revealed more sharply the gap between us: his was history's most traumatized generation of Jews, mine the least.

—Yossi Klein Halevi, Israeli journalist, author, and son of a Holocaust survivor, *Memoirs of a Jewish Extremist* (1995)

Every man is his own ancestor, and every man is his own heir. He devises his own future, and he inherits his own past.

—Dr. Morris Mandel, columnist, *The Jewish Press*, December 26, 1997

He yearned to package for each of the children, the grandchildren, for everyone, that joyous certainty, that sense of mattering, of moving and being moved, of being one and indivisible with the great of the past, with all that freed, ennobled. Package it, stand on corners, in front of stadiums and on crowded beaches, knock on doors, give it as a fabled gift.

—Tillie Olsen, novelist, *Tell Me a Riddle* (1960)

I wish there were some award for the myriad nameless Jewish immigrants—our parents and grandparents—who never attained celebrity but who have provided a substantial part of the bone and flesh and robust spirit of our community. I often marvel at their courage in pulling up roots in the old country and their sacrifices in sinking new roots in the American soil.

—David Sarnoff, businessman and pioneer in the broadcasting industry, receiving an award from the Hebrew Immigrant Aid Society in 1959, quoted in *Sarnoff: An American Success* by Carl Dreher (1977)

Every child born into a Jewish family represents a blessed link in the long chain of Jewish life stretching back to Abraham and Sarah. The soul is seared by the thought of the generations that, because of the Nazi Holocaust, will not be born.

> —Dr. Ruth K. Westheimer, author and sex therapist, "What Being Jewish Means to Me," part of a series produced by the American Jewish Committee, 1997

Thanks, old father, for the Jewish awareness you drummed into me. You gave me the best thing you had.

> —Herman Wouk, writer, *Inside, Outside* (voice of I. David Goodkind) (1985)

My ambition is to be a good ancestor.

> —Herbert Zipper, composer, conductor, and Austrian-born Holocaust survivor, reflecting at age ninety-two about his life's journey, quoted in the *Los Angeles Times*, April 9, 1997

❖ GERMANY (POST-WAR) ❖

(see also World War II)

The path for the new Germany is clear. The Jewish people pray that you will prove that the world has nothing to fear; that you will follow the path away from your worst traditions and toward the best traditions of which you are so capable. The great challenge is to build a Germany firmly rooted in peace and respect for universal human values.

> —Edgar M. Bronfman, chairman of The Seagram Company Ltd. and president of the World Jewish Congress, from a 1990 speech given in the presence of German Chancellor Helmut Kohl and other notables, *The Making of a Jew* (1996)

Even though I had thought that the book [*Hitler's Willing Executioners*] would be well received in Germany once people were exposed to its arguments, I did not imagine that it would turn out as it has. All of this says a great deal that is positive about contemporary Germany. For Germans to confront this horrific part of their past is enormously unpleasant. That so many are willing to do so is yet another indication of how transformed the Germany of today is compared to 1933 or 1945. In this sense, Germany is the great cultural and political success story of the postwar period.

> —Daniel Jonah Goldhagen, political scientist and author, quoted in an interview with Maurice Wohlgelernter, *Society*, January–February 1997

I said, come on. You must be kidding. He wouldn't be that stupid. That insensitive. . . .He was like a superstar going on television to endorse a product that would rot your teeth.

> —Bill Graham, rock music impresario who owned the Fillmore East and Fillmore West theaters and was a refugee from Nazi-occupied Europe, commenting on President Reagan's decision to visit Bitburg to lay a wreath at a cemetery where SS officers were buried, *Bill Graham Presents,* written with Robert Greenfield (1992) (Graham responded with a full page ad in protest and he organized a rally in San Francisco against the visit; shortly after, his office was firebombed and destroyed by vandals who left swastika graffiti behind—they were never caught.)

As a Jew who lost most of his family during the Holocaust, to go to Germany is an act of forgiveness. Those Germans who were not yet alive, or who were children during the Holocaust, do not need forgiveness. Those who are old enough to need it, neither I nor anyone else can forgive.

> —Rabbi Arthur Hertzberg, author and professor of the humanities, "Why I Have Not Visited Germany," *Reform Judaism*, Winter 1997

"We knew, we just knew, all America, that this day would come," said President Bush in November 13 about the amazing events in Berlin. It's nice of him to include us all, but let me confess that I certainly didn't know it would come. And if he knew, he kept it a wonderful surprise. Conservative doctrine had been that it would never come . . . The conservative view has never been that a contained communism could collapse of its own internal contradictions.

> —Michael Kinsley, columnist, *The New Republic*, December 4, 1989

I will not have died unfulfilled if it does not happen in my lifetime.

> —Henry A. Kissinger, speaking on the prospect of the reunification of Germany, interviewed on *This Week With David Brinkley*, ABC-TV, November 19, 1989

Jews have a task regarding the new Germany. It is not to oppose reunification or to begrudge German prosperity. It is to prevent the forgetting of Auschwitz.

—Michael Wyschograd, professor of philosophy, "Two Germanys Into One," *Hadassah*, May 1990

Collective punishment is not a basis for foreign policy.
> —Michael Wyschograd, "Two Germanys into One," *Hadassah*, May 1990

❖ GOD ❖

(see also Faith, Prayer, Spirituality)

You've got to be very close to God, you have to know Him very well to blaspheme Him. Only a deeply religious person can despise God, shake his fist at God and abuse Him. A blaspheming Jew is a believing Jew. And the camps were composed of these Jews in great numbers. . . . Being an atheist in the camp was no easy thing.
> —Anonymous Holocaust survivor who worked on clearance detail of the gas chamber, quoted in *The Faith and Doubt of Holocaust Survivors* by Reeve Robert Brenner (1980)

I call myself an atheist although I know deep in my heart that God exists. It is just that I refuse to give Him the satisfaction of acknowledging it.
> —Anonymous Holocaust survivor, quoted in *The Faith and Doubt of Holocaust Survivors* by Reeve Robert Brenner (1980)

For me, encountering God has meant addressing God directly in my own words and seeking a direct reply in any form describable as divine revelation— God becoming manifest to humans. However, establishing such a connection is almost impossibly difficult, not necessarily because God is inaccessible—quite the contrary—but because I am. I hesitate to make the approach, feeling unworthy, daunted by the prospect of absolute vulnerability, unprepared no matter when it is, fearful of raw unmediated truth, and, absurdly, embarrassed by the lack of parity between me and the One I am about to address.
> —Arlene Agus, scholar, teacher and activist, "Afterword—Meeting God's Gaze" in *Beginning Anew: A Woman's Companion to the High Holy Days*, edited by Gail Twersky Reimer and Judith A. Kates (1997)

I do not suggest that God "wills" tragedy, injustice, painful choices or evil into being, but I do believe that these, too are part of the flow of godliness in the universe, and part of what God is all about. Even within darkness and evil, deepest despair and most painful decision making, there is God.

—Rabbi Leila Gal Berner, congregational rabbi and composer of Jewish music, "Our Silent Seasons" in *Lifecycles 1*, edited by Rabbi Debra Orenstein (1994)

The great achievement of Israel is not so much that it told mankind of the one, real God, the origin and goal of all that exists, but rather that it taught men that they can address God . . . that man can say Thou to Him, that we human beings can stand face to face with Him, that there is communion between God and man.

—Martin Buber, theologian, 1948 remarks, quoted in *Martin Buber: Jewish Existentialist* by Malcom L. Diamond (1960)

It's really a very meaningful religion irrespective of whether you believe in God or not. The mitzvahs make sense even if you could prove black and white there is no God. This is just a meaningful way of life.

—Rabbi Ephraim Z. Buchwald, educational director of Lincoln Square Synagogue in New York City, speaking to his beginner Bible class, quoted in *Tradition in a Rootless World* by Lynn Davidman (1991)

Spiritual seeking is the human drive to make meaning out of the fact of existence. We name what we seek "God." By creating holiness/wholeness in life, we reveal the face of God.

—Rabbi Meryl M. Crean, upon ordination from the Reconstructionist Rabbinical College, *RRC 1996 Annual Report*

Judaism is a man's religion not only in substance and in practice but in its symbolic theology. God is male. Israel in relation to God is female: the bridegroom God and the Virgin Israel. The Shekhinah, the Divine Presence, represents the female potency within God. The Torah is female, the Sabbath is female. In relation to them, God is male. In the books of the Prophets and, of course, in the Song of Songs, marriage and sexual relations symbolize the ties between God and Israel, Israel and the Sabbath, Israel and Torah.

—Lucy S. Dawidowicz, author and teacher of modern Jewish history, "On Being a Woman in Shul" in *The Jewish Presence: Essays on Identity and History* (1977)

I believe the presence of God is revealed through our relationships — relationship to family, friends, God, community, and self.

—Rabbi Mona Decker, upon ordination from the Reconstructionist Rabbinical College, *RRC 1996 Annual Report*

I cannot conceive of a God who rewards and punishes his creatures, or has a will of the kind that we experience in ourselves.

> —Albert Einstein, Nobel Prize-winning theoretical physicist and humanist, "The World as I See It" in *Ideas and Opinions: Albert Einstein* (1982)

If we are to succeed in preserving Jewish faith, we will have to unbracket the question of God somewhat and redeem God, as it were, from both the silence to which He is condemned by our secular culture and the trivialization to which He is subjected by many fundamentalists.

> —Arnold Eisen, professor of Jewish thought, "Saving the Remnants of Jewish Faith" in *New Traditions 2*, Spring 1985

Over a period of time, I came to realize that there is a wide range of Jewish belief. There's no one thing that I could say that all Jews believe, other than that Jews believe in one God . . . if they believe in God.

> —Darlene Feldstein, a Jew by choice, quoted in *Finding a Home for the Soul: Interviews with Converts to Judaism* by Catherine Hall Myrowitz (1995)

When I pray, I speak to God. When I study, God speaks to me.

> —Rabbi Louis Finkelstein, president of The Jewish Theological Seminary of America from 1940, and chancellor from 1951–1972, quoted in *Conservative Judaism: The New Century* by Neil Gillman (1993)

To the extent that I am able to, I would like to be a vessel for bringing God's awareness before the world. The most precious of God's creation is mankind, and therefore, to be of service to mankind is perhaps the most worthwhile thing a person can do in life . . . If I can give a person a sense of God, then I have given the person a sense of how to value the essence of his own transcendent being.

> —Rabbi Gedaliah Fleer, teacher and lecturer on Jewish thought and mysticism, quoted in *In the Service of God: Conversations with Teachers of Torah in Jerusalem* by Shalom Freedman (1995)

Indeed, it is from within immanence itself that we rediscover transcendence: God is so profoundly and ineffably present in each moment, in every place, and in a special way in each human soul that the encounter with that presence leads us right back to transcendent mystery.

> —Rabbi Arthur Green, professor of Jewish thought and former dean and president of Reconstructionist Rabbinical College, "Judaism for the Post-Modern Era," the Samuel H. Goldenson Lecture, delivered December 12, 1994, at the Hebrew Union College-Jewish Institute of Religion, Cincinnati

The affirmation of God's existence is not a cold, factual statement. It is the conscious recognition of the ethical import of life . . . The moral attributes of God are holiness, justice, mercy, love and faithfulness. The knowledge of these is derived from the ideals for which men strive. In ascribing such attributes to God, we imply that God is the ideal, the pattern and inspirer of all morality.

—Rabbi Mordechai M. Kaplan, founder of the Reconstructionist movement, *Judaism as a Civilization* (1934)

Jewish education is inconceivable without reference to God. Either God or the Torah as the law of God is the central theme of practically all Jewish writings before the nineteenth century, and religion is the central interest of all but the recent events of Jewish history.

—Rabbi Mordechai M. Kaplan, *Judaism as a Civilization* (1934)

As for the mystery of God. . . . If I could understand God, I would be God. The Kotzker Rebbe once said: "A God that any Tom, Dick or Harry can understand, phooey. I don't need such a God."

—Steven T. Katz, Jewish philosopher, author, and professor of Near Eastern studies, quoted in *The God I Believe In* by Joshua O. Haberman (1994)

What always bothers me about Judaism is that the rabbi never says: "What do you believe?" He says, "Come on and get on the train like everyone else!" Yet for me, God is a very personal commitment.

—Alfred Kazin, author and literary critic, quoted in *Jerusalem Report*, February 19, 1998

We experience the reality of God in our own lives, but we experience it vicariously as well when we examine the history of the Jewish people. No one who reads the story of our 3,000 years of tribulation and accomplishment can deny that God makes a difference in the world.

—Rabbi Harold S. Kushner, author and rabbi emeritus of Temple Israel in Natick, Mass., *When Children Ask About God* (1971)

To our children, Aaron Zev and Ariel Ann, who have taught me more about God than I have taught them.

—Rabbi Harold S. Kushner, dedication in his book *When Children Ask About God* (1971)

You say, "I don't believe in God." And I respectfully ask, "What makes you think it matters to God?" You don't have to believe in psychoanalysis to have an unconscious either.

—Rabbi Lawrence Kushner, author and spiritual leader of Congregation Beth El in Sudbury, Mass., "Trout Fishing," *Tikkun*, July/August 1995

Encounter with God is the fulfillment of the mitzvot [sacred obligations]. If I washed today at half past six in the morning and went to the synagogue to fulfill the prayer duty, that was my encounter with God.

—Yeshayahu Leibowitz, Judaic scholar and professor of biochemistry, 1992 remarks, quoted in *The God I Believe In* by Joshua O. Haberman (1994)

If you can get to the point where you're not suffused with self-pity, then you've probably done 51 things right to every 49 things you did wrong. I think self-pity is the ultimate spiritual disease because it's anger against God. That means that there's no respect for God, and the moment there's no respect for God, we're in a lot of trouble.

—Norman Mailer, author, *Booknotes* interview with Brian Lamb, *C-SPAN*, June 25, 1995

Without human participation, God remains incomplete, unrealized. It is up to us to actualize the divine potential in the world. God needs us.

—Daniel C. Matt, professor of Jewish mysticism, *The Essential Kabbalah: The Heart of Jewish Mysticism* (1995)

If children get a love of God in their hearts they'll keep that love through their lives. Why is it that there are so few Catholic converts to Communism? It is because they learned the love of God when they were children. Why don't Jews and Protestants do the same thing?

—Louis B. Mayer, motion picture executive, speaking in Haverhill, Mass., where his film career began, at a Chamber of Commerce dinner in his honor, April 1954, quoted in *An Empire of Their Own* by Neal Gabler (1988)

What is so great about the fact that there is one God? Suppose there are 10 gods? Or 20 gods? Or none. . . . But if there is one creator God, there is a tremendous consequence. You and I are brothers and the Haitians are my brothers and sisters. Now that is a major difference that you don't get without the concept of God, and that is particularly Jewish.

—Rabbi Marshall T. Meyer, human rights activist, founder of the Seminario Rabinico Latinoamericano, and spiritual leader of B'nai Jeshurun in New York City, interviewed by Jonathan Perlman in the documentary *Being Jewish*, cited in *The Jewish Advocate*, January 12–18, 1996

By looking at the order of the world, we can infer purpose and from purpose we begin to get some knowledge of the Creator, the Planner of all this. I look at God through the works of God's hands and from those works imply intentions. From these intentions, I receive an impression of the Almighty.

> —Arno Penzias, 1978 Nobel laureate in physics, quoted in *The God I Believe In* by Joshua O. Haberman (1994)

The love of God and the love of human beings are two sides of the same coin.

> —Chaim Perl, congregational rabbi and author, quoted in *In the Service of God: Conversations with Teachers of Torah in Jerusalem* by Shalom Freedman (1995)

These images of God—lover, friend, companion, cocreator—are more appropriate metaphors for the God of the covenant than the traditional images of lord and king. Defining God's power not as domination but empowerment, they evoke a God who is with us instead of over us, a partner in dialogue who ever and again summons us to responsible action.

> —Judith Plaskow, author and professor of religious studies, *Standing Again at Sinai: Judaism from a Feminist Perspective* (1990)

Patriarchal theology . . . supports patriarchy as a religious and legal system. When the Torah is thought of as divinely revealed in its present form, the subordination of women is granted the seal of divine approval. When God is conceived of as male, as a king ruling over his universe, male rule in society seems appropriate and right.

> —Judith Plaskow, *Standing Again at Sinai: Judaism from a Feminist Perspective* (1990)

That there are morons who are religious is no more an argument against God than that there are morons who are lawyers is an argument against law.

> —Dennis Prager, author and radio talk show host, *Dennis Prager Show*, KABC Radio, Los Angeles, December 1994

The commandments are the link, the holy wiring through which a connection can be made between man and God. The better the connection, the more meaningful the love. The postcard from across the ocean with the message, "Thinking of you, Love, Harold," is simply not enough when it comes to God. Great distances—and could there be a greater distance than the distance between man and God?—require meaningful actions, not only thoughts. The Torah's commandments are the means by which it is possible to keep in contact with God, an ever-present reality not just in one's thought, but in one's heart, soul and might.

> —Rabbi Shlomo Riskin, founder of yeshiva in Efrat, Israel, and founding rabbi

of Lincoln Square Synagogue in New York City, "How to Love God with All One's Heart, Soul, Might: Parshat V' Etchanan," *Jewish Sentinel*, August 11, 1995

Not only are we God's partners—God is our partner too.

> —Rabbi Zalman Schachter-Shalomi, leader of Jewish renewal movement, *Paradigm Shift* (1993)

Hasidism denied in principle the existence of a purely secular sphere in life of no significance to the religious task of man. What appears to be profane and without relevance to religion, in fact contains a specific religious demand on man. . . . Thus religion is not a beaten track in a circumscribed sphere. New paths open up wherever one looks, and God is at the end of every path.

> —Gershom Scholem, professor of mysticism, "Martin Buber's Hasidism," *Commentary*, October 1961

When I was in prison, I was given a very simple choice: "Agree to say what we ask you to say, and you can go to Israel." . . . They felt if I'd do it, I would lose that which I had found for myself and I would again be a slave. . . . There is a God of moral values which simply was not part of their culture, a God who really exists objectively and dictates to you the way to live if you choose it. . . . I was lucky, I had a chance to compare both ways of life, life without God, a fully materialistic life, and the kind of life when you are doing what you feel will satisfy your sense of what ought to be. And that is how I came to God.

> —Natan Sharansky, former refusenik, quoted in *The God I Believe In* by Joshua O. Haberman (1994)

You must know that we've already been in this world before. Because, as far as God is concerned, it doesn't make sense for Him to send a soul into the world only once. Maybe in a previous incarnation, I was a rabbi somewhere. Because the fact is that my tongue constantly rattles around verses and sayings of our Sages of Blessed Memory, which I know without even having studied them. Can you explain the world without God? Whenever I'm in trouble, I look up at the sky and pray. Since I'm in trouble most of the time, I never stop praying. Not a regular prayer from a prayer book. A personal conversation between me and the Creator. Mostly I plead with Him, but sometimes I also complain. I often tell Him that I don't justify His acts. Not a day goes by without a sharp dialogue between us. In many cases, He responds to my prayers and gives answers to my distress. Sometimes the plot of my story is stuck like a cart in the mud, and I don't know how to get it out. I prostrate myself, hesitate, sometimes put in a prayer to Him, and suddenly a heavenly illumination, and the cart slides out of the swampy mud. The belief that man is the master of his fate is as far from me as east is from west. God is silent, speaks in acts; and we on earth have to decipher his secrets. We long for faith as much as we yearn for sex. Our great hope is free choice, divine gift . . .

> —Isaac Bashevis Singer, Nobel-Prize winning Yiddish writer, in conversation with his son, quoted in *Journey to My Father* by Israel Zamir (1994)

God is an American.

> —Howard Stern, radio talk show host, quoted in *George*, April/May 1996

If God as some now say is dead, He no doubt died of trying to find an equitable solution to the Arab-Jewish problem.

> —I. F. Stone, journalist, *New York Review of Books*, August 3, 1967

If God had wanted us to be robots, He would have provided us with all the answers beforehand and so deprived us of any opportunity for freedom of choice. But the moment God wanted us to be human beings and have the Divine Image, Tzelem Elokim, God had to leave us a gray area where we are able to shape our own world and life through our own free choice.

> —Rabbi Daniel Tropper, founder and director of the Gesher Foundation, quoted in *In the Service of God: Conversations with Teachers of Torah in Jerusalem* by Shalom Freedman (1995)

God is involved in man's destiny—good or bad. To thank Him for Jerusalem and not question Him for Treblinka is hypocrisy.

> —Elie Wiesel, author, "Prayer and Modern Man" in *Rabbi Joseph H. Lookstein Memorial Volume* (1980)

Reconstructionist Jews conceive of God as the ultimate cosmic force: that force which stands behind all creativity, all striving for justice, the will to love and the pursuit of harmony. God is not a being or a thing, but a force in motion; the very essence of the creative process that empowers our universe and ourselves.

> —Rabbi Avi Winokur, "Authentic Jews: A Reconstructionist Response," *The Jewish Week*, February 5, 1993

Bashevis Singer discovered, contrarily, that those who abandoned God went straight to the devil. The human being might be driven, as he himself had been driven by his reason, to doubt the sanctity of God's law, but it was dangerous folly to think that reason could ever provide a substitute for God's law. The more human beings believed in their own power, the greater the evil they would commit. Bashevis Singer ceased to believe that God had revealed himself to the Jews at Sinai, but he never stopped believing in the devil. The devil's Torah was to persuade man that he was God.

> —Ruth R. Wisse, professor of Yiddish and comparative literature, reflecting on the death of Isaac Bashevis Singer, *Forward*, August 8, 1991

Perhaps what God seeks is not request but relationship, and we must learn to redirect our hearts to seek out not the goods that God could offer but to seek God.

> —Rabbi David J. Wolpe, author, *Why Be Jewish?* (1995)

❖ GREAT DEPRESSION ❖

Ownership of a Model T, even if shared with the finance company, was more than entertaining: it inclined one to accept things as they were.

> —Irving Bernstein, labor historian, describing the workers mood in the 1920s just prior to the Great Depression, quoted in *The Great Depression* by Robert S. McElvaine (1984)

Naturally, no right-thinking man will blame [President] Hoover. After all he was only elected to be in the White House for four years. But that's no consolation for the rest of us who'll probably be in the poorhouse for the rest of our lives.

> —Eddie Cantor, entertainer, *Caught Short! A Saga of Wailing Wall Street* (1929)

Paul Revere's ride was tame compared to the wild gallop the market took when everything tumbled. . . . The only thing that stood up was a person's hair. The night of the worst crash I was too frightened to go to my home in Great Neck [New York]. I went instead to one of the larger hotels in New York City and asked the clerk for a room on the nineteenth floor. The clerk looked up at me and asked: "What for? Sleeping or jumping?"

> —Eddie Cantor, entertainer, *Caught Short! A Saga of Wailing Wall Street* (1929)

Nothing breeds humor better than adversity. Maybe I even overcompensate today, but there's no better feeling than to look into my wallet and see real money.

> —Bill Dana, comedian, recalling growing up during the Great Depression, quoted in *The Jewish Comedy Catalog* by Darryl Lyman (1989)

Even at the depth of the economic depression when I was a boy, one still felt idealism, Americanism. If you grew up more or less on the Left, as I did, you believed the perfectibility of your social vision, that it was a struggle but by golly we would end poverty, we would end racism, we would solve the problems, and all it took was doggedness, organization, and refusing to quit.

> —Jules Feiffer, cartoonist and writer, quoted in *On the Edge of Darkness* by Kathy Cronkite (1994)

Why shouldn't the American people take half my money from me? I took all of it from them.

> —Edward A. Filene, Boston retail executive, expressing the 1935 pro-New Deal business view, quoted in *The Great Depression* by Robert S. McElvaine (1984)

Stock prices have reached what looks like a permanently high plateau.

> —Irving Fisher, economist, observation made on October 15, 1929, two weeks before the stock market crashed, quoted in *The Great Depression* by Robert S. McElvaine (1984)

Mostly as you go through life you see giants become men but in the New Deal days men became giants.

> —Abe Fortas, Washington, D.C., attorney, commenting on the Depression, 1981, quoted in *Abe Fortas: A Biography* by Laura Kalman (1990)

By the time I graduated in 1932, . . . we were in the midst of the worst depression we've ever had. The major problems of the country were economic, and it's natural that I would have been interested.

> —Milton Friedman, economist and author, reflecting on his decision to be an economist, *Booknotes* interview with Brian Lamb, C-SPAN, November 20, 1994

I remember vividly the flash of insight that turned me into a socialist during my college years. When I was an adolescent in New York City in the 1930s, I saw around me unemployed men eager to work but finding no jobs. . . . This situation is not only tragic, it's stupid. Under such circumstances, the notion of an economy planned by governmental authority seemed commonsensical, not ideological.

> —Irving Kristol, social critic, editor and publisher, *Neoconservatism: The Autobiography of an Idea* (1995)

I specialized in foreclosures, an astute choice in 1932. It was fast, dirty work. . . . Without warning, we would swoop down on some storekeeper, cobbler, or dressmaker at closing time and declare the city was locking his doors because the poor fellow had proved himself completely unable to save his business. Wives and children were always weeping in the background—it was a sad business.

> —Irving "Swifty" Lazar, show business agent, *Swifty: My Life and Good Times*, written with Annette Tapert (1995)

It was the illness that prepared him best. Roosevelt had taken command of it and had learned how to take command of a people in panic. He taught them that strength (like "fear itself") can become a self-fulfilling prophecy. Crippled himself, he taught a nation crippled by fear how to walk.

> —Max Lerner, professor, author, and columnist, reflecting on the presidency of Franklin D. Roosevelt, "Wounded Titans" in *Notre Dame Magazine*, Autumn 1984, reprinted in *Wounded Titans: American Presidents and the Perils of Power*, edited by Robert Schmuhl (1996)

He was an amiable man with many philanthropic impulses, but he is not the dangerous enemy of anything . . . a pleasant man who, without any important qualifications for the office, would very much like to be President.

> —Walter Lippmann, journalist, describing New York Governor Franklin Roosevelt early in the election year as a potential Democratic candidate in the 1932 presidential election, quoted in *The Great Depression* by Robert S. McElvaine (1984)

. . . a series of historical accidents.

> —Paul Samuelson, economist, reflecting on the origins of the Depression, quoted in *The Great Depression* by Robert S. McElvaine (1984)

❖ GROWING UP ❖

I'm a public school brat. I went through the whole bloody system, starting in 1942, with a couple hours of kindergarten. I ate wooden blocks. The fiber was delicious. An Irish spinster lady pulled my hair in the first grade because I'd picked up this lousy habit at Hebrew school of starting sentences on the right side of the page. . . . Took me a whole season to learn where the margin was.

> —Jerome Charyn, novelist, *Metropolis: New York as Myth, Marketplace and Magical Land* (1986)

I was in my father's synagogue on Rosh Ha-Shonah and I can recall sitting next to my father listening to the rabbi's sermon—which I did not understand. I must have been eight years old or so. But at one point in the sermon, the rabbi said that at this time of year God opens the book of life, a book with everyone's name in it, and decides who will live and who will die.

I remember wondering as the rabbi made that statement how God organized this book. Alphabetically, or by family? I imagined it to be by family, and to this day I visualize it in that way. In fact, I hope someday to be God's librarian for those books.

> —Arthur Kurzweil, genealogist, author, editor, and publisher, *From Generation to Generation: How to Trace Your Jewish Genealogy and Family History* (1994)

Having polio wasn't a reason for me to play. I was learning in spite of having polio. I wanted to separate my abilities from my disabilities.

> —Itzhak Perlman, violinist, quoted in *Parade*, interview with James Brady, November 26, 1995

Life is truly a ride. We're all strapped in and no one can stop it. When the doctor slaps your behind, he's ripping your ticket and away you go. As you make each passage from youth to adulthood to maturity, sometimes you put your arms up and scream, sometimes you just hang on to that bar in front of you. But the ride is the thing. I think the most you can hope for at the end of life is that your hair's messed, you're out of breath, and you didn't throw up.

> —Jerry Seinfeld, comedian, *SeinLanguage* (1993)

You know who I had a crush on when I was in school? Bobby Fischer. He was a year younger than me, but I would have lunch with him every day and he would sit there, laughing hysterically, reading MAD magazine . . . He was always alone and very peculiar. But I found him very sexy. I was 16 and he was 15. He was the chess champion then.

> —Barbra Streisand, singer, actress, producer, and director, recalling her high school in Brooklyn and classmate Bobby Fischer, who became the world chess champion, interview with Lawrence Grobel in *Playboy*, October 1977

Pleasure was not the principle of our home. We were abstemious with laughter; I learned early that to laugh before breakfast was to cry before dinner.

> —Diana Trilling, essayist and critic, *The Beginning of the Journey: The Marriage of Diana and Lionel Trilling* (1993)

❖ GULF WAR ❖

(see also Israel)

If it hadn't been for Menachem Begin, Saddam Hussein would have had nuclear weapons in the Gulf War, and I'd be writing this column from heaven.

> —Ze'ev Chafets, Israeli journalist, "My 25th Anniversary," *Jerusalem Report,* August 13, 1992

It is misleading to define great conflicts in terms of their proximate causes.

> —Abba Eban, former foreign minister and Israeli ambassador to the United Nations, "What is the War About?" *Jerusalem Report,* February 21, 1991

Two nights before, I sat in a West Side restaurant in Manhattan and was struck by the normalcy of it all—actually by the abnormal normalcy of it all. There was not the slightest hint that the well-dressed, well-groomed, well-fed, well-mannered, over-pampered, thirtysomething crowd around me was living in a country at war. Two hours earlier, people back home had been in sealed rooms with gas masks and plastic bags over their heads, and here I was in a country at war, deciding between brochettes of lamb, filet of duck, and salmon steaks with light cream sauce and capers. . . . Our children go back to school in a country that has no direct part in this war but which is very much at war. And I go down for breakfast in a country at war in which war is hardly felt at all.

> —Hirsh Goodman, Israeli journalist, "Report From Another Front," *Jerusalem Report,* February 21, 1991

First, let me make one comment about this stress syndrome. After World War II, I separated hundreds of Marines who had hit the beaches of Iwo Jima, Tarawa and Okinawa, and had been in hand-to-hand bayonet fighting. That's stress. When they got back to be separated from the service, they had two things on their mind, and the second one was going home. Not one of them had all this "stress" business. I never heard one of the hundreds of them say: "I have arthritis, I have memory loss, I have skin rashes," and all the other stuff. I have no faith in that stress theory.

> —Dr. Edward S. Hyman of New Orleans, who testified before a Congressional committee about the reality of the "Persian Gulf Syndrome" among veterans of the Gulf War at a time when others denied its existence and attributed it to stress, quoted in *Lifestyles,* Summer 1996

We even evaluate wars according to their effect on our self-esteem: Vietnam was a downer. The Persian Gulf War, like a good self-help program, cured us of our "Vietnam syndrome" and "gave us back our pride". . . . Whether or not the war was necessary, whether or not the victory was real, we shouldn't consider it a great success because it gave us parades and a proud Fourth of July. The culture of recovery is now insidious: now the moral measure of a war is how it makes us feel about ourselves.

> —Wendy Kaminer, author, *I'm Dysfunctional, You're Dysfunctional: The Recovery Movement and Other Self-Help Fashions* (1992)

By thrilling to the devastation Hussein has wreaked on others they show the kind of polity to which they aspire.

> —Martin Peretz, editor-in-chief and publisher of *The New Republic*, commenting on the Palestinians' support for Saddam Hussein in Iraq prior to the outbreak of the Gulf War, *The New Republic*, October 8, 1990

A war that lasted three hours and culminated in three months of parades.

> —Mort Sahl, political humorist; from Sahl's one-man show, "Mort Sahl's America, Part II," in Cambridge, Mass., quoted in *The Jewish Advocate*, May 23–29, 1997

Our restraint was our contribution. And the people in Washington know just how important it was.

> —Yitzchak Shamir, Prime Minister of Israel, on Israel's decision not to fire a shot in the Gulf War, quoted in *Jerusalem Report*, March 7, 1991

No country has ever brought a country to its knees by sanctions alone.

> —Stephen J. Solarz, United States Congressman (D-N.Y.), interviewed on *Larry King Live*, CNN, September 3, 1990

People should realize that they get on each other's nerves a bit more now. Do a lot of hugging and kissing, even if it doesn't lead to a sexual encounter.

> —Dr. Ruth K. Westheimer, author and sex therapist, who was in Israel for a one-week support mission during the Iraqi Scud attacks when Israelis found shelter in sealed rooms, quoted in *Jerusalem Report*, February 21, 1991

Buchanan's vicious comment, prior to the allied attack on Iraq, [was] that "only two groups, the Israel Defense Ministry and its amen corner in the United States, are beating the drums for war." . . . Should this comment not, in fact, have rightfully been classified as unadulterated anti-Semitism? . . . Words have consequences. So when infamous words can turn—have turned—into guns, gas, and ovens, they become a clear and present danger.

> —Maurice Wohlgelernter, professor of English literature, reacting to comments by conservative columnist Patrick Buchanan regarding the American role in the conflict, letter to the editor, *Commentary*, September 1992

❖ Healing ❖

One afternoon, when Bryan was due for a treatment [for cancer], he developed a bad cold. This infection made giving him an anesthetic too risky. My father-in-law sat down with him and explained: "Bryan, I have to give you this treatment. There is no way to put it off. Because you have a cold, I can't take away your pain by giving you the anesthetic. But whenever I have to put in the medicine, I am going to hold you very tight in my arms. I love you very much and I will hold you close whenever the pain comes." And so it was. Somehow, they both got through it.

> —Rabbi Tsvi Blanchard, senior teaching fellow at the National Jewish Center for Learning and Leadership (CLAL), writer, psychologist, recalling his father-in-law, a pediatrician and anesthesiologist, "The Story of Bryan" in *Chosen Tales: Stories Told by Jewish Storytellers*, edited by Peninnah Schram (1995)

When you have a chance to heal one person, you are not healing just one person. It's not finite. At that moment you can reach beyond yourself, reaching that love of God which was before Creation. Infinite. When you walk up to a person and give them a good word, when someone is heartbroken and you give them a good word, when you utter some words—sometimes they are your words, sometimes they are Mashiach's [Messiah's] words. In one second, you can cure that person, you can give him back his self-confidence.

> —Rabbi Shlomo Carlebach, "Shlomo on Love," transcribed by Rivka Haut, *Connections*, July 1985

One of the most difficult lessons that those who love a sick person must learn is that they can't bring about survival. But they can do a great deal to affect the will to survive.

> —Paul Cowan, journalist, "In the Land of the Sick," *The Village Voice*, May 17, 1988

The inhabitants of the land of the sick speak a common language. We can discuss fears we barely admit to others. We can indulge ourselves in bleak jokes we don't dare tell people we love. We're there for one another.

> —Paul Cowan, "In the Land of the Sick," *The Village Voice*, May 17, 1988

People have called it a brave decision, a righteous decision, a courageous decision. To us, it was simply the right thing to do at the time.

> —Stephen Flatow, father of twenty-year-old Alisa Flatow (a Brandeis University junior who was killed in a 1995 terrorist attack on a bus going to the Gaza Strip), speaking of the family's decision to donate Alisa's organs, quoted in *Long Island Jewish World*, November 24–30, 1995

Healing is about what the illness teaches us.

> —Debbie Friedman, composer, liturgist, performer, and singer, quoted in *Moment*, June 1996

An illustration of the estrangement of our people. . . . Rarely does one find a prayerbook or Bible near the bedside of a Jewish patient. But ever so often the rabbi is petitioned, "Pray for me."

> —Sol Landau, author, *Length of Our Days: Focus on Judaism and the Personal Life* (1961)

The greatest therapy can be to recognize the tremendous strength of the soul that lies within us despite the weakness of our extremities.

> —Betsy Leib-Feldman, diagnosed with Lyme disease, quoted in the *Detroit Jewish News*, November 14, 1997

I have made death's acquaintance. . . . Death has given me some new information about life, all of which has made me better at it than I was before. And with some more practice, I could get better still. If I don't have a recurrence of cancer and die soon, all I've lost is a breast, and that's not so bad.

> —Betty Rollin, journalist, *Am I Getting Paid for This?* (1982)

If I have a car accident, don't take me to an herbalist.

> —Andrew Weil, M.D. and alternative medicine advocate, quoted in "Andrew

Weil, Shaman, M.D." by Larissa MacFarquhar, *The New York Times Magazine*, August 23, 1997

If the universal experience of illness were addressed by the Jewish community, I think any number of people would find their way back to a Jewish connection.

—Rabbi Simkha Weintraub, rabbinic director of the Manhattan-based National Center for Jewish Healing, quoted in *Newsday*, May 7, 1996

Patients vary enormously. Some will do almost anything rather than alter their lives to increase their chances for a cure. When I offer them a choice between an operation and a change in lifestyle, eight out of ten say, "Operate. It hurts less. That way all I have to do is get a babysitter for the week I'm in the hospital."

—Bernie S. Siegel, surgeon, teacher, author, and president of the American Holisitic Medicine Association, *Love, Medicine and Miracles* (1990)

The all too common failure to interact fruitfully with patients comes from the way a physician is taught to be a mere mechanic. In medical school we learn all about the disease, but we learn nothing about what the disease means to the person who has it.

—Bernie S. Siegel, *Love, Medicine and Miracles* (1990)

❖ HEROES ❖

Superman was the ultimate assimilationist fantasy. The mild manners and glasses that signified a class of nerdy Clark Kents was, in no way, our real truth. Underneath the schmucky facade there lived Men of Steel! Jerry Siegel's accomplishment was to chronicle the smart Jewish boy's American dream. Acknowledge that, and you can better understand the symbolic meaning of the planet Krypton. It wasn't Krypton that Superman came from; it was the planet Minsk or Lodz or Vilna or Warsaw.

—Jules Feiffer, illustrator, "The Minsk Theory of Krypton," *The New York Times Magazine*, December 29, 1996

The danger of setting aside one day a year to commemorate a national hero is that he may not be heard from on the other 364. [Martin Luther] King's most famous and stirring oration, electrifying when it was delivered in front of the Lincoln Memorial, now has become an annual pageant rather than the moral imperative it was.

—Paul Greenberg, editorial page editor of the *Pine Bluff Commercial* and syndicated columnist, "The Plague of Forgetfulness," *The Washington Times*, January 15, 1997

I have few heroes and no idols.

—Mayor Edward I. Koch of New York City, "Compassion and Common Sense in Government" in *His Eminence and Hizzoner: A Candid Exchange*, coauthored with John Cardinal O'Connor (1989)

Most of us, the majority of us, are not heroes, nor will we ever be. But there is an anonymous kind of heroism of which we are all capable, and that is made of searching out these sparks of holiness, these rarefied instants of sanctity and enshrining them in our active memories so that they can nurture our impoverished souls and bodies when we feel overwhelmed with loneliness and that insatiable hunger for meaning.

—Rabbi Marshall T. Meyer human rights activist, founder of the Seminario Rabinico Latinoamericano, and spiritual leader of B'nai Jeshurun in New York City, Yom Kippur (Kol Nidre) sermon at B'nai Jeshurun, 1989

I found that I could relate a lot easier to a guy who had no superpowers, who put on a cape and a mask, who worked hard to perfect his mind, spirit and body, and decided that one person could make a difference in the world. And if he was shot, he would bleed. It was always a risk. . . . Batman just made a lot of sense to an 8-year-old. It was my greatest wish to one day write for Batman comics.

—Michael Ulsan, executive producer of the Batman film series, quoted in *Lifestyles*, New Year 1996

I went to the folklore department and convinced them that comic books were modern American folklore. I did this by asking them if they could tell me the story of Moses. They said, "A kid is born to a family, there is trouble brewing, destruction is imminent, they put him in a little basket, they float him down the river, he is adopted by a family of a different race, and he grows up under these conditions to be a great hero." Then I said, "Now tell me the story of Superman." And they said, "Well, the planet Krypton is about to explode, the family puts their infant son into a little rocket ship, they send him off to Earth, he grows up among human beings and becomes a great hero." There was a pause and the next thing they said was, "We'll sponsor you."

—Michael Ulsan, quoted in *Lifestyles*, New Year 1996

❖ History ❖

Of course the same ignorance applies to much of American history, and nobody seems worried that, say, the survivors of Pearl Harbor are dying. But there aren't "scholars" popping up to deny that Pearl Harbor was bombed.

> —Jonathan Alter, journalist, reporting on a recent poll revealing an ignorance about the Holocaust among Americans, *Newsweek*, December 20, 1993

But perhaps the most striking and frightening aspect of the German flight from reality is the habit of treating facts as though they were mere opinions.

> —Hannah Arendt, German-born American philosopher and social critic who was forced to flee Germany in 1933 (she moved to Paris and in 1941 to the United States), "Germany 1950," *Commentary*, October 1950

Untimely death reminds us how history assesses public figures who die too soon. In the making of historical reputations, there are advantages and opportunities to brevity.

> —Daniel J. Boorstin, historian, "JFK: His Vision Then and Now," *U.S. News & World Report*, October 24, 1988, quoted in *Covering the Body: The Kennedy Assassination, the Media, and the Shaping of Collective Memory* by Barbie Zelizer (1992)

John Kennedy was president of the United States for two years and ten months. Had their terms been similarly truncated, Franklin Roosevelt would be remembered as an inspiring failure; Woodrow Wilson as an accidental interlude in decades of Republican rule and American isolationism; Abraham Lincoln as the man who allowed a peaceful separation to become a bloody dismemberment of the Union. One cannot apply customary canons of historical judgment to so abbreviated a span.

> —Richard Goodwin, an advisor and speechwriter in the Kennedy and Johnson administrations, *Remembering America* (1989)

Our Jewish experience leads us to be more aware of dangers than of opportunities. This tendency has to be transcended if we are to emerge into a future different from the recent past.

> —Abba Eban, former foreign minister and Israeli ambassador to the United Nations, "The Partner Fantasy," *Jerusalem Post*, July 14, 1989

History's logic is often perverse.

—Mark A. Heller, columnist and senior research associate at the Jaffe Center for Strategic Studies, Tel Aviv, noting the irony that the new need for collective soul searching following the murder of Rabin is an outgrowth of Rabin's greatest military victory in 1967, *Jerusalem Post*, November 17, 1995

Even those of us who have predicted events more accurately than others must be humbled by the complexities, contingencies and ambiguities of history.

—Sidney Hook, philosopher and educationist, quoted in *Midstream*, October/November 1990

In a sense we are all accomplices of history, a sentiment which if not qualified would lead to the absurd view that the oppressors and their victims are both guilty. There are degrees of guilt, degrees of ignorance, and degrees of responsibility, which failure to recognize makes moral judgment meaningless.

—Sidney Hook, quoted in *Midstream*, October/November 1990

My interest has been in history, and historians have on the whole been less shocked by foolishness, cruelty, lack of compassion, missed opportunities, and various tragedies than sociologists and students of political science, simply because historians have been preoccupied with what actually happened rather than what should have happened.

—Walter Z. Laqueur, "How Has the United States Met Its Major Challenges Since 1945?" a symposium, *Commentary*, November 1985

In this relativistic time we live in, Holocaust denial is turned into an opinion, and everyone's opinion is of equal validity. That's like asking whether slavery happened.

—Deborah E. Lipstadt, author of *Denying the Holocaust* and professor of Jewish studies, quoted in *Newsweek*, December 20, 1993

On this we disagree, at the root of the matter: Museum or drama? Ritual or creativity? Total orientation toward the past—"What was is what will be"—in which every question has an answer from the holy books, every new enemy is simply the reincarnation of an ancient one, every new situation is simply the reincarnation of an old and familiar one—or not? Can it be that history is not a spinning wheel but a twisting line, which, even if it has loops and curves, is essentially linear, not circular?

—Amos Oz, Israeli novelist and essayist, *In the Land of Israel* (1983)

❖ HIV/AIDS ❖

(see also Healing, Illness)

We don't have education on AIDS in the same way we don't have any about teen pregnancy because, thank God, we don't have those problems.

> —Isaac Abraham, member of Brooklyn's Satmar Hasidic community, quoted in "Dying of Shame" by Vince Beiser, *Jerusalem Report,* February 23, 1995

There are a small but growing number of people [in the Orthodox world] who take the position that HIV/AIDS exists and must be dealt with. It's like the way they've dealt with issues like alcoholism or domestic violence over the last 20 years. The community originally said, "We don't have it." Then it was, "We have it but we can take care of it." Finally it was, "We need some external resources to help us deal with this." It hasn't happened yet with AIDS, but I think that issue is on the same trajectory.

> —Pinhas Berger, director of program development at New York's Jewish Board of Family and Children's Services, quoted in "Dying of Shame" by Vince Beiser, *Jerusalem Report,* February 23, 1995

I get angry—really angry—when people talk about why they are still around. About their good attitudes. About eating carrots, being vegetarians. About "I love life," "I found my spirit," and my inner soul. It's an insult to all those beautiful people who died.

> —Ivan Bernstein, HIV positive, quoted in *The Gravest Show on Earth: America in the Age of AIDS* by Elinor Burkett (1995)

What your life presents is a dilemma also for the rest of us. It seems to me we have a responsibility to create a world in which it's possible for human beings to live as they are, and be present fully as who they are. And somewhere there is a responsibility on us to make it possible for you to be able to live among us as who you are in your human situation, and feel accepted and loved by us.

> —Rabbi Tsvi Blanchard, philosopher and psychologist, in conversation with a guest who was contemplating whether to reveal to his family and friends that he is HIV-positive, "Moral Dilemmas: What Would You Do?" *The Oprah Winfrey Show,* January 14, 1994

Being ill like this combines shock—this time I will die—with a pain and agony that are unfamiliar, that wrench me out of myself. It is like visiting one's own funeral, like visiting loss in its purest and most monumental form, this wild darkness, which is not only unknown but which one cannot enter as oneself.

> —Harold Brodkey, novelist who died of AIDS in January 1996, "This Wild Darkness," *The New Yorker*, February 5, 1996

In Orthodox communities, it's still seen as not our problem, so there hasn't been a push to get it out in the open. But Orthodox Jews are affected, of course.

> —Joan Entel, an Orthodox woman who is senior social worker for HIV/AIDS cases at the Long Island Jewish Medical Center, quoted in "Dying of Shame" by Vince Beiser, *Jerusalem Report*, February 23, 1995

I consider myself a spiritual person and I have gotten through mainly because of my deep-seated belief in God and belief that there must be a reason . . . Part of my upbringing, being raised Jewish, is that no matter what you've done, you're still a child of God; judgments are not called for.

> —Mary Fisher, former aide to President Gerald R. Ford, daughter of prominent GOP fundraiser Max Fisher, mother of two sons, and AIDS activist who is HIV positive, quoted in the *Jewish Bulletin of Northern California*, August 2, 1996

When people I knew started dying of AIDS, I couldn't bring myself to rip up their Rolodex cards, so I started saving them, and I ended up with hundreds of cards with a big rubber band around them. It was very, very disturbing.

> —David Geffen, entertainment executive and high-profile supporter of AIDS-related causes, quoted in "King David," *US*, April 1997

People can't turn the page on me.

> —Alison Gertz, white teenager from an affluent family who contracted the AIDS virus from a single heterosexual encounter in 1982, statement in 1988, quoted in *Last Night in Paradise* by Katie Roiphe (1997)

I'm not going to be alive much longer, so I'm planning my demise and memorial service. I've always admired the Jewish religion and I want to acknowledge that I'm Jewish. The only way now is through a memorial service which ties me to my background and who I am.

> —Sheldon Golub, a fifty-two-year-old with AIDS, recalling his meeting with rabbis who were reaching out to patients with AIDS, quoted in "AIDS— How Can Judaism Help?" *Hadassah*, August/September 1992

In your letter you ask me to reconsider my "decision with regard to the UJA-Federation Campaign." In furtherance of this request you state that you are "assisting one out of every four AIDS patients in our community." If for no other reason—and there are others—I would not contribute a dollar to UJA. These AIDS victims, almost without exception, have incurred their disease as an outcome of their unnatural, immoral, dangerous sexual behavior. What is more, many of them are gays—radical homosexuals—who advocate teaching schoolchildren that homosexuality is normal.

> —Howard L. Hurwitz, director of the Family Defense Council, from his letter to Stephen D. Solender, Executive Vice President of the UJA-Federation of New York, *The Jewish Press*, July 4, 1997

My friends, surely as God is in heaven so is God with patients on ward 5B [in San Francisco General Hospital]. As surely as God's light shines above this ark, it shines above their beds. But God has no other hands but ours. If the sick are to be healed, it is our hands, not God's, that will heal them. If the lonely and frightened are to be comforted, it is our embrace, not God's, that will comfort them.

> —Rabbi Robert Kirschner of Temple Emanu-El in San Francisco, from a 1985 sermon that led to the establishment of an AIDS relief fund in the congregation, quoted in *Tough Choices: Jewish Perspectives on Social Justice* by David Saperstein and Albert Vorspan (1992)

Often, circumstances demand ingenuity and innovation. Let's take the AIDS situation as an illustration. We're urging the use of condoms as one aspect of "safer sex," and we're urging the use of clean needles . . . to help control the spread of this virulent and devastating disease. We can't tell people: "Just Say No." New York City is not fantasyland.

> —Mayor Edward I. Koch of New York City, "Compassion and Common Sense in Government" in *His Eminence and Hizzoner*, coauthored with John Cardinal O'Connor (1989)

If this article doesn't scare the shit out of you we're in real trouble. If this article doesn't rouse you to anger, fury, rage and action, gay men may have no future on this earth. Our continued existence depends on just how angry you get.

> —Larry Kramer, one of the founders of the Gay Men's Health Crisis, attempting to mobilize New York City's gay community, referring to an article in *New York Native*, quoted in *The Gravest Show on Earth: America in the Age of AIDS* by Elinor Burkett (1995)

There was a vacuum—someone had to fill it. I hate injustice. . . . I saw the potential for social disaster associated with a condition that was of unknown origin, progressive, irreversible, transmissible, and that occurred in a minority group that was stigmatized.

—Mathilde Krim, research biologist and virologist who founded the AIDS Medical Foundation in 1982, quoted in *New York*, April 25, 1988

In this situation, panic is never justified, but fear is justified, and sometimes I share it.

—Mathilde Krim, quoted in *New York*, April 25, 1988

When history measures to what extent we have the right to call ourselves civilized, it will be on the basis of how we handle this situation.

—Mathilde Krim, quoted in *New York*, April 25, 1988

Someone always survives the unsurvivable. Someone must share the experience. . . . I was a woman infected with HIV when they thought women didn't get AIDS. I am a Jewish woman who discovered her faith by finding her God. I am a human being who is experiencing a miracle every day I am alive.

—Sherri Lewis, singer and AIDS activist who is HIV-positive, "Living with HIV," *The Jewish Advocate*, July 26–August 1, 1996

By the time you're finished with the judgments, you're still standing there with the diapers in one hand and the rubber gloves in the other. AIDS is the only disease where people ask you how he got it. Because of its implications, AIDS can follow a woman even after her husband has died.

—Ruth Rothbart Mayer, social worker who runs support groups in New York for women whose husbands died of AIDS or are HIV-positive (her husband died of AIDS), quoted in "AIDS—How Can Judaism Help?" *Hadassah*, August/September 1992

Every age has its defining illness, the one that really makes its way into people's nightmares, the one that seems to tell us, with an eloquence beyond words, the story of our particular social decline. . . . In this case the AIDS virus appeared just in time to offer a vivid critique of the hedonism that we were already in the process of becoming disenchanted with.

Katie Roiphe, author, *Last Night in Paradise* (1997)

By the time these kids began thinking about sex, the fatal virus had already become part of the buying and selling of colorful sweaters and scarves, part of business as usual. The fact that some people die from sex is a thought that teenagers are used to. Ask anyone under twenty when she first learned about AIDS, and she will say she always knew about it.

—Katie Roiphe, commenting on the 1990s generation of high school kids and

Benetton's advertising promoting AIDS awareness, *Last Night in Paradise* (1997)

Let me tell you something. If you think there were no white, upper-class Jewish businessmen who pulled up in their Lincoln Continentals and exchanged needles, you're wrong.

—Mary Ann Siegel, administrative assistant of the Michigan Jewish AIDS Coalition, recalling her previous work with a needle-exchange program in Detroit's inner city, "It Takes a Village" by James D. Besser, *The Jewish Journal of Greater Los Angeles*, October 18–24, 1996

It's easy for us to look at someone sick and feel compassionate. It's harder to anticipate down the road when the truck coming to plow down your children is invisible.

—Robert Zielony, director of the HIV/AIDS Prevention and Education Program for the Jewish Board of Family and Children's Services, quoted in "One Man's Mission" by Hillary Kessler, *Jerusalem Report*, February 23, 1995

I wouldn't be doing a good job of pikuach nefesh (saving lives) if I didn't speak out on what I perceive to be happening in our community. I don't like it when people die when they don't have to.

—Robert Zielony, quoted in "One Man's Mission" by Hillary Kessler, *Jerusalem Report*, February 23, 1995

❖ HOLIDAYS ❖

(see also Jewish Observance)

Precisely because of our human value and worth, because what we do is of ultimate value, we have to be deprived of normal raiment, normal nourishment, normal pride for a day—and be reminded that we are not granted an infinite amount of time in which to grab hold of what really matters in life.

—Arnold Eisen, professor of Jewish thought, discussing Yom Kippur, "Remember Us for Life," *Tikkun*, September/October 1990

It's time to blow our own horn.

—Advertisement appearing in California newspapers placed by Chabad-Lubavitch, encouraging Jews to prepare for the high holidays, 1996

We want festivals to bring the family together, which seems difficult enough in America today. But if only the family comes together, without including the poor, the stranger, the widow and the depressed, we do not yet have the right kind of happiness.

> —Rabbi Eliezer Finkelman of Congregation Beth Israel in Berkeley, Calif., "Torah Thoughts," *Jewish Bulletin of Northern California*, May 24, 1996

Purim is the balance to Passover; it is the humor that admits that the Shabbat is still a dream. To act as if Shabbat and the final redemption are fact would be insane; but not to affirm the totality of hope would be a sellout. Purim offers an alternative: humorous affirmation. Thus Purim's laughter preserves integrity and sanity together. This is Purim's remarkable role in Jewish history.

> —Rabbi Irving Greenberg, author, scholar, and founder of the National Jewish Center for Learning and Leadership (CLAL), *The Jewish Way: Living the Holidays* (1988)

Thanksgiving seems made to order for Jews. . . . It is celebrated by eating, and Jews eat rather than drink. . . . And what comes out of the mouth on Thanksgiving is equally Jewish — both the message and the tone. Thanksgiving is the great point of intersection between Judaism and the sacral tradition of America.

> —Milton Himmelfarb, critic, "The Twelve Weeks of Christmas," 1963, quoted in "We Gather Together" by Carol Kur, *Moment*, November 1977

On Yom Kippur, as on no other day, we can live wholly in only one world, the better to create for ourselves the emotional cerebral tallis [prayer shawl] in time.

> —Frances Degan Horowitz, president of the Graduate School and University Center of the City University of New York, "On Yom Kippur," *Judaism*, Summer 1995

Tonight many a Jew marks a touchy reunion with a good friend who he has neglected for a long time — namely religion! We really have no better friend, and he is waiting for us although we seem to have forgotten him for quite a while. It is like a homecoming, a reunion after a year of separation.

> —Rabbi Ezekiel Landau, rabbi of the Hebrew Immigrant Aid Society (HIAS) and spiritual leader of the American Congregation of Jews from Austria, delivering his Kol Nidre sermon in 1958, quoted in *Bridging Two Worlds* by Sol Landau (1968)

To walk along Park Avenue on Yom Kippur in dressy clothes and the requisite sneakers . . . induced in me a state of morbid self-consciousness: everyone could tell I was Jewish, as clearly as if I was wearing a yellow star.

—Daphne Merkin, "Dreaming of Hitler," *Esquire*, August 1989

Rosh Hashanah initiates "aseret yemei teshuvah," commonly translated as "the Ten Days of Repentance." I would like to suggest that for these days to have new dimensions of meaning we translate aseret yemei teshuvah as the ten days of searching and twisting and turning, of wrestling with our souls and trying desperately to find new meaning to our existence.

—Rabbi Marshall T. Meyer, human rights activist, founder of the Seminario Rabinico Latinoamericano, and spiritual leader of B'nai Jeshurun in New York City, Interview on ABC radio, September 28, 1986

Puritanical America needed a good moral excuse to enjoy itself. In order to enjoy a good Falstaffian feast once a year, there had to be the moral and religious excuse of Thanksgiving.

—Zero Mostel, actor, delivering the Theodore Spencer Memorial Lecture at Harvard University, May 20, 1962, quoted in *Zero Mostel: A Biography* by Jared Brown (1962)

One can say that the festivals act as lodging for travelers making their way through the year. These festival inns are special accommodations not sorely for rest or retreat from the world, but also places to halt and take our bearings to make sure we are traveling and not just going around in circles.

—Michael Strassfeld, director of programming at Ansche Chesed in New York City and author (who later became a rabbi), *The Jewish Holidays: A Guide and Commentary* (1985)

You might call this day the Pearl Harbor of Jewry.

—Herman Wouk, author, reflecting on Tisha B'Av (the ninth day of the hebrew month of av, an observance and day of fasting marking the destructions of both temples in Jerusalem, as well as other mournful periods in Jewish history), *This Is My God* (1959)

The two festivals [Chanukah and Christmas] have one real point of contact. Had Antiochus succeeded in obliterating Jewry a century and a half before the birth of Jesus, there would have been no Christmas.

—Herman Wouk, author, *This Is My God* (1959)

The Hagadah [the book that contains the story of the exodus from Egypt for use at the Passover seder] is the model for our rescue. It is a history book that links the past to the present and a primer for teaching the free about the absence of freedom. Important as it may have been in sustaining Jewish souls during times of persecutions, people facing pogroms or Nazis had no special need for its message. We do. Today, more than any other time in history, there are masses of Jews who, to paraphrase the Haggadah, don't even know how to ask questions.

> —Carmela Efros Kalmanson, president of Hadassah, "The Haggadah Idea," *Hadassah,* April 1990

Passover is a table set for meaningful tears.

> —Rabbi Ben Kamin, senior rabbi at the Temple-Tifereth Israel in Cleveland, *Thinking Passover* (1997)

Passover sighs with relief when the telling of the Story liberates you to tell your story.

> —Rabbi Ben Kamin, *Thinking Passover* (1997)

My parents put potato peels on the seder plate. "These," my father would explain at the beginning of the seder, "remind us of Auschwitz, where any inmate who was able to get hold of potato peels was fortunate. In the camps, potato peels were food."

> —Menachem Z. Rosensaft, founding chairman of the International Network of Children of Jewish Holocaust Survivors and a member of the U.S. Holocaust Memorial Council, quoted in *Jewish Telegraphic Agency,* April 14, 1995

There is going to be a seder tonight for the Jewish boys in Guadalcanal. A few months ago, it didn't look that way . . . I couldn't have imagined that in a few months I'd be standing here, before a microphone, talking about Passover, or that Guadalcanal would be completely in American hands with Jewish men among the troops there holding seder out in the open air to celebrate both our victory on Guadalcanal and the victory of the children of Israel who fought for freedom against Pharaoh.

> —Sgt. Barney Ross, prizefighter, who was injured during the 1943 assault on Guadalcanal, speaking on U.S. Army radio, 1944, quoted in *Jewish Telegraphic Agency,* April 14, 1997

❖ HOLINESS ❖

(see also Spirituality)

Judaism doesn't see holiness as a holier-than-thou concept. A holy person is not someone distinguished with a halo and wings, rather merely an average person reaching exceptional heights, dedicating himself to a lifetime of effort and growth.

> —Rabbi Eli Glaser, associate director for the Washington, D.C., office of Aish HaTorah, quoted in *Washington Jewish Week*, May 8, 1997

As a Reform Jew, I look at kedushah [holiness] as a process. We are never there, but always reaching.

> —Rabbi Michael L. Kramer, rabbi in Maryland, "A Personal Statement" in *Rabbis and Vegetarianism: An Evolving Tradition* (1995)

I believe that God is the source of holiness and sanctity in the Universe. I believe that men and women and children can draw constantly closer to that Source when we exercise our capacities to say no to, and to translate our no, to destruction, hatred, egotism, prejudice, untrammeled possessiveness, uncontrolled megalomania. The sacred is that dimension of being which propels us into the search for love, awe, and reverence. . . . which allows us to create for the morrow a world that is better than yesterday. . . . the power of decision to ensure, as much as we are able, that there will be a morrow.

> —Rabbi Marshall T. Meyer, human rights activist, founder of the Seminario Rabinico Latinoamericano and spiritual leader of B'nai Jeshurun in New York City, Sermon, Yom Kippur (Kol Nidre) at B'nai Jeshurun, 1989

❖ HOLOCAUST ❖

(see also Eichmann Trial)

We wish to inform you of the greatest murder of all time—the murder of more than three million Polish Jews. Brothers! The remnant of Polish Jewry live in the conviction that your have offered us no assistance during the most terrible days of our history. Heed us! This is our last appeal to you!

> —The Warsaw Ghetto National Council telegram sent to the leaders of Amer-

ican Jewry, January 1943, quoted in *Pillar of Fire: The Rebirth of Israel—A Visual History* by Yigal Lossin, translated by Tsvi Ofer, edited by Carol Halberstadt (1983)

Cain slew Abel in anger, but he never tortured him. Cain had a personal attachment to his brother, but we are strangers to our murderers.

—Simon Wiesenthal, Vienna-born Holocaust survivor and Nazi hunter, *The Sunflower* (voice of the character Josek) (1976)

The Holocaust is a central event in many people's lives but it has also become a metaphor for our century. There cannot be an end to speaking and writing about it.

—Aharon Appelfeld, Israeli novelist, quoted in *The New York Times*, November 15, 1986

In the aftermath of Nazi Germany we must once and for all understand that culture and crematoria are not mutually exclusive. Scientific progress does not ensure moral protection, nor can secular humanism produce saints. People will always find reasons to justify any kind of behavior.

—Rabbi Benjamin Blech, congregational rabbi and assistant professor of Talmud, *Understanding Judaism: The Basics of Deed and Creed* (1991)

Our age abhors the unexplained event. Better a dozen theories than one obstreperous fact. We are in the way of killing true knowledge by premature understanding.

—Solomon F. Bloom, "Dictator of the Lodz Ghetto," *Commentary*, February 1949

Worst of all is our eternal nauseating gratitude to those goyim who behave with the most elemental kind of decency expected by one human being of another. It is an obscenity that we should think it natural and proper to give medals to goyim who saved the lives of Jews in World War II. Has there ever been any other nation on earth which found it natural and right to give awards to people of other nations for treating them like human beings?

—Aviva Cantor, founding member of the Jewish Liberation Project, editor of the *Jewish Liberation Journal* in which this article appeared in November 1970, "The Oppression of America's Jews" in *Jewish Radicalism: A Selected Anthology*, edited by Jack Nusan Porter and Peter Dreier (1973)

What can be said of a world in which a multitude of men and women seem to believe in all sincerity that Jews are not wronged if only physical violence is restrained, no matter how great the contumely and insult and humiliation and dishonor!

> —Benjamin Cardozo, United States Supreme Court justice, from a letter to Rabbi Jacob Weinstein, March 28, 1933, quoted in *The World of Benjamin Cardozo* by Richard Polenberg (1997)

Arafat is not Hitler. . . . The knowledge of the Holocaust should enhance our power of discernment.

> —Emil L. Fackenheim, philosopher, reflecting on those who perceive Arafat as Hitler, quoted in an interview with Micha Odenheimer, *Washington Jewish Week,* 1989

One thing my father told me before we separated, "Don't forget where you come from. When all this is over, go home." Those few words are the only reason I survived.

> —Harry Joseph Feldinger, survivor of Auschwitz, quoted in *When They Came to Take My Father: Voices of the Holocaust,* photographs by Mark Seliger, edited by Leora Kahn and Rachel Hager (1996)

No one knows for certain how many non-Jews risked their lives to save Jews during the Holocaust. . . . Rescue activity demanded utmost secrecy. Lives depended on it. Many rescuers were discovered and killed. Some sheltered a Jew for a night; others hid several people for years. Some made single, one-time gestures; still others were part of an anonymous network that searched for hiding places, papers, good coupons, and money for Jews. The parting words between some Jews and the Christians who saved them were "Promise that you will never tell anyone my name. Don't ever write to me. Good luck."

> —Eva Fogelman, psychotherapist, lecturer and author who is founding director of the Jewish Foundation for Christian Rescuers, *Conscience and Courage: Rescuers of Jews During the Holocaust* (1994)

We have to emphasize the volunteerism of the killers. They essentially chose to kill Jews.

> —Daniel Jonah Goldhagen, political scientist and author, quoted in an interview with Maurice Wohlgelernter, *Society,* January–February 1997

One of the reasons that we have so many photographs of the Holocaust is because the Germans took photos. And they took them, obviously, not to indict themselves but rather, to memorialize their deeds.

> —Daniel Jonah Goldhagen, interview with Maurice Wohlgelerter, *Society,* January–February 1997

It's frightening to think about the relevance of our museum. I think we would have liked it to be less relevant.

> —Elaine Heumann Gurion, Deputy Director of the U.S. Holocaust Memorial Museum, quoted in book review of *Preserving Memory: The Struggle to Create America's Holocaust Museum* by Edward T. Lilienthal, *The Jerusalem Post*, October 20, 1995

If I should go to Poland or Germany, every stone would remind me of contempt, hatred, murder, of children killed, of mothers burned alive, of human beings asphyxiated.

> —Rabbi Abraham Joshua Heschel, author, activist, and theologian (who never returned to Poland, Germany, or Austria after he left Warsaw in 1939), *Israel: An Echo of Eternity* (1969)

The Mengele twins became the most exclusive club in the world.

> —Irene Hizme, Holocaust survivor who was part of Mengele's experiments in Auschwitz, quoted in *When They Came to Take My Father: Voices of the Holocaust*, photographs by Mark Seliger, edited by Leora Kahn and Rachel Hager (1996)

I have to hope that no one will ever be able to look at the Holocaust with complete objectivity, but it will take several generations before audiences can confront re-creations of it as they confront a film on any profoundly grave subject.

> —Stanley F. Kaufmann, film critic, "On Films: A Predicament," *The New Republic*, December 11, 1995

I die peacefully, but not complacently; persecuted, but not enslaved; embittered, but not cynical; a believer, but not a supplicant; a lover of God, but no blind amen-sayer.

> —Tsvi Kolitz, journalist, filmmaker, playwright, and professor, "Yossel Rakover Speaks to God" (a story set in 1943 in the Warsaw ghetto, first published in Yiddish in "El Diario Israelita" in Buenos Aires, September 25, 1946), reprinted in *Yossel Rakover Speaks to God: Holocaust Challenges to Religious Faith* (1946)

I did not come to this country to save myself or to seek positions of personal power. Rather, I am here so that, with your help, we can save our brothers and the centers of Torah learning all over Europe! On the other side of the ocean our brothers are waiting for our help; only you, the Jews of America, are able to help them. Do it now! Save them!

> —Rabbi Aharon Kotler, rabbinical scholar and founder of the Beth Midrash

Gevoha in Lakewood, N.J., 1940s quoted in Be'er Hagolah Institute publication, c. 1990

The image of The Nazi is great and grotesque in our minds, but the Nazis in person turn out to be quite small and often ludicrous. . . . In the newsreel coverage of the trial we saw a harassed, uncomprehending crew of unshaven individuals — without dignity, fanaticism, obsessive hate, or the statue that large-scale wickedness often bestows, In comparison with John Dillinger, Hermann Goering looked like an indigent pickpocket.

— Irving Kristol, social critic, discussing the Nuremberg trials, "What the Nazi Autopsies Show," *Commentary,* September 1948

You cannot divert a tiger from devouring his prey by adopting resolutions or sending cables. You have to take your gun and shoot him.

— Richard Lichtheim, a representative of the World Jewish Congress in Switzerland and a hero for informing the world of the genocide, 1942 statement quoted in "America, FDR, and the Holocaust" by William J. vanden Heuvel, *Society,* September/October 1997

I believe we must eliminate the words Holocaust revisionism from our vocabulary, and call this movement Holocaust denial, because denial is what it is. Revisionism is the denier's own language.

— Deborah E. Lipstadt, author and professor of modern Jewish studies, addressing the Hadassah National Convention, July 1992

In these apartments, unpainted for more than 50 years, one may still see the outlines of mezuzahs on doorposts. One's hand can glide the same wrought iron bannisters. Look at the blue and white tile on the stairway landings, once so crowded, and this is what ghetto Jews saw in 1941. Once upon a time a Jew walked on this marble stoop and was home.

— Jonathan Mark, journalist, "Poland Without Tears," *The Jewish Week,* May 13-19, 1994

If you had been in the American government 50 years ago, we would not be sitting around this table today.

— Benjamin Meed, president of the American Gathering of Holocaust Survivors, addressing Stuart Eizenstat, U.S. diplomat, at a meeting about the investigation of Nazi gold, quoted in *Jewish Telegraphic Agency,* June 1997

. . . no one, myself included, dreamed then that Hitler's vow to destroy the Jews would ever be literally carried out. In a way, I suppose, it should be chalked up to the credit of normal decent men and women that we couldn't believe that such a monstrously evil thing would ever actually happen—or that the world would permit it to happen. It was simply that we couldn't conceive of what was then still inconceivable. Today, however, no horror is inconceivable to me anymore.

> —Golda Meir, prime minister of Israel, recalling Germany in the 1930s, *My Life* (1975)

My fellow survivors, touched by the madness of our nightmare, we have tried to live normal lives. Scarred by the acid of barbarous hatred, we have tried to give love to our children. Forgotten by a silent world, we have tried to avoid cynicism and despair. Despite all we have known, we affirm life—despite the most ferocious of efforts to steal it from us. While we shall never forget, we will not live with hate.

> —Ernest W. Michel, executive vice-president of New York UJA–Federation and chairman of the World Gathering of Holocaust Survivors, speaking at the World Gathering at Yad Vashem in Jerusalem, June 13, 1981, quoted in *Promises to Keep* (1993)

The Treasury's responsibility . . . gives us a front-row view of those eighteen terrible months of inefficiency, buck-passing, bureaucratic delay and sometimes what appeared to be calculated obstructionism. With sinking hearts we battled for action against the eternal stretching out of memoranda, committees, conferences—all devouring precious time while innocent people perished miserably in concentration camps and gas chambers.

> —Henry Morgenthau, Jr., secretary of the treasury in the FDR administration, quoted in *Justice in Jerusalem* by Gideon Hausner (1966)

The world that once was no longer is. Gone are the holy communities, the sainted Jews, the children and their mothers, the rabbis, the libraries of thousands of sacred books adding up to hundreds of millions, the holy Torah schools and Friday night candlesticks and Saturday night spice boxes. A world that no historian, sociologist, anthropologist, writer will ever be able to reconstruct—not even a hair of it, a shadow.

> —Rabbi Ephraim Oshry, survivor of the Kovno ghetto who was a rabbinical authority there and rabbi of Beth Hamedrash Hagadol in New York City, *Response from the Holocaust* (1983)

While you were going to theaters, we were already here.

> —Judy Perlaki, Holocaust survivor who was brought to Auschwitz from a town in Hungary, recalling remarks to newcomers to Auschwitz from some of the Polish and Czech Jews already there, quoted in "The Last Days of Auschwitz," *Newsweek*, January 16, 1995

What it did affect in me was not Jew versus the world. It was people are not basically good—that was, to me, the important effect that the Holocaust had on me. I don't believe it was an aberration. And Rwanda and Cambodia and Armenia and communism and Nazism and Bosnia right now confirm murder and torture are in the human soul.

> —Dennis Prager, author and talk show host, interview with Brian Lamb on *Booknotes*, C-SPAN, February 4, 1996

Every year now, another novelist, historian, photographer finds a new corner to turn, still another story, still another voice. Our revenge is our testimony. Our testimony is among our most remarkable creations. It enables us to hold together, to go on.

> —Anne Roiphe, author "The Legacy of Memory" in *When They Came to Take My Father: Voices of the Holocaust*, photographs by Mark Seliger, edited by Leora Kahn and Rachel Hager (1996)

It would have been our pleasure to be bombed.

> —Celia Rosenberg, Holocaust survivor brought to Auschwitz from Hungary, quoted in "The Last Days of Auschwitz," *Newsweek*, January 16, 1995

We have a situation in Europe today which gives us very little reason for optimism. We have a continent on which five-sixths of the Jewish population has been exterminated. We have a continent on which there are some 1,250,000 Jews left—Jews who are living under the most distressing conditions. It may be said, using a Biblical phrase, that there is not a Jewish home in Europe today in which there is not one dead. And there are many Jewish homes in which there is not one living.

> —Joseph J. Schwartz, Chairman of the European Executive Council of the American Jewish Joint Distribution Committee, briefing the executive committee in New York on the catastrophe in Europe and the need for resources, June 20, 1945, quoted in *The Secret Alliance* by Tad Szulc (1991)

A Jew in Warsaw today is a curiosity. People look around in surprise when they see a Jew walking on the streets. The attitude of the general population seems to be "What, is he still alive?"

> —Joseph J. Schwartz, from a 1946 report, quoted in *The Secret Alliance* by Tad Szulc, (1991)

Indeed it seems plausible to me to divide my life into two parts, before I saw those photographs (I was twelve) and after.

> —Susan Sontag, critic, describing viewing photographs of the concentration camps, *On Photography* (1970)

Official Washington's capacity for finding excuses for inaction is endless, and many people in the State and War departments who play a part in this matter can spend months sucking their legalistic thumbs over any problem. So many things that might have been done were attempted too late.

>—I. F. Stone, journalist, from his weekly column in *The Nation*, June 10, 1944

The liberated are treated far worse than the defeated.

>—I. F. Stone, journalist, from his weekly column in *The Nation*, October 6, 1945, regarding the poor treatment of displaced persons in Europe

The danger is that if nothing but the Holocaust exists in Jewish life, we'll become a morbid people, a sick people. We shouldn't do that. There is a statute of limitations on morbidity. . . . But without it, Jewish life would also be false. How can one lead a Jewish life today and not learn something about it?

>—Elie Wiesel, author and Nobel laureate, quoted in *The New York Times*, March 5, 1997

I believe the Holocaust is a uniquely Jewish event. Never before has there been such a tragedy, and never again will there be such a thing. I don't think it could happen again because it is such a unique event.

>—Elie Wiesel, speaking at a Jewish Week luncheon, November 9, 1995

One thing I had learned: no deed was so awful that its wickedness could not be surpassed.

>—Simon Wiesenthal, Vienna-born Holocaust survivor and Nazi hunter, *The Sunflower* (1977)

Are you absolutely satisfied that "deportation" means "extermination"?

>—Rabbi Stephen S. Wise, activist and leader, speaking in 1942 to Professor Paul Guggenheim of the Institute des Hautes Etudes, legal advisor to the World Jewish Congress, quoted in *Israel in the Mind of America* by Peter Grose (1983)

The noble efforts of the government of the United States to welcome refugees to this country, within the limits of the quota laws, are deeply appreciated by American Jews. But there remains still the grave problem of the millions of Jews who must remain in Eastern and Central Europe and undergo an oppression whose barbarism has no parallel in the history of living men. It is no exaggeration to say that if this oppression is permitted to continue, Jewish life in Europe will be destroyed.

>—Rabbi Stephen S. Wise, letter to Frank Murphy (mayor of Detroit), April

12, 1938, quoted in *Radio Priest: Charles Coughlin, the Father of Hate Radio* by Donald Warren (1996)

Ours is the last generation that will ever meet a Holocaust survivor.

—Rabbi David Woznica, director of the 92nd Street Y's Bronfman Center for Jewish Life in New York City, quoted in *92nd St. Y Review*, Spring 1996

There is no salvation to be extracted from the Holocaust, no faltering Judaism can be revived by it, no new reason for the continuation of the Jewish people can be found in it. If there is hope after the Holocaust, it is because to those who believe, the voices of the Prophets speak more loudly than did Hitler.

—Michael Wyschograd, professor of philosophy, "Faith and the Holocaust: A Review Essay of Emil Fackenheim's God's Presence in History," *Judaism*, Summer 1971

To argue that one is asserting only the uniqueness of the Holocaust and not that it is a greater or more tragic crime than all others, simply won't do because the uniqueness which is asserted . . . turns out to be morally decisive and just an attribution of abstract uniqueness. It is necessary to recognize that, from any universally humanistic framework, the destruction of European Jewry is one notable chapter in the long record of man's inhumanity against man, a record which compels the Holocaust to resign itself to being, at most, a first among equals.

—Michael Wyschograd, "Faith and the Holocaust: A Review Essay of Emil Fackenheim's God's Presence in History," *Judaism*, Summer 1971

HOLOCAUST SURVIVORS

My father was not born a survivor. He had a life before the Holocaust and he certainly had a life after.

—Rositta Erlich Kenigsberg, executive vice-president of the Holocaust Documentation and Education Center of the North Miami campus of Florida International University, quoted in "A Child's Act of Faith" by Helen Mintz Belitsky, *Lifestyles*, Summer 1996

I think the notion of "survivor guilt" is a misconception. I believe reports of sorrow, of mourning, of grief, of yearning, of wishing that they had not survived. Because to tell you the truth, surviving is a hell of a lot harder than dying. When you're dead, you're dead. You don't sit around with memories of other people's deaths.

—Magda Denes, psychoanalyst and author, interview in conjunction with publication of *Castles Burning: A Child's Life in War* (1997)

My cousins were American-born Jews: very Middle-Western, kind generous people, who also shrank from me a little. You understand, the concentration camp experience is nothing that endears you to people.

> —"Elena," recalling meeting her relatives in 1945, quoted in *New Lives* by Dorothy Rabinowitz (1976)

I never expected to survive. I just lucked out. Equally committed people with equally good cover finished in the Danube. It was a daily lottery with death. And I happened to win.

> —Congressman Tom Lantos (D-Calif.), Holocaust survivor who was rescued by Raoul Wallenberg, quoted in *When They Came to Take My Father: Voices of the Holocaust*, photographs by Mark Seliger, edited by Leora Kahn and Rachel Hager (1996)

Survivors can sit down and talk about carrots or flowers and somehow, the conversation ends with the Holocaust.

> —Benjamin Meed, survivor of the Warsaw Ghetto and president of the American Gathering of Holocaust Survivors, quoted in *When They Came to Take My Father: Voices of the Holocaust*, photographs by Mark Seliger, edited by Leora Kahn and Rachel Hager (1996)

It was years before we could ask a policeman for directions. Why? Because he was wearing a uniform. For a long time it took great courage just to answer a knock on the door of our apartment.

> —Benjamin Meed, from remarks delivered at the U.S. Capitol, April 16, 1996, quoted in the *New York Post*, April 18, 1996

In the years just after the war . . . the survivors were not at all prepared for the questions that were asked of them, nor were they familiar with the idea of a survivor image, much less obedient to one—as many years later, some of them became. One learned that it was quite possible he would be asked . . . by what means he had purchased his life; and often those who were asked these questions learned that such questioning . . . [was] proof to them that they and their experiences were utterly incomprehensible to all those who had not been part of it.

> —Dorothy Rabinowitz, *New Lives* (1976)

It [the Holocaust] is like a crazy bass that is playing all the time. I have learned to play the fiddle above it so that there should be some harmony to my life. There isn't a second, however, that I'm not aware of it.

> —Fredrick Terna, artist and survivor of Lipa, Theresienstadt, and Auschwitz, quoted in *When They Came to Take My Father: Voices of the Holocaust,* photographs by Mark Seliger, edited by Leora Kahn and Rachel Hager (1996)

The survivors are a very special species, the most endangered species in history. At the beginning, they used to meet at weddings, at the births of the children, then bar mitzvahs and weddings. Now they meet at funerals.

> —Elie Wiesel, quoted in *The New York Times*, March 5, 1997

HOLOCAUST—SECOND GENERATION

Children of Holocaust survivors are called the "Second Generation" because everything earlier exists only in memory. There are no things from before our parents came here, and yet the weight in memory of the absent family farms or silver candlesticks or embroidered table linen is formidable.

> —Lori Hope Lefkovitz, author and professor of literature, "Inherited Holocaust Memory and the Ethics of Ventriloquism," *Kenyon Review*, Winter 1997

Sometimes I thought I carried a terrible bomb. I had caught glimpses of destruction. In school, when I had finished a test before time was up or was daydreaming on my way home, the safe world fell away and I saw things I knew no little girl should see. Blood and shattered glass. Piles of skeletons and blackened barbed wire with bits of flesh stuck to it the way flies stick to walls after they are swatted dead. Hills of suitcases, mountains of children's shoes. Whips, pistols, boots, knives and needles.

> —Helen Epstein, journalist and author, *Children of the Holocaust* (1979)

Reality had overtaken fantasy: the Dracula story seemed tame compared to what had actually happened to Jews in Transylvania.

> —Yossi Klein Halevi, journalist and author, *Memoirs of a Jewish Extremist* (1995)

When I think of what my mother was going through at my age—do you realize her head was shaved completely? She had nothing to eat, she was running around in the snow without shoes, and here I am, state queen at the Miss America contest—it's really unbelievable.

—Connie Lerner, Miss North Carolina of 1972, who is the daughter of Holocaust survivors, competing in the Miss America Pageant, quoted in *The Lonely Days Were Sundays: Reflections of a Jewish Southerner* by Eli N. Evans (1993)

The trouble with imbibing the black draft of the Holocaust so early was that it unfairly upped the ante: How unbearable could anything be if it wasn't being in a concentration camp?

—Daphne Merkin, novelist and essayist, "Dreaming of Hitler," *Esquire*, August 1989

We must never forget, that's what they learned in school, and Mummy said it too. Mummy didn't buy anything that came from Germany, except a nail file by mistake once. In Israel they had lots of Volkswagens because Germany gave them out of guilt, but Judith's family would never buy one. They are the cars Hitler invented. Some rich Jews drove Mercedes. Judith's Hebrew principal said: Your grandmother's teeth are in a Mercedes.

—Nessa Rapoport, author, *Preparing for Sabbath* (1981)

❖ HOMOSEXUALITY ❖

(see also Gay and Lesbian Jews)

It's ironic that if you were getting hired by somebody, you couldn't be asked what your sexual orientation is. But in any election, it's important who you are and what you are. When the voters vote for someone, it's like they're bringing you into their family.

—Karen Burstein, unsuccessful candidate for both New York State attorney general and Manhattan Surrogate's Court, quoted in *New York*, January 13, 1997

If I could have had a vote, why would I have chosen to put myself through all this stuff?

—David Geffen, entertainment executive reflecting on his sexual history, quoted in "King David," *US*, April 1997

Some believers—Catholic, Protestant, Jewish—say that "we hate the sin and love the sinner." I think it's fair to say that many of those committing the alleged sin are not so much interested in being loved as in being respected. In this case, love is not as important as respect and equality.

—Mayor Edward I. Koch of New York City, "The Mayor" in *His Eminence and Hizzoner,* coauthored with John Cardinal O'Connor (1989)

I certainly think of myself with pride and dignity and I like my differences. I don't like having to confront hate because I walk down the street holding my boyfriend's hand.

—Larry Kramer, playwright, quoted in *Singular Voices: Conversations with Americans Who Make a Difference* by Barbaralee Diamonstein (1997)

No matter how categorical scripture seems to be, though, one never assumes that a subject is closed.

—Rabbi Tsvi Marx, director of applied education at the Shalom Hartman Institute for Advanced Study in Jerusalem, quoted in *Jerusalem Report,* April 6, 1995

I was born of heterosexual parents, I was taught by heterosexual teachers, in a fiercely heterosexual society, with TV ads and newspaper ads fiercely heterosexual, a society that puts down homosexuality; then why am I homosexual if I'm affected by role models? I should have been a heterosexual. And no offense meant, but if teachers are going to affect you as role models, there'd be a lot of nuns running around the streets today.

—Harvey Milk, activist, campaigning against California Proposition 6 that would deny homosexuals their jobs in public schools, 1978, quoted in *The Times of Harvey Milk,* 1984 documentary

People are very emotional. They don't want to listen. Look what happened in Germany. Now, Anita Bryant already says that Jews and Moslems are going to hell. You know she's got a shopping list.

—Harvey Milk, statement during the 1978 statewide campaign against California's Proposition 6, quoted in *The Times of Harvey Milk,* 1984 documentary

This bill is about targeting scapegoats, and as a people who have been the quintessential scapegoats of Western civilization, we stand with our gay and lesbian brothers and sisters in saying that this bill is immoral and unjust.

—Rabbi David Saperstein, director of the Reform Action Center, from written testimony submitted in opposition to a law proposed by opponents of same-sex marriages, "The Defense of Marriage Act," quoted in *Forward,* May 24, 1996

Luckily, coming out in the open isn't as difficult in a metropolitan area like Detroit. My parents were aware by the time I graduated college, but for them, it was like a lefty versus a righty.

—Jeffrey Seller, producer of the Broadway musical *Rent,* quoted in *The Detroit Jewish News,* May 30, 1997

This case is about the limits of government power. . . . The power invoked here, I think we must be clear about it, is the power to dictate in the most intimate and, indeed, I must say, embarrassing detail how every adult, married or unmarried, in every bedroom in Georgia will behave in the closest and most intimate personal association with another adult. . . . Robert Frost once said that home is where, when you go there, they have to take you in. I think constitutionally home is the place where, when the government would tell you in intimate detail what you must do there and how you must behave there, they have to give you a better reason why than simply an invocation of the majority's morality.

—Laurence Tribe, professor of law, presenting arguments to the United States Supreme Court in the case of Bowers v. Hardwick (1986) that challenged a Georgia law, passed in 1816 making sodomy a crime, quoted in *May It Please The Court* edited by Peter Irons and Stephanie Guitton (1993)

Since Judaism opposes sins rather than the sinner, even those guilty of homosexual practices should not be ostracized or branded as "politically subversive." They should rather be accorded the kind of sympathy and compassion which is due to all those who fail to live up to the stringent demands of Judaism.

—Rabbi Walter Wurzburger, rabbi of Congregation Shaaray Tefila, Lawrence, N.Y., former president of the Synagogue Council of America, and editor of *Tradition,* "Preferences Are Not Practices," *Judaism,* Fall 1983

To be sure, Judaism condemns homosexuality as a perversion. But there is no need to exaggerate the seriousness of the violation by charging it, to boot, for all sorts of social ailments afflicting temporary society.

—Rabbi Walter Wurzburger, "Preferences Are Not Practices," *Judaism,* Fall 1983

[Roy Cohn] lived in a closet that was the oddest in history—a closet with neon lights—but he maintained it fiercely.

—Sidney Zion, journalist and author, *The Autobiography of Roy Cohn* (1988)

Roy [Cohn] understood the difference between de facto and de jure. He could do anything he liked as long as he didn't admit it. A confession had the force of law—de jure. The rest was gossip—de facto. I watched him play this for twenty years. He never admitted it to me, either.

> —Sidney Zion, *The Autobiography of Roy Cohn* (1988)

❖ HOPE ❖

I try to maintain hope—or at least the memory of hope—when I am consumed with fear or despair. I believe that hope is part of the will to live: it allows people to choose forms of treatment that are painful, risky, and promising; it enables people to fight fear with enthusiasm for family and friends, for books and ideas.

> —Paul Cowan, journalist, "In the Land of the Sick," *The Village Voice*, May 17, 1988

The art is to ransom sacred moments—the messages of the past—and to deposit them in the bank of eternity. Only then will we be able to recharge our batteries of courage and intergrity to battle for a morrow with hope.

> —Rabbi Marshall T. Meyer, human rights activist, founder of the Seminario Rabinico Latinoamericano, and spiritual leader of B'nai Jeshurun in New York City, talk at Ebenezer Baptist Church in Atlanta on Dr. Martin Luther King's birthday, 1991

I waited with that kind of crazy kind of expectation that comes when there is no hope, waited for the dream to come back from wherever it had gone to hide.

> —Arthur Miller, playwright, *The American Clock* (voice of the character Lee about his life in the 1930s) (1980)

❖ HUMAN RIGHTS ❖

I note that others share with me the notion that everyone should be treated as though created in the image of God. But to take that seriously should have some political consequences: namely, to increase their power, their ability to make free choices, their sense of dignity. If your guiding value is on the importance of giving to Palestinians full rights to make choices, have their voices respected and full power to shape their own lives. I don't think you'd end up with some of the facts on the ground such as they have been described here.

> —Rabbi Tsvi Blanchard, psychologist and philosopher, quoted in "Jerusalem Roundtable Panel Discussion," *Tikkun*, May 15, 1997

What can we say about an organization [the U.N.] whose Commission on Human Rights annually condemns Israel for every crime in the book, and refuses to denounce the massacres in Uganda and Cambodia? . . . If the Commission on Human Rights' main function is to cover up rather than expose such violations, tyrants and dictators throughout the world will sleep easier, their barbarism in a sense legitimized by the United Nations itself.

> —Yehuda Z. Blum, Permanent Representative of Israel to the United Nations, excerpt from address at the 65th National Commission meeting of the Anti-Defamation League of B'nai Brith, New York, November 17, 1978, *For Zion's Sake* (1987)

Following the weekend massacre [of Chinese dissidents in Tiananmen Square], I had my associate call a number of those who are the most vocal in condemning the United States, Israel, and other Western democracies. . . . Not surprisingly, several of these perennial democracy-bashers were unavailable for comment: They were indisposed, incommunicado, incognito, incoherent, in the bathroom, or in Timbuktu.

> —Alan M. Dershowitz, law professor, appellate lawyer, activist, and author, *Contrary to Popular Opinion* (1992)

Human rights will never become a reality until the world insists on a single standard of compliance, regardless of who the perpetrators and the victims are.

> —Alan M. Dershowitz, *Contrary to Popular Opinion* (1992)

According to tradition, whoever forgets one segment of the Torah commits a great sin. How much more is a person guilty if he remains careless to the agony of one human being.

> —Rabbi Abraham Joshua Heschel, author, activist, and theologian, "What Happens to Them Happens to Me," *United Synagogue Review*, Winter 1964

In this moment of history, so pregnant with hope and promise . . . I respectfully suggest that we must not be afraid of the light—and of where the light can take us.

> —The Honorable Max M. Kampelman, head of U.S. Delegation to the Copenhagen meeting of the Conference on the Human Dimension, Plenary, June 29, 1990, cited in *Challenging the Kremlin: The Soviet Jewish Movement for Freedom 1967–1990* by Edward R. Drachman (1991)

If one were to transcribe every phrase in the Hebrew Bible that deals with righteousness, justice, honesty, the need to care for the poor, the orphan, the widow, the needy; if one were to include the important and painstaking investigation of how to adjudicate property in the courts according to the Talmud, one would be faced with hundreds upon hundeds of pages of some of the most exalted ideas and concepts in the history of mankind.

—Rabbi Marshall T. Meyer, human rights activist, founder of the Seminario Rabinico Latinoamericano, and spiritual leader of B'nai Jeshurun in New York City, talk at Congregation Ahavas Israel, Grand Rapids, Mich., April 25, 1987

To speak in the accents and with the passion of the biblical Prophets is hardly to invent a new theology. It seems to me that if indeed we are neither prophets nor the children of prophets, we are the descendants of those who preferred the desert to slavery, who understood that God wants all peoples to be free, and who brought the message of ethical monotheism to the world. . . . There is simply no way of permitting the abuse of human rights in the name of, or with the approval of, Judaism. Nor is there any way in reading the texts that permits us to look the other way and thus be guilty of sins of omission or acquiescence.

—Rabbi Marshall T. Meyer, talk at Hebrew University, January 21, 1992

Why can't you, as a human being, see that these people are permitted to live?

—Henry Morgenthau, U.S. Ambassador to Turkey, addressing Hans Freiherr von Wangenheim, the German ambassador to Turkey at a 1913 meeting in an attempt to spare the lives of Armenian civilians prior to the Armenian massacres (1915–1923), *Ambassador Morgenthau's Story* (1918) cited in *The History of the Armenian Genocide* by Vahakn N. Dadrian (1997)

Oh, what a joy simply to dream that one day a President of the United States will put his arm around that good man, the Dalai Lama, smile pleasantly into the camera and say, "Well, the Chinese Communists can just stick it in their ears."

—A. M. Rosenthal, columnist, *The New York Times*, March 14, 1990

Israel faces certain severe challenges. We all understand that. But when it comes to preserving human rights, Amnesty International can't pull punches.

—Joshua Rubenstein, regional director of Amnesty International in Boston, quoted in *The Jewish Advocate*, July 12, 1996

❖ IDEALISM ❖

In the Roosevelt years, we really thought we could change the world. Would you make a sacrifice for Bush? You live your own life today, . . . and you try to be part of the human values that *Casablanca* stood for.

> —Howard Koch, one of the screenwriters of *Casablanca*, quoted in *Round Up the Usual Suspects: The Making of Casablanca* by Aljean Harmetz (1992)

Idealism is usually associated with the good guys, but I'll tell you, whoever is the Imperial Wizard of the Ku Klux Klan is as much an idealist in his mind as anyone else who believes deeply in his convictions and is willing to die for them or have others killed for them. These people don't expose their prejudices to a healthy doubt.

> —Roman Polanski, film director, interview with Larry Dubois in *Playboy*, December 1971

Self-interest is a powerful root from which all sorts of idealism can grow.

> —Michael Walzer, author and philosopher, quoted in *Values, Interests and Identity: Jews and Politics in a Changing World*, edited by Peter Y. Medding (1995)

When there are people going hungry, they must come first; their well-being must take precedence over all ideals—no, their well-being must become our ideal.

> —Elie Wiesel, *Somewhere a Master* (1981)

❖ IDEOLOGY ❖

Helping people stretch their ideological tolerance seems to be a constant but thankless task at all ends of the spectrum.

> —Rabbi Saul Berman, professor of Judaic studies, article in *The Rabbinate as Calling and Vocation: Models of Rabbinic Leadership* (1991)

I recently re-read *The Fountainhead* and while I still have great affection for it and recommend it to anyone taking a plane trip, I am forced to conclude that it is better read when one is young enough to miss the point.

> —Nora Ephron, author, screenwriter, and director, *Wallflower at the Orgy* (1968)

A heresy does not shrink from publicity. It welcomes it. Not so a conspiracy. The signs of a conspiracy are secrecy, anonymity, the use of false names and labels, and the calculated lie. . . . In general, whoever subverts the rules of a democratic organization and seeks to win by chicanery what cannot be fairly won in the process of free discussion is a conspirator.

> —Sidney Hook, philosophy professor and polemicist who broke with Communism in the early 1930s, *Heresy Yes, Conspiracy No* (1953)

It's inevitable. [Yitzchak] Shamir, when he was prime minister, said it very honestly: "Israel is an ideological state." Well, I don't believe anymore in ideologies. I've seen what happened. Ideologies of any kind have always been an affliction.

> —Alfred Kazin, author and literary critic, commenting on the gulf between Diaspora Jews and Israel, quoted in *Jerusalem Report*, February 19, 1998

An orthodoxy has far greater staying power than a counterculture. And even when it does succeed, it creates, willy-nilly, a new orthodoxy of its own.

> —Irving Kristol, social critic, editor, and publisher, *Neoconservatism: The Autobiography of an Idea* (1995)

There are two sides to every issue. One side is right and the other is wrong, but the middle is always evil.

> —Ayn Rand, writer and philosopher, interview with Alvin Toffler in *Playboy*, March 1964

❖ ILLNESS ❖

(see also Healing)

On September 11, 10 days before my 47th birthday, I was diagnosed with leukemia. Until that day, I had assumed that health and sickness were separate, distinct terrains. I've since learned that those boundaries don't really exist. Instead, the world is composed of the sick and the not-yet-sick.

> —Paul Cowan, journalist, "In the Land of the Sick," *The Village Voice*, May 17, 1988

The artist who painted "The Country Doctor" would scarcely recognize the modern bedside, crowded with so many new faces. Ethicists and committees, administrators and risk managers; legions of lawyers, judges, legislators, and politicians; reporters and right-to-lifers: never before has being sick been such a committee affair.

> —Nancy Dubler, attorney, head of the Division of Legal and Ethical Issues in Health Care at Montefiore Medical Center, New York, *Ethics on Call,* written with David Nimmons (1992)

I have heard that at Bellevue people with AIDS are shown the ICU while they are relatively healthy so they can see what it is like to be connected to a mechanical ventilator. They are asked to decide if they want to be intubated. We should all be required to take this tour, and not only for our own sake. John Mazelli's [a patient in the ICU] life is going to end, not with a bang and not with a whimper, and not with fire or ice, but with a hose down his throat and the hiss and rattle of a breathing machine in his ears and an unlimited, unobstructed view of the ceiling. He will wither under the twenty-four-hour grow-lights. It might take a while. This while is what will be referred to as his life.

> —Sue Halpern, author, "23 Hours Back of Beyond," *Migrations to Solitude* (1992)

From a distance, this kingdom of the sick seems to be an aberrational place, a hateful, twilight-zone country off the charts, the kind of distant land that ancient mariners feared as abounding with monsters. So foreign, yet so near. But it's a real place with real people and sooner or later we all get there.

> —Robert Lipsyte, author and journalist, *In the Country of Illness* (1998)

Raped of a sense of future, much of the fabric underpinning my sense of security is badly tattered. The dailiness of my days' routines is no less pleasurable but is totally devoid of meaning without either a sense of future or a vertical connection. The U'netaneh Tokef (prayer recited during Rosh Hashana and Yom Kippur that states that "repentance, prayer and charity cancel the stern decree") sounds like the clarion call: Only to the extent that we live in alignment with the Aysbishter (God), will we have the fortitude to endure our ordeals. And it is in the performance of these very acts of repentance, prayer and kind deeds that we bring the Aybishter close and thereby somewhat sweeten the bitterness of the decree.

> —Shira Ruskay, lawyer and Social Work Coordinator of Visiting Nurse Service of New York Hospice, on her experience with cancer, *Sh'ma,* September 19, 1997

My work, my life, is all with the sick—but the sick and their sickness drives me to thoughts which, perhaps, I might otherwise not have. So much so that I am compelled to ask, with Nietzsche: "As for sickness, are we not almost tempted to ask whether we could get along without it?"—and to see the questions it raises as fundamental in nature. Constantly my patients drive me to question, and constantly my questions drive me to patients.

> —Oliver Sacks, neurologist and author, *The Man Who Mistook His Wife for a Hat and Other Clinical Tales* (1985)

❖ IMAGINATION ❖

What is imagination but a reflection of our yearning to belong to eternity as well as to time?

> —Stanley Kunitz, poet, introductory essay to *Passing Through: The Later Poems* (1995)

Imagination is the bridge between God and humans. It is not the locus of fiction, but the locus of truth. God speaks to us through the imagination.

> —Rabbi Ira Stone, author and rabbi of Beth Zion/Beth Israel Synagogue in Philadelphia, *Seeking the Path to Life: Theological Meditations on God and the Nature of People, Love, Life and Death* (1992)

❖ IMMIGRATION ❖

(see also Anti-Semitism, World War II)

We lived then on the first floor of a small house in Kiev, and I can still recall distinctly hearing about a pogrom that was to descend on us. I didn't know then, of course, what a pogrom was, but I knew it had something to do with being Jewish and with the rabble that used to surge through town, brandishing knives and huge sticks, screaming "Christ Killers!" as they looked for the Jews, and who were now looking to do terrible things to me and my family.

> —Golda Meir, who emigrated from Eastern Europe to the United States with her family, quoted in *A Different Mirror—A History of Multicultural America* by Ronald Takaki (1993)

The most ignorant immigrant on landing, proceeds to give and receive greeting, to eat, sleep, and rise, after the manner of his own country; wherein he is corrected, admonished, and laughed at, whether by interested friends or the most indifferent strangers; and his American experience is thus begun.

> —Mary Antin, author, *The Promised Land* (1912)

The individual, we know, is a creature unknown to the statistician.

> —Mary Antin, *The Promised Land* (1912)

What if the creature with the untidy beard carries in his bosom his citizenship papers? What if the cross-legged tailor is supporting a boy in college who is one day going to mend your state constitution for you? What if the ragpicker's daughters are hastening over the ocean to teach your children in the public schools? Think, every time you pass the greasy alien on the street, that he was born thousands of years before the oldest native American; and he may have something to communicate to you, when you two shall have learned a common language.

> —Mary Antin, *The Promised Land* (1912)

On arriving in this country, the immigrants discover that they are not only valueless, but that they are a hindrance, and sometimes a nuisance, in the eyes of his fellow-men. . . . Were it given to us, by some kind of spiritual X-rays, to perceive the fractures in the souls of men, we would be . . . horrified by the sight of the untold numbers of mangled human souls which are writhing in inexpressible suffering in the midst of our Jewish immigrant population.

—Israel Friedlander, scholar and activist, 1915 statement quoted in *Practical Dreamer: Israel Friedlander and the Shaping of American Judaism* by Baila Round Shargel (1985)

"Luft—giebt mir luft." He spoke only Yiddish. The new country had given the Plague before the language. For the sweatshop . . . had made him weak; his weakened body could make no fight; the Plague came in and fed swiftly. Still on through the winter he had worked over the machine in the sweatshop, infecting the garments he sewed—feverish, tired, fearful—to buy food and coal. . . . And now on this last day of life, ten times he had whispered to his brother, begging him to care for the wife and the three little children. The struggle is now ended. . . . The smothered whisper is forever hushed. "Breath—breath—give me breath." It speaks the appeal of thousands.

—Ernest Poole, a settlement house worker who won the first Pulitzer Prize for fiction; from a story describing an immigrant's death from tuberculosis, "The Plague in Its Stronghold," 1903

It was one of these letters from America, in fact, which put the notion of emigrating to the New World definitely in my mind. An illiterate woman brought it to the synagogue to have it read to her, and I happened to be the one to whom she addressed her request. The concrete details of that letter gave New York tangible form in my imagination. It haunted me ever after.

—Abraham Cahan, author and editor, *The Rise of David Levinsky* (1917)

For my father, the material advantages of America were of secondary importance. He saw in his own emigration to the Golden Land a symbolic act. He was going along with his own people; the folk writer, as he liked to call himself, would journey with his own folk; he would be with them, with his pen and his heart, as he had been with them all these years in Kasrilevka and Yehupetz.

—Marie Waife-Goldberg, daughter of Sholem Aleichem (the family left Russia in late December 1905), *My Father, Sholem Aleichem* (1968)

Within a month the new arrivals had jobs, a flat, and they were saving money for the other members of the Roskolenko tribe left over in Zareby Koscielne. And that was the way a minor portion of the street in New York City was settled, the unions built, new trades learned, new children born, new shuls [synagogues] attended. The studious traveled even farther. Those who could afford to study and manage to work their way into the professions left the pushcarts and sweatshops to their fathers—for America made professional bargains. For all of us soon learned that the green dollar did not grow on green trees. It came via Ellis Island, heartbreak, bad health, and pain.

—Harry Roskolenko, author, "America the Thief" in *The Immigrant Experi-*

ence: *The Anguish of Becoming American*, edited by Thomas C. Wheeler (1971)

As an immigrant boy, I was tossed into the bewildering whirlpool of a metropolitan slum area, to sink or swim . . . I learned the hard way what a helping hand, a sympathetic word, a reasonable opportunity can mean in giving hope to a new arrival in this wonderful land.

—David Sarnoff, pioneer in the broadcasting industry, receiving an award from the Hebrew Immigrant Aid Society, 1959, quoted in *Sarnoff: An American Success* by Carl Dreher (1977)

By systematic exploitation of the defendants' alien blood, their imperfect knowledge of English, their unpopular social views, and their opposition to the war, the District Attorney invoked against them a riot of political passion and patriotic sentiment and the trial judge connived in the process.

—Felix Frankfurter, Boston attorney, "The Case of Sacco and Vanzetti, A Critical Analysis," 1927, excerpted from *Law and Literature*, edited by Ephraim London (1960)

A few years before *Casablanca*'s premiere a proposal to admit 20,000 German children aged fourteen or younger outside the annual German quota had failed in the United States Congress. Viewers of *Casablanca* were faced with no such moral dilemma.

—Daniel J. Steinbock, "Refuge and Resistance: *Casablanca*'s Lessons for Refugee Law," *Georgetown Immigration Law Journal*, December 1993

As we boarded the ship [departing Hamburg] there was somewhat of an atmosphere of tension. . . . After all, we had lost our homeland and I don't have to tell you what the circumstances were. . . . The boat began to sail and we were . . . happier than we'd ever been to be getting out of there. We took various possibilities into consideration but we never considered what actually happened then. . . . What we could not understand was how America, so huge a country, would not allow us in somewhere, anywhere.

—Herta Fink-Hurtig, passenger on the SS *St. Louis* who was returned in 1939 to Holland and subsequently to a concentration camp after the ship was turned away from all shores, quoted in *Pillar of Fire: The Rebirth of Israel— A Visual History* by Yigal Lossin, translated by Tsvi Ofer, edited by Carol Halberstadt (1983)

This is called the "St. Louis gambit." . . . The suggestion is that we should have moved six million people. . . . At that point in time or even today, we cannot accept everybody who wants to come here. To have a totally cavalier attitude about what the public thinks . . . and let ivory tower, inside-the-beltway eggheads decide how many come in . . . you're asking for trouble.

> —Dan Stein, Executive Director of FAIR (Federation for American Immigration Reform), a restrictionist group calling for a moratorium on immigration, responding to a question from Leon Botstein, president of Bard College, about whether the public opinion polls in 1933–1939 that were against admitting Jewish refugees were an adequate answer to the situation, quoted on *Firing Line*: "Immigration Debate," broadcast on PBS, June 16, 1995

All the speeches were highly emotional, decrying the horrible and awesome character of a Nazi regime and expressing pity for the Jews. And every speech had one common denominator: "However, my country cannot take them in." . . . I remember saying that I hoped to live to see the day when no one will have to pity the Jews.

> —Golda Meir, Histadrut delegate to the Evian Conference, an international conference on the refugee question convened by the U.S., quoted in *Pillar of Fire: The Rebirth of Israel—A Visual History* by Yigal Lossin, translated by Tsvi Ofer, edited by Carol Halberstadt (1983)

Puppet show . . . even the strings were visible.

> —Congressman Emanuel Celler (D-N.Y.), condemning the Bermuda Conference on refugees convened by British and American leaders, quoted in *Free World*, July 1943, cited by Deborah E. Lipstadt, *Modern Judaism*, February 1982 (The conference's location in Bermuda made it impossible for anyone to monitor proceedings.)

I think it is about time we stopped confusing the experience of being an immigrant, or an immigrant's son with the experience of being Jewish.

> —Alfred Kazin, author and literary critic, 1944 statement quoted in "American Jewish Writers and Their Judaism" by Harold U. Ribalow, reprinted in *Jews in the Modern World, Volume 2*, edited by Jacob Fried (1962)

I guess I'm a sucker for irony. I enjoy being an immigrant—it feels so Jewish.

> —Stuart Schoffman, columnist, commenting on being an American oleh (immigrant) to Israel, *Jerusalem Report*, April 21, 1994

The fact of the matter is that the Jews are on the march. The trouble is that they have nowhere to go.

> —Joseph J. Schwartz, Chairman of the European Executive Council of the American Jewish Joint Distribution Committee, briefing the executive committee in New York on the catastrophe in Europe and the need for resources, June 20, 1945, quoted in *The Secret Alliance* by Tad Szulc (1991)

Most of the refugees had a secret hope that Hitler would be defeated and they could go back home. I never had that hope. This was home. I had a clear-cut vision: "This is where I am going to die."

> —Billy Wilder, director who fled Nazi Europe, quoted in *Round Up the Usual Suspects: The Making of Casablanca* by Aljean Harmetz (1992)

Fourteen months of life in America have made a new human being out of me. I have been given a new lease on life. . . . The people of Port Huron offered me a home in the truest sense of the word. I will always be indebted to that town.

> —Ernest W. Michel, executive director emeritus of UJA-Federation of New York and survivor of Auschwitz, who was a refugee to the United States after the war in 1946, *Promises to Keep* (1993)

Rescue for the shattered remnant of European Jewry lies only in emigration. . . . Were the hope of emigration to die within them, then all would indeed be lost to them. A civilized world cannot long defer the realization of this hope.

> —Isaac L. Asofsky, executive director of Hebrew Immigrant Aid Society (HIAS), reporting on the situation of Jewish displaced persons in Europe, January 7, 1947

My coming to America has demoted me in a way, thrown me back to the ordeal of a beginner in writing, in life, in my struggle for independence. I had a taste of what it would be for someone to be born old and to grow younger with the years instead of older, diminishing constantly in rank, in experience, in courage, in widsom of maturity.

> —Isaac Bashevis Singer, Nobel Prize–winning Yiddish writer, *Love and Exile* (1984)

Harry, I am worried about the heavy Yiddish accent with twenty million Americans watching and listening.

> —David Dubinsky, retired president of the ILGWU, when asked by journalist Harry Golden why he wouldn't appear on Edward R. Murrow's *Person to Person* show, quoted in *Ess, Ess Mein Kindt* by Harry Golden (1966)

If one believes America's historic role is to provide a home for "huddled masses yearning to breathe free," then it failed in its performance of its historic task at this critical juncture in history. However, the truth of the matter is that, while this may have been the role America once played, by 1920 — and certainly in 1940 — this was no longer the case. In the hearts of most Americans, and on the pages of their newspapers and magazines, was engraved another statement, one which gave much truer expression to their feelings: we are genuinely sorry about European Jewry's condition and suffering—if all that is reported is really true—but you must understand that our doors are closed and shall remain so.

—Deborah E. Lipstadt, author and professor of modern Jewish history, "America News Media and the Holocaust," *Modern Judaism*, February 1982

I still love America even though it has nothing to do with the kingdom of my childish imagination. And immigration, it has become a piece of memory that I will never forget. It proved that all people are looking for the paradise but most of us don't get to find it—or just don't find it—because there's no such place.

—Raimonda Kopelnitsky, teenager who lived in the Ukraine until she was twelve when she emigrated to the United States with her parents and brother in 1989, *No Words to Say Goodbye* (1994)

It's the plight of the alien who's learned perfectly how to imitate the natives. I think the sense of being from somewhere else, of being a Jew in another culture, is the main thing about my work.

—Mike Nichols, film director who was born in Berlin in 1931 (his family fled from the Nazis to the United States in 1939), quoted in *Jerusalem Report*, December 16, 1993

An immigrant's patriotism—how old-fashioned the word now sounds—is not a sentiment in the abstract. It is a comparative judgement, America viewed against every place else.

—Martin Peretz, editor-in-chief, *The New Republic*, June 29, 1992

One of them is a Democrat and the other Republican. But when it comes to understanding America's roots and the dangers to them, you can't tell these guys apart—my happy thought for the day.

—A. M. Rosenthal, columnist, commending Mario Cuomo (Democratic Governor of New York) and Rudolph Giuliani (Republican Mayor of New York City) for taking a pro-immigrant position during a wave of anti-immigrant sentiment throughout the United States, "Hunt Them Down," *The New York Times*, October 4, 1994

No one ever loved this country more deeply. He thought America a truly golden land, a Gan Eden [garden of eden], a haven, a heaven of endless promise. "Why here you can talk, you can argue, you can disagree, you can call a mayor a crook—you can even complain to a policeman!"

—Leo Rosten, author, recalling his father, an immigrant from Poland, *People I Have Loved, Known or Admired* (1970)

No matter how dispassionate, objective, or scholarly, all work in this field inevitably rests on moral principles. When we talk about immigration, we perforce enter into considerations of life saving; family relationships; basic economic opportunity; competing claims by groups to scarce resources; levels of responsibility to family, fellow citizens, and strangers; human rights inherent in the person regardless of ties to others; and other basic moral questions. It is impossible to address or even frame questions in this field without the guidance of an ethical value system, even if it is an unconscious one.

> —Gary E. Rubin, director of national affairs of the American Jewish Committee, "Are There Too Many People in the Lifeboat?" paper delivered at conference "Babel and Beyond: Ethics, Opportunity and Power in a Multicultural Society," Starkoff Institute of Ethics and Contemporary Moral Problems of Hebrew Union College-Jewish Institute of Religion, Los Angeles, October 14, 1991

Immigration is not an affirmative-action policy. Aliens around the world do not have inherent rights to enter, so there is no need to choose entrants in proportion to their representation in the international population. Immigration is a national decision, which we make according to our feelings of closeness with various groups abroad. But, given the different definitions of closeness with various groups abroad, all conceptually valid, how do we rank order our preferences for entry?

> —Gary E. Rubin, "Are There Too Many People in the Lifeboat?" 1991

Assimilation, if it is to succeed, must be a voluntary process, by both the assimilating immigrants and the assimilated-to natives. Assimilation is a human accommodation, not a mechanical production.

> —Peter D. Salins, professor of urban affairs and author, *Assimilation, American Style* (1997)

Actually, I was worried about the expense, but there was no question that we were going to accept. I had a strong, simple feeling about the invitation, and it struck a sympathetic chord in Lionel. My father had come to America from Poland when he was a boy of eighteen, without a penny, and knowing no English. He peddled macaroons on the Staten Island Ferry while he learned the language, and now for his daughter to be invited to the White House — well, I owed him the acceptance of that invitation.

> —Diana Trilling, essayist and critic who, with her husband Lionel Trilling, was a guest at the White House dinner given by President and Mrs. Kennedy for the Nobel laureates in 1962, "Washington Memoir: A Visit to Camelot," *The New Yorker*, May 2, 1997

By chance, my first day of classes was "treat day." Other students had brought cookies and candy to swap at the mid-morning snack, but I had nothing. . . . Shirley Newman — my first American friend — made her way toward my desk and shyly put down a piece of candy. One by one, the other girls followed until my desk was covered with treats. I nearly wept with gratitude — my first experience of American generosity. I was glad that at least I did know how to say "Thank you."

> —Lillian Vernon, founder, chairman, and CEO of the specialty catalog company that bears her name, talking about her first day of school in America, *An Eye for Winners* (1996)

❖ INTERMARRIAGE ❖

(see also Conversion, Marriage)

We can only say that some mixed marriages are happy, others unhappy. But then many marriages between Jew and Jew, Christian and Christian are not successful either. It is true, however, that in some mixed marriages the differences between man and wife create unhappiness. Therefore we cannot take it upon ourselves to advise the young man regarding this marriage. This he must decide for himself.

> —Response from newpaper advice columnist, 1908, reprinted in *A Bintel Brief; Sixty Years of Letters from the Lower East Side to the Jewish Daily Forward*, edited by Isaac Metzker (1971)

However fearful of a Christian society contemporary Jews may claim to be, they have in dangerously increasing numbers been voting otherwise with their feet. One of the ironies of the demographic crisis . . . is that the very Jewish groups who most loudly profess their anxiety about Christians are, with a frequency never before seen in all of Jewish history, marrying them.

> —Elliot Abrams, author and president of the Ethics and Public Policy Center in Washington, D.C., *Faith or Fear: How Jews Can Survive in a Christian Culture* (1997)

As a whole the Jewish community has not yet decided whether to treat interfaith couples as problems or people: as pariahs or as men and women who are not yet committed Jews.

> —Paul Cowan, journalist and author, with Rachel Cowan, rabbinical student, *Mixed Blessings: Marriage Between Jews and Christians* (1987)

If interfaith couples are invited into the Jewish community they may well join. If they're told their love is heresy they'll probably flee.

> —Paul Cowan with Rachel Cowan, *Mixed Blessings: Marriage Between Jews and Christians* (1987)

We're such a small number. I agree that conversion is the key. We have to divide up the waterfront in terms of our tasks. It's appropriate for there to be such a strong stance against intermarriage from Orthodoxy, but there's also a place for greater outreach. We need multiple responses, the whole range; and our denominational structure allows for that.

> —Blu Greenberg, author, teacher, and activist, quoted in "Roundtable on Intermarriage," *Tikkun*, January/February 1997

Rabbis who do not officiate at intermarriages are not passing judgement on choices of partners people make. Many of us spend hours in counseling with couples at whose weddings we will not officiate, seeking to become the rabbis for their marriages, not "officiants" for their weddings.

> —Rabbi Richard Hirsh of Evanston, Ill., letter to the editor, *The New York Times*, July 20, 1995

The rate of intermarriage in my books is even greater than intermarriage in America.

> —Susan Isaacs, author, quoted in *Forward*, July 26, 1996

Intermarriage [marriage to an uncoverted spouse] is like an infectious disease. If it penetrates a family, and if the victim is not isolated, then its contagion spreads, causing the spiritual death of countless Jewish children.

> —Rebbetzin Esther Jungreis, teacher and activist, quoted in *The Jewish Press*, April 11, 1997

A friend of mine who runs a Hillel foundation at one of the major universities in the United States sends a letter out to the parents of all the Jewish freshman as the year begins. It is folded over and the top fold says, "How to make sure that your child marries a Jew," and you open it up and it says, "Live in the 16th century."

> —Rabbi Harold S. Kushner, author and rabbi emeritus of Temple Israel in Natick, Mass., interviewed by Jonathan Perlman in his documentary *Being Jewish*, quoted in the *Boston Advocate*, January 12–18, 1996

To put it in a crude way, the Jewish community is not in a position to be picky. We'll take anybody we can get, we'll help them in any way we can.

—Rabbi Lawrence Kushner, author and spiritual leader of Congregation Beth-El in Sudbury, Mass., quoted in "Roundtable on Intermarriage," *Tikkun*, January/February 1997

We must say to young people: "Intermarriage poses a dire threat to the future of the Jewish community, and it also threatens your spiritual well-being. On some level, you will be lonely because you will be unable to share community, values, or history." In other words, we must say: "More than contributing to the survival of our people, choose a Jewish spouse for your own good."

—Deborah E. Lipstadt, author and professor of modern Jewish studies, addressing the Hadassah National Convention, July 1992

Jewish leaders need to understand that the choice of a non-Jewish partner isn't necessarily a statement of alienation from Judaism—although failure to welcome intermarried couples into Jewish institutions often engenders resentment and causes such families to turn away from participation in Jewish life.

—Ellen Jaffe McClain, teacher and author of *Embracing the Stranger*, letter to the editor, *The New York Times*, July 20, 1995

I wanted a new thing—happiness. I was not a girl representing a race. I was not a Jewish maiden responsible to a race. . . . I was not Biblical Rebecca sorrowfully pleading for her race. I was American, now, just as he was.

—Leah Morton (pseudonym of Elisabeth G. Stern), author, *I am a Woman—And a Jew* (1926), quoted in *The Wonders of America: Reinventing Jewish Culture, 1880–1950* by Jenna Weissman Joselit (1994) (The main character was preparing to marry a non-Jew.)

Intermarriage points to the continuous dialectic between distinctiveness and similarity. It poses the question of how to reconcile mutual love with the love for one's tradition. Expectations of mutual self-revelation lead to the disclosure of ethnic and religious differences. Yet in our embrace of the victory of love over tradition, we have come to overlook the persistence of meaning, symbols, and attachments to our ancestral heritage.

—Ester Perel, psychotherapist, talk presented at the Paul Cowan Memorial Conference on Intermarriage, Conversion and Outreach at the City University of New York, October 24, 1989, reprinted in *Journal of Jewish Communal Service*, 1990

The issue is not intermarriage. The issue is whether or not Judaism is important to the Jew. If Judaism is important, no arguments against intermarriage are necessary. If Judaism isn't important, no arguments against intermarriage are effective.

> —Dennis Prager, author and radio commentator, *Moment,* February 1993

A bird and a fish could fall in love, but where would they build a nest?

> —Tevye, from *Fiddler on the Roof,* a musical written by Joseph Stein, based on Sholem Aleichem's Tevye stories (1964)

Interracial and interreligious marriages are a good thing, and certainly the latter, because I'm involved in one. Some say you can't change your grandfather. But you can forget your grandfather, and lots of Americans have, and I think that's a good thing, often.

> —Abigail Thernstrom, author, quoted in *Forward,* January 9, 1998

The future of American Jewry is a proposition that we are voting on with our own behavior. My feeling is that if you are voting no, even if you wish the rest of us well, then I am under no obligation to treat your simcha [joyous occasion] as one the community should celebrate.

> —Jonathan S. Tobin, editor, *The Jewish Ledger,* West Hartford, Conn., from an editorial about the refusal of his paper to print interfaith wedding announcements (where no religious conversion took place), quoted in *The New York Times,* July 12, 1995

❖ INTERNATIONAL AFFAIRS ❖

(see also Politics, Government, and Leaders; World War I, World War II)

Together they represented seventy nations in the greatest assemblage of royalty and rank ever gathered in one place and, of its kind, the last. The muffled tongue of Big Ben tolled nine by the clock as the cortege left the palace, but on history's clock it was sunset, and the sun of the old world was setting in a dying blaze of splendor never to be seen again.

> —Barbara W. Tuchman, historian, describing the May morning in 1910 when nine kings rode in the funeral of King Edward VII of England; *The Guns of August* (1962)

[Theodore Roosevelt] was the first President who knew that the United States had come of age—that not only were they no longer colonies of Europe, and no longer an immature nation on the periphery of western civilization, but that they had become a world power. He was the first to realize what that means, its responsibilities and its dangers and its implication, and the first to prepare the country spiritually and physically for this inescapable destiny. . . . Theodore Roosevelt began the work of turning the American mind in the direction which it had to go in the Twentieth Century.

> —Walter Lippmann, journalist, quoted in *Walter Lippmann and the American Century* by Ronald Steel (1980)

. . . The elevation of Adolph Hitler to the Chancellorship of the Reich came as a surprise even to close observers of the German scene, and probably, also to Hitler and his followers. . . . And yet, when the history of the preceding thirteen years is studied it is discerned that these events were but inevitable links in a chain, the forging of which was begun with the scarcely noticed launching of the National Socialist movement in 1920. It is now evident that the course and propaganda of that movement during the succeeding years could have led to no other result, especially under the circumstances which attended the accession to power of the leaders of the movement.

> —Summary of Year's Events, *American Jewish Year Book 1933–1934*

In view of what has been proposed by the Committee of Jewish Delegations in Paris, we can only pray, that God grant us protection from our enemies as best we can.

> —Jacob Henry Schiff, banker and philanthropist, reacting to a proposal that the Jews should seek representation as a nation in the Council of the League of Nations, August 29, 1920, quoted in the *American Jewish Year Book 1921–1922*

He is surrounded by judicious men . . . Hindenburg . . . and von Papen. And responsibility generally puts curbs on the folly and viciousness even of the most irresponsible demagogue.

> —Editorial in B'nai Brith's official magazine, March 1933, on whether the new Chancellor of Germany, Adolf Hitler, would ever actually have real power, quoted in *B'nai Brith: The Story of A Covenant* by Edward E. Grusd (1966)

[I would not] insult the flag of pirates by comparing it to the swastika.

> —Benjamin Cardozo, United States Supreme Court justice, reacting to a ruling by Magistrate Louis B. Brodsky that resulted from an incident arising out of demonstration against the *Bremen*, a German passenger liner that flew the swastika flag, July 1935, quoted in *The New York Times*, September 18, 1935, cited in *The World of Benjamin Cardozo* by Richard Polenberg (1997)

I think FDR too hoped that wouldn't get into the war but at the same time he illustrated . . . the principle of polarity. . . . You've got to do the opposite at the same time. . . . To do the contradictory is a tough problem; namely with might and main to try to prevent from coming to pass the very situation in relation to which you're making preparations. That's what we have to do in life so much. You build a fire-proof house and nevertheless take out fire insurance.

> —Felix Frankfurter, United States Supreme Court justice, quoted in *Felix Frankfurter Reminisces*, recorded in talks with Dr. Harlan B. Phillips (1960)

[U.S. Secretary of State John Foster Dulles] always managed to make his moral principles coincide with his material gains. Whenever he wrestled with his conscience, he tended to win.

> —Abba Eban, former foreign minister and Israeli ambassador to the United Nations, *The New Diplomacy: International Affairs in the Modern Age* (1983)

Our internationalism actually contained a good measure of anticommunism — that is internationalism sold in the name of anticommunism. Inevitably there was what Toynbee calls historical transference — we took on some of the coloration of their [the Soviet Union's] society. As they were secretive, we ourselves became more secretive; as Stalin was the most paranoid of figures, some of that paranoia inevitably took root here.

> —David Halberstam, journalist and author, *The Next Century* (1991)

If diplomacy is dramatic and histrionic, it is more likely to evoke passion than reason.

> —Abba Eban, *The New Diplomacy: International Affairs in the Modern Age* (1983)

It is true that ever since Adam and Eve ate the apple in the Garden of Eden mankind has never abstained from any folly of which it is inherently capable.

> —Abba Eban, *The New Diplomacy: International Affairs in the Modern Age* (1983)

A dangerous pernicious doctrine. [If Vietnam were] to become the one determining factor in U.S. foreign policy halfway across the globe in totally different circumstances, the result must be war everywhere or paralysis everywhere. [There is] no inherent reason why one cannot criticize the abuse of power in Vietnam and the abdication of power elsewhere.

> —Theodor Draper, professor of history, commenting on the suggestion that there must be consisitency, i.e., if one must be "all hawk or all dove" when

taking positions on the Vietnam War and the Six-Day War, "Israel and World Politics," *Commentary*, August 1967

Judging the war in Vietnam to be reactionary, we oppose United States policy there. But that is surely no reason to claim that this binds us to a policy of inflexible abstentionism in other circumstances. . . . It is all a matter of where, in what way, toward what end, and within what limits? Our hope therefore is that the mideast crisis will in no way diminish opposition to the Vietnam War.

— Irving Howe, author and professor of English, and Stanley Plastrik, on whether one must be "consistent" in oppposing one war (Vietnam) and not another (The Six-Day War), "After the MidEast War," *Dissent*, July–August 1967

We had had a hero. He was a young good-looking man with a beautiful wife, and he had won the biggest poker game we ever played, the only real one — we had lived for a week ready to die in a nuclear war. Whether we liked it or not. But he had won. It was our one true victory in all these years, our moment; so the young man began to inspire a subtle kind of love. His strength had proved stronger than we knew.

— Norman Mailer, author, recalling President Kennedy and the 1962 Cuban Missile Crisis, *Some Honorable Men: Political Conventions 1960–1972* (1976)

After the past year's events in Eastern Europe and the Soviet Union, who can say that progress in the Middle East is impossible?

— Eugene V. Rostow, foreign policy analyst, *The New Republic*, April 23, 1990

In international affairs, foreign nations and peoples trust this administration at their own risk.

— A. M. Rosenthal, op-ed columnist, referring to Bush administration policies toward loan guarantees to Israel, the demonstrations in Tiananmen Square, and the response to the Kurdish refugees after the Gulf War, *The New York Times*, September 17, 1991

The United States should not be ashamed of either the military or the moral power it wields. The international community relies on the United States to lead, and even when the United States is not using its power, other states often assume that it is acting behind the scenes. By actually leading, the United States merely lives up to its reputation.

— Morris B. Abram, U.S. permanent representative to the United Nations in Geneva, "The United Nations, The United States, and International Human Rights" in *U.S. Policy and the Future of the United Nations*, edited by Roger A. Coate (1994)

No longer are we necessarily a people that dwells alone, and no longer is it true that the whole world is against us; We must overcome the sense of isolation that has held us in its thrall for almost half a century. We must join the international movement towards peace, reconciliation and cooperation that is spreading over the entire globe these days—lest we be the last to remain, all alone, in the station.

> —Yitzhak Rabin, Israeli prime minister, opening speech to the Knesset, 1992, quoted in the *Washington Post*, November 5, 1995

Wars are not self-starting. They may "break out," like an accidental fire, under conditions difficult to analyze and where the attribution of responsibility seems impossible. But usually they are more like arson than accident: war has human agents as well as human victims.

> —Michael Walzer, author, *Just And Unjust Wars: A Moral Argument with Historical Illustrations* (1977)

Self-determination is nothing more than a code word for the right to be ruled by a dictator of your own race.

> —Sidney Zion, journalist, *Trust Your Mother but Cut the Cards* (1993)

This is the heart of the State Department's view of global strife—everything can be reduced to failure to communicate. If the Palestinians only understood the pain and fears of the Israelis, goes the reasoning, and if the Israelis only understood the sense of victimhood of the Palestinians, then peace would break out all over. But that is not the nature of the conflict. This is not couples therapy.

> —Mona Charen, columnist, commenting on a plan put forth by the State Department that Arafat should visit the U.S. Holocaust Memorial Museum during a visit to Washington, *The Washington Times*, January 21, 1998

Mr. Arafat is a man who calmly ordered the murder of Israeli schoolgirls just a few years ago. If he tours the [Holocaust] museum, it would be only to take notes.

> —Mona Charen, columnist, *The Washington Times*, January 21, 1998

The media, especially television, report what is currently happening but are not very interested in covering anticipated events. If we were to contact the media to tell them that a possible 10,000 people could be murdered in country X tomorrow, I doubt that such a prediction would receive much attention. On the other hand, if we were to contact our friends in the media and tell them that 10,000 people are being murdered today in country X, we would elicit much more interest.

—Lionel Rosenblatt, president of Refugees International, an advocacy organization on behalf of refugees and displaced persons around the world, "The Media and the Refugee," included in *From Massacres to Genocide: The Media, Public Policy, and Humanitarian Crises,* edited by Robert I. Rotberg and Thomas G. Weiss (1996)

The key events of the last decade, which failed to obey the standard rules of change, are a premonition of things to come. Classic political instruments, such as armies, parties, or even superpowers have had no role to play at all. Thus, communism collapsed in the Soviet Union without aid from the Red Army—neither for those who supported it, nor for those who wished to rid themselves of it. As the Soviet Union was overthrown, the army remained . . . on the sidelines. . . . The same is true of apartheid in South Africa. Also, what happened in the Israeli-Palestinian conflict is very similar. It began in the darkness of calm Norwegian nights, without a single gunshot. . . . Conversely, traditional political instruments have proven completely ineffective in Bosnia, Somalia, or Burundi. . . . Is is merely chance, or are we observing the first signs of a new world that works according to rules yet unknown to us?

—Shimon Peres, Israeli foreign minister, "The End of the Hunting Season in History" *New Perspectives Quarterly,* Fall 1995, reprinted in *At Century's End: Great Minds Reflect on Our Times,* edited by Nathan P. Gardels (1995)

❖ INTIFADA ❖

(see also Israel)

The [American TV] networks show the agony of occupation but, to make an intelligent judgement, one must also ask why the territory was occupied. Televison is an astigmatic medium, and they don't apply the corrective lens to get it into focus.

—Morris B. Abram, Chairman of the Conference of Presidents of American Jewish Organizations, quoted in *Israel in Medialand,* compiled and edited by Eliyahu Tal (1988)

The question that I must ask you is, what do you see as an alternative? Not one of our critics so far had come forward with such an alternative. Not one of them, indeed, can point to the solution of similar situations in other countries without resorting to force. . . . If you criticize our methods of achieving law and order as many in Israel do, you should at least advise us what the alternative is. Should we resort to the methods used not so long ago in the U.S. on the campuses such as Kent State, or in Watts County (34 dead), Newark (26 dead) and other centers of racial or political unrest?

> —Chaim Herzog, president of Israel, from his letter to American Rabbi Alexander Schindler, January 25, 1988, quoted in *Israel in Medialand*, compiled and edited by Eliyahu Tal (1988)

When Israeli soldiers swing clubs around rioters, TV gets a lot of what it likes best—great moments. They shock the viewers. They compel attention. When action is the essence of the story, as it is most simply in something like a sports event or an earthquake, the moments can add up to a truth. In the West Bank and Gaza riots, the moments may have added up to a lie.

> —Mortimer B. Zuckerman, editor-in-chief, *U.S News and World Report*, February 1, 1988

They use the phrase "moderate Arabs" which is an oxymoron. The fact is: They want it all.

> —Robert Asher, AIPAC (American Israel Public Affairs Committee) chairman, speaking at the 29th annual AIPAC policy conference, Washington, D.C., quoted in *Long Island Jewish World*, May 27, 1988

This is a continuation of a war that is at least 60 years old. This war is being represented on network television as some sort of children's crusade, or an act of civil disobedience, or a modern-day version of the Palestinian David fighting the Israeli Goliath. This war is being sugar coated in the United States by professors and Mahatma Gandhi impersonators who go on television to depict that all they want is an end to the occupation and for the beginning of coexistence.

> —Tom Dine, executive director of AIPAC (American Israel Public Affairs Committee), speaking at its 29th annual policy conference in Washington, D.C., quoted in *Long Island Jewish World*, May 27, 1988

The present confrontation in the territories is marked by the fact that the young Palestinians have succeeded in turning the conflict between us into a truly popular war. In that war, armed, uniformed Israeli soldiers are pitted against Palestinian civilians with stones and Molotov cocktails in their hands, but with murder in their eyes and hearts.

> —Yosef Goell, Israeli columnist, *Jerusalem Post*, March 10, 1988

Who said, "Violence does not help"? . . . Of course violence helps. It helps to force an issue onto the headlines and consciousness of the world. It makes people talk about the issue. And then, if the violence is accompanied by clever propaganda, it helps remarkably well. . . . This is true for all people whether their cause is right or wrong. And of course, the Arab cause is wrong. But it does not remove the essential reality of the very great effectiveness of violence.

> —Rabbi Meir Kahane, founder of the Jewish Defense League, *The Jewish Press*, 1988

Israel is not yet a pariah among nations because so many Israelis are using their political rights to fiercely and openly oppose what their government is doing to make it a pariah among nations. But, if as is likely, the Likud bloc led by Yitzhak Shamir takes complete control of the government in November, it is going to be very difficult for the human-rights forces in Israel to prevent their nation from being increasingly compared with that undeniable pariah nation, South Africa.

> —Nat Hentoff, journalist, *The Village Voice*, May 17, 1988

The intifada does not fall within the definition of terrorism.

> —Rita Hauser, attorney who led the Jewish delegation that met with Yasir Arafat in Stockholm in December 1988 where they accepted the PLO's right to continue the intifada while renouncing terrorism, quoted in *Washington Jewish Week*, December 15, 1988

Beating Jews is unimportant; but when a Jew is beating—this is news.

> —Yitzhak Rabin, Israeli defense minister, responding to criticism from abroad about his order to the Israel Defense Forces to use batons against violent Palestinian demonstrators, quoted in *Ma'ariv* (Israeli daily newspaper), March 2, 1988

Of course, Israel's brutalities in the occupied territories are not nearly so barbaric as the traditional means of suppressing dissent in most Arab states. But are Israel's methods these last 18 months worthy of being called Jewish?

> —Nat Hentoff, journalist, quoted in *Long Island Jewish World*, May 19, 1989

The violence in the territories and the whole uprising is not about human rights or civil rights or economic demands. Its purpose, its goal is a far-reaching political one that, in my humble opinion, to my mind, can endanger Israel's future and security. Therefore, we must block the uprising, we must overcome their way—or at least their illusion that in this way they will achieve what Israel can never accept.

—Yitzhak Rabin, Israeli defense minister, quoted in *The Jewish Week*, May 26, 1989

We know that the Jews overseas are upset. Tell them for us that we like doing this even less than they like watching it on TV.

> —Rami, Israeli soldier, speaking to Martin Gallanter, national director of the Friends of the Israel Defense Forces, quoted in the *Baltimore Jewish Times*, April 7, 1988

This isn't like Vietnam, where you resolve a situation and walk away. Neither side is going anywhere.

> —Rabbi David Hartman, founder and director of the Shalom Hartman Institute for Advanced Jewish Studies in Jerusalem, quoted in "Why Israel Needs a Gentle Intifada Victory," *Time*, July 24, 1989

Look at this! This is not an instrument of protest, this is an instrument of murder. . . . The veneer of civilization is very thin.

> —Rabbi David Hartman, who was riding in a taxi in Jerusalem when a chunk of Jerusalem stone the size of an avocado, heavy and jagged, hit him in the face, quoted in *Time*, July 23, 1990 (He keeps the stone on the windowsill in his office.)

The Intifada is the only war Israel has waged in which total victory could mean defeat . . . Israel's choice is not between tranquility and letting the Intifada stabilize at a certain level, but between "Intifada-type" violence and unrestrained terrorism.

> —Ehud Ya'ari, Israeli journalist, *Jerusalem Report*, April 2, 1992

The Middle East memory bank is empty again. It goes belly up every time Israel gets rough with its enemies. When this happens, the world is born yesterday, or tomorrow.

> —Sidney Zion, journalist, *Trust Your Mother but Cut the Cards* (1993)

❖ ISRAEL ❖

(see also Zionism)

If our cause is wholly just and righteous, we are bound to find just and righteous and peaceful means of conciliation. We shall ally ourselves with the best of our Arab fellows, to cure what is diseased in us and in them. Arukat bat-ammi and also Arukat ha-goyim — the healing of my people and the healing of the nations.

> —Henrietta Szold, founder of Hadassah, speaking in 1922, quoted in *Henrietta Szold: Record of a Life* by Rose Zeitlin (1952)

I went to Palestine in 1947. In order to get a visa, I had to get false papers. An orthodox friend helped, with the approval of her mother who said, "To go to Eretz Yisrael, you could lie." I arrived in Haifa Harbor on an unconverted troop ship. When we sighted land, we all gathered on the deck and sang Hatikvah [Zionist anthem]. It was a moment. . . . I worked as a cook on a kibbutz. I learned to throw a grenade, to shoot a rifle, to crawl along the ground in order to deliver messages. I took part in creating a state. It remains for me the thing that reaches into my soul most.

> —Yocheved Muffs, Jewish communal professional involved in education, Zionism, interfaith understanding, Holocaust studies, and civil rights, from a conversation, 1998

In Tel-Aviv in May 1948 — Jerusalem was then under siege and isolated — as I pondered the dangers of an independence declaration and the odds against us, I recalled the men and women of London during the blitz. And I said to myself: "I have seen what a people is capable of achieving in the hour of supreme trial. I have seen their spirit touched by nobility. This is what man can do. This is what the Jewish people can do."

> —David Ben-Gurion, Israel's first prime minister, from a series of talks with Moshe Pearlman, *Ben-Gurion Looks Back* (1965)

I had read my [George] Washington . . . What struck me so deeply was the nature of Washington's army — they were underfed, under-armed, with no proper clothing and meager transport. They could have been called a rabble. Yet, they had the stronger will — and they were victorious. I don't say there is not a limit to the odds that can be faced and overcome. I do say however, that the will of the people and the spirit and morale of its army are immeasurably powerful factors in war and can be decisive.

> —David Ben-Gurion, from a series of talks with Moshe Pearlman, as he recalls anticipating war as Israel announced statehood, *Ben-Gurion Looks Back* (1965)

Israel is the crudest and hardest place one can live today. It is also a place where one hears the young sing at night, and even the old ones talk about the future.

> —Cornell Capa, author and photographer, 1948, *Israel: The Reality* (1969)

Never in history have blockade and peace existed side by side. From May 24 onward, the question of who started the war or who fired the first shot became momentously irrelevant. There is no difference in civil law between murdering a man by slow strangulation or killing him by a shot in the head.

> —Abba Eban, Israeli ambassador to the United Nations, commenting on Egypt's decision to create a blockade, speech to the U.N. General Assembly, June 19, 1967, immediately after the end of the Six-Day War

We discussed a good deal about whether Nasser really wanted to do what he did, whether he was eagerly seeking a way out of the dilemma that he himself had created . . . I'm not an expert on Nasser's unconscious mind and from the point of view of a legal system, it doesn't really make a difference. The legal system operates . . . on the assumption that people intend the natural consequences of what they do. . . . These events occurred, we saw them occur, they had certain legal consequences, political consequences, military consequences, and we put together a program for responding to them as best we could.

> —Eugene V. Rostow, fellow at the U.S. Institute of Peace who was undersecretary of state for political affairs in 1967, speaking in 1992 at a conference on the 25th anniversary of the war, quoted in *The Six-Day War: A Retrospective*, edited by Richard B. Parker (1996)

The Jewish people have never in its history passed through an hour of such danger. It's entire existence is gravely threatened. The people of Israel have the privilege to give their lives to preserve the very existence of the nation. The best that we in America can do is to support them with our money. This day is our great opportunity, one that may never repeat itself, to help save Klal Yisrael [the people of Israel].

> —Saul H. Lieberman, professor of Talmud, issuing a statement announcing his personal donation to the Israel Emergency Fund, June 1967, quoted in *American Jewish Year Book 1968*

There is an allegation that in 1967 Israel was ready for war . . . that Israel had "laid a trap" for Nasser . . . and the whole thing was premeditated by Israel. . . . Anybody who was in Israel at the time . . . knows Israel was caught unprepared. There was a deep sense of crisis in Israeli society and a deep confusion at the top. There were clashes between generals and ministers, a feeling of sudden emergency. The Israelis didn't know which fire to put out first. . . . The premeditated conspiracy version is simply wrong.

> —Shimon Shamir, fellow at the U.S. Institute of Peace who was an officer in Israeli military intelligence in 1967, speaking at a 1992 conference on the 25th anniversary of the war, quoted in *The Six-Day War: A Retrospective*, edited by Richard B. Parker (1996)

The Six-Day War had made an indelible impression on me as it did on most Soviet Jews, for, in addition to fighting for her life, Israel was defending our dignity. . . . A basic eternal truth was returning to the Jews of Russia—that personal freedom wasn't something you could achieve through assimilation. It was available only by reclaiming your historical roots.

> —Natan Sharansky, former refusenik, *Fear No Evil* (1988)

I think it must have been this way for many of my generation, that the Israeli-Arab collision was a moment of truth. For the first time in my grown-up life, I really understood what an enemy was. For the first time, I knew what it was to be us against the killers. . . . Two weeks ago, Israel was they; now Israel is we. . . . I have lost the purity of the untested.

> —Nancy Weber, author, "The Truth of Tears," *The Village Voice*, June 15, 1967

The Temple Mount is in our hands. Repeat. The Temple Mount is ours.

> —Mordechai Gur, command of the parachute brigade capturing Jerusalem's Old City in the Six-Day War, quoted in his obituary, *Jerusalem Post*, July 21, 1995

I was walking down the street listening to a transistor radio when I first heard that the Israelis, the Jews, had reached the Wailing Wall . . . No one was watching me, but I wept anyway. Sometimes even the tear-glands know more than the mind.

> —Nancy Weber, "The Truth of Tears," *The Village Voice*, June 15, 1967

The paratroopers, who conquered the Western Wall, leaned on its stones and wept, and as a symbol this was a rare occasion, almost unparalled in human history. Such phrases and cliches are not generally used in our Army but this scene on the Temple Mount beyond the power of verbal description revealed as though by a lightning flash deep truths.

> —Yitzhak Rabin, chief of staff of the Israel Defense Forces, accepting an honorary doctorate from the Hebrew University, June 28, 1967, reprinted in *The Arab-Israeli Reader*, edited by Walter Z. Laqueur (1969)

I know that even the terrible price which our enemies paid touched the hearts of many of our men. It may be that the Jewish people never learned and never accustomed itself to feel the triumph of conquest and victory and therefore we receive it with mixed feelings.

> —Yitzhak Rabin, accepting an honorary doctorate from the Hebrew University, June 28, 1967, reprinted in *The Arab-Israeli Reader*, edited by Walter Z. Lacquer (1969)

The suggestion that everything goes back to where it was before the 5th of June is totally unacceptable . . . It is a fact of technology that it is easier to fly to the moon that to reconstruct a broken egg.

—Abba Eban, Israeli foreign minister and ambassador to the United Nations, speaking to the U.N. General Assembly, June 19, 1967

The Arab states can no longer be permitted to recognize Israel's existence only for the purpose of plotting its elimination.

—Abba Eban, speaking to the U.N. General Assembly, June 19, 1967

Zionism's dream, the "ingathering of the exiles," has been achieved, though in an ironic form; it is the Arab exiles who are back.

—I. F. Stone, *The New York Review of Books*, August 3, 1967

While Divine promise gives us a right to the Land of Israel, it does not inhibit us from a partial exercise of that right in the name of higher ends, such as peace and the preservation of our unique and particular peoplehood.

—Abba Eban, "Two Years Later," *Jerusalem Post Magazine*, June 6, 1969

Who can forget those days before the Six-Day War when every free-world capital saw massive rallies in support of Israel? From London to Warsaw the common man supported Israel in its fight to live. Even the leftists backed Israel, although one can only feel that the left would have rather avoided the subject entirely. But Israel's victory lost her any left-wing support she had . . .

—M. J. Rosenberg, journalist, "To Uncle Tom and Other Jews," *The Village Voice*, February 13, 1969, reprinted in *Jewish Radicalism: An Anthology*, edited by Jack Nusan Porter and Peter Dreier (1973)

I've worked hard for you and I've never asked anything for myself. But I'm asking you now. Please send the Israelis what they need. You can't let them be destroyed.

—Max M. Fisher, business executive and philanthropist, from a letter to President Richard Nixon, October 9, 1973, during the first days of the Yom Kippur War, quoted in *Quiet Diplomat: A Biography of Max M. Fisher* by Peter Golden (1992)

Those Arabs who dwell and who dwelt for years in Eretz Yisroel are indeed part of the Arab people or nation and we respect and recognize that definition. But they are not "Palestinians," for there never was such a concept. . . . As individuals who arrived and lived in the Land of Israel while there was no Jewish state, they are free to live and prosper. Under claim of national right, they are entitled to nothing.

—Rabbi Meir Kahane, founder of the Jewish Defense League, *Our Challenge* (1974)

The guiding principle behind the attitude of the Arabs in 1936 and 1937, however, was exactly what it has been ever since: Decisions are made not on the basis of what is good for them, but on the basis of what is bad for us.

> —Golda Meir, recalling the Arab rejection of the recommendation of the Peel Commission to partition Palestine into two states, *My Life* (1975)

Both as a spectacle and as a political event, Sadat's astonishing voyage to Jerusalem and his address to the Knesset stand out as one of the climactic experiences of this generation.

> —Abba Eban, former foreign minister and Israeli ambassador to the United Nations, *New Diplomacy: International Affairs in the Modern Age* (1983)

The balance of my world was about to change. I suspended disbelief.

> —Ernest W. Michel, executive director of UJA-Federation of New York, watching television as President Anwar Sadat of Egypt was about to arrive in Jerusalem from Cairo, November 19 1977, *Promises to Keep* (1993)

The rhetoric and literature of rejection would live on elsewhere, but in November 1977 it lost its dogmatic force and could no longer claim to be the only normative Arab doctrine. On the same day Israelis came to look upon peace not as a utopian fantasy, but as a concrete and vivid reality.

> —Abba Eban, *The New Diplomacy: International Affairs in the Modern Age* (1983)

My sense of solitariness stemmed from the secretive nature of my role as special counsel. My effectiveness depended on my keeping out of the headlines. Together with Bob Lipshutz [counsel to President Carter], I had fashioned an informal and unpublicized back-door channel connecting the White House and the Kirya, Israeli government compound. Both sides claimed it had been invaluable in furthering the peace process. But, irony of ironies, no one knew about it beyond the inner circles in each capital.

> —Leon H. Charney, New York lawyer who was instrumental in negotiating the 1979 Camp David peace treaty between Israel and Egypt, *Special Counsel* (1983)

We must never forsake that vision, that human dream, that unshakable faith.

> —Menachem Begin, prime minister of Israel, as Israel and Egypt signed the Camp David accord on the White House lawn, March 26, 1979

There is now an element of criticism in the American Jewish attitude towards Israel. It's no longer "Israel right or wrong" perhaps because we are not as right as we used to be, perhaps because the leaders no longer excite the same unquestioned fidelity as the original leaders of the Ben-Gurion era. I think that is a favorable development. I've written and spoken against the idea that we should deny the legitimacy of dissent on the grounds that "the goyim might be listening." If they do listen, I think they are likely to have respect for the new pluralism and diversity of expression. Under these circumstances, when we do show solidarity it will have more meaning.

—Abba Eban, member of Knesset, *Moment*, June 1980

Middle East politics would be a lot less confusing and agonizing if anti-Zionism and anti-Semitism were, as so many want to believe, entirely separate issues. Which is to say that things would be a lot simpler if the Israelis weren't Jews.

—Ellen Willis, author, *Beginning to See the Light: Pieces of a Decade* (1981)

What makes Beirut such a wild and crazy and absurd place to live is not that people get killed. It's that they get killed playing tennis or they get killed taking their kids to school or they get killed playing golf.... Life was always secure enough for you to go about your day but never secure enough for you to be sure that day wouldn't be your last.

—Thomas L. Friedman, former *New York Times* bureau chief in Beirut and Jerusalem and author, *Booknotes* interview with Brian Lamb, C-SPAN, September 19, 1989

We played at a field hospital near Beirut, and that was very moving. Sure, there was shelling all around us, but I felt no fear. Somehow, when you're with Israelis, you feel immortal.

—George Segal, actor, recalling entertaining the Israeli troops during the 1982 war in Lebanon, quoted in *Lifestyles*, New Year 1996

Goyim kill goyim, and they immediately come to hang the Jews.

—Menachem Begin, prime minister of Israel, after the 1982 massacre in the Palestinian refugee camps of Sabra and Shatilla, carried out by Lebanese forces with some Israeli soldiers stationed nearby, quoted in *Speaking Freely* by Nat Hentoff (1997)

[One] should think more carefully about Menachem Begin. How he came to be what he is. And who is responsible for that. This man, who sounds like vinegar, and is accused of execrably bad taste for talking about "goyim killing goyim" ... The Begin government's share of the responsibility for the deaths being clear, nonetheless it is interesting that everyone did come to hang the Jews while worldwide indignation was still fresh and ferocious after the massacre. But for a significant period of time, hardly any attention was paid to the actual killers, the Christians, the followers of the Prince of Peace among the Lebanese forces. But I'm sure this did not surprise Mr. Begin.

> —Nat Hentoff, journalist and author, reflecting on the aftermath of the massacres in Sabra and Shatila, *The Village Voice*, October 1982, *Speaking Freely* (1997)

So, after a lifetime of fighting for a place where Jews will be free from the goyim and their murderous craziness. . . . Menachem Begin looks out the window of his home and sees Jewish pickets calling him a murderer in Lebanon. Some of them have backgrounds much like his, but they came out different. Fear of the treacherous goyim did not freeze them, as it had Begin. But they—and we—should see Menachem Begin, and remember him, as a prisoner of those eternal goyim. Because not for a moment has he been free of them in his head. And they finally brought him down.

> —Nat Hentoff, *Speaking Freely* (1997)

You think in the Diaspora it's normal? Come live here. [Israel] is the homeland of Jewish abnormality. Worse: now we are the dependent Jews, on your money, your lobby, on our big allowance from Uncle Sam, while you are the Jews living interesting lives, comfortable lives, without apology, without shame, and perfectly independent. . . . We are the excitable, ghettoized, jittery little Jews of the Diaspora, and you are the Jews with all the confidence and cultivation that comes of feeling at home where you are.

> —Philip Roth, novelist, *The Counterlife* (voice of the character Shuki Elchanan) (1986)

Anybody who goes to Israel, aside from all the memorials and the plaques, should see Israel the way Israelis see Israel. We don't go to Masada every day. We don't go to Yad Vashem. We face low income neighborhoods. Development towns. Battered women. Go and see the day-to-day life in order to wake up and see that the State of Israel is not a dream anymore but a reality like any other.

> —Avrum Burg, Israeli political scientist, interview in *New Traditions 3*, Summer 1986

We believe that the forces for peace that are at work in Israel are not naive, unsophisticated parties that are playing into the hands of our would-be exterminators, but rather that they represent the individuals steeped in Jewish and world history who have learned their lessons well: that no nation can continue to exist based upon the oppression and exploitation of others; that all colonialism in the last analysis finally disappears from the earth, that no nation can thrive by the means of sheer military power and strength.

> —Rabbi Marshall T. Meyer, human rights activist, founder of the Seminario Rabinico Latinoamericano, and spiritual leader of B'nai Jeshurun in New York City, talk at peace rally in New York City, April 24, 1988

I thought long and hard before deciding to enter politics. It was the quality and the ideals of the younger Knesset generation that decided it for me. In five or ten years, you'll see this new generation getting startling results.

> —Benjamin Netanyahu, Israel's United Nations ambassador, deciding to leave his post in order to enter electoral politics with the Likud party, "The Right Stuff, Israeli Style," *Hadassah*, November 1988

Israel knows it must cope with the PLO. Before it does so, however, it wants to know with which PLO: the one in Arabic or in English. It could mean the difference between life and death.

> —Editorial, *The Jewish Week*, May 9, 1989

Perhaps he [U.S. Secretary of State James Baker] really wanted peace for the Middle East and for Israel, but what he wanted more was to bring it off.

> —Moshe Arens, Israeli foreign minister, *Broken Covenant: American Foreign Policy and the Crisis between the United States and Israel* (1989)

We need no urging to make peace. We pay for the absence of peace the highest price of all—the lives of our sons.

> —Moshe Arens, quoted in the *New York City Tribune*, May 23, 1989

The man has absolutely no political glitz at all, none. Americans, non-Jews and Jew, like Israeli leaders to be a little romantic.

> —A. M. Rosenthal, columnist, referring to Prime Minister of Israel Yitzhak Shamir, *The New York Times*, August 18, 1989

There is a basic imbalance in the relationship between Israelis and American Jews. . . . Deeply committed American Jews spend the better part of their working and/or leisure hours thinking about, working on behalf of, and worrying about the State of Israel. Few Israelis spend more than a few minutes a year worrying about the future of American Jews.

> —Joyce R. Starr, author, *Kissing Through Glass* (1990)

It is irrelevant whether we like or don't like Israelis. The point is, it's Israel that we like, we love, we care about, and want to support.

—Sara Tobin, an American who lived in Israel for seven years, quoted in *Kissing Through Glass* by Joyce R. Starr (1990)

We are not here only to play the role of the heroes and to fight and to get our children killed just so someone can walk on Independence Day in New York with his chest full of air. This is not what we see as our role in this relationship.

—Shmuel Ben-Tovim of the Israel Forum, quoted in *Kissing Through Glass* by Joyce R. Starr (1990)

In Jerusalem, this is the time of the shtarkers [tough guys].

—William Safire, columnist, discussing the prospect of Likud's Yitzhak Shamir forming a government of the right, *The New York Times*, June 11, 1990

Sadat's trip to Israel, in November 1977, was as amazing as a visit from Mars. . . . For the rest of his life, Sadat kept his word; and, in death, that word became his legacy. Because of it, Israel is no longer surrounded by enemies. Because of it, Israelis can dare hope that peace is possible.

—Ze'ev Chafets, Israeli journalist, reflecting on the 10th anniversary of the Sadat assassination in Cairo, *Jerusalem Report*, October 10, 1991

I find it inconceivable that in a situation where there are disagreements between Israel, the only democracy in the Middle East, and the surrounding states with totalitarian governments that have attacked Israel time and again, the United States will be completely neutral. Between Israel and Syria, how can the United States take a neutral position?

—Moshe Arens, Israeli minister of defense, quoted in *Jerusalem Report*, December 19, 1991

The United States' national interest and Israel's are not identical; therefore Israel need not let Washington set policy for it. But it is quite another thing for the prime minister [Shamir], defending Israel's all-out settlement campaign, to say that he will not be intimidated by opposition from gentiles. This denigration . . . dismisses the extraordinary, ongoing American support for Israel with the implication that, deep down, America is a bunch of goyim who have no concern for Jews.

—Rabbi Irving Greenberg, author, scholar, and founder of National Jewish Center for Learning and Leadership, (CLAL), "A Decent Respect," *Jerusalem Report*, Feb, 27, 1992

To think of all Palestinians as terrorists is as logical as equating all Jews with the Jewish Defense League. To understand Palestinians, we first have to speak with them, learn about their hopes and fears.

> —Albert Vorspan and Rabbi David Saperstein, leaders in the Reform movement, *Tough Choices: Jewish Perspectives on Social Justice* (1992)

I have probably engendered as much animosity on the Arab side as on the Israeli side because I don't work on the basis of sentiment—theirs or mine. What matters to me is, can you construct a process in which interests can be mediated?

> —Daniel Kurtzer, deputy assistant secretary of state, one of the Bush Administration's top Mideast policy advisors, quoted in *Newsweek*, June 1, 1992

In America they check your bags when you go out of a store. In Israel, they check when you go in.

> —Shoshana Hyman, twenty-four-year-old teacher from Brooklyn, recalling the different mindset of life in Israel, "Ticket to a Jewish Future," *Hadassah*, August/September 1992

One thing is clear: Since it is a consequence of the Arab war against Israel, the occupation by Israel of this territory could not retroactively be its cause.

> —Ruth R. Wisse, professor of Yiddish and comparative literature, "Fatal Naïveté" *Jerusalem Report*, April 22, 1993

I don't deny that I was more optimistic about rapid progress when I first took office. But I repeat: The Arab countries and Israel have passed the point of no return in making peace.

> —Yitzhak Rabin, Israeli prime minister, quoted in *Jerusalem Report*, July 15, 1993

The fact that Rabin and Peres are ready to make concessions to the PLO is not evidence that the PLO has changed—it is merely evidence that Labor and its leftwing allies have been working overtime to condition the Israeli public to the idea that the PLO must eventually be accepted and given a state. Slowly but surely, over the course of Labor's first year in power, they broke down the taboos.

> —Dr. Irving Moskowitz, member of the Board of Governors of America for a Safe Israel, commenting on the Oslo Accords, quoted in the *Stamford Jewish Ledger*, September 3, 1993

I did not boycott the event but went to the White House. The Israelis had been the principal victims of PLO terrorism, so it was enough for me that Peres and Rabin shook Arafat's hand. Realpolitik is sometimes a little too real for me.

—Arlen Specter, U.S. Senator (R-Pa.), commenting on the 1993 ceremony on the White House lawn at which Rabin and Peres each shook Arafat's hand, *Middle East Quarterly*, March 1997

Describing the Israeli-Palestinian conflict as a tragic clash between right and right, I maintain that we do not want a Shakespearean conclusion, with poetic justice hovering over a stage littered with dead bodies. We may now be nearing a typical Chekhovian conclusion for the tragedy: the players disillusioned and worried, but alive.

—Amos Oz, Israeli novelist, essayist, and peace activist, "To Prevail Over Our Past," *Time*, September 20, 1993

The awarding of the Nobel Peace Prize to Yasir Arafat—who more than anyone else alive contributed to the spread of international terrorism, . . . is without question the lowest point in the history of the prize, and one which vitiates it of any moral worth.

—Benjamin Netanyahu, Israeli political leader (Likud), *Fighting Terrorism: How Democracies Can Defeat Domestic and International Terrorism* (1995)

It is difficult for many outside of Israel to accept the failings built into the Oslo Accords, especially since so many hopes for peace have been vested in these agreements.

—Benjamin Netanyahu, *Fighting Terrorism: How Democracies Can Defeat Domestic and International Terrorism* (1995)

Sarah sought to keep Issac and Ishamel apart. She failed. The descendants of Isaac and Ishamel are destined to dwell together in one small part of the world.

—Rabbi Samuel Z. Glaser, rabbi emeritus of the Elmont Jewish Center on Long Island and professor of psychology, excerpt from sermon, 1993

As a Jew and an Israeli, as a man and as a human being, I am humiliated by the shame brought upon us by this lowly killer.

—Yitzhak Rabin, Israeli prime minister, speaking to the Knesset after the 1994 massacre of Palestinians by Baruch Goldstein at the Tomb of Abraham in Hebron, quoted in the *Chicago Tribune*, November 6, 1995

If Israel can bring itself to recognize the PLO, it can certainly recognize Reform Judaism.

—Rabbi Ammiel Hirsch, executive director of the Association of Reform Zionists of America, quoted in *Jerusalem Report*, April 20, 1995

If the Reform movement wants to raise $2 million, it might consider whether the money would be more effectively spent on encouraging aliyah [emigration to Israel], on schools, or on other outreach efforts presenting a spiritual alternative to Orthodoxy. But then, it's so much more fun to fight for the rights of a minority that hardly exists—especially when you can do it long distance.

—Gershom Gorenberg, Israeli journalist, discussing the Reform movement campaign to raise $2 million to fight for religious equality in Israel, *Jerusalem Report*, April 20, 1995

For the rest of the world, the "Hebron massacre" means Purim 1994. But for Jews here it means 1929. In a city consecrated to the graves of ancient ancestors, the dead of 1929 are virtual contemporaries. Hebron's Jews see their own relentless militancy as a response not only to current Arab terrorism but also to 1929—as though, having brutalized the passive Jews who once lived among them, Hebron's Arabs have now gotten the Jews they deserve.

—Yossi Klein Halevi, Israeli journalist, recalling the sixty-seven unarmed Hebron Jews murdered by local Arabs in 1929, destroying the centuries-old Jewish community, "Side by Side in Hatred," *Jerusalem Report*, June 15, 1995

I didn't come to Efrat like a thief in the night. It was Yitzhak Rabin who came [to Lincoln Square Synagogue in New York City] in 1981 and said everyone should leave and go to Efrat.

—Rabbi Shlomo Riskin, founder of yeshiva in Efrat, Israel, and founding rabbi of Lincoln Square Synagogue in New York City, at a press conference responding to whether Efrat is a "disputed" territory, July 14, 1995, quoted in *The Jewish Week*, July 20, 1995

I consider these efforts an attempt to tear the nation apart.

—Yitzhak Rabin, Israeli prime minister, criticizing an ongoing settler campaign against the extension of Palestinian self-rule in the West Bank, quoted in *Jewish Telegraphic Agency*, August 3, 1995

I don't understand American Jews. They want to sit in Brooklyn and defend Hebron and Shechem from there?

—Shimon Peres, Israeli foreign minister, at news conference, referring to demonstrations in New York expressing solidarity with protesting Israeli settlers, quoted in *Jewish Telegraphic Agency*, August 4, 1995

Please take a good hard look. The sight you see before you at this moment was impossible, was unthinkable just two years ago. Only poets dreamed of it, and to our great pain, soldiers and civilians went to their death to make this moment possible.

> —Yitzhak Rabin, Israeli prime minister, at the White House for the signing of the second key Israel-PLO (Oslo II) Accord instituting Israeli withdrawal and Palestinian self-government on the West Bank, quoted in *The New York Times*, September 29, 1995

Abandoning these places is treason and murder and the [Israeli] government is committing treason and murdering.

> —Rabbi Moshe Levinger, founder of the Jewish settlement in Hebron, quoted in *The New York Times*, September 29, 1995

The Israelis and Palestinians are so closely intertwined in such a small area that after the divorce, they will still wake up every day in the same bed. . . . Let us hope they can continue to confound the skeptics.

> —Mortimer B. Zuckerman, editor-in-chief, editorial, *U.S. News & World Report*, October 9, 1995

Jerusalem is an operation left open. It never healed. There are a lot of infections; strange doctors get involved that shouldn't.

> —Yehuda Amichai, Israeli poet, quoted in "The Holy City's Non-Prophet Poet," *The Washington Post*, October 25, 1995

We can barter craziness. I give up a little craziness. You give up a little craziness.

> —Yehuda Amichai, reflecting on the peace process, quoted in "The Holy City's Non-Prophet Poet," *The Washington Post*, October 25, 1995

Look how God works . . . the government wanted to withdraw from Hebron? So something happens like the Purim event in the makhpelah [Tomb of the Patriarchs] and thousands of Jewish soldiers are forced to come here. You see? Even if they want to, they can't give up our father's grave.

> —Dr. Ya'akov Ben-Taria, who moved to Hebron after Baruch Goldstein's death left Hebron's five hundred Jews without a doctor, speaking of plans for Israeli withdrawal from Hebron in "Side by Side in Hatred" by Yossi Klein Halevi, *Jerusalem Report*, June 15, 1995

People are outraged? What can I do? We're not in the business of satisfying everybody.

> —Shimon Peres, Israeli foreign minister, in an interview with American Jewish

media, on the signing of the Israeli-Palestinian (Oslo II) accords, quoted in
The Jewish Week, October 6, 1995

You are the only Jews whom it is permissible to loathe and revile without being accused of anti-Semitism.

—Jerold H. Auerbach, professor of history, "An Open Letter to the Jews of Hebron," *The Jewish Advocate,* October 27, 1995

The day is coming when your government will decide that the new Middle East requires your expulsion from Hebron. . . . When that happens, if not sooner, Israel will have traded its biblical birthright for a mess of post-Zionist pottage.

—Jerold S. Auerbach, "An Open Letter to the Jews of Hebron," *The Jewish Advocate,* October 27, 1995

We must not distort history by pretending that the present peace is the source of terrorism and insecurity. There is no blueprint for absolute security.

—Rabbi David Hartman, founder and director of the Shalom Hartman Institute for Advanced Jewish Studies in Jerusalem, quoted in *The Jewish Week,* November 3, 1995

I lost a child in the Lebanese war, a beautiful son-in-law, a pilot, a human being of great integrity who taught me about the futility of trying to solve our conflict with the Palestinians by bombing them into submission.

—Rabbi David Hartman, quoted in *The Jewish Week,* November 3, 1995

Meanwhile, the Rabin government . . . is at least destroying one important pillar of anti-Semitism—the belief that all Jews are smart.

—A. M. Rosenthal, columnist and former editor of *The New York Times,* quoted in *Lifestyles,* Pre-Spring 1996

A Jew who can have a pizza delivered via a cellular phone is not a Jew with a lost identity. That is a Jew who is free.

—Rabbi Ben Kamin, senior rabbi, Temple-Tifereth Israel in Cleveland, responding to a *New York Times* column on Israel's emerging and opulent culture, letter to the editor, *The New York Times,* November 2, 1995

As you travel over the vast expanses of this [American] continent, it is very difficult to understand the intensity of feeling and investment over very small pieces of land. . . . In the conflict between Israelis and Arabs you have wounded civilizations—the Arabs have been wounded in their dealings with the West, and an insecure Jewish people have gone through terrible disasters and traumas.

There is no end to the Jewish quest for security and there is no end for the Arab quest for redress and dignity. It is very difficult to reconcile the two.

> —Itamar Rabinovich, Israeli ambassador to the United States, quoted in "In the Eye of the Hurricane" by Felipe Serra, *Lifestyles,* New Year 1996 (written before the assassination of Prime Minister Yitzhak Rabin in November 1995)

Every so often, I meet an Israeli who tells me that he is not a supporter of this [Israeli] government and its policies and then adds something like, "But please finish the negotiations before my son is drafted."

> —Itamar Rabinovich, Israeli ambassador to the United States, 1995 interview, *Lifestyles,* New Year 1996

Nearly five years remain till the end of the century. The [Oslo] peace process with Syria, Lebanon, and the Palestinians will need all five years. . . . We will not embark on a religious and fraternal war. Yes, we will debate; yes, we will stand our ground, but this will be done as a civilized nation, whose future is before it. We have the power in these five years to make Israel a normal state and—despite all the cynicism—to really make it a light unto the nations and a great hope.

> —Shimon Peres, Israeli prime minister, speaking at a special session of the Labor party's central committee in the aftermath of the Rabin assassination, quoted in the *Jerusalem Post,* November 14, 1995

Since that time, political discourse in Israel has been infused with a kind of mysticism increasingly subversive of tolerance, compromise, and the culture of democracy itself.

> —Mark A. Heller, columnist and senior research associate at the Jaffe Center for Strategic Studies, Tel Aviv, recalling the Six-Day War, *Jerusalem Post,* November 17, 1995

Essentially, the settlement . . . creates a Palestinian state de facto but not de jure leaving policy makers with the conundrum of having to deal with a state that's not a state, a government that's not a government, situated in a capital that's not a capital, ruled by a president who is not a president and populated in part by pockets of Jewish settlers who, as Israelis, use the services of embassies in Tel Aviv. Or as one Western diplomat put it to me recently: "What a bloody mess."

> —Hirsh Goodman, Israeli journalist, "One Embassy Down, One to Go," *Jerusalem Report,* November 16, 1995

In calling Israel's strategic withdrawal a "peace process," the Labor government had tried to camouflage the harsh political realities of decisions it believes its citizens would not otherwise accept. Like the leader who promises bread to a land of famine, or water to a people in the desert, politicians who promise Israelis peace are appealing to a craving so great that it can sweep reasoned doubt away.

> —Ruth R. Wisse, professor of Yiddish and comparative literature, "Making War With the Word 'Peace,'" *The Weekly Standard*, November 20, 1995

Judaism cannot save Israel. Judaism can save only Judaism, and the souls of believing Jews. Israel will have to save Israel; and it can begin by recoiling from all forms of the sacralization of politics, right and left, and affirming, for the sake of the Jewish state and the Jewish religion, a stringent separation of synagogue and state, and warning the God-intoxicated radicals in its midst that their dangerous drunkenness will have to give way before the values of democracy and the requirements of law.

> —Leon Wieseltier, literary editor of *The New Republic*, letter to the editor, *The New York Times*, November 23, 1995

All Israelis see when they talk of American olim [immigrants to Israel] are Kahane Chai and Baruch Goldstein.

> —Avraham Burg, representative of the Jewish Agency, speaking to a forum at the General Assembly of the Council of Jewish Federations in Boston, quoted in the *Jerusalem Post*, November 17, 1995

The question cannot be who wants peace; the question is who is mature enough and sensible enough and practical enough and tough enough to translate the dreamy desire into a plan, a program, a practice.

> —Leonard Fein, columnist, *Forward*, December 8, 1995

It is given that Shimon Peres is a clever man. But unlike Mark Anthony's famous eulogy at Caesar's burial, it cannot be said of Peres that he is an "honorable man." Like Caesar, Peres wants to remain in power, but here the similarity ends. Caesar was a proud and loyal Roman. He knew, loved, and admired his people and their culture. Peres has not such pride in being a Jew, nor admiration for his Jewish people or their heritage. He is neither a believer in Judaism, nor does he share in the belief of the Jewish prophets as to his people's ordained destiny.

> —Ruth Matar, chairwoman of Women in Green, "Is Peres an Honorable Man?" *The Jewish Press*, April 19, 1996

Beyond defense, the so-called West Bank is the heart of Israel, it's the Bible. Again, a picture is worth a thousand years, three thousand years. Check yesterday's *New York Times*. On Page One, Arafat and Clinton. On Page Three, an old Jew lying on the ground of a Hebron market with a Palestinian knife in his back. A Jew can't live in Hebron, this is the message of Shimon Peres, who kvells over Arafat in the Oval Office and dares not say kaddish over this old Jew in Hebron.

> —Sidney Zion, journalist, *New York Daily News*, May 3, 1996

The very idea that Shimon Peres is now Israel's Prime Minister makes the free world quiver with anxiety and makes Israelis tremulous.

> —Toby Willig, Zionist activist, letter to the editor, *The Jewish Press*, May 24, 1996

In less than 75 years, Israel went from galut to galut [exile to exile]. This is why Israelis are now suing for peace with those committed to their destruction. They couldn't bear the looks they were getting from the outside world, and had to look for a baron to protect them from the hands of the mighty.

> —Midge Decter, author, speaking on panel discussing "What Went Wrong" at an International Zionist Convention organized by Americans for a Safe Israel, quoted in *The Jewish Voice*, May 1996

In 1964, when the Jews did not have the Old City, the PLO didn't want it. In 1968, we had just gotten it back. Now they want to take Jerusalem from us, because we have it. PLO nationalism, which should be taken seriously, wants to replace Zionism. We cannot go on without Jerusalem which is the way they want it.

> —Emil L. Fackenheim, philosopher and Holocaust survivor, speaking at an International Zionist Convention organized by Americans for a Safe Israel, quoted in *The Jewish Voice*, May 1996

We had our Holocaust and our answer is, we are in Jerusalem, witnesses to resurrected hope, and not just for us. Peace will come to Jerusalem if Christians and Moslems come to pray there, not despite the Jewish return, but because of it.

> —Emil L. Fackenheim, speaker at an International Zionist Convention organized by Americans for a Safe Israel, quoted in *The Jewish Voice*, May 1996

Even if Yasser Arafat put on tallit and tefillin, they wouldn't believe him.

> —Avraham Sela, research fellow at Hebrew University's Truman Institute for

the Advancement of Peace, referring to the Israeli right-wingers, quoted in *Jewish Bulletin of Northern California*, May 24, 1996

We're talking generations before we can talk about a new Middle East. . . . It's not like between France and Spain, we have to be prepared for everything.

> —Avraham Sela, research fellow at Hebrew University's Truman Institute for the Advancement of Peace, quoted in *Jewish Bulletin of Northern California*, May 24, 1996

Benjamin Netanyahu's ideology is not extreme nationalism. It is extreme skepticism. He will negotiate but not on the thin threads of hope.

> —Charles Krauthammer, columnist, quoted in *The Jewish Press*, May 24, 1996

I thank God for the privilege of living at a time when I can travel to Jerusalem, be nourished by her being and drink from the cup of her dreams. Ours is a blessed generation.

> —Marlene Post, national president of Hadassah, quoted in *Long Island Jewish World*, May 17, 1996

The Election of Shimon Peres Will Mean the End of Israel As We Know it.

> —Editorial, *The Jewish Press*, May 24, 1996

Many of our fears are justified; after all, we're not surrounded by the Salvation Army.

> —David Grossman, Israeli author, assessing Prime Minister Benjamin Netanyahu's victory over Peres, "Across the Spectrum," *Time*, June 10, 1996

The greatness of Rabin and Peres was that they said we are strong enough now to be a little weaker, to take a calculated risk.

> —David Grossman, "Across the Spectrum," *Time,* June 10, 1996

What is frightening to me is Peace Now's belief that Jews can live anywhere in the world except in locations of historic and spiritual significance to the Jewish people.

> —Rabbi David Eliezrie, director of the North County Chabad of Yorba Linda, Calif., quoted in *The Jewish Journal of Greater Los Angeles*, June 14, 1996

The Oslo agreements are interim agreements—meant to be gauged as they go along. Israelis had three years to gauge their land-for-peace deal with Arafat. They judged that for three years they gave land and got no peace. Unless the

Palestinians reciprocate their obligations—and their primary obligation is to stop killing Jews—the "peace process" cannot continue.

— Charles Krauthammer, columnist, *New York Daily News*, July 1, 1996

The key difference between Peres and Netanyahu was not about land for peace. It was about whether the Palestinians had to deliver the peace and security they promised in return for the real territory, real authority, real assets that Israel had delivered.

— Charles Krauthammer, *New York Daily News*, July 1, 1996

Israel was not founded to dig tunnels under the Moslem quarter in Jerusalem, or in order to rebuild the Jewish quarter in Hebron. Israel was created in order to enable the Jewish people to exist as a free nation, in harmony and peace with its neighbors and the rest of the world. This goal is now attainable, but there are some among us who are pushing Israel into a new type of war for new goals.

— Amos Oz, Israeli novelist and essayist, "An Unholy War," *The New York Review of Books*, November 14, 1996

... the opening of the tunnel and the current Israeli policy over Hebron represent nationalistic and religious autism rather than legitimate security considerations.

— Amos Oz, "An Unholy War," *The New York Review of Books*, November 14, 1996

Autonomy will lead inevitably to a Palestinian state—de facto even if not formalized. The longer this reality is avoided, the less it can be used to enhance Israel's security.

— Henry A. Kissinger, former U.S. secretary of state, quoted in the *Jerusalem Post*, December 6, 1996

In six months in office, [Prime Minister Netanyahu] has found time to visit the graves of dead rebbes from Brooklyn, but has not managed to find five minutes to meet with Reform and Conservative leadership.

— Rabbi Eric H. Yoffie, president of Reform movement synagogue organization, Union of American Hebrew Congregations, quoted in *The New York Times*, December 15, 1996

I've said that George Bush, without necessarily meaning to be, was the best foreign friend Israel ever had. . . . I get a lot of raised eyebrows with that.

—Edgar M. Bronfman, chairman of The Seagram Company Ltd. and president of the World Jewish Congress, *The Making of a Jew* (1996)

Prime Minister Netanyahu told a joint session of Congress in July that he would like to see it end. That hasn't made my job on the Foreign Operations Subcommittee to keep the aid any easier.

—Arlen Specter, U.S. Senator (R-Pa.), stating his view of U.S. financial aid to Israel, interview, *Middle East Quarterly*, March 1997

In the early years of the state, we delighted in army hymns and parades. We were trying to negate the Holocaust by showing how different we were from Europe's Jews who had supposedly gone like sheep to slaughter. But with each new war, our need to prove our courage has lessened. Not since the Six-Day War have we as people glorified battle; today we sing of war only as tragedy.

—Yossi Klein Halevi, Israeli journalist, *The Jerusalem Report*, March 6, 1997

Of course we have the right to build in Har Homa [in Jerusalem]. I have the right to eat a pint of Haagen-Dazs every morning for breakfast, but that doesn't mean it's sensible to do so. . . . The idea is not to teach them who's boss. The idea is to create a peace for all our children. The sensible and moral implementation of Israel's considerable power continues to be the central dilemma of the Jewish state. A bulldozer can prove as deadly as a tank.

—Stuart Schoffman, Israeli journalist, commenting on the decision of the Israeli government to proceed to build on the site of Har Homa, disputed territory in Jerusalem, *JUF News*, April 1997

Twenty years after Sadat's dramatic flight to Jerusalem—to break what he called the "psychological block"—the block is still there. It weighs heavier than it did in 1977.

—Amos Elon, Israeli journalist and author, *The New York Times Magazine*, May 11, 1997

In other countries, leftist intellectuals often criticize their governments for not doing enough for peace. In Egypt, they accuse it of doing too much.

—Amos Elon, *The New York Times Magazine*, May 11, 1997

Much has been lost through this dangerous policy, but it is not too late to turn it around. May God give Israel's leaders the good sense to get us out of this mess.

—Rabbi Shmuel M. Butman, Lubavitch leader, reacting to the latest developments in implementing the terms of the Oslo II accords, quoted in *The Jewish Press*, June 27, 1997

It is Israel's great misfortune that the people with whom it must somehow live are the Palestinians, so miserably led and so resolutely unable to bring forth a better leadership. . . . But wish it away and will the morrow be host to the Palestinians replaced by, say, Canadians and Belgians? Hardly. The Palestinians are who they are, and making peace with them is not a concession . . . [it is] hard-nosed self-interest.

—Leonard Fein, columnist, *The Jewish Advocate*, August 8, 1997

Who could have believed back in June 1967 that 30 years later Jews would be verbally and physically accosting each other over the right to pray by the Western Wall?

—Joseph R. Rackman, attorney and columnist, *Long Island Jewish World*, September 26, 1997

Israel is far too important to be left to Israelis.

—Rabbi Eric H. Yoffie, leader of the Union of American Hebrew Congregations, Shabbat sermon at the UAHC convention, quoted in the *Baltimore Jewish Times*, November 14, 1997

Some say that the only reason for y'ridah [leaving Israel] is if you are a rabbi going to save lost souls, but I think the reverse has to happen. People from America who are involved in the progressive aspects of the Jewish community need to come here and get Israelis involved. Zionism is not enough to carry this country into the next century.

—Erika Meitner, graduate student in Israel on a fellowship from Dartmouth College who is a member of Women of the Wall (an international organization advocating equal access for women's prayer groups at the Western Wall), quoted in *Lifestyles*, New Year 1998

Those who care about Israel's future must bring the same zeal we brought to building and securing the state to the struggle for assuring that it remains true to its founding vision: the promise of a state based, as stated in the Declaration of Independence, on "freedom, justice and peace . . . that will guarantee freedom of religion and conscience."

—David Arnow, psychologist, past president of New Israel Fund and a vice-president of UJA-Federation of New York, 1998

❖ JEWISH EDUCATION ❖

(see also Education, Jewish Survival)

*W*here, we usually ask these principals, is it written that yeshiva education is reserved for the Harvard bound? Or even the Yeshiva University and Stern [College] bound? Here's a real news flash: Not every Jewish child is academically talented, inclined or motivated at the age of 13. But every Jewish child is entitled to a Jewish education, regardless of past performance. . . . How dare we turn that option into a selection process that only the most academically qualified survive?

> —Editorial, *The Jewish Voice*, May 1966

How ironic. Students were the catalysts who mobilized the American Jewish community to take up the banner of Soviet Jewry. Now Jewish students in what was known as the Soviet Union receive funding, conduct educational seminars, organize on a regional and national basis, send a record number of students to Israel and are in the WUJS (World Union of Jewish Students). American Jewish students and the American Jewish community must look for inspiration to a community whose Jewish identity was ravaged by 70 years of Communist rule. We should be ashamed. What good is raising billions if we cannot produce Jewishly literate students? How dare we bask in the glow of our political power without noticing the exiting shadows of young Jews on the walls of our synagogues, schools, community centers and homes?

> —Yosef I. Abramowitz, journalist, commenting on the neglect by American Jewry of the 360,000 unaffiliated Jewish students on campus, *Moment*, February 1992

In my experience it was a drunken Hebrew school teacher drilling kids to pronounce Hebrew in a Hebrew school nobody wanted to go to so you could take part in a dreadful ceremony called a bar mitzvah to which people came to give you idiot presents that you wanted to retreat from out of sheer embarrassment because you consider them offensive.

> —David Antin, professor of visual arts, "Writing and Exile," *Tikkun*, September/October 1990

He [Rabbi Joseph Soloveitchik, known as the Rav] was a person old in years, but when he walked into that classroom, he was so young in spirit, and when he studied a piece of Talmud [with us] the commentaries came alive, it wasn't like learning that Maimonides lived in the 1200s—you felt as if Maimonides was in the room. What he was able to do in that classroom was remove the shackles of time from the talmudic dialogue.

> —Rabbi Kenneth Brander, congregational rabbi in South Florida, quoted in *Forward,* May 24, 1996

Jewish decision-making and Jewish policy formulation are directly enabled by Jewish learning and the elementary truth is that when adult Jews deeply and seriously study Jewish tradition, the Judaization of our institutions will be axiomatic.

> —Ronald A. Brauner, president of the Foundation for Jewish Studies and professor of Judaic Studies, "Thou Shalt Teach Them Diligently to Thy . . . Self" in *Being Jewish in a Gentile World* (1995)

We are the most Jewishly illiterate generation we've ever had. Let's admit that. We're affluent and successful but Jewishly illiterate.

> —Shoshana S. Cardin, chairman of the United Israel Appeal, speaking at the Council of Jewish Federation's General Assembly, Boston, November 1995

The right yeshiva is a place where there is so much love that it's awesome. God gave us Torah with so much love, so if I want to give over the Torah to my children it has to be done in that same way.

> —Rabbi Shlomo Carlebach, 1993 interview with Michael Lerner, *Tikkun*, 1997

The beauty of a Jewish education is that you learn to argue if you pay attention. . . . Part of my education was in having teachers who had seen too much death to argue for the fun of it.

> —Andrea Dworkin, author and activist, "Israel: Whose Country Is It Anyway?" *Ms.,* September/October 1990

I am convinced that Yeshiva College is of great importance for the preservation of the Jewish tradition and for the deeper spiritualization of the Jewish youth in general. The Jew who has gone through such a school is inwardly so rich, and so firm, that he is able to face the psychic dangers to which he is exposed in a non-Jewish atmosphere. If the majority of the German Jews had been trained in such a manner, one would have found among them today more dignity and less of despair and suicide.

> —Albert Einstein, Nobel Prize-winning theoretical physicist and humanist, speaking at a 1935 Yeshiva University commencement, quoted in *Bernard Revel: Builder of American Jewish Orthodoxy* by Aaron Rothkoff (1972)

Many American Jews went to Hebrew school, after all, and have not entirely recovered. The shuls of their youth were probably full of rote performances and self-righteous struts. They may have fled at bar and bat mitzvah, never to return—and allowed themselves to walk the streets as adults with an adolescent's view of Judaism, something they would never permit in any other remotely important area of life.

> —Arnold Eisen, professor of Jewish thought, *Tikkun*, January/February 1993

Our children know who they are. The first things they learn are blessings over food, not "Mary had a little lamb."

> —Fayge Estulin, who was sent with her husband by the Lubavitcher Rebbe to Los Angeles to work with Jewish immigrants from Russia, quoted in *The Invisible Thread: A Portrait of Jewish American Women* by Diane Bletter (1989)

Growing up, I loved K'tonton, about a Jewish Tom Thumb who would spin on a runaway Chanukah top or ride the back of a bird to an island where the animals would celebrate the holidays with him. It is the "Twilight Zone" approach, such as taking a fantasy subway and getting off in the middle of the Battle of Jericho, that involves a child in great events.

> —Eli N. Evans, author and president of the Charles H. Revson Foundation, *The Lonely Days Were Sundays: Reflections of a Jewish Southerner* (1993)

When we examine Halakha [Jewish law] according to our best ethical understanding, we are not evaluating Torah by secular values. Our ethical principles are also a part of Torah.

> —Tikva Frymer-Kensky, professor of biblical studies, "Toward a Liberal Theory of Halakha," *Tikkun*, July/August 1995

Given the skills contemporary Jewish communities rely on and the practices they hold dear, Hebrew schools should revise their curricula to emphasize fundraising and party-throwing.

—Rabbi Michael Goldberg, author, *Why Should Jews Survive? Looking Past the Holocaust Toward a Jewish Future* (1995)

If you stop your Jewish education before you reach your complete intellectual sophistication, then you will think about your secular issues in a sophisticated way, but you'll analyze Jewish topics immaturely. The only way to pursue a meaningful Jewish life is to keep studying.

—Judith Hauptman, professor of Talmud, quoted in *The Invisible Thread: A Portrait of Jewish American Women* by Diana Bletter (1989)

We should not have to break the bank to save ourselves and our people.

—Samuel C. Heilman, professor of sociology and Jewish studies, commenting on the rising cost of Jewish education, *Stamford Jewish Ledger*, December 10, 1993

I watched my students grow in dignity as they understood that Judaism was not ethnic guilt, the food at Zabar's and the insistence of their grandmothers in Florida that they should not marry out. They saw Judaism, most of them for the first time, as an important, leading element in Western civilization.

—Rabbi Arthur Hertzberg, author and professor, recalling his teaching at Dartmouth College in the religion department, quoted in *The Jewish Week*, July 26, 1996

When we read and study Jewish texts, we are involved in another task as well: an attempt to understand those who came before us. What did the rabbis of the past believe and care about? What did the Jews of the Middle Ages feel as they wrote their poetry and philosophy? What did the Hasidim of the 18th century need to create their own religious path? We can study the Jewish classics in the manner that we read the Greeks, the Romans, the ancient Chinese and that would be fine. Except for us there is something different here too, something beyond an inquiry into history. These, after all, are our predecessors. We trace these works the way we follow the lines on a family tree. It is where we came from. And like a relative one may not know very well we feel a kind of obligation to pause a moment to see who this member of the family really is. In that sense to study these texts is a debt we feel we owe to our ancestors and our collective past.

—Barry W. Holtz, author and professor of education, *Finding Our Way: Jewish Texts and the Lives We Lead Today* (1990)

We don't teach them about Torah, we teach them Torah.

> —Eugene Korn, an administrator at the Shalom Hartman Institute, a think tank of Orthodox, Conservative, Reform and non-Jewish scholars, quoted in *The Jewish Week,* 1996

Ignorance will have done more to "solve the Jewish question" than did the Holocaust.

> —Rabbi Norman Lamm, president of Yeshiva University, *Torah Umadda: The Encounter of Religious Learning and Worldy Knowledge in the Jewish Tradition* (1990)

I am happy to hear that you are now a high school Bible teacher. If so, be careful and do not come in and deliver "sermonettes," rather let the students work on, search through, discover and analyze texts. . . . This teaches students to engage in a close reading and will bring them to love and respect the text of the Bible. May God enlighten your eyes and may you be successful in this holy work.

> —Professor Nehama Leibowitz, noted Israeli Bible scholar, from a letter sent to a former student, Rabbi Nathaniel Helfgot, in 1989, quoted in "Recalling a Master Teacher" by Nathaniel Helfgot, *The Jewish Week,* April 18, 1997

Jewish study is not a solitary endeavor, carried out by a lonely scholar in his cubicle. Once the Torah was brought down from heaven, the attainment of truth has been the responsibility of human beings, teaching and learning from each other.

> —Richard N. Levy, Hillel regional director, *Religious Education,* May/June 1974

I was not in competition with Tifereth Jerusalem or with Torah Voda'ath [referring to two traditional yeshivas] but with Horace Mann and Ethical Culture.

> —Rabbi Joseph H. Lookstein, rabbi of Kehilath Jeshurun, lecturer, and founder of the Ramaz School in New York City, describing his decision in the 1930s to establish Ramaz School as a demonstration of the viability of synthesis between Jewish and American culture, quoted in *New York's Jewish Jews: The Orthodox Community in the Interwar Years* by Jenna Weissman Joselit (1990)

It was the setting for meeting the learned Jewish women of Jerusalem who would be my role models. They provided compelling evidence that the world of traditional sacred learning was not absolutely and inherently masculine. They demonstrated that I could define my religiousness not by just the output of my kitchen or by my daily deeds, but by the activities of my critical intelligence. They stretched the boundaries of my learning and, consequently, the boundaries of my faith.

> —Vanessa Ochs, writer, commenting on studying Jewish texts in Jerusalem, *Words on Fire: One Woman's Journey into the Sacred* (1990)

Jewish educators are the Rodney Dangerfields of our community. . . . We pay them low wages and expect them to provide our offspring with the kind of knowledge of and love of Yiddishkeit that used to be in the purview of parents and grandparents.

> —Gary Rosenblatt, editor and publisher, *The Jewish Week*, July 26, 1996

The truth is that we get what we pay for, and by refusing to deal boldly with the ongoing crisis in the quality and quantity of Jewish education nationwide, we as a community are making a statement, whether we realize it or not.

> —Gary Rosenblatt, *The Jewish Week*, July 26, 1996

It would be a fatal policy for us to neglect the instruction of our girls in a true conception of the tenets of our faith. . . . It is not against the dicta of rabbis to teach religion to girls.

> —Albert Lucas, secretary of the Union of Orthodox Jewish Congregations of America, quoted in the *Hebrew Standard*, June 26, 1903

We ought to admit that with all the babble about Jewish continuity and the flood of cleverly written programs to achieve it, the only thing that really works is education, and not education about secular pursuits with Jewish labels. Bellow, Malamud, Miller, and Roth may be Jewish, but their works will not guarantee that our grandchildren will be Jewish. Nor, with suitable apologies to the prophets of pluralism, will applications of Jewish veneer to essentially non-Jewish pursuits.

> —Nosson Scherman, general editor of Mesorah Publications, "Tapping an Unperceived Need," *Sh'ma*, September 19, 1997

Jewish education is not limited to the classroom by any manner or means. It must penetrate every other room and activity of the temple's life.

> —Rabbi Alexander M. Schindler, president of the Union of American Hebrew Congregations (Reform) speaking at the National Association of Temple Educators Convention, December 26, 1988, cited in *The Jewish Condition: Essays on Contemporary Judaism Honoring Rabbi Alexander M. Schindler* (1996)

For Torah to be perpetuated among the Jewish people, precedence must be given to Jewish women. Giving such prominence to women may appear questionable in view of several traditional attitudes. Those attitudes, however, are narrow and restrictive when judged by the objective standard of Torah law and certainly may be considered so within the context of the application of these standards to contemporary society.

> —Rabbi Menachem Mendel Schneerson, Lubavitcher Rebbe, "A Woman's Place in Torah," *Sichos in English* (1990), quoted in *Judaism: An Anthology of the Key Spiritual Writings of the Jewish Tradition, 3rd edition*, edited and interpreted by Rabbi Arthur Hertzberg (1990)

I cite the statement of the English philosopher John MacMurray: "All thought presupposes knowledge".... Consider this statement within the Jewish context! Who among the Jews finds himself unable to think and to express his thoughts about Jewish affairs despite the absence of knowledge about Jewish matters? How many of us today, subjected to the light touch of Jewish education in this country, if any, have acquired sufficient knowledge to arrive at conclusions and opinions about Jewish life, by the same standards that we apply to other areas of knowledge?

> —Judah J. Shapiro, "The Jewish Community and the Synagogue in Perspective," presented at the annual meeting of the National Conference of Jewish Communal Service held in St. Louis, May 28, 1956, quoted in the *Journal of Jewish Communal Service*, Fall 1956

Jews cannot afford their current ignorance in a period when Judaism and Zionism are vilified as a rationale for murderous anti-Semitism. To cope with the anti-Jewish threats of the present, Jews must know Jewish history and Jewish teaching.

> —Marie Syrkin, author and professor, *Tikkun*, Fall 1986

I contend that the pupils of most supplementary Jewish schools heave a sigh of relief after bar and bat mitzvah and stop attending classes because the present system and method of Hebrew instruction has not engaged their capacity of intelligent understanding.

> —Dr. Trude Weiss-Rosmarin, author, lecturer, and editor, editorial, *The Jewish Spectator*, March 1970

Too many of us can name the mother of Jesus, but not the mother of Moses; we know the author of *Das Kapital*, but not the author of the *Guide for the Perplexed*... our challenge then is this: to lift up a whole generation of Reform Jews from the crippling ignorance that is all too often their companion, and to help them become competent and literate Jews.

—Rabbi Eric H. Yoffie, president of the Union of American Hebrew Congregations (Reform), speaking at Sabbath morning services at the UAHC convention in Dallas, November 1997

How can we have a Zionist revival when our children are not learning the basics?

—Herb Zweibon, chairman of Americans for a Safe Israel, referring to when he asked several area yeshivas for copies of their "Zionist curriculum" and was told they had none, quoted in *The Jewish Voice,* May 1996

❖ JEWISH IDENTITY ❖

(see also Jewish Survival)

Norma Rae, a southern mill worker, upon meeting a Jew for the first time: What makes you different?

Reuben Warshafsky, a labor organizer: History.

—From the film *Norma Rae,* written by Harriet Frank, Jr., and Irving Ravetch, (1979)

We are Jews by virtue of our acceptance of Judaism. We consider ourselves no longer a nation. We are a religious community, and neither pray for nor anticipate a return to Palestine nor a restoration of any of the laws concerning the Jewish state. . . . Our nation is the United States of America. Our nationality is America. Our flag is the "Stars and Stripes." Our race is Caucasian.

—Principle #2 from "Basic Principles of Congregation Beth Israel," published in 1943 in Houston, Tex., to guide the congregation and its members, cited in *Critical Documents of Jewish History,* edited by Ronald H. Isaacs and Kerry M. Olitzky (1995)

I am the son of my parents. I have no choice. The stamp is on my face. I could become a Muslim or a Christian, but the way I look and my identity card will still say "Jew."

—Soviet Jewish émigré, an engineer from Moscow in the 1970s, interviewed by the William E. Wiener Oral History Library of the American Jewish Committee, quoted in *A Special Legacy: An Oral History of Soviet Jewish Émigrés in the United States* by Sylvia Rothchild (1985)

If you have a quarter or an eighth of Jewish blood you are considered Jewish. It's just as it is in America with blacks. If they have a drop of black blood they are black.

— A forty-five-year-old Soviet émigré physician, commenting on whether it is possible to be "half a Jew" in Russia, interviewed by the William E. Wiener Oral History Library of the American Jewish Committee, quoted in *A Special Legacy: An Oral History of Soviet Jewish Émigrés in the United States* by Sylvia Rothchild (1985)

The Jewishness of the newcomers reflects a different cultural, historical and political experience from American born Jews — differences that need to be understood, respected and built upon, principles and guidelines for the Federated system regarding resettlement of Soviet Jews in the United States.

— Council of Jewish Federations Task Force on Acculturation and Integration, excerpt from statement May 1991

I drive a BMW. I have four mink coats, a safe-deposit box full of jewelry. And most of the time I don't have a dime in my pocket. I don't want anyone to think I'm a "JAP." Who am I kidding?

— Unidentified single Jewish woman, quoted in "Voices for Change: Future Directions for American Jewish Women," the report of the National Commission on American Jewish Women, November 1995

Yes, I am a Jew. I always knew that I was. Both my parents were, although they never talked about it. My mother went to church all the time, and we children were baptized. But every Friday night she lit Shabbat candles in jars and hid them under the table.

— Raul, a New Mexican "hidden Jew," quoted in "My Cousin the Nun" by Rena Varon Down, *Bridges*, Winter 1998

Each of us are part of a continuum that began with Abraham and continued through Joseph and Moses and the prophets and King David and Ruth and Esther and Hillel and Rabbi Akivah and Maimonides and the Vilna Gaon and the Baal Shem Tov and Martin Buber and Sholom Aleichem and Sigmund Freud and Theodor Herzl and Albert Einstein and David Ben-Gurion and Anne Frank and Louis Brandeis and Barbra Streisand. And you.

— Joseph Aaron, editor of the *Chicago Jewish News*, reflecting on the perspective of those in "Generation X," quoted in *The Jewish Advocate*, November 3, 1995

To the many values and many facets that make up who I am, I now add the knowledge that my grandparents and members of my family perished in the worst catastrophe in human history . . . So I leave here tonight with the certainty that this new part of my identity adds something stronger, sadder and richer to my life.

> —Madeleine Albright, U.S. Secretary of State, commenting while touring the Old Jewish Cemetery in Prague and the adjacent Pinkas synagogue (inscribed on the walls are names of Holocaust victims), quoted in *The Jewish Week*, July 18, 1997

The Sephardi Mediterranean from which I come is a world of many languages and no borders. My father's family speak Ladino among themselves; my mother's speak French. Most of them have a "foreign" accent in every language they speak, though they speak very fluently. Contained in this trace of an accent, in this shred of difference, is the nature of their identity: belonging everywhere, but not quite.

> —Gini Alhadeff, journalist, *The Sun at Midday* (1997)

When people ask me why I identify as a Sephardic Jew (and not simply as a Jew), I explain that the Sephardim are invisible in this culture, that we are almost unknown by the majority of the Jews here, and that we have a long and proud history. Indeed, Sephardic history is a history of incredible survival through Inquisition, Diaspora and the Holocaust.

> —Rita Arditti, feminist scholar, "To Be a Hanu" in *The Tribe of Dina: A Jewish Woman's Anthology*, edited by Melanie Kaye Kantrowitz and Irena Klepfisz (1986)

The events of recent years have proved that the "excepted Jew" is more the Jew than the exception; no Jew feels quite happy any more about being assured that he is an exception. The extraordinary catastrophe has converted once again all those who fancied themselves extraordinarily favored beings into quite ordinary mortals.

> —Hannah Arendt, German-born American philosopher and social critic who was forced to flee Germany in 1933 (she moved to Paris and in 1941 to the United States), "The Moral of History," 1946, in *The Jew as Pariah: Jewish Identity and Politics in the Modern Age*, edited by Ron H. Feldman (1978)

Jews brought up in the cauldron of Central European anti-Semitism understood where being Jewish got you. If such a Jew found it convenient first to abandon and then not reclaim his Jewishness, and preferred the advantageous simplicity of being an "ordinary" Czech, I would not cast a stone at him. Indeed, I would be glad to shake his hand, acknowledging that I don't know whether, in his circumstances, I would have behaved differently.

> —Louis Begley, lawyer and novelist, responding to news stories about Secre-

tary of State Madeleine Albright's discovery of her Jewish lineage, quoted in "In Patriotism's Name," *The New York Times*, February 12, 1997

When you hang your shingle out, and say you're the American Jewish Theater, there are certain people, including a portion of the American Jewish community, who don't want to come. They feel uncomfortable, like there's chicken fat on the seats. They think: "Why do I need to go back and deal with this stuff? It's issues of the past." So when somebody walks through the door, there's a drama that's already begun.

—Stanley Brechner, artistic director, American Jewish Theater, quoted in "Seeking a Theater Varied as a Rainbow," *The New York Times*, February 23, 1997

For too many years, we have expressed ourselves, not by learning Judaism and the pride that comes from that, but by writing checks for Israel and feeling pride in that country and its mighty army. We face extinction in the Diaspora, that's the real threat.

—Edgar M. Bronfman, chairman of The Seagram Company Ltd. and president of the World Jewish Congress, *The Making of a Jew* (1996)

I'm Jewish. Count Basie's Jewish. Ray Charles is Jewish. Eddie Cantor's goyish. B'nai Brith is goyish; Hadassah, Jewish. Marine Corps—heavy goyim, dangerous. Koolaid is goyish. All Drake's cakes are goyish. Pumpernickel is Jewish, and, as you know, white bread is very goyish. Instant potatoes—goyish. Black cherry soda's very Jewish. Macaroons are very Jewish—very Jewish cake. Fruit salad is Jewish. Lime jello is goyish. Lime soda is very goyish. Trailer parks are so goyish that Jews won't go near them.

—Lenny Bruce, comedian, quoted in *The Essential Lenny Bruce*, edited by John Cohen (1967)

Next to being the children of God, our greatest privilege is being the brothers of each other.

—Martin Buber, philosopher, commenting to American Jewry in 1951 on his first visit to the United States, quoted in *American Jewish Year Book 1966*

For me, "In the beginning" was Auschwitz.

—Melvin Bukiet, novelist, describing how his worldview is influenced by his being the son of a Holocaust survivor, quoted in *The Jewish Week*, August 11, 1995

For more than 40 years, Israelis have debated the question, "Who is a Jew?" At the moment, as far as immigration is concerned, the answer seems to be, "Who isn't?"

> —Ze'ev Chafets, Israeli journalist, regarding the provisions of the Israeli Law of Return, *Jerusalem Report,* June 13, 1991 (The law determines immigration policy; under its provisions, any Jew, half-Jew, or quarter-Jew can come to Israel along with his or her spouse and other close relatives, thus adopting for immigration purposes the broad "Nuremberg" criterion, rather than according to Jewish law)

Even for the chosen there were two sides to the coin: the joy of election and the pain of entrapment. Even being chosen had its dualities. Because one thing it means to be chosen is this: Being chosen means you have no choice.

> —Robert Cohen, novelist, *The Here and Now* (voice of the character Sam Kornish) (1996)

I am an American and a Jew. I live at once in the years 1982 and 5743, the Jewish year in which I am writing this book. I am Paul Cowan, the New York-bred son of Chicago-born, very successful parents; and I am Saul Cohen, the descendant of rabbis in Germany and Lithuania.

I see the world through two sets of eyes, my Americanized ones and my Jewish ones. . . . Sometimes I think that makes me quite conflicted. Sometimes I think it makes my life seem wonderfully rich and varied. I do know this: that my mind is enfolded like a body in a prayer shawl, by my ancestral past and its increasingly strong hold on my present . . .

I am not alone. Indeed, I believe my story, with all its odd, buried, old-world family mysteries, with its poised tension between material wealth and the promise of spiritual wealth, is the story of much of my generation, Jew and Gentile alike.

> —Paul Cowan, journalist, *An Orphan in History* (1982)

The paradigm today is no longer one of being, but of meaning; the question no longer how, but why: Why be a Jew?

> —Rabbi Rachel Cowan, director, Jewish Life Program, The Nathan Cummings Foundation, "The New Spirituality in Jewish Life" in *The Nathan Cummings Foundation Annual Report 1994*

I am a deeply committed Jew. Though I am also an American, a civil libertarian, an academic, and many other things, my primary identification is as a Jew. I believe I will always be an American—and I hope I'm not like those German Jews who believed before World War II that they would always be

German. I believe that I will always be a civil libertarian, an academic, and all the other things that now characterize me. But I know I will always be a Jew.

> —Alan M. Dershowitz, law professor, appellate lawyer, activist, and author, *The Vanishing American Jew* (1997)

There is no problem. I'm a Jew. It touches my poetry, my life in ways I can't describe. Why should I declare something that should be so obvious?

> —Bob Dylan, singer and songwriter, responding to questions at Mount Zion Yeshiva in Jerusalem about why he shied away from a personal, direct, unmistakable declaration, 1971, quoted in *No Direction Home: The Life and Music of Bob Dylan* by Robert Shelton (1986)

The term ultra-orthodox is despicable and it is time for the Jewish community to stop using it. The term indicates that in the realm of normal political and religious discourse, my judgments are beyond the pale—"ultra." In truth this so-called ultra is representative of the historic norm of religious Judaism.

> —Rabbi David Eliezrie, director of the North County Chabad of Yorba Linda, Calif., quoted in *The Jewish Journal of Greater Los Angeles*, June 14, 1996

When I was growing up as the only Jew in my high school, I discovered that I was representing all the Jewish people in everything I did. I was changed by that experience. I knew they would judge all the Jewish people by the few Jews they knew.

> —Eli N. Evans, author and president of the Charles H. Revson Foundation, *The Lonely Days Were Sundays: Reflections of a Jewish Southerner* (1993)

Two hundred years after the Emancipation, Judaism has finally become, in fact as well as theory, an option. We now truly enter the age of Judaism-by-consent. And the question, therefore, becomes: To what have we consented when we say "I do"?

> —Leonard Fein, author and activist, "American Pluralism and Jewish Interests" in *The Jewish Condition*, edited by Aron Hirt-Manheimer (1995)

When I was a child I knew the history of the State of Israel backward and forward; I spoke fluent Hebrew; celebrating the holidays rejuvenated me. Today I have cultural amnesia. I fear my right hand must surely have lost its cunning because I live in a world where my identity is not reflected back to me. So I try, with the rest of my generation, to nourish my Jewish soul.

> —Jyl Lynn Felman, author and professor, "Why I Want to Be a Rabbi"—response on her rabbinical school application—in *The Tribe of Dina: A Jewish Woman's Anthology*, edited by Melanie Kaye Kantrowitz and Irena Klepfisz (1984)

When anybody asks me, you understand, I am a Jew; when I question myself, I am not so sure.

> —Leslie A. Fiedler, critic, quoted in "American Jewish Writers and Their Judaism" by Harold U. Ribalow in *Jews in the Modern World, Volume 2,* edited by Jacob Fried (1962)

Life throws us some crazy pitches.

> —Tony Fossas, Cuban-born major league pitcher commenting upon discovering his Jewish identity, quoted in *Long Island Jewish World,* March 14–20, 1997

They Don't Make Jews Like Jesus Anymore

> —Kinky Friedman, singer, songwriter, and author, title of country-western song

"You're asking how it felt that we were "multiple outsiders" in Johnstown? Did we feel insecure? I tell you . . . [compared to Eastern Europe] it was a much more secure insecurity.

> —Louise G., an immigrant from the Ukraine to a small steel town in Pennsylvania prior to World War II, quoted in *Insecure Prosperity: Small Town Jews in Industrial America, 1890–1940* by Eva Morawska (1996)

I got away with my ideas in the South because no southerner takes me—a Jew, a Yankee, and a radical—seriously. They mostly think of a Jew as a substitute Negro, anyway.

> —Harry Golden, North Carolina journalist, quoted in *The Lonely Days Were Sundays: Reflections of a Jewish Southerner* by Eli N. Evans (1993)

There were Jews at Princeton, of course, but nobody seemed Jewish. At Columbia even the non-Jews had seemed Jewish.

> —Rebecca Goldstein, novelist, *The Mind Body Problem* (voice of the character Renee Feuer) (1983)

My final assumption is that Jews are trans-geographical, that wherever fate may have placed them, they are one family, accountable to each other.

> —Hirsh Goodman, Israeli journalist, *Jerusalem Report,* September 22, 1994

Despite outward cynicism, ours is a generation of Jews who desperately want to make a difference. We want to know that our lives and our loves, our triumphs and our trials, our dreams and our fears are not for naught.

—Rabbi Daniel Gordis, vice-president of the University of Judaism and author, *Does the World Need the Jews?* (1997)

Whenever you are a part of a minority group, it is human instinct to over-compensate and to hide flaws; in hiding flaws, however, we hide some of our humanity. We have this ideal self-image in our head: "Jews are — — —" or "Jews should be. . . ." Rarely does it reflect who we are at the core. We don't think we're capable of violence or whoring around or even addiction.

> —Dan Gottlieb, psychologist and host of National Public Radio's "Family Matters," regarding the murder of a young Jewish woman allegedly by her Jewish husband, *Jewish Telegraphic Agency*, May 30, 1997

I realized I never disliked being Jewish. I just didn't like being disliked for being Jewish.

> —Mary Rodgers Guettel, arts patron and daughter of composer Richard Rodgers, reflecting on her first visit to Israel as part of the Anti-Defamation League's Mission to the Arts in 1994, quoted in *Lifestyles*, Summer 1996

American Jews may be the descendants of not very learned, poor immigrants, but they are Jews, and thus they know that being Jewish is indissolubly connected to moral responsibility and to the inner life of the spirit.

> —Rabbi Arthur Hertzberg, author and professor, *The Jews in America: Four Centuries of an Uneasy Encounter* (1989)

My own perception of myself is definitely not as a "Jewish Woman Writer" but as a writer, a woman and a Jew. Remember Saul Bellow's interview after the Nobel Prize when he said he was not a Jewish American writer, but a writer who was American and Jewish? I feel quite strongly that he was right in making the distinction.

> —Laura Z. Hobson, author, quoted in "Remembering Laura Z. Hobson" by Julia Wolf Mazow, *Lilith*, Summer 1986

As Jews, many of us will look at her differently from now on. Before any of the recent revelations, Jews by and large rejoiced at her appointment. Here was a woman whose world view meshed with our own. That high regard is unlikely to change. Now, however, a touch of pride—deep down, she's one of us—mixes with sadness, because she did not become who she is as one of us. And that is lost forever.

> —Lisa Hostein, editor of *Jewish Telegraphic Agency*, commenting on Secretary of State Madeleine Albright's acknowledgment of her Jewish roots, *Hartford Jewish Ledger*, February 14, 1997

The older we get, the more Jewish we become in my family. My mother's father declared himself an atheist in his communist youth, so we never belonged to a synagogue or had bat mitzvahs. But we wind up in Hebrew homes for the aged and in cemeteries with Hebrew letters over the gates.

—Erica Jong, novelist and poet, "How I Got to Be Jewish" in *American Identities: Contemporary Multicultural Voices* (1984)

I have come to believe that after the Holocaust there is no place for ambivalent Jewishness.

—Erica Jong, *Fear of Fifty* (1994)

One who knows where he came from and where he is going is free of all fear of contempt by others and its most dangerous result—self-hatred.

—Rabbi Meir Kahane, founder of the Jewish Defense League, *Our Challenge* (1974)

Buddhism doesn't start off on what you must believe; it says, here's what Buddha says, how about you? That appeals to Jewish sensibilities. For many Jews, the relaxation of clinging to an identity is a relief. It can feel like a burden if there's no inner context for you. You need to know why you're doing these things.

—Rodger Kamenetz, author, responding to observations that many Jews turn to Buddhism for answers, quoted in the *Baltimore Jewish Times*, November 7, 1997

The Jews are my unconscious.

—Alfred Kazin, author and literary critic, *New York Jew* (1978)

My mother was an Orthodox Jew and my father an orthodox socialist.

—Alfred Kazin, quoted in *Jerusalem Report*, February 19, 1998

In a culture where Ralph Lauren and Lorne Greene (of "Bonanza" fame) have managed to make themselves better known for dressing up as cowboys than for being Jews, the goal of not seeming Jewish, or at least not seeming too Jewish, has been one of the central facts of American Jewish life.

—Michael Kimmelman, arts reporter, "Too Jewish? Jewish Artists Ponder," a review of a new exhibition at the Jewish Museum in New York titled "Too Jewish," *The New York Times*, March 8, 1996

In the secular world I had been given everything that society tells me is the thing to have, and I wasn't happy. I realized that what makes us happy are not those [material] things. What makes us happy are the things that Torah inculcates into the Jewish soul.

> —Joel Klein, bond fund manager, commenting on his decision in 1991 to study in Israel at the yeshivah Ohr Somyach and become a "ba'al teshuva" (someone not raised in a Torah-observant home who decides to explore a traditional Jewish lifestyle), quoted in *JUF News* (Chicago), April 1997

But history has frequently forced Jews to cope with fragments and, as a result, we have learned how to create new contexts, new structures, new wholes—this process as in the case of Yiddish itself sometimes taking centuries. It is, I think, part of our resilience, part of our great capacity to transform when we have the will.

> —Irena Klepfisz, poet, "Secular Jewish Identity" in *The Tribe of Dina: A Jewish Woman's Anthology*, edited by Melanie Kaye Kantrowitz and Irena Klepfisz (1986)

I am proud to be a Jew because it is an art to be a Jew, because it is hard to be a Jew.

> —Tsvi Kolitz, journalist, filmmaker, playwright, and professor, "Yossel Rakover Speaks to God," a story set in 1943 in the Warsaw ghetto, first published in Yiddish in "El Diario Israelita" in Buenos Aires, September 25, 1946, reprinted in *Yossel Rakover Speaks to God: Holocaust Challenges to Religious Faith* (1995)

Too often, the Judaism we teach and the institutions that we run appear to be speaking exclusively to the demand side of Jewish identity. We ask people to observe "X" or "Y," we solicit people, we make demands on them before we create a ground for response. We need to remember that Jewish identity is dialectical. It is demand and promise, mitzvah and grace, conditional and unconditional, Sinai and Zion. As a teacher, I try to keep the dialectic alive.

> —Rabbi Irwin Kula, president-elect of CLAL, *Sh'ma*, January 21, 1994

In the 50s and 60s, we made people feel Jewish by talking about Israel and the Holocaust. In the 90s and the 21st century, we have to make people take Israel and the Holocaust seriously by teaching them to be serious Jews.

> —Rabbi Harold S. Kushner, author and rabbi emeritus of Temple Israel in Natick, Mass., interviewed in *92 St. Y Review*, Winter 1995

In our age, one would expect a little less secrecy and self-consciousness, but conditioned reflexes, as Pavlov taught us, persist for a long time. Or is it that, having prepared (or having been bequeathed) a certain legend about our origins, converts find it embarrassing to change it? These, then, are the mysteries of the human heart; perhaps it is best not to try to delve into them too deeply, especially from afar.

> —Walter Z. Laqueur, author, commenting on Secretary of State Madeleine Albright's acknowledgment of her Jewish roots, *The New Republic*, March 10, 1997

None of us can be defined simply as being members of one group or another. . . . And all of us, ultimately, will join one of the most despised, neglected and abused groups within our society—the old and the sick. As Jews we know the frailty and unreliability of acquired status and privilege. It may be here today and gone tomorrow. We know the perils of being defined by others and of being stigmatized. We know the pain and the invisibility, the fickleness of friends and the conformity of enemies.

> —Gerda Lerner, professor of history, author, and pioneer in the field of women's history, *Why History Matters* (1977)

It seems that I have been journeying to the mountain of God all my life and would have wandered past if God had not intervened. I am no longer deceived that the black face that stares at me from the mirror is the totality of my being.

> —Julius Lester, professor of Judaic studies, history, and English, "Here Am I," *New Traditions*, Spring 1984

To be a Jew in America at the end of the twentieth century is to fight an uphill battle to preserve the values that have preserved the Jewish community since the beginning of time. One of those values is concern for the other.

> —Norman Linzer, professor of social work, "Self and Other: The Jewish Family in Crisis" in *Crisis and Continuity: The Jewish Family in the 21st Century*, edited by Norman Linzer, Irving N. Levitz, and David Schnall (1995)

There are two types of Jews in this world: the mathematical and the literary, those who crunch numbers and those who tell stories.

> —Dr. Joseph Lowin, director of cultural services at the National Foundation for Jewish Culture, *Hebrewspeak: An Insider's Guide to the Way Jews Think* (1995)

When a Jew dies, who asks if he is a Jew? He is a Jew, we don't ask. There are many ways to be a Jew. So if somebody comes to me and says, "Rabbi, shall we call such a man Jewish who lived and worked among the gentiles and sold them pig meat, trayfe, that we don't eat it, and not once in twenty years come inside a synagogue, is such a man a Jew, rabbi?" To him I will say, "Yes, Morris Bober was to me a true Jew because he lived in the Jewish heart." Maybe not to our formal tradition—for this I don't excuse him—but he was true to the spirit of our life—to want for others that which he wants also for himself.

> —Bernard Malamud, novelist and short story writer, *The Assistant* (1957)

Being a Jew seemed so beautiful to me, as it still does; as a child, the beauty was heightened, the way so many aspects of identity seem fantastical. Even the moon seems personal to children. As a young girl, I viewed being Jewish like getting your period: I couldn't wait to come into it! . . . adult . . . dreamy . . . sophisticated . . . full of ineffable pain, blood, sex, inevitability . . . grown up, like smoking or kissing . . . cool . . . a series of exquisite burdens.

> —Deb Margolin, performance artist, *"Oh Wholly Night" and Other Jewish Solecisms*, 1996

I am Jewish precisely because I am not a believer. Because I associate from early childhood the courage not to believe with being Jewish.

> —Elaine Marks, professor of European literature, quoted in "American Jews and the Problem of Identity" by Edward S. Shapiro, *Society*, September/ October 1997

Judaism is my mother tongue. Through Judaism I encounter others, see creation, perceive time (and timelessness), and search for and find my own place in this world.

> —Rabbi Vivie Mayer, commenting upon ordination from the Reconstructionist Rabbinical College, *RRC 1996 Annual Report*

People should not have to justify their existences. The Jew has a certain feeling that he has to justify his existence. He carries in him a kind of burden. He has to prove before God, or the rest of the world, that he has a reason for living. There are millions of people—bless them—who don't carry that burden around, raise good children, and live good lives.

> —Yehudi Menuhin, violinist, quoted in *Conversations with Menuhin* by David Dubal (1992)

I never met a Jewish girl or woman who didn't take it as the highest accolade to hear it observed that she didn't look Jewish.

> —Daphne Merkin, novelist and essayist, "Dreaming of Hitler," *Esquire*, April 1989

The extent of (these) Jews' evident disinterest in their own heritage puzzled me initially, just because they seemed so tolerant—so curious—about everything else, from Zen Buddhism to deconstructionism. Only the arcana of Jewish life struck them as humdrum . . . their disregard for an almost six-thousand-year-old tradition was nothing short of dazzling.

> —Daphne Merkin, commenting on "closet" Jews, "Dreaming of Hitler," *Esquire*, April 1989

In an age when the middle-class Gentile intellectual begins to understand a little more of what it means to be a Jew, the Jews themselves, especially the middle-class intellectual outsiders, are more confused than ever.

> —Rabbi Alan W. Miller, spiritual leader of the Society for the Advancement of Judaism (Reconstructionist) in New York City, *God of Daniel S: In Search of the American Jew* (1969)

All right, Judaism can't be all things to all people, but I insist that every Jew has the right to construct his own ark, set sail, trim his vessel as he sees the mountain rising in the distance.

> —Mark Jay Mirsky, novelist, *My Search for the Messiah: Studies and Wanderings in Israel and America* (1977)

Beginning in late 1936 my interests began to change. . . . I can discern in retrospect more than one reason for these changes. I had had a continuing smoldering fury about the treatment of Jews in Germany. . . . I had relatives there.

> —J. Robert Oppenheimer, physicist, excerpted from his written reply to letters of charges from the Atomic Energy Commission, March 4, 1954, quoted in *J. Robert Oppenheimer: Shatterer of Worlds* by Peter Goodchild (1981)

If we blow into the narrow end of the shofar, we will be heard far. But if we choose to be Mankind rather than Jewish and blow into the wider part, we will not be heard at all; for us America will have been in vain.

> Cynthia Ozick, novelist and essayist, "Toward a New Yiddish," 1970 in *Art & Ardor* (1983)

Early in my career, people would say to me, "You're a Jewish actor." I took offense because I wanted to play everything. And indeed the theatre never typecast me as a Jew. I was Che Guevara, I was Georges Seurat, I was anybody. I was never Jewish. And yet, it took me quite a while, and maybe the birth of my sons, and maybe my marriage, maybe experiencing the anti-Semitism that I denied as a boy, to make me finally realize that everybody I play is Jewish. It is how I look at the world.

> —Mandy Patinkin, singer and actor, quoted in *The Jewish American Family Album*, edited by Dorothy Hoobler and Thomas Hoobler (1995)

Our new Secretary of State [Madeleine Albright], as existentially American as she has become, seems not to understand that in our country very little onus attaches to Jews and to Jewishness. Her spinning of her past was, therefore, pointless. Why could she not have simply said, when asked, "Yes, although I am not a Jew myself, I descend from Jews." Like Barry Goldwater and Michael Blumenthal and Caspar Weinberger and James Schlesinger and Robert Mossbacher and God only knows how many other good Christians. The Jews would not have claimed her. . . . And the gentiles would not have disdained her. No one would have cared much at all.

> —Martin Peretz, editor-in-chief, *The New Republic*, March 10, 1997

Being Jewish is sort of what it is being a New Yorker to me. Jewish culture, history, Jewish neuroses, Jewish food, whatever—it's very rich stuff that gives texture to your life.

> —Neil Postman, media critic and professor, quoted in *Growing Up Jewish in America: An Oral History* by Myrna Katz Frommer and Harvey Frommer (1995)

My belief is that I wasn't born into Judaism by accident, and so I needed ways to honor that. From a Hindu perspective, you are born as what you need to deal with, and if you just try and push it away it's got you in terms of your mind.

> —Ram Dass, author who was born Richard Alpert, became a Hindu, and came to accept the Torah on a par with the Hindu Vedas, quoted in "Return Tripping" by Ira Rifkin, *Jerusalem Report*, April 2, 1992

Alienated for so long from other Jews, deeply divided about my own homosexuality, I have felt myself twice strange: Jewish in the gay community, gay in the Jewish community. In each, different, lesser, ashamed.

> —Lev Raphael, author, "To Be a Jew" in *Journeys and Arrivals* (1996)

I feel the pull of the ancient rituals and I pull back. . . . Despite myself the distances close. I am not such a stranger to this place.

> —Anne Roiphe, novelist and essayist, *Generation Without Memory* (1981)

The sad lesson of the past thirty years is that, in the final analysis, we shall stand and fall together. To speak figuratively, in the shower rooms it will little matter that one fellow was once Albert Shanker and the other was Mark Rudd. Their destinies and fates are intertwined, for better or for worse. If we haven't learned that, we have learned nothing.

> —M. J. Rosenberg, journalist, "To Uncle Tom and Other Jews," *The Village*

Voice, February 13, 1969, reprinted in *Jewish Radicalism: An Anthology*, edited by Jack Nusan Porter and Peter Dreier (1973)

I had, I learned, become the Marxist so as not to be the Jew—the permanent scapegoat I thought that my father was.

— Harry Roskolenko, author, "America the Thief" in *The Immigrant Experience: The Anguish of Becoming American*, edited by Thomas C. Wheeler (1971)

I have always been far more pleased by my good fortune at being born a Jew than my critics may begin to imagine. It's a complicated, interesting, morally demanding and very singular experience, and I like that. I find myself in the historic predicament of being Jewish, with all its implications. Who could ask for more?

— Philip Roth, novelist, from an interview by George Plimpton in *The New York Times Book Review* when *Portnoy's Complaint* was reviewed there, 1969, reprinted in *Reading Myself and Others* by Philip Roth (1975)

I grew up among a group of Jews who wished, more than anything else, I think, to be invisible. . . . I was brought up without any reason to be proud of being Jewish and then was told to be proud; without any reason for shame, and then saw that people were ashamed.

— Muriel Rukeyser, poet, quoted in "American Jewish Writers and Their Judaism" by Harold U. Ribalow, 1944, reprinted in *Jews in the Modern World, Volume 2*, edited by Jacob Fried (1962)

The Judaization of Soviet Jews in this country is a mixed bag. For the most part, we can't or we shouldn't really expect to make them more Jewish than we make our own constituents, our own American Jews. Why demand more from them?

— Carmi Schwartz, former executive vice president, Council of Jewish Federations (CJF), quoted in *A CJF Oral History Project: The Response of the North American Federations to the Emigration of Jews from the Former Soviet Union to the United States and Israel, Volume I* (1991)

I have no problem saying this; I've been doing it for thirty years. I am first and foremost a Jew, only then an Israeli.

— Ariel Sharon, a Likud member of the Israeli Knesset and former defense minister, quoted in the *Jerusalem Post*, November 3, 1995

It wasn't until I actually left New York that I understood what it was to be a Jew. . . . Only when I went to graduate school at Northwestern University did

I go through a terrible period of culture shock; women with blue hair and white gloves, and churchbells and serene people and no one shouting.

> —Mark Siegel, lobbyist and political consultant, quoted in *Jewish Times* by Howard Simons (1988)

When a Jew doesn't know whether she is Ashkenazic or Sephardic, it's usually a good indicator that she has no idea that we are a multicultural people, and this has the effect of intensifying the sense of Sephardic erasure I already feel.

> —Shoshana Simons, a self-described "mixed salad" Sephardic/Ashkenazic Jew born in London and living in Burlington, Vt., "In Search of Fritada," *Bridges*, Winter 1998

I was a Polish Jew and I thought anything could happen. You were an American Jew and you thought nothing could happen.

> —Isaac Bashevis Singer, Nobel Prize-winning Yiddish writer, speaking to Lucy S. Dawidowicz about her journey from New York to Vilna in the summer of 1938, quoted in *Midstream*, August/September 1990

Jews were not put here just to fight anti-Semitism.

> —Rabbi Joseph B. Soloveitchik, Talmudic scholar, professor, and author, responding to Edgar Bronfman's request for advice upon being elected president of the World Jewish Congress, 1981, quoted in *The Making of a Jew* by Edgar M. Bronfman (1996)

I am the next generation of nothing. A Greek, a Jew, I could be anything. We share dead languages, a Mediterranean view, a soccer match in the stadium. But after school I learn an aleph bet while the streets of Athens fill with boys. No special tutorials or ritual incantations; they are what they were born.

> —Cameron Stracher, novelist and lawyer, *The Laws of Return* (voice of the character Colin Stone) (1996)

Jewishness was like sex. It was absolutely taboo as a subject for discussion with either of my parents. By example rather than by word, they raised the three of us to be anti-Semitic. One did not go to a Jewish school or country club or summer resort. Our loyalty and our duty were not to Jews but to the family and its traditions.

> —Donald B. Straus, retail executive, member of the Straus family that owned Macy's department store, quoted in *Merchant Princes* by Leon Harris (1979)

My mother is Jewish, my father isn't. . . . I feel least Jewish when with Jews, and most Jewish with non-Jews. I may not have a home in either house, but I am blessed with the offers of guest bedrooms in each.

> —Jeffrey Sweet, playwright, quoted in *Fruitful and Multiplying*, edited by Ellen Schiff (1996)

Being a Jew is like walking in the wind or swimming; you are touched at all points and conscious everywhere.

> —Lionel Trilling, critic, from a 1928 journal entry, quoted in "At Journey's End," interview with Joseph A. Concotti, *Jerusalem Report*, December 30, 1993

I went to Israel in 1992, which really woke in me that it was nothing to be ashamed of. It's embarrassing to admit that you're ashamed of being Jewish all your life. At the end it was not prejudice but an ignorance, a hole where the Judaism should be.

> —Alfred Uhry, playwright, who grew up in the South, quoted in "Remembering Prejudice, of a Different Sort," *The New York Times*, February 23, 1997

My grandfather was born in Jerusalem, my father was born in Yugoslavia, my mother in Bulgaria. I was born in Greece, my wife in Germany, my son in Israel, and my daughter in America. This is what it is to be a Jew.

> —Unnamed man at a gathering of Holocaust survivors from Greece, quoted in *When They Came to Take My Father: Voices of the Holocaust*, photographs by Mark Seliger, edited by Leora Kahn and Rachel Hager (1996)

I know I paid my price for my fascination with being a Jew. One's horizons shrink. There is the ever present danger of parochialism. One's creative efforts miss universality. But I couldn't help it; the shirt is closer than the jacket.

> —Bruno Weiser Varon, former Israeli diplomat, journalist, and professor at Boston University, *Professions of a Lucky Jew* (1994)

Our generation of Jews, this crisis Judaism doesn't attract us. It's all negative. I'm not gonna be a Jew because six million Jews died in the Holocaust. I'm not going to be a Jew because Israel's threatened.

> —Rabbi Neil Weinberg, quoted in *Embracing the Stranger* by Ellen Jaffe McClain (1995)

Your Jewishness in America is a Jewishness that is on the bookshelves; you don't have a land, a language, a daily reality that is any way Jewish. No wonder you fight so hard to insist on the "right line" about what Jewish values are — because you think if one book is missing from the bookshelf maybe you won't have a Jewish library anymore. Whereas here [Israel] there is a fully textured

Jewish life; and that allows me to be more free. So if on some point Moses is wrong, I can reject that part of Moses. If the biblical Joshua was wrong, I am free to reject him, without worrying whether I am really still Jewish or if I have lost my Jewish identity.

> —A. B. Yehoshua, Israeli author, quoted in "A Conversation with A. B. Yehoshua" by Michael Lerner, *Tikkun*, September/October 1990

I can't, Jerry, I'm a Kohen.

> —Abner "Longy" Zwillman, Jewish mob boss, explaining why he refused to go into the funeral chapel to pay his respects to his friend Hymie Kugel, quoted in *But—He Was Good to His Mother* by Robert A. Rockaway (1993)

❖ JEWISH OBSERVANCE ❖

(see also Holidays, Ritual)

Regardless of their definition, secular or religious, all forms of contemporary Jewish life must arise out of a confrontation with the past. Whether one lives in harmony with tradition or in tension with it, one must contend with that tradition. Comprehending the Halakhah [Jewish law] is necessary for a Jewish life, whether one seeks to follow Jewish law or depart from it.

> —Rachel Biale, author, *Women and Jewish Law* (1984)

There are small things attached to far greater objects, holding them in place and ensuring that they give light to the whole community. What is a little mitzvah? And who can tell how much effect its removal may have on the total picture? Some years ago, the thirteenth space launch of the U.S. shuttle program met disaster. Scientists combed the debris and found that a faulty O-ring was responsible. That small item caused the death of the astronauts and millions in dollars in damage. Who is to judge what is small and what is large, what is less and what is more important? So, too it is with mitzvot. We dare not judge. What we deem insignificant may bear light to the whole world.

> —Rabbi Benjamin Blech, congregational rabbi and assistant professor of Talmud, *Understanding Judaism: The Basics of Deed and Creed* (1991)

I feel there is not enough love between people, their emphasis is not on loving. . . . You walk in orthodox circles, who's called an orthodox person? His wife wears a sheytl [wig] and buys glatt [by the strictest standards] kosher meat. I never heard somebody say, "This man is really orthodox, have you ever seen the way he talks to people, the way he talks to children?" We need both, God needs the whole thing.

—Rabbi Shlomo Carlebach, dialogue with host Robert L. Cohen, "Yedid Ne-fesh" radio broadcast, November 1979

Reform has gone from being a religion that says we don't keep kosher and all the rest of it to one that says that anything within the Jewish tradition is available, and we will take what we find meaningful.

—Rabbi Daniel Freelander, one of the authors of a study of Reform congregations, quoted in *Jerusalem Report*, April 20, 1995

Like most American Jews, I find myself able to observe only a tiny fraction of the Torah's commandments. Unlike some, I believe the commandments are binding. When I fail to perform a religious obligation, I don't want a soothing Reform or Conservative authority to tell me I am in luck—that particular obligation had been dropped from the new edition and I am free to ignore it. I am not free to ignore it and commit a sin when I fail to do it. I acknowledge my failings and recall that God is merciful. . . . This infantile insistence that religious ritual conform to you rather than the other way around is the essence of modern American culture, and is strangling Judaism.

—David Gelernter, author and professor, quoted in "American Jews and the Problem of Identity" by Edward S. Shapiro, *Society*, September/October 1997

He is the type of Jew seen less and less in today's metropolitan area Orthodox congregations. He is the infrequent Sabbath worshipper who drives to services on holy days but stealthily parks his car around the corner from shul [synagogue] so as not to embarrass himself nor offend his more observant neighbors. His kitchen at home is kosher insofar as biblically forbidden foods are never or rarely served (someone should study the phenomenon of the "chazer pot" in otherwise kosher kitchens), and meat and milk meals and dishes are kept separate.

—Jeffrey S. Gurock, professor of American Jewish history, *American Jewish Orthodoxy in Historical Perspective* (1996)

Indeed, if you rent a room in which to live a settled life, and then rent another room in a hotel as a tourist, you are certainly living a "double life." But if you rent two rooms in one apartment, you have not a double life but a broad life. A multitude of diverse points, one above the other, certainly implies [an undesirable] multiplicity, but when all the points are arranged around one central point, you have a circle. That, my dear friend, is your obligation in the world: to place in the center of your life the "One" . . . and every new point that you acquire will simply serve to broaden the circle, and this will in no way injure your sense of unity.

> —Rabbi Yitzchak Hutner, former head of Brooklyn's Mesivta Chaim Berlin, commenting in a written response to a student who inquired whether pursuing a secular career meant he was living a double life, published in *Sefer ha-Zikaron le'Maran ha-"Pahad Yitzchak,"* edited by Yosef Buksbaum (1983)

But if Jews are not to exaggerate the importance of the dietary practices, neither should they underestimate the effect those practices can have in making a home Jewish. If the dietary folkways are capable of striking a spiritual note in the home atmosphere, Jews cannot afford to disregard them. . . . Since the main purpose of these practices is to add Jewish atmosphere to the home, there is no reason for suffering the inconvenience and self-deprivation which result from a rigid adherence outside the home.

> —Rabbi Mordechai M. Kaplan, founder of Reconstructionism, *Judaism as a Civilization* (1934)

I'm grateful that I've found Reform Judaism because otherwise I might have rejected Judaism altogether. I've found a way to be Jewish that doesn't feel restricting to me. I have the spirituality and sense of tradition, but I'm allowed to make choices. I can light candles on Friday night the way my mother did, but then I can take my family out to eat at Taco Bell.

> —Pearl Kleinberger of Seattle, quoted in *The Invisible Thread: A Portrait of Jewish American Women* by Diana Bletter (1989)

I wanted to do this. I knew that somehow it is always possible—if you work extremely hard—to arrive at the wonderful place where the portion changes from total strangeness to being wholly and simply part of you. There is no way to chant (well) unless you live and breathe the portion like part of yourself. This is one of the things that most engages me in learning to chant Torah. From point zero you go to complete intimacy and out of that intimacy, you are able to bring the voice of Torah to life for others.

> —Sonia Kovitz of Congregation Tifereth Israel, Columbus, Ohio, "On Chanting Torah," *Sh'ma*, May 12, 1995

You can't force people to do what they don't want to do, to feel what they don't feel. If someone wills one thing, you cannot tell it to will another. It has to come from within.

> —Yeshayahu Leibowitz, Judaic scholar and professor of biochemistry, quoted in "Of Thorns, Idols and Prophecy," *Hadassah*, May 1990

The first thing I told them was that I couldn't work on Yom Kippur, or the two days of Sukkot, or the two days Shemini Atzeret and Simchat Torah. The telephone lines to Washington were buzzing that night to find out what kind of nut had been provided to them.

> —Nathan Lewin, attorney, recalling Yom Kippur 1963, when he was working for the U.S. Justice Department's Criminal Division, and he and his family were dispatched to Nashville to prosecute Teamster president Jimmy Hoffa, quoted in *Lifestyles*, New Year 1998

Jewish life needs many things. But one stands out above all others—non-Orthodox religiosity. We need to concentrate on developing widespread non-Orthodox religiosity even more than we need to concentrate on anti-Semitism. We know how to fight anti-Semitism; we don't know how to keep most non-Orthodox Jews Jewish.

> —Dennis Prager, author and radio commentator, *Moment*, June 1992

Non-Orthodox Jews must take Judaism as seriously as Orthodox Jews do. Most do not. For example, when it comes to many Jewish practices, the motto of many Reform Jews is, "I don't have to, I'm Reform"—an attitude that renders Reform Judaism an excuse rather than an affirmation.

> —Dennis Prager, *Moment*, June 1992

The countercultural aesthetic that shaped the havurah [informal prayer group] depended on expressive individualism that featured the activism of all participants. Expressive individualism in turn was the product of the American culture that gave rise to American Judaism and promoted Jewish secularism.

> —Riv-Ellen Prell, anthropologist, *Prayer and Community: The Havurah in American Judaism* (1989)

It's how the Hasidim celebrate Judaism, which is different than anything else, and it doesn't feel as genuine to American Jews. If Hasidism wasn't sexist and separatist, people would be hard-pressed to come up with any argument against it.

> —Oren Rudavsky, filmmaker who cowrote and directed, with Menchem Daum, the film *A Life Apart: Hasidism in America*, quoted in *Lifestyles*, New Year 1998

Judaism is not a religion which does not oppose itself to anything in particular. Judaism is opposed to any number of things. . . . It permeates the whole of your life. It demands control over all your actions, and interferes even with your menu. It sanctifies the seasons, and regulates your history, both in the past and in the future. Above all, it teaches that disobedience is the strength of sin.

—Rabbi Solomon Schechter, president of The Jewish Theological Seminary of America, inaugural address, November 20, 1902, quoted in *Conservative Judaism: The New Century* by Neil Gillman (1993)

Religion itself cannot survive when it makes no demands upon its adherents. . . . too many of our people want an easygoing religion, one which does not interfere with their leisure, their sleep, or their television; which calls for no study and no observance, which does not challenge or disturb them . . . no religion ever survived in that kind of emotional and intellectual vacuum—and Judaism least of all.

—Rabbi Abba Hillel Silver, reform rabbi and Zionist leader for more than fifty years, until his death in 1963, quoted in *Length of Our Days* by Sol Landau (1961)

Halakhic man [someone who lives according to Jewish law] does not quiver before any man; he does not seek out compliments, nor does he require public approval. If he sees that there are fewer and fewer men of distinguished spiritual rank about, then he wraps himself in his mantle and hides away to the four cubits of Halakhah. He knows that the truth is a lamp unto his feet and the Halakhah a light unto his path.

—Rabbi Joseph B. Soloveitchik, Talmudic scholar, professor, and author, *Halakhic Man* (1984)

When halakhic man approaches reality, he comes with his Torah, given to him from Sinai, in hand. He orients himself to the world by means of fixed statutes and firm principles. An entire corpus of precepts and laws guides him along the path leading to existence.

—Rabbi Joseph B. Soloveitchik, *Halakhic Man* (1984)

A religious person has not only intellectual involvement or cultural involvement, he also has an involvement of self, of living it, not only knowing about it. . . . It's the difference between reading a description of a country and being there. . . . If you read [Baedeker Guides] you know about every town and when the railway station was built and how many inhabitants are in the town. So you have knowledge and a kind of vicarious experience. But when you are there you relate to the same phenomena in a very different way. That is the basic difference between knowing about something and living it.

—Rabbi Adin Steinsaltz, Talmudic scholar, interview in *Moment*, October 1988

When I am at functions in the Jewish community, people usually know that my hat means I am Orthodox. Just as my hat tells them something about me, their reaction to my hat tells me something about them.

—Susan Rubin Weintrob, "Why I Wear a Hat," *The Jewish Press*, June 27, 1997

The Jewish immigrant had a saying, "When the boat is halfway to America, throw overboard your prayer shawl and phylacteries." To some, this meant a release from a galling yoke; to others, a sad yielding to the facts of the new world. In America, in those days, you worked on Saturday or you didn't eat.

—Herman Wouk, author, *Inside, Outside* (voice of I. David Goodkind) (1985)

❖ JEWISH ORGANIZATIONS ❖

The basis for Jewish association in the past has been anti-Semitism, religion, nostalgia, history, Yiddishkeit and nationalism. None of them seem to work anymore.

—Phil Baum, executive director, American Jewish Congress, *The Jewish Week*, August 26, 1994

All the old structures we had were for the old crises. Where are we going now?

—Phil Baum, *The Jewish Week*, August 26, 1994

Israel is here to stay. It is not in conflict with our American citizenship and loyalties. . . . It is an indivisible part of Jewish life. It may become the most important factor in the future development of the Jew in this world not rivaling but complementing the American Jewish community. Let us use Israel programmatically.

—Graenum Berger of the Federation of Jewish Philanthropies in New York, from "Programming Around Israel," presented at the Annual Meeting of the National Association of Jewish Communal Service, May 29, 1956, *Journal of Jewish Communal Service*, Fall 1956

Hadassah, alone within the whole Zionist movement, carries the legacy of Henrietta Szold. Ideologies come and go but orphans and the sick and the socially or psychologically disabled will be with us forever; Zionism will come to mean this thing or that—or in a happier world, maybe nothing—but the 318,000 members of Hadassah . . . will not be left looking for ways to concretize their attachment to it.

—Midge Decter, author "The Legacy of Henrietta Szold," *Commentary*, December 1960

What is necessary is a Jewish sense of humor to reduce to size our conceptions of yesteryear, and to recognize that immortality does not apply to organizations and institutions. We must recognize that going out of business is an essential quality of community service — not change for the sake of change, but change because it is necessary and good.

> —Ralph I. Goldman, executive vice-president of the American Jewish Joint Distribution Committee, presentation at the International Conference of Jewish Communal Service, Jerusalem, August 1981

You have to speak to American Jews in superlatives before they will listen. Cool, balanced analysis makes no impression on them, and exaggeration is almost indispensable.

> —Nahum Goldmann, president of the World Jewish Congress, quoted in *Israel in the Mind of America* by Peter Grose (1983)

It's just as well that the Conference of Presidents of Major American Jewish Organizations has come out in favor of the peace process. Had it not, it may have had to fight the next war without Israel.

> —Hirsh Goodman, Israeli journalist, *Jerusalem Post*, September 22, 1994

Indeed, the JDL [Jewish Defense League] was the most fully American of any organization, for it tested, without anxiety, the limits of American tolerance toward Jews. We relied on the basic restraint of the police even as we provoked them, trusted in the protection of the American government even as we threatened its interests.

> —Yossi Klein Halevi, Israeli journalist and author, *Memoirs of a Jewish Extremist* (1995)

No movement has ever failed so completely.

> —Samuel Kassow, historian, referring to the demise of the Bund (having allied themselves with the failed ideology that turned on them in the Soviet Union, they found themselves in Eastern Europe at the time of the Holocaust), at a commemoration of the Bund's centennial at the Greater Hartford Jewish Community Center, jewishworldreview article by Jonathan S. Tobin, posted on the Internet, February 6, 1998

They gave the Jewish workers a sense of dignity, of worth and hope. They gave them a sense they were not alone.

> —Samuel Kassow, historian, paying tribute to the Bund for its trade unions, for helping to transform Yiddish from a colloquial jargon into a literary culture, and noting the powerful impact made by Bundist immigrants on

American Jewish, jewishworldreview article by Jonathan S. Tobin, posted
on the Internet, February 6, 1998

Is it necessary that this Committee represent the riffraff and everybody? If
the Committee represents the representative and high class Jews of America,
that is enough.

> —Adolf Kraus, president of Jewish fraternal order B'nai Brith, commenting on
> the formation of the American Jewish Committee, 1906, quoted in *Israel in
> the Mind of America* by Peter Grose (1983)

I did that because we're not one people. We are all Jews; we do not behave
with the same mind. We need to strive to be there for each other and build a
peoplehood that takes into account our diversity culturally, our diversity of religious practice, our diversity of language. We understand that no matter where
you are, you can walk into any Jewish community and know that there'll be
somebody there for you, that you're part of a family—like Sister Sledge sang in
the mid-70s. "We are family" is a better slogan, and if they'd let us, I'd use the
song. In a family, you don't like all your cousins; you're not all in love with
each other 24 hours a day.

> —Bernie Moscovitz, leader of the National United Jewish Appeal, on his de-
> cision to drop the slogan "We Are One" from UJA, quoted in *Lifestyles,*
> New Year 1998

There is only one venue left to the American people where all of our people
can meet and talk, tragically, and that's the venue we call Federation. No one
denomination will voluntarily walk into another denomination's synagogues and
be openly accepted, warmly accepted. This body, which is essentially a creation
of American Jewry, is the only place that we have left to us, where all the tribes
of Israel will still meet and talk.

> —Chaim Potok, author, from a speech at the annual meeting of the Jewish
> United Fund/Jewish Federation, Chicago, September 11, 1997, quoted in
> the *Baltimore Jewish Times,* November 27, 1997

AIPAC [American Israel Public Affairs Committee] proudly proclaims that
it is now one of Washington's most powerful lobbies, suggesting that what matters is not Israel's standing in Washington, but AIPAC's.

> —M. J. Rosenberg, former editor of the AIPAC newsletter, *The Near East
> Report, The Jewish Week,* January 23, 1998

The one unifying force in Jewish life is not celebrating the Shabbat or
contributing to UJA [United Jewish Appeal] but rather stifling a yawn at a public

event where the only people still smiling at the end are those who are being honored or who have undergone a lobotomy.

> —Gary Rosenblatt, editor of the *Baltimore Jewish Times*, "Why Is Jewish Life Dull?" *Jewish Bulletin of Northern California*, March 19, 1993

[Zionist men] withheld their appreciation of her personality, never gave her the place she deserved in their councils. Had only the Zionist men appreciated her as we women did! She stood above them all in organizing ability, judgment, leadership. Her democratic organization of Hadassah, which now had thousands of members and covered a network of cities, was afterward made the model of American Zionist organization.

> —Jessie Sampter, Zionist activist, discussing the attitude of Zionist men to Henrietta Szold and Hadassah, quoted in *The Journey Home: Jewish Women and American Century* by Joyce Antler (1997)

Communal services operate on a very conservative basis—there is a resistance to change. One of the most telling arguments for maintaining a service is that it has always existed. History seems to justify continuation. Only changes are challenged.

> —Isidore Sobeloff, executive vice president, Jewish Welfare Federation of Detroit, delivering the keynote address at the National Conference of Jewish Communal Service, May 27, 1956, in St. Louis, quoted in *Journal of Jewish Communal Service*, Fall 1956

Since World War II, and especially since the creation of the State of Israel, Jews have been able to have their cake and eat it too. They have become increasingly active in American politics, and Jewish organizations brag about their political influence while maintaining a strong aversion to religion in public life. Jews have been able to present themselves as a secular interest group.

> —Fredelle Z. Spiegel, "Hobby Called Judaism," *Jerusalem Report*, December 30, 1993

We have not taken anything from the men's organization. Adam's lost rib leaves no gap, and in its place was found a full grown woman and helpmate.

> —Henrietta Szold, founder of Hadassah, commenting on the role of a separate Zionist organization for women, from *The Maccabean*, February 1917, quoted in *The Journey Home: Jewish Women and American Century* by Joyce Antler (1997)

We have never asked the Congress to do something that we have not been willing to do first.

> —Mark Talisman, director of the Washington Action Office of the Council

of Jewish Federations, citing the Jewish community's cooperation with the federal government agencies in the Council of Jewish Federations matching grant program to provide assistance to refugee resettlement in the United States, quoted in the *Jewish Exponent*, October 16, 1992

In every institution—whether it is a synagogue, a Hebrew school, a hospital—we find the identical situation. The women members are allotted no say and almost no representation at all when it comes to basic decisions affecting the policies of the institution.

—Dr. Trude Weiss-Rosmarin, author, lecturer, and editor, editorial, *The Jewish Spectator*, August 1936

Who is the man of the year? Whoever gives $200,000. Who is the woman of the year? Elizabeth Taylor. Why? Jewish organizations really live for the sake of being mentioned in *The New York Times.*

—Dr. Trude Weiss-Rosmarin, quoted in "Remembering Trude" by Estelle Gilson, *The Jewish Spectator*, Fall 1989

Not relief, but redress, not palliatives but prevention, not charity but justice.

—Rabbi Stephen S. Wise, Jewish leader and activist, stating the goals of the American Jewish Congress at a March 1916 meeting in Philadelphia, *Challenging Years* (1951)

American Jewish life is organized as a benevolent plutocracy. The players in the dollar dominated society passionately want egalitarianism in the larger non-Jewish society, but not in their own organizations. It is a process designed to depress idealistic young Jews, the one group Jewish organizations are desperate to attract and keep.

—Nicholas Wolfson, professor of law, quoted in the *Hartford Jewish Ledger*, March 17, 1995

❖ JEWISH SURVIVAL ❖

(see also Assimilation, Jewish Education)

The only answer capable of ensuring Jewish continuity in America lies in Judaism: in a religious faith that instructs the believer to remain a Jew, faithful to the covenant. For unless the community is based on faith in God, what possible purpose could there be for concern about its survival?

—Elliot Abrams, author and president of the Ethics and Public Policy Center in Washington, D.C., *Faith or Fear: How Jews Can Survive in a Christian Culture* (1997)

All it takes to sustain Jewish life in America are 500 good Jews.

—Salo Baron, historian, in conversation with Rabbi Stephen S. Wise, 1930s

As human beings, as Jews, as parents who have brought children into this world, we must fight the battle—all the battles—as long as we draw breath. This is our legacy, and we must pass it on to those who will follow. There has to be a reason the Jews have survived to the last half of the twentieth century to become stronger than ever before. It must be that we have a purpose, and I believe that purpose still is to be "a light unto the nations."

—Edgar M. Bronfman, chairman of The Seagram Company Ltd. and president of the World Jewish Congress, *The Making of a Jew* (1996)

There is an empirical principle in Jewish life. And that principle is that a Jew can maintain his or her Jewish identity for three or four generations. However, after three, four generations of giving up the rites and rituals of Judaism, giving up kosher, giving up Shabbat, they blend into the regular society. And they're basically lost.

—Rabbi Ephraim Z. Buchwald, founder and director of the National Jewish Outreach Program, interviewed in the film *Jewish Soul, American Beat*, produced, directed, and written by Barbara Pfeffer (1997)

Instead of sending out the ocean liner (to bring Jews back), we have been sending out the rowboat.

—Rabbi Ephraim Z. Buchwald, quoted in *The Jewish Press*, February 28, 1997

Survival of Jewry is not in and of itself sufficient to justify loyalty to Judaism or on which to base the will to remain a Jew. If being a Jew has no meaning, then the survival of Jewry as a distinct people or faith is of no consequence.

—Rabbi Hayim Halevy Donin, former rabbi of Congregation B'nai David in Southfield, Mich., and professor of Judaic studies who moved to Jerusalem, *To Be a Jew* (1972)

If we are serious about saving the remnants of Jewish faith in this time, we will need to engage Jews in Jewish ritual, the study of Jewish texts and the knowledge of Jewish languages, and, most important, to strengthen deeply-fragmented communities.

—Arnold Eisen, professor of Jewish thought, "Saving the Remnants of Jewish Faith" in *New Traditions 2*, Spring 1985

I was speaking in Ann Arbor, Michigan, the other day, and the last question addressed to me was: "What about a Jew who is not prepared to go on aliyah, but who wants to respond to the Holocaust with a vibrant Jewish life?" I said he should have one more child than he had planned on.

> —Emil L. Fackenheim, professor of philosophy, interview in *New Traditions* 3, Summer 1986

My friends, let me suggest to you that the principal enemy of Jewish continuity in this country is not assimilation, is not anti-Semitism, is not even intermarriage; our principal enemy is boredom.

> —Leonard Fein, author and activist, remarks at the Council of Jewish Federations General Assembly held in Seattle in November 1996

Eating gefilte fish will not assure the continuity of the Jewish people. There has to be religious observance. If this generation does not get involved, 10 or 15 years from now there won't be 60- or 70-year-olds sitting in temple.

> —Roger Fisher, a founder of the "Connections" program on Long Island that tries to bring together Jews in their 30s and 40s, quoted in "Donations to a Jewish Philanthropy Ebb" by Karen W. Arenson, *The New York Times,* December 27, 1995

While some of you believed that the sickness of Judaism can only be cured by a radical operation, I am convinced that such an operation is unnecessary and even dangerous, and that all the patient needs is proper care and treatment which would enable him to regain his innate powers of resistance and reject in a natural and painless way the injurious elements which at present endanger his health and his very life.

> —Israel Friedlander, scholar and activist, 1917, quoted in *Practical Dreamer: Israel Friedlander and the Shaping of American Judaism* by Baila Round Shargel (1985)

Why should Jews survive? Whatever responses there may be, God is the one that matters: Jews should survive because they are the linchpin in his redemption of the world.

> —Rabbi Michael Goldberg, author, *Why Should Jews Survive? Looking Past the Holocaust Toward a Jewish Future* (1995)

We once associated barbed wire barricades and intricate security precautions with Israel. Now we find these concerns on the agenda of Jewish institutions in a number of countries throughout the world. All are on the front lines. More than ever, the concept of "All of Israel is responsible one for another" must be applied.

—Ralph I. Goldman, executive vice-president of the American Jewish Joint Distribution Committee, presentation at the International Conference of Jewish Communal Service, Jerusalem, August 1981

Jewish leadership in the United States has a large responsibility for the future of world Jewry, and it has exercised the responsibility for the last generation with great commitment and enormous dignity. That leadership also has the prime responsibility for the survival of its own community, and here the American Jewish leaders are on the bridge of a very leaky ship. Before my eyes is the terrifying image of the *Titanic*. In my nightmare, it is sinking not while the band plays but while in its main dining room a very successful black-tie fund-raiser is being conducted.

—Rabbi Arthur Hertzberg, author and professor, *Moment*, 1975

Today, American Jews find themselves remarkably free from danger but in the midst of temptation—temptations of the most philistine and the most sophisticated sort. The future of American Jewry depends, first, on a rejection of the false idols of our times; second on a willingness to "bend the knee and bow in worship" only to the Holy One, blessed be He; and finally, on the ability to demonstrate and articulate reasonably the nobility and profundity of the religion into which we have had the good fortune to be born.

—William Kristol, editor and publisher of *The Weekly Standard*, quoted in *Moment*, December 1997

Torah, as the source of all Jewish learning, is necessary to the survival of Jews as a distinct group, and more critical to the flourishing of Judaism in an open society than in a closed one. To be a Jew in a ghetto requires no knowledge, not even much commitment. An insulated society communicates and enforces its own rules . . . However, an open society is by definition one in which the citizen is subject to all kinds of competing ideas and ideals and is free to engage in the commerce of values, concepts and lifestyles.

—Rabbi Norman Lamm, president of Yeshiva University, *Torah Umadda: The Encounter of Religious Learning and Worldy Knowledge in the Jewish Tradition* (1990)

We are entering a new era in the history of the Jew. . . . The salvation of Judaism is in the American-born Jew.

—Leo N. Levi, president of B'nai Brith, 1900, quoted in *B'nai Brith: The Story of a Covenant* by Edward E. Grusd (1966)

To maintain Jewish life and preserve the traditional values that served to perpetuate the group until the present requires the erection of boundaries high enough to foster a distinctive Jewish culture and identity. Modern Jews are not yet ready to erect boundaries that will, in effect, distinguish them and their culture and values from those of other Americans.

> —Norman Linzer, professor at the Wurzweiler School of Social Work, Yeshiva University, "Self and Other: The Jewish Family in Crisis" in *Crisis and Continuity: The Jewish Family in the 21st Century*, edited by Norman Linzer, Irving N. Levitz, and David Schnall (1995)

To the question "to be or not to be," each nation must make its own reply in its own way, and Jews neither can nor should ever depend on anyone else for permission to stay alive.

> —Golda Meir, prime minister of Israel, *My Life* (1975)

. . . 5,000 people who had never been to a Chanukah party in their lives showed up and sang and danced, bumbling their way through the blessings and candlelighting and nobody slapped them for being bad Jews. Everybody said it was the greatest thing that ever happened and it was. . . . I would love to see that kind of simple rebirth happening in North America.

> —Bernie Moscovitz, leader of the National United Jewish Appeal, recalling a mission to Kiev and Odessa in 1994–95, quoted in *Lifestyles*, New Year 1998

Only God can write the report card on who has done, or is doing, more for the survival of Jews and Judaism. Our effort to replace Him is arrogance.

> —Rabbi Emanuel Rackman, chancellor of Bar Ilan University, author and columnist, *The Jewish Week*, November 16, 1990

If Jewish leaders fear a loss of continuity, why aren't they doing more to help Jewish families? . . . Jewish leaders should be worrying about the third children that committed Jewish women aren't having.

> —Nessa Rapoport, author, "Five Words for Jewish Leaders: You Still Don't Get It," *Tikkun*, January/February 1993

There was hardly a generation in the Diaspora that did not consider itself the final link in Israel's chain. Each always saw before it the abyss ready to swallow it up.

> —Simon Rawidowicz, author and professor, "Israel: The Ever-Dying People" in *Studies in Jewish Thought*, 1974

We need to revive the self-confidence and sense of purpose of American Jewry. We are the most prosperous and have the most freedom of any Jews in 2,000 years. What are we going to do with it? It can't be that we came all this way simply to expire.

—Robert S. Rifkind, president of the American Jewish Committee, quoted in *The Jewish Week*, August 4, 1995

The observance of the Sabbath, the keeping of the Dietary laws, the laying of tefillin, the devotion to Hebrew Literature and the hope for Zion in Jerusalem are all things as absolutely necessary for maintaining Judaism in America as elsewhere.

—Rabbi Solomon Schechter, scholar who left his position at Cambridge University to assume the presidency of The Jewish Theological Seminary in 1902, letter to Dr. Raisin, February 10, 1905, reprinted in *American Jewish Year Book 1906*

Life is short; the problems before modern Judaism are great; and small, very small indeed is the number of those among us who are working unselfishly for the highest interests of our race and our faith.

—Dr. Isadore Singer, quoted in *The American Hebrew*, May 31, 1901

Jews will continue to beat the paths to cults until we show them the beauty of Judaism. Incredible! The people who gave the world spiritual values now have the biggest problem of any group keeping their own in the spiritual fold!

—Rabbi Yaakov Spivak, columnist, *The Jewish Press*, April 11, 1997

We must create a Jewish people that is not driven into Jewishness by antagonism, but rather, is drawn by the excitement of better living.

—Michael Steinhardt, philanthropist, "Stopping the Drift: An Entrepreneurial Vision for Jewish Renewal," speech at a Hillel conference in Baltimore, reprinted in *Forward*, April 10, 1988

I have never understood Jews who abandon Jewry. They simply walk out of an unending drama in which they are assured of good parts.

—Bruno Weiser Varon, former Israeli diplomat, journalist, and professor at Boston University, *Professions of a Lucky Jew* (1994)

A community which understands that change is one thing and progress quite another and which is willing to make both happen can succeed and will survive.

—Leonard Zakim, executive director of the Anti-Defamation League of Boston, "A Turning Point" in *At the Crossroads: Shaping Our Jewish Future*, published by the Wilstein Institute of Jewish Policy Studies (1995)

❖ JOURNALISM ❖

If I had the authority I would institute a law that all public liars, newspaper men, that is, who handle truth carelessly, should be treated as common thieves, and the publishers of their fabrications as dealers in stolen goods.

> —Ashmedai, journalist, "If I Were Censor," *American Jewish Chronicle*, May 11, 1917

If the Messiah had arrived in Baltimore the only way it would have been covered in the *Jewish Times* was if he'd sent in a press release.

> —Chuck Buerger, former publisher of the *Baltimore Jewish Times*, who transformed the paper from a mom-and-pop weekly "bulletin board" that relied on press releases, quoted by Gary Rosenblatt (former editor of the *Baltimore Jewish Times*), *The Jewish Week*, November 15, 1996

Are you going to print that?

> —Daniel Burros, a KKK leader and Nazi who was born of Jewish parents and had a Bar Mitzvah, questioning *New York Times* reporter McCandlish Phillips, quoted in *One More Victim* by A. M. Rosenthal and Arthur Gelb (1967) (On October 31, 1965, the story appeared in *The New York Times* and Burros committed suicide.)

There was, on the [New York] *Times*, an obvious sense of shock and unhappiness that a story in the paper had been the ostensible cause of a man's suicide, but almost to a man, reporters and editors believed that the decision to print the story had been not only correct but professionally and ethically unavoidable.

> —A. M. Rosenthal and Arthur Gelb, *New York Times* editors, *One More Victim* (1967)

Talk to the readers like you would talk to your bubbe [grandmother].

> —Abraham Cahan, author and editor of the *Forward* for nearly fifty years, quoted in *Forward*, 100th anniversary issue, May 16, 1997

He had been out here almost two whole weeks, time enough to absorb the conventional wisdom. . . . The reporter is not an expert, you say? Nonsense. His opinions and judgments are the daily fare of more than a million American readers. That makes him an expert by definition. The point is that experts don't necessarily know anything, and usually they are wrong.

—Ze'ev Chafets, Israeli journalist, recalling a conversation with a newly arrived foreign correspondent assigned to Jerusalem, *Jerusalem Report*, March 7, 1991

I've received very angry calls from leading Republicans and even lost a friendship here and there over what I've written. . . . But I hate seeing journalists using their platform to reward friends and skewer enemies.

—Mona Charen, syndicated columnist, *George*, May 1997

"Ultra" is not a term of endearment. . . . Journalists see "ultra" only when looking rightward.

—Don Feder, columnist, "In Israel and Here: Devout Under Fire," *Boston Herald*, January 26, 1995

To catch a trend at just the right moment is the most important thing we can do.

—Max Frankel, executive editor, *The New York Times*, "The Top 20 New Yorkers," *New York*, April 25, 1988

The intimidation [of foreign correspondents in Lebanon by the PLO] was there, it was real, and anyone who denies that fact is simply fooling himself. . . . I think neither the press critics nor the press itself has been honest about this issue. The press critics have taken the view that all of us were intimidated, hence none of us wrote the truth, hence the truth didn't get out, hence Israel's image in the world was skewed. The press took the view, "Intimidated? Me? Intimidated macho me? Why, bullets bounce off my chest." But that's equally disingenuous. In fact the truth is somewhere in between.

—Thomas L. Friedman, former *New York Times* bureau chief in Beirut and Jerusalem, *Moment*, June 1985

Israel demands to be judged by different moral standards. It makes a moral claim to the U.S. We don't give Syrians three billion dollars a year. . . . We give Israel money because it's the 51st state in the very best sense of the word, that it is like us, that it's a society that is worth supporting, and it is truly a friend in need and it's a value worth preserving. So when we in the press judge Israel by a different yardstick than we judge the Syrians I find nothing particularly surprising about that. To the contrary, I say God save us from the day when I cover Syria like I cover Israel.

—Thomas L. Friedman, *Moment*, June 1985

The virtue of my method is that nobody thinks they're the source; but everyone thinks they know who the source is.

—Thomas L. Friedman, *New York Times* foreign affairs columnist, quoted in "The Tourist With an Attitude" by David B. Green, *Jerusalem Report*, March 9, 1995

Media are mobile spotlights, not passive mirrors of the society; selectivity is the instrument of their action.

—Todd Gitlin, journalist, *The Whole World Is Watching: Mass Media and the Making and the Unmaking of the New Left* (1980)

Who knows where today's anchorpersons are from, and what difference would it make if we did? . . . It is not ideas or insights that mark the modern communicator, but a blend of careful coiffure and sincerely antiseptic manner. . . . The political column is now said to be a dying art, and Personal Journalism is something that was practiced in the 19th Century—as though any journalism that ever affected us was not personal.

—Paul Greenberg, editorial page editor, *Pine Bluff Commercial*, and syndicated columnist, essay based on his acceptance speech on receiving an award at the University of Kansas, February 10, 1988, in which he warns of the "Blanding of American Journalism," *Entirely Personal* (1992)

The pressure on the political press to decide what's going to happen before it happens—it's like shingles, you can't get rid of it. I don't know what the impulse is. We never learn, we're always wrong . . . maybe we need a twelve-step program for political journalists to take it one primary at a time.

—Jeff Greenfield, television journalist and syndicated columnist, interviewed after the New Hampshire presidential primaries, *Later With Bob Costas*, February 1992

Once you leave the world of totalitarian governments, where there's one channel and one newspaper, you must engage the audience. And to that extent, it's always been entertainment. But recently, stories which are intriguing and fascinating and titillating, but have no greater value, have definitely leeched into the news business. This kind of information intrigues people, but at the end of the day, do we really care who Donald Trump marries; or about Woody Allen and Mia Farrow; or Amy Fisher?

—Jeff Greenfield, interviewed by Gary S. Lipman, *92nd St. Y Review*, Fall 1995

General, we are not your corporals. We will continue to call Ambassador Lodge and General Harkins until you put us on the choppers and we will call them at any damn hour of the day that we have to because that is our job. We are not going to take your word for anything that happens if there is the remotest chance that we can see it for ourselves. We are here for the *Times*, and the AP and the UPI and *Time* magazine, and they chose us to be here.

> —David Halberstam, *New York Times* correspondent in Vietnam, comment-
> ing to Brigadier General Richard Stilwell, chief of operations, South Viet-
> nam, 1963, quoted by Harrison E. Salisbury in *Heroes of My Time* (1993)

The byline is a replacement for many other things, not the least of them money.

> —David Halberstam, *The Best and the Brightest* (1969)

I can cover the My Lai massacre, Kent State massacre. And nobody ever called me a self-hating American. If you report on the Temple Mount massacre [in Jerusalem], you get labeled a self-hating Jew.

> —Don Hewitt, creator and executive producer of the CBS series *60 Minutes*,
> responding to remarks allegedly made by CBS former chief Laurence Tisch
> four years earlier, quoted in the *Baltimore Jewish Times*, April 26, 1996

[Broadcast journalism is] becoming a lost art and may all but vanish by the end of the century . . . The kind of tasteful and important journalism that made CBS News, ABC News and NBC News giants in the news business is, for the most part, gone and nobody seems to care.

> —Don Hewitt, speaking to members of the Institute for Public Relations Re-
> search and Education, quoted in *The Washington Times*, October 13, 1997

Nobody in my circle of friends believed that being a sportswriter was hard work. But you had to do a first edition story, a second edition story, a late story—three different stories in a day. It was a repetitive experience. You were always unsettled. In your suitcase. Out of your suitcase. In a sense, you're a foreign correspondent. You're on duty twenty-four hours a day. If someone falls off a curb and breaks his leg, it's your problem to report that.

> —Roger Kahn, journalist and author, quoted in *Bums* by Peter Golenbock (1984)

Some people collect Chinese porcelain, some collect Persian rugs. I collect decades. I love wandering, rummaging through old decades in search of glitter and litter, integrity and trash, gibberish and substance.

> —Bernard Kalb, former foreign correspondent for CBS, NBC, and *The New
> York Times*, from his remarks at a Columbia Graduate School of Journalism
> awards ceremony, January 26, 1995, *Columbia Journalism Review*, March/
> April 1995

If you believe, as we all do, that the press is the sentinel of democracy, the sentinel, for the most part is AWOL.

Bernard Kalb, from his remarks at a Columbia Graduate School of Journalism awards ceremony, *Columbia Journalism Review*, March/April 1995

This is the new journalism—issues packaged in anecdotes that may or may not be true. As an occasional, alternative approach to news and analysis, it is affecting; as the predominant approach, it is not just trite but stupefying. If all issues are personalized, we lose our capacity to entertain ideas, to generalize from our own or someone else's experiences, to think abstractly. We substitute sentimentality for thought.

—Wendy Kaminer, author, *I'm Dysfunctional, You're Dysfunctional: The Recovery Movement and Other Self-Help Fashions* (1992)

Unfortunately, in our line of work, everybody else's poison tends to be our meat. . . . I fear that if several of you showed up in my driveway to gauge my reaction to the slaughter of my wife on a commuter train or the rape of my daughter in some alley, I might lose some of my enthusiasm for the First Amendment.

—Ted Koppel, television journalist, December 10, 1993 broadcast, quoted in *Nightline: History in the Making and the Making of Television*, written with Kyle Gibson (1996)

The technological tail is wagging the editorial dog.

—Ted Koppel, "The Worst Is Yet to Come," *The Washington Post*, April 3, 1994

I think it was probably the first time that a large American audience saw, on network television, Palestinians and Israelis speaking in a sense past one another, but at least as equals, as equal human beings, with equal standing on the stage and equal standing in the audience. And I think after that, it may have been a little more difficult for people just to dismiss Palestinians as a caricature.

—Ted Koppel, recalling the live 1988 *Nightline* broadcast from the Jerusalem Theater featuring Israeli and Palestinian panelists on a program with a live audience, *Nightline: History in the Making and the Making of Television*, written with Kyle Gibson (1996)

On-camera, I rarely change my demeanor in deference to the stature of the guest. Were my respect for the rank, fame, or accomplishments of a guest to impede my line of questioning, the discussion would suffer. And there are a few exceptions to that—a sitting President is one, the Pope is another. Except for those, I approach almost every guest as if, until midnight, we are on equal footing.

—Ted Koppel, *Nightline: History in the Making and the Making of Television*, written with Kyle Gibson (1996)

If A. B., a non-Jew, commits a crime, the Associated Press dispatches furnish the public with the news without any reference as to whether he is a Methodist, a Catholic, or whatever Christian denomination. If, however, A. B. happens to be a Jew, then almost invariably the news item informs us that A. B., a Jew, committed an offense. Is there any good reason for making such a distinction?

> —Adolf Kraus, president of B'nai Brith, from a 1908 letter written to Melville E. Stone, head of the Associated Press, quoted in *B'nai Brith: The Story of a Covenant* by Edward E. Grusd (1966)

Jews are news. It is an axiom of journalism. An indispensable axiom, too, because it is otherwise impossible to explain why the deeds and misdeeds of dot-on-the-map Israel get an absurdly disproportionate amount of news coverage around the world.

> —Charles Krauthammer, columnist, "Judging Israel," *Time*, February 26, 1990

If the morning papers can't match the drama of Cable News Network anchor Bernard Shaw describing how he hid under his bed in a Baghdad hotel room, they can offer a bit of perspective, a historical record, plus such useful details. . . . Some liken it to fans devouring the Monday sports section after already having watched the Redskins game.

> —Howard Kurtz, media reporter for *The Washington Post*, "Newspapers, Getting It Late but Right," reprinted in *The Media and the Gulf War: The Press and Democracy in Wartime*, edited by Hedrick Smith (1992)

Half the battle for the future of the Middle East will be won on the day when news about this part of the world will be relegated from page 1 to page 16 in *The New York Times* and other leading newspapers.

> —Walter Z. Laqueur, author and historian, "Is Peace in the Middle East Possible?" *The New York Times Magazine*, August 27, 1967

Say what you will about West Bank settlements, but let's be precise with language. Not every Jewish residence on the West Bank is a settlement. In modern Middle East parlance a settlement is something that sprung up since the 1967 war. . . . The settlement of Beit Schneerson [established in 1819] existed before 29 of the 50 states were admitted to the Union. For the [New York] *Times* to call something a settlement and not tell readers that it is 178 years old—even older than the *New York Times*—is just to muddy the situation rather than illuminate it.

> —Jonathan Mark, journalist, "Media Watch" column, *The Jewish Week*, January 17, 1997

Here in New York, there is a side of Zionist machismo that expresses itself in Jews proudly threatening to cancel their subscriptions to *The New York Times*, or some other newspaper, because it is not supportive of the Likud position and is therefore "anti-Israel"—even when the anti-Israel opinion is shared by at least half of everyone actually living in Israel.

—Jonathan Mark, *The Jewish Week*, January 17, 1997

Libel seldom causes as much public indignation as it does private anguish.

—Louis Nizer, attorney, *My Life in Court* (1961)

The New Republic does not judge every political matter by whether it is good for the Jews.

—Martin Peretz, editor-in-chief of *The New Republic*, letter to the editor, *Time*, March 21, 1994

I had long known it was impossible for a journalist to convey a hundred percent of the truth, but I didn't realize to what extent the truth is distorted, both by the intentions of the journalist and by neglect. I don't mean just the interpretations of what happened; I also mean the facts. The reporting about Sharon and the murders were virtually criminal. . . . The victims were assassinated two times: once by the murderers, the second time by the press.

—Roman Polanski, film director, commenting on press coverage surrounding the murder of his wife, actress Sharon Tate, by members of the Charles Manson family, 1969, interview with Larry Dubois in *Playboy*, December 1971

Early on in my life as diplomat, I discovered what I had known all along: there's no such thing as "off the record."

—Itamar Rabinovich, Israeli ambassador to the United States, quoted in *Lifestyles*, New Year 1996

I've spent a large portion of my years as a journalist trying to get people to talk, and they keep talking, and I keep being amazed when they do. I think part of the reason is, simply, that most people like to talk about themselves and a reporter is one of the few people they're likely to run across who seems to want to listen.

—Betty Rollin, journalist, *Am I Getting Paid for This?* (1982)

The problem is not that the facts were repressed but that their publication spurred little action, or even interest, among readers.

—Gary Rosenblatt, editor and publisher, reporting on the findings of a three-day academic conference on "Journalism and the Holocaust, 1933–1945" at Yeshiva University in New York City, *The Jewish Week*, October 27, 1995

When the background noise of being executive editor faded and I began writing, things that I'd been interested in, but didn't realize how much, began rising in my consciousness, and one of them was Israel.

> —A. M. Rosenthal, columnist and former editor of *The New York Times*, quoted in *Lifestyles*, pre-Spring 1996

To him, the morning paper renewed the newness of life each day, without fail: a glorious bazaar, a circus of wonders and follies, a forum, a sideshow, a school, a stage.

> —Leo Rosten, author, recalling his father, *People I Have Loved, Known or Admired* (1970)

In Vietnam, there was no front. What front there was, reporters and soldiers had equal access to. I think they [the military establishment] were naive and expected that we were to be a kind of cheerleading squad. Well, journalism had changed. Warfare had changed.

> —Morley Safer, *60 Minutes* correspondent who opened the CBS News Saigon bureau in 1965 and served two tours in Vietnam, *Booknotes* interview with Brian Lamb, C-SPAN, May 6, 1990

The importance and power of the media cannot be overemphasized. The reporting of an arrest always exceeds the reporting of an acquittal.

> —Robert L. Shapiro, defense attorney, 1993 article in *The Champion*, the magazine of the National Association of Criminal Defense Lawyers, reprinted in *Columbia Journalism Review*, September/October 1994

It's fitting to commemorate the guys who died trying to tell their stories. . . . It's probably a good thing for people both inside and outside the business who think that all it takes are stand-ups and eye contact.

> —Bob Simon, CBS News Chief Middle East correspondent, commenting on the memorial to slain journalists funded by the Freedom Forum near Arlington Cemetery, quoted in *USA Today*, May 24, 1996

You get more information from *The New York Times* and *The Washington Post* than from most intelligence sources. At most classified briefings on Capitol Hill, half the stuff is familiar from that morning's paper; the other half we read in the next morning's paper.

> —Senator Arlen Specter (R-Pa.), former chair of the Senate Intelligence Committee, interview in *The Middle East Quarterly*, March 1997

When I reported back that Joanne Woodward was at least as interesting as her husband [actor Paul Newman] . . . my male editor said that I couldn't write it that way. *Journal* readers would be threatened by interesting wives.

> —Gloria Steinem, author and activist, recalling a writing assignment for *Ladies Home Journal*, in "Life Between the Lines," *Outrageous Acts and Everyday Rebellions* (1983)

One encountered a sense of excitement, of adventure, and of relief that a long-expected storm had finally broken. As for the newspapermen, myself included, we all acted a little like firemen at a three-alarmer.

> —I. F. Stone, journalist, commenting on the Japanese attack on Pearl Harbor in his weekly column in *The Nation*, December 13, 1941, reprinted in *The War Years 1939–1945*

Have you ever seen so many sad faces on TV? Reporting the Israeli election was no fun for most of the journalists who told us about Netanyahu's stunning victory last week—and it showed.

> —Jonathan S. Tobin, executive editor of the *Connecticut Jewish Ledger*, commenting on American response to Benjamin Netanyahu's election victory over Shimon Peres, *Long Island Jewish World*, June 14, 1996

Anyone who has been in television as long as I have knows only too well that the prime-time merchants in our business have almost always viewed news programs with undisguised disdain. They resented the existence of documentaries and the like because they were the traditional loss leader, the soft underbelly in an otherwise lucrative prime-time schedule. Among other things, the enduring success of *60 Minutes* has jabbed a thumb in the eye of that conventional wisdom. Yet even though I've lived through it and been a part of it, I really never expected to see the day when a news broadcast would consistently challenge the most popular entertainment shows in the weekly ratings. However, that is what happened and I think it will continue to happen. After all, unlike *Dallas* and *The A-Team*, we don't have to worry about running out of plots or exhausting our story line.

> —Mike Wallace, television journalist, *Close Encounters* written with Gary Paul Gates (1984)

Imagine being paid for something you would do for nothing.

> —Walter Winchell, columnist, talking about receiving his first payment for an article in *Billboard*, quoted in *The Men Who Invented Broadway* by John Mosedale (1981)

❖ JUSTICE ❖

I think the two greatest contributions of Judaism to the world are the values of justice and compassion. We can disagree about the content of these values — is an eye for an eye really justice — but the quest to balance these values has been the overarching theme of Jewish life. And what I find especially impressive is that justice is not the natural human condition. Power is. Revenge is much more natural than justice.

> —Alan M. Dershowitz, law professor, appellate lawyer, activist, and author, quoted in *92nd St. Y Review*, Spring 1996

There is no commandment to hate the enemy in any Jewish source I have ever read or heard of. Again, Christian polemics frequently make Jewish "justice" into "vengeance," a polemic that has had its effects to this day. When in 1961 the most horrendous criminal ever to be tried by a Jewish court was brought for trial to Jerusalem, the Canadian Broadcasting Corporation featured a nationwide television program. It was entitled: "The Eichmann Trial — Justice or Vengeance?"

> —Emil L. Fackenheim, professor of philosophy, "The Ethics of Judaism/ Justice," *The Jewish Spectator*, Fall 1989

Throughout all history, indeed, the natural inequality of human beings has justified razing a whole city to revenge the murder of one privileged person . . . "An eye for an eye" is a fundamental conception of social justice. No society has ever got further than this principle in its actual administration of justice (despite all the talk about a higher "law of love") and many, even today, are still not up to it.

> —Maurice Friedman, professor of religious studies, philosophy, and comparative literature, "Hasidism and the Love of Enemies," 1964, in *The Challenge of Shalom*, edited by Murray Polner and Naomi Goodman (1994)

Social justice should have nothing to do with personal likes and dislikes.

> —Sam Levenson, humorist and author, *Everything but Money* (1966)

Admittedly, there are those who describe Nazi war criminal trials as revenge for the past. If such people consider legal action against mass murderers as acts of vengeance, how, one must ask, would they define justice?

> —Lawrence D. Lowenthal, executive director of the American Jewish Committee, Greater Boston Chapter, *Boston Globe*, August 29, 1993

❖ KABBALAH ❖

(see also Meditation, Spirituality)

A talmudic adage says that there are as many ways to Truth as there are human faces. Thus the Kabbalah may assume any shape or form. Depending on the "receiver," it may appear as an angel, a holy fool, a Torah scholar, or a beautiful woman. It may be embodied in a book, a song, a dance, or a conversation with God. As with all spirtiual traditions, Kabbalah cannot really be taught; it must be experienced.

—Perle Besserman, author, teacher, and descendent of the Baal Shem Tov, *Kabbalah and Jewish Mysticism* (1997)

It would be a great mistake to regard Kabbalah's elaborate visions of heavenly palaces and supernatural beings as anything more than symbolic waystations on the path to the One.

—Perle Besserman, *Kabbalah and Jewish Mysticism* (1997)

One of the primary texts of the Kabbalah, the Zohar, cries out to humankind, saying, "You beings on earth who are in deep slumber, awaken! Who among you has labored to turn darkness into light and bitterness into sweetness?" It pleads with us, "Stop sleeping! Wake up! What are you waiting for?"

—Rabbi David Cooper, author, teacher of Jewish meditation, and director (with his wife) of the Heart of Stillness Hermitage in Colorado, *God Is a Verb: Kabbalah and the Practice of Mystical Judaism* (1997)

Each particle in our physical universe, every structure and every being, is a shell that contains sparks of holiness. . . . Our opportunities to raise sparks are boundless. The choices we make for our activities, the interactions we have with our family, friends . . . even strangers, the way we spend our leisure time, the books we read . . . everything in daily life presents sparks locked in husks awaiting release.

> —Rabbi David Cooper, *God Is a Verb: Kabbalah and the Practice of Mystical Judaism* (1997)

Emptiness is the first step in going within and touching God. When you empty your mind of clutter, your heart of expectations, and your body of excess stimulations, you become an empty vessel ready to receive God. Only if you are empty can you reflect God's image, echo God's voice, and be filled with God's light.

> —Rabbi Shoni Labowitz, author, lecturer, creator of healing rituals, and co-rabbi (with her husband) of Temple Adath Or in Fort Lauderdale, Fla., *Miraculous Living: A Guided Journey in Kabbalah Through the Ten Gates of the Tree of Life* (1996)

As you walk the path of Intention, landscapes of light open to sanctuaries of silence. In stillness the silence welcomes you to explore the inner chambers of your being. Silence invites you to refuel your energy, clear your mind, relax your body, and return to the Source of your Divine nature. In silence, all becomes clear.

> —Rabbi Shoni Labowitz, *Miraculous Living: A Guided Journey in Kabbalah Through the Ten Gates of the Tree of Life* (1996)

The world is teeming with God. Since God is in everything, we can serve God through everything.

> —Daniel C. Matt, author and professor of Jewish mysticism, *Moment*, February 1997

The revival of Kabbalah is a revival of fragments, each with its own face. It is still too early to tell how much light these fragments will be able to hold, but at no time perhaps since the early years of the Hasidic movement have so many people been thinking so deeply about Kabbalah and its meaning for our age, people now trying to absorb the light of Kabbalah into the busy stream of contemporary life.

> —Rabbi Micha Odenheimer, journalist and activist, "Jerusalem Mystics," *Moment*, February 1997

❖ KADDISH ❖

(see also Jewish Observance)

I am the only woman in the room, and, with one or two exceptions, I will remain so for the next eleven months. . . . I would learn that, from certain quarters, when I rose to speak the Mourners' Prayer, there would be a silence at each of the four or five places where the congregation was required to say Amen. The prayer was, therefore, regarded as null and void, my father dishonored.

> —Esther M. Broner, novelist who said Kaddish for her father in an Orthodox synagogue, *Mornings and Mournings: A Kaddish Journal* (1994)

I came into the world as a Jew and I want to leave it as a Jew.

> —Felix Frankfurter, justice of the United States Supreme Court; quoted by a former law clerk who said Kaddish at his funeral and explained the Jewish tradition of Kaddish to other mourners, quoted in the *American Jewish Year Book, 1966*

Kaddish gives voice to why Jews should survive: They are the hope of the world.

> —Rabbi Michael Goldberg, author, *Why Should Jews Survive? Looking Past the Holocaust Toward a Jewish Future* (1995)

When others rise to recite the kaddish, the feeling of having been individually victimized by our loss is blunted. We are not alone in our dark period. We see death in a larger context, as part of the mystery of human existence in which are interwoven and inseparable the good and the bad, happiness and sorrow, life and death. Through the saying of the kaddish, we both honor the dead and help heal the living.

> —Dr. Jack Shechter, professor of Bible, "Saying Kaddish," *Direction*, Spring 1993

To do this in Manhattan is to discover once again that the orthodox Jews keep this thing together. There is no minyan [quorum of ten] without them, and I travel each day from New York to Prague to Pinsky to Sharmgun, depending on the hour I awake. These little shuls [synagogues], these shtetls from long ago and far away, they are my home for 11 months.

> —Sidney Zion, journalist, reflecting on saying Kaddish for his mother, quoted in *The Jewish Week*, December 1993

One night in the summer Rabbi Goldberg called and said we needed three more. Frank Sinatra was in the place, and he took Sammy Cahn and a couple of Jews in his party. This was the Kaddish walk of all time; if Damon Runyan was around it'd have been a musical.

> —Sidney Zion, recalling saying Kaddish in 1982 at the Actor's Temple on 47th Street in Manhattan, around the corner from his restaurant, Broadway Joe, quoted in *The Jewish Week*, December 1993

❖ KOREAN WAR ❖

Most people want peace, but there are some on Wall Street who are afraid of it. Even the *Wall Street Journal* criticizes them. "War itself is a terrible thing, but we find more terrible yet the fact that there are men walking around who talk of peace as if it were terrible."

> —Dorothy G. Horowitz, letter to her husband Mel, a young M.A.S.H. surgeon on the Korean front, April 1, 1953, *We Will Not Be Strangers: Korean War Letters Between a M.A.S.H. Surgeon and His Wife*, edited by Dorothy G. Horowitz (1997)

By doing vascular repairs we save not only limbs, but money. Every leg amputation costs the government $100,000 by the time the pt.[private] lives to 50 years old.

> —Mel Horowitz, a M.A.S.H. surgeon on the Korean front, writing to his wife Dorothy, March 20, 1953, *We Will Not Be Strangers: Korean War Letters Between a M.A.S.H. Surgeon and His Wife*, edited by Dorothy G. Horowitz (1997)

❖ LABOR ❖

The Jewish Working Girl's Vacation Society has for the last 6 years maintained at the seashore a vacation house for working girls in which, for $3 a week, girls, worn with the year's labor in shop or factory, have enjoyed the benefits of sea bathing, fresh, bracing air, and well-prepared food.

> —Fund-raising notice in *The American Hebrew*, June 7, 1901

Finally, after a half year of doing battle, peace reigns again in the garment industry. . . . During the first week of the conflict, the manufacturers demanded that the Amalgamated [Clothing Workers] cease to exist, and they did everything in their power to destroy the union. But the Amalgamated showed that this was impossible.

> —Headline article in the [Yiddish] *Forward* reporting that "The Garment Workers' Struggle Is Over," 1921, "Looking Back," *Forward*, May 31, 1996

As an industry develops into a larger unit, the chances of the individual being able to protect himself diminish. Self-protection is possible only where real freedom of contract exists. The only freedom the individual worker has is to leave and go to another employer. But if that is the only alternative and the other employer is equally as large, then the worker passes from pillar to post, and he has no protection at all.

> —Louis D. Brandeis, Boston attorney and future U.S. Supreme Court justice, speaking before the United States Commission on Industrial Relations, January 23, 1915, quoted in *An American Primer*, edited by Daniel J. Boorstin (1995)

The sit-down strike satisfied the urge for recognition of the depersonalized and alienated automobile worker. Looking at the idle machine beside which he sat, he could believe, for the first time, perhaps, that he was its master rather than its slave.

> —Sidney Fine, labor historian, recalling the sit-down strike by workers that began in Flint, Mich., on December 30, 1936, quoted in *The Great Depression* by Robert S. McElvaine (1993)

We regard the minimum wage rate as one of the most, if not the most, anti-black laws on the statute books.

> —Milton and Rose Friedman, economists and authors, *Free to Choose: A Personal Statement* (1980)

Competition for his services—that is the worker's real protection.

> —Milton and Rose Friedman, *Free to Choose: A Personal Statement* (1980)

The system of petty, nagging tyrannies that prevailed before the strike was either maddening or fatal to self-respect. There were fines and abuses, there were insults and favoritism, with all the subtle influences degrading to womanhood. Under such conditions the human worker sinks into a mere drudge at infinite cost to the human soul.

> —Samuel Gompers, president of the American Federation of Labor, "Struggles in the Garment Trade," *American Federationist*, March 1913

Capitalist and laborer are both men; let them but meet as men and they will soon realize how closely akin they are. Cutting each other's throats will bleed them both to death . . . it will bleed society in the process.

> —Senator Jacob K. Javits (R-N.Y.), *Javits: The Autobiography of a Public Man*, written with Rafael Steinberg (1981)

Girls, what have we to lose! We are humble in our demands. In return for our youth and our labor we want a little more leisure so that we may rest for the next day, a little more food so that we may live a few years longer, and a little more joy so that we may keep faith with humanity.

> —Sonya Levien, union member who became a writer, quoting the protagonist "Little Old Girl" in her story "The Veteran" as she addressed a crowd in the Union Hall in New York City, *Metropolitan*, March 1913

You girls, you supposedly ignorant immigrants, untaught, unfed and unloved, you are the pioneers that are paving the way for a better race—with your last cent you are purchasing economic freedom for the scabs of our trade, with your lives you are paying for the freedom of those others who are too smug or selfish to know that they, too, are slaves. And it is up to you to have the pride and endurance of pioneers. You, the minute women of this age, unite and stand for a better world for womanhood!

> —Sonya Levien, quoting the protagonist "Little Old Girl" in her story "The Veteran" as she addressed a crowd in the Union Hall, *Metropolitan*, March 1913

It would be absurd to assume the minimum-wage legislation is a kind of omnibus for paradise. To fix a "living standard" would be a great advance over what we have, but by every civilized criterion it is a grudging and miserable thing. In those moments of lucidity . . . it seems like a kind of madness that we should have to argue and scrape in order that we may secure to millions of women enough income to "live". . . . Not a wage so its women can live well, not enough to make life a rich and welcome experience, but just enough to secure existence and drudgery in grey boardinghouses and cheap restaurants.

> —Walter Lippmann, journalist, *The New Republic*, March 27, 1915

The labor movement was never just a way of getting higher wages. What appealed to me was the spiritual side of a great cause that created fellowship. You wanted the girl . . . who worked beside you to be treated as well as you were, and an injury to one was the concern of all.

> —Rose Schneiderman, women's labor leader and advocate from 1904 through the 1950s, quoted in "Our True Legacy: Radical Jewish Women in America" by Janet Zandy, *Lilith*, Winter 1989

It is easy—and absolutely wrong—to say that such progress was inevitable, that things get better by themselves. Only because trade unions organized and demanded and insisted and fought for these changes did they come about.

> —Louis Stulberg, president of the International Garment Workers Union, speaking at his induction as a Fellow of Brandeis University, March 6, 1969, quoted in *Out of the Sweatshop*, edited by Leon Stein (1977)

It was the Triangle fire that decided my life's course.

> —Fannia Cohn, trade union activist, from a letter—about the horrific 1911 fire in which 146 women garment workers lost their lives—to E. G. Lindeman, February 7, 1933, Fannia Cohn Papers, The New York Public Library, cited in *The Jewish People in America, Volume III* by Gerald Sorin (1992)

. . . saw girl after girl appear at the reddened windows, pause for a terrified moment, and then leap to the pavement below, to land as a mangled, bloody pulp.

—Louis Waldman, socialist labor lawyer and eyewitness to the Triangle fire, *Labor Lawyer* (1944)

The workers who had died . . . were not so much the victims of a holocaust of flame as they were the victims of stupid greed and criminal exploitation.
—Louis Waldman, *Labor Lawyer* (1944)

I would be a traitor to these poor burned bodies if I came here to talk good fellowship. We have tried you good people of the public and we have found you wanting. . . . This is not the first time girls have been burned alive in the city. Every week I must learn of the untimely death of one of my sister workers. Every year thousands of us are maimed. The life of men and women is so cheap and property is so sacred. There are so many of us for one job it matters little if 146 of us are burned to death.
—Rose Schneiderman, organizer for the International Ladies Garment Workers Union (ILGWU) and the Women's Trade Union League, speaking at the memorial meeting held at the Metropolitan Opera House on April 2, 1911, quoted in *The Survey*, April 8, 1911

The lesson of the hour is that while property is good, life is better; that while possessions are valuable, life is without price. Because life is sacred, we realize today the indivisible oneness of human welfare. These women and these men will have died in vain unless we today highly resolve that my brother's wrong is my wrong. I am not merely the keeper of my brother and my sister, but the justice-dealing brother to all men and women in God's world.
—Rabbi Stephen S. Wise, Jewish leader and activist, remarks at a meeting of twenty philanthropic organizations at the headquarters of the Women's Trade Union League on the day after the tragic fire in 1911, quoted in *Rabbi and Minister: The Friendship of Stephen S. Wise and John Haynes Holmes* by Carl Hermann Voss (1964)

❖ LANGUAGE ❖

(see also Books, Literature, Writing)

The word is hard to translate. "Good deed" sounds too pious and solemn, "duty" too much like something one ought to do but doesn't really want to do. Perhaps the best translation is this, that to do a mitzve is to behave like a mensch. But then, "human being" is not quite the right translation for the Yiddish mensch either.

—Emil L. Fackenheim, philosopher, reflecting on the meaning of the word "mitzve," "The Ethics of Judaism: On Being a Mensch," *The Jewish Spectator*, Fall 1989

[It was a word I had] used all my life, and in my act for years, and no one thought anything of it.

—Jackie Mason, comedian, explaining his use of the words "fancy shvartzer" in describing New York Mayor David Dinkins in a room full of reporters, quoted in "Notes on Shvartzer" by Richard Goldstein, *The Village Voice*, October 19, 1989

I think the selection and arrangement of words is, in a small way, a moral choice. In preferring a particular verb, in avoiding cliches and idioms, or in using them upside down, you make a decision that may have at least a microscopic ethical consequence. Words can kill: this we know only too well. But words can, in small measure, also sometimes heal.

—Amos Oz, Israeli novelist and essayist, from "Peace and Love and Compromise," acceptance speech for the German Publishers Peace Prize in Frankfurt, October 1992, excerpted in *Harper's*, February 1993

We can give ourselves over altogether to Gentile culture and be lost to history, becoming a vestige nation without a literature; or we can do what we have never dared to do in a Diaspora language: make it our own, our own necessary instrument, understanding ourselves in it while being understood by everyone who cares to listen or read.

—Cynthia Ozick, novelist and essayist, "Toward a New Yiddish," 1970, in *Art & Ardor* (1983)

We choose our clothes more carefully than we choose our words, though what we say about and to others can define them indelibly. That is why ethical speech—speaking fairly of others, honestly about ourselves, and carefully to everyone—is so important. If we keep the power of words in the foreground of our consciousness, we will handle them as carefully as we would a loaded gun.

—Rabbi Joseph Telushkin, author, lecturer, and spiritual leader of the Synagogue for the Performing Arts in Los Angeles, *Words That Hurt, Words That Heal: How to Choose Words Wisely and Well* (1996)

❖ LAW ❖

We cannot put constitutions together like prefabricated henhouses.

> —Albert P. Blaustein, law professor whose expertise was in drafting constitutions for nations in transition—he believed that for a constitution to work, it must reflect a country's culture and history—quoted in his obituary, *The New York Times*, August 23, 1994

The wrongs of aggrieved suitors are only the algebraic symbols from which the court is to work out the formula of justice.

> —Benjamin Cardozo, future U.S. Supreme Court justice, describing the function of the court in his publication "The Jurisdiction of the New York State Court of Appeals," 1903, quoted in *The World of Benjamin Cardozo* by Richard Polenberg (1997)

[A conviction for a rape in New York State required that the woman] oppose the man to the utmost limit of her power. A feigned or passive or perfunctory resistance is not enough. It must be genuine and active and proportioned to the outrage. The record discloses a situation where conflicting inferences may be drawn whether resistance in that sense was offered.

> —Benjamin Cardozo, justice in the New York State Court of Appeals, per curiam opinion, People v. Raymond Carey, in which they set out the requirements of a woman's behavior in order for a defendant to be convicted of rape in New York, 1918, quoted in *The World of Benjamin Cardozo* by Richard Polenberg (1997)

It is when the colors do not match, when the references in the index fail, when there is no decisive precedent, that the serious business of judging begins. He must then fashion law for the litigants before him. In fashioning it for them, he will be fashioning it for others.

> —Benjamin Cardozo, justice in the New York State Court of Appeals, *The Nature of the Judicial Process* (1921)

This is the first time in my life I have addressed a jury on behalf of a defendant in a criminal case. When I went to law school, little did I dream that my first time in this role would be in my own behalf.

> —Roy M. Cohn, lawyer, addressing a federal court jury in New York City charged on a five-count criminal indictment, December 9, 1969, *A Fool for a Client* (1971) (He was acquitted of all charges.)

A greater percentage of you will become criminal defendants than will be defense lawyers.

> —Alan M. Dershowitz, law professor, appellate lawyer, activist, and author, speaking to his criminal law class at Harvard Law School about the tendency of the school to turn out corporate lawyers, quoted in "Trying to Save Leona," *New York*, March 12, 1990

There is no one I would not defend, if it came to him being without a defense.

> —Alan M. Dershowitz, quoted in *Boston*, November 1995

An appeal lawyer is like a good insurance policy you hope you never have to use.

> —Alan M. Dershowitz, quoted in *Boston*, November 1995

The myth that Jewish law was always the same, and that all of Halakhah [Jewish law] was handed down at Sinai, was designed to prevent Jews from recognizing the mutable nature of the very human institution that is Judaism.

> —Alan M. Dershowitz, *The Vanishing American Jew* (1997)

When I was in CCNY [City College of New York] I took an aptitude test. The results said I should be a lawyer first, an investment banker second, and third, a used-car salesman. I got something that combines all three.

> —Joseph Flom, last surviving name partner in the corporate law firm of Skadden, Arps, Slate, Meagher & Flom, reflecting on the skills required to be a lawyer specializing in mergers and acquisitions, quoted in *Skadden: Power, Money, and the Rise of a Legal Empire* by Lincoln Caplan (1993)

I may be wrong about this, but I do believe that in some of this Court's decisions there has been a tendency from time to time . . . to forget the realities of what happens downstairs, of what happens to those poor, miserable, indigent people when they are arrested and they are brought in these strange and awesome circumstances before a magistrate, and then later on they are brought before a court; and there, Clarence Earl Gideon, defend yourself.

> —Abe Fortas, counsel for petitioner before the U.S. Supreme Court in *Gideon v. Wainright*, regarding the question of whether a criminal defendant can get a fair trial without a lawyer, 1963, quoted in *May It Please the Court*, edited by Peter Irons and Stephanie Guitton (1993)

A man may live—even in the aquarium of public office—without revealing and, indeed, without discovering his essential convictions. But for a Justice of this ultimate tribunal, the opportunity for self-discovery and the occasion for self-revelation are usually great. Judging is a lonely job, in which a man is, as near as may be, an island entire. The moment is likely to come when he realizes that he is, in essential fact, answerable only to himself.

> —Abe Fortas, former Supreme Court justice, tribute to his mentor Justice William O. Douglas, *The New Republic*, August 21, 1965

We are never in doubt. We always do the right thing. Sometimes we have to do it 5-4.

> —Abe Fortas, reflecting on the Supreme Court in an address at the Yale Law School banquet, April 2, 1966, quoted in *Fortas: The Rise and Ruin of a Supreme Court Justice* by Bruce Allen Murphy (1988)

A criminal trial is not a game in which the state's function is to outwit and trap its quarry. The state's pursuit is justice, not a victim.

> —Abe Fortas, discussing the issue of trying to safeguard the rights of the accused from certain discovery procedures employed by the state (*Giles v. Maryland*), 1967, quoted in *Fortas: The Rise and Ruin of a Supreme Court Justice* by Bruce Allen Murphy (1988)

What is the worth of identification testimony even when uncontradicted? The identification of strangers is proverbially untrustworthy.

> —Felix Frankfurter, jurist in Boston, *The Case of Sacco and Vanzetti: A Critical Analysis* (1927)

All systems of law, however wise, are administered through men, and therefore may occasionally disclose the frailties of men. Perfection may not be demanded of law, but the capacity to correct errors of inevitable frailty is the mark of a civilized legal mechanism.

> —Felix Frankfurter, *The Case of Sacco and Vanzetti: A Critical Analysis* (1927)

American criminal procedure had its defects. That we know on the authority of all who have made a special study of its working. But its essentials have behind them the vindication of centuries.

> —Felix Frankfurter, *The Case of Sacco and Vanzetti: A Critical Analysis* (1927)

As judges we are neither Jew nor Gentile, neither Catholic nor agnostic. We owe equal attachment to the Constitution and are equally bound by our judicial obligations whether we derive our citizenship from the earliest or latest immigration to these shores. . . . As a member of this Court I am not justified in writing my private notions of policy into the Constitution, no matter how deeply I may cherish them or how mischievous I may deem their disregard. . . . It can never be emphasized too much that one's own opinion about the wisdom or evil of a law should be excluded altogether when one is doing one's duty on the bench.

> —Felix Frankfurter, justice of the United States Supreme Court, from his 1946 opinion in a case involving a salute to the flag, quoted in *American Jewish Year Book 1966*

When the law contradicts what most people regard as moral and proper, they will break the law—whether the law is enacted in the name of a noble ideal such as equality or in the naked interest of one group at the expense of another.

> —Milton and Rose Friedman, economists and authors, *Free to Choose: A Personal Statement* (1980)

Generalizations about the way women are, estimates of what is appropriate for most women no longer justify denying opportunity to women whose talent and capacities place them outside the average description.

> —Ruth Bader Ginsburg, U.S. Supreme Court justice, from her opinion for the Court ordering the Virginia Military Institute to admit women, June 1996, quoted in *The New York Times Magazine*, October 5, 1997

Laws as protectors of the oppressed, the poor, the loner, is evident in the work of my Jewish predecessors on the Supreme Court. The Biblical command "justice, justice shalt thou pursue" is a strand that ties them together.

> —Ruth Bader Ginsburg, address to the annual meeting of the American Jewish Committee, May 1995, as adapted in an ad in the committee's "What Being Jewish Means to Me" series

Intelligence has always been the one attribute of man that appealed to me more strongly than any other. And since you happen to possess more of it than any other man whom I have had the pleasure of meeting, this alone would cause me to bow down in abject hero worship. But, sir, I appreciate the other great qualities that bring you to undertake our case. Courage, surely.

> —Nathan F. Leopold, teenager on trial with Richard Loeb for the kidnap and murder of young Bobby Franks on May 21, 1924, from a letter to attorney Clarence Darrow in appreciation of his decision to represent them at trial, *Life Plus 99 Years* (1957)

The reason pro bono is both the challenge and the test is not subtle in the least. If the legal profession does not stand for equal justice under law, then it is hard to see what it does stand for.

—Sol M. Linowitz, attorney, diplomat, and author, *The Betrayed Profession: Lawyering at the End of the Twentieth Century*, written with Martin Mayer (1994)

The most frightening measure of what the legal profession has lost is that most Americans do not even remember the trust that society once placed in its lawyers. If a new Alexis de Tocqueville came to America today to study its laws and customs, he could never come up with the idea that the lawyers were the country's natural aristocracy.

> —Sol M. Linowitz, *The Betrayed Profession: Lawyering at the End of the Twentieth Century*, written with Martin Mayer (1994)

The result surely would have been different if there were blacks on the jury, or the jurors were less homogenous in terms of their background. And there is no doubt that a more heterogeneous jury would have been selected if the trial had been kept in L.A.

> —Barry Scheck, professor of law who was a commentator for Court TV during the Rodney King case, *The New Republic*, May 25, 1992 (Two years later he was part of the defense team representing O. J. Simpson in which similar issues arose.)

The truth of the matter is, the law as a profession is unsatisfying most of the time. To be able to create a space where you feel that, on a day-to-day basis, everything you do is directed toward achieving social justice is rare indeed.

> —Barry Scheck, lawyer who, along with Peter Neufeld, created and ran the Innocence Project at Yeshiva University's Benjamin N. Cardozo School of Law, specializing in helping to free innocent convicts using DNA testing, quoted in *New York*, January 2, 1995

I puzzle on it all the time. We come from a cultural tradition that's extremely legalistic. And you could probably argue that this tradition tends to select those who are better at manipulating rules.

> —Scott Turow, lawyer and novelist, discussing why there are so many Jewish lawyers, in an interview in *Jerusalem Report*, November 14, 1996

❖ LEADERSHIP ❖

Rarely in history does a creator achieve his reward. Moses was allowed to see the land from afar but not to enter it. Herzl died on alien soil while the dream of his life was still far from fulfillment. Weizmann was granted by the historic providence of the Jewish people to see the fruits of his life's work.

> —David Ben-Gurion, first prime minister of Israel, reflecting on his proposal in 1948 that Chaim Weizmann be named the first president of the State of Israel, from a series of talks with Moshe Pearlman, *Ben-Gurion Looks Back* (1965)

We seek a leadership construed not primarily in terms of the accomplishment of plans but equally in terms of its humanizing effect on the people being led.

> —Rabbi Eugene B. Borowitz, professor of education and Jewish religious thought, "Tzimtzum: A Mystic Model for Contemporary Leadership," *Religious Education*, November/December 1974

Dominance reflects strength; leadership must be earned.

> —Henry A. Kissinger, former Secretary of State and National Security Advisor to President Nixon, from his eulogy for Nixon, Yorba Linda, Calif., April 27, 1994, C-SPAN broadcast of the funeral ceremonies for the late Richard Nixon

There is nothing new under the sun or under the ballroom lights. Each generation has wailed over the absence of adequate leadership since it is only in retrospect and with some historical perspective that a leadership can be properly evaluated.

> —Philip M. Klutznick, lawyer, public official, and national president of B'nai Brith, *No Easy Answers* (1961)

It is relatively easy for a leader to appropriate the rhetoric of Dr. King, to speak of "The Dream" in abstract, often sentimental terms, as if those words had no specific meaning and implied no moral mandate for society. It is much harder for a leader to unpack the content of that dream and to remind a nation that we have betrayed and trampled on its meaning.

> —Jonathan Kozol, author, "Memos to Clinton," *Tikkun*, January/February 1997

I don't know what would have happened if a public opinion poll was taken when Moses left Egypt. My impression is that he may not have enjoyed a majority.... Shall we go after the Golden Calf because it's the will of the majority, or should we go to the promised land because that is our destiny?

> —Shimon Peres, Israeli foreign minister, commenting on the signing of the Israeli-PLO (Oslo II) accords in an interview with American Jewish media, quoted in *The Jewish Week*, October 6, 1995

What does it take to be a Jewish leader in America these days? Clearly, the greatest leader in Jewish history [Moses] wouldn't stand a chance. He wasn't wealthy; his best-known asset was humility, which would not have moved him up the ranks of board memberships very quickly; and he wasn't an orator—in fact, he stuttered.

> —Gary Rosenblatt, editor and publisher, *The Jewish Week*, June 13, 1997

A nation needs its guides and shepherds, its scouts and leaders of the flock, who will carry out the function of leadership: the ability to feel and the power to think.

> —Rabbi Adin Steinsaltz, Talmudic scholar, *The Strife of the Spirit* (1988)

The Lubavitcher rebbe, his memory should be a blessing, did not need medals, nor did he need honors. It was an honor to be in his presence. It was an honor to listen to him. It was an honor to be seen by him. Few have brought hope and fervor to so many men and women who were deprived of both.

> —Elie Wiesel, author and Nobel laureate, speaking at a Washington, D.C., dinner in honor of the late Rebbe Menachem Mendel Schneerson and the unveiling of the Congressional Gold Medal, the highest civilian honor, awarded to the rebbe on the first anniversary of his death, June 28, 1995, quoted in *The Jewish Week*, July 7, 1995

❖ LIBERALS AND CONSERVATIVES ❖

(see also Politics, Government, and Leaders)

There are three not-sapos-tas that have hurt liberals. You're not supposed to say that the free enterprise system is wonderful and has worked better than any other. You're not supposed to say that in our era, certainly since the fall of Hitler, Communism has been by far the worst system of government in the world, or that most people who are in prison are bad people.

> —Barney Frank, U.S. Congressman (D-Mass.), speaking one month after

Democrat Michael Dukakis lost his run for the presidency against George Bush, quoted in "A Liberal's Liberal Tells Just What Went Wrong" by E. J. Dionne, Jr., *The New York Times*, December 22, 1988

I'm not a conservative. I have never been a conservative. We are radicals. We want to get to the root of things. We are liberals in the true meaning of that term—of and concerned with freedom. We are not liberals in the current distorted sense of the term—people who are liberal with other people's money.

— Milton Friedman, economist and author, *Booknotes* interview with Brian Lamb, C-SPAN, November 20, 1994

The editors of the liberal *Tikkun* and the conservative *Commentary* have more in common respectively with Jesse Jackson and Ronald Reagan than either of them has with Maimonides—or with me.

— Rabbi Michael Goldberg, author, *Why Should Jews Survive? Looking Past the Holocaust Toward a Jewish Future* (1995)

With his Jewish immigrant ancestry, Goldwater could never share the right's nativism. Nor could he share its isolationism. In his first autobiography, Goldwater wrote that he came to fear Hitler well before the outbreak of the war because he recalled how his ancestors had been driven from Poland by anti-Semitism.

— John B. Judis, journalist, "The Alrightnik of Arizona," *The New Republic*, November 28, 1988

A lot of people who shake their fists and say, "That Ron Kuby is a son of a bitch! How can he represent that scum!" have become clients. You know that saying, "A conservative is a liberal who's been mugged"? Well, my position is that a liberal is a conservative who's been indicted.

— Ronald Kuby, attorney and longtime associate of William Kunstler, quoted in *George*, 1996

Liberals aren't evil people but their ideas are.

— Rabbi Daniel Lapin, founder and president of Toward Tradition, a national organization of Jewish conservatives, quoted in "Conservative Jews Rally for Political Exodus," *Insight*, October 27, 1997

Remember, we are in favor of all things nuclear: power, bombs and families.

— Rabbi Daniel Lapin, speaking at a conference in Washington, D.C., September 22, 1997, broadcast on C-SPAN

Liberalism used to be a vision of justice; it has increasingly become, outside the economic sphere, the dogma of those who want to do whatever they damn well please.

> —Martin Peretz, editor-in-chief, "Why Dukakis Lost," *The New Republic*, November 28, 1988

A lot of people say this derives from the Prophets. I think that's a lot of crap.

> —Norman Podhoretz, former editor of *Commentary*, discussing the view that Judaism is indistinguishable from liberalism, quoted in "As Right as Ever" by Edward R. Silverman, *Jerusalem Report*, June 15, 1995

Liberal? I was incoherent and radical. I was even a feminist and I'm very embarrassed about it . . . If you grow up as a Jew and a woman in New York City, you are a liberal until you go away and think things through.

> —Lisa Schiffren, speechwriter for Vice President Dan Quayle who wrote the speech attacking *Murphy Brown*, recalling her earlier politics in high school, quoted in *New York*, August 3, 1992

As tolerant folk who want to live and let live, liberals trust that all human problems are amenable to negotiated solutions, that all people are united in a spirit of brotherhood, and that history itself is a record of progress.

> —Ruth R. Wisse, professor of Yiddish and comparative literature, *"If I Am not for Myself": The Liberal Betrayal of the Jews* (1992)

❖ LIFE IN AMERICA ❖

A convention of Jewish farmers is without doubt one of the most beautiful phenomena of Jewish life in America.

> —*Tageblatt*, November 30, 1914

My real close friends are Jewish, my after dark friends in general are Jewish, but my daytime friends are gentile.

> —A housewife in Park Forest, Ill., quoted in "The Origin of a Jewish Community in the Suburbs" by Herbert J. Gans in *The Jews: Social Patterns of an American Group*, edited by Marshall Sklare (1958)

They must have missed those "Hogan's Heroes" reruns.

> —Jonathan Alter, journalist, reporting on the results of a survey revealing that

more than fifty percent of high school students didn't know what the word "Holocaust" meant and that a quarter of all adults didn't know that it was in Germany that the Nazis first came to power, *Newsweek*, December 20, 1993

It might be suggestive of what happened in this town of Washington to remind you—and remind myself—that the year before I came here, in 1950, I remember trying to have lunch with a black friend of mine, George Weaver, a man who ten years later became Assistant Secretary of Labor. When I tried to make a lunch date with him through a phone call from New York, and I suggested that we go to the Statler, he said "no," and then I suggested the Occidental and he said "no," and I finally realized what was going on and I was very embarrassed, and I said, "OK George, tell me where we can have lunch," and we ended up in a small Chinese restaurant. That was only thirty years ago.

> —Hyman Bookbinder, Washington, D.C., representative of the American Jewish Committee, quoted in *Moment*, May 1981

In 1955 my father died with his ancient mother still alive in a nursing home. The old lady was ninety and hadn't even known he was ill. Thinking the shock might kill her, my aunts told her that he had moved to Arizona for his bronchitis. To the immigrant generation of my grandmother, Arizona was the American equivalent of the Alps, it was where you went for your health. More accurately, it was where you went if you had the money. Since my father had failed in all the business enterprises of his life, this was the aspect of the news my grandmother dwelled on, that he had finally had some success. And so it came about that as we mourned him at home in our stocking feet, my grandmother was bragging to her cronies about her son's new life in the dry air of the desert.

> —E. L. Doctorow, novelist, "The Writer in the Family" (voice of the character Jonathan) in *Lives of the Poets* (1984)

The "has been" disappeared from the cafe and this meant that he was no longer among the living. The New World was to him a table without a cloth somewhere in the corner of a cafe.

> —Ossip Dynow, "The Has Been," *American Jewish Chronicle*, May 18, 1917

The American lives even more for his goals, for the future, than the European. Life for him is always becoming, never being.

> —Albert Einstein, Nobel Prize–winning theoretical physicist and humanist, interview in *Berliner Tageblatt*, July 7, 1921, relating his impressions of America, *Ideas and Opinions: Albert Einstein* (1982)

In the voting booth, an American is alone with his mind and his soul. No one threatens him. Even at that point in history, no one—not J. Edgar Hoover nor Senator McCarthy—no one dared threaten the American worker in the voting booth.

> —Howard Fast, author, who became a member of the Communist Party at the peak of his career, 1944–1957, *Being Red: A Memoir* (1990)

For commuters, home is a place to eat and sleep.

> —Don Feder, columnist, "Whatever Happened to the Idea of Community?" *Boston Herald*, November 25, 1993

When I dial the phone after 10 P.M., all I get is an answering machine. After machine after machine. When my mother died, I got three machines in a row. . . . Convenience. Everything is open twenty-four hours except the human spirit.

> —Jyl Lynn Felman, author, *Tikkun*, July/August 1996

I was as fascinated as everyone else by Houdini's fabled escapes. One day I was roaming about with my Bauman cousins, Seymour, my own age, and Jack, a few years younger. We decided to tie Jack up to a tree, like Houdini, and see if he could escape. And then, incomprehensibly, we ran off and left him. Jack must have escaped, because he grew up to be a top Santa Monica anesthesiologist.

> —Sid Fleischman, author and magician, *The Abracadabra Kid: A Writer's Life* (1996)

I don't think you want my band to play here. I think we better fold up right now. I'm not telling anybody to come in the back door.

> —Benny Goodman, jazz musician, responding to the hotel manager's request that the black band members not enter through the front door and through the ballroom—and instead enter through the kitchen—the night they were to open at the New Yorker, quoted in *Swing, Swing, Swing: The Life and Times of Benny Goodman* by Ross Firestone (1993)

For Jews, it is akin to the tales in general American culture of George Washington's honesty after he chopped down the cherry tree or Abraham Lincoln's decision to walk miles to return a penny. Koufax's famed decision made the impression that it did because it suggested to us that one could be both an American and a Jewish hero at the same time.

> —Rabbi Daniel Gordis, dean of the Rabbinical School, University of Judaism, discussing Sandy Koufax's decision not to play in the first game of the 1965

World Series because of Yom Kippur, *Does the World Need the Jews?* (1997)

On any given weekend there are more people in houses of worship than attend major-league baseball games all year long.

> —Jeff Greenfield, television journalist and syndicated columnist, quoted in *The Jewish Week*, August 1994

This is my first trip to the United States. Americans are very polite, but trying to relate to them is like kissing through glass.

> —David Grossman, Israeli author, quoted in *Kissing Through Glass* by Joyce R. Starr (1990)

Barbie gives a little girl the ability to project her dreams of the future in a very positive way.

> —Ruth Mosko Handler, cofounder, with her husband Elliot, of Mattel and inventor of the Barbie doll, named for their daughter Barbara, quoted in *The Jewish Journal of Greater Los Angeles*, July 26, 1996

Andy Warhol's remark that in the future everyone will be famous for fifteen minutes delineates the quintessential American dilemma. We can all become famous, but perhaps not stay famous. And once having known that fame, how will we live out the rest of our lives?

> —Erica Jong, novelist and poet, *Fear of Fifty* (1994)

My generation had Doris Day as a role model, then Gloria Steinem—then Princess Diana. We are the most confused generation.

> —Erica Jong, quoted in *People*, March 7–14, 1994

In *Playboy* magazine a long interview with me was printed. (And for those who want to know why I, a rabbi, allowed the interview, the answer is: Think of all the Jewish readers of *Playboy*, and who needs the teachings of JDL more than they?)

> —Rabbi Meir Kahane, founder of the Jewish Defense League, *The Story of the Jewish Defense League* (1975)

I remember taking my mother to see the musical *Fiddler on the Roof*. My mother was born in a village very much like Anatevka, the setting for *Fiddler*. And when it was over, and we were back out on the street, I said, "Ma, how did you enjoy it? Did it bring back memories?" "It was wonderful," she said, "Only I don't remember so much singing and dancing."

> —Alan King, comedian, *Name-Dropping*, written with Chris Chase (1996)

I take people up on their invitations. I don't own any property—except for a burial plot in New Jersey.

> —Edward I. Koch, former mayor of New York City, quoted in *The New York Times Magazine*, August 10, 1997

The truth is that money is everything here and everything else doesn't matter as much. In Russia, friends were everything because of the way of life where you couldn't get much with money and because of the time you spent with your friends because there was nothing to do, just talk. In a way it's boring, but you never have to worry about tomorrow, and the future. Here, tomorrow is why you live, or what you worry about.

> —Raimonda Kopelnitsky, teenager who lived in Ukraine until she was twelve in 1989 and emigrated to the United States with her parents and brother, *No Words to Say Goodbye* (1994)

My grandmother came to this country when she was fifteen years old, a young girl arriving from Galicia. She carried with her a single suitcase, and in that suitcase she had packed her few belongings, including photographs of her parents and of her childhood home. When she arrived here and came in through Ellis Island she was met by her brother, a much older brother who had emigrated earlier. And the first thing that brother did when he met her was to take her suitcase and throw it into New York Harbor. He told her that she was an American now and that she had to leave the Old Country behind.

> —Aaron Lansky, founder and president of the National Yiddish Book Center, at the dedication of the Center's new building in Amherst, Mass., June 15, 1997

O wasteful America! We boast we are a clever people, yet go on juggling with youth and its dreams.

> —Sonya Levien, writer, from a story describing the union's efforts against conditions in the sweatshops, "The Veteran," *Metropolitan*, March 1913, quoted in *Out of the Sweatshop*, edited by Leon Stein (1977)

No man who owns his own house and lot can be a Communist. He has too much to do.

> —William Levitt, builder who revolutionized the process of home building via mass production to provide single-unit housing for middle-class citizens

in "Levittown" in the 1950s, quoted in *The Fifties* by David Halberstam (1993)

L.A.'s a city where the rules of civility are turned upside down, where the waiters introduce themselves within seconds and tell their life stories, but where next-door neighbors are so guarded that they never stop by even to say hello. Starbuck's is the perfect L.A. metaphor, a destination without even the commitment of a full meal.

> —Marlene Adler Marks, managing editor, *Jewish Journal of Greater Los Angeles*, July 5, 1996

The popular culture is now as unavoidable as any airborne pollutant. To say that if you don't like it you should just tune it out makes as much sense as saying that if you don't like the smog, stop breathing.

> —Michael Medved, author and media commentator, *Hollywood vs. America* (1992)

I was born and bred in New York City. In those years, the 1950s and 1960s, we called it "the City": no other modifier than the definite article was needed. There was only one City, and I grew up as close to the center of Jewish life outside of Israel as you could get.

> —Deborah Dash Moore, professor of religion, "I'll Take Manhattan: Reflections on Jewish Studies" presented at a symposium of the American Jewish Historical Society, May 27, 1995

We feel the necessity of enjoying ourselves and so we must attempt to do so while we wear this hairshirt. If we go to the opera, it is not for enjoyment, but to be improved. If we visit European cities, it is to be cultured, not to enjoy ourselves. . . . Everything else we do is because it is tax deductible.

> —Zero Mostel, actor, Theodore Spencer Memorial Lecture at Harvard University, May 20, 1962, quoted in *Zero Mostel: A Biography* by Jared Brown (1989)

What's amazing is that my son will probably feel the same way about camp for the rest of his life. I know I do, and most everyone else who went to camp seems to as well. No subject I've written about in my journalistic career has prompted the outpouring of joyous confessionals from readers that camp does.

> —Frank Rich, columnist, anticipating visiting day at his son's summer camp, *The New York Times*, July 20, 1996

I find that I am suddenly living in a country in which the Jew has come to be—or is allowed for now to think he is—a cultural hero.

—Philip Roth, novelist, speech at Loyola University (Chicago) for a symposium, "The Needs and Images of Man," 1961, reprinted in *Reading Myself and Others* (1975)

Instead of writing, people are calling; instead of communicating, they're "staying in touch."

—William Safire, columnist, speech at Syracuse University, May 13, 1978, included in *Lend Me Your Ears: Great Speeches in History*, edited by William Safire (1992)

When the toilet bowl flushed like Niagara, when a suburban homeowner killed his wife and children, and when a Jew was made a member of President Theodore Roosevelt's cabinet, the excited exclamation was: "America! America!"

—Delmore Schwartz, poet and fiction writer, *America! America!* (1940)

The change upon our scene that would be most bewildering to a person of the 19th century is not the illumination of our cities by electricity, not our horseless carriages, not our flying birds. It is the pervasive presence and movement of television. It appears to me that television would yield to our imaginary visitor of another century an object of greatest admiration and concern, at once a most awesome and available miracle of the century.

—Solomon Simonson, actor, public radio broadcaster, television producer and director, rabbi, lawyer, and professor of communications, *Crisis in TV* (1966)

None of the old philosophers and thinkers could have foreseen an epoch such as this one: the helter-skelter epoch. Work in haste, eat in haste, speak in haste. Even die in haste.

—Isaac Bashevis Singer, Yiddish writer, *Enemies, A Love Story* (1972)

We live in strange times . . . Some people go to a spa and pay $300 a day for not eating.

—Elie Wiesel, Nobel laureate and author, quoted in *The Christian Science Monitor*, December 10, 1996

American girls want everything. And I was no exception.

—Ellen Willis, essayist, *Beginning to See the Light: Pieces of a Decade* (1981)

By the time the Republicans made their pitch for the patriarchal family, the entire country of Oprah-watching women knew exactly what the injustices and dangers of that family structure looked like.

> —Naomi Wolf, author, *Fire With Fire: The New Female Power and How It Will Change the 21st Century* (1993)

❖ LITERATURE ❖

(see also Books, Language, Poetry, Writing)

Rereading is a delight for which there is no substitute. Anyone who says that he doesn't need to read Dante or Rabelais or Cervantes or Shakespeare or look again at Giotto or the dome of Florence Cathedral is living in a fool's paradise because the greatness of the experience of having lived these years is to be able to see anew, to see something new in all these works.

> —Daniel J. Boorstin, Librarian of Congress, author, and historian, *Booknotes* interview with Brian Lamb, C-SPAN, December 6, 1992

There was another aspect of Anne Frank's diary that pleased me . . . the fact was that Anne Frank didn't in the least appear to think that the Holocaust— although it howled like the hungriest of wolves right at her doorstep—devoured the intensity of all other, private experience. . . . The reality in her own mind was as valid as the life-threatening reality external to her mind . . . you could be living right in the eye of the Nazi storm and still take your own little angst seriously.

> —Daphne Merkin, novelist and essayist, "Dreaming of Hitler," *Esquire*, August 1989

Literary history and the present are dark with silences: some the silences for years by our acknowledged great; some silences hidden; some the ceasing to publish after one work appears; some the never coming to book form at all.

> —Tillie Olsen, author, *Silences* (1978)

The literary Tevye . . . was very real for us. We were so fond of him that we often forgot he was fictional and regarded him as a member of the family, sorrowing with him in his troubles and rejoicing in his moments of happiness. We were always affected by his genuine warm humanity that knew no bounds, whether directed toward his creator in heaven or his horse on earth.

> —Marie Waife-Goldberg, *My Father, My Sholem Aleichem* (1968)

Literature and prayer have much in common. Both take everyday words and give them meaning.

> —Elie Wiesel, author, "Prayer and Modern Man" in *Rabbi Joseph H. Lookstein Memorial Volume* (1980)

The weight of fiction, too, depends on the possibility of outrage. Who is left today to be outraged? In the America of O. J. Simpson, who can object to Philip Roth?

> —Ruth R. Wisse, professor of Yiddish and comparative literature, review of Philip Roth's *Sabbath's Theater* in *Commentary*, December 1995

❖ LONELINESS ❖

People are lonesome. I'm lonesome. It's strange to be in a body. So what I'm doing—what we're all doing—on a day like today is saying, "Touch me, sleep with me, talk to me."

> —Allen Ginsberg, poet, reflecting on participation in a Be-In, quoted in *Allen Ginsberg in America* by Jane Kramer (1968)

It's easier actually to be alone than to be in the presence of that which arouses the need but fails to address it. . . . If one cannot win over loneliness, at least one can learn that it's not fatal. Such knowledge becomes a strength, an ally, a weapon.

> —Vivian Gornick, essayist and author, *Approaching Eye Level* (1996)

❖ LOVE ❖

Love is as difficult to describe as God himself.

> —*Etikete*, a 1912 Yiddish compendium of manners and morals, quoted in *The Wonders of America: Reinventing Jewish Culture, 1880–1950* by Jenna Weissman Joselit (1994)

It occurred to me that I had stepped into something like magic—into a soft, limelit world where time stops, and where one thinks of miracles, and of quiet beauty, and of how the things we want most in life are so rarely given that when they are granted we seldom believe it, and don't dare touch, and, without knowing, sometimes turn them down.

—Andre Aciman, author and professor, "Cat's Cradle," *The New Yorker*, November 3, 1997

People fall in love with a person's body, with who they know, with the way they dress, with their scorecards. With everything but their real selves, which is what you need to love if you're to be happy together.

—Bob Dylan, singer and songwriter, quoted in *No Direction Home: The Life and Music of Bob Dylan* by Robert Shelton (1986)

More and more I come to the conclusion that a personal love is not for one who dedicates himself to an ideal. Somehow it is like serving two Gods . . . no man could be satisfied to give all of himself. And to receive in return only a small part of the woman he loves. And how is she to give all when every nerve of her pulls toward the impersonal, the universal love? And so she must forswear the one for the other. No, there can be no personal life for me.

—Emma Goldman, anarchist and a founder of the women's rights movement, 1911 letter to Leon Malmed, quoted in *Emma Goldman: An Intimate Life* by Alice Wexler (1984)

Superficial feelings come and go; physical attractions are merely temporary; true love is a decision based on judgment.

—Sol Landau, author, *Length of Our Days: Focus on Judaism and the Personal Life* (1961)

Love is not to be condemned and so degraded, but to be exercised and mastered. . . . Let not your soul, if it is ardent, become contaminated and disordered by false shames and a false sense of sin. Love in itself is the source of loveliness and wisdom if it is gratified without falsehood and without abandoning the sterner elements of life. Natural things are made sinful only by a mistaken notion that they are so. Account love, then, as inevitable and lovely, but remain master of your soul and of yourself and of the larger purposes which you were born to fulfill.

—Ludwig Lewisohn, writer, musing on what he would say to a son, *Upstream: An American Chronicle* (1922)

There is one other fundamental difference between love and hate. Love is always a refuge. Hate is never a refuge. Only a mentally sick person can find refuge in his hates. But love is the enduring sanctuary of life. Life may rob you of many things. It often does. But it can never bereave us of love itself. That remains.

—Rabbi Abba Hillel Silver, rabbinic leader, from a December 22, 1940, sermon, quoted in *Therefore Choose Life: Selected Sermons, Addresses, and Writings of Abba Hillel Silver, Volume One*, edited by Herbert Wiener (1967)

To say "I love you" one must know first how to say the I.

—Ayn Rand, writer and philosopher, interview with Alvin Toffler in *Playboy*, March 1964

A human being must love someone, otherwise he or she goes out like a candle.

—Isaac Bashevis Singer, Nobel Prize–winning Yiddish writer, *Meshugah* (1995)

❖ LUCK ❖

Mazel is the imp of metaphysics.

—Rebecca Goldstein, *Mazel* (voice of the character Sasha) (1995)

My first piece of advice is to "be lucky." That's not always easy, but one of the tricks is to recognize opportunity when it knocks.

—Edgar M. Bronfman, chaiman of The Seagram Company Ltd., and president of the World Jewish Congress, *Good Spirits: The Making of a Businessman* (1988)

❖ MARRIAGE ❖

(see also Love, Families)

Love comes after marriage, and then the hardest thing is to stay away from each other during the time when you are not permitted.

— Lubavitch housewife and activist, quoted in *Hasidic People* by Jerome Mintz (1994)

It's not necessary to have a philosopher for a wife; a little common sense is far better than a university education and modern theories.

— *Etikete*, a 1912 Yiddish compendium of manners and morals, quoted in *The Wonders of America: Reinventing Jewish Culture, 1880–1950* by Jenna Weissman Joselit (1994)

A woman has a greater need for love than a man — and concomitantly, a greater need for security. Being loved is part of a woman's natural life in the same way it is a part of man's. To make her personality attractive and seductive is imperative, we repeat, for purposes of security. In the past she could, perhaps, feel safe after she had married and then sometimes risk neglecting her charms; but today, with the present rise in divorce, the woman who depends on a man for her means of support and social position must continue to pay attention not only to her intellect but also to what may be called narcissistic pursuits, that is personal enhancement and better appearance.

— Rabbi Menachem M. Brayer, psychiatrist and author, *The Jewish Woman in Rabbinic Literature: A Psychosocial Perspective* (1986)

That's where the conflict is — we want for a wife a combination kindergarten teacher and a hooker.

—Lenny Bruce, comedian, quoted in *The Essential Lenny Bruce*, edited by John Cohen (1966)

The I-Thou relation is most fully realized in love between man and wife. Here arises what Buber calls the exemplary bond, two people revealing the Thou to each other. Love involves the recognition and confirmation of the other in his or her uniqueness, and to this end, marriage affords the greatest length of time and greatest degree of intimacy.

> —Malcolm L. Diamond, professor of religion, *Martin Buber: Jewish Existentialist* (1960)

As a general rule my wife does not give me any advice about cooking, and I do not give her any advice about the law. This seems to work quite well on both sides.

> —Martin Ginsburg, tax attorney and professor who is married to Justice Ruth Bader Ginsburg, speaking with his wife on a panel on balancing public and private life at Wheaton (Ill.) College, May 1997, quoted in *The New York Times Magazine*, October 5, 1997

Simply stated, Judaism says that marriage is the ideal human condition and a basic social institution dating back to creation. It is said that when Adam and Eve were married, presumably in the Garden of Eden, God was the best man.

> —David C. and Esther R. Gross, editors and authors, *Under the Wedding Canopy: Love and Marriage in Judaism* (1997)

Two nicer people they don't come; I hope it will blow over like little gray clouds.

> —Jennie Grossinger, owner and hostess of Grossinger's Resort, commenting on the breakup of the marriage of Eddie Fisher and Debbie Reynolds, who had been guests at her hotel, 1957, quoted in *A Summer World* by Stefan Kanfer (1989)

I think she loves him the way any man would want to be loved, for his strengths and his weaknesses, with wide-open eyes. She knows better than anyone who he is, and she loves him.

> —Mandy Grunwald, former media strategist for Bill Clinton, discussing the Clintons' marriage amid the allegations of Bill's Clinton's infidelity, quoted in *The New York Times*, January 26, 1998

Marriage is a form of ownership. I don't like fusion. I think it's dangerous. I think you lose personal power.

> —Goldie Hawn, actress (who was married and divorced twice, and has lived

with actor Kurt Russell since 1983), quoted in *The New York Times*, December 1, 1996

Although an atheist, I know I have been blessed.

— Nat Hentoff, journalist and author, reflecting on his marriage of thirty-seven years to Margot Hentoff, *Speaking Freely* (1997)

To have a soulmate, you have to have a soul.

— Rabbi Shmuel Irons, head of the Kollel Institute in Oak Park, Mich., quoted in "The Deepest Connection" by Lynn Meridith Cohn, *Detroit Jewish News*, May 23, 1997

For, while the cry . . . rings with the woman that isn't married to some man and ought to be, the real tragedy of the hour is the woman who is married to him and oughtn't to be . . . The direction of the compass has changed for woman; it does not point only to the home. The ideal marriage with its peace and security is welcome in any age.

— Sophie Irene Loeb, social and civic reformer and reporter for the *New York Evening World*, from a 1915 symposium on women's suffrage, quoted in *The American Jewish Woman: A Documentary History* by Jacob R. Marcus (1981)

Fidelity is rooted in love. The object of love is not only "union" but unity. It represents a life of truth, such as loving husbands and wives can perceive and share. It is unity in the full sense of the word. To reach that stage of complete oneness calls for unreserved absorption, both physical and spiritual. It is the job of a lifetime.

— Dr. Morris Mandel, columnist, *The Jewish Press*, May 23, 1997

The position of the Jewish wife is enviable. It is not left to the whim of the husband to determine her status and her rights. There are laws governing their mutual relations down to the minutest detail. They are dictated by the utmost tenderness and refinement, revealing the reverent attitude toward womankind that is characteristic of a home-and-family-loving people. . . . The justice and ethical import of most of these laws are so evident that they speak for themselves and reflect glory on the people who accepted these laws so far advanced that to this day the world at large has been unable to improve upon them.

— Deborah M. Melamed, author, *The Three Pillars: A Book for Jewish Women* (1927)

In the modern ideology of intimacy, the spouses stand in the center of the marriage, replacing the extended family and culture. Society has chosen Romeo and Juliet over the Montagues and the Capulets.

> —Ester Perel, psychotherapist, talk presented at the Paul Cowan Memorial Conference on Intermarriage, Conversion and Outreach at the City University of New York, October 24, 1989, reprinted in the *Journal of Jewish Communal Service*, 1990

I always thought that any woman who got him for a husband was going to get a supreme catch.

> —Carol Pollard, older sister of spy Jonathan Pollard who was sentenced to life for espionage, recalling her brother, 1986, quoted in *Territory of Lies* by Wolf Blitzer (1989)

I wanted someone to share my sandwich with. And it had to be marriage and not just living together because I didn't want him (or me) to eat and run.

> —Betty Rollin, journalist, commenting on her decision to remarry, *Am I Getting Paid for This?* (1982)

I was twenty-one and my husband was twenty-four when we married. Jewish girls didn't go to work after they were married. My mother-in-law was scandalized. What will the neighbors say? I said: "To hell with the neighbors."

> —Dora Rosenzweig, age ninety-four, quoted in *American Dreams: Lost and Found* by Studs Terkel (1980)

The real test is not whether we could be crucified to save mankind but whether we can live with someone who snores.

> —Bernie S. Siegel, surgeon, teacher, and president of the American Holisitic Medicine Association, discussing forgiveness, *Love, Medicine and Miracles* (1990)

In the actual conduct of our lives, the two of us, in fact, silently accepted the premise that my first responsibility was to my home and family. Had this been put in words, I daresay that even as far back as the 30s and 40s I would have protested it. But so long as it was not formulated, I was able to deceive myself that it was as a matter of free will and competence that I took on the tasks of the home—they were easier for me to do than they would have been for Lionel and I was better at them. . . . Lionel wanted as much for me in self-realization—but he would have hated that word!—as he wanted for himself. I wanted as much for him as he wanted for himself and more than I wanted for myself. There was nothing special about this. It was the way that nice girls were raised.

—Diana Trilling, essayist and critic, *The Beginning of the Journey: The Marriage of Diana and Lionel Trilling* (1993)

A wedding is supposed to be about small-scale messianism. A lover, like the Messiah, has the power to take everything wrong and make it right again.

—Dr. Ruth K. Westheimer, author and sex therapist, and Jonathan Mark, journalist, *Heavenly Sex: Sexuality in the Jewish Tradition* (1995)

There is an inherent, irreducible risk in loving: it means surrendering detachment and control, giving our lovers the power to hurt us by withdrawing their love, leaving or wanting someone else. The marriage contract appeals to our self-contradictory desire to negate that risk, nullify that power . . . contrary to its myth, the institution supports our fear of love rather than our yearning for it.

—Ellen Willis, essayist, "The Family: Love It or Leave It" in *Beginning to See the Light: Pieces of a Decade* (1981)

❖ MEANING OF LIFE ❖

Three great mysteries there are in the lives of mortal beings: the mystery of birth at the beginning; the mystery of death at the end; and, greater than either, the mystery of love. Everything that is most precious in life is a form of love. Art is a form of love, if it be noble; labor is a form of love, if it be worthy; thought is a form of love, if it be inspired.

—Benjamin Cardozo, jurist (later named to the U.S. Supreme Court), officiating at a 1931 wedding, quoted in *Cardozo* by Andrew L. Kaufman (1998)

Toklas: Gertrude, what is the answer?

Stein: Alice, what is the question?

—Gertrude Stein and Alice B. Toklas, at Stein's deathbed, 1945, attributed

❖ MEDITATION ❖

(see also Kabbalah, Prayer, Spirituality)

While the majority of Americans are not theologically sophisticated, they are profoundly sophisticated about professional development, sexual matters, interpersonal dynamics, and psychology. This has translated into a demand for tools of personal transformation that, while not necessarily theologically complex, have great potential to help a person spiritually and psychologically and give them direct access to the Divine.

> —Avram Davis, author and founder and codirector of Chochmat HaLev in Berkeley, Calif., a renewal center for Jewish meditation and learning, "Introduction: The Heart of Jewish Meditation" in *Meditation From the Heart of Judaism: Today's Teachers Share Their Practices, Techniques, and Faith,* edited by Davis (1997)

The purpose of the higher forms of meditation is to break through the masks that deceive us, the lies that hinder us, the ephemeral that depresses us. They seek to move us through normal reality (while never leaving it behind) to actually experiencing the Divine. Additionally, it's important to remember that for Jews, interacting with the world is a component of experiencing the Divine.

> —Avram Davis, "Introduction: The Heart of Jewish Meditation" in *Meditation From the Heart of Judaism: Today's Teachers Share Their Practices, Techniques, and Faith,* edited by Davis (1997)

Chanting within the context of contemplative silent practice creates a space in which the power of the chant deepens and evolves, allowing its potential to unfold in the silence. My intention is not for the chant to continue in the silence, but rather for the chanter to use the chant as a doorway into the depths and the vast expanse of the silence.

> —Rabbi Shefa Gold, teacher of meditation, "That This Song May Be a Witness: The Power of Chant" in *Meditation From the Heart of Judaism: Today's Teachers Share Their Practices, Techniques, and Faith,* edited by Avram Davis (1997)

As some of the many Jewish students and devotees of Eastern traditions come home to their own ancestral roots, as we hope and pray they will, we should also hope that they bring with them some of the techniques of meditation and understandings of the human heart that Judaism could well absorb in this new era, much as in prior ages we made room for Plato and Aristotle or Kant and Hegel.

> —Rabbi Arthur Green, professor of Jewish thought at Brandeis University, former dean and president of Reconstructionist Rabbinical College, "Judaism for the Post-Modern Era," the Samuel H. Goldenson Lecture, delivered at the Hebrew Union College-Jewish Institute of Religion, Cincinnati, December 12, 1994

I'd been impressed by a quality Tibetans call "quiet mind." I knew I didn't have one. My mind was more Philip Roth novel than meditation manual. It had voices within that raged and insinuated, shouted and mocked in general echoes of a fierce family argument.

> —Rodger Kamenetz, author and professor of English, *Stalking Elijah* (1997)

For many people, the main difficulty of meditating is that it's scary to open the closets of the mind. You don't know exactly where you're going and you don't know whether it is worthwhile. . . . My own meditation has led me to a certain amount of equanimity and helped me to become a more responsive and a less reactive person.

> —Rabbi Jonathan Omer-Man, founder and director of Metivta, a school of Jewish wisdom and meditation in Los Angeles, "Noble Boredom: How to View Meditation," in *Meditation From the Heart of Judaism: Today's Teachers Share Their Practices, Techniques, and Faith*, edited by Avram Davis (1997)

❖ MEMORY ❖

The only lasting Holocaust memorial is a prayer. . . . We observe the destruction of the Temple not with dramatic candle lighting ceremonies and prominent guest speakers but with the fast of Tisha B'Av and a liturgy. Without hoopla, the Ninth of Av will be observed as it has been observed for two thousand years. Let us be guided by this so as to make sure that the Destruction of our time will be remembered.

> —Rabbi Joshua Berkowitz, rabbi of Congregation Agudath Shalom in Stamford, Conn., *The Jewish Spectator*, Summer 1981

If there is any substitute for love, it's memory. To memorize, then, is to restore intimacy.

> —Joseph Brodsky, Russian-born poet exiled to the United States in 1972 who won the Nobel Prize in 1987 and was appointed poet laureate of the United States in 1991, from his eulogy of Nadezhda Mandelstam, widow of the great Russian poet, included in *The Book of Eulogies*, edited by Phyllis Theroux (1997)

I'd rather live in the moment than some kind of nostalgia trip, which I feel is a drug, a real drug that people are mainlining. It's outrageous. People are mainlining nostalgia like it was morphine. I don't want to be a drug dealer.

> —Bob Dylan, singer and songwriter, describing his attitude to those fans who want him to continue performing his old songs exactly the way he recorded them, quoted in *Newsweek*, March 20, 1995

You've been to the hospitals and must surely have noticed those names sandblasted into the marble over the entrance to the nifty new wings, or seen the plaques in the temples, under every window in the sanctuary. The sanctuary? The toilets—the stalls and the urinals. Trees in Israel, waves in Waikiki, moonlight in Vermont. For a people wary of blowing God's horn—saying His name, I mean—we're not so reluctant to memorialize the monikers and to-do's of our loved ones. Not a sparrow falls, as it were.

> —Stanley Elkin, novelist and professor, *The Rabbi of Lud* (1987)

What is painful to one generation is insight for the next.

> —Eli N. Evans, author and president of the Charles H. Revson Foundation, *The Lonely Days Were Sundays: Reflections of a Jewish Southerner* (1993)

To the next generation, Hitler might as well be Genghis Khan.

> —Abraham H. Foxman, national director of the Anti-Defamation League, quoted in "Letting Go—A Personal Inquiry" by Philip Weiss, *New York*, January 29, 1996

We Jews stress the value of memory, for it permits us to span time. Sometimes, though, memory imprisons us in the belief that the past is destined to be repeated. We have become captives of martyrdom. We view ourselves as incapable of ever being fully integrated into a society of nations, even as we seek to be a nation like all other nations.

> —Rabbi Samuel Z. Glaser, rabbi emeritus of the Elmont Jewish Center on Long Island and professor of psychology, excerpt from sermon, 1992

You can't go back forty years musically any more than you can put together the New York Yankees of Joe DiMaggio and Lou Gehrig.

> —Benny Goodman, jazz musician, from an interview in *The New Yorker* promoting his return to Carnegie Hall on January 18, 1978, to celebrate the 40th anniversary of his now-legendary 1938 concert, quoted in *Swing, Swing, Swing: The Life and Times of Benny Goodman* by Ross Firestone (1993)

The presence of people we love, or indeed even just "people" is a small sliver of the presence of God. In Hebrew the word for "presence" and the word for "face" are the same; the very same word for the external facade and for the deepest innerness. The convex and the concave, male and female sacred space, public and private worlds, one is the reverse of the other, and the same word is used for both. For presence is the projection of the soul of the person on to physical space. "Your presence lingers on . . . ." What is presence but the expression of the soul of people, their mark after they themselves have vanished.

—Freema Gottlieb, author and professor, "The Visitor," *The Jewish Quarterly*, Autumn 1995

For great-grandchildren the lives of their parents' grandparents are a sliver of memory that for their children will not even exist.

—Richard Grossinger, anthropologist, author, publisher, and grandson of Jennie Grossinger, founder of the resort, *The Story of Grossinger's* (1997)

We rarely discover, we remember before we think; we see the present in light of what we already know. We constantly compare instead of penetrate, and we are never entirely unprejudiced. Memory is often a hindrance to creative experience.

—Rabbi Abraham Joshua Heschel, author, activist, and theologian, *Man Is Not Alone* (1951)

The anniversary of his death is May 13. He was superstitious. He always numbered page 13 as 12a. Since he died, every "May 12a" has been observed according to his will.

—Bel Kaufman, writer, speaking of her grandfather Sholem Aleichem, quoted in *Growing Up Jewish in America: An Oral History* by Myrna Katz Frommer and Harvey Frommer (1995)

In his will, my grandfather stipulated: Take care of your grandmother. Preserve your Yiddishkeit. I don't want any monuments. If people read my books, that will be my best monument. Read one of my merriest stories aloud in whatever language is most convenient.

—Bel Kaufman, quoted in *Growing Up Jewish in America: An Oral History* by Myrna Katz Frommer and Harvey Frommer (1995)

My mother knew I wouldn't be observant, kosher. The only thing she asked of me was that wherever I am, I say Yizkor for her. I'm in my eighties, and I still do that.

—Al Lewis, television personality, quoted in *Growing Up Jewish in America: An Oral History* by Myrna Katz Frommer and Harvey Frommer (1995)

There's magic in memory. You can stop and replay it at almost any point, rubbing old images together for sparks of new meaning.

—Leo Melamed, financier, *Escape to the Futures*, written with Bob Tamarkin (1966)

Memory is humankind's faculty to treasure in the recondite prisms of one's mind those smiles, glances, tears, anxieties and love that inform the celebration of the past.

> —Rabbi Marshall T. Meyer, human rights activist, founder of the Seminario Rabinico Latinoamericano, and spiritual leader of B'nai Jeshurun in New York City, Holocaust Service, Duke University, April 9, 1987

Memory is the arsenal of glories lived and lost, of untranslated dreams, of securities and insecurities, of ingenuousness untrammeled, of virgin youth unbesmirched by the world's all-too-frequent ugliness.

> —Rabbi Marshall T. Meyer, Holocaust Service, Duke University, April 9, 1987

The real rift is no longer between Jew and Arab but rather between past-oriented people on both sides.

> —Amos Oz, Israeli novelist, essayist, and peace activist, commenting on the Oslo agreements, "To Prevail Over Our Past," *Time*, September 20, 1993

My prayers, memories, and supplications will in time form the content of the stories that I will tell my children about how, most of all, prayerful remembering is what makes us Jewish. Indeed, there is no redemption in the stories of the Holocaust or in the story of Tisha B'Av. There is only memory of suffering which binds us to each other, to respective and collective histories, and perhaps, in the telling, ultimately to the sadness and suffering of God himself.

> —Dr. Eugene L. Pogany, cofounder of Dor L'Dor, a counseling practice involved with religious/cultural/historical development as it impacts on psychological health, "Exile and Memory: Reflections on Tisha B'Av," *Cross Currents*, Winter 1996

The Jewish past only became precious when it was perceived to have been lost forever.

> —David Roskies, professor of Jewish literature, keynote address at *Hadassah* magazine's 13th annual Harold U. Ribalow book award ceremony, November 29, 1995

And then there was the great classic, matzo brei, pieces of matzo soaked in milk, squeezed into a delectable mess, and fried to golden curls and flakes—one of the dishes that evokes piercing darts of nostalgia in every Jewish breast and stories of childhood Passovers complete with lightly drunken uncles.

> —Kate Simon, author, *Bronx Primitive: Portraits in a Childhood* (1982)

❖ MEN AND WOMEN ❖

(see also Relationships)

I've tried not to let my gender become an issue. But I am reminded of it every time someone is unwilling to have a serious conversation with me. The dismissiveness comes from where you'd least expect it. I've had some of my most substantive talks with Orthodox rabbis. . . . But from liberals, I get machismo.

> —Ambassador Colette Avital, Israeli consul general in New York, interview with Letty Cottin Pogrebin, *Moment*, October 1996

In the tradition I was born into, and in which I live today, men and women don't shake hands with each other. They do not allow themselves to be alone in a locked room unless they are married or related by blood. In so doing, they maintain a sensitivity that others have lost. And for this they are to be envied.

> —Rabbi Manis Friedman, dean, Beis Chanah Institute, St. Paul, Minn., *Doesn't Anyone Blush Anymore?* (1990)

The purpose of the separation [between men and women] in the synagogue isn't to handcuff people to keep them from misbehaving. The purpose is to preserve and protect our sense of sexuality, which we can squander if we're not careful.

> —Rabbi Manis Friedman, *Doesn't Anyone Blush Anymore?* (1990)

In a toss-up between having Anne Frank or Eva Braun as a date, it was clear to me who these men would choose.

> —Daphne Merkin, novelist and essayist, "Dreaming of Hitler," *Esquire*, August 1989

If women's and men's styles are shown to be different, it is usually women who are told to change. I have seen this happen in response to my own work.

> —Deborah Tannen, professor of linguistics and author, *You Just Don't Understand: Women and Men in Conversation* (1990)

To support a woman, promise permanence or fidelity, or take responsibility for the children one fathered might be bourgeois, but to expect the same woman to cook and clean, take care of the kids and fuck on command was only natural.

—Ellen Willis, journalist, recalling some of the chauvinistic aspects of the counterculture, *Beginning to See the Light: Pieces of a Decade* (1981)

Seizing legislative and economic power is not the same as getting help with the dishes.

—Naomi Wolf, author, *Fire with Fire: The New Female Power and How It Will Change the 21st Century* (1993)

❖ MESSIAH ❖

We want Moshiach [Messiah] now!

—Lubavitch slogan, 1980s

While the idea of the rebbe as the Messiah has enormous significance for the Lubavitcher community, it hasn't changed anyone's plans for the summer.

—Rabbi David Hartman, founder and director of the Shalom Hartman Institute for Advanced Jewish Studies in Jerusalem, commenting on the belief within the Lubavitcher Hasidic community that the ninety-year-old rebbe, Rabbi Menachem Mendel Schneerson, might be the Messiah, quoted in *Newsweek*, April 27, 1992

The idea of Elijah is a good thing for us in the 1990s. How often do we just open the door, dream a little, and surreptitiously check to see if a magical cup needs replenishing or not? How often do we just wonder if there's something out there that is more than what we can plainly see?

—Rabbi Ben Kamin, senior rabbi at the Temple-Tifereth Israel in Cleveland, *Thinking Passover* (1997)

The thing I love most about being Jewish is waiting for the Messiah! That is what I love the most . . . waiting, waiting, like so much of life . . . we Jews are waiting for the Messiah. Now many people believe the Messiah has already come, but we Jews are waiting . . . I love that the book is still open on the question of the identity of Moshiach [Messiah] . . . we Jews are sitting on the fire escape, having a smoke, noticing who goes by. I've noticed lots of people: Eleanor Roosevelt, George Balanchine, Martin Luther King, Nadine Gordimer, Fred Rogers, Richard Pryor, Cruz Irizarry, the woman who takes care of my kids when I'm working, the UPS man who's so nice about carrying in the boxes and setting them down wherever you need, the sexy guys from the cable company . . . it's like a big Halloween party, life is a costume party in which anyone may come forward from behind the masks and reveal themselves as Moshiach.

—Deb Margolin, performance artist, *"Oh Wholly Night" and Other Jewish Solecisms*, 1996

The avoiding of the twin pitfalls of despair and utopianism gives Jewish messianism its power. It is certainly the single most valuable concept which the Hebraic religion had bequeathed the world. Of course, the price we pay for this extraordinary idea is the possibility of its distortion.

> —Rabbi Seymour Siegel, professor of theology, "Theology for Today," *Conservative Judaism*, Summer 1974

Ich leb far Moschiach tzu kumen. [Now I believe the Messiah is coming.]

> —Isaac Bashevis Singer, Nobel-prize winning Yiddish writer, beginning his talk at the University of Texas-Austin, after being introduced—in Yiddish— by a gentile professor of Jewish studies, Robert King, 1979

With a broad hint that the "Era of Moshiach" is upon us, the Lubavitch advertisers invite us to jump on the bandwagon, and "Be part of it!" Both religion and politics are trivialized by this manipulation of hope. The advertisement promises Jews Redemption like a giveaway benefit of a Thanksgiving Day sale. Jews have maintained their disciplined religious civilization too long through too much painful history for it to be degraded by such cheapened rhetoric.

> —Ruth R. Wisse, professor of Yiddish and comparative literature, *Forward*, November 1, 1991

❖ MIKVAH ❖

(see also Jewish Observance)

When a woman goes to the mikvah she is putting the state of separation behind her and beginning anew. The focus is not on erasing sins or changing outward identity, but rather on moving from the state of individuality to another, higher, identity. We dissolve our egos in the "womb," returning to the original waters. We prepare to unite with our husbands by symbolically entering the Garden of Eden, when Adam and Chava [Eve] were freshly created, as "one flesh."

> —Tamar Frankiel, author and scholar of comparative religion and American religious history, "To Number Our Days" in *Total Immersion: A Mikvah Anthology*, edited by Rivkah Slonim (1996)

If you'd like more excitement in your life, test the waters.

—Advertisement appearing in California newspapers placed by Chabad-Lubavitch, 1996

❖ MONEY ❖

(see also Business, Economics)

Can anyone imagine Moses, Jesus, or Gandhi armed with the money-bags of Carnegie?

—Albert Einstein, Nobel Prize-winning theoretical physicist and humanist, *On Wealth* (1934)

Our economy demands the possession and the use of money but does not require the religion of the Golden Calf.

—Rabbi Ezekiel Landau, spiritual leader of the American Congregation of Jews from Austria, remarks from his 1958 Kol Nidre sermon, quoted in *Bridging Two Worlds* by Sol Landau (1968)

In America we have this idea that things are either serious or amusing. And money is supposed to be serious. But we all know that the teachers we remember from college are the ones who could bring a serious subject to life. Besides, I've always taken the position that it's just your money—it's not your life.

—Louis Rukeyser, host of television show *Wall Street Week*, celebrating its 25th anniversary, quoted in *USAir Magazine*, July 1996

❖ MORALITY ❖

(see also Ethics)

It is not the possession of material goods per se that is seen in Judaism as being evil. Rather, it is the method of obtaining them and the use thereof that represent an almost unlimited challenge to morality.

—Meir Tamari, director of the American Association for Jewish Business Ethics, international lecturer, and consultant, *The Challenge of Wealth: A Jewish Perspective on Making and Spending Money* (1995)

Jewishness is more than a matter of ethnic identity and Judaism more than a perfunctory performance of ritual. . . .Judaism has something to say—and to teach—about all moral issues.

> —Rabbi J. David Bleich, professor of Talmud, "The Karen Quinlan Case: A Torah Perspective," *Jewish Life*, Winter 5736 (1976)

If we insist that public life be reserved for those whose personal history is pristine, we are not going to get paragons of virtue running our affairs. We will get the very rich, who will contract out the messy things in life; the very dull, who have nothing to hide and nothing to show; and the very devious, expert at covering their tracks and ambitious enough to risk their discovery.

> —Charles Krauthammer, columnist, *Time*, September 10, 1984

The public is entitled to a high ethical standard, but where is the line between unethical behavior and normal human frailty? There is no perfect answer, only further discussion.

> —Madeleine M. Kunin, Governor of Vermont (the third Democrat, the first woman and the first Jew to hold that office), speaking at Temple Israel in Great Neck, New York, quoted in *Long Island Jewish World*, May 27–June 2, 1988

Hypocrisy is a greatly underrated virtue. It was much better when people just pretended to be good, because then they had to behave themselves in public. Who cares what they did in private? . . . People say, "Would you vote for a man who cheated on his wife?" Why not? If you need open-heart surgery, you don't care if your doctor cheats on his wife.

> —Fran Lebowitz, essayist, *George*, April/May 1996

I'm tough on everybody who calls me. To me, the point of all the calls is to have people get by their own needs and feelings . . . and to have nobler bases upon which to make decisions.

> —Dr. Laura Schlessinger, syndicated radio host and author, quoted in *Detroit Jewish News*, July 19, 1996

The rules of morality are not a burden. They are great teachers instructing us as to the real content of love. They are fences—fences of roses according to our tradition—which direct us toward the right. Without discipline, no creativity, even in morality, is possible.

> —Rabbi Seymour Siegel, professor of theology, "Theology for Today," *Conservative Judaism*, Summer 1974

In the Jewish world, the greatest accomplishments of life are most often done in private, in the home where no one sees, in the privacy of one's own heart and mind, where moral strength and determination, coupled with an ability to turn one's back on the ever-present temptation of sin and passion, are private battles to be waged and won. The ability to say "no" to sin, passion and temptation is an achievement performed in secret.

> —Rabbi Pinchas Stolper, executive director of Orthodox Union, *The Sacred Trust* (1997)

It did not require great ethical sophistication to distinguish right from wrong when witnessing black children in Birmingham being killed in church bombings and assaulted by police equipped with attack dogs, fire hoses, and electric cattle prods. It was not difficult to salute those fighting to win the elementary right to vote and to condemn those who sought to frustrate that right . . . The certainties of yesterday have become the uncertainties and conflicts of today, especially when one right collides with another right.

> —Albert Vorspan and Rabbi David Saperstein, leaders in the Reform movement, *Tough Choices: Jewish Perspectives on Social Justice* (1992)

In moral life, ignorance isn't all that common; dishonesty is far more so.

> —Michael Walzer, author, *Just and Unjust Wars: A Moral Argument With Historical Illustrations* (1977)

❖ MOVIES ❖

(see also Entertainment)

I went to see the movie on closing night of the New York Film Festival and it brought tears to my eyes, because all the Jewish intellectuals who call me "Dirty Al, the Pornographer," stood up and applauded Larry's film.

> —Al Goldstein, publisher of *Screw* magazine, commenting on the film *The People vs. Larry Flint*, quoted in *New York*, February 10, 1997

In going from the spectacular to the real the movies are losing something for which they will not be compensated until they go on from the real to the symbolic. The danger in the commonplace is dullness. People want to be thrilled.

> —Albert Lewin, filmmaker who wrote and directed *The Moon and Sixpence* and other films, from Lewin's papers at the University of Southern California, 1924, quoted in *Botticelli in Hollywood* by Susan Felleman (1997)

Both the screen's first and latest heartthrobs—Theda Bara and Winona Ryder—are Jews; but how would one know if one did not know?

The position of the Jew as a minority in films is closer to that of the Gay than that of the Black; his or her identity is, to a large extent, capable of being either concealed or revealed.

> —David Mamet, playwright, novelist, essayist, screenwriter, and director, "The Jew for Export," *The Guardian*, April 30, 1994

In the world of Billy Wilder, you can always rest assured that the situation is definitely hopeless—but not serious.

> —Walter Matthau, actor who starred in several of Billy Wilder's films, from *Billy Wilder: The Human Comedy*, documentary broadcast on PBS in 1998

The film must go from significant episode to more significant episode in a constantly mounting pattern. It's an exciting form. But it pays a price for this excitement. It cannot wander as life wanders, or pause as life always pauses, to contemplate the incidental or the unexpected. The film has a relentless form. Once you set it up, it becomes your master, demanding and rather terrifying. It has its own tight logic, and once you stray from that straight and narrow path, the tension slackens—or, you might say, the air is let out of the balloon.

> —Budd Schulberg, novelist and screenplay writer, "Why Write It if You Can't Sell It to Pictures?" *Saturday Review*, September 3, 1955

I am anonymous, and I have forgotten myself. It is always so when one goes to the movies, it is, as they say, a drug.

> —Delmore Schwartz, poet and fiction writer, *In Dreams Begin Responsibilities* (1938)

Every time you have a project like *[In the Presence of Mine Enemies]*, it's hard to get it done well. What you get is "we've done World War II things" or "we've done the Holocaust." There's always a thousand reasons not to do it. It takes the dedication of a team of people who feel the material is worthwhile.

> —Joan Micklin Silver, filmmaker, on making the film *In the Presence of Mine Enemies*, set in the Warsaw Ghetto shortly before the uprising, quoted in *The Jewish Week*, April 18, 1997

I have a pretty good imagination. I've made a fortune off my imagination. My imagination is dwarfed by the events of 1940 to 1945. Just dwarfed.

> —Steven Spielberg, film director, reflecting on the making of *Schindler's List*, quoted in *Newsweek*, December 20, 1993

Schindler's List must never be looked upon as *the* Holocaust story; it is only *a* Holocaust story.

> —Steven Spielberg, at the European premiere of *Schindler's List,* quoted in *Newsweek,* March 14, 1994

If there's one thing I hate more than not being taken seriously, it's to be taken too seriously.

> —Billy Wilder, filmmaker, director and writer, from *Billy Wilder: The Human Comedy,* documentary broadcast on PBS, 1998

Don't bore people. . . . If you have anything worthwhile to say, better be very sure that it is wrapped in chocolate so they will swallow it.

> —Billy Wilder, from *Billy Wilder: The Human Comedy,* documentary broadcast on PBS, 1998

❖ MUSIC ❖

(see also Arts)

Society's greatest fear is not for its heroes, but of them. We put them in jail when they're alive and build monuments to them when they're dead. [Freed] lived to be scorned, reviled and sentenced to prison, his penalty for inventing the term rock and roll and then infecting America with it.

> —Al Aronowitz, music critic, reflecting on Freed's involvement in the 1950s payola scandal in which links between radio airplay, record promotion, and the mob were first uncovered, "Murray the K's Entitled," *Fusion,* July 1972, quoted in *Big Beat Heat* by John A. Jackson (1991)

It could be argued that a tune of Rav Shlomo Carlebach or Rebbe Nachman of Bratslav is more convincing than any academic discourse.

> —Reuven Ben Dov, quoted in "Arguments for Piety," *Jerusalem Post,* June 5, 1997

Language leads a double life; it has a communicative function and an aesthetic function. Music has an aesthetic function only. . . . In other words, a prose sentence may or may not be a part of a work of art. But with music there is no such either-or; a phrase of music is a phrase of art. It may be good art or bad art, lofty or pop art, or even commercial art, but it can never be prose in the sense of a weather report.

> —Leonard Bernstein, conductor, The Charles Eliot Norton Lectures, 1973,

The Unanswered Questions: Six Talks at Harvard by Leonard Bernstein (1976)

I offered him $6500 for two shows.

> —Sid Bernstein, music promoter, recalling a conversation with Brian Epstein, manager of the Beatles, asking if the Beatles would appear at Carnegie Hall, 1963, quoted in *The Beatles: The Authorized Biography* by Hunter Davies (1968)

The simple truth is that no composer worthy of the name has ever written anything merely to be "as great as" or "better than" some other composer. He writes in order to say something of his own—to put down some expression of his own private personality. If he succeeds, the results should be listened to by his countrymen even though they may not be "as great as" or "better than" the music of the immortals. At any rate, it is the only way we shall ever have a music of our own.

> —Aaron Copland, composer, *The New Music 1900–1960* (1969)

Composers are in danger of being put out of their own house. The writing of music has begun to attract a new type of individual, half engineer and half composer.

> —Aaron Copland, *The New Music 1900–1960* (1969)

In our group we have both secular and religious members. The only concession we have to make [to the Orthodox members]—and we are glad to do so—was the substitution of "Hashem" for God's name. A love of singing good Jewish music does wonders for reconciling religious differences.

> —Carol Davidson, musical director and conductor of the Hebrew Union College Cantorial Student Ensemble and Community Choir, quoted in "New Roles for Jewish Women" by Livia Bitton-Jackson, 1988, *Events and Movements in Modern Judaism*, edited by Raphael Patai and Emanuel Goldsmith (1995)

It was so sad. I had a breakdown! I broke down . . . one of the very few times. I went over my whole life, my whole childhood. I didn't talk to anyone for a week. If it wasn't for Elvis and Hank Williams, I couldn't be doing what I do today.

> —Bob Dylan, singer and songwriter, recalling his reaction to the death of Elvis Presley in 1977, quoted in *No Direction Home: The Life and Music of Bob Dylan* by Robert Shelton (1986)

I guess listening to me is like reading a newspaper. I wanna be entertaining as well as truthful.

> —Bob Dylan, quoted in *No Direction Home: The Life and Music of Bob Dylan* by Robert Shelton (1986)

He saw the coming importance of the Beatles, but he rejected my view that they were going to be the biggest thing in the world. He agreed in the end, but his producer later told me that Sullivan had said it was ridiculous to give a British group top billing when a British group had never made it big in the States before.

> —Brian Epstein, manager of the Beatles, recalling his discussions with Ed Sullivan to book the Beatles for two of his shows with top billing on both shows, quoted in *The Beatles: The Authorized Biography* by Hunter Davies (1968)

Yeah boy, that was really something. That same week I did a show with Merle Haggard. Ain't too many singers can say that.

> —Kinky Friedman, writer and singer of country tunes (including songs with Jewish themes such as "Ride 'Em Jewboy"), recalling a concert in Brooklyn with Hasidic singer Rabbi Shlomo Carlebach, quoted in *Members of the Tribe* by Ze'ev Chafets (1988)

Carrying a man's cello is like carrying his wife.

> —Abe Fortas, attorney and close friend of Pablo Casals, recalling buying first-class tickets in 1961 on a flight from Puerto Rico to New York for himself and Casals's cello, which needed repair, quoted in *Fortas: The Rise and Ruin of a Supreme Court Justice* by Bruce Allen Murphy (1988)

Let's face it, rock and roll is bigger than all of us.

> —Alan Freed, 1950s deejay who introduced the new sound "rock and roll" on his radio shows, interview with television commentator Mike Wallace, 1958, quoted in *Big Beat Heat* by John A. Jackson (1991)

Given a fondness for music, a feeling for rhyme, a sense of whimsy and humor, an eye for the balanced sentence, an ear for the current phrase, and the ability to imagine a performer trying to put over the number in progress — given all this, I would still say it takes four or five years collaborating with knowledgeable composers to become a well-rounded lyricist.

> —Ira Gershwin, lyricist, quoted in *Ira Gershwin: The Art of the Lyricist* by Philip Furia (1996)

A good lyric should be rhymed conversation.

> —Ira Gershwin, quoted in *Ira Gershwin: The Art of the Lyricist* by Philip Furia (1996)

I'm 44; what do I know about what teenagers like?

> —Danny Goldberg, president of Atlantic Records, quoted in "The Goldberg Variations" by Ann Hornaday, *New York*, October 3, 1994

I didn't just ask for good musicianship; I insisted on it. Nothing less than perfection would do; I lived that music, and expected everybody else to live it, too.

> —Benny Goodman, jazz musician known as the "King of Swing" in the 1940s and 1950s, quoted in *Swing, Swing, Swing: The Life and Times of Benny Goodman* by Ross Firestone (1993)

In music, it sometimes happens that the less you know, the better off you are.

> —Benny Goodman, quoted in *Swing, Swing, Swing: The Life and Times of Benny Goodman* by Ross Firestone (1993)

As great as the music was, the ongoing conversation was really about something more than solos and songs. Listening to rock and roll was learning a secret language. There was something conveyed by the attitude of the bands and their records that stood apart from their music, and the way you spoke the language told people how you felt about the world. When you first met someone, the conversation turned immediately to music because once you knew which bands a person listened to, you knew if you were going to get along.

> —Fred Goodman, journalist and former *Rolling Stone* editor, *The Mansion on the Hill* (1997)

I don't know where Woody would be tonight if he were alive; but I can guarantee you he wouldn't be here.

> —Arlo Guthrie, folksinger, speaking at the Rock and Roll Hall of Fame induction dinner—where his father Woody Guthrie was posthumously honored in 1988—held at the Waldorf-Astoria where a table for eight cost $10,000, quoted in *The Mansion on the Hill* by Fred Goodman (1997)

When I kissed my first girl, I wasn't listening to Pete Seeger or Woody Guthrie.... I was listening to the Everly Brothers.... And I still love them.

> —Arlo Guthrie, interview with Linda Ellerbee, *Later with Bob Costas*, 1991

A C-major chord in Israel is the same as a C-major chord in Syria and the same as a C-major chord in Burundi.

> —Marvin Hamlisch, pianist and composer, commenting on the power of music to unite people, quoted in *The Jewish Advocate*, August 23, 1996

Nothing else more than that rip-off of black music made me more ashamed of being white than anything, not even the "woman who came in on Thursdays." But all of a sudden, some dude came struttin' up from down in the South somewhere . . . He sang from inside out and yet he was white!

> —Abbie Hoffman, activist, recalling Elvis Presley, *Woodstock Nation* (1969)

I've had many thrills in my life, but this remains one of the top ones. . . . No matter how many songs I've written, the moment the orchestra leader gives the downbeat to the first musical interpretation, it is almost like, you know, spanking the newborn baby!

> —Sammy Kahn, songwriter, quoted in *They're Playing Our Song*, edited by Max Wilk (1973)

The question is not whether there is a hype but whether there is anything beneath the hype.

> —Jon Landau, critic for *Rolling Stone*, commenting on the MGM campaign to promote several bands from "Bosstown" (Boston), quoted in *The Mansion on the Hill* by Fred Goodman (1997)

[Jerusalem of Gold] is the one song of our generation that will last into the next millennium. First of all, it's a great tune; and has so entered everyone's subconscious that whenever you see Jerusalem printed in gold or referred to as golden, which is always, it's because of Naomi Shemer [the song's composer]. Whenever we perform the song, people sing the refrain, get chills, and thank us for allowing them to re-experience the emotion.

> —Matthew Lazar, conductor of the Zamir Chorale, commenting on the song "Jerusalem of Gold," quoted in "A Song for Jerusalem" by Jonathan Mark, *The Jewish Week*, May 31, 1996

In the '20s and '30s, poor Jews looked to the shul [synagogue] for their spiritual life but also their opera, their Broadway! Now they want to go home at 11 and take a nap.

> —Jacob Mendelson, former student, recalling Moshe Ganchoff, the last cantor and composer of the "Golden Age," upon his death at age ninety-two on August 11, 1997, quoted in "Moshe Ganchoff, Cantor's Cantor" by Naomi Giszpenc, *Forward*, August 27, 1997

The music, if such a word can be used, was torture for me . . . what they didn't realize was that they [the audience] were in a serious condition of being manipulated. It was disturbing to see all these young people so numbed, imitating the gestures of the group onstage, their emotions being taunted for commercial gain.

> —Yehudi Menuhin, violinist, recalling his experience at a rock concert, quoted in *Conversations with Menuhin* by David Dubal (1992)

That is the good thing about a musician, that he must learn, and he can't avoid learning, that if he plays a note out of tune, no one else has played it.

> —Yehudi Menuhin, quoted in *Conversations with Menuhin* by David Dubal (1992)

The girls gave their hearts and souls to them, and the guys were very jealous. [John] Lennon and [Paul] McCartney were always afraid they were going to be attacked, not by terrorists, but by irate boyfriends.

> —Bruce Morrow, New York deejay "Cousin Brucie" of WABC radio, discussing reactions of fans to the Beatles in 1964, quoted in *The Bergen Record*, November 19, 1995

You ain't heard nothin' yet.

> —Jakie Rabinowitz/Jack Robin in the film *The Jazz Singer*, played by Al Jolson, based on Samuel Raphaelson's play, 1927

When Elvis died, we had a real day of mourning here. It was like Tisha B'Av. They had made an idol of him, a God of him.

> —Fagie Schaffer, landlord of the Memphis apartment rented by Gladys and Vernon Presley and their teenage son Elvis, commenting on the 20th anniversary of his death, "Elvis the Shabbos Goy," by Eric J. Greenberg, *The Jewish Week*, August 22, 1997

I also feel lost when the program tells you right at the top that Papegeno is in love with Sarstro but is thwarted by Monostatos, who in turn falls in love with Pamina. Somehow I just can't warm up to people whose parents gave them these names. I'm a Joe and Sam kind of guy.

> —Neil Simon, playwright, commenting on opera, *Live! Everything Entertainment*, October 1997

For people who thought the South African music was unusual or exotic or strange, it was no more exotic than rock and roll was to me sitting on the back porch filling out the Yankee lineup.

—Paul Simon, singer and songwriter, commenting on the music on his album *Graceland*, interviewed by Ed Bradley on CBS-TV's *60 Minutes*, 1995

Art is craft, not inspiration.

—Stephen Sondheim, composer, interviewed by host James Lipton on "Inside the Actors Studio" on Bravo cable network, September 1996

Judaism is a revelation of a nomadic people. One of its important concepts is that there is little in the physical realm to grab onto. The central things you can grasp are spiritual concepts. Being a musician leads the mind and the spirit to a state of truth-singing, truth-seeing, truth-seeking.

—Michael Tilson Thomas, music director of the San Francisco Symphony, principal guest conductor of the London Symphony Orchestra, and grandson of Boris and Bessie Thomashefsky, founding members of the Yiddish Theater in America, quoted in *JUF News*, January 1996

[It is] a Scottish lament written by a Jewish guy from the Bronx.

—Jay Ungar, composer of "Ashokan Farewell," the fiddle tune that was the theme of the PBS documentary *The Civil War*, quoted in *The New Yorker*, March 11, 1991

Music, too, is portable. A shofar, a violin, a clarinet could be packed and carried whether one was fleeing an Egyptian or a Cossack.

—Paul Wieder, "Why Do Jews Choose Music?" *MetroWest Jewish News*, July 11, 1996

❖ Names ❖

(see also Jewish Identity)

In fact, he had my new name picked out for me; it was to be Leonard S. Burns; my heart sank, my stomach turned over, I did lose a night's sleep over it, I tossed and turned and thought about it, and I reported to him the next morning, no sir, I'm sorry—I will have to make it with the name Leonard Bernstein or not at all.

> —Leonard Bernstein, conductor of the New York Philharmonic, recalling that conductor Serge Koussevitzky thought Bernstein's name was an obstacle, that it would never be on a poster at Carnegie Hall, in *The Gift of Music*, a television documentary about Leonard Bernstein broadcast on PBS, September 22, 1996

We all played the game of deciding what name would lead me to fame and fortune. "Norman Dems" was considered. I wanted a last name that started with "D" that wasn't Danielovitch or Demsky. Somebody suggested "Douglas." I liked it. The first name took longer. Finally, someone suggested "Kirk." It sounded right. I liked the crisp "k" sound. I didn't realize what a Scottish name I was taking.

> —Kirk Douglas, actor who was born Issur Danielovitch, *The Ragman's Son* (1988)

Mrs. stands to the right of me, and Miss stands to the left. Me is a ghost somewhere in the middle.

> —Doris Fleischman, writer and publicist who kept her own name after marriage, "Notes of a Retiring Feminist" in *American Mercury*, 1948, quoted in *Jewish Women in America*, edited by Paula E. Hyman and Deborah Dash Moore (1997)

He talked to me . . . like a warm friend. He said that now that I had started life . . . "this is a good time to change your name. Frankfurter—you know, there's nothing the matter with it, but it's odd, fun-making. . . . Give yourself an appropriate name." I said, "Thank you very much," but I thought I'd better get along with what circumstances had given me and he thought that was very foolish.

> —Felix Frankfurter, U.S. Supreme Court justice, recalling the advice of a junior partner at a firm where he interviewed for a job after Harvard Law School, quoted in *Felix Frankfurter Reminisces,* recorded in talks with Dr. Harlan B. Phillips (1960)

My father was very proud of me . . . and there was no way I wanted him to say, "Hey, did you hear that fellow on the air, Marty Manning. That's my son."

> —Marty Glickman, sports broadcaster, recalling his rejection of the idea of changing his name when he began his broadcast career, quoted in *Ellis Island to Ebbets Field* by Peter Levine (1992)

Most of my classmates carried the names of murdered grandfathers.

> —Yossi Klein Halevi, Israeli journalist and author who is a son of a Holocaust survivor, *Memoirs of a Jewish Extremist* (1995)

Hewitt? Hewitt? I imagine there's a Horowitz under there somewhere.

> —Rabbi Arthur Hertzberg, president of the American Jewish Congress, upon being introduced to *60 Minutes* producer Don Hewitt in 1975, quoted in *Close Encounters* by Mike Wallace and Gary Paul Gates (1984)

The mark of who knew Mother was what they called her. She made a decision early on, that Ann Landers was a professional name and that she was really Eppie. This was a contrast to the way Popo had chosen to go. She became Abby to everyone, including her husband.

> —Margo Howard, daughter of Eppie Lederer (advice columnist Ann Landers) and niece of advice columnist "Dear Abby," *Eppie: The Story of Ann Landers* (1982)

"You don't know how much trouble this is going to bring you," one grandmother said recently. "You haven't seen how rough it will be for you with such a Jewish name." Then she ticked off for me a list of immigrant's sorrows: the slurs, the exclusions, the jobs lost, the being so different. To her it is still 1908, the goyim can't pronounce her name and somehow it's her own fault.

> —Jeremy Kalmanofsky, rabbinical student who was named Jeremy Kaplan at birth, "Name Dropping," *Hadassah*, March 1993 (At age twenty-four, he

legally changed his last name to the original name of his immigrant grandparents.)

How did he respond on the night his daughters came home and announced they had a new name? "America," he must have said, or similar words of resignation. But I do not think this change went gently on his soul. I imagine it was one of those moments that made him sorry he ever came to this cruel goldene medine, this golden country that steals a man's name.... But what could he do? His children had to go to school. He bent.

—Jeremy Kalmanofsky, "Name Dropping," *Hadassah*, March 1993

What a pity that Jewish parents should ignore beautiful Hebrew names, so rich in associations, and select those that help to disguise the Jewish character of the bearer.... It seems to require a little courage to bear their English equivalent. A boy so named may be subject to petty annoyance from ignorant companions. So Moses is changed to Monroe, while Isaac appears as Irving; Samuel becomes Stanley and Miriam is called Marjorie. It would seem that only a Lincoln can afford to be called Abraham, or a president's wife be known as Abigail.

—Deborah M. Melamed, author, *The Three Pillars: A Book for Jewish Women* (1927)

All of the Abrahams on the paper went through a second journalistic circumcision.

—A. M. Rosenthal, journalist, recalling how *New York Times* editors were sensitive about Jewish names when he began his career, quoted in *Lifestyles*, pre-Spring 1996

Yeah, that's what Jerry Lewis said when I met him making *Ship of Fools* on the Paramount lot. He said, "Segal, you kept your name." I hadn't even thought about that.

—George Segal, actor, quoted in *Lifestyles*, New Year 1996

Every Jew who has ever stepped into a synagogue or temple knows that we have two names: the outside name with which we go through life, and the inside name, the Jewish name, used in blessings and Torah call-ups, marriage and divorce ceremonies, and on tombstones.... It is a far-drifted Jew who has forgotten his or her inside name.

—Herman Wouk, author, *Inside, Outside* (voice of I. David Goodkind) (1985)

❖ NATIONALISM ❖

Out of deep attachments to fellow Jews and an almost inchoate theological memory—Judaism's classic teaching that no loyalty, other than to God, should be absolute—Jewry has developed a model to take the poison out of nationalism. The vaccine against virulent nationalism is multiple loyalties. By their behavior, Jews teach the world that moral obligations do not stop at national borders.

> —Rabbi Irving Greenberg, author, scholar, and founder of National Jewish Center for Learning and Leadership (CLAL), quoted in *Washington Jewish Week*, May 8, 1997

It is because we—more than the Jewish leftists and liberals—understand and respect the reality of Arab nationalism, that we realize the futility of expecting the nationalist to give up his dream. Would we give up our dream? Would we lose our hope? Neither will the Arab nationalist.

> —Rabbi Meir Kahane, founder of the Jewish Defense League, *Our Challenge* (1974)

No nationalist was ever bought by an indoor toilet and electricity in his home. And that is exactly what those who preach peace through materialism are doing.

> —Rabbi Meir Kahane, *Our Challenge* (1974)

❖ NEIGHBORHOODS ❖

There are two reasons villages get formed in Rockland. One is to keep the Hasidim out and the other is to keep the Hasidim in.

> —Paul W. Adler, chairman of Rockland County's Jewish Community Relations Council (N.Y.), quoted in *The New York Times*, January 13, 1997

It's like they moved Brooklyn in a mass migration.

> —Warren Adler, novelist, on the topic of all the former New Yorkers retired to southern Florida, *Never Too Late for Love* (voice of the character Solly Lebow) (1995)

There is no fringe in Borough Park. There are 100,000 Jews in Borough Park.... Even Baruch Goldstein didn't live here. He's from Bensonhurst.

> —Noach Dear, member of the New York City Council as representative of Borough Park and Flatbush in Brooklyn, quoted in the *Jerusalem Post,* November 17, 1995

Hibbing, Minnesota, was just not the place for me to stay and live. There really was nothing there.... The only thing you could do there is be a miner, and even that kind of thing was getting less and less... I didn't want to die there. As I think about it now, though, it wouldn't be such a bad place to go back and die in. There's no place I feel closer to now

> —Bob Dylan, singer and songwriter, speaking of his hometown, interview with Nat Hentoff in *Playboy,* March 1966

Being Jewish in the South is like being Gentile in New York.

> —Eli N. Evans, author and president of the Charles H. Revson Foundation, *The Lonely Days Were Sundays: Reflections of a Jewish Southerner* (1993)

I believe that no one born and raised in the South, even if one moves away physically, can escape its hold on the imagination. I was touched in childhood by its passions and myths, by its language and literature, by the heartbeat of its music, by the rhythm of its seasons and the beauty of its land, by the menacing fear of violence, by the complexities of race and religions, by the intensity of its history and the turbulence of its politics, by its sunlight and its shadow, illusions and mysteries. With such entanglements a native son remains irredeemably and endurably Southern. So it has been with me, immersed in the endless fascinations and dense matrix of Southern history entwined with Jewish roots, resonating in my soul forever.

> —Eli N. Evans, *The Provincials* (1973)

If you are committed to your faith, there is no culture shock. Postville and Crown Heights [Brooklyn] are one and the same.

> —Rabbi Feller, one of 150 Lubavitcher Jews living in Postville, Iowa (population 1,512), quoted in "Strangers in a Strange Land," *Chicago Tribune Magazine,* January 28, 1996

... A community where there were enough Jews to be noticed, but not enough to be close enough to a majority. That's where you get the anti-Semitism, when you're a noticeable minority.

> —Barney Frank, U.S. Congressman (D-Mass.), recalling growing up in Bayonne, N.J., "Newt's Nemesis," *Jerusalem Report,* April 6, 1995

Here, people work out their antagonisms and their dreams.

> —Max Frankel, executive editor of *The New York Times*, quoted in *New York*, April 25, 1988, describing New York City

Bronx neighborhoods were by day female worlds; the only men were the elderly, or the storekeepers who became somehow a target for the remaining coquetry in the lives of these otherwise sedate women. There was a difference between my mother dressed and my mother at home in housedress and slippers. My mother dressed was a woman with a firm step, decisive, on stage, as it were, conscious of her persona, playing her part in the neighborhood. And, of course, each of the neighbors had her part, her assigned role in the loosely formed constellation of acquaintances and friends who met together as they shopped, or sat together in little clusters in front of the house.

> —Ruth Gay, author, *Unfinished People: Eastern European Jews Encounter America* (1997)

It was Brooklyn and The Bronx, eye to eye at last.

> —Bill Graham, rock music impresario who owned the Fillmore East and Fillmore West theaters, commenting on meeting Barbra Streisand on the set of *A Star Is Born*, quoted in *Bill Graham Presents*, written with Robert Greenfield (1992)

Our Father in Heaven, look with favor as we gather together this morning as a symbol of our community. . . . May this sacred spot [recall] the countless number of immigrants who came here seeking the promised land of equality . . . and the pursuit of happiness.

> —Rabbi Eli Greenblatt, an immigrant to the U.S. from Argentina, at the ceremony to celebrate the 70th anniversary of the opening of the Cyclone at Coney Island in Brooklyn, quoted in *The Jewish Week*, July 11, 1997

To live in a suburb but to do so with other Jews who Americanized their Jewishness seemed a way of being like other Americans without having altogether to leave the Jewish orbit.

> —Samuel C. Heilman, professor of sociology and Jewish studies, "Starting Over: Acculturation and Suburbia, the Jews of the 1950s" in *Portrait of American Jews: The Last Half of the Twentieth Century* (1995)

On the beach, athletes who stood on their heads balanced on the abdomen and knees of supine girlfriends were so prevalent as to hardly command more than a glance. . . . Pinochle games played by elderly Jewish men with vigorous gestures and impassioned discussions were more exciting spectator sports as we tried to learn the subtleties of the game and figure out what these characters from the Old World were gloating and disputing about. Portable radios made their appearance with huge batteries in large cases that seemed to weigh half a hundred pounds.

—Joseph Heller, novelist, *Now and Then: From Coney Island to Here* (1998)

Had anyone asked me growing up if I was Jewish, I would have replied, "Isn't everyone?"

—Donna Karan, fashion designer and executive, reflecting on being born and raised in Woodmere, one of the "Five Towns," on Long Island, quoted in *Jerusalem Report*, April 6, 1995

Have you ever lived in the suburbs? I haven't, but I've talked to people who have, and it's sterile. It's nothing. It's wasting your life.

—Edward I. Koch, mayor of the city of New York, interview with Peter Manso in *Playboy*, April 1982

Where you gonna find a good lox and bagel sandwich? No! A good kosher beef sandwich? No! You go where you have what you want. So they migrated. And they left us old folks here to ponder the future, and dream about the past.

—Leslie Kornfeld, age seventy-nine, president of Ahavath Rayim Synagogue in Greenwood, Miss., talking about how most of the young Jews have left the once-thriving community, *Holding On: Dreamers, Visionaries, Eccentrics and Other American Heroes* by David Isay, photographs by Harvey Wang (1995)

We're not moving from this place. If we're not safe here, then no one will be safe anywhere! Besides, you walk down the street, you see a building and you say, "This used to be a shul." Then you come to another one and you say the same thing. You come to the Intervale Jewish Center and you don't say, "This used to be a shul." Do you know why? Because this still is a shul!

—Moishe Sacks, elderly baker and leader of the congregation of the Intervale Jewish Center in the South Bronx, quoted in *The Miracle of Intervale Avenue* by Jack Kugelmass (1996)

My parents live in Florida now. They moved there last year. They didn't want to move to Florida, but, they're in their seventies, and that's the law. You know how it works, they got the leisure police. They pull up in front of the old people's house with a golf cart, jump out. "Let's go, Pop. White belt, white pants, white shoes, get in the back. Drop the snow shovel right there. Drop it."

—Jerry Seinfeld, comedian, *SeinLanguage* (1993)

Looking back on it, I think I assumed that the real Jews were in New York. In fact, New York was a code word for Jewish in Kansas City, in the way Lincoln was a code word for black—so that blacks went to the movies at the Lincoln and Jews bought bagels at the New York bakery. New York was also where the real baseball players were—the Kansas City Blues were a farm club of the New York Yankees—and I suppose I saw the situation as somewhat analogous. We were farm club Jews.

—Calvin Trillin, columnist and author, *Messages From My Father* (1996)

❖ NONVIOLENCE ❖

For I cannot help withstanding evil when I see that it is about to destroy the good. I am forced to withstand the evil in the world just as the evil within myself. I can only strive not to have to do so by force. I do not want force. But if there is no other way of preventing the evil destroying the good, I trust I shall use force and give myself up into God's hands.

—Martin Buber, theologian, "A Letter to Gandhi," 1930s, quoted in *Martin Buber: Jewish Existentialist* by Malcolm L. Diamond (1960)

In the face of this new threat to humanity, it would be suicide to advocate nonresistance. He who has witnessed the atrocities of the Hitler Reich has no choice but to arm. I'm no longer an unconditional pacifist but a realistic one.

—Albert Einstein, Nobel Prize–winning theoretical physicist and humanist, 1930s, quoted by Richard Bank, *Midstream*, October/November 1990

If ever a people was a people of non-violence through century after century, it was the Jews. I think they need learn but little from anyone in faithfulness to their God and their readiness to suffer while they sanctify His name.

—Rabbi Judah L. Magnes, communal leader and first president of the Hebrew University of Jerusalem, from a letter to Mahatma Gandhi, November 26, 1938, referring to an article by Gandhi in *Harijan*, reprinted in *Modern Jewish Thought*, edited by Nahum N. Glatzer (1977)

I have seen enough unnatural deaths to last a lifetime. I know that I, like other men and women, have no choice but to die—only once but sometime. I do however, have a choice as to whether I will die with human blood on my hands. I am deeply tired of and sickened by killing.

—Rabbi Steven S. Schwarzschild, who fled Nazi Germany with his family in the 1930s, *Roots of Jewish Non-Violence* (1971)

❖ NUCLEAR ARMS ❖

My fellow citizens of the world . . . we are here to make a choice between the quick and the dead. . . . That is our business. . . . Behind a black portent of the new atomic age lies a hope which, seized upon with faith, we can work our salvation. . . . We must elect World Peace or World Destruction.

> —Bernard Baruch, financier and statesman, testimony before the Atomic Energy Commission, June 14, 1946

We helped in creating this new weapon in order to prevent the enemies of mankind from achieving it ahead of us, which, given the mentality of the Nazis, would have meant inconceivable destruction and the enslavement of the rest of the world. We delivered this weapon into the hands of the American and British people as trustees of the whole of mankind, as fighters for peace and liberty. . . . The war is won but the peace is not.

> —Albert Einstein, Nobel Prize–winning theoretical physicist and humanist, from an address at the Nobel Anniversary Dinner, December 10, 1945

To say that we have avoided nuclear war for forty years may be only to congratulate ourselves just before going over the precipice. . . . Men live as if they will not die and nations and societies go on as if they cannot be horribly destroyed in an instant by a few bombs.

> —Nathan Glazer, sociologist, "How Has the United States Met Its Major Challenges Since 1945? A Symposium," *Commentary*, November 1985

To justify the awful possible conclusion of this process, we are impelled to make Soviet Russian reality and intentions and ideology even more awful than they are. We are forced into a process of demonization in order to justify the hell our conflict may lead to.

> —Nathan Glazer, "How Has the United States Met Its Major Challenges Since 1945? A Symposium," *Commentary*, November 1985

Growing up, I had naturally assumed that any genocidal threat against me would be "Jewish." But somehow, I'd forgotten about the Bomb. Annihilation had become non-discriminatory.

> —Yossi Klein Halevi, Israeli journalist and author, *Memoirs of a Jewish Extremist* (1995)

We are taught that an individual who has the ability to prevent a murder from taking place and chooses to ignore the opportunity is in violation of the prohibition, "Do not stand (idly) by the blood of your fellow." It is incumbent upon us to exercise our democratic rights and halachic [Jewish legal] obligations by pressuring our political system to freeze its nuclear buildup and truly begin the process of removing the sin of the lethal nuclear capacity from our midst.

> —Rabbi Samuel Intrator, "Tikkun Haolam: The Nuclear Issue," *Connections*, October 1985

If atomic bombs are to be added to the arsenals of a warring world, or to the arsenals of nations preparing for war, then the time will come when mankind will curse the names of Los Alamos and Hiroshima. . . . The peoples of this world must unite, or they will perish. This war that has ravaged so much of the earth, has written these words. The atomic bomb has spelled them out for all men to understand.

> —J. Robert Oppenheimer, physicist, speaking at a 1945 party in his honor upon his resignation from the work at Los Alamos, quoted in *Oppenheimer: Years of Risk* by James W. Kunetka (1982)

. . . The atomic clock ticks faster and faster. We may anticipate a state of affairs in which two great powers will each be in a position to put an end to the civilization and life of the other, though not without risking its own. We may be likened to two scorpions in a bottle, each capable of killing the other, but only at the risk of its own life. . . . This prospect does not make for serenity.

> —J. Robert Oppenheimer, from an article in *Foreign Affairs*, July 1952, quoted in *Oppenheimer: Years of Risk* by James W. Kunetka (1982)

Having lived through a pilot project for the destruction of humanity, I know that the unthinkable is possible, and that it is at least as realistic to expect of man the worst as it is to expect the best. I have no packaged program of remedies, but I have an enhanced perception of perils. Must everyone have an Auschwitz first? Or can those who experienced only normal life also understand that the sacrifices required to cope with some of the world's problems are much less than they supposed; but that the dangers involved in ignoring any of them are infinitely greater than they imagine.

> —Samuel Pisar, international lawyer and Holocaust survivor, *Of Blood and Hope* (1980)

Suddenly, the whole world is Jewish.

> —Elie Wiesel, Nobel laureate and author, commenting that the nuclear specter makes humankind worry about survival in the same way Jews have worried for centuries, quoted in "The Haggada Idea" by Carmela Efros Kalmanson, *Hadassah*, April 1990

❖ PATRIOTISM ❖

*W*hen the class read, and it came my turn, my hands shook and the book trembled in my hands. I could not pronounce the name of George Washington without a pause. Never had I prayed, never had I chanted the songs of David, never had I called upon the Most Holy, in such utter reverence and worship as I repeated the simple sentences of my child's story of the patriot.

> —Mary Antin, writer, *The Promised Land* (1912)

It required no fife and drum corps, no Fourth of July procession, to set me tingling with patriotism. Even the common agents and instruments of municipal life, such as the letter carrier and the fire engine, I regarded with a measure of respect.

> —Mary Antin, *The Promised Land* (1912)

My contribution to an America that has done everything for me.

> —Sam Bernstein, merchant from Russia, commenting about his son Leonard Bernstein, after the conductor's triumphant debut leading the New York Philharmonic in 1943, in place of Bruno Walter, who was ill, quoted in *The Gift of Music*, a television documentary about Leonard Bernstein, broadcast on PBS, September 22, 1996

I'm the happiest combination you can think of. I'm a Russian poet, and an English essayist and citizen of the United States.

> —Joseph Brodsky, Russian-born poet exiled to the United States in 1972 who won the Nobel Prize in 1987 and was appointed poet laureate of the United

States in 1991, reacting to the news of his 1987 Nobel Prize, quoted in his obituary, *The Washington Post,* January 29, 1996

The thing I shall always remember is how you felt about the United States. You kept telling me there was no better place to live than America. And I could never appreciate this unless I was a Jew who had lived in Europe. . . . Well, Pop, I just wanted you to know, as far as your children are concerned, you made the right decision when you left Poland. . . . So let the tall ships sail and the fireworks explode. . . . If you were here you would say, "It's probably a good thing people remember what a great place this country is, even if it's going to cost the city a lot of money."

> —Art Buchwald, columnist and humorist, from his column "Letter to Pop," written to his deceased father on July 4, 1976, quoted in *This I Believe: Documents of American Jewish Life* by Jacob Rader Marcus (1990)

I cannot for the life of me figure out why anyone would want to serve in the military, but if people who happen to be gay want to serve their country they should have the right to do so.

> —David Geffen, entertainment executive, quoted in *The Mansion on the Hill* by Fred Goodman (1997)

We never felt we were unpatriotic. To me the country is the land and the people, not necessarily the guy who happens to be president.

> —Abbie Hoffman, activist, from a speech on the student antiwar movement delivered at the University of South Carolina, September 16, 1987, *The Best of Abbie Hoffman* (1989)

People have looked at Jews' contribution to art, literature and science. But stereotypically, Jews are considered weak people. I just wanted to see how many of us are here, in Arlington Cemetery.

> —Ken Poch, attempting to compile a list of Jewish veterans buried at Arlington National Cemetery, quoted in *Washington Jewish Week,* August 1994

Not for one second during my German-speaking childhood did any of us— my parents, my sister, or I—doubt our Americanness. We took our Americanness for granted and were proud to be Americans. My national ancestors were not Otto Von Bismarck or Frederick the Great, but George Washington and Thomas Jefferson. I thought *Father Knows Best* was about my family.

> —Peter D. Salins, professor of urban affairs and author whose parents immigrated to the United States from Germany in 1938, *Assimilation, American Style* (1997)

I am going back to America sometime, someday not too long. I am already homesick for America. I never knew it was so beautiful. It was like a bachelor who goes along fine for 25 years and then decides to get married. That is the way I feel about America.

> —Gertrude Stein, speaking to an Associated Press reporter in Paris, quoted in *When You See This Remember Me: Gertrude Stein in Person* by W. G. Rogers (1948)

❖ PEACE ❖

If we want to live in peace with the Arabs, as much as we need an army to make war, we need an army to make peace. The army to make peace — give me five thousand free tickets to bring holy hippies from Los Angeles and San Francisco, to bring them here, and we will go to every Arab house in the country and bring them flowers and tell them that we want to be brothers with them. We will bring musicians and we will play at every Arab wedding and we want them to bring their bands to play at our weddings. We have to live together.

> —Rabbi Shlomo Carlebach, statement in Israel after the Six-Day War in 1967, retold in 1993 interview with Michael Lerner, *Tikkun,* September–October 1997

There is always time to choose war. It is never too late to choose killing. How often in history have we given peace a chance to show its power?

> —Rabbi Marshall T. Meyer, human rights activist, founder of the Seminario Rabinico Latinoamericano, and spiritual leader of B'nai Jeshurun in New York City, speaking at Ebenezer Baptist Church in Atlanta on Martin Luther King's birthday, 1991

The Bible also deals with peace of a temporal, prosaic kind: "And Abraham said to Lot [his nephew]: Let there be no conflict between me and you . . . for we are brothers. Behold, the whole land is before you, please part from me. If you go left, I will turn right, and if you turn right I will go left." This, I think, is a model of pragmatic peace in an imperfect world: precisely for people to remain on brotherly terms with each other, it is sometimes necessary to define their respective places. While aspiring to a loving union, we must nevertheless work within the boundaries of our human limitations.

> —Amos Oz, Israeli novelist and essayist, from "Peace and Love and Compromise," a speech delivered while accepting the German Publishers Peace Prize in Frankfurt, October 1992, excerpted in *Harper's,* February 1993

As far as we are concerned, democracy, and that includes Palestinian democracy, is the best and probably the only ultimate guarantee for a real and durable peace.

> —Shimon Peres, prime minister of Israel, addressing a joint session of Congress on December 12, 1995, quoted in "In Congress, Peres Again Appeals to Syria for a Mideast Peace" by Serge Schmemann, *The New York Times*, December 13, 1995

Peace is not just a prayer. It is at first a prayer, but it is also the realistic aspiration of the Jewish people.

> —Yitzhak Rabin, Israeli prime minister, speaking—for the last time—at a peace rally in Tel Aviv, moments before his assassination, November 4, 1995

We should not let the land flowing with milk and honey become a land flowing with blood and tears.

> —Yitzhak Rabin, speaking at the signing of the Israeli-Palestinian Interim Agreement in Washington, D.C., September 28, 1995

Peace has no borders.

> —Yitzhak Rabin, speaking at the signing of the Israeli-Palestinian Interim Agreement in Washington, D.C., September 28, 1995

Peace! Here is a noun that functions against its own purpose. As long as we think of "having peace," we treat peace as a product, a commodity and not as an incremental and mutual process.

> —Rabbi Zalman Schachter-Shalomi, leader of the Jewish renewal movement, *Tikkun*, premiere issue, Fall 1986

❖ PHILANTHROPY ❖

There are Jewish millionaires in this country who have not contributed one single cent to the relief fund during the long period of the war. There are others who have waxed fat and rich in the last 3 years and whose contributions to the relief fund amount to practically nothing. There are men who pose as Jewish philanthropists and whose contribution to the relief fund is miserably out of proportion not only to their capital but even to their income.

> —Editorial, *American Jewish Chronicle*, May 17, 1917

We help 4.5 million people a year. One at a time.
> —Advertisement for UJA-Federation of New York, 1996

The congregation was forced to switch gears, from the intense involvement of many individuals joined in a community of public prayer, to the sullen passivity of unwitting TV viewers coerced into watching a Jewish version of the Home Shopping Channel.
> —Alice Chasen, executive editor of *Tikkun*, describing the experience of an Israel Bond appeal during the final hours of Yom Kippur, "Shul and Spirit," *Tikkun*, November/December 1994

Charity is increasingly impersonal. A solicitation arrives in the mail and a check goes out in a postage paid envelope. Those [Salvation Army] kettles . . . provide the opportunity to reach into pockets or purses and make spontaneous offerings, to get the warm glow that comes from giving to a real person and getting a sincere "God bless you" in return.
> —Don Feder, columnist, "This Army Figures to Make Us Care," *Boston Herald*, December 6, 1995

The first rule of giving money is this: never give money to any charity or institution in Israel that isn't building an Israel you'd want your children to live in.
> —Thomas Friedman, columnist, *The New York Times*, October 9, 1997

I think anybody with a drop of Jewish blood should show up. Your heritage will be taken into account if you make a pledge. For example, if you are only half Jewish, you only have to pay half the pledge. If you are a quarter Jewish, you only have to pay a quarter of the pledge.
> —Alan C. Greenberg, chairman of Bear Stearns, urging attendance at a fundraising meeting for Israel in a memo to senior management dated January 1991, *Memos From the Chairman* (1996)

It is not so much the gloves, but telling people they count.
> —Meyer Michael Greenberg, New Yorker who, for thirty years, went to the Bowery between Thanksgiving and Christmas to give away pairs of gloves, quoted in his obituary, *The New York Times*, June 21, 1995

The highest form of charity is to help others help themselves—which means creating jobs. I know my father would be most proud of me, not for winning a Super Bowl, but for creating jobs in Israel.
> —Robert Kraft, owner of the NFL's New England Patriots, commenting upon opening a new plant for his business, Carmel Container Systems, Ltd., in Israel, quoted in *Lifestyles*, New Year 1998

The Torah says that he who teaches his friend's son Torah, it is as if he gave birth to him. Here's a woman who for 101 years was childless and now becomes a mother to a whole community. Not only now, but for generations to come.

> —Rabbi Norman Lamm, president of Yeshiva University, regarding a $22 million bequest from Anne Scheiber to Yeshiva University, a school she never attended, to help women she never met, quoted in her obituary, *The New York Times*, December 2, 1995 (Scheiber left a job at the Internal Revenue Service in 1944 and invested her five thousand dollars savings in the stock market.)

As an additional safeguard against self-pity in our home, Mama kept several charity boxes marked "For the Poor." We gave to the poor regularly. It made us feel rich.

> —Sam Levenson, humorist and author, *Everything but Money* (1966)

The New York Jewish community helped us. Now let's show that we are also people who can help.

> —Ella Levine, director of the Russian division of UJA-Federation of New York, speaking at the division's gala at the Plaza Hotel, quoted in *Forward*, May 24, 1996

You can't decide whether we should fight or not. We will. . . . You can only decide one thing: whether we shall be victorious in this fight.

> —Golda Meir, Israeli party leader sent to America on an emergency fundraising mission, speaking at a 1948 Chicago conference, quoted in *Kissing Through Glass* by Joyce R. Starr (1990)

When one of the senior UJA officials was asked what the formula is for such great success, he replied, "First you need 2,000 years of Jewish suffering." He had a point.

> —Ernest W. Michel, executive director emeritus of UJA-Federation of New York, *Promises to Keep* (1993)

My views on charity are very simple. I do not consider it a major virtue and, above all, I do not consider it a moral duty. There is nothing wrong in helping other people, if and when they are worthy of the help and you can afford to help them.

> —Ayn Rand, writer and philosopher, interview with Alvin Toffler in *Playboy*, March 1964

Wealth has replaced wisdom as a symbol of leadership, particularly in the last 100 years. It has been noted that in the early 20th century, men of affluence in a community lined up to see the rabbi; now, rabbis line up to see the philanthropist.

> —Gary Rosenblatt, editor and publisher, *The Jewish Week*, June 13, 1997

I am a great believer that institutions which deserve support will find supporters and when the time comes that an institution is not needed it should not be hampered by endowment funds to prevent it from going out of existence.

> —Julius Rosenwald, son of poor Jewish immigrants from Germany who, with his family's help in 1895, bought an interest in and managed Sears, Roebuck and Co., 1923, quoted in *Inside American Philanthropy* by Waldemar A. Nielsen (1996)

Shall we devote the few precious days of our existence only to buying and selling, only to comparing sales with the sales of the same day the year before . . . only to seek pleasures and fight taxes, and when the end comes to leave as little a taxable estate as possible as the final triumph and achievement of our lives? Surely there is something finer and better in life, something that dignifies it and stamps it with at least some little touch of the divine. My friends, it is unselfish effort, helpfulness to others that ennobles life, not because of what it does for others but more what it does for ourselves. In this spirit we should give not grudgingly, not niggardly, but gladly, generously, eagerly, lovingly, joyfully, indeed with the supremest pleasure that life can furnish.

> —Julius Rosenwald, quoted in *Inside American Philanthropy* by Waldemar A. Nielsen (1996)

[His] legacy is not only what he contributed but how he contributed — showing that if you apply vision, idealism, business sense and a belief in Jewish values, you can influence history through charity.

> —Natan Sharansky, former refusenik, tribute to philanthropist Ludwig Jesselson, "A Classic Jewish Pursuit," *Jerusalem Report*, May 6, 1993

[American Jews] have given money for various funds as uncaringly as cows give milk.

> —Moshe Shertok, Jewish Agency executive, 1943, quoted in *Israel in the Mind of America* by Peter Grose (1983)

My real expertise is in simplicity. I present people with simple projects they can do immediately. I want to give them the sense that they can have an enormous effect on people's lives, and it can begin with a single act.

> —Danny Siegel, volunteer fund-raiser who collected $1,300,000 (in seventeen

years) for small and deserving grassroots charities in the U.S. and Israel,
quoted in "Mitzva Poet," *Hadassah*, March 1993

Our greatest strength is our greatest weakness. We serve Jews in need
wherever they are, which is our strength. While that sometimes involves building buildings, it more often means providing support and services that are not
as visible.

> —Jeffrey Solomon, senior vice president and chief operating officer of UJA-
> Federation of New York, quoted in "Target Practice" by Stewart Ain, *The*
> *Jewish Week*, December 27, 1996

I never have regrets about having spent a lot of money trying to make things
better.

> —George Soros, international executive, financier and philanthropist, quoted
> in *The New York Times*, July 12, 1997

It was always my intention to give back to the Jewish community any money
I received from *Schindler's List*.

> —Steven Spielberg, film director, who founded the Righteous Persons Foun-
> dation after making *Schindler's List* and donated $650,000 to create the
> Fund for Jewish Documentary Filmmaking at the National Foundation for
> Jewish Culture, quoted in *The Jewish Week*, July 26, 1996

I became a humanitarian when my characters started eating people.

> —Steven Spielberg, who created the films *Jaws* and *Jurassic Park*, accepting
> a Human Relations Award at the American Jewish Committee dinner,
> quoted in *Jewish Telegraphic Agency*, February 7, 1997

The Almighty has been good to us. You can only eat three meals a day.

> —Irving Stone, founder-chairman of American Greetings, the world's largest
> publicly held greeting card company, quoted in *Cleveland Jewish News*,
> January 12, 1996

The big problem with UJA is that it was built all these years on emotion.
With that emotional impact gone, it has lost its impact. People don't like the
corporate concept of UJA. They want to touch their gift.

> —Morris Talansky, executive vice-chairman of Shaare Zedek Hospital in Je-
> rusalem, commenting on the shifting philanthropic trend of designated giv-
> ing, quoted in "Target Practice" by Stewart Ain, *The Jewish Week*,
> December 27, 1996

Wealthier families are expected to, and sometimes do, contribute more money than their less affluent neighbors. Consequently, their names are pasted all over buildings, rooms, memorial this-and-that in the synagogue. Somehow it is assumed that by giving more, they are more important, better qualified for honors and leadership than the ordinary Jew-in-the-pew.

> —Rabbi Andre Unger, author, lecturer, and rabbi of Temple Emmanuel in Woodcliff Lake, N.J., quoted in "The Politics of Piety," *The Jewish Spectator*, Spring/Summer 1989

A $100-a-head dinner dance is small potatoes to an investment banker but a big drain for a schoolteacher. An old-age pensioner's check of fifty dollars buys a lot less than fifty thousand from the owner of a chain of supermarkets, but subjectively, and thus ethically, represents a far greater sacrifice. One pays for a year's supply of paper clips, the other picks up the tab for the principal's yearly salary.

> —Rabbi Andre Unger, quoted in "The Politics of Piety," *The Jewish Spectator*, Spring/Summer 1989

One of the most pleasant characteristics of mankind is the ability to care about other beings that you don't know.

> —Leslie Wexner, business executive who is the son of immigrant parents and creator, with his mother, of the Wexner Foundation in 1973, quoted in *Inside American Philanthropy* by Waldemar A. Nielsen (1996)

The way to think about giving in general is, you never know when your lease expires. I'd like to feel that I've always met my obligations, personal ones and community ones. I'd like to check out with 10 cents and have seen the good happen while I was on earth.

> —Leslie Wexner, quoted in *Inside American Philanthropy* by Waldemar A. Nielsen (1996)

American Jews are, with the exception of African-Americans, the most liberal group in American politics. They regularly buy into the egalitarian policies of the most liberal components of the Democratic party. They bemoan what they view as the hierarchical, elitist, political and economic positions of Pat Robertson, Newt Gingrich and their followers. But look at the organized Jewish world. The naked influence of the dollar is everywhere, without veil or shame. People are rated by the amount of their annual gift and honored commensurately.

> —Nicholas Wolfson, professor of law, quoted in the *Hartford Jewish Ledger*, March 17, 1995

The community seemed hell-bent on making a hero out of the Big Giver, no matter how lacking in knowledge or how unobservant in ritual life he might be.

> —Melvin Urofsky, historian, *We Are One! American Jewry and Israel* (1978)

❖ PLURALISM ❖

(see also Denominations)

Once we didn't classify Jews as heart Jews, head Jews or stomach Jews. Once a Jew loved his traditions and felt quite comfortable under them.

> —Goldie Stone, liaison communal worker for the immigrants, from her autobiography, response to a question as to whether she was a "stomach Jew" by a Jewish host who wanted to prepare some bacon for her, 1912, quoted in *The American Jewish Woman: A Documentary History* by Jacob R. Marcus (1981)

The hate-mongering against the word orthodox may come from a revulsion to the "A" word. That word is "Absolute". . . . Many are so appalled by it, that the only thing they are absolutely sure of, is that there are not absolutes. And with that certainty they have discarded not only much that was dark and evil, but much that is timeless and valuable. And they have despised men of good conscience, and their own brothers.

> —Yitzchok Adlerstein, professor of Jewish studies, *Sh'ma*, January 6, 1989

It seems, at this point, we do not have to be as concerned with anti-Semitism from the outside as we do with anti-religiousness from the inside.

> —Sharlene Balter, Los Angeles resident, protesting the newspaper's characterization of the Orthodox community, letter to the editor, *Jewish Journal of Greater Los Angeles*, June 14–20, 1996

What concerns liberals about the orthodoxies is not that, given the power, they will be intolerant, only that, because of their central beliefs, they can, in principle, generate extremism, zealotry and fanaticism. And these, simple human experience has taught us, desecrate God's name while claiming to exalt it, and therefore are among the most reprehensible of human sins.

> —Rabbi Eugene B. Borowitz, editor and professor of education and Jewish religious thought, *Sh'ma*, January 6, 1989

We are not "one people".... We go our separate ways. Sometimes we interact, usually only in times of crisis. The gap . . . is wide and will continue to widen until and unless the right-wing Orthodox fundamentalists stop vilifying the rest of us. Short of that we will survive without one another.

> —Rabbi Balfour Brickner, senior rabbi emeritus of the Stephen Wise Free Synagogue in New York City, *The Jewish Week*, April 18, 1997

The price the Jewish people pays for Israel's political arrangement is not only the insult the arrangement flings at religious Jews of non-Orthodox or of modern Orthodox persuasion; it is also the injury it does to Judaism itself.

> —Leonard Fein, political scientist and columnist, *Forward*, May 31, 1996

I propose that things in common are much more important than distinctions.

> —Allen Ginsberg, poet, quoted in *Allen Ginsberg in America* by Jane Kramer (1968)

Pluralism is more than tolerance. Without saying that anything goes or that all are the same, without yielding its own standards, the pluralist group affirms that the others, despite their limits and even misdeeds, make a contribution to Clal Yisrael, which God wants and which the group alone cannot make.

> —Rabbi Irving Greenberg, author, scholar, and founder of National Jewish Center for Learning and Leadership (CLAL), *The Jewish Week*, October 6, 1995

The truth is, I would feel more at home with the Pope than with a Reform rabbi.

> —Rabbi Abraham B. Hecht, president of the Rabbinical Alliance of America (Orthodox), commenting on his willingness to be in a room with Conservative and Reform rabbis for a private visit with Pope John Paul II for a chance to teach the "Seven Laws of Noah," quoted in *The Jewish Week*, October 6, 1995

We're not talking about a democratic vote. We're talking about religious law.

> —Rabbi David Hollander, member of the executive board of the Union of Orthodox Rabbis, commenting on the group's conclusion that Reform and Conservative movements aren't Judaism, quoted in the *Baltimore Jewish Times*, March 28, 1997

By reason of the prevailing diversity in world outlook, there has to be room in Jewish religion for different versions of it.

—Rabbi Mordechai M. Kaplan, founder of Reconstructionism, *The Principles of Reconstructionism and Questions Jews Ask*, (1956), reprinted in *Modern Jewish Thought* edited by Nahum N. Glatzer (1977)

From my own vantage point as a part of Centrist Orthodox Judaism, I am terrified at the prospect of such disunity. I believe fervently in the middle position. I believe in respect for varying opinions, which also includes respect for those who hold those opinions. I believe in moderation in expressing our views and in acting upon them.

> —Rabbi Haskel Lookstein, rabbi of Kehilath Jeshurun and principal of the Ramaz School in New York City, speaking at the annual meeting of the New York Board of Rabbis, December 18, 1985, accepting the organization's presidency, "Mending the Rift: A Proposal," *Moment*, March 1986

There are few places left in the religious Jewish world where one can find mutual respect and love on the part of one Jew for another despite religious disagreement. Indeed, looking at the Jewish religious community in America these days I understand, as never before, the frightening words of the Sa'adia Gaon that we recite at selichot services on the eve of Rosh Hashanah: "Paninu l'yemin v'ein ozer; l'smol v'ein somech"—"I turn to the right and there is no support; to the left and there is no encouragement."

> —Rabbi Haskel Lookstein, speaking at the annual meeting of the New York Board of Rabbis, December 18, 1985, "Mending the Rift: A Proposal," *Moment*, March 1986

My rabbi says that whatever you do, someone's not going to eat in your kitchen.

> —David Mamet, playwright, novelist, essayist, screenwriter, and director, commenting at a public dialogue with Cynthia Ozick in New Rochelle, N.Y., December 15, 1997

Unity is not uniformity. A healthy Jewish civilization requires people of different religious, cultural and political viewpoints who embrace a common principle and respect one another's right to express the principle in different ways.

> —Marlene Post, president of Hadassah, quoted in *Long Island Jewish World*, June 20, 1997

Religious freedom is an ideal of Judaism. Religious coercion is not. If coercion was approved or applied at any time in our millennial history it was not because the Bible suggested it.

—Rabbi Emanuel Rackman, chancellor of Bar-Ilan University, author, and columnist *The Jewish Week*, April 7, 1989

The polarization between orthodox and heterodox Jews has reached catastrophic proportions. We cannot even hear each other clearly. Our anxiety that someone will coerce us away from our deepest commitments makes us shy of really hearing even the most irenic propositions.

—Rabbi Zalman Schachter-Shalomi, leader of the Jewish renewal movement, *Tikkun*, premiere issue, Fall 1986

American Jewish pluralism will not just go away; while it breeds acrimony, it has also become a means of modern Jewish survival, and one that offers a wide range of options to a diverse and opinionated public. Whatever the weaknesses of Reform Judaism, for example, it has encouraged many to retain a modicum of Jewishness.

—Robert M. Seltzer, professor of Jewish history, "American Jews & Their Judaism," *Commentary*, March 1994

The Sephardic world has lived for hundreds of years with the concept of one Jewish people, one halachah [code of Jewish law] and one synagogue, albeit with a larger measure of tolerance and acceptance of each individual's ability to keep the mitzvot [sacred obligations]. This concept has kept us united.

—Edwin Shuker, executive director of the American Sephardic Federation, letter to the editor, *The Jewish Week*, July 26, 1996

American Judaism is divided into some thousands of fragments of so and so many square blocks each, centered in more or less richly endowed synagogues with two rabbis or one with a simple Hazan [cantor], "scapegoats" held responsible by the boards of trustees for the size and income of the respective congregations.

The main cause for this unfortunate splitting of American Judaism, and of the disastrous vestry-politics which has already ruined so many congregations, transformed synagogues into concert houses . . . is the more or less sincere fight between what one generally calls Orthodoxy and Reform.

—Dr. Isadore Singer, quoted in *The American Hebrew*, May 31, 1901

I believe in pluralism. For me a Jew is a Jew is a Jew.

—Elie Wiesel, Nobel laureate and author, speaking at a *Jewish Week* luncheon in New York, November 9, 1995

Where are the successors of Haim Greenberg, Stephen Wise, Louis Marshall and Abraham Heschel? If there is none, it is because there is no audience worthy of them, because we have condemned our heritage of dissent and non-conformity. Ahavat Yisrael [loving other Jews] means the willingness to share even those problems which cannot be solved, to respect fellow Jews in Gush Emunim [Israeli settler movement], and even in the Jewish Defense League. It means remembering what halbanat panim [the prohibition against publicly shaming others] is. And it means remembering that all Jews are brothers and sisters and must treat each other that way.

> —Rabbi Arnold Jacob Wolf, activist and rabbi of Kam Isaiah Israel Congregation in Chicago, speaking at the annual Rabbinical Assembly (Conservative) convention, 1977

If Israel fails we die, but if we fail because we tried to be more McCarthyite than McCarthy, then Israel dies too.

> —Rabbi Arnold Jacob Wolf, speaking at the annual Rabbinical Assembly convention, 1977

❖ POETRY ❖

(see also Books, Language, Literature, Writing)

All you need is an olive tree, a few nuns, a muezzin screaming, a little bit of Holocaust, falafel and some Sabbath candles. . . . Put it together and cook and you have a poem. It helps to have a dead grandfather in Poland . . . it's so easy to write bad poetry about Jerusalem; it's a terrible mixture of schmaltz and wars.

> —Yehuda Amichai, Israeli poet, offering a recipe for a poem about Jerusalem, quoted in "The Holy City's Non-Prophet Poet," *The Washington Post*, October 25, 1995

American poetry is this country's greatest patrimony. It takes a stranger to see some things clearly. This is one of them, and I am that stranger. . . . Books find their readers. And if they will not sell, well, let them lie around, absorb dust, rot and disintegrate. There is always going to be a child who will fish a book out of the garbage heap. I was such a child, for what it's worth.

> —Joseph Brodsky, Russian-born poet exiled to the United States in 1972 who won the Nobel Prize in 1987 and was appointed poet laureate of the United States in 1991, from his address at the Library of Congress in which he

suggests that the government help subsidize the publication of American poetry, "The Poet on Trial," *The New Yorker,* February 12, 1996

Like I'm beginning to see my poetry as a kind of record of the times—my impressions of what's going on, like what's going on in terms of how my being responds to it. I don't know. It may not last, but I think it's maybe useful in that it helps clarify the present.

> —Allen Ginsberg, poet, quoted in *Allen Ginsberg in America* by Jane Kramer (1968)

It disturbs me that twentieth century American poets seem largely reconciled to being relegated to the classroom—practically the only habitat in which most of us are conditioned to feel secure. It would be healthier if we could locate ourselves in the thick of life, at every intersection where values and meanings cross, caught in the dangerous traffic between self and universe.

> —Stanley Kunitz, poet, introductory essay to *Passing Through: The Later Poems* (1995)

Poetry, I have insisted, is ultimately mythology, the telling of the stories of the soul.

> —Stanley Kunitz, introductory essay to *Passing Through: The Later Poems* (1995)

❖ POLITICS, GOVERNMENT, AND LEADERS ❖

(see also International Affairs)

I will not be a party to any attacks upon your personal integrity or personal life. We seem to have different views regarding the philosophy of government and on that alone am I willing to contend against you.

> —Bernard Baruch, financier and statesman, from a letter sent to President Herbert Hoover, 1928, quoted in *American Jewish Year Book 1929–1930*

There's something wrong when some Orthodox rabbis and Ku Klux Klansmen can endorse the same candidate.

> —Douglas Bloomfield, columnist, quoted in *Long Island Jewish World,* March 8, 1996

And do we have to hear about the sex lives of our presidents? . . . It is getting to the point that a eunuch has a better chance of getting elected.

> —Kirk Douglas, actor and author, *Climbing the Mountain* (1997)

American democracy is at its best in its talent for transfer of power.

> —Abba Eban, former foreign minister and Israeli ambassador to the United Nations, *Abba Eban: An Autobiography* (1977)

He went to see places where elected officials never go, and he went to listen, not to hold forth. And after he listened and learned, he acted.

> —Peter Edelman, legislative aide to Senator Robert F. Kennedy from 1965 to 1968, discussing Kennedy, quoted in *RFK: Collected Speeches*, edited by Edwin O. Guthman and C. Richard Allen (1993)

What the American people have to ask themselves is whether the system we've stumbled into for selecting candidates for the presidency produces the best leadership for the nation or just people with the stamina to get through the experience.

> —Eli N. Evans, author and president of the Charles H. Revson Foundation, *The Lonely Days Were Sundays: Reflections of a Jewish Southerner* (1993)

You look at any picture of a politician with some girls around him and at least some of them will be mine. . . . If I really came out and talked I could have stopped NAFTA.

> —Heidi Fleiss, Hollywood madam, quoted in *National Review*, February 21, 1994

Bob Dole could have picked Herzl and he would lose in the Jewish community.

> —Ira Forman, executive director of the National Jewish Democratic Council, commenting on the selection of Jack Kemp as Bob Dole's running mate, quoted in *Jewish Telegraphic Agency*, August 13, 1996

Let us remember Lyndon Johnson's greatness. Let us remember his love for people. . . . Let us remember the fullness of his understanding of his nation, of its roots, its meaning, its mission. Let us remember that he was determined that his nation should fulfill and not frustrate its destiny. . . . Above all, let us remember that he was a large man, of enormous strength and intense dedication. He was a man alive, vital, eager, restless, warm and passionate. He was American. . . . Let us not lose our way. Let us honor him by continuing the ascent which he began.

—Abe Fortas, Washington, D.C., attorney, from his eulogy for former president Lyndon Johnson, quoted in *The New York Times*, January 25, 1973, cited in *Fortas: The Rise and Ruin of a Supreme Court Justice* by Bruce Allen Murphy (1988)

It's not the same thing as having a bias against Ivy Leaguers. The world hasn't tortured or killed Ivy Leaguers.

—Abraham H. Foxman, national director of the Anti-Defamation League, commenting on the revelation that President Nixon directed top White House staff to "persecute" perceived Jewish tax cheats, quoted in *The Jewish Week*, January 17, 1997

I do not recall the date of [President] Wilson's "neutral in thought and deed." That was a silly remark to make, that you should be neutral, that you should stop thinking, that you shouldn't analyze what were the contending forces and which ones you wanted to prevail. If that's what "neutral in thought" meant, it was silly. If it didn't mean that, it was a deception. That doesn't mean that I don't think Wilson was right in not hurling us into war . . . until the country was educated.

—Felix Frankfurter, U.S. Supreme Court justice, quoted in *Felix Frankfurter Reminisces*, recorded in talks with Dr. Harlan B. Phillips (1960)

Surely half the population is more than a special interest group.

—Betty Friedan, author and activist, supporting the proposed Equal Rights Amendment to the U.S. Constitution, *The Second Stage* (1981)

Experience shows that once a government undertakes an activity, it is seldom terminated.

—Milton and Rose Friedman, economists and authors, *Free to Choose: A Personal Statement* (1980)

This one-sided "compact between the generations," foisted on generations that cannot give their consent, is a very different thing from a "trust fund." It is more like a chain letter.

—Milton and Rose Friedman, *Free to Choose: A Personal Statement* (1980)

No one in his right mind would argue that a Jew ought to vote for a Jew when he knows his coreligionist is clearly the inferior man, or that an Irishman ought to call for a policy which he knows is bad for the rest of his countrymen. But the time for nervousness about ethno-religious politics is over. . . . There is something ironic in anyone claiming to vote his religious and cultural heritage and at the same time insisting that it has nothing to do with forming attitudes on social and political policy. More realistic was the view of Woodrow Wilson who, when he was told what a pity it was that so great a man as Justice Brandeis should be a Jew, replied, "But he would not be Mr. Brandeis if he were not a Jew."

> —Lawrence H. Fuchs, professor of political science, *The Political Behavior of American Jews* (1956)

There is none, period. A Jew is running for president. My reaction is: So what?

> —Jerome A. Chanes, codirector for domestic concerns at the National Jewish Community Relations Advisory Council, when asked whether there would be a "favorite son" attitude among Jewish voters to the presidential candidacy of Senator Arlen Specter, quoted in *Jewish Telegraphic Agency*, April 5, 1995

Sometimes America's politics are more poetry than prose and more music than poetry: Here were the members of the country's political leadership, gathered en masse, ritually marking their acceptance of the great fact of modern American political life—the fact that the flawed, furiously human Richard Nixon, a man of dark nightmares and optimistic dreams, was part of each of them, as mysterious to them as he was to himself.

> —Leonard Garment, author and former counsel to Presiden Nixon, commenting on Nixon's funeral, *Crazy Rhythm* (1997)

In politics there are probably no innocents; there are only people who are not guilty as charged.

> —Suzanne Garment, author, *Booknotes* interview with Brian Lamb, C-SPAN, November 17, 1991

The options for action open to the United States government were pitifully few. But even the possibilities barely came up for discussion. Roosevelt's guilt, the guilt of American Jewish leadership and of the dozens and hundreds of others in position of responsibility, was that most of the time, they failed to try.

> —Peter Grose, author, quoted in *Kissing Through Glass* by Joyce R. Starr (1990)

Why should we want a Jewish president? If the economy should falter, they will blame the Jews, not just the president. Those who disagree with his politics will attribute his views to his religion. A practicing Jew as president could evoke rage among those who contend that America is a Christian nation. There is truth in this argument and it is possible that a Jewish president might bend over backwards to prove impartiality in conflicts between Israel and its Arab neighbors. . . . We are probably better off without a Jewish president and give our support to the candidates who are just, moral and good for America, but the idea is irksome. The unspoken truth is, a Jew is unelectable as a candidate for the presidency.

> — Rabbi Rafael G. Grossman, president of the Rabbinical Council of America, *The Jewish Press*, May 24, 1996

My mourning for Adlai Stevenson began before his death.

> — Nat Hentoff, journalist and author, *Speaking Freely* (1997)

Nothing is more natural than the ties of like people with each other. One knows where one is with that. . . . If [that] Republican candidate had had it explained to him that the Jewish businessmen of Memphis were voting as they did because they saw in the Goldwater movement a threat to themselves as Jews, as well as a threat to liberal values, even he might have understood. What no one can understand is claptrap — like a denial of anything specifically Jewish about the way all those individual businessmen, who happened to be Jews, also happened to vote differently from the Gentile businessmen.

> — Milton Himmelfarb, author, commenting on the 1964 presidential election, when Goldwater opposed Johnson, "How We Are," *Commentary*, January 1965

Remember a guy named Lyndon Johnson? He was so predictable when Yippie! began. And then pow! . . . He did the one thing no one had counted on. He dropped out. "My God," we exclaimed. "Lyndon is out-flanking us on our hippie side."

> — Abbie Hoffman, activist, *Revolution for the Hell of It* (1968)

The United States political system was proving more insane than Yippie! Reality and unreality had in six months switched sides. It was America that was on a trip; we were just standing still. How could we pull our pants down? America was already naked. What could we disrupt? America was falling apart at the seams.

> — Abbie Hoffman, activist, commenting after the assassination of Senator Robert Kennedy, *Revolution for the Hell of It* (1968)

New left guerrillas are nothing more than guerrillas with tenure.

> — Irving Howe, author and critic, in conversation with Kenneth Libo, New York City, 1970

When I could not show up for a speaking date at all, or when I had to decline an invitation, I always sent a telegram. These telegrams became a standing joke with my staff and my friends. It was said that a new definition of a minyan is nine Jews and a telegram from Jacob Javits.

> —Jacob K. Javits, U.S. Senator (R-N.Y.), *Javits: The Autobiography of a Public Man*, written with Rafael Steinberg (1981)

On more than 90 percent of the issues facing the country and the state, the janitor's son from the Lower East Side and the grandson of the richest man in America saw eye to eye.

> —Senator Jacob K. Javits, recalling the 1962 questionnaire completed by Javits and New York Governor Nelson Rockefeller on policy matters, *Javits: The Autobiography of a Public Man*, written with Rafael Steinberg (1981)

I remember once back around 1955, when a prep school boy took me out in his car, and we went up to a secluded street in Riverdale and started necking. Then he said something about how Nixon was his ideal and I said, "Take me home," I was completely turned off.

> —Erica Jong, novelist and poet, interview with Gretchen McNeese in *Playboy*, September 1975

I hadn't wanted Reagan to win; I'd voted for Carter without hesitation. But as I waited for him to show up, and looked at the outgoing Democratic officials gathered on the stage I realized there was not one of these people I wasn't happy to see go.

> —Mickey Kaus, journalist, recalling the crowd in a Washington, D.C., hotel, waiting for President Jimmy Carter to arrive and concede his defeat by Ronald Reagan in the 1980 presidential election, *The End of Equality* (1992)

[The late President Nixon] stood on pinnacles that dissolved into precipice. He achieved greatly and he suffered deeply. But he never gave up.

> —Henry A. Kissinger, former secretary of state and national security advisor to President Richard Nixon, from his eulogy at the Nixon Library in Yorba Linda, Calif., April 27, 1994

During the last campaign, I used to say to voters, "It may be that as a result of everything I've done, a lot of you will get together and throw me out. That's OK. I'll get a better job, but you won't get a better mayor."

> —Edward I. Koch, mayor of the city of New York, interview with Peter Manso in *Playboy*, April 1982

In matters on which I have no opinion—and there are lots of such matters, although I think people find that hard to believe—I am willing to listen and learn and, as a result of a consensus, adopt a position. But in adopting a position involving what I perceive to be morality in a very strict sense— . . . you couldn't persuade me, you couldn't change my mind; you can throw me out of office but you won't get me to change my positions on matters of morality.

> —Edward I. Koch, "Compassion and Common Sense in Government," chapter in book cowritten with John Cardinal O'Connor, *His Eminence and Hizzoner: A Candid Exchange* (1989)

Rarely, whether in America or elsewhere, have romantic love and summit power been found together. In our witless sense of perfectionism we dream of their somehow miraculously working together. They haven't and don't. The deepest yearnings of the heart are incompatible with the steepest demands of power.

> —Max Lerner, professor, author, and columnist, reflecting on the marriage of Franklin and Eleanor Roosevelt, "Desire and Power in the White House," 1984, in *Wounded Titans: American Presidents and the Perils of Power,* edited by Robert Schmuhl (1996)

The moral for politicians is: Put not your faith in a past lover who feels wounded, strapped for cash, and starved for recognition in an overnight celebrity market.

> —Max Lerner, commenting on revelations about Governor Bill Clinton's personal life during the primaries, from his column dated February 2, 1992, reprinted in *Wounded Titans: American Presidents and the Perils of Power,* edited by Robert Schmuhl (1996)

You will only succeed if you can build a politics of meaning, a politics based on a sense of shared purpose and moral vision.

> —Michael Lerner, author and editor, "Memo To Clinton: Our First Hundred Days," *Tikkun,* January/February, 1993

If [President] Bill Clinton had an affair with a 21-year-old intern, he should and will suffer the consequences. But after this story is over, we should draw the line on our obsession with the sex lives of politicians. The fact remains that the correlation between our leaders' Puritanism and their statesmanship is zero.

> —Anthony Lewis, columnist, *The New York Times,* January 26, 1998

Once you touch the biographies of human beings, the notion that political beliefs are logically determined collapses like a pricked balloon.

> —Walter Lippmann, journalist, *A Preface to Politics* (1913)

They think like Republicans, they talk like Republicans, they act like Republicans, and yet they vote Democrat.

> —Frank Luntz, Republican pollster, discussing the party affiliation of most American Jews, quoted in the *Washington Jewish Week*, March 1995

Well, I think President Eisenhower is a bit of a woman. . . . He's very passive. . . . If we're entering a crisis, he's not exactly the kind of man, I believe, who would have any imagination, any particular grasp of how to change things.

> —Norman Mailer, novelist, 1957 interview with Mike Wallace on *Night Beat*, quoted in *Close Encounters* by Mike Wallace and Gary Paul Gates (1984)

The thought cannot be tolerated that the citizens of this country shall form racial or religious groups in the exercise of their civic and political functions. The citizens of the United States constitute one people and there can be no divergent interests among them so far as government is concerned.

> —Louis Marshall, lawyer and president of the American Jewish Committee, Report of the American Jewish Committee, November 18, 1923

The key is to advertise your positions only if the public agrees with them.

> —Dick Morris, political strategist, *Behind the Oval Office* (1997)

One nice, mid 1930s day, my mother asked me to take a folding chair and go to Southern Boulevard and sit. In about two hours, President Franklin D. Roosevelt would drive by. She wanted a reserved front-row sight of him. In an hour and a half, she came for her seat under the IRT elevated-subway tracks. Thunder above and hurrays in Yiddish, Russian, Polish and English below. He arrived, waved to my mother and, in a slow minute, passed. It turns out that Roosevelt was the President my neighborhood had come to this country for.

> —Grace Paley, author, "Tough Times for a City of Tenants," *The New York Times*, January 25, 1998

Our own endorsement of the Democratic ticket was, as the Talmud puts it in a gloss on the story of the Jewish holiday Purim, "not out of love of Mordechai but out of repugnance for Haman."

> —Martin Peretz, editor-in-chief, "Why Dukakis Lost," *The New Republic*, November 28, 1988

My metaphor for this administration is coitus interruptus. George Bush can't consummate anything. Since coitus interruptus is well known to breed anxiety, the country is suffering from an anxiety attack.

—Norman Podhoretz, editor-in-chief of *Commentary*, quoted in *The Atlantic Monthly*, October 1992

There is no correlation between fidelity and ability to lead a country or city or dogcatcher. I wish there were but there isn't. Great leaders have had affairs and miserable people who have done great harm have been faithful. So what? That doesn't mean "so what" on fidelity, fidelity is very important: between the person, his spouse, himself, and his God. But not me outside of that relationship, it's none of my damn business. We're a country of voyeurs.

—Dennis Prager, author and radio commentator, *The Dennis Prager Show*, KABC Radio, Los Angeles, December 1994

I'd differentiate between ethics and morals, although the words often overlap. I think of ethics as being the difference between good and bad, and morality the difference between right and wrong. Morality is internalized—private decision-making—and ethics externalized—a person's conduct in dealing with the world. I'm determinedly uninterested in private morality, except when it spills over into the public area. But I'm very interested in political ethics.

—William Safire, columnist, interview with Victor Gold, *Washingtonian*, August 1991

[President Ronald Reagan] won because he ran against Jimmy Carter. If he had run unopposed he would have lost.

—Mort Sahl, comedian and satirist, commenting on the Reagan landslide in his presidential race against President Jimmy Carter, 1981, attributed

The problem we face is that we're too accepted. If Ruth Messinger were the first Jewish woman running for mayor years ago, she could have reached out to all the sectors of the Jewish community. . . . Twenty years ago, Ed Koch was a very Jewish guy running for mayor, and there had only been one Jewish mayor before. There was a reason for Jews to vote on an ethnic basis. Now we have a Jewish public advocate, a Jewish city comptroller, a Jewish speaker of the state Assembly. There's no particular drive for Jews to rally behind a Jewish candidate.

—Henry Sheinkopf, Democratic political consultant, regarding the 1997 New York mayoral race in which Ruth Messinger challenged incumbent Rudolph Giuliani, quoted in "Rudy, the Cops and the Election," by J. J. Goldberg, *The Jewish Week*, August 22, 1997

The government is its own worst enemy, the way it does not level with the American people.

—Arlen Specter, U.S. Senator (R-Pa.), interview, *Middle East Quarterly*, March 1997

It's time to turn the feminist adage around. The political is personal.

—Gloria Steinem, author and activist, *Revolution from Within* (1992)

I read his speeches, the ones before and the after. The ones he gave before the murder of his brother are often pragmatic. The ones delivered afterwards are strikingly lyrical and sometimes prophetic: They move you deeply. Is it a new man who is speaking to us? . . . Battered by destiny, he wanted to show his solidarity with victims everywhere.

—Elie Wiesel, Nobel laureate and author, remembering Senator Robert F. Kennedy, quoted in *RFK: Collected Speeches*, edited by Edwin O. Guthman and C. Richard Allen (1993)

Male blindness to women's reality leads to faulty politics.

—Naomi Wolf, author, *Fire with Fire: The New Female Power and How It Will Change the 21st Century* (1993)

I can't prove it with polls, but I'd lay 20-to-1 that more Jews say Kaddish for Richard Nixon than ever voted for him.

—Sidney Zion, *New York Daily News*, October 20, 1995

In Washington, the notion seems to be that if a scandal is big enough, the people will not understand, and if it involves enough politicians in both parties, there is no scandal at all. In other words, everybody will be blamed, so nobody will be blamed. This is intolerable.

—Mortimer B. Zuckerman, editor-in-chief, on the failure of the savings and loan institutions, *U.S. News & World Report*, May 7, 1990

❖ POLLARD CASE ❖

(see also Israel, Diaspora)

Since Pollard was never formally tried the facts of the case may never be fully known. But Pollard's treatment has been so anomalous that it only seems right to demand some kind of public accounting from the government.

—David Biale, professor of Jewish history, commenting on the incarceration of Pollard, who was caught in 1985 after passing top-secret documents to Israel while working in U.S. Naval Intelligence, *Tikkun*, May/June 1997

It is essential to distinguish between Pollard (and his most ardent supporters) and the case itself. One need not feel great sympathy for his ideology or his actions to sense that, on the human level, he has paid his price.

—David Biale, *Tikkun*, May/June 1997

Pollard, who gave secret information about Iraq and other Arab states that threatened Israel, was wrong to do so, no matter what his motivation. And it was both stupid and wrong of the Israelis to employ him. But if convicted Soviet superspy Aldrich Ames—whose treachery reportedly ended in the deaths of U.S. agents—can speak freely to the press, why can't Pollard?

—Richard Z. Chesnoff, columnist, *New York Daily News*, May 23, 1997

The Pollard case is a nightmare-come-true for American Jews. In Pollard, the Israelis created an anti-Semitic stereotype—an American Jew of confused loyalties who sold out his country. Indignation and shame are felt in equal measure.

—Richard Cohen, *Washington Post* columnist, 1987, quoted in *Jewish Power* by J. J. Goldberg (1996)

Though Pollard considered himself Judah Maccabee, Americans familiar with the case viewed him as Judas Iscariot.

—Hirsh Goodman, Israeli journalist, *Jerusalem Report*, April 21, 1994

Another Nelson Mandela? A modern-day Nathan Hale? No, it's Jonathan Jay Pollard, the poster boy for American Jews who feel there is an anti-Semite lurking in every shadow.

—Arthur M. Horwitz, publisher, *Detroit Jewish News*, January 10, 1997

There are enough people in our government who are not Jewish who will use this. And they will be more difficult to deal with. On the other hand, there are enough people in our government who are Jewish who will be very reluctant to do certain things that are perfectly legitimate for fear that they will be misunderstood.

—Philip M. Klutznick, Secretary of Commerce during the Carter Administration, quoted in *Territory of Lies* by Wolf Blitzer (1989)

If Israel feels Pollard has been treated unfairly, it knows how to get him an early release. There's no doubt that if he were a Soviet spy, he'd be out by now. I don't feel it's a matter for the American Jewish community. If Israel caught an American spy, it shouldn't be the American immigrants who get him out. The Israeli government can't pass this off on the American Jewish community.

—Arthur Liman, corporate lawyer, quoted in *Jerusalem Report*, June 13, 1991

The ugly battles between the various family members and factions claiming to speak for Jonathan Pollard have squandered numerous opportunities for assistance, while turning potential friends into enemies. . . . Even if it is true that Jonathan Pollard was put in jail by those who hated him, there can be little question that he is being kept in jail by those who claim to love him.

—David Luchins, senior assistant to Senator Patrick Moynihan (D-N.Y.), from a letter to Larry Dub, Pollard's lawyer, in response to a request by Dub that Luchins distance himself from the case, quoted in "Campaign to Free Pollard Moves to Israel," *Forward*, September 19, 1997

I was faced with a cruel dilemma in which I thought I had to choose between the law and my conscience. The danger that I perceived to Israel's existence was so acute that I instinctively chose action over reflection. I now know that was wrong. I should have made the effort to discover a legal solution to the predicament I faced. For this error in judgment I am profoundly sorry.

—Jonathan Pollard, former U.S. Navy intelligence analyst, from a letter to his parents in June 1991, from Marion, Ill., federal prison, quoted in "Release Pollard: He's Served Enough" by Rabbi Haskel Lookstein, *Newsday*, October 25, 1995

I don't know if you read any of his [Graham Greene's] books, but he happens to be one of my favorite authors. There's a character, an international correspondent, who characterizes an acquaintance of his—an American diplomat—by saying, "I've never met a man who had better motives for all the trouble he's caused." And I suspect that that aptly characterizes both my motives and my subsequent involvement in this affair.

—Jonathan Pollard, interview with Wolf Blitzer on November 20, 1986, in the Petersburg, Va., federal penitentiary, where he was awaiting his sentencing on espionage charges, quoted in *Territory of Lies* by Wolf Blitzer (1989)

In retrospect, I wish that I had thought about alternative courses of action. They were available. If I saw something that was wrong, I should have exhausted the legal processes that were at my disposal. They are called the chain of command. . . . But instead, I broke faith and took the law into my own hands . . . I ruined and brought disgrace upon my family. I have inadvertently strained relations between two otherwise amicable nations. And in spite of the fact that I neither intended nor wanted to take monetary compensation for my actions on behalf of the Israelis, I did. And there is no way around the fact that I crossed a line.

> —Jonathan Pollard, addressing Judge Aubrey E Robinson, Jr. at his sentencing, quoted in *Territory of Lies* by Wolf Blitzer (1989)

My case is not just about one man's freedom. It is about equal justice for all citizens in America, and it is about the fate of the Jewish community in America. It is about whether or not Israel can secure equal treatment as an ally. These are not small issues.

> —Jonathan Pollard, letter to the editor, *The Jewish Press*, February 28, 1997

You know what? I am, all in all, a failure. I am an agent who failed. True, there were mitigating circumstances. I was not trained for my mission; I wasn't a professional. I made a lot of mistakes. But that doesn't change a whole lot. History will remember me as one who failed, as one who did not fulfill his mission. And that is really a shame.

> —Jonathan Pollard, interview with Ben Caspit for March 28 [Israeli daily] *Ma'ariv*, reprinted in English translation, *MetroWest Jewish News*, June 5, 1997

The Pollard case will not end with his release. It is like the Rosenberg case or the Alger Hiss case. Historians will be writing about it 50 years from now.

> —Hershel Shanks, editor, *Moment*, February 1993

Many people now say that Jonathan [Pollard] was legally wrong but morally right in what he did.

> —Rabbi Avi Weiss, senior rabbi of the Hebrew Institute of Riverdale, professor of Judaic studies, and president of Coalition for Jewish Concerns, quoted in *The Jewish Week*, December 10, 1993

As Pollard now serves his twelfth year in Federal prison, with no release in sight, it would be useful to recall what this case was initially about: benefit to Israel, not harm to the United States. It would also be useful to evaluate whether the allegations of harm the government made only after winning a guilty plea from Pollard can withstand the scrutiny of a decade's hindsight.

> —David Zweibel, director of government affairs and general counsel of Agudath Israel of America, who was "of counsel" on the amicus curiae brief submitted in support of Jonathan Pollard's 1991 appeal to the U.S. Court of Appeals for the D.C. Circuit, *Middle East Quarterly*, June 1997

❖ POVERTY ❖

There were rooms in these houses where the sun never shone. There were rooms in which children slaved over bundles of garment work, breathing in the foul air that made them tubercular before they were grown up. . . . Fifty-three years ago, the International Ladies Garment Workers' Union was officially organized to war against the sweatshop. . . . Now, fifty years later, the garment workers return to their place of origin. We have wiped out the sweatshop. Now we return to wipe out the slum.

> —David Dubinsky, president of the International Ladies Garment Workers
> Union (ILGWU), remarks at the groundbreaking ceremony for an ILGWU
> housing project on the Lower East Side of New York, November 21, 1953,
> quoted in *Justice*, December 1, 1953, cited in *Out of the Sweatshop*, edited
> by Leon Stein (1977)

In my experience, middle-class Americans do not feel at ease around poor people. Even people of high ideals who care about the needy experience discomfort in the presence of the needy themselves.

> —Rabbi Eliezer Finkelman, rabbi of Congregation Beth Israel in Berkeley,
> Calif., quoted in *Jewish Bulletin of Northern California*, May 24, 1996

There are other issues facing this country right now, but the hunger of a three-year-old who doesn't deserve to be hungry outweighs in my judgment all other harms that can happen.

> —Barney Frank, U.S. Congressman (D-Mass.), quoted in *Esquire*, June 1988

When a poor man knocks at your door and says, "I'm hungry," and your first thought is, "Why can't you get a job?", you've invaded his privacy. Why would you need to know why he can't get a job? He didn't come to discuss his inabilities or bad habits; he came to discuss his hunger. If you want to do something about it, feed him.

> —Rabbi Manis Friedman, rabbi and dean of Bais Chana Institute in St. Paul,
> Minn., *Doesn't Anyone Blush Anymore?* (1990)

In the years that followed it became fashionable, even mandatory, to speak of the "failure" of the Great Society. But the Great Society did not fail. It was abandoned.

> —Richard Goodwin, advisor and speechwriter in the Kennedy and Johnson
> administrations, who created the concept and speech that introduced "The

Great Society" in a speech delivered by Lyndon Johnson on May 24, 1964,
Remembering America (1989)

We've always had rich and poor. But money is increasingly something that
enables the rich, and even the merely prosperous, to live a life apart from the
poor. And the rich and semi-rich increasingly seem to want to live a life apart,
in part because they are increasingly terrified of the poor, in part because they
increasingly seem to feel that they deserve such a life, that they are in some
sense superior to those with less. An especially precious type of equality—equality not of money but in the way we treat each other and live our lives—seems
to be disappearing.

—Mickey Kaus, journalist, *The End of Equality* (1992)

We were on welfare for a year. . . . New York City bought me my first pair
of glasses.

—Larry King, radio and television talk show host, recalling the struggle of his
widowed immigrant mother to raise her family, quoted in *Jewish Times* by
Howard Simons (1988)

Knowledge carries with it certain theological imperatives. The more we
know, the harder it becomes to grant ourselves exemption.

—Jonathan Kozol, author, *Time*, December 11, 1995

I don't think the problem is that we have insufficient information or cleverness. . . . The problem is that we lack the moral and theological will to act on
what we know.

—Jonathan Kozol, quoted in the *Los Angeles Times*, November 8, 1995

The last thing people want to see outside the marquee of *Les Miserables*
is the real miserables, the children on the sidewalk, after they leave their $250
tickets.

—Jonathan Kozol, quoted in the *Los Angeles Times*, November 8, 1995

To the rich all poor people look alike. To me, they were individuals—not
all good and kind and noble, but individuals.

—Sam Levenson, humorist and author, *Everything but Money* (1966)

I'm always comparing Delancey Street to Harvard: They're very snooty
about taking the top two percent, and we're equally snooty about finding the
bottom two percent.

—Mimi Silbert, cofounder of Delancey Street Foundation, a San Francisco–

based self-help organization offering rehabilitation programs, *Biography*, August 1997

Another basic principle . . . is the insistence upon individual consideration of the needy, rather than indiscriminate handling of them as so many "faces in the crowd." The indigent remains a dignified individual, with his own needs and drives, his own sensibilities and rights, strengths and weaknesses. The essence of the religious commandment is "to assist a poor person according to his needs"—in other words, selectively, not uniformly. Regimentation or massive institutionalization are not in keeping with this spirit.

— Isadore Twersky, author and professor of Hebrew literature and philosophy, "Some Aspects of the Jewish Attitude Toward the Welfare State" in *Poor Jews: An American Awakening*, edited by Naomi Levine and Martin Hochbaum (1974)

The prophetic books reaffirm the values of the Exodus story: indeed, no other body of literature is so likely to press people who take it seriously toward an identification with the poor and oppressed, and toward a suspicion not so much of wealth and power as of the moral complacency and arrogance that commonly accompany them. And suspicion also has its everyday uses.

— Michael Walzer, author and philosopher, *Values, Interests and Identity: Jews and Politics in a Changing World*, edited by Peter Y. Medding (1995)

Kids should not be penalized because of their parents' income.

— Dr. Larry Wolk, pediatrician who developed and runs the nonprofit organization Rocky Mountain Youth, treating more than 100,000 children, many homeless and poor, quoted in "Gift of Caring," *People*, August 18, 1997

❖ POWER ❖

What has moved many in our generation to despair is neither the ubiquity nor the decisiveness of power but rather the recognition that almost everywhere we see power in action we see it abused.

— Rabbi Eugene B. Borowitz, professor of education and Jewish religious thought, "Tzimtzum: A Mystic Model for Contemporary Leadership," *Religious Education*, November/December 1974

Modern times brought democracy into human relationships. . . . By contrast, the best a previous generation had been able to do to humanize man's will to power was to appeal to his better nature, to beg the mighty to act with mercy.

> —Rabbi Eugene B. Borowitz, "Tzimtzum: A Mystic Model for Contemporary Leadership," *Religious Education*, November/December 1974

Those who deny control are using that word "control" in a very restricted sense. They mean that these particular individuals have not definitely said, "This thing shall be done and this thing shall not be done." But, as a matter of fact, control is exercised and exercised to an extraordinary degree by the existence of a great power whom people believe and usually have reason to believe would be pleased and displeased with the adoption or rejection of a given course. Great power controls without issuing orders.

> —Louis D. Brandeis, Boston attorney and future U.S. Supreme Court justice, speaking before the United States Commission on Industrial Relations, January 23, 1915, quoted in *An American Primer*, edited by Daniel J. Boorstin (1995)

Clark Clifford and I get more done in one day on the telephone than they do in 20 years of law-review writing.

> —Abe Fortas, Washington, D.C., attorney, quoted in "In Washington, You Just Don't Not Return a Call From Abe Fortas" by Victor Navasky, *The New York Times Magazine*, August 1, 1971, cited in *Fortas: The Rise and Ruin of a Supreme Court Justice* by Bruce Allen Murphy (1988)

The Holocaust made it overwhelmingly clear that Jewish powerlessness was no longer compatible with Jewish survival.

> —Rabbi Irving Greenberg, author, scholar, and founder of National Jewish Center for Learning and Leadership (CLAL), in *A New Era in Jewish History* (1985)

Despite the continuing attack on the law as racist, the Law of Return is staunchly upheld by Israelis because it is the most sensitive indicator that Jews are masters in their own land, that they exist by right and not by sufferance or by tolerant goodwill.

> —Rabbi Irving Greenberg, "A New Era in Jewish History" (1985)

I think the greatest legacy of the 1960s was the general feeling that not only can you fight the powers that be, but you can win.

> —Abbie Hoffman, activist, 1986, *The Best of Abbie Hoffman* (1989)

Power in Jewish life comes from knowledge.

> —Francine Klagsbrun, columnist and author, speaking at conference "In

Search of Ourselves: The Power of Jewish Women," November 1995, sponsored by Hadassah and the Barnard Center for Research on Women

Eye contact was different. No one looked through or past me. Everyone looked at me. Neither men nor women allowed their eyes to stray toward someone more interesting, important or fun. It was me they wanted to talk to. And it was they who wanted to be heard. Remember this, I warned myself. It will evaporate like rain in a dry heat.

—Madeleine M. Kunin, three-term governor of Vermont who served as Deputy Secretary of Education in the Clinton administration, reflecting on her experience at a party while serving as governor, National Public Radio interview with Susan Stamberg, April 16, 1994

Finally, it is not the reality, but the dream of Israel that animates us all. What is amazing is that we live in an era when we can do something about it. It is an era of unprecedented power for Jews, and ultimately we will be held accountable, not only to God, but to ourselves for what we do with this opportunity.

—Joseph R. Rackman, attorney and columnist, *Long Island Jewish World*, September 26, 1997

Power can be taken, but not given. The process of the taking is empowerment in itself.

—Gloria Steinem, author and activist, "Far From the Opposite Shore," 1978, *Outrageous Acts and Everyday Rebellions* (1983)

To see the Poor People's March on Washington in perspective, remember that the rich have been marching on Washington ever since the beginning of the Republic. They came in carriages and they come on jets. They don't have to be put up in shanties. Their object is the same, but few respectable people are untactful enough to call it handouts.

—I. F. Stone, journalist and author, "The Rich March on Washington All the Time," *I. F. Stone B-Weekly,* May 13, 1968, reprinted in *Polemics and Prophecies 1967–1970* (1989)

I come here as rarely as possible. Everybody here likes and wants power. . . . The congressman wants to be senator. The senator wants to be vice president. The vice president wants to be president. I have met many of them and, in my official functions, was favorably impressed by them. But outside of my functions, when you heard people talk, it was about who was up and who was down.

—Elie Wiesel, Nobel laureate and author, discussing Washington, D.C., quoted in the *Chicago Tribune*, November 26, 1995

The anniversary of Zionism is the anniversary of the Jewish preference for power over self-pity. What the early Zionists could not have known, but what we can know, is that power becomes dangerous when it refuses to let self-pity go. The stronger we are, the weaker we are: this has been the ridiculous premise of those Israelis and American Jews with an un-Zionist appetite for apocalypse, who are not satisfied to think empirically about danger. But in truth, the stronger we are, the stronger we are; and the strong, too, have enemies. Let us be pleased with our muscles, but let us not think with them.

—Leon Wieseltier, literary editor, "Washington Diarist," *The New Republic*, September 8 & 15, 1997

❖ PRAYER ❖

(see also Meditation)

To the Kabbalah, prayer is a vehicle for self-transformation. It is not begun with the hope of changing Hashem's mind to give us things we haven't received. It is cultivating our own willpower to establish a direct connection to Hashem so that we can change ourselves and become capable of receiving what has been waiting for us all along.

—Rabbi David Aaron, director of the Isralight Institute, *Endless Light* (1997)

God forbid this should come to pass. A daughter of Israel may not participate in such worthless ceremonies that are totally contrary to Halacha [Jewish law]. We are shocked to hear that "rabbis" have promoted such an undertaking which results in the desecration of God and his Torah. We forewarn all those who assist such "Minyonim" that we will take the strictest measures to prevent such "prayers," which are a product of pure ignorance and illiteracy. We admonish these "orthodox rabbis": Do not make a comedy out of Torah.

—Agudath HaRabanim [Union of Orthodox Rabbis] statement about women's prayer groups, *The Jewish Press*, December 10, 1982

I think of the passionate responses of my heart as an ongoing, spontaneous prayer, and I recognize my moment-to-moment attempts to stay alert and balanced as my natural response to finding myself in a life, in a world, in a universe far beyond my control or comprehension. As a Buddhist, I name this recollecting of myself mindfulness. As a Jew, I think of it as t'shuvah (return).

—Sylvia Boorstein, author, meditation teacher, and psychotherapist, *That's Funny, You Don't Look Buddhist: On Being a Faithful Jew and a Passionate Buddhist* (1997)

As people of the Book, whose most revered prayer is the Shema—the command to hear and heed the words which have shaped the religious beliefs of over half the world's population—we Jews cannot underestimate the power of words.

—Annette Daum, staff person for the reform movement's Task Force on Equality of Women, who compiled a glossary of substitute terminology for the prayer book (e.g. replacing "Heavenly Father" with "Heavenly One"), quoted in *Jewish and Female: Choices and Changes in Our Lives Today* by Susan Weidman Schneider (1984)

Jews commonly assume that, like breathing, one should be able to pray automatically. When they find that they cannot do this, they are disconcerted and annoyed. Prayer, however, is a skill; it does not usually come spontaneously to people. Some people do indeed have a gift for being able to pray, but most of us require extensive training and practice to master the skill of prayer.

—Dr. Elliot Dorff, professor of philosophy, *Knowing God: Jewish Journeys to the Unknowable* (1992)

To me, kavannah, intention in prayer, means meaning what you say. I can't have kavannah with words that are inappropriate. Many Jews today don't relate to a Lord God King of the World. It doesn't make sense for us to be praying as if we did. Metaphors have impact.

—Marcia Falk, author, poet, scholar, translator, and liturgist who re-creates traditional prayers in contemporary, gender-free language, *The Book of Blessings* (1996)

Blessings intensify life by increasing our awareness of the present even while awakening our connections to the past.

—Marcia Falk, *The Book of Blessings* (1996)

We never pray as individuals, set apart from the rest of the world. The liturgy is an order which we can enter only as part of the Community of Israel. Every act of worship is an act of participating in an eternal service, in the service of all souls of all ages.

—Rabbi Abraham Joshua Heschel, author, activist, and theologian, *Man's Quest for God* (1954)

Words are not made of paper. Words of prayer are repositories of the spirit. It is only after we kindle a light in the words that we are able to behold the riches they contain. It is only after we arrive within a word that we become aware of the riches our own souls contain.

> —Rabbi Abraham Joshua Heschel, *Man's Quest for God* (1954)

Prayer as a personal conversation with God clearly does not include mumbling, nor monotones, nor speed reading. It does not include an obligation to spend great amounts of time reciting fixed texts, especially when those texts are not intelligible, or when they do not convey a sincere message to God.

> —Rabbi Seth Kadish, teacher in Israel, *Kavvana: Directing the Heart in Jewish Prayer* (1997)

When she prayed an exuberant calmness, a glow would come over my mother that I never saw at any other time. Her eyes would be blazing; her cheeks would seem fuller, and she had full cheeks. It was as if she had a direct link to God.

> —Herb Kalisman, publisher, quoted in *Growing Up Jewish in America: An Oral History* by Myrna Katz Frommer and Harvey Frommer (1996)

The language of prayer should help us to an experience, not get in the way. Perhaps the most powerful language for Jews today is silence: we need more shohin—more emptying—in our prayer experience.

> —Rodger Kamenetz, author and professor of English, *Stalking Elijah* (1997)

People who pray at home pray because they want to be sure God hears them. I don't think there's a God, and God's not going to hear me. I love to pray because I love the community of Jews praying together. I love to be in that number. As "When the Saints Go Marching In" says, I long to be in that number.

> —Sherwin Nuland, author and professor of medicine, quoted in *Singular Voices: Conversations With Americans Who Make a Difference* by Barbaralee Diamonstein (1997)

Jewish prayer addresses the many things that concern us. If we look at the subject matter in the psalms, we find that they are filled with the concerns of ethics, war, enemies, relationship with God, fear, protection, wonder. The psalms actually provide us with the opportunity—and the permission—to say things we would otherwise feel uncomfortable saying.

> —Carol Ochs, author and professor of philosophy, and Kerry M. Olitzky, rabbi, author, and Jewish educator, *Jewish Spiritual Guidance: Finding Our Way to God* (1997)

To become a master of prayer involves breaking, at least for a few precious moments, the norms for "proper" behavior, whose first principle is the constant, vigilant awareness of oneself as a social animal.

—Rabbi Micha Odenheimer, journalist and director of the Israeli Association of Ethiopian Jews, *Jerusalem Report,* May 19, 1994

And as forests and deserts have disappeared from most of our lives, so has prayer. Or rather, it has been repressed, as sexuality was repressed in previous generations and heresies in still earlier ones. People may still pray, but prayer— wild, heartrending prayer—is almost never represented in mainstream culture. You don't hear it on the radio or see it on TV, in movies or in literary creations. If you do it is seen as slightly shameful or embarrassing, or as reflecting despair or even madness. . . . We have driven prayer into the fringes.

—Rabbi Micha Odenheimer, *Jerusalem Report,* May 19, 1994

I kissed the holy books when I closed them (as Orthodox Jews do) not because I thought I should but because I chose to acknowledge them as sacred and because the act itself felt beautiful. The impulse came from deep inside, where a sense of reverence was growing. Each service I attended gave me more understanding, beauty, more belief, and connection. Prayer, once foreign and contemptible, enriched my life.

—Lev Raphael, author, "To Be a Jew" in *Journeys and Arrivals* (1996)

I didn't write my diary last night because I was keeping Yom Kippur as I have never kept it before. Not only did I fast, as I have done many times before, but I didn't write or lift a finger to work. I spent last evening and all day today in the chapel. I read Hebrew with its English translation hour after hour. I followed the services closely. I tried and tried to pray—to get some divine sooth- ing inspiration. . . . I didn't pray for anything in particular; yet I prayed. I wanted to feel near to God. I didn't succeed. I just wanted to feel near Him, to tell him that I understood what He was doing and that I'd make the most of life regardless of what happened. Sometimes I felt that He heard me, but then I knew that He didn't hear—or else, He wasn't interested.

—Captain Hyman Samuelson, Jewish officer in charge of African-American troops in New Guinea during World War II, diary entry September 27, 1944, New Guinea, as cited in *Love, War, and the 96th Engineers (Colored),* edited by Samuelson and Gwendolyn Midlo Hall (1995)

When a button reading "It's not just tallis envy" was circulated at a Jewish feminist conference in 1974, everyone had a good chuckle. Many of the women who were gathering together in separate prayer and study groups were wearing some variation of a tallit. Now, ten years later, in havurot [informal prayer groups] and many other services, you can count on seeing at least a few women wearing the standard tallit, the large-size wraparound version or alternative model—sometimes a fringed shawl or a handwoven serape.

> —Susan Weidman Schneider, editor of *Lilith* and author, *Jewish and Female: Choices and Changes in Our Lives Today* (1984)

Many of those who, for ideological reasons, had ceased to pray, could not repress their emotional attachment to the prayers themselves.

> —Rabbi Adin Steinsaltz, Talmudic scholar, *The Strife of the Spirit* (1988)

Prayer is that dimension of language which begins in the human heart and carries that voice through the imagination to God. Ideal prayer returns to the human heart from the responsive heart of God.

> —Rabbi Ira Stone, author and rabbi of Beth Zion/Beth Israel Synagogue in Philadelphia, *Seeking the Path to Life: Theological Meditations on God and the Nature of People, Love, Life and Death* (1992)

The substance of language and the language of silence—that is prayer.

> —Elie Wiesel, Nobel laureate and author, "Prayer and Modern Man" in *Rabbi Joseph H. Lookstein Memorial Volume* (1980)

Prayer was meant to engage man and God in eternal dialogue. Thanks to prayer, we know that God is present, better still: that God is presence.

> —Elie Wiesel, "Prayer and Modern Man" in *Rabbi Joseph H. Lookstein Memorial Volume* (1980)

Appreciating beauty is an act of devotion.

> —Rabbi David J. Wolpe, assistant to the chancellor of The Jewish Theological Seminary, *The Jewish Week*, July 26, 1996

For the ordinary worshiper, the rewards of a lifetime of faithful praying come at unpredictable times, scattered through the years, when all at once the liturgy glows as with fire. Such an hour may come after a death, or after a birth; it may strike after a miraculous deliverance, or on the brink of evident doom; it may flood the soul at no marked time, for no marked reason. It comes, and he knows why he has prayed all his life.

> —Herman Wouk, author, *This Is My God* (1959)

✤ PREJUDICE ✤

I only wanted to lead my life according to those standards I believe to be right, and the "sins" that are combined in me aren't aimed at irritating, provoking, defying anyone. They arise out of reality, logic, out of being consistent. I'm a Negro and that's a reality. I'm a convert to Judaism because in Judaism I found the religious faith I was looking for, the solution to a spiritual crisis that was troubling me, and so that was an act of logic. I married a beautiful blonde because I loved her and she loved me, so that was completely being consistent. Nothing else. I never thought, "I'll convert to Judaism in order to annoy the Catholics, the Methodists, the Presbyterians, and the rest." I never said, "I want to marry a beautiful white woman." All I said was, "I'll marry the woman I fall in love with, and she will bear my children." That's all.

> —Sammy Davis, Jr., entertainer, 1964 interview with Oriana Fallaci, *The Penguin Book of Interviews*, edited by Christopher Silvester (1993)

The Anti-Defamation League does not believe in laws prohibiting prejudice, but we do believe decent people must speak out against it and make it unfashionable and unacceptable. We believe a balance must be struck between the extremes of unchallenged bigotry and political correctness. True, we cannot and should not insist that an individual think in a certain way. At the same time, having learned from the Holocaust what bigotry and hate can engender, we cannot be so quick to dismiss the hurtful power and potential of words.

> —Abraham H. Foxman, National Director of the Anti-Defamation League, letter to the editor, *Harper's*, August 1995

I remember Emmett Till, who I think was about my age, a black kid from Chicago who was killed in Mississippi—lynched. And I remember being in high school and seeing a *Life* magazine spread on that and just being furious. It's probably bigotry that bothers me most. Bigotry and undeserved poverty.

> —Barney Frank, U.S. Congressman (D-Mass.), quoted in *Esquire*, June 1988

I would not be writing about a young student worrying about whether he could get into a good medical school because he's Jewish; I would not be writing about a landlord or real estate broker asking a direct question like,"Are you of the Hebraic persuasion?" . . . No, I couldn't write those scenes now in 1982. But what if Phil [in *Gentleman's Agreement*] were black or Puerto Rican or Mexican-American and trying to rent or buy a house in certain neighborhoods? What about his getting into those good medical schools or renting an apartment or finding a job if he was known to be gay, and refusing to remain a closet gay? Alas, if I were writing this book at this very minute and merely changed the word Jew to black or Puerto Rican or gay or Mexican-American, I could leave most of the scenes intact.

> —Laura Z. Hobson, writer, whose book *Gentleman's Agreement* was made into a film starring Gregory Peck as a gentile reporter who poses as a Jew, *Laura Z: A Life—Years of Fulfillment* (1989)

Every card in the American deck is a race card. That's the nature of life in America.

> —Ronald Kuby, lead attorney representing plaintiff Darrell Cabey in the civil trial of subway gunman Bernhard Goetz, *Newsday*, April 18, 1996

The time has come to stop making apologies for black America, to stop patronizing black America with that paternalistic brand of understanding which excuses and finds reasons for the obscenities of black hatred.... Farrakhan is subtly but surely creating an atmosphere in America where hatreds of all kinds will be easier to express openly, and one day, in some as yet unknown form, these hatreds will ride commuter trains into the suburbs. By then it will be too late for us all.

> —Julius Lester, professor of Judaic studies, history and English, commenting when Louis Farrakhan addressed a rally in New York, *The New Republic*, October 1985, recalled by journalist Jim Sleeper after the December 7, 1993, Long Island Railroad massacre of commuters by gunman Colin Ferguson, *The New Republic*, January 1994

A white father may still not want a black man for a son-in-law, but he's dying to vote for a black man because then he can solve the problem of the major guilt trip he's been on his whole life. He can march around his house the next day looking at mirrors with pride that he is staring at the face of an unprejudiced man. This is the reason for Colin Powell's amazing popularity.

> —Jackie Mason, comedian, quoted in the *Los Angeles Times*, November 1, 1995

The hatred I still feel for Negroes is the hardest of all the old feelings to face or admit, and it is the most hidden and the most overlarded by the conscious attitudes into which I succeeded in willing myself... I know it from the insane rage that can stir in me at the thought of Negro anti-Semitism; I know it from the disgusting prurience that can stir in me at the sight of a mixed couple; and I know it from the violence that can stir in me whenever I encounter that special brand of paranoid touchiness to which many Negroes are prone. This then is where I am; it is not exactly where I think all other white liberals are, but it cannot be so very far away either.

> —Norman Podhoretz, editor, "My Negro Problem—And Ours," *Commentary*, February 1963

We used to think it was ironic that whenever we sold a lot of white sheets we knew that there was going to be a Klan meeting.

> —Dale M. Schwartz, attorney in Atlanta whose family ran a small department store in Winder, Ga., in the 1950s, quoted in *Jewish Times* by Howard Simons (1988)

Stereotypic thoughts are a natural way of organizing one's experience. Suppressing them in the discourse may be politically satisfying and helpful to maintaining order, but it won't make stereotyping obsolete, because for all their destructive power, stereotypes are also useful. They are half-truths, but half a truth is better than none when you are trying to map your landscape, however crudely. The real question is whether you can put those stereotypes aside when confronted with closer evidence that doesn't support them.

> —Philip Weiss, journalist, "Letting Go—A Personal Inquiry," *New York*, January 29, 1996

❖ PROHIBITION ❖

(see also Alcohol)

How much business Father and his brothers did with bootleggers was never clear, although Father insisted that everything they did was perfectly legal. One thing was certain: when American Prohibition was lifted, the Bronfman name was tarnished by lawsuits brought by the U.S. government against Canadian companies that had dealt with bootleggers. Though Father didn't let it stop him from building his own empire, he was deeply and permanently wounded by the impugning of his reputation.

> —Edgar M. Bronfman, chairman of the The Seagram Company Ltd., *Good Spirits: The Making of a Businessman* (1998)

People wanted booze, they wanted dope, they wanted to gamble and they wanted broads. For a price, we provided them with these amusements. We only gave them what they wanted.

> —Herschel Kessler, former Detroit gangster, quoted in *But—He Was Good to His Mother* by Robert A. Rockaway (1993)

❖ PSYCHOLOGY ❖

A philosopher once said, "If a man finds himself, he has a mansion in which he can live for the rest of his life." I would like to add to that: if a man does not find himself, he can build mansion after mansion and try to compensate for the loss of self, but he will not find a home. The soul is not at home in the ego.

—Rabbi David Aaron, director of the Isralight Institute, *Endless Light* (1997)

Whether it's personal or political, cynicism is the best solution that one can come up with to protect oneself from humiliation. . . . Cynicism is an attempt to make sense of the world in order to make the best of it and protect yourself from the ever-present dangers of relaxing your guard.

—Michael J. Bader, psychotherapist, presentation at the Summit on Ethics and Meaning, Washington, D.C., April 1996

Male psychologists, psychiatrists, and social workers must realize that as scientists they know nothing about women; their expertise, their diagnosis, even their sympathy is damaging and oppressive to women. . . . For most women the psychotherapeutic encounter is just one more power relationship in which they submit to a dominant authority figure.

—Phyllis Chesler, author and professor of women's studies, quoted from a paper presented at the annual convention of the American Psychological Association, Miami Beach, Fla., September 1970

As I stepped onto the platform at Worcester to deliver my "Five Lectures upon Psychoanalysis," it seemed like the realization of some incredible daydream. Psychoanalysis was no longer a product of delusion—it had become a valuable part of reality. . . . In Europe I felt like an outcast, here I saw myself received by the best men as their equal.

—Dr. Sigmund Freud, recalling when he spent one month in the United States and lectured to a gathering of psychologists at Clark University, 1909, quoted in *The People's Almanac* by David Wallechinsky and Irving Wallace (1975)

The question would imply that women are some separate species. I'm more interested in what the question implies—that women are strange creatures no one understands, and what could they possibly want? It's men saying: "I work, bring home money, I don't drink, I don't beat you—so what do you want from me? We're doing everything we can and women still aren't satisfied." It's that kind of silly question.

> —Sophie Freud, psychologist and professor of social work at Simmons School of Social Work Boston, who is the granddaughter of Sigmund Freud, stating her reaction to her grandfather's famous query, "Of Women and Men, A Conversation with Sophie Freud" by Margaret Pantridge, *Boston*, February 1992

People who go through years of therapy spend too much time completely occupied with themselves. It would be better for them to stop relying on therapy, and just do something good for a change.

> —Rabbi Manis Friedman, rabbi and dean of Bais Chanah Institute, St. Paul, Minn., *Doesn't Anyone Blush Anymore?* (1990)

Analysts all seem to be Talmudists who flunked out of Seminary.

> —Erica Jong, novelist and poet, *Fear of Flying* (1973)

Analysis is surrender—and who wants surrender? No one. We fight till we have no other option, till the pain is so great that we must.

> —Erica Jong, *Fear of Fifty* (1994)

Outside a church or court of law the difference between sickness and sin may be merely semantic. Sickness, however, is more marketable than sin: readers who find it satisfying and useful to be diagnosed as the victims of disease would probably resent being called evil. Inner child doctrine assures us that no one is unforgivable; everyone can be saved. What looks at first like a therapeutic view of evil turns out to be religious instead: Codependency theory replaces the Freudian subconscious with its unholy impulses and drama of inner conflict with the peaceful, happy vision of the child within. Because no one is inhabited by evil or "unhealthy urges," because inside every addict is a holy child yearning to be free, recovery holds the promise of redemption.

> —Wendy Kaminer, author, *I'm Dysfunctional, You're Dysfunctional, The Recovery Movement and Other Self-Help Fashions* (1992)

The Nazis are human: that is what the psychiatrists tell us. We always knew that, though it does no harm to have it confirmed.

> —Irving Kristol, social critic, "What the Nazi Autopsies Show," *Commentary*, September 1948

Psychoanalyzed men are liberated from the despotism of the unconscious. They are able to choose, no longer vassals of the tyrants within them. They are strong enough to moderate the ferocity of their demands, upon themselves or upon others. They are free, at last, to face the inescapable frustrations and suffering of living.

—Leo Rosten, author, *People I Have Loved, Known or Admired* (1970)

He [Freud] had tried to alleviate human suffering, to understand things that had not yielded their secrets to healers, and shamans and physicians down the centuries. But he was, in the last analysis, dedicated to analysis itself. He exemplified the scientist's respect for what is. He turned emotions into materia medica. He charted the dark ocean of the unconscious.

—Leo Rosten, *People I Have Loved, Known or Admired* (1970)

Of course, the brain is a machine and a computer—everything in classical neurology is correct. But our mental processes, which constitute our being and life, are not just abstract and mechanical, but personal, as well—and, as such, involve not just classifying and categorizing, but continual judging and feeling also. If this is missing, we become computer-like.

—Oliver Sacks, neurologist and author, *The Man Who Mistook His Wife for a Hat and Other Clinical Tales* (1985)

Modern therapy promotes self-centeredness. Everything is rational or relative. I'm not. My morality is based on the Old Testament and the Talmud. Whenever I can I try and push people toward religion.

—Dr. Laura Schlessinger, radio therapist and author, quoted in "The Just Do-It Shrink" by Rebecca Johnson, *The New York Times Magazine*, November 17, 1996

It's what I do for a living: debugging human intuition.

—Dr. Amos Tversky, cognitive psychologist who researched how people make decisions about risks, benefits, and probabilities, quoted in his obituary, *The New York Times*, June 6, 1996 (In 1988, he received a lot of attention when he published a study during the National Basketball Association playoffs showing that contrary to popular belief, there are no "hot hands" or "streaks" in basketball.)

The major critique that can be leveled against est [Erhard Seminars Training] is—not that it is simplistic (there may be virtue in that), not that it is mass production (every great system of thought demands a popularizer)—but that it is fundamentally inconsistent. Authoritarianism will not breed personal autonomy but, on the contrary, always stifles freedom. It is sophistry to claim, as est presumably does, that a product of personal responsibility may emerge from a procedure of authoritarianism. Which, after all, is the product and which the procedure?

> —Irvin D. Yalom, author and professor of psychiatry, commenting on est, the mass produced, large group approach to personal change founded by Werner Erhard, which was very commercially successful in the 1970s, *Existential Psychotherapy* (1980)

❖ RABBIS ❖

(see also Synagogues)

*W*anted: At Congregation Tifereth Israel (Progressive Orthodox) an experienced Hebrew pedagogue, who is capable of preaching in English. [Des Moines, Iowa]

> —Advertisement in *The American Hebrew*, June 7, 1901

There is no direct halakhic [Jewish legal] objection to the acts of training and ordaining women to be a rabbi, preacher and teacher in Israel.

> —Final report of the Commission for the Study of the Ordination of Women as Rabbis, Rabbinical Assembly (Conservative), 1979

He's the "Seinfelder Rav."

> —Congregant of B'nai Yeshurun, in Teaneck, New Jersey, likening the rabbi's pulpit style to that of comedian Jerry Seinfeld, quoted in the *Jerusalem Post*, October 8, 1995

He (the preacher) must be the teacher plus something else. That something else is his personality. He must be subjective. He must put into his discourses, under proper control, his whole being, his body, soul, and mind. All that mysterious quality we name personal magnetism, eloquence, soulfulness, must pass from the depths of his being to that of his hearers. . . . It is the man behind the sermon, not the verbiage or rhetoric, that counts.

> —Rabbi Henry Berkowitz, *Intimate Glimpses of the Rabbi's Career* (1921)

A rabbi is someone who helps Jews to open their own doors and sing their own songs in the company and community of others.

—Rabbi Brian Field, 1994 graduate of the Reconstructionist Rabbinical College, college brochure, 1994

A newly-ordained rabbi, twenty-five years old and fresh from the seminary, acquires his first pulpit. What does the congregation want of him? Not alone to attend to his ritual and pastoral duties but to do a bit of fund-raising; to be host and socialite; to join the local Rotary; to serve on an unmanageable variety of boards and committees; to organize whatever needs organizing; to be the Jewish stand-in at civic affairs; and generally to become an all-purpose community leader overnight.

> —Philip M. Klutznick, lawyer, public official, and national president of B'nai B'rith, *No Easy Answers* (1961)

I became a congregational rabbi out of a deep belief that synagogues hold the potential for perpetuating Jewish life by nurturing Jews where they live, by creating and instilling a sense of rootedness in the traditions of our people and a sense of belonging to that people.

> —Rabbi Joy Levitt, rabbi of Reconstructionist Synagogue of the North Shore on Long Island, "Will Our Grandchildren Be Jewish?" *Journal of Jewish Communal Service*, Summer 1992

People come to the synagogue burdened with problems. They are frightened by the conditions of life. They are lonely and depressed. They need guidance and moral support. Furthest from their mind is a text and clever manipulation of it. . . . The task of the Jewish preacher . . . is to rebuke like a Hosea, lament like a Jeremiah and comfort like an Isaiah.

> —Rabbi Joseph H. Lookstein, rabbi of Kehilath Jeshurun, lecturer, and founder of the Ramaz School in New York, 1930s, quoted in *New York's Jewish Jews: The Orthodox Community in the Interwar Years* by Jenna Weissman Joselit (1990)

The religion in which the Jewish ministry should be trained must be specifically and purely Jewish, without any alloy or adulteration. Judaism must stand or fall by that which distinguishes it from other religions.

> —Rabbi Solomon Schechter, president of The Jewish Theological Seminary of America, inaugural address, November 20, 1902, quoted in *Conservative Judaism: The New Century* by Neil Gillman (1993)

[When I first came to America] I got my first job in Tujunga. I took three buses and spent two and one half hours to get there. I could not find the address of the Rabbi. I looked around the neighborhood and saw a man in Bermuda shorts sitting by a pool. I showed him the note that said I am looking for Rabbi

Rosenbaum. He said, "I'm Rabbi Rosenbaum." If he would have told me he just came from Mars, it would have been much easier to believe.

> —Elieser Slomovic, professor of rabbinics born in Czechoslovakia, interview in *Directions*, Spring 1993

In theory at least, a Jewish community could carry on its whole spiritual and religious life without the services of a rabbi, who, being learned in the Torah and Jewish law, has merely to help the members of the community when a religious problem arises.

> —Rabbi Adin Steinsaltz, Talmudic scholar, *The Strife of the Spirit* (1988)

❖ REALITY ❖

I've never felt Truth was Beauty. Never, I've always felt that people can't take too much reality. I like being in Ingmar Bergman's world. Or in the world of the New York Knicks. Because it's not this world. You spend your whole life searching for a way out. You just get an overdose of reality, you know, and it's a terrible thing.

> —Woody Allen, actor, writer, and director, quoted in "The Imperfectionist" by John Lahr, *The New Yorker*, December 9, 1996

Reality was but a creature formed from one of the intellect's own ribs, from language.

> —Rebecca Goldstein, novelist, *The Mind Body Problem* (voice of the character Renee Feuer) (1983)

The materialist says that only appearance is real. The mystic (or realist in the medieval sense) says there is a reality beyond appearance. Appearance, in fact, may not only be not a clue to reality, but a barrier. How many senses do we need to perceive reality? None; since many more than five would still not suffice. The beginning of knowledge is blindness, deafness, the absence of taste, touch, smell.

> —Albert Lewin, filmmaker who wrote and directed *The Moon and Sixpence* and other films, 1951, Lewin's papers at the University of Southern California, quoted in *Botticelli in Hollywood* by Susan Felleman (1997)

❖ RECONCILIATION ❖

(see also Peace)

Those who say we should forgive and forget, have nothing to forgive and nothing to forget. I cannot forgive. I cannot forget.

> —John Klein, Holocaust survivor and partisan fighter, quoted in *When They Came to Take My Father: Voices of the Holocaust*, photographs by Mark Seliger, edited by Leora Kahn and Rachel Hager (1996)

I never blamed anybody but the terrorist who drove the van into her bus. . . . One day I'll have my reconciliation, my conversation with God, but right now I take solace in that she is in a much better place.

> —Stephen Flatow, father of twenty-year-old Alisa Flatow (a Brandeis University junior who was killed in a 1995 terrorist attack on a bus going to the Gaza Strip), quoted in *Long Island Jewish World*, November 24, 1995

We must work for reconciliation among the peoples, between the races, between labor and management, but we must also work for it in the undramatic situations in our lives—in the everyday.

> —Maurice Friedman, professor of religious studies, philosophy, and comparative literature, "Hasidim and the Love of Enemies," 1964, in *The Challenge of Shalom*, edited by Murray Polner and Naomi Goodman (1994)

The key to convincing the other side that reconciliation is possible is to give an unequivocal signal of turning one's back on the past.

> —Rabbi Irving Greenberg, author, scholar, and founder of National Jewish Center for Learning and Leadership (CLAL), "Peace After Fratricide," *Jerusalem Report*, December 30, 1993

It is possible to imagine a world from which forgiveness is absent. But that world, it seems, would have to be either more human (one in which no wrongs are committed or suffered), or less human—a world in which resentment and vengeance would not only have their day, but would continue to have it, day after day after day. Neither of these, as it happens, is the world we inhabit. . . . The issue then is not whether forgiveness should have a place in our life, but only what place it should have.

—Berel Lang, author and professor of philosophy and humanistic studies, *Tikkun*, March/April 1996

I believe that I will not have fulfilled my duty if I do not here serve as spokesman for many of the need to beg forgiveness from HaRav Shlomo Carlebach. We did not relate to him with enough respect; we did not value him sufficiently; we did not stand strong enough to guard the honor which he never sought but was truly entitled to. I ask forgiveness and pardon in the name of those who are present here, and in the name of the many who should have been present here but did not come. They will come, however, and they will come to value this great soul who moved among us. A soul from the world of nobility and purity, the world of awe, of melody, and of intimacy with the divine.

—HaRav Yisrael Meir Lau, Chief Rabbi of Israel, speaking at the burial of Rabbi Shlomo Carlebach in Jerusalem, October 1994 (19 Cheshvan 5755), quoted in *Kol Chevre*, newsletter of the Shlomo Carlebach Foundation, special yohrziet (memorial) issue, November 1995

Once in a while, by chance, a Japanese and an American would meet. The Japanese would hold out his hand and the American, tentatively, somewhat reluctantly, would take it. Some hoped the commemoration would serve as a reconciliation of old enemies, but that was not to be. On this battlefield during these days, the Americans were reconciling themselves to the death of their friends and to their own survival. To ask more was to ask too much.

—Arnold H. Leibowitz, author and attorney specializing in the law of U.S. territorial relations, commenting on the commemoration of the 50th anniversary of the brutal Battle of Peleliu, September 12–15, 1994, *Embattled Island: Palau's Struggle for Independence* (1996)

My dear friends, when you have two views you don't have to have two peoples.

—Shimon Peres, prime minister of Israel, speaking at a memorial tribute to Yitzhak Rabin, Madison Square Garden, December 10, 1995

Right here, right now, in front of me, I want you to look at each other in the eye and ask for forgiveness for anything [hurtful] you ever said or did to each other, knowingly or unknowingly. . . . I need to know there is peace among my children.

—Jack Rosenfeld, retired eighty-year-old businessman, speaking to his three adult children on his deathbed, quoted in *Jewish Bulletin of Northern California*, September 20, 1996

❖ RED SCARE ❖

(see also Communism)

The teaching profession as a whole was frightened into submissiveness. At one point, a bunch of us had written to Albert Einstein and said, "What shall we do?" He wrote back, "Become plumbers, become anything, but do not sign the loyalty oath." To us, it was the beginning of American fascism.

> —Frances Eisenberg, public school teacher attacked by the California State Committee on UnAmerican Activities in 1946 and blacklisted in 1954, quoted in *Red Scare: An Oral History* by Griffen Fariello (1995)

Mr. Speaker, we are making history, regrettable history, in finding innocent people guilty of contempt without trial, without jury, and without benefit of counsel. I believe we are turning our backs upon our glorious past if we pass this resolution. We thereby throw overboard the right of free speech, the right of security of one's property and person, and the right of castle. . . . I predict that our action will come back to plague us.

> —Emanuel Celler, U.S. Congressman (R-N.Y.), commenting on the vote in the House of Representatives to declare Howard Fast and others in contempt of Congress, *The Congressional Record*, April 16, 1946

They [the FBI] visited all my neighbors and I found that out because next door to us there was a family of refugees from Germany. They were German Jews who had escaped from Hitler. The FBI asked them if I had meetings in my house or if they ever saw strange cars coming out. She said, "Look, this is a community-minded woman. She collects for the Community Chest." Then they said, "Please don't tell her that we were here." She said she saw them go across the street to good neighbors of ours, whose children played with our children. . . . Nobody told me except this woman; she said she would have no truck with it. She invited Sam and me over there and said, "I'm telling you this because this was the way it started in Germany."

> —Ruth Goldberg, a Progressive Party candidate for president of her local PTA in New York City, 1947, quoted in *Red Scare: An Oral History* by Griffen Fariello (1995)

The blacklist started for me in 1948. They didn't have to come and tell me, I just knew—the telephone stopped ringing. I had been getting assignments pretty regular and now I was not. But I knew this was coming. They were afraid to hire any of us who were on that list. There was nothing my agent could do. He worked for me as long as I was acceptable.

—Howard Koch, screenwriter who shared an Academy Award in 1942 for writing *Casablanca*, quoted in *Red Scare: An Oral History* by Griffen Fariello (1995)

There are some things you do in order to live with yourself.

—Abe Fortas, Washington, D.C., attorney, commenting on the decision of his law firm, Arnold, Fortas & Porter, to represent clients accused in loyalty cases, "Arnold, Fortas, Porter and Prosperity" by Louis Casses, *Harper's,* November 1951, cited in *Abe Fortas: A Biography* by Laura Kalman (1990)

I am ready and willing to testify before the representatives of our Government as to my own opinions and my own actions, regardless of any risks or consequences to myself. . . . But to hurt innocent people who I knew many years ago in order to save myself is, to me, inhuman and indecent and dishonorable. I cannot and will not cut my conscience to fit this year's fashions.

—Lillian Hellman, playwright, excerpt of a letter to Congressman John Wood, chairman of the Committee on Un-American Activities, May 19, 1952, reprinted in her memoir *Scoundrel Time* (1976)

There are no issues—no specific points to be determined—except that the accused had thought, done and read, and everybody with whom he has ever seen or with whom he has ever talked, are within the scope of inquiry. There are no standards of judgments, no rules, no traditions of procedure or judicial demeanor, no statute of limitations, no appeals, no boundaries of relevance and no finality. In short, anything goes; and anything frequently does.

—Abe Fortas, attorney, discussing the impact of President Truman's executive order 9835 that directed the head of each department in the executive branch to establish at least one loyalty board to investigate the loyalty of its employees, "Outside the Law," *Atlantic Monthly,* 1953

Many innocent people have been ensnared by these [Communist front] organizations. . . . Only those exceptional souls who have never made a mistake or have never been fooled can shut the gates of understanding and charity against all members of such groups and pronounce a blanket judgment against them.

—Sidney Hook, philosopher and educationist who broke with Communism in the early 1930s, *Heresy Yes, Conspiracy No* (1953)

I had to submit the names of everybody in every category to an executive of Young & Rubicam and nobody could be engaged by me finally or a deal made and consummated, before a clearance or acceptance came back from Young & Rubicam . . . approximately 33%, perhaps a little higher, came back politically rejected.

> —David Susskind, producer, testifying at a 1962 trial about the existence of blacklists in the industry, recalling his role as producer of *Appointment with Adventure* in 1955–56, quoted in *Zero Mostel: A Biography* by Jared Brown (1989)

I as an individual employer can refuse to hire anybody because I don't like the color of his tie. I can refuse to hire anybody because I don't like his speech, I don't like the way he dresses. That is my privilege as an American, but that isn't blacklisting. That doesn't mean that I send around a list to all the employers that this man will go to, and they all agree that they can't hire this man. That is what is evil about it.

> —Louis Nizer, lawyer, from his summation to the jury while representing radio personality John Henry Faulk in his 1962 suit against those who blacklisted him, *Fear on Trial* by John Henry Faulk (1981)

It's part of the history of this country, and a lot of kids don't even realize that blacklisting ever existed.

> —Zero Mostel, actor, discussing his participation in the 1976 film *The Front*, quoted in *Zero Mostel: A Biography* by Jared Brown (1989) (Many contributors to the film, including Mostel, had been victims of the blacklist.)

The language of hysteria was acceptable in the highest places.

> —Alfred Kazin, author and literary critic, *New York Jew* (1978)

Perhaps one way of describing certain Stalinists was as people ready to believe anything.

> —Irving Howe, literary critic and author, *A Margin of Hope: An Intellectual Biography* (1982)

There have been periods of detente with the Soviet Union, but never really with the American Left.

> —Carl Bernstein, author and former reporter for *The Washington Post*, recalling the impact of the Red Scare on his politically progressive parents and their family, *Loyalties: A Son's Memoir* (1989)

I know that the blacklist wrecked some lives but I'm not easily wrecked.

> —Zero Mostel, actor who invoked the Fifth Amendment when called to testify before the House Committee on Un-American Activities, quoted in *Zero Mostel: A Biography* by Jared Brown (1989)

Long ago, I lost my faith in anyone's objectivity, including my own.

> —Howard Fast, novelist who joined the Communist Party in 1943 and broke from it thirteen years later, *Being Red: A Memoir* (1990) (He was blacklisted and imprisoned in 1950 for failure to "name names" for the House Committee on Un-American Activities.)

I was born in 1914, and no one with a brain in his head or a shred of social consciousness could have matured during the two decades following my birth without being well aware of the Communists and the Communist Party.

> —Howard Fast, *Being Red: A Memoir* (1990)

If I were to seek some testament to leave to my grandchildren, proving that I had not lived a worthless existence but had done my best to help and nourish the poor and oppressed, I could not do better than to leave them this FBI report.

> —Howard Fast, *Being Red: A Memoir* (1990)

. . . there is little doubt that a significant part of the intellectual elite lent its support to an idea that turned out to have the most destructive consequences of European history—more murderous in the number of victims it claimed than even Hitler's Third Reich. Nor is there any doubt that their criticism of Communist theory and practice could once have made a difference by exposing and condemning its crimes and demanding an end to them.

> —Ruth R. Wisse, professor of Yiddish and comparative literature, *Jerusalem Report*, August 13, 1992

I have thought most earnestly of the alternative suggested. Under the circumstances this course of action would mean that I accept and concur in the view that I am not fit to serve this government, that I have now served for some twelve years. This I cannot do.

> —J. Robert Oppenheimer, nuclear physicist, from a 1953 letter in response to an offer that he terminate his contract as a consultant to the Atomic Energy Commission, and thereby avoid explicit charges of disloyalty, quoted in *Oppenheimer: Years of Risk* by James W. Kunetka (1982)

If it is a question of wisdom or judgment, as demonstrated by actions since 1945, then I would say one would be wiser not to grant clearance.

> —Edward Teller, physicist who immigrated to the United States in 1935, was a member of the team that produced the first nuclear chain reaction in 1941, and worked on the atomic bomb project at Los Alamos from 1943 to 1945, responding to the question—at a 1954 Atomic Energy Commission hearing—of whether it would endanger the common defense and security

to grant clearance to fellow physicist Oppenheimer, quoted in *J. Robert Oppenheimer: Shatterer of Worlds* by Peter Goodchild (1981)

It's ridiculous to think you can deny Oppenheimer access to atomic se-crets—you'd have to chop his head off!

> —Dr. Raymond Kaufman, professor of mathematics and physics and former research physicist at the Rand Corporation, commenting about the denial of security clearance to J. Robert Oppenheimer, conversation at a perfor-mance at Lincoln Center of the drama "In the Matter of J. Robert Oppen-heimer," Spring 1971

This committee isn't set up to show the agencies are doing what they're supposed to do; our job is to find the weak spots. . . . We just aren't concerned with what you do most of the time; it's the mistakes that interest us.

> —Roy M. Cohn, attorney, referring to his role as counsel to Senator Joseph McCarthy in the Voice of America investigation, 1953, quoted in *Senator Joe McCarthy* by Richard H. Rovere (1959)

The more McCarthy yells, the better I like him. He's doing a job to get rid of all the "termites" eating away at our democracy. . . . [I wish] there was some way we could give every American a trial of Communism. I wish it would be like running water, and we could turn the faucet on for about thirty days and then turn it off and back to our American way.

> —Louis B. Mayer, film executive, speaking at a Chamber of Commerce din-ner in April 1954 in his honor in Haverhill, Mass., where his film career began, quoted in *An Empire of Their Own* by Neal Gabler (1988)

I despised McCarthy, his tone, his innuendo, his smears, and his inability to back any of it with fact. He was a disgrace to the body politic, and I said so at every opportunity.

> —Barry Gray, radio broadcaster, *My Night People: 10,001 Nights in Broad-casting* (1975)

It seemed impossible in public to admit doubts, divisions, nuances, contra-dictions, hesitations, lost illusions. . . . Communism had indeed invaded the highest places. Alger Hiss was obviously incapable of telling the whole truth about himself; the Rosenbergs in the death house wrote the crudest Party slogans to each other in the form of personal letters. . . . McCarthy could hardly admit that his goal was . . . to inflame the populace in unashamed Hitler fashion, to gain constant publicity and prominence for himself. . . . The demand for orthodoxy suffocated me. Almost anywhere you looked now, the lies of Stalinists and the blood lust of super-Americans yelled down everything else.

> —Alfred Kazin, author and literary critic, *New York Jew* (1978)

This anti-Communist hysteria, while in many ways understandable in the light of Stalin's behavior, was aggravated by the wild charges of Senator Joseph McCarthy, until it grew to such proportions that it became a national disgrace.

> —Iphigene Ochs Sulzberger, daughter of the founder of *The New York Times* and wife, mother, and mother-in-law of *Times* publishers, quoted in *Iphigene* by Susan W. Dryfoos (1981)

A question has been floating over me for 35 years, as in a cartoon balloon. It asks: "Why would a nice Jewish boy from the Bronx, the son of a renowned liberal Democratic judge, choose to make his name by prosecuting the Rosenbergs and working for Joe McCarthy?"

> —Roy M. Cohn, attorney appointed—at age twenty-six—chief counsel to Senator Joseph McCarthy's Communist-hunting subcommittee, quoted in *The Autobiography of Roy Cohn* by Sidney Zion (1988)

I was to discover that . . . there was a ravaging, boundless hatred that would only become more vituperative after McCarthy died (in 1957) and I was the only symbol of the evil incarnate left to kick around. I say this without complaint but with bemusement over the virility of the anti-McCarthy, anti-Cohn virus, which seems to be genetically transmitted by liberals.

> —Roy M. Cohn, quoted in *The Autobiography of Roy Cohn* by Sidney Zion (1988)

McCarthy's carnival-like four year spree of accusations, charges and threats touched something deep in the American body politic, something that lasted long after his own recklessness, carelessness, and boozing ended his career in shame. McCarthyism crystallized and politicized the anxieties of a nation living in a dangerous new era. He took people who were at worst guilty of political naiveté and accused them of treason. He set out to do the unthinkable, and it turned out to be surprisingly thinkable.

> —David Halberstam, author and journalist, *The Fifties* (1993)

ROSENBERG TRIAL

We should not admit, even by implication, that there is group responsibility for this crime.

—Rabbi S. Andhil Fineberg, head of the American Jewish Committee's Staff Committee on Communism, taking the position that the Rosenbergs' Jewish background was "utterly irrelevant" to the charges against them and should be excluded from press accounts of the case, 1951, quoted in *Jews Against Prejudice* by Stuart Svonkin (1997)

It is not in my power, Julius and Ethel Rosenberg, to forgive you. Only the Lord can find mercy for what you have done. . . . For the crime for which you have been convicted, you are hereby sentenced to the punishment of death, and it is ordered . . . you shall be executed according to law.

—Judge Irving R. Kaufman, presiding judge in United States v. Rosenbergs and Sobell, addressing the Rosenbergs at their sentencing, April 5, 1951, quoted in *Invitation to an Inquest* by Walter and Miriam Schneir (1965)

I can see grave implications in an action which in effect would be a claim that the fact of his [Judge Irving Kaufman's] Jewishness rendered him incapable of exercising his judicial responsiblity dispassionately. . . . For all these reasons I could not, in all conscience as president of the American Jewish Committee recommend that our organization take any action whatsoever with respect to this matter [of clemency].

—Jacob Blaustein, president of the American Jewish Committee, from a letter in response to physicist Felix Bloch's letter in support of clemency, May 1, 1951, quoted in *Jews Against Prejudice* by Stuart Svonkin (1997)

The Rosenbergs still have a chance to save their necks by making full disclosure about their spy ring—or Judge Kaufman, who conducted the trial so ably, has the right to alter the death sentence. . . . Their lives remain in their own hands—if they talk, they can still save themselves.

—Leonard Lyons, *New York Post* columnist, from his columns after Judge Kaufman sentenced the Rosenbergs to death, *New York Post*, April 1951

As the leader of a great group of veterans of the Jewish faith, I especially resent the efforts to make an issue of the religious identification of the defendants. We despise equally those who would callously use the Rosenbergs to injure the Jews and those who would callously use the Jews to help the Rosenbergs.

—Jesse Moss, national commander of the Jewish War Veterans, from a 1952 letter to Judge Irving Kaufman, quoted in *Jews Against Prejudice* by Stuart Svonkin (1997)

We are the first victims of American Fascism.

—Ethel Rosenberg, from a letter written to her attorney on the night of her execution, June 19, 1953, quoted in *Invitation to an Inquest* by Walter and Miriam Schneir (1965)

To be writing an opinion in a case affecting two lives after the curtain has been rung down upon them has the appearance of pathetic futility. But history also has its claims.

> —Felix Frankfurter, U.S. Supreme Court justice, writing three days after the execution of the Rosenbergs, June 22, 1953, quoted in *Invitation to an Inquest* by Walter and Miriam Schneir (1965)

To a child the connection was unavoidable: if they could be executed, what was to prevent the execution of one's own parents, particularly one's own mother? The Rosenbergs had been married on June 18, 1939, the same day as my mother and father. . . . The Rosenbergs too were progressive people — and they were going to die for it; they were going to fry.

> —Carl Bernstein, author and former reporter for *The Washington Post*, remembering the impact of the Rosenberg trial, on his family, *Loyalties: A Son's Memoir* (1989)

The Rosenberg case resulted in my first exposure to bitter controversy. The case itself was dramatic and important but uncomplicated. . . . After the trial, to some, the Rosenbergs became a cause celebre. . . . Hundreds of thousands of dollars were raised by national committees studded with the usual bleeding hearts. Of course, no such committees were organized for prison-camp or torture chamber victims of Communist oppression.

> —Roy M. Cohn, member of the team of prosecutors in the trial of Julius and Ethel Rosenberg, *A Fool for a Client* (1971)

The trial of the Rosenbergs became a definitional ceremony in which opposing versions of American Jewish identity competed for ascendancy.

> —Deborah Dash Moore, historian, quoted in *Jews Against Prejudice* by Stuart Svonkin (1997)

There was never any question about Julius; [Judge] Kaufman told me before the trial started that he was going to sentence Julius Rosenberg to death.

> —Roy M. Cohn, prosecutor of the Rosenbergs, quoted in *The Autobiography of Roy Cohn* by Sidney Zion (1988)

This is the striking part about the Rosenberg case: Julius Rosenberg was both guilty and framed. . . . I got this directly from Roy Cohn [one of the prosecutors]. . . . I believe that they manufactured evidence to prove that a guilty person was guilty. They couldn't get away with that today.

—Alan M. Dershowitz, law professor, appellate lawyer, activist, and author, quoted in *Chronicle: Trial of Julius and Ethel Rosenberg*, A&E network, 1988

When your family is disrupted in that very harsh way and not in an accident or something quick, but something where they were subjected to it inch by inch in the glare of publicity particularly . . . and the whole issue, for a while, being afraid to tell people my last name. . . . That created a lot of self-hatred. A few times I denied who I was when I was a young child. Those were great difficulties and I'm sure they left scars.

> —Michael Meeropol, oldest son of Julius and Ethel Rosenberg (ten years old when they were executed) who is a professor of economics, quoted in *Chronicle: Trial of Julius and Ethel Rosenberg*, A&E network, 1988

The government got away with murder because our attorneys were that bad. Murder, literally.

> —Morton Sobell, codefendant in the Rosenberg atom spy case who was found guilty and sentenced to thirty years in prison (he served eighteen and one-half years), quoted in *Red Scare: An Oral History* by Griffen Fariello (1995)

❖ RELATIONSHIPS ❖

(see also Friendship, Romance)

My grandmother knew what she was talking about when she said, "If you have to stand on your head to make somebody happy, all you can expect is a big headache."

> —Ilene Beckerman, author, *What We Do for Love* (1998)

To me, it is a very vivid thing. The sense of being an atom in all this vast universe without any other atom traveling the same daily orbit is annihilating. It doesn't help me much to know that atoms more or less akin are traveling orbits not very distant with feelings of atomic friendship. Even a little separation is a big one when only atoms are involved.

> —Benjamin Cardozo, justice of the New York State Court of Appeals, reflecting on the meaning of the word "loneliness" and describing himself as a "lone bachelor" in a letter to his cousin Annie Nathan Meyer, July 20, 1929, quoted in *The World of Benjamin Cardozo* by Richard Polenberg (1997)

You can't attack a man who warmly shook your hand two minutes before — at least I can't.

> —Felix Frankfurter, U.S. Supreme Court justice, recalling his encounter with Chaim Weizmann before they were both going to speak (and disagree), quoted in *Felix Frankfurter Reminisces*, recorded in talks with Dr. Harlan B. Phillips (1960)

Never be afraid to talk to your enemy. If you are good you can always find out more about them than they can about you. If you are not good keep your mouth shut. When the FBI visits you they already know the answers to the questions anyway. Never attribute more intelligence to your enemy than to yourself and your brothers. Always trust your brothers and yourself.

> —Abbie Hoffman, activist, *Revolution for the Hell of It* (1968)

Criticism should leave a person with the idea that he has been helped.

> —Dr. Morris Mandel, columnist, *The Jewish Press*, May 30, 1997

Let's face it: if you're romantically involved, you're financially involved.

> —Sylvia Porter, columnist, author, and financial advisor, *Sylvia Porter's Love and Money* (1983)

The romantic stories currently buzzing through our phone lines have no clear progression or obvious endings. Relationships come together and dissolve in a general atmosphere of haziness and impermanence. People live together and move out. They sleep together for indefinite periods. They marry later. They travel light.

> —Katie Roiphe, author, *Last Night in Paradise* (1997)

I said that it had never occurred to me that he'd rather be shooting hoops than in bed with me, and he said that, yes, in fact, sometimes he would prefer to play basketball, and that in terms of absolute value, sex and sports were equally meaningless to him, they were just two different ways to have fun.

> —Elizabeth Wurtzel, author, *Prozac Nation* (1994)

Lifelong commitments to one's children are often experienced as among the few lifelong relationships available in America.

> —Laurie Zoloth-Dorfman, author and ethicist with a practice in clinical bioethics, *Tikkun*, July/August 1995

❖ RELIGION ❖

Yes, it's a comforting faith, very much so.
> —Roseanne Arnold, actress, reflecting on her Jewish identity, *Larry King Live* televison interview, March 2, 1994

Here's the thing with me and the religious thing. This is the flat-out truth: I find the religiosity and philosophy in the music. I don't find it anywhere else. Songs like "Let Me Rest on a Peaceful Mountain" or "I Saw the Light"—that's my religion. I don't adhere to rabbis, preachers, evangelists, all of that. I've learned more from the songs than from any of this kind of entity. The songs are my lexicon. I believe the songs.
> —Bob Dylan, singer and songwriter, quoted in *Newsweek*, October 6, 1997

Everything that the human race has done and thought is concerned with the satisfaction of deeply felt needs and assuagement of pain. One has to keep this constantly in mind if one wishes to understand spiritual moments and their development.
> —Albert Einstein, Nobel Prize-winning theoretical physicist and humanist, quoted in *The New York Times Magazine*, November 9, 1930

For science can only ascertain what is, but not what should be, and outside of its domain value judgments of all kinds remain necessary. Religion, on the other hand, deals only with evaluations of human thought and action; it cannot justifiably speak of facts and relationships between facts.
> —Albert Einstein, quoted from "Science, Philosophy and Religion, a Symposium," published by the Conference on Science, Philosophy and Religion and Their Relation to the Democratic Way of Life, 1941

Religion should unite men as its name implies but can do so only through acceptance of diversity of opinions and action [emphasizing that acceptance of diversity must not be passive, but must derive from a thorough and objective examination of variable alternatives, based on] the doctrine that one arrives at truth through reasoned agreement.
> —Rabbi Louis Finkelstein, president of The Jewish Theological Seminary, speaking at commencement 1972 (the year of his retirement after thirty-two years), quoted in "The Finkelstein Era" by Michael Greenbaum in *Tradition Renewed: A History of the Jewish Theological Seminary of America,* edited by Jack Wertheimer (1997)

The essential religious experience is that of Isaac walking with his father, Abraham, to his expected death. Its essence is not the sacrifice of Isaac but the shared experience in which the self is submerged to the needs of another.

> —Rabbi Samuel Z. Glaser, rabbi emeritus of the Elmont Jewish Center on Long Island and professor of psychology, excerpt from sermon, 1990

Christianity and Islam are serious religions, spiritually dignified. You don't have to become Jewish to be related to God.

> —Rabbi Irving Greenberg, author, scholar, and founder of National Jewish Center for Learning and Leadership (CLAL), quoted in *In the Service of God* by Shalom Freedman (1995)

A person cannot be religious and indifferent to other human beings' plight and suffering.

> —Rabbi Abraham Joshua Heschel, author, activist, and theologian, "What Happens to Them Happens to Me," *United Synagogue Review*, Winter 1964

No religion is an island. We are all involved with one another. Spiritual betrayal on the part of one of us affects the faith of all of us.

> —Rabbi Abraham Joshua Heschel, "No Religion Is an Island" in *Moral Grandeur and Spiritual Audacity* (1996)

You can be a Jew who does some Buddhist practices, such as meditation, and it can help your practice. But can you be a serious Buddhist? I don't know. I'm skeptical.

> —Rodger Kamenetz, author, poet, and professor of English, quoted in the *Baltimore Jewish Times*, November 7, 1997

Religion frequently asks us to believe without question, even (or especially) in the absence of hard evidence. Indeed, this is the central meaning of faith. Science asks us to take nothing on faith, to be wary of our penchant for self-deception, to reject anecdotal evidence. Science considers deep skepticism a prime virtue. Religion often sees it as a barrier to enlightenment.

> —Carl Sagan, author and professor of astronomy and space sciences, "Religious Leadership and Environmental Integrity" in *The Jewish Condition: Essays on Contemporary Judaism Honoring Rabbi Alexander M. Schindler*, edited by Aron Hirt-Manheimer (1995)

Formal religion can no longer be dismissed as a medieval relic, as we did in our emancipated youth.

> —Marie Syrkin, author and professor, *Tikkun*, Fall 1986

There is in every religious community the potentiality of growth and development. That can take place provided there is an intention to want to overcome one's parochialism and isolationism.

> —Rabbi Marc Tanenbaum, activist on behalf of human rights and interreligious understanding, "The Future of Jewish-Christian Relations," speech given at the Rabbinical Assembly Convention, 1985

❖ REPENTANCE ❖

Writing this column over the years has given me a much greater understanding of human weakness, and I have learned that each of us is capable of doing something completely irrational and totally out of character at some point in our lives. This doesn't mean we are intentionally trying to hurt others. It simply means we are human.

> —Eppie Lederer, advice columnist also known as Ann Landers, apologizing to readers for offensive remarks she made about Pope John Paul II and others of Polish origin, quoted in the *Chicago Tribune*, December 10, 1995

For it is a spiritual disquiet, much more than a guilty feeling, that makes us feel the urge to take a look back. Indeed, we feel we are no longer the right person in the right place, we feel we are becoming outsiders in a world whose scheme of things escapes us.

> —Adin Steinsaltz, Talmudic scholar, *The Strife of the Spirit* (1988)

One of the biggest hurdles in therapy is for the patient to learn how to confront a shattered or tarnished past, the sins of yesterday. This is not to suggest that anything goes, but, as the Book of Ruth teaches, that everything passes, becomes transformed. Dust turns to diamonds, water to wine—this is a tradition as concerned with the forgiven as with the forbidden.

> —Dr. Ruth K. Westheimer, sex therapist, and Jonathan Mark, journalist, *Heavenly Sex: Sexuality in the Jewish Tradition* (1995)

Repentance is the mechanism for rebalancing lives that have been distorted by mistakes or by sin.

> —Rabbi David J. Wolpe, author, *Why Be Jewish?* (1995)

❖ REVELATION ❖

The greatness of the moment at Sinai is that God made His love for us manifest through Torah, that we might return that love by doing His will.

> —Ronald A. Brauner, president of the Foundation for Jewish Studies and professor of Jewish studies, "Making Love at Sinai" in *Being Jewish in a Gentile World* (1995)

We often wonder whether God still speaks to us today. If we understood revelation as our own perception of God's hand in history, then the establishment of the state of Israel constitutes a magnificent act of God, and entails a bold revelation: Keep the state of Israel and sustain it. We are privileged to live in the time when the voice of God speaks more clearly than at any time since Sinai.

> —Edward L. Greenstein, professor of Bible, quoted in *The Jewish Holidays*, edited by Michael Strassfeld (1985)

❖ RITUAL ❖

(see also Jewish Observance, Holidays)

All our traditions and rituals are ways the Jewish people has devised to respond to God's "I am" which we heard at Sinai or which we hear at every moment our hearts are open, so fulfilling those commandments is somehow God's will, even though the human role in devising them is one I don't deny.

> —Rabbi Arthur Green, professor of Jewish thought, interview with William Novak, *Kerem*, Spring 1995

You can't bow your head down for the Aleinu prayer or look up to see if there are stars at the end of Shabbat before Havdalah without losing your lid. Try to dance at a wedding and you find yourself dancing with one hand placed firmly on the top of your head.

> —Rabbi Richard Israel, Jewish educator and Hillel director, *The Kosher Pig and Other Curiosities of Jewish Life* (1994)

Ritual has the potential to heal and warm; to glorify God and reify human devotion; to make objects and places sacred; to create community; to permeate the membrane between religion and peoplehood and bond one person into the whole. Ritual physicalizes the spiritual and spiritualizes the physical.

—Letty Cottin Pogrebin, author and activist, *Deborah, Golda and Me* (1992)

. . . To practitioners of a religion, the history of a ritual is often as important as its origin. Origins reflect what a ritual was, not necessarily what it is. A practice may continue to be observed for centuries for exactly the same reason that its observance began; its content and message may remain unchanged. In Jewish history, however, this is rare.

—Rabbi Joel Roth, professor of Talmud, *Moment*, February 1992

I like weddings because just like in the theater, the ritual works. There's never a time when you don't cry. It's not just the romance—it's the history, it's the grandparents, it's the hope for the future.

—Wendy Wasserstein, playwright, quoted in "Vows," *The New York Times*, June 21, 1998

❖ ROMANCE ❖

(see also Dating, Love)

Timid clients, especially the younger ones with fussy American ideas, sulk and get stubborn when they first put themselves into [Mr.] Rubin's hands. . . . They insist on working a certain amount of romance into the thing, for which Rubin blames poets, songwriters and the movies. Pin him down and he'll concede a pinch of romance is O.K.

—Meyer Berger, journalist, from his portrait of Louis Rubin, proprietor of Rubin's Prominent Matrimonial Bureau, *The New Yorker*, June 11, 1938, quoted in *The Wonders of America: Reinventing Jewish Culture, 1880–1950* by Jenna Weissman Joselit (1994)

Women use romance and passion to sweeten you up. A man is no more the victim of that passion. You give me a woman who can cook and sew and I'll take that over passion any day. I'd like to find a mate. But I can't spend any time with a woman if we're not friends.

—Bob Dylan, singer and songwriter, 1978, quoted in *No Direction Home: The Life and Music of Bob Dylan* by Robert Shelton (1986)

Let's face it, everyone is the one person on earth you shouldn't get involved with.

—Nora Ephron, author, screenwriter, and director, quoted in *Time*, January 27, 1992

Love does not make the world go round, looking for it does.

—Herb Gardner, playwright, *Conversations With My Father* (voice of the character Charlie), 1991

It always seemed to me that making love to a Jewish girl would be like making love to your sister.

—Groucho Marx, actor and comedian, commenting on never having been romantically involved with a Jewish woman, interview with Charlotte Chandler in *Playboy*, March 1974

Does a man have control over his lust? Life is an overflowing sea. Every affair enriched my life and my creativity. No, I'm not sorry. I'm a bachelor, a bachelor in my soul. Even if I married a whole harem of women, I'd still act like a bachelor. Every woman who passes by on Broadway is a riddle to me. I'd like to stop her in the street and ask, "Excuse me, ma'am, where are you from? Do you believe in God? In free choice? In reincarnation? What are your relations with your husband?" I've got an ability to decipher the dots of pain in their lives. My stories get their shape not only from the terrific landscape I describe but mainly from real characters, mostly from women.

—Isaac Bashevis Singer, Nobel Prize-winning Yiddish writer, in conversation with his son Israel Zamir, *Journey to My Father, Isaac Bashevis Singer* (1994)

❖ SABBATH ❖

(see also Jewish Observance)

Rekindle an old flame.

> —Advertisement appearing in California newspapers placed by Chabad-Lubavitch, reminding Jews about keeping the Sabbath, 1996

Business worries? Rest on the Sabbath & G-d Will Do the Rest

> —Slogan on a poster carried in a March for the Sabbath on New York's Lower East Side by the orthodox in the 1950s, cited in *Conservative Judaism: The New Century* by Neil Gillman (1993)

Do you know what it meant to me when I was called to the [Sabbath] candles last Friday? . . .To this day, when the heat of the candles is on my face, I circle the flame and cover my eyes and then I feel again my mother's hands on my smooth cheeks.

> —"Basha," member of the Aliyah Senior Citizens' Center in California, quoted in *Number Our Days* by Barbara Myerhoff (1978)

The observance of Shabbat, due to its frequency of recurrence and its apparently negative focus, often becomes a matter of habit, devoid of substantial meaning. Yet for many people outside of the religious community, the experience of Shabbat has been a major factor in their reentry into religious life. The first of these facts demands, and the second implies, the existence of a new level of awareness of the meaning of Shabbat in our lives.

> —Rabbi Saul Berman, professor of Jewish philosophy, "The Extended Notion of the Sabbath," *Judaism*, Summer 1973

Club Med advertises itself as the "antidote to civilization," and that's what Shabbat is for me. It's time for me to stop doing and concentrate on just being.

> —Diana Bletter, photographer and author, *The Invisible Thread: A Portrait of Jewish American Women* (1989)

We walked because it was Shabbat. I am not usually a keeper of the Sabbath, but I am when I represent the Jewish people.

> —Edgar M. Bronfman, chairman of The Seagram Company Ltd. and president of the World Jewish Congress, recalling a visit to Bucharest, *The Making of a Jew* (1996)

We could give the American Jewish community an island of time. You cannot have quality time without quantity time and Shabbos makes it possible.

> —Rabbi Ephraim Z. Buchwald, founder and director of the National Jewish Outreach Program, initiating a "Shabbat Across America" program on the weekend of April 4, 1997, quoted in *The Jewish Press*, February 28, 1997

Elvis refused to take money. He said it was his pleasure to help us keep our Sabbath.

> —Jeanette Fruchter, Memphis resident who, with her husband Rabbi Alfred Fruchter, was the upstairs neighbor of teenage Elvis Presley, who would turn off the electricity or light the gas for them on the Sabbath, recalling the singer on the 20th anniversary of his death, quoted in "Elvis the Shabbos Goy" by Eric J. Greenberg, *The Jewish Week*, August 22, 1997

Once it's Shabbat, we let go of all things that didn't work in the past week and try to bring forward our best selves.

> —Gila Gevirtz, author of *Partners with God* (1995), written to help eight- and nine-year-old children understand that they can have a personal relationship with God, quoted in *Jewish Telegraphic Agency*, January 1, 1997

I would like to see there be a silent Kabbalat Shabbat service in our cities, where the beginning of the holy day is marked with candle lighting, a period of wordless chanting, a long time of silent awareness of the change of light in that mysterious hour ...

> —Rabbi Arthur Green, professor of Jewish thought, "Judaism for the Post-Modern Era," the Samuel H. Goldenson Lecture, delivered December 12, 1994, at the Hebrew Union College-Jewish Institute of Religion, Cincinnati

What could be better? You get to sing, debate, have food served to you. Shabbat indeed looked wonderful—from a man's perspective.

> —Andrea Gurwitt, visiting the home of a Hasidic family in Jerusalem, in "The

Seduction of Certainty: Losing Feminist Daughters to Orthodoxy," *On the Issues*, Winter 1996

Judaism teaches us to be attached to holiness in time, to be attached to sacred events, to learn how to consecrate sanctuaries that emerge from the magnificent stream of a year. The Sabbaths are our great cathedrals; and our Holy of Holies is a shrine that neither the Romans nor the Germans were able to burn.

> —Rabbi Abraham Joshua Heschel, author, activist, and theologian, *The Sabbath* (1951)

I have a lot of followers in Har Nof, in Jerusalem. The neighborhood where they live is ninety-seven percent Orthodox. But the other three percent here have rights too. So I told my supporters, don't close the street to traffic on Shabbes—let those who want to drive, drive. We can make Shabbes here without stopping the traffic. You see, "Shabbes" used to be the most beautiful word in the Jewish vocabulary. And the stone throwers have turned it into a curse, a threat. When a Jew hears the world "Shabbes" he should think of flowers, not stones.

> —Grand Rabbi Levi Horowitz (Bostoner rebbe) of the New England Chasidic Center, quoted in *Members of the Tribe* by Ze'ev Chafets (1988)

Sometimes, when I'm working hard at the office and it's getting late, a colleague who might have known nothing about Shabbes before he met me will say, "Go home already, the sun is going down."

> —Judith Kramer, resident of Brooklyn, quoted in *The Invisible Thread: A Portrait of Jewish American Women* by Diana Bletter (1989)

Friday night's dinner was a testimonial banquet to Papa. For that hour, at least, he was no longer the oppressed victim of the sweatshops, the harassed, frightened and unsuccessful breadwinner, but the master to whom all heads bowed and upon whom all honor was bestowed. He was our father, our teacher, our wise man, our elder statesman, our tribal leader.

> —Sam Levenson, humorist and author, *Everything but Money* (1966)

For me to reclaim Shabbat requires no classes, no conversion. It is my birthright, my legacy. I know the script, the lines, the text, the tunes (I often hum my favorites on the way to the gym). . . .But I'm afraid to commit to the Sabbath Bride, who could seem so stern, so demanding in my youth. Most weekends, I resist her advances. But there are other Saturdays, increasing in number, when, moving from observation to observance, I postpone my errands, forget about my workout, put on a skirt, and go to shul. On such Saturdays, my heart is light and my spirits soar.

> —Martha Mendelsohn, journalist, "Observing the Sabbath," *Tikkun*, May/June 1996

Free to break the Sabbath, I no longer give myself a break. . . . As an adult, there's no day when I don't shlep home heavy bags or ignore the laundry. Who is freer on Saturday mornings? My husband and I, weighed down by pounds of groceries, or the shul-goers, holding each other's hands?

> —Martha Mendelsohn, "Observing the Sabbath," *Tikkun*, May/June 1996

Keeping Shabbat is an incredible value because how many things connect us back to the beginning of time?

> —Rabbi Julie Schonfeld, spiritual leader of the Society for the Advancement of Judaism in New York City and actress, quoted in "A Rabbi With All Varieties of Jewish Experience" by Gustav Niebuhr, *The New York Times*, September 14, 1996

I do love Manischewitz wine at Shabbat time!

> —Alicia Silverstone, actress, quoted in "Hollywood Princess," *Vanity Fair*, September 1996

For the Catalog the only Sabbath worthy of its name is one that included homemade hallah and cake, as well as homemade wine, homemade chicken soup, homemade gefilte fish, homemade cholent, homemade kugel, homemade tzimmes, and homemade kreplach. And it goes without saying that . . . it is even more insistent on the lighting of homemade candles.

> —Marshall Sklare, sociologist, criticizing *The Jewish Catalog*, a how-to book published in 1973, modeled on the then popular *Whole Earth Catalog*, reflecting the 1960s counterculture, "The Greening of Judaism," *Commentary*, December 1974

From the twenty-five hours of Shabbat we can learn a rhythm for our turning, a rhythm we can dance to even in the moments of a tiny Shabbat in the midst of our workaday lives.

> —Rabbi Arthur Waskow, author and activist, *Down-to Earth Judaism: Food, Money, Sex, and the Rest of Life* (1995)

What makes time and life into a spiral instead of a straight line or a circle is setting aside time for reflection, rest, renewal. That renewal time — Shabbat, the Sabbath — is the curve that moves the spiral forward.

—Rabbi Arthur Waskow, *Godwrestling Round 2: Ancient Wisdom, Future Paths* (1995)

For me it is a retreat into restorative magic . . . the telephone is silent. I can think, read, study, walk, or do nothing. It is an oasis of quiet. When night falls, I go back to the wonderful nerve-racking Broadway game. Often I make my best contribution of the week then and there. . . . My producer one Saturday night said to me, "I don't envy you your religion, but I envy you your Sabbath."

—Herman Wouk, author, *This Is My God* (1959)

❖ SCIENCE ❖

The most beautiful experience we can have is the mysterious. It is the fundamental emotion which stands at the cradle of true art and true science. Whoever does not know it and can no longer wonder, no longer marvel, is as good as dead, and his eyes are dimmed.

—Albert Einstein, Nobel Prize-winning theoretical physicist and humanist, "The World as I See It," *Ideas and Opinions: Albert Einstein* (1982)

The benefits that the inventive genius of man has conferred on us in the last hundred years could make life happy and carefree, if organization had been able to keep pace with technical progress. As it is, in the hands of our generation these hard-won achievements are like a razor wielded by a child of three.

—Albert Einstein, "The 1932 Disarmament Conference," *The Nation*, September 23, 1931, reprinted in *The Nation, 1865–1990*, edited by Katrina vanden Heuvel (1990)

The natural aim of technology was to make intuition obsolete.

—Norman Mailer, author, *Of a Fire on the Moon* (1969)

But when you come right down to it the reason that we did this job is because it was an organic necessity. If you are a scientist you cannot stop such a thing. If you are a scientist you believe that it is good to find out how the world works; that it is good to turn over to mankind at large the greatest possible power to control the world and to deal with it according to its lights and its values.

—J. Robert Oppenheimer, physicist, speaking to five hundred members of the newly created Association of Los Alamos Scientists, November 2, 1945, quoted in *Oppenheimer: Years of Risk* by James W. Kunetka (1982)

The notion of DNA as a text makes it possible to imagine natural selection as an author in deep time, writing at the rate of perhaps a letter every few centuries to produce the instruction books for all the living things we are among today. . . . Each living person's DNA is rich in specific passages derived from a particular genealogy. Yet at the same time we can be sure that the texts we find will all refer to the same past, a past of branching descent. We must begin to see the texts of an individual and the texts common to members of a species as a form of literature, to approach them as one would approach a library of precious, deep, important books.

> —Robert Pollack, author and professor of biological sciences at Columbia University who worked for several years with James Watson, co-discoverer of DNA's structure, *Signs of Life: The Language and Meaning of DNA* (1994)

Alisa's heart is alive and beating in Jerusalem.

> —Yitzhak Rabin, Israeli prime minister, visiting the New Jersey family of Alisa Flatow, whose family donated eight of her organs, including her heart, to six Israeli patients after she was murdered in a suicide-bombing in Gaza, quoted in *Jerusalem Report*, June 1, 1995

Everybody starts out as a scientist. The job of a science popularizer is to penetrate through the teachings that tell people they're too stupid to understand science.

> —Carl Sagan, author and professor of astronomy and space sciences, quoted in his obituary, *The Washington Post*, December 21, 1996

Science or religion?—which will survive? Why, both—if man is to survive. Without religion, science is a dreadful destroyer, a machine that will crush the very man who invented it; for the mind let loose in the world, unrestrained by ethical and moral consideration, uninspired by purpose, is so much dynamite in the hands of a child. Religion without science is a helpless thing, subject to all the dangers of superstition, subject to constant degeneration, because with the mind atrophied and the intellect left untrained, a man remains permanantly incomplete. Science and religion are friends. God created His world by wisdom, and the beginning of wisdom is the fear of the Lord.

> —Rabbi Abba Hillel Silver, rabbinic leader, from his sermon at The Temple, March 22, 1925, quoted in *Therefore Choose Life: Selected Sermons, Addresses, and Writings of Abba Hillel Silver, Volume One*, edited by Herbert Wiener (1967)

❖ SEX ❖

A boy will have guilt feelings about masturbation. I try to give him a sense that he is only a human being. He should practice self-control within his limits. I don't condone it. I can't condone it. It's not accepted from a religious point of view, but whatever I say to a boy, I have to see if it is destructive or constructive. If he comes in feeling like two cents, I must make certain he doesn't go out feeling like one cent. I give practical advice, to play sports. After a while I get him to face the fact that human beings are not angels.

> —Borough Park counselor, quoted in *Hasidic People* by Jerome Mintz (1994)

One of the most subtle phases of female psychology with respect to her normal erotic life is her shyness: the natural demureness or coquettish sexual caution of woman. This characteristic has been variously emphasized, distorted, and perverted to appear as something of an affectation. However, it is so deeply rooted in the female constitution that it is typical of the woman of all races and cultures.

> —Rabbi Menachem M. Brayer, psychiatrist and author, *The Jewish Woman in Rabbinic Literature: A Psychosocial Perspective* (1986)

Woman cannot understand sexual intercourse without love, and this love is the dominating factor in the life of the woman; it is, in fact, the whole of her life, the essential purpose of her life. This is what makes her a woman.

> —Rabbi Menachem M. Brayer, *The Jewish Woman in Rabbinic Literature: A Psychosocial Perspective* (1986)

There is, of course, a difference in weight between evidence of particular acts and evidence of habitual prostitution. But it is a difference in weight only. The truth remains that once chastity has been yielded, that honor has been lost, and that the great motive which inspired resistance even until death, has gone. To deny this is to ignore a truth which all history and all literature and all experience proclaim.

> —Benjamin Cardozo, justice of the New York State Court of Appeals, per curiam opinion, *People v. Raymond Carey*, which set out the requirements of a woman's behavior in order for a defendant to be convicted of rape in New York, 1918, quoted in *The World of Benjamin Cardozo* by Richard Polenberg (1997) (The case also addressed the question of whether a woman's past sexual experiences, referred to as "acts of misconduct" with men other than the alleged rapist should be admissible.)

To be aware of the sexual possibilities inherent in every relationship is not sick; it's a mark of humanity. We need to remember that this is God's world, and He created many nice things in it. Some of them he lets us have, and some things we can't have because they aren't ours to have.

> —Rabbi Manis Friedman, rabbi and dean, Beis Chanah Institute, St. Paul, Minn., *Doesn't Anyone Blush Anymore?* (1990)

Sex is like a double-edged sword; it releases our spirit and it binds it with a thousand threads, it raises us to sublime heights and thrusts us into the lowest depths. What people will do to each other in their intimate relations they never could or would do to their friends.

> —Emma Goldman, anarchist and a founder of the women's rights movement, 1931 letter to Stella Ballentine, quoted in *Emma Goldman: An Intimate Life* by Alice Wexler (1984)

Men love me because I'm their fantasy. They think I'm getting laid; they think I'm living this wild extroverted life. The truth is I fall asleep watching Ted Koppel. I'm not a night person.

> —Al Goldstein, publisher of *Screw* magazine, *New York*, February 10, 1997

I certainly had those fantasies when I was 23 or 24 years old, of wanting anonymous sex. Or thinking I wanted it. But, of course, whenever it was offered to me, or when I would wake up in bed with somebody who was an unspeakable idiot, I would think, who needs it? Probably the "zipless fuck" [a fling with a total stranger] is better as a fantasy than a reality.

> —Erica Jong, novelist and poet, commenting on the phrase from her novel *Fear of Flying*, interview with Gretchen McNeese in *Playboy*, September 1975

The perfect fit, even when you find it, may not be the perfect companion.

> —Erica Jong, *Fear of Fifty* (1994)

Can we afford to continue living under the tyranny of beauty and muscles and big tits and big dicks and clonedom and youth? Can we afford not to begin working hard toward eroticizing intelligence, kindness, responsibility, devotion, achievement, respect—skills and qualities that are far more sexy, far more lasting, and far more important for our survival than big pecs and biceps and a washboard stomach?

> —Larry Kramer, playwright, speaking at Gay Pride Day, June 26, 1983, *Reports From the Holocaust: The Making of an AIDS Activist* (1990)

When I first got into this work, I thought a woman should remain a virgin until she married or died, whichever came first. . . . Well, I changed my mind about that.

— Eppie Lederer, advice columnist also known as Ann Landers, 1981, quoted in *U.S. News & World Report*, October 23, 1995

I hope you realize that it is always easier to lure a married man than a single one. So don't take too much credit for that conquest.

— Groucho Marx, from a letter to his daughter dated September 4, 1947, quoted in *Love, Groucho: Letters from Groucho Marx to His Daughter Miriam*, edited by Miriam Marx Allen (1992)

In sex, we experience a temporary oneness with each other and with the universe. We perceive our connection to a world without end, to a sense of omnipotence and immortality.

— Rabbi Levi Meier, Jungian therapist, biblical scholar, and chaplain, *Ancient Secrets* (1996)

When a husband and wife are committed to being apart—for the good and greater growth of each—their reunion will be all that much sweeter. Such is age-old wisdom, and such is the advice of the Bible.

— Rabbi Levi Meier, *Ancient Secrets* (1996)

What is normal? What is off? Once you put the extremes aside, where do you draw the line? How, for that matter, do you locate the center? We know only that heterosexuality has ceded its automatic right-of-way; that the dark continent of sadomasochism has been domesticated into a household state of mind; and that the gender-true convention of the man on top and all it implies no longer holds sway even in Dubuque.

— Daphne Merkin, novelist and essayist, *The New Yorker*, December 27, 1993

When I was young, sex seemed to many of us like traveling: you could see the insides of different apartments, eat breakfast in coffee shops in other neighborhoods, and generally see the way other people lived their lives—and then slip back into your own. It was an experiment, an escape, a way of playing at being something you were not.

— Katie Roiphe, author *Last Night in Paradise* (1997)

The massive late-sixties assault upon sexual customs came nearly twenty years after I myself hit the beach and began fighting for a foothold on the erotic homeland held in subjugation by the enemy. I sometimes think of my generation of men as the first wave of determined D-Day invaders, over whose bloody, wounded carcasses the flower children subsequently stepped ashore to advance triumphantly toward the libidinous Paris we had dreamed of liberating as we inched inland on our bellies, firing into the dark. "Daddy," the youngsters ask, "what did you do in the war?" I humbly submit they could do worse than read *Portnoy's Complaint* to find out.

> —Philip Roth, novelist, interview conducted by the Italian critic Walter Mauro, reprinted in *Reading Myself and Others* by Philip Roth (1975)

Sexuality is the human counterpart of divine creation. Just as God created out of the passionate engagement of his Love, so, too, do human beings create life out of the passionate engagement of their love.

> —Rabbi Ira Stone, author and rabbi of Beth Zion/Beth Israel Synagogue in Philadelphia, *Seeking the Path to Life: Theological Meditations on God and the Nature of People, Love, Life and Death* (1992)

Now, I don't want you to go to the JCC tomorrow and sit around and masturbate, but it's the only plausible means of satisfaction when there's no partner.

> —Dr. Ruth K. Westheimer, author and sex therapist, addressing an audience at Congregation Emanu-El in San Francisco on "Sex After Sixty" as part of the Festival of Natural Living, quoted in *Jewish Bulletin of Northern California*, July 19, 1996

We know that there is no biological difference between sex with an abuser and sex with a lover. The difference is emotional and spiritual. Just as Moses and the magicians performed the same act but with different motivations—as did Tamar, Ruth, and other Bible characters—it becomes evident that one person can use sex and the appearance of love to keep you enslaved, while another can use sex and love to be your redeemer, setting you free.

> —Dr. Ruth K. Westheimer, sex therapist, and Jonathan Mark, journalist, *Heavenly Sex: Sexuality in the Jewish Tradition* (1995)

❖ SIN ❖

Give your lungs a religious experience.

> —Slogan of anti-smoking campaign of the National Jewish Outreach Program

The law is plain and simple . . . it is forbidden for people to smoke in a house of study so long as there is even one non-smoker who is disturbed by it, even though he may not be harmed or fall ill because of it. This is truer still when one could be apprehensive about the sickness or harm which could be caused by it, even when there are smokers who claim that this ruling will lead them to squandering time which should be spent in Torah study.

—Rabbi Moshe Feinstein, Talmudic authority, "Hoshen Mishpat," quoted in *Judaism: An Anthology of the Key Spiritual Writings of the Jewish Tradition, 3rd Edition*, edited and interpreted by Arthur Hertzberg (1983)

Judaism takes our souls seriously, so it takes our sins seriously. Not every mistake is a sin, but equally, not every sin is a "mistake." We are in God's image, and just as we celebrate the nobility of our virtues, we must acknowledge the gravity of our wrongs.

—Rabbi David J. Wolpe, author, *Why Be Jewish?* (1995)

❖ THE SIXTIES ❖

They found their individuality in conformity.

—Don Feder, columnist "Remembering Woodstock in Horror," *Boston Herald*, June 23, 1994

I could have called it Temple Israel, but no one would have come.

—Rabbi Shlomo Carlebach, recalling the House of Love and Prayer, his Jewish outreach center in the late 1960s in San Francisco, quoted in "Jewish Soul Man" by Robert L. Cohen, *Moment*, August 1997

It's too late to know and it's too soon to tell.

—Arlo Guthrie, folksinger and songwriter, responding to the question of whether the 1960s meant anything, interview with Linda Ellerbee on *Later With Bob Costas*, 1991

It wasn't planned. It just happened.

—Arlo Guthrie, interview with Linda Ellerbee on *Later With Bob Costas*, 1991

Cops are our enemy. Not each one as a person, naked, say. We're all brothers when we are naked. . . . But cops in uniform are a different story. Actually, all uniforms are enemies.

—Abbie Hoffman, activist, *Revolution for the Hell of It* (1968)

Can it happen again? No way. It is never going to happen again. The music is never going to be that good, the sex is never going to be that free, the dope is never going to be that cheap. . . . We're never going to have the affluence. . . . The combination of affluence, demographics, the resistance to the 1950s that was there — all those elements are not going to happen again.

> —Abbie Hoffman, reflecting on the 60s, *The Best of Abbie Hoffman* (1989)

The stage was set: The [Vietnam] war, the Kennedy tragedy. We were broken up as a nation. The Beatles made us smile again.

> —Bruce Morrow, New York deejay "Cousin Brucie" of WABC radio, commenting on the 20th anniversary of the Beatles' first visit to the United States, quoted by UPI, February 6, 1984

The country owes a debt of gratitude to the tatterdemalion army of Yippies, hippies and peaceniks — and to their leaders David Dellinger, Tom Hayden and Jerry Rubin — who frightened the Establishment into such elaborate security precautions in Chicago. They made opposition to the war visible.

> —I. F. Stone, journalist, "When a Two-Party System Becomes a One-Party Rubber Stamp," *I. F. Stone Bi-Weekly*, September 9, 1968, after the violent demonstrations at the Democratic National Convention in Chicago, reprinted in *Polemics and Prophecies 1967–1970* (1989)

The last time I saw Dave Dellinger he was trying to convince me that Abbie [Hoffman] was killed by a CIA plot; this is someone who has not really made a successful transition.

> —Lee Wiener, one of the seven defendants in the Chicago Seven conspiracy trial, quoted in *The New York Times*, August 2, 1996

It was easy to be a self-righteous antimaterialist if you had never known anxiety about money; easy to sneer at the security of marriage if you had solicitous middle-class parents.

> —Ellen Willis, writer, *Beginning to See the Light: Pieces of a Decade* (1981)

I wish I was retired. I'd spend the rest of my life gratis just working among these kids and find out what the problem is. . . . Listen, legalizing marijuana may not be a good thing, but to make a whole generation criminals is a worse thing. . . . Nobody could get involved with half a million youngsters and be the same afterward as he was before.

> —Max Yasgur, dairy farmer in Bethel, N.Y., who agreed to make his fields available for what was to be the Woodstock Music Festival in August 1969, quoted in "Dusk in the Catskills" in *A Summer World* by Stefan Kanfer (1970)

❖ SOVIET JEWRY ❖

(see also Activism)

A movement is seriously being considered . . . for the removal of the Jews from Russia. . . . If the plans for such a movement are put into effect, the Society over which I preside will take an active part.

> —Adolf Kraus, president of B'nai B'rith, from a letter to Count Witte (Russia's prime minister) in February 1906 (in the previous October, pogroms broke out in far separated Russian communities, apparently the result of planned action), quoted in *B'nai B'rith: The Story of a Covenant* by Edward E. Grusd (1966)

[We need to be] properly prepared to receive many hundreds of thousands of Jews from the countries of the Soviet bloc. . . . Our reply to the Soviet campaign of slander cannot be made in the form of expressions of indignation and protest. . . . Our reply must be one of deeds.

> —Golda Meyerson, Israeli labor minister (later known as Golda Meir), speaking at an Israel Bonds dinner in Brooklyn at the time of the Doctors' Plot in the Soviet Union, quoted in *Jewish Telegraphic Agency*, April 3, 1953 (Stalin accused doctors of a conspiracy to murder members of his government, arousing fears of anti-Jewish purges. After Stalin died on March 5, 1953, the trial never took place and the charges were dropped.)

We are a recently founded organization of university students from all parts of the United States, who have joined together in a completely non-affiliated, self-supported group to aid Soviet Jewry . . . [a group that refused to] remain silent as did so many of our parents when the Nuremberg laws were being promulgated. . . . We felt that the time for action had arrived, even though we might incur the displeasure of the organizations who claimed to represent the Jewish masses in this matter.

> —Jacob Birnbaum, founder of the Student Struggle for Soviet Jewry (SSSJ), who believed that the Jewish establishment should be pressured into taking action by the grassroots, letter to labor leader David Dubinsky, September 2, 1964, *The Struggle for Soviet Jewish Emigration 1948–1967* by Yaacov Ro'i (1991)

We shall protest—we shall march—and we shall overcome.

> —Morris B. Abram, president of the American Jewish Committee, speaking

at a rally sponsored by the New York Conference on Soviet Jewry at Madison Square Garden, June 1965

It would be a foolish prophet who would dare to predict the spiritual end of Soviet Jewry.... It would be even more foolish and dangerous to rely on miracles.

— Abraham Ribicoff, U.S. Senator (D-Conn.), describing the crisis of Soviet Jewry in an address to the American Jewish Conference on Soviet Jewry, Washington, D.C., April 5–6, 1964

The Jew cannot be a Jew but neither can he be a non-Jew.

— Elie Wiesel, author, *The Jews of Silence* (1966)

They are the bone of our bone, flesh of our flesh.... We are all part of a covenant people who share a common history, faith, culture, language and tradition.... The bar of history would not forgive our inaction.

— Rabbi Seymour J. Cohen, president of the Synagogue Council of America, speaking at a week-long Eternal Light Vigil in Washington, D.C., September 1965

The door was locked with the key in it and we had to put the Haggada under the table if anyone knocked.

— Bella Yeselson of New York, remembering a family seder in Leningrad, USSR, quoted in "Seders in Freedom," *Hadassah*, April 1990

Is it slander that in the multi-national Soviet State, only the Jewish people can not educate its children in Jewish schools? Is it slander that there is no Jewish theatre in the USSR? Is it slander that in the USSR there are no Jewish papers?... Perhaps it is slander that for over a year I have not succeeded to obtain an exit permit for Israel?... But even this isn't the heart of the matter. I don't want to be involved in the national affairs of a state in which I consider myself an alien.... I want to live in Israel. My wish does not contradict Soviet law.

— Boris Kochubiyevsky, refusenik from Kiev who was denied exit permission and put on trial for "anti-Soviet slander," from his 1968 letter to Soviet Premier Brezhnev, cited in *Challenging the Kremlin: The Soviet Jewish Movement for Freedom 1967–1990* by Edward R. Drachman (1991)

Would it not be better, more humanizing, and more just, were the Soviet Union to wipe out anti-Semitism and to accord its Jews the same rights of cultural autonomy and expression it gives all its other nationalities? The Russian Jews have fought for Russia, bled for the Revolution, made no small contribution to Russian literature and thought; why should they be cast out? This would be a spiritual catastrophe for Russia as well as Jewry even though it would supply another flow of desperate refugees to an Israel already short of Jews if it is to expand as the Zionist militants hope to expand it.

> —I. F. Stone, journalist, *The New York Review of Books*, August 3, 1967

[It is] the devotion of Jews like you that give the Jewish people strength to face the great challenges of our times.

> —Nehemia Levanon, Israeli diplomat, from his 1967 letter to Jacob Birnbaum, quoted in *The Struggle for the Soviet Jewish Emigration, 1948–1967* by Yaacov Ro'i (1991)

We are confronted with a paradox here. We are not wanted here, we are being completely oppressed, forcibly denationalized, and even publicly insulted in the press—while at the same time we are forcibly kept here. As the Lithuanian proverb goes, "He beats and he screams at the same time."

> —Letter from twenty-six Lithuanian Jews to Comrade A. Snietskus, First Secretary of the Central Committee of the Lithuanian Communist Party, which appeared in *The Washington Post* and *The New York Times* on October 30, 1969, quoted in *Redemption: Jewish Freedom Letters From Russia*, edited by Moshe Dector (1969)

It is wrong to generate too much activity on behalf of Russian Jewry, because this could endanger the very existence of three million Jews.

> —Nahum Goldmann, president of the World Jewish Congress, expressing his disagreement with the strategy of public campaigns on behalf of Soviet Jews, 1969, quoted in *They Did Not Dwell Alone: Jewish Emigration From the Soviet Union 1967–1990* by Petrus Buwalda (1997)

It was the American Jewish leadership through their public advocacy and private initiatives that brought the American government and the American public into the issue of Soviet Jewry, so that Soviet Jewry was not strictly an American Jewish communal issue, it became an American issue.

> —Carmi Schwartz, former executive vice president, Council of Jewish Federation, November 21, 1991, quoted in the *CJF Oral History Project: The Response of the North American Federations to the Emigration of Jews from the Former Soviet Union to the United States and Israel, Volume I* (1991)

"The ten circles of hell"

> —David Zilberman, Soviet émigré, describing the experience and difficulties encountered by Soviet Jews wishing to emigrate from the Soviet Union, quoted in the *Jerusalem Post*, December 1, 1971

To understand the problems of an average Jew in Russia you have to imagine a rabbit surrounded by wolves, trying somehow to live with them in the same forest.

> —Moshe S., a fifty-five-year-old painter from Odessa, interviewed by the William E. Wiener Oral History Library of the American Jewish Committee, 1970s, quoted in *A Special Legacy: An Oral History of Soviet Jewish Émigrés in the United States* by Sylvia Rothchild (1985)

We didn't have one friend. We didn't have a single relative or an acquaintance to share a word with. We were the so-called Soviet Jews, and we saw cars speeding by with bumper stickers that said "Save Soviet Jewry," but nobody was willing to save us.

> —Leonid K., a Soviet émigré, commenting on the initial adjustment to American society, interviewed by the William E. Wiener Oral History Library of the American Jewish Committee, 1970s, quoted in *A Special Legacy: An Oral History of Soviet Jewish Émigrés in the United States* by Sylvia Rothchild (1985)

My reasons for emigration had nothing to do with material things. It's true that there were five of us living in two rooms, but that meant nothing to us because everyone lived like that. You have to understand that it's very difficult to change your language, your culture and your habits. A reasonable person doesn't give up his friends and relatives for the sake of a bigger apartment and the chance to eat strawberries in January.

> —Boris F., a computer analyst from Kharkov, interviewed by the William E. Wiener Oral History Library of the American Jewish Committee, 1970s, quoted in *A Special Legacy: An Oral History of Soviet Jewish Émigrés in the United States* by Sylvia Rothchild (1985)

You can say things the administration can't say. You can raise issues we can't raise. Go ahead and raise them.

> —Henry A. Kissinger, member of the National Security Council, speaking to Jack Stein and Max Fisher, July 25, 1973, before Stein and Fisher went to lunch at the Russian Embassy in Washington, D.C., with Soviet Ambassador Anatoly Dobrynin, quoted in *Quiet Diplomat: A Biography of Max M. Fisher* by Peter Golden (1992)

If we allow this to continue, if you, our brothers, forsake us, we will be the last of the Jews of this land, the last witnesses, the last of the Jews who in silence bury the Jew within them. And know this, brothers who leave without having spoken to us, that so much silence is breaking my heart, that hope has deserted me. Know that it is more than I can bear, it is more than I can bear . . .

—Elie Wiesel, author, *Zalman and the Madness of God* (voice of the rabbi) (1974)

For those who doubt the efficacy of the amendment, I suppose the simple response is: What was the alternative? The alternative was to do nothing and leave it entirely in the hands of the Soviets, to associate no cost at all with beastly behavior and no benefits with doing the right thing.

> —Richard Peele, Assistant Secretary of Defense for international security policy, regarding the Jackson-Vanik amendment, quoted in *Jewish Times* by Howard Simons (1988) (The amendment linked most-favored-nation status and other trade benefits with a liberalized Soviet emigration policy.)

I went, and met all the old timers [refuseniks]—Sharansky, Slepak, Lerner—and I promised myself that I wouldn't leave this office until Sharansky, Slepak and Lerner were out.

> —Zeesy Schnur, executive director of the Coalition to Free Soviet Jewry, recalling a trip to the Soviet Union in 1976, quoted in *Long Island Jewish World*, May 27, 1988

We must take our souls. That's the main thing we'll bring with us. Everything else is nothing.

> —Vladimir Slepak, refusenik, receiving word that the Soviet Union granted his request to emigrate to Israel seventeen years and seven months after first applying for exit permission, 1977, quoted by columnist Cal Thomas, *New York Daily News*, October 26, 1987

I am not an outstanding person. I am a simple Jew with a simple ordinary strength . . . I think many of you, many other Jews, being in my situation could do the same.

> —Vladimir Slepak, 1977, quoted in *A Refusenik Diary*, documentary (1988)

We made it, guys, even if we had to crawl here on our hands and knees, we made it.

> —Masha Slepak, former refusenik, approaching the Western Wall in Jerusalem with her husband Vladimir and their son, 1977, quoted in *A Refusenik Diary*, documentary (1988)

The Russians never quite knew what to do with their Jews. Autocratic Tzars saw the Jews as a problem which could only be solved by assimilation or banishment. But Jews who assimilated were accused of trying to take over the power in their fatherland and Jews who emigrated were regretted as a serious economic loss or labeled as treacherous revolutionaries.

> —Chaim Potok, author, *Wanderings* (1978)

We call on you, the Jews of the West, those who spend their efforts on paperwork of endless conferences . . . in defense of Soviet Jewry. . . . And we say: "Enough, brothers and sisters, of chewing over our despair while lunching at 'Lindy's.' Enough of the flaming cocktail party declarations and touching 'twin-Bar-Mitzva' shows. . . . The time has come to sound the alarm. There have been enough expressions of concern — the hour has come for some practical action. . . . The above is not an expression of base ingratitude or a reproach against your passivity, but a call for concrete action, since Russia always understood only concrete deeds and a practical approach. . . . Who, if not you, can help us remove the stone from the mouth of the well."

> —"An Appeal for Urgent Action by Distraught Refuseniks," December 23, 1984, quoted in *Challenging the Kremlin: The Soviet Jewish Movement for Freedom 1967–1990* by Edward R. Drachman (1991)

Let's base ourselves on reality, on the number of people who in fact have applied to leave. Let's talk about them and not about some mythical figure that has been thought up by some kind of organization which simply doesn't like either the Soviet Union or Soviet Jews, even though it calls itself an organization for Soviet Jews or something like that. . . . Let's see how many people all in all want to leave and we'll very easily find out what the truth is.

> —"Samuel," deputy director of the Anti-Zionist League in Moscow, responding to American TV host Phil Donahue's citing of the National Conference of Soviet Jewry's estimate of 380,000 Jews who want to emigrate from the Soviet Union, "Donahue in Russia," broadcast February 11, 1987, Museum of Television and Radio archives (Donahue was meeting with "content" Jews that the Kremlin wanted the world to see; the Soviet authorities chose the guests, and they spoke with the approval of the party and the government.)

We want to say hello to your countrymen, to all you Americans who are ready to listen to us, to understand our tragic situation, the desire to leave for Israel. That is our position, not your agreement with [Soviet] radio.

> —Unidentified refusenik in conversation with talk show host Phil Donahue, explaining why the refuseniks refused to tape a segment with Donahue after the show was promised fifty refusenik participants but was later permitted to include only twenty-five, "Donahue in Russia," broadcast February 11, 1987, Museum of Television and Radio archives

A few hours ago I was almost a slave in Moscow. Now I'm a free woman in my own country. It is the moment of my life.

> —Ida Nudel, former refusenik, commenting on her arrival in Israel from the Soviet Union on October 15, 1987, quoted in *Lilith*, Winter 1987–88

My former existence is now nothing but a history, removed from me and somehow living its own life. And now I have the luxury of doing something I couldn't allow myself for years: forgetting. Forgetting, finally, the exact wording of the punishments, the conversations with my interrogators, the names of my guards. Forgetting the cold of the punishment cells and the weakness of my starving body.

> —Natan Sharansky, former refusenik, *Fear No Evil* (1988)

The position that the majority of us took was that the Soviet Jews were entitled to decide where they wanted to live. We may have preferred that they go to Israel, but we were not going to rescue them from an oppressive society, bring them into a free one, and then make their first personal decision for them. Nor once they entered the United States were we going to allow them to become destitute.

> —Martin S. Kraar, executive vice-president of the Council of Jewish Federations, discussing the explosive debate in 1988–89 between American Jews and Israelis about the destination of Soviet Jews who were finally given permission to emigrate from the Soviet Union, quoted in *Quiet Diplomat: A Biography of Max M. Fisher* by Peter Golden (1992)

The American Jewish community is opposed to forcing anyone to live where he doesn't want to live. The community will not support coercion.

> —Morris B. Abram, president of the National Conference of Soviet Jewry, quoted in *The Washington Post*, October 23, 1988

Israel does not exist to allow Jews to go from one Diaspora to another. We cried to Gorbachev to let the Jewish people go—not to Brighton Beach or to Chicago, but to Jerusalem.

> —Uri Gordon, head of aliyah department of the Jewish Agency for Israel, 1988, quoted in *Kissing Through Glass* by Joyce R. Starr (1990)

I believe that Jews should have the right to move anywhere they want. But they should not use Jewish public funds to do it.

> —Mendel Kaplan, chairman of the Jewish Agency Board of Governors, 1988, quoted in *Quiet Diplomat: A Biography of Max M. Fisher* by Peter Golden (1992)

A public relations disaster waiting to happen.

> —Micah Naftalin, director of the Union of Councils for Soviet Jewry, a grassroots network for advocacy on behalf of Soviet Jews, commenting on the Israeli government's proposals to counter the "drop-out" phenomenon—that of Soviet Jews who emigrate with an Israeli visa and change their destination to the United States, 1988, quoted in *They Did Not Dwell Alone: Jewish Emigration from the Soviet Union, 1967–1990* by Petrus Buwalda (1997)

It's easy to forget us, but we must not be cast aside. Only noise will get us out.

> —Natasha Stonov, refusenik since 1979, commenting after a three-day fast in March 1989, concerned that the permission granted to some high-profile cases should not lull the advocates on their behalf, quoted in "Soviet Jewish Women Fast for Right to Emigrate" by Masha Hamilton, *Los Angeles Times*, March 10, 1989

There is a lot of talk about glasnost and perestroika. Well, for people who have received permission to leave, it is very good, but we are still here, so for us it's not so good.

> —Igor Uspensky, refusenik (with his wife Inna) in Moscow since 1979, quoted in *Long Island Jewish World*, May 27, 1988

It seemed to me she did not know the Soviet life or the life of Soviet Jews at all, because she was waiting for some terrible cases about how they tried to kill me or hang me and my family.

> —Alexander Rabechev, émigré, describing his interview with the Immigration and Naturalization Service, October 24, 1988, in Rome, Italy, *Washington Jewish Week*, December 15, 1988 (Rabachev was denied refugee status to enter the United States on the grounds that the liberalizing trends in the Soviet Union mean that Soviet Jews should no longer enjoy a presumption of well-founded fear of persecution.)

What I saw around me [was] that the common folks do hate Jews, period. You go to the store and stand in line; someone cuts the line and you speak up . . . the response is, "And what do you want, you kike, you Jew. . . . Go to your Israel." And that's constantly in the streets.

> —Leonard Slepak, refusenik who was released by the Soviet authorities years before his parents, Vladimir and Masha Slepak, *A Refusenik Diary*, documentary, 1988

It is possible that Soviet Jewry had really entered the final phase of its existence, but this phase is a long process and we must be concerned to do something for those who stay as well as those who leave.

> —Mikhail Chlenov, ethnographer who was among the founders of the Congress of Jewish Organizations and Communities (the Va'ad) in the USSR, "Should Soviet Jews Leave?" *Tikkun*, September/October 1990

Tell me, why are people who are not my relatives so concerned about me?

> —Rafael Zaitsef, new immigrant to Israel from the Soviet Union, quoted in "Immigrants at Midnight," *Hadassah*, April 1990

I would like to say thank you to Pamyat, for they uncovered this disease, this cancer. They wear no mask in words or acts. They stand for the hidden part of the iceberg.

> —Yuri I. Sokol, Soviet Jewish activist, commenting on Pamyat's anti-Semitic message, quoted in "The Jewish Museum Packs Them In" by Scott Shane, *Baltimore Sun*, August 30, 1988 [Pamyat is an "informal" (not politically sanctioned) Russian nationalist and virulently anti-Semitic political activist group in the Soviet Union, one of many "informal" groups that sprung up under glasnost.]

It's not going to be easy. There will be plenty of problems, but you're among family now. You're on your way home.

> —Natan Sharansky, former refusenik, speaking on video played on El Al Flight 363 to Tel Aviv carrying Jews emigrating from the Soviet Union to Israel, quoted in *U.S. News and World Report*, May 7, 1990

We didn't come here . . . for the luxuries. . . . If we could survive the war [World War II] in the Soviet Union, we could survive any hardship. What we couldn't take was the constant pain you feel inside when you are insulted as a Jew.

> —Rachel Rapaport, retired surgeon from Leningrad and recent émigré to Israel, quoted in *U.S. News and World Report*, May 7, 1990

The ultimate purpose in rescuing and resettling Jews from the Soviet Union in North America is to help them live in a free society, to be reunited with the Jewish people and to live enriched lives as members of the American Jewish community. The cultural and communal integration of these new Jewish Americans into American Jewish communities has the potential to greatly enhance American Jewish life and help insure its future.

> —Council of Jewish Federations Task Force on Acculturation and Integration, excerpted from statement May 1991

We initiated an operational process that dealt with the real, not with the ideal, with the feasible, with the "do-able," not necessarily the desirable or what some people may have wanted.

> —Carmi Schwartz, former executive vice-president of Council of Jewish Federations (CJF), discussing the change in policy that permitted refugees with immediate relatives in the U.S. to be processed in Moscow (all other Soviet Jewish émigrés would travel directly to Israel from the Soviet Union, eliminating the route through Western Europe), quoted in *A CJF Oral History Project* (1991)

Circumstances have changed. . . . There are no more doors to open in the former Soviet Union—and no more debates about which doors to close; the passion surrounding the issue has evaporated. Zionism's claim that Israel is the only option for Jews was proven correct: For all practical purposes America's doors are closed at the very moment that the number of refugees seeking a haven has skyrocketed.

> —Natan Sharansky, "When Worlds Collide," *Jerusalem Report*, February 27, 1992

Walter's [Annenberg] pledge was a real spark. I made the announcement, and by the time coffee was poured $58 million was pledged to Operation Exodus.

> —Max M. Fisher, business executive and philanthropist, recalling the March 1990 UJA breakfast as part of a fund-raising campaign, Operation Exodus, for the express purpose of settling Soviet Jews in Israel, quoted in *Quiet Diplomat: A Biography of Max M. Fisher* by Peter Golden (1992)

More and more I began to feel that something was wrong in the society in which I had grown up and in which you could not even be apolitical, you were forced to participate. That was unbearable for me. I hated that system, the antihumanism of it more than its anti-Semitism.

> —Yuri Zieman of Boston, former refusenik, reminiscing in an October 30, 1993, interview, quoted in *They Did Not Dwell Alone: Jewish Emigration From the Soviet Union 1967–1990* by Petrus Buwalda (1997)

Those were my best years. I saved many people. I watched the prisoners, helped them in their special circumstances. The KGB won against me physically—they kept me there. But I won spiritually.

> —Ida Nudel, former refusenik now living in Israel, "The Bitter New World of Ida Nudel," interview with Yossi Klein Halevi, *Jerusalem Report*, December 30, 1993

Our government will sell Jews or not sell Jews, will let them go or not, depending on what it gets in return. Jews are a card in the political game.

> —Natasha Rapoport, quoted in *Lenin's Tomb* by David Remnick (1993)

Those who do manage to come here . . . come to our shores as strangers. Even when they have family, they come as strangers. But we also have a Jewish tradition for that. We are to look after the stranger; we are to look after the ger [stranger], as well as we look after our own family. It's our Jewish tradition, as we are told in the story of Rebecca when she welcomed the stranger. Her father's tents were open and the strangers were fed and housed. That is our responsibility, yours and mine, and we cannot be tired because it's 1993 and they have been coming for fifteen and twenty years. . . . We have to have the patience to understand their trauma. . . . When they complain, we get impatient; but Jews have complained before, here and elsewhere. We have to be stronger than that.

> —Shoshana S. Cardin, chairman of the National Jewish Center for Learning and Leadership (CLAL) and past president of the Conference of Presidents of Major American Jewish Organizations, from her paper presented at the Council of Jewish Federations General Assembly in Montreal, November 18, 1993, "Jewish Communal Responsibilities For Soviet Refugees in the Post–Cold War Era"

This was not an easy decision, because we're dealing with people's lives. But it is the right decision. We did this knowing that it's always possible that the situations can change. It's about recognizing progress when progress takes place.

> —Mark Levin, executive director of the National Council of Soviet Jewry, the leading agency representing the American Jewish establishment on the issue of Soviet Jewry, commenting on the NCSJ decision to back President Clinton's position to certify Russia in compliance, for the first time, with the terms of the 1974 Jackson-Vanik amendment, quoted in *Jewish Telegraphic Agency*, September 22, 1994

Even though the number of refuseniks is very low compared to years ago, the battle is not over, and we should not abandon our soldiers in the field. When you're so close, you don't give up.

> —Glenn Richter, national coordinator of the Student Struggle for Soviet Jewry, reacting to Clinton's decision to declare Russia in compliance with terms of the Jackson-Vanik amendment, quoted in *Jewish Telegraphic Agency*, September 22, 1994

I have no sense of what's going to happen. I don't think everyone is going to move out in the next three or five years, but then again, I wouldn't advise building a new synagogue.

> —Rabbi Ya'akov Bleich, American-born chief rabbi of Ukraine's approximately 500,000 Jews, quoted in *Jewish Telegraphic Agency*, September 22, 1994

In Russia they called us zhid (kike). Here they call us Russians.

> —Unidentified Soviet Jewish émigré, voicing oft-made comment by Soviet Jewish émigrés, quoted in *The Jewish Week*, August 4, 1995

Jacob Birnbaum will be revered as a modern day Judah Maccabee.

> —Micah Naftalin, executive director of the Union of Councils for Soviet Jewry, acknowledging the pioneer organizer, activist, and advocate for Soviet Jewry, quoted in *The Jewish Week*, December 27, 1996

My colleagues and I have come a long way to reach this occasion and this building. . . . My grandfather is buried in Siberia, where he was exiled and murdered because of his Zionist activities. At this moment, I'm thinking: I wish my grandfather could, even for a second, see me standing here, after all the persecution, repression and assimilation, speaking here in Hebrew, in the Israeli Knesset, in the State of Israel.

> —Yuri Shtern, former Soviet Jewish dissident and a member of the Israeli Parliament, quoted in *The New York Times*, July 26, 1996

Every time I would arrive at a new prison, the warden would tell me to forget about Israel and that I would never see it as long as I lived.

> —Yuli Edelstein, Israeli minister of immigrant absorption who served nearly three years in Soviet prison camps before emigrating to Israel in 1987, quoted in *The New York Times*, July 26, 1996

As a tool, Jackson-Vanik [amendment] should always be in the toolshed.

> —Mark Talisman, former aide to the amendment's House sponsor Rep. Charles Vanik (D-Ohio) when it originally passed in 1973, considering the current instability in the former Soviet Union, quoted in *MetroWest Jewish News*, June 12, 1997

The efforts to absorb so many newcomers into Israeli society no longer captivates the imagination of American Jews, and that is a shame.

> —Gary Rosenblatt, editor and publisher, "Between the Lines," *The Jewish Week*, November 3, 1995

❖ SOVIET UNION ❖

Pandemonium broke out. Everyone was howling and weeping and it was somehow expected of me to cry too, but—to my shame then: now I think to my honor—I couldn't. When I got home my mother was also crying. I looked at her with some astonishment, until my father suddenly gave me a wink. Then I realized for sure that there was no particular reason for me to get upset over Stalin's death.

> —Joseph Brodsky, Russian-born poet exiled to the United States in 1972 who won the Nobel Prize in 1987 and was appointed poet laureate of the United States in 1991, recalling Stalin's death in 1953 when he was twelve years old in Russia, in conversation with writer Solomon Volkov, *The New Yorker*, February 12, 1996

There was baby Lenin, looking like a cherub in his blond curls. Then Lenin in his twenties and thirties, bald and uptight, with that meaningless expression on his face which could be taken for anything, preferably a sense of purpose. This face in some way haunts every Russian and suggests some sort of standard for human appearance because it is utterly lacking in character.

> —Joseph Brodsky, recalling the ubiquitous images of Lenin, *The New Yorker*, February 12, 1996

I was a link in a chain that went from Khrushchev to me to Amos Manor to Allen Dulles to Eisenhower. I didn't make history, but I touched it for a few hours.

> —Victor Grayevsky, recalling his role as a thirty-one-year-old Polish journalist who unwittingly obtained the West's first copy of the top secret document of Khrushchev's secret speech denouncing Stalin to the 20th Communist Party Congress, quoted in "The Man Who Touched History" by Abraham Rabinovich, *Jerusalem Post*, November 17, 1995 (He shared the speech with the Israeli embassy in Poland and his copy was transmitted to Washington by the Shin Bet head Amos Manor; based on this information, the complete text was published in *The New York Times*. This episode is recognized as one that elevated Israel within the international intelligence community.)

I was planning to immigrate to Israel and I looked on what I intended to do now as if I were coming to it with a bouquet of flowers.

> —Victor Grayevsky, quoted in "The Man Who Touched History" by Abraham Rabinovich, *Jerusalem Post*, November 17, 1995

Nazi Germany destroyed the lives of millions, Soviet Communism, the souls. . . . The Communists destroyed the souls of the survivors within their power.

> —Rabbi Jacob Neusner, author and professor of Jewish studies, *Long Island Jewish World*, April 11, 1997

I think the main difference is the number of corpses left behind.

> —David Remnick, journalist and author, comparing Lenin and Stalin, *Book-notes* interview with Brian Lamb, C-SPAN, July 25, 1993

In the Soviet world there has always been a dichotomy between freedom from want and freedom from fear.

> —Daniel Schorr, senior news analyst for National Public Radio, *Christian Science Monitor*, December 22, 1995

You must understand not just the two languages but also the two mentalities, not only translate words, but also ideas and understanding.

> —Natan Sharansky, former refusenik whose knowledge of English enabled him to provide translations at press conferences organized by refuseniks and other Soviet dissidents in the 1970s, quoted in *They Did Not Dwell Alone: Soviet Emigration from the Soviet Union, 1967–1990* by Petrus Buwalda (1997)

The Soviet system could be stable only if it had full control over the brains of the people. In fact it was a very insecure system. And that is why even the existence of one person, whose public sayings were his own and his right, was a danger for them. That is why they made such an effort not only to put you in prison but to make you say publicly that you were wrong and they are right.

> —Natan Sharansky, quoted in *They Did Not Dwell Alone: Jewish Emigration from the Soviet Union, 1967–1990* by Petrus Buwalda (1994)

There's never been a Russian revolution where Jewish blood wasn't spilled.

> —Alexander Shmukler, member of the Soviet Jewish Vaad Organization, speaking at the August 24 funeral of Ilya Krichevski, a Jew killed resisting the August 1991 coup, quoted in *Jerusalem Report*, September 5, 1991

Three more showers! I can't wait to get the hell out of here.

> —Robert Strauss, ambassador to Russia, interviewed during the last days before completing fifteen months of service, quoted in *The New Yorker*, December 28, 1992

Materially and morally, Russia looks like an experiment in ugliness, as if engineers had been competing for seventy years to see how much damage they could do to communities and families and individuals, to a society and an economy.

> —Ruth R. Wisse, professor of Yiddish and comparative literature, *The New Republic*, February 3, 1997

❖ SPACE PROGRAM ❖

There are problems on Earth, just as there have been since the first human was eaten by a saber-toothed tiger. There were rats and sewage problems back in Genoa when Christopher Columbus was growing up. Their muddy streets probably had some hellacious potholes. Columbus' generation also had some trouble getting decent health care. Scurvy was a problem, so was the plague. They didn't have CAT scans or laser surgery or intensive care units—which by the way, got their starts because of the space program.

> —Daniel Goldin, administrator of the National Aeronautics and Space Administration, remarks to his NASA colleagues, quoted in *Lifestyles*, Spring 1997

Last night a group of us weirdoes sat up all night and watched what has to be the greatest TV show, in fact, the "Greatest Show on Earth".... One tries not to be cynical; after all, they are jumping around on the fuckin' moon and no matter what you think of PIG NATION, you have to admit that it does have a good special effects department.

> —Abbie Hoffman, activist, *Woodstock Nation* (1969)

It was a Twentieth Century audience when all was said, and quick in its sense of fashion. By an hour and a half of the moon walk they were bored— some were actually slipping out. All over the room was felt the ubiquitous desire of journalists for the rescue of a drink. Boredom deepened. Now the mood was equal to the fourth quarter of a much anticipated football game whose result had proved lopsided.... More and more reporters departed.

> —Norman Mailer, novelist, commenting on covering the Apollo 11 moon landing from NASA in Houston, *Of a Fire on the Moon* (1969)

It was their last night before the moon landing. They were obliged to wonder whether two of them would sleep tomorrow on the moon or sleep forever. Yet calmly they went to sleep. So recorded the monitors on the ground. There are souls whose health it is to sleep upon the edge of profound uncertainty, men whose greatest calm resides in the edge of danger. Who indeed can understand the psychology of astronauts?

> —Norman Mailer, *Of a Fire on the Moon* (1969)

A kind of technological Pearl Harbor.

> —Edward Teller, physicist, commenting on the success of Sputnik, the satellite launched by the Soviet Union on October 4, 1957, an event that caught the American public off guard, quoted in *The Fifties* by David Halberstam (1993)

❖ SPIRITUALITY ❖

(see also Holiness, Meditation, Prayer)

What is a Chasid's dance but one long, sustained attempt to arch away into suspended ascension, beyond the laws of bodies, a thing of air and light and fire?

> —Rebecca Goldstein, novelist, *Mazel* (1995)

Am Yisrael [the Jewish people] has a spiritual resilience that is never lost and with a little bit of love and perseverance, in an instant, our sons and daughters can come back.

> —Rebbetzin Esther Jungreis, founder of Hineni and columnist, *Jewish Press,* July 18, 1997

Ultimately I see spiritual growth as climbing a ladder. You climb slowly, step by step. With each step you take you solidify your footing, then move on to the next step. Each step you take up the ladder nourishes your soul. In time, you will feel completely nourished and connected to God. You will have truly met God.

> —Rabbi Harold S. Kushner, author and rabbi emeritus of Temple Israel in Natick, Mass., "God's Fingerprint on the Soul," *Handbook for the Soul,* edited by Richard Carlson and Benjamin Shields (1995)

Spiritual interpretation depends on a subtle form of awareness, through which we learn to connect the events in the world to the role God plays in them. Our life in the world and our life with God are inextricably intertwined.

> —Carol Ochs, author and professor of philosophy, and Kerry M. Olitzky, rabbi, author, and Jewish educator, *Jewish Spiritual Guidance: Finding Our Way to God* (1997)

All agree that the physical world as we see it is only secondary and peripheral to the spirit. The essence of creation and the true reality is spiritual, but people do not fully appreciate the greatness of the supernatural. A miracle thus shows them their error in this regard.

> —Rabbi Menachem Mendel Schneerson, who would become the Lubavitcher Rebbe, from a letter written to the previous Lubavitcher Rebbe, 1932

❖ Sports ❖

It's goin', goin', gone.

> —Mel Allen, Yankee broadcaster, giving his unique home run call, quoted in his obituary, *Forward*, June 21, 1996

The Yankees fired me that time. The fans never did.

> —Mel Allen, broadcaster for the New York Yankees from 1939–1964, quoted in "How About That Mel?" by Mike Lupica, *New York Daily News*, June 18, 1996

Lou patted me on the thigh and said, "Kid, I never listened to the broadcasts when I was playing, but now they're what keep me going." I went down the steps and bawled like a baby.

> —Mel Allen, recalling an encounter with Lou Gehrig in 1940 when Gehrig was stricken with amyotrophic lateral sclerosis, quoted in Allen's obituary, "Golden Voice of Yankees," *The New York Times*, June 17, 1996

I saw strong men weep this afternoon, expressionless umpires swallow hard, and emotion pump the hearts and glaze the eyes of 61,000 baseball fans in Yankee Stadium. Yes, and hard-boiled news photographers clicked their shutters with fingers that trembled a bit. It was Lou Gehrig Day at the stadium, and the first 100 years of baseball saw nothing quite like it.

> —Shirley Povich, journalist covering sports for *The Washington Post*, from his reporting of Lou Gehrig's famous farewell, July 4, 1939, quoted in *Covering the Bases* by Benedict Cosgrove (1997)

One of the announcers—I think it was Ralph Kiner, who had seen me bat and field—said, "Hey, he's got a good motion." That meant as much to me as winning the Academy Award.

> —Woody Allen, actor and director, quoted in *The New York Times*, November 2, 1995

It was the single most important rule change in the last fifty years.

> —Red Auerbach, coach of the Boston Celtics, referring to the debut of the
> 24-second shot clock in the NBA, October 30, 1954 (the 1954–55 Celtics
> became the first team to average 100 points per game), quoted in *The NBA
> at 50*, edited by Mark Vancil (1996)

At least, when I coached, we had a great psychological edge. People would
come into Boston with a great defeatist complex. They thought we were doing
something to them. We weren't doing anything . . . but as long as they believed
that, it gave us a competitive edge. . . . We had a good team in those days for
many years. The opposition was going to get beat anyway and this was just an
alibi as to why they'd get beat.

> —Red Auerbach, former coach and general manager of the NBA Boston Cel-
> tics, commenting on how the Boston Garden intimidated opposing clubs,
> interview with Hillel Kuttler, *Jerusalem Post*, October 17, 1995

There's no such thing as a starter. It's not important who starts. What's
important is who's finishing. I inaugurated the sixth man idea and it became
so popular. When you make a team in the NBA, that's it—you make it. When
you figure you're one of twelve guys on any team, you're one of the great
basketball players in the world, so how bad can you be?

> —Red Auerbach, interview with Hillel Kuttler, *Jerusalem Post*, October 17,
> 1995

I don't feel sorry for myself. I knew sooner or later I'd have to pay the
piper. . . . But I'll tell you who I do feel sorry for—all those guys who never
heard the music.

> —Bo Belinsky, baseball player (a left-handed pitcher for the Los Angeles An-
> gels who pitched a no-hitter against the Baltimore Orioles in 1962), antici-
> pating the end of his playing career, quoted in *Baseball Anecdotes* by Daniel
> Okrent and Steve Wulf (1989)

His own grandmother died on the Sunday of the Cleveland-Boston Braves
World Series. That's how he dates most things: baseball games, horse races,
championship fights. But never football, though he watches a good deal of it
on television. I think the only game he ever went to was with me, the Redskins
and the Giants in 1955. We did a lot of fighting before he relented. At halftime
they played "Dixie." He said he would never go again until they integrated the
team.

> —Carl Bernstein, journalist, describing his father, *Loyalties: A Son's Memoir*
> (1989)

I remember it as if it were yesterday. It was October 6—the opening day of the 1965 World Series. . . . It was a courageous act for Koufax to abstain from playing in an era that preferred to sanitize difference. . . . Koufax taught me that I could hope to take an active part in American life without compromising my religious convictions. This lesson has remained and has solidified my commitment to make it accessible to all people.

> —Rabbi Lee Bycel, dean of the Hebrew Union College-Jewish Institute of Religion, remembering Sandy Koufax's decision not to pitch in the first game of the World Series because it was on Yom Kippur, *Jewish Bulletin of Northern California*, September 20, 1996

Koufax was not known as either a religious or civil rights leader; his personal decisions were not calculated to have an impact on others. He was a great baseball player and a Jew, but who could have imagined that his not playing would inspire a generation of youth to embrace their distinctive identity. . . . I learned that October in 1965 the power of personal acts.

> —Rabbi Lee Bycel, *Jewish Bulletin of Northern California*, September 20, 1996

There is only one area where Jews play a key role in American sports—management. There isn't a single major league that cannot mount a minyan [quorum of ten] of team owners. And the NBA, dominated by commissioner David Stern, is a veritable Council of the Elders of Zion. There is nothing wrong with this—indeed, Jewish owners make a real contribution to the health and prosperity of American sports. Still, it isn't much fun to sit in the stands and root for the Pistons' Bill Davidson, say, to make another million bucks.

> —Ze'ev Chafets, Israeli journalist, "Jews Can't Jump," *Jerusalem Report*, July 15, 1993

Wait a minute! Wait a minute! Sonny Liston is not coming out! Sonny Liston is not coming out! He's out. The winner and the new heavyweight champion in the world is Cassius Clay.

> —Howard Cosell, television and radio sports commentator, calling the fight between Sonny Liston and Cassius Clay (Muhammad Ali), ABC radio broadcast, February 25, 1964

We have the only shomer Shabbat [Sabbath observant] ice hockey program in the city; We have the only Hebrew-speaking hockey team in the world.

> —Ben Epstein, a criminal attorney who coaches the Kehilath Jeshurun Barak (Lightning), a team sponsored by Kehilath Jeshurun in New York City, quoted in *The Jewish Week*, July 11, 1997

I ought to be out there, I should be out there . . . and I'm not.

> —Marty Glickman, sports broadcaster and former track-and-field Olympic contender, recalling watching his American teammates mount the victory stand while the "Star Spangled Banner" played, Munich 1936, quoted in *Ellis Island to Ebbets Field* by Peter Levine (1992)

As I walked into the stadium, I began to get so angry. I began to get so mad. It shocked the hell out of me that this thing of forty-nine years ago could still evoke this anger. . . . Not about the German Nazis. . . . That's a given. But anger at Avery Brundage and Dean Cromwell for not allowing an eighteen-year-old kid to compete in the Olympic games just because he was Jewish.

> —Marty Glickman, recalling his return visit to Berlin's Olympic stadium, quoted in *Ellis Island to Ebbets Field* by Peter Levine (1992)

I'd watch him with hungry eyes as he walked to a car. When I say that I worshipped Babe Ruth I'm putting into words what every New York kid felt in those days.

> —Hank Greenberg, baseball Hall of Famer, "How to Hit a Home Run," *Collier's*, April 22, 1939

They'll be serving sushi at Wrigley Field any day now if they haven't started already. If there's hope for baseball, it lies with the minors.

> —Paul Greenberg, editorial page editor of the *Pine Bluff Commercial* and syndicated columnist, "Goodbye, Comiskey: The Romance of Baseball" in *Entirely Personal* (1992)

What it came down to in Manila wasn't the heavyweight championship of the world. Ali and [Joe] Frazier were now fighting for something more important than that. They were fighting for the championship of each other, and it was an epic battle. . . . Both men gave it everything they had. . . . And if you do what we do for a living, you wanted to be at ringside for that fight.

> —Jerry Izenberg, sportswriter, recalling the Ali-Frazier fight in Quezon City, outside Manila, October 1, 1975, quoted in *Muhammad Ali: His Life and Times* by Thomas Hauser (1991)

I can't tell you what I went through for defending him. All the cancellations of my newspaper column, the smashed car windows, the bomb threats, the thousands of letters from army war veterans talking about Jews like me and concentration camps. I think I must have been in a different army from these guys when I was in Korea.

> —Jerry Izenberg, sportswriter, remembering the controversy over Muhammad

Ali's decision not to comply with his draft notice to serve in Vietnam, quoted in *Muhammad Ali: His Life and Times* by Thomas Hauser (1991)

Red Barber was an indelible part of my life. . . . Like with the players, we had our argument over announcers. Who was best, Mel Allen versus Red Barber versus Russ Hodges. The big complaint Yankee fans had against Barber was that he didn't get excited enough. This was because Mel Allen openly rooted for the Yankees. I remember listening with such hatred of Mel Allen when he would talk about Joe Page coming in. It was as though Mel himself was a Yankee.

> —Larry King, radio and television talk show host, quoted in *Bums* by Peter Golenbock (1984)

When we [the Dodgers] played the Yankees, it was us poor Dodger fans against the rich. . . . And the Yankee fans didn't scream. They clapped, like at the opera.

> —Larry King, radio and television talk show host, quoted in *Bums* by Peter Golenbock (1984)

Al Campanis, from everything I understand, you're a very decent man and highly respected man in baseball. I confess to you, before we began this program, baseball is not one of my areas of expertise. I'd like to give you another chance to dig yourself out, because I think you need it.

> —Ted Koppel, television journalist, interviewing Al Campanis, a vice-president of the Los Angeles Dodgers and director of player personnel, April 6, 1987, after Campanis said that he believed that black baseball men may not have "some of the necessities" to be field managers or general managers, *Nightline: History in the Making and the Making of Television*, written with Kyle Gibson (1996)

It's nice to have this honor. It's great to be inducted into anything, because it makes you realize what you've done, and other people realize what you've done.

> —Aaron Krickstein, professional tennis player, on his induction into the Michigan Jewish Sports Hall of Fame, quoted in the *Detroit Jewish News*, November 14, 1997

The German Olympic Committee was making an attempt to make amends, and I thought, I can't hold the sins of the fathers and grandfathers against the new generation. After all, many of them hate what Hitler, and the Nazis did too.

> —Margaret Lambert, track-and-field star who was barred, as a Jew (known as

Gretel Bergmann) from the German Olympic team in 1936, speaking on
the occasion of an invitation to join the German team at the 1996 Olympics
in Atlanta, quoted in *The New York Times,* July 20, 1996

My mother would be so impressed when Jake Pitler would walk off the
field in the seventh inning of a game, when it got dark because it was Yom
Kippur. She would say, "That's a good Jewish man."

> —Jack Newfield, journalist, recalling the 1940s when Jake Pitler, the first base
> coach, became the Brooklyn Dodgers' Jewish presence, quoted in *Bums* by
> Peter Golenbock (1984)

Once Pete Hamill and I were having dinner and . . . I said to Pete, "Let's
try an experiment. You write on your napkin the names of the three worst
human beings who ever lived, and I will write the three worst, and we'll compare." Each of us wrote down the same three names and in the same order:
Hitler, Stalin, Walter O'Malley.

> —Jack Newfield, quoted in *Bums* by Peter Golenbock (1984)

It seems to me that the very idea of the World Series, and the All-Star game,
is that they are special things, played at a special time, and if you're working,
you plan if you can go late to lunch so you can get a couple of innings in, or
you have a radio hidden somewhere, or the messengers bring the word in.

> —Joel Oppenheimer, poet, columnist, and ardent fan of the New York Mets,
> *The Wrong Season* (1973)

One of the loveliest ploys I've heard about was Fischer, who long ago converted from Judaism, showing up in Spassky's room wearing a yarmulke, because
he had heard that the Russians wouldn't let Spassky wear one in public.

> —Joel Oppenheimer, recalling the 1972 World Championship Chess Tour-
> nament between Bobby Fischer of the U.S. and Boris Spassky of the Soviet
> Union, *The Wrong Season* (1973)

On Tuesday, September 5, the Olympics finally died in the blood of seventeen people. I would not have written that line that day, but now, some time
after, it seems clearer and clearer that this is precisely what happened—even if
there are new games at Montreal.

—Joel Oppenheimer, recalling the 1972 terrorist attack in the Olympic Village in Munich against Israeli athletes, *The Wrong Season* (1973)

They tell me Jack was not a gentle man; did they expect Ernie Banks smiling all day long? It takes a long time to enjoy what you are fighting to hold onto—and I mean no disrespect to Banks, it's just that I think by now we don't call superstars "nigger." In 1947 we did.

> —Joel Oppenheimer, recalling baseball player Jackie Robinson, *The Wrong Season* (1973)

In an America so divided between black and white, between insured and uninsured, between those who've returned to Jesus and those who haven't, between those who want the air clear and those who want to live free and die free, between those who only feel safe when a gun is near and those who prefer to carry wallets in their inside pockets, it's a good thing we have the same heroes.

> —Anne Roiphe, novelist and essayist, "New Yorker's Diary," *New York Observer*, August 28, 1995

So the little boys at the table with the baseball cards are learning boy talk, the common conversation of men on trains, in elevators, in schoolyards. They are being initiated into an America where everyone knows that Tom Landry was the head coach of the Dallas Cowboys and we all start out dreaming of playing in the majors.

> —Anne Roiphe, "New Yorker's Diary," *New York Observer*, August 28, 1995

We came to say to all the world, "Here we are, you have to remember this."

> —Oshrat Romano, daughter of an Israeli athlete slain at the 1972 Munich Olympics, who attended the 1996 Atlanta Olympic Games along with thirteen other children of the slain athletes, quoted in the *Baltimore Jewish Times*, July 26, 1996

To see him climb in the ring sporting the six-pointed Jewish star on his fighting trunks was to anticipate sweet revenge for all the bloody noses, split lips, and mocking laughter at pale little Jewish boys who had run the neighborhood gauntlet.

> —Budd Schulberg, novelist and screenwriter, "The Great Benny Leonard," *Ring*, May 1980

In the twelfth inning, Boston's catcher, Carlton Fisk, hit a home run and Boston won the game. The series would go to a seventh game, and we—that is, Boston, and I—were still in it. At the time it was the most important thing in the world and that moment remains something I will never forget. . . . Now I was a baseball fan. . . . It wasn't that I converted, but rather that I returned to baseball.

> —Howard Senzel, author, describing the sixth game of the 1975 World Series between the Boston Red Sox and the Cincinnati Reds, *Baseball and the Cold War* (1977)

In the sense that the self is the sum total of all experience, these little baseball memories have the same weight in determining who I am as, say, the answers to: Where were you when the lights went out in New York City? When John Kennedy was shot? During the Cuban Missile Crisis? Yuri Gagarin's space flight? Or any of what the papers call "the happenings and events that made today history"?

> —Howard Senzel, *Baseball and the Cold War* (1977)

The papers knew more about baseball than anyone. When it came to politics, the papers were both ignorant and given to telling lies. They deliberately contorted themselves to see every event through the eyes of the richest people in town. . . . Accuracy in the sports page was always essential; elsewhere in the paper it was not.

> —Howard Senzel, *Baseball and the Cold War* (1977)

At first he was going to sue me. He didn't really know whether it was making fun of him or not. . . . His point was, "Why are they saying, 'Where have you gone Joe DiMaggio . . .' I'm doing a Mr. Coffee commercial, I'm very much here. . . .'" He obviously hadn't begun to think of himself as a metaphor.

> —Paul Simon, singer and songwriter, commenting on Joe DiMaggio's reaction to appearing in the lyrics to Simon's 1968 song "Mrs. Robinson," interviewed by Ed Bradley on CBS-TV's *60 Minutes*, 1995

The perception that we [Jews] are exclusively scholars is totally blown out of proportion. I'm not the exception to the rule. I'm not a freak.

> —Mark Spitz, winner of nine Olympic gold medals in swimming, quoted in *Jerusalem Report*, July 15, 1993

Always remember something. At the beginning of the 1980s, we were at the bottom of the food chain. You heard three things about our league: too rich, too black, too much drugs. One thing we never lose sight of around here is how far we've come in a relatively short time.

> —David Stern, commissioner of the National Basketball Association, reflecting

on the popularity of pro basketball, quoted in "Air Stern" by Mike Lupica,
Esquire, December 1995

Understand one thing. Nothing happens without the Game. We can talk
about labor relations and relationships with owners and between the teams, and
marketing and globalization. But we've also got the best game. Everything we
do emanates from that.

> —David Stern, quoted in "Air Stern" by Mike Lupica, *Esquire*, December
> 1995

When basketball is spoken, no translation is needed. It has become an
independent international language.

> —David Stern, quoted in *The NBA at 50*, edited by Mark Vancil (1996)

Throwing [Bob] Cousy out of the Boston Garden is like telling the Pope
he's got to leave Rome. Cousy's smiling, and he got his jacket and walks out.
The place goes wild. . . . We need extra police to get out of there. It was a hell
of a debut. But you know what? I earned Cousy's respect. And I didn't mind
the jeering—that's what you call recognition.

> —Earl Strom, "dean" of the National Basketball Association referees, recalling
> his first NBA season as referee at a Boston Celtics game, quoted in "The
> Right Call" by Jeff Coplan, *The New Yorker*, October 1, 1990

Some of the best calls are the ones you don't make.

> —Earl Strom, quoted in "The Right Call" by Jeff Coplan, *The New Yorker*,
> October 1, 1990

A crucial call had to be made, and damn the crowd.

> —Earl Strom, recalling a championship-round game between the Portland
> Trailblazers and the champion Detroit Pistons when he made the last call
> of his career, "The Right Call" by Jeff Coplan, *The New Yorker*, October
> 1, 1990

He was more impressed with that than with my getting the Nobel Prize.
So of course, I accepted.

> —Elie Wiesel, author and Nobel laureate, recalling his son's reaction to his
> being asked by the baseball commissioner to throw out the first ball in a
> 1986 World Series game between the New York Mets and the Boston Red
> Sox, "Is Elie Wiesel Happy?" by Yosef I. Abramowitz, *Moment*, February
> 1994

I don't think anybody who covered Ali ever stops thinking about him.

— Vic Ziegel, sportswriter, recalling Muhammad Ali, quoted in *Muhammad Ali: His Life and Times* by Thomas Hauser (1991)

Anti-Semitism didn't kill the Jews in basketball, just small hands.

— Sidney Zion, journalist, *New York Daily News*, May 14, 1996

❖ SUFFERING ❖

What an unfortunate creature God put together that can learn only through unbearable pain.

— Howard Fast, author, *Being Red: A Memoir* (1990)

When a disaster befalls us, we have the option to withdraw or to attempt to transform the experience into a teacher for ourselves, our friends, our families, and our communities. Our personal disaster may not only be our gift, it may sometimes be another's gift as well. It is our obligation to discover these gifts and give them to others.

— Debbie Friedman, composer, liturgist, and performer, "Shattered and Whole" in *Lifecycles, Volume 2*, edited by Rabbi Debra Orenstein and Rabbi Jane Litman (1997)

If God is testing us, He must know by now that many of us fail the test. If He is only giving us burdens we can bear, I have seen him miscalculate far too often.

— Rabbi Harold S. Kushner, author and rabbi of Temple Israel in Natick, Mass., *When Bad Things Happen to Good People* (1981)

You know, I changed my life to become closer to God. And then my son is tortured, dying. I didn't, I still don't understand it. I don't understand how that happens.

— Marc Weiner, comedian and children's puppeteer, talking about his son's severe birth defects (the boy died before he turned five), quoted in "Of God and Weinerville" by Ellen Pall, *The New York Times Magazine*, December 10, 1995

❖ SYNAGOGUES ❖

(see also Rabbis)

I stopped going even to High Holidays when I was in the seventh grade because it was apparent to me that the mink coat was more important than the service—who had the biggest diamond, who had the most stuff.

> —Unidentified single Jewish woman, quoted in "Voices for Change: Future Directions for American Jewish Women," report of the National Commission on American Jewish Women, November 1995

Beyond passivity, there is often boredom at the heart of our service; with Hebrew a foreign language to many Jews, the Humash [Five Books of Moses] remains a closed book (literally and figuratively). Torah reading time is often a period to attend to personal needs or to schmooze with a friend or relative. Yet, when the Torah reading intersects with a key life cycle moment (naming a baby, celebrating an aufruf, becoming a bar or bat mitzvah), the act of hearing these words read is the most powerful and inexpressible Jewish moment for those same Jews who were, but a moment ago, bored by the same practice.

> —Rabbi Bradley Shavit Artson, rabbi of Congregation Eilat in Mission Viejo, Calif., *Sh'ma*, May 12, 1995

The effect America has had on our religious perspective is that of looking through an enormous magnifying glass over a single word on a printed page, thereby distorting its true proportion. . . . Imagine a long list of all the concepts, practices, and institutions that constitute Orthodox Judaism in the modern age. We in America have laid a great magnifying glass over the word "shul" [synagogue].

> —Joshua Berman, "Balancing the Bimah: The Diaspora Struggle of the Orthodox Feminist," *Midstream*, August/September 1990

Stained souls need cleansing and failed ambitions need some consolation. Missed opportunities and awkward foul-ups need second chances; spirits in disrepair need some time to rest and recuperate. We need each other. That's what synagogue (temple, shul, whatever you call it) is really all about.

> —Ronald A. Brauner, president of the Foundation for Jewish Studies and professor of Judaic studies, "From the Ordinary to the Extraordinary" in *Being Jewish in a Gentile World* (1995)

The pulpit is a most powerful instrument, both because of what the rabbi can do with it and because of what it can do to the rabbi.

—Rabbi Reuven Bulka, congregational rabbi and founding editor of the *Journal of Psychology and Judaism* quoted in *The Rabbinate as Calling and Vocation: Models of Rabbinic Leadership*, edited by Rabbi Basil Herring (1991)

The hollowness in the heartland of American Jewish life can't simply be laid, in self-righteous indignation, at the feet of congregants who don't see the inside of a shul from one fall to the next. In the year 5755, despite the fact that the materialism and spiritual morbidity of middle-class congregational Judaism has been well-documented . . . and chronicled memorably in American-Jewish fiction, we continue to elevate members of our community for the wrong reasons, thereby driving away untold numbers of the young of my generation and now, I fear, the next, from a Judaism thus defined.

—Alice Chasen, executive editor of *Tikkun,* "Shul and Spirit," *Tikkun,* November/December 1994

I don't lead a perfect Jewish life by any means, but the shul has always been there. It's just a part of my life. To lose it would be just like losing a member of my family—I can't put it any other way.

—Joe Erber, an auxiliary police officer who is acting rabbi of Ahavath Rayim Synagogue in Greenwood, Miss., talking about the dwindling Jewish community, in *Holding On: Dreamers, Visionaries, Eccentrics and Other American Heroes* by David Isay, photographs by Harvey Wang (1995)

[Some] synagogues are like religious 7-11s. When American Jews get a craving for something sweet and gooey—a bar or bat mitzvah, a wedding, a baby-naming—they drop in, plunk down their money, savor their choice, and then drive away, until the craving overcomes them again. The "members" of such synagogues are essentially nothing more than consumers. . . . And the rabbi? He or she takes the role of counter help whose job it is to keep the individual customers satisfied so they keep coming back to this particular franchise outlet rather to that other religious Stop 'N Shop down the street.

—Rabbi Michael Goldberg, author, *Why Should Jews Survive? Looking Past the Holocaust Toward a Jewish Future* (1995)

What does being a "family congregation" mean? Does it mean that no single, divorced or widowed Jews are welcome? . . . Or does it mean that if I go bankrupt or my health insurance runs out, the congregation will be that place where, in Robert Frost's words, "when you go there, they have to take you in"?

—Rabbi Michael Goldberg, *Why Should Jews Survive? Looking Past the Holocaust Toward a Jewish Future* (1995)

The Jewish family formerly from Brooklyn, where it rarely entered through temple or synagogue doors, has become a more dependable regular at Sabbath services and absorbed in the men's club and sisterhood as well—now that it lives in Rockville Center [a Long Island suburb].

—Philip M. Klutznick, lawyer, public official, and national president of B'nai B'rith, *No Easy Answers* (1961)

When someone says to me, "I tried to get involved in your synagogue, but I found it to be full of petty, small-minded hypocrites," I can usually resist the temptation to tell him, "That's all right, there's always room for one more." What I say instead is, "A synagogue that admitted only saints would be like a hospital that admitted only healthy people. It would be a lot easier to run, and a more pleasant place to be, but I'm not sure we would be doing the job we are here to do."

—Rabbi Harold S. Kushner, author and rabbi emeritus of Temple Israel in Natick, Mass., *Who Needs God* (1989)

There is much too much emphasis on numbers. The effectiveness of the synagogue is measured by the size of the membership, attendance at services. The rabbi's effectiveness, too, is judged largely by the number of worshipers he attracts. These are the criteria of rabbinic leadership about which synagogue boards are concerned. Very little is said about the number of people who have become committed Jews and whose lives have been touched by the message of Judaism, who have been transformed as a result of synagogue affiliation.

—Sol Landau, author, *Length of Our Days: Focus on Judaism and the Personal Life* (1961)

A prominent Christian lawyer of another city has told me that he entered this building at the beginning of a service on Sunday morning and did not discover that he was in a synagogue until a chance remark of the preacher betrayed it.

—Rabbi Judah L. Magnes, speaking to his reform congregation, Temple Emanu-El, 1911, quoted in *A History of the Jews* by Paul Johnson (1987)

Reading Kissinger's memoirs, I learned the basics of shuttle diplomacy. The first thing Kissinger did was, before getting both parties to sit down together in the same room, he had to get them to agree that a room is a room. In this case I had to find out whether there was anything that all the parties would agree upon.

—Moishe Sacks, elderly baker and leader of the congregation of the Intervale Jewish Center in the South Bronx, discussing how to handle different factions within the congregation, quoted in *The Miracle of Intervale Avenue* by Jack Kugelmass (1996)

Far from being an island of sanity amidst the raging passions, or a refuge from the suspicions and jealousies and downright vendettas that checker Jewish existence, synagogues all too often become the arena, the battleground, of individual and collective madness.

—Rabbi Andre Unger of Temple Emmanuel in Woodcliff Lake, N.J., author and lecturer, "The Politics of Piety," *Jewish Spectator*, Spring/Summer 1989

❖ TELEVISION ❖

(see also Entertainment)

I plead guilty to the stridency. But when you have 90 seconds to relay the history of the universe and the destiny of our world, you have to talk fast.

> —Dr. Martin Abend, professor of political geography, recalling his years (1960s–1970s) as a New York City television commentator who often attacked liberals, quoted in "The Raging Bull of Channel 5," *New York*, January 14, 1991

A quiz-show investigation without [Charles] Van Doren is like Hamlet without anyone playing Hamlet.

> —Felix Frankfurter, Supreme Court justice, offering advice to his former law clerk, Richard Goodwin, who was an investigator for the congressional committee looking into the quiz show scandals, 1959, quoted in *The Fifties* by David Halberstam (1993)

You can't do the Mideast in two and a half minutes, no matter how good you are. The pictures are so strong, so powerful, that there is no other side.

> —Fred Friendly, former president of CBS News, quoted in *Israel in Media-land*, compiled and edited by Eliyahu Tal (1988)

All public reality's a script, and anybody can write the script the way he wants. . . . Whoever controls the language, the images, controls the race. Power all boils down to whether [U.S. Secretary of Defense Robert] McNamara gets up on the right side of the bed. And who's McNamara anyway? He's a lot of TV dots.

—Allen Ginsberg, poet, quoted in *Allen Ginsberg in America* by Jane Kramer (1968)

Film was so powerful that a reporter was well advised to get out of the way and let the pictures do the talking. . . . The images were so forceful that they told their own truths and needed virtually no narration.

—David Halberstam, journalist and author, commenting on the impact of television news on reporting the story of the confrontation at Central High School in Little Rock, Ark., *The Fifties* (1957)

To me the important thing about Charles Van Doren is it shows what television could do; that it could take overnight someone who had never been on television, no one knew his name, and within two weeks make him into a national hero, someone who could run for the presidency. . . . They did it, and brought Van Doren out and the whole nation fell in love with him.

—David Halberstam, reflecting on the quiz show scandals in the 1950s and the popularity of contestant Charles Van Doren, *Booknotes* interview with Brian Lamb, C-SPAN, July 11, 1993

Little Rock was, before Vietnam, our first great television battleground. It was not that what we were seeing was new; it was the seeing itself.

—David Halberstam, commenting on the historic confrontation in which white mobs assaulted nine black teenagers trying to enroll in Central High School in Little Rock, Ark., 1957, "And Now, Live From Little Rock," *Newsweek*, September 29, 1997

I liked the goyim [gentiles] on television. They seemed decent, familiar, human people: people like Ricky Ricardo, the handsome husband on "I Love Lucy," who reminded me of my father because he too spoke an eccentric English and came from Cuba.

—Yossi Klein Halevi, Israeli journalist and author, whose father was a survivor of the Holocaust who immigrated to the United States, *Memoirs of a Jewish Extremist* (1995)

If I hear a viewer at home saying to his wife, "Hey, Mildred, you got any idea what these guys are talking about?" then we're off track.

—Don Hewitt, creator and executive producer of the CBS television show *60 Minutes*, quoted in *The New York Times*, May 19, 1997

I do not inhabit the America I see on television. Guns, crime, murder, incest, lust—these are not my neighbors. And even when the crime figures are going down, television, because of its instant magnification of reality, offers up a constant portrait of America that does not at all resemble the America we live in.

> —Bernard Kalb, former foreign correspondent for CBS, NBC, and *The New York Times*, speaking at a Columbia Graduate School of Journalism awards ceremony, quoted in *Columbia Journalism Review*, March/April 1995

You do have a certain name ID with .01 percent of the American people. This morning I got into a cab and the driver, some right-wing immigrant, said, "Mr. Kristol, it's really great to have you in my cab." You can see why Pat Buchanan thinks he can run for president. You go through the airport and someone says, "You were great on *Crossfire*" and you say, Hey, I'm famous. You can deceive yourself that you really have influence because you're on television, when all you're doing is being a pundit. You're like one of those guys on Hollywood Squares.

> —Irving Kristol, social critic, commenting on the effect of appearing on television talk shows, quoted in *Hot Air: All Talk All the Time* by Howard Kurtz (1996)

I wake up every morning of my life, read the newspapers and think, oh God, why aren't we on the air now . . . to comment about all of this, to get some of the humor that exists in everything in life out of all of this that is now so seriously and agitatedly considered.

> —Norman Lear, television producer, *Straight Talk with Roger Ailes*, America's Talking Cable network, October 9, 1995

Basically, America is so bottom line, short-term oriented, certainly network television is; the name of the game is "Give me a hit at 8:30 Tuesday night" and every other value is damned.

> —Norman Lear, *Straight Talk with Roger Ailes*, America's Talking Cable network, October 9, 1995

Family hour is dead. The safe haven we once counted on has now turned into a broadcast bordello.

> —Joseph I. Lieberman, U.S. Senator (D-Conn.), speaking at a Senate hearing regarding television network broadcasting, quoted in *Insight*, June 16, 1997

The conscious eye of the nation would be there to witness this event. By television they would witness it. That would be an experience like getting conceived in a test tube.

> —Norman Mailer, novelist, anticipating the first moon landing, *Of a Fire on the Moon* (1969)

On the one hand we're told that an hour of television programming does nothing to shape the sentiments of the public and on the other we're asked to believe that the brief spots that interrupt this program are powerful enough to change perceptions of anything from canned goods to candidates.

> —Michael Medved, author and media commentator, reflecting on the hypocrisy of network executives of commercial television, *Hollywood vs. America* (1992)

News meant interviewing people with whom you had no appointment, but rather catching them on the run—occasionally as they fled a burning building. News meant emergencies, and in emergencies, you don't think; you do. And you do fast. Slapping a news story together, getting it edited, written and ready for air was in itself an emergency. When you did that you had to skip a lot of things: things like digesting the material; mulling it over; rethinking a point; rewriting; expanding; pondering.

> —Betty Rollin, journalist, reflecting on being a local television reporter, 1972, *Am I Getting Paid for This?* (1982)

My impression is that policy-makers utilize print journalism primarily as a source of background information and ideas. Television, on the other hand, makes them aware of the issues to which they must react immediately whether they want to or not.

> —Lionel Rosenblatt, president of Refugees International, an advocacy organization on behalf of refugees and displaced persons around the world, "The Media and the Refugee" in *From Massacres to Genocide: The Media, Public Policy, and Humanitarian Crises*, edited by Robert I. Rotberg and Thomas G. Weiss (1996)

When I first started to bring humor to the subject of money, I was told by the television experts that I was very foolish to try this, because money supposedly isn't funny. But I realized early on that if you were going to get people interested in a show like this, you'd have to do it with a little flair.

> —Louis Rukeyser, host of television show *Wall Street Week*, celebrating the 25th anniversary of the show, quoted in *USAir Magazine*, July 1996

Now we add radio sight to sound. It is with a feeling of humbleness that I come to the moment of announcing the birth in this country of a new art so important in its implications that it is bound to affect all society. It is an art which shines like a torch in a troubled world. It is a creative force which we must learn to utilize for the benefit of all mankind.

> —David Sarnoff, business executive and pioneer in the broadcasting industry, speaking at the opening of the New York World's Fair in April 1939 to

announce the beginning of regular television service by NBC, quoted in
Sarnoff: An American Success by Carl Dreher (1977)

My name is Jerry Seinfeld and I am a bad actor. But I think I have proven
convincingly that you can do very well when you surround yourself with spectacular talent.

> —Jerry Seinfeld, comedian, speaking at the Screen Actors Guild award cere-
> mony, quoted in *US*, May 1997

Although the potential force of the medium of television is hardly as overwhelming as atomic energy, the two have one dread and one power in common:
they leave no cave for privacy. There is no escape from either the pursuing
bomb or the omnipresent television. The bomb and television can ferret out
the most singular hermit and will reach into the most outlandishly rugged ter-
rain. . . . The coincidence of their simultaneous appearance in human history
foreshadows an ominous cooperation between the atom and television, incipient
partners in war and propaganda.

> —Solomon Simonson, actor, public radio broadcaster, television producer and
> director, rabbi, lawyer, and professor of communications, *Crisis in TV* (1966)

I would tell you that the suicide rate in this country, if it weren't for
TV, would be higher. We keep saying that our company's motto is we do
not make anything for Beverly Hills or the Bel Air circuit. We make it for
people out there. . . . TV is so much closer to them than the movies. You're
in your home watching it. You can take any big TV star and have him walk
down the street with four movie stars and see where the people run to.
They'll run to that TV star. He's there every week for them. He's a member
of the family.

> —Aaron Spelling, television producer of *Mod Squad, Dynasty, Melrose Place,
> Charlie's Angels, Love Boat, Fantasy Island,* and other shows, quoted in *US,*
> December 1996

What is being lost is the magic of the word. I am not an image person.
Imagery belongs to another civilization: the caveman. Caveman couldn't express
himself so he put images on walls.

> —Elie Wiesel, Nobel laureate and author, quoted in the *Chicago Tribune,*
> November 26, 1995

❖ Terrorism ❖

I used to need bodyguards to protect me from Arab terrorists. Now, I need bodyguards when I go to a synagogue.

> —Colette Avital, Israeli consul general in New York, quoted in *The New York Times*, November 13, 1995

One good thing about America is that someone sworn to destroy me in the Middle East can talk to me in a symposium here.

> —David Burns, former student at the University of South Florida, where Ramadan Abdullah Shallah taught before being named head of the terrorist group Islamic Jihad, quoted in *The Jewish Week*, November 13, 1995

Terror or no terror, the Israeli people will still be around. . . . It won't be Zionist fervor that keeps them here, but the same thing that keeps Canadians in Canada and Belgians in Belgium—it's home.

> —Larry Derfner, journalist, "Future Shock," *The Jewish Week*, July 7, 1995

I cannot consider the individual rights of a Palestinian detainee in an Israeli jail as a separate issue from protecting the lives of bus passengers. Nor do I have the luxury of examining this question from an abstract moral perspective. If applying limited physical pressure to a suspected terrorist can spare even one parent the pain of losing a son or a daughter, I am all for it. In the meantime, I pray that the conditions that give rise to the need for such methods will speedily come to an end.

> —Stephen Flatow, attorney from New Jersey whose daughter Alisa was killed by an Islamic Jihad suicide bomber on a bus in Israel in 1995, quoted in *The New York Times*, May 19, 1997

Even though there may be a conspiracy of evil in this world, there is here and in this world a conspiracy of goodness that will overcome.

> —Rabbi Marc Gellman, rabbi of Temple Beth Torah in Dix Hills, Long Island, speaking at a memorial service on Fire Island, L.I., attended by more than six hundred family members of the two hundred thirty people killed in an explosion on TWA Flight 800 (at the time it was believed to be the result of terrorism), quoted in *The Jewish Week*, July 26, 1996

We've lost the capacity for fear in the kind of world we live in today.

> —Victor Gerwitz, Lubavitcher Jew from Crown Heights who emigrated from

Argentina, quoted in "New York Jews Warier of Terrorism," *The New York Times*, July 30, 1994

Before the Oslo process, the apologists for terror said there was terror because there was no peace process. During the Oslo process, the explanation for terror was that it was the work of extremists who wanted to stop the process. So now what do they say? . . . The mind is left with the horrible conclusion that this type of terror occurs no matter what anyone does — a thought that is excruciatingly difficult to deal with.

> —Herb Keinon, Israeli columnist, writing after thirteen people were killed in a terrorist blast in Jerusalem's Mahaneh Yehuda market, *Jerusalem Post*, July 21, 1997

I am not claiming there's a cover-up. But to go after someone who kills Jews is not something [for officials] to get enthusiastic about.

> —Sergio Kiernan, Argentine journalist, referring to the July 14, 1994, bomb in Buenos Aires that destroyed the site of the Argentine Israelite Mutual Aid Association, quoted in the *Jerusalem Post*, July 21, 1995 (Eighty-six people died and one hundred twenty were wounded in the worst attack on Jews in the Diaspora since World War II.)

Death may be around any corner in Israel.

> —Anthony Lewis, columnist for *The New York Times*, reprinted in *The Dallas Morning News*, September 6, 1997

Israel has mourned her Olympic loss alone for 24 years. We now hope that the rest of the Olympic community will join us in recognizing the tremendous loss.

> —Aryeh Mekel, Israel consul general in Atlanta, commenting about a speaking tour in the American South by relatives of the eleven athletes killed at the 1972 Munich Olympic Games at the time of the 1996 Olympics in Atlanta, quoted in *Jerusalem Report*, August 8, 1996

You all know that I am not religious and I often have sharp opinions regarding religion, but I hope that in your prayers on Friday night you include a prayer for the protection of the State of Israel and for its citizens. . . . We are scared.

> —Tal Muscal, student at George Washington University spending his junior year at Hebrew University, writing via e-mail to friends in the U.S. during a series of suicide bombings in Israel, quoted in *The Washington Post*, March 9, 1996

Another Sunday morning, another Bus 18. . . . I truly beg of you, please make sure that all of GW, that all of Washington, knows what is going on here—if not for the sake of showing a presence, then for the sake of mourning.

> —Tal Muscal, quoted in *The Washington Post*, March 9, 1996

Fighting terror is not a "policy option"; it is a necessity for the survival of our democratic society and our freedoms.

> —Benjamin Netanyahu, leader of the Likud party, *Fighting Terrorism: How Democracies Can Defeat Domestic and International Terrorism* (1995)

There was a city long ago that experienced destruction, despair and desolation. . . . One city came back from desolation more beautiful, more holy, more together than ever before. And the name of that city was Jerusalem. And so our city, our community, our Oklahoma City will come back in greater closeness, with greater beauty, with greater love.

> —Rabbi David Packman, remarks at the prayer service for the victims of the 1995 Oklahoma City bombings, CNN live broadcast, April 23, 1995

This killer emerged from a small and limited political framework. He grew up in a swamp whose roots are overseas.

> —Yitzhak Rabin, Israeli prime minister, speaking to the Knesset, February 28, 1994, after Dr. Baruch Goldstein committed the massacre of Muslims at prayer in Hebron's Tomb of the Patriarchs, quoted in *Newsweek*, March 14, 1994

I stand before the world as an Israeli and as a Jew, with my head hung in shame. Never in my worst dreams did I imagine myself addressing you in such circumstances.

> —Yitzhak Rabin, speaking to the Knesset, February 28, 1994, quoted in *The Economist*, March 5, 1994

It is impossible to question a terrorist over a cup of coffee.

> —Yitzhak Rabin, speaking at a meeting at which an Israeli ministerial committee rejected his request to grant extended interrogation powers to the Shin Bet, Israel's domestic security service, quoted in *Jewish Telegraphic Agency*, August 7, 1995

Closure surely is a balm for grief, and we can only hope that the mutilated families will find it. But if the rest of us are now lulled into complacency by a well-conducted trial's fair outcome, that's not closure—it's amnesia. Timothy McVeigh didn't come from nowhere.

> —Frank Rich, columnist, writing after Timothy McVeigh was convicted for

murder in the 1995 terrorist blast in Oklahoma City, *The New York Times*, June 5, 1997

We are all in this together.

> —Geraldo Rivera, television journalist, speaking as master of ceremonies of the 25th anniversary commemoration of the May 30, 1972, terrorist attack by the Japanese Red Army at Lod Airport which left twenty-five dead, among them fifteen Puerto Rican Christian pilgrims and twelve Israelis, quoted in *The Jewish Week*, July 11, 1997

In those early United Nations years there was a feeling of safety, would you believe it. Nobody dreamt that there might be a bomb in the United Nations garage, a killer in the corridor or a sniper in the hotel across the street. Now, any important delegate who walks around without armed guards is not brave but a fool. Terrorism has stolen the life from many diplomats and the freedom of movement, contact and mind from the others.

> —A. M. Rosenthal, columnist, "The U.N. at Fifty," *The New York Times*, October 22, 1995

I can close my eyes and see the bus coming. The door opens and I get on. I hope I get on. You just do it. It's like a phone call you don't want to make. You dial the phone. You say "Hello" and then you are doing it. You get on the bus.

> —Ayalah Scher, seventeen-year-old New York City student planning to spend her high school senior year in Israel, speaking after the funeral services for a schoolmate killed in the bombing of a bus in Israel, quoted in *New York Daily News*, March 3, 1996

We are angry and ashamed. For Baruch Goldstein was one of ours.

> —Hershel Shanks, editor, reflecting on the 1994 mass killing, "Massacre at Hebron," *Moment*, April 1994

We have no doubt that many of the victims hated us. We have no doubt that some of them would have murdered us if they had had the chance. But that is beside the point. This is not how you should die and we are ashamed that it has been at the hands of one of ours. More than that, we understand the rage of the families and survivors. We too would be enraged.

> —Hershel Shanks, "Massacre at Hebron," *Moment*, April 1994

I was crying before the plane landed, wondering, is my kid on that bus? But then later, I was listening to the radio. In 10 minutes, I heard about three people shot to death in Brooklyn . . . a murder suicide in the Bronx, this lunatic

Leary who blew up the subway . . . this other guy who killed a woman and stole her earrings . . . and I should be worried about sending my kid to Israel? . . . If you die here, you die alone. If you die in Israel, you belong to the country.

> —Mrs. Stone, mother of Chaim Stone of Monsey, N.Y., whose son returned to the U.S. on the day of the bus bombing in Israel, quoted in the *New York Daily News*, March 3, 1996

❖ THEATER ❖

(see also Arts, Writing)

By what right can Mr. Levin dictate to a parent how his daughter shall be presented to the world. . . . Mr. Levin's attacks are only undignified and irritating. He would please us far more by . . . leaving poor Anne Frank to develop into whatever sort of symbol she can.

> —Philip Gillon, columnist, commenting on the disagreement between writer Meyer Levin and Otto Frank (Anne's father) over the stage production of *The Diary of Anne Frank, Jerusalem Post*, April 4, 1960

The actual psychological effect of omitting such a passionate Jewish speech from the stage . . . who can imagine it? The attitude is that the Jew would assimilate and disappear. To take out "Jewish suffering" and put in "all people suffer" is to equalize the Holocaust with any kind of disaster. If you do this, you unhook the search for meaning, you unhook the wrong to the Jews. . . . And you end up with what they're using now. The bottom line reads: "The Jews did worse to the Arabs in Palestine than the Nazis ever did to the Jews." It's been stated that way by any number of leaders in the United Nations.

> —Meyer Levin, writer, who was involved in a decades-long disupte over whether his material was plagiarized for the stage production of *The Diary of Anne Frank*, speaking to reporter Ira Berkow in 1976, on the omission of specific reference to Jews in Anne Frank's lines, quoted in *An Obsession With Anne Frank* by Lawrence Graver (1995)

The big problem with Fiddler was selling it. It was felt to have limited appeal. I've been quoted as having had a producer say to me: "I like it very much, but what do I do when I run out of Hadassah benefits?"

> —Sheldon Harnick, lyricist who, with composer Jerry Bock, created the musical score for the Broadway show *Fiddler on the Roof,* quoted in *Lifestyles*, New Year 1998

I cannot pretend that I was without talent, but such gifts as I possessed were raw and undisciplined. It was one thing to have a flair for playwriting or even a ready wit for dialogue. It is quite another to apply these gifts in the strict and demanding terms of a fully articulated play so that they emerge with explicitness, precision, and form. All this and a great deal more I learned from George Kaufman. And if it is true that no more eager disciple ever sat at the feet of a teacher, it is equally true that no disciple was ever treated with more infinite patience and understanding.

> —Moss Hart, playwright, recalling his collaboration with playwright George Kaufman on Hart's *Once in a Lifetime*, 1930, *Act One* (1960)

The thing that's hardest about a play is that it has only so many pages, so many hours of time, and you have to find a way of making people sit there, surrounded by all the other people in the audience, and lose themselves.

> —Larry Kramer, playwright, quoted in *Singular Voices: Conversations With Americans Who Make a Difference* by Barbaralee Diamonstein (1997)

If I know the life of the character I am doing, I can use my inventiveness to eliminate or supplement an element of the character, and so create a spontaneity every night, every performance.

> —Zero Mostel, actor, quoted in *Zero Mostel: A Biography* by Jared Brown (1989)

I say to myself, "Will Sholem Aleichem like what I'm doing?"

> —Zero Mostel, stating his standard for performing as Tevye in *Fiddler on the Roof*, quoted in *Zero Mostel: A Biography* by Jared Brown (1989)

Perhaps if I had been Louis Picon's son I would have had a classical education and been a scholar. Instead, as the wardrobe mistress' daughter, I got a love of the stage because there I could make believe I was all the things I could never be in real life.

> —Molly Picon, actress in Yiddish theater, *Molly!* (1980)

Of course, acting paid a person well—when a person had a job. But you could no more count on getting an acting job than you could count on a homer in the bottom of the ninth.

> —Betty Rollin, journalist, *Am I Getting Paid for This?* (1982)

We always ask ourselves when we evaluate a play, are the Jews going to come and are the gays going to come. Because without them we won't have a show.

—Jeffrey Seller, producer of the musical *Rent*, quoted in "The Man Who Believed in Rent" by Curt Schleier, *The Jewish Week*, July 11, 1997

If politics are all about spin and imagery, then maybe plays are all about the truth.

—Wendy Wasserstein, playwright, quoted in "Of Plays About Politics and Politicians at Play," a conversation with Christopher Durang in *The New York Times*, October 6, 1996

❖ TRIAL OF O. J. SIMPSON ❖

(see also Fame and Celebrity, Law)

I'm not paid for my opinions. I'm hired to be an advocate.

—Alan M. Dershowitz, law professor, appellate lawyer, activist, author, and member of Simpson's defense team (who would have handled any appeals), responding to the question of whether he still thought that O. J. Simpson was innocent, quoted in *Boston*, November 1995

I have a policy of never participating in any victory celebration when my client has won if there is a victim. There have been two horribly murdered people, children without a mother. There is a man who spent almost a year and a half in prison. This is a case where there are victims. This is not a cause for joy. It is a tremendous relief that it is over.

—Alan M. Dershowitz, quoted in *The Washington Times*, October 4, 1995

I was deeply offended. To me the Holocaust stands alone as the most horrible human event in modern civilization. And with the Holocaust came Adolf Hitler, and to compare this man in any way to a rogue cop in my opinion was wrong.

—Robert L. Shapiro, defense attorney for Simpson, commenting on defense attorney Johnnie Cochran's final argument in which he compared a key prosecution witness, retired police detective Mark Fuhrman, to Adolf Hitler, quoted in *The Washington Times*, October 4, 1995 (following Simpson acquittal)

The Jewish outrage at a black man making reference to Hitler seemed a bit overdone, especially since many Jews seem to make far more outrageous

Hitler comparisons with far less criticism. Ben Gurion compared Begin to Hitler. Several Israeli politicians and American rabbis have compared Rabin to Hitler.

> —Alan M. Dershowitz, "The Jewish Bigotry Unleashed by O. J.," *Jerusalem Report*, November 16, 1995

The fact is that Johnnie Cochran did not compare Mark Fuhrman to Hitler. He compared their views.

> —Alan M. Dershowitz, "The Jewish Bigotry Unleashed by O. J.," *Jerusalem Report*, November 16, 1995

For those who say that Hitler is proprietary to the Jews, he isn't.

> —Charles Lindner, a Jewish lawyer who helped defense attorney Johnnie Cochran fashion his closing argument, reported by Tom Tugend, *Jerusalem Post*, October 17, 1995

My position was always the same—that race would not and should not be part of this case. I was wrong. Not only did we play the race card, but we dealt it from the bottom of the deck.

> —Robert L. Shapiro, defense attorney for O. J. Simpson, quoted the day after the verdict of not guilty in the criminal trial in the *Chicago Tribune*, October 4, 1995

June 13, 1994, was the worst nightmare of my life. This is the second.

> —Fred Goldman, father of murder victim Ron Goldman (murdered on June 13, 1994), speaking after the jury acquitted Simpson of the charges of murder, quoted in *Newsweek*, October 16, 1995

We never caught up with the appetite of the audience.

> —Jeff Greenfield, television journalist and syndicated columnist, interviewed on the *Oprah Winfrey Show*, broadcast January 2, 1996

When one team has considerably more money than the other, the varsity ends up playing the junior varsity. That's been the black experience going to court.

> —Norman Mailer, author, "Black and White Justice," *New York*, October 16, 1995

It was an enormous achievement of civilization to transcend group identities and locate human dignity and responsibility in the individual. The regression to a race/class/gender mentality is yet further evidence of the de-moralization that afflicts our society—the demoralization that occurs when individuals are deprived of their moral character, their responsibility as individual moral agents.

—Gertrude Himmelfarb, author, quoted in *The Weekly Standard*, October 16, 1995

If we had God booked and O. J. was available, we'd move God.

—Larry King, radio and television talk show host, quoted in *Newsweek*, October 16, 1995

❖ TRUTH ❖

In an academic institution, truth must be a primary value. In making free speech the central issue in these cases, truth became irrelevant.

—Nathan Glazer, sociologist, "Levin, Jeffries, and the Fate of Academic Autonomy," *The Public Interest*, Summer 1995

Truth is highly subjective to people whose central experience is victimization: the details, the facts of any particular instance of oppression, don't matter to those who are sure of their oppression in general.

—Wendy Kaminer, author, *I'm Dysfunctional, You're Dysfunctional: The Recovery Movement and Other Self-Help Fashions* (1992)

Emotions are not tools of cognition. What you feel tells you nothing about the facts; it merely tells you something about your estimate of the facts.

—Ayn Rand, writer and philosopher, interview with Alvin Toffler in *Playboy*, March 1964

If there is such a thing as truth it is as intricate and hidden as a crown of feathers.

—Isaac Bashevis Singer, Yiddish writer, *A Crown of Feathers* (1970)

Truth can be found everywhere, even on the lips of drunkards, in the noisiest of taverns.

—Elie Wiesel, Nobel laureate and author, *Somewhere a Master* (1981)

❖ TWENTIETH CENTURY ❖

At eighty-two, I've lived through virtually the entire century. . . . In my life, more dreadful things occurred than at any other time in history. Worse than even the days of the Huns.

> —Isaiah Berlin, Oxford historian and philosopher, quoted in *At Century's End: Great Minds Reflect on Our Times* compiled from *New Perspectives Quarterly* edited by Nathan P. Gardels (1995)

The twentieth century ideals of America have been the ideals of the Jew for more than twenty centuries.

> —Louis D. Brandeis, attorney and judge, later appointed to the Supreme Court, "A Call to the Educated Jew," *Menorah Journal*, 1915

Nothing in my childhood prepared me for the violent and bewildering times in which I was to live and for the radical changes which have occurred in the human condition.

> —Walter Lippmann, journalist, from an unpublished autobiographical fragment, July 1, 1959, quoted in *Walter Lippmann and the American Century* by Ronald Steel (1980)

The century would seek to dominate nature as it had never been dominated, would attack the idea of war, poverty and natural catastrophe as never before. Yet the century was now attached to the idea that man must take his conception of life out to the stars. It was the most soul-destroying and apocalyptic of centuries.

> —Norman Mailer, novelist, *Of a Fire on the Moon* (1969)

Future historians will record that we of the 20th century had the intelligence to create a great civilization, but not the moral wisdom to preserve it.

> —Dr. Morris Mandel, columnist, *The Jewish Press*, June 6, 1997

In Poland, little more remains of the Jewish golden age than a fur hat in a museum. After a century of pogroms, poverty, purges, Nazis and Communists, whole Jewish populations have been reduced to small plaques nailed to stucco walls on the edge of town.

> —Jonathan Mark, journalist, "Poland Without Tears," *The Jewish Week*, May 13, 1994

The twentieth century is waning. . . . Our duty is, with renewed vigor, to enter it [the 21st century] wisely, having plumbed the meaning of our own experience—the experience of people who have endured the depths and witnessed the peaks of the twentieth century—and then to produce our own ethical will, a testament to what we seek to preserve and what we believe wants change, a testament we can then pass on to the new generations that follow ours.

—Albert Vorspan and Rabbi David Saperstein, leaders in the Reform movement, *Tough Choices: Jewish Perspectives on Social Justice* (1992)

❖ United Nations ❖

The U.N. vote to repeal its repugnant resolution equating Zionism with racism is a bit like Lady Macbeth washing her hands. It will take a lot more than scrubbing to remove the stain.

> —Douglas Bloomfield, columnist, writing after the U.N. General Assembly voted overwhelmingly to rescind the 1975 resolution equating Zionism with racism, *Jerusalem Post*, January 25, 1992

The U.N. Resolution [equating Zionism with racism] is an attack on a people, crafted into ideology . . . Bigotry is at its most dangerous when it is molded into an appealing package, and sold as something noble.

> —Sholom Comay, president of the American Jewish Committee, quoted in "Anti-Zionism: The Sophisticated Anti-Semitism" by Kenneth S. Stern, a publication of the American Jewish Committee, September 1990

Hitler would have felt at home on a number of occasions during this past year, listening to the proceeding of this forum.

> —Chaim Herzog, Israeli president, from his speech before the U.N. General Assembly during the debate of the "Zionism Is Racism" resolution, November 10, 1975 quoted in the *Jerusalem Post*, November 17, 1995 (At the conclusion of his remarks he demonstratively tore up the text of the resolution before the General Assembly.)

I do not come to this rostrum to defend the moral and historical values of the Jewish people. They do not need to be defended. They speak for themselves. They have given to mankind much of what is great and eternal. They have done for the spirit of man more than can readily be appreciated by a forum such as this one.

> —Chaim Herzog, from his speech before the U.N. General Assembly during the debate of the "Zionism Is Racism" resolution, quoted in the *Jerusalem Post*, November 17, 1995

I am mindful at this moment of the Jewish people throughout the world wherever they may be, be it in freedom or in slavery, whose prayers and thoughts are with me at this moment.

> —Chaim Herzog, from his speech before the U.N. General Assembly during the debate of the "Zionism Is Racism" resolution, quoted in the *Jerusalem Post*, November 17, 1995

He would rather face the U.N. condemnation of Israel with the Iraqi nuclear reactor destroyed than face an operating Iraqi reactor and no U.N. condemnation of Israel.

> —Jon Kimche, Israeli journalist, speaking of Israeli Prime Minister Menachem Begin, quoted in *Midstream*, October/November 1990

I've attacked the U.N. I've called it a monument to hypocrisy. I called it a cesspool. Nothing wrong with that. But I always treated the people there very courteously.

> —Edward I. Koch, former mayor of New York City, criticizing Mayor Rudolph Giuliani's decision to have an assistant ask Yassir Arafat to leave a Lincoln Center concert held for one hundred forty heads of state, their spouses, and other ambassadors during the celebration of the U.N.'s 50th anniversary, quoted in *The Jewish Week*, November 3, 1995

❖ URBAN LIFE ❖

(see also Neighborhoods)

He emerged from the hotel and walked up Eighth Avenue. Two men were mugging an elderly lady. My God, thought Weinstein, time was when one person could handle that job. Some city. Chaos everyplace. Kant was right: The mind imposes order. It tells you how much to tip. What a wonderful thing, to be conscious! I wonder what the people in New Jersey do.

> —Woody Allen, film director, writer, and actor, "No Kaddish for Weinstein" in *Without Feathers* (1975)

When I was in high school and very much fascinated by literature, I went to the 92nd Street Y and I heard T. S. Eliot and Carl Sandburg and Robert Frost read. I was absolutely blown away by the idea that these giants were appearing at this facility where someone like me with no social standing, no access, could pay a few bucks, take a bus and sit in the presence of these important literary figures.

> —Jeff Greenfield, television journalist and syndicated columnist, interviewed in the *92nd St. Y Review*, Fall 1995

For a New York politician of my generation, I was born and brought up in the right place. Manhattan's Lower East Side—the twentieth-century equivalent of a log cabin—was the first home in America for masses of hopeful immigrants from Europe, and for them and generations of their children it was the cradle of a great adventure.

> —Jacob K. Javits, U.S. Senator (R-N.Y.), *Javits: The Autobiography of a Public Man*, written with Rafael Steinberg (1981)

Trying on other lives is the privilege of the actor, the novelist, the schizophrenic—and the subletter.

> —Philip Lopate, essayist and author, "Reflections on Subletting" in *Against Joie de Vivre: Personal Essays* (1989)

The fire escape was our viewing balcony . . . and it became our minute bedroom on hot nights when we slept folded on each other tight as petals on a bud, closed from the perilous stairs by a high board.

> —Kate Simon, *Bronx Primitive* (1982)

Oh please God, please let there be a subway somewhere near here.

> —Neil Simon, playwright, voice of the character Eugene Jerome, on a training march through a swamp in a Mississippi army boot camp in 1945, *Biloxi Blues* (1985)

❖ VEGETARIANISM ❖

(see also Food)

Life has become too precious in this era for us to be involved in the shedding of blood, even that of animals, when we can survive without it. This is not an ascetic choice, we should note, but rather a life-affirming one. A vegetarian Judaism would be more whole in its ability to embrace the presence of God in all creation.

— Rabbi Arthur Green, professor of Jewish thought, *Seek My Face, Speak My Name* (1992)

Vegetarianism is an ideal way to actualize the Torah's vision of a world in which the divine spark in all creation is respected and revered.

— Rabbi Bonnie Koppell, "Vegetarianism" in *Rabbis and Vegetarianism: An Evolving Tradition* (1995)

The major Jewish dietary laws rest on a single premise: Eating meat is a moral compromise. There is a difference between eating a hamburger and eating a bowl of cereal. For one of them, a living creature had to be killed. Should we ever become so casual about the eating of meat that we lose sight of that distinction, a part of our humanity will have shriveled and died.

— Rabbi Harold S. Kushner, author and rabbi emeritus of Temple Israel in Natick, Mass., *To Life* (1993)

❖ VIETNAM WAR ❖

How sad. How bitter that the sons of our liberators should now be the ones to do something like this.

> — Survivor of Bergen-Belsen concentration camp, speaking of the My Lai massacre, quoted in *New Lives* by Dorothy Rabinowitz (1976)

General George Armstrong Custer said today in an exclusive interview with this correspondent that the Battle of Little Big Horn had just turned the corner and he could now see the light at the end of the tunnel. "We have the Sioux on the run," General Custer told me. "Of course we will have some cleaning up to do, but the Redskins are hurting badly and it will only be a matter of time before they give in."

> — Art Buchwald, columnist and satirist, column dated February 6, 1968, inspired by the Tet offensive begun on January 31, a turning point in the war, quoted in *The Best and the Brightest* by David Halberstam (1972)

In releasing the Pentagon Papers I acted in the hope I still hold: that truths that changed me could help Americans free themselves and other victims from our longest war.

> — Daniel Ellsberg, government official prosecuted for leaking the Pentagon Papers, a secret government study on U.S. involvement in Vietnam, May 1973, quoted in *Famous Trials: Cases That Made History* by Frank McLynn (1995)

We should take or make an early opportunity to state, emphatically, that we're going to see this through to a successful conclusion.

> — Abe Fortas, advising President Lyndon Johnson in the fall of 1967, quoted in *Abe Fortas: A Biography* by Laura Kalman (1990)

During Vietnam, Dad didn't want his sons to go to war. Just like Dan Quayle's father. The only difference was Dad didn't want anyone else's son to go to Vietnam. So he demonstrated against it.

> — Al Franken, comedian and writer, *Rush Limbaugh Is a Big Fat Idiot and Other Observations* (1996)

I cannot help but sympathize with the President's policy in Vietnam. It is unthinkable to pull out, as many of my friends suggest. Perhaps we shouldn't be there, but we are there and in a fight.

— Harry Golden, journalist, *Ess, Ess, Mein Kindt* (1966)

I was interviewing people of all ranks at precisely the same moment many of them were examining not merely the failure of so tragic a policy, but their own participation in it.

— David Halberstam, journalist and author, commenting on the timing of his book about America's engagement in Vietnam, *The Best and the Brightest* (1972)

Without meaning to, and surely without design, he's become a barometer for 30 years of change in American history. Look at the way the country has changed. Today, you'd be hard pressed to find anybody—the guy would have to be a dyed-in-the-wool Nazi—who doesn't feel that Ali's stand on Vietnam was understandable and basically justified.

— Jerry Izenberg, sportswriter, recalling the controversy over Muhammad Ali's decision not to comply with his draft notice to serve in Vietnam, quoted in *Muhammad Ali: His Life and Times* by Thomas Hauser (1991)

Then there is the defeat of the United States in Vietnam—and let there be no mistake, it is a defeat. Who will be blamed for the humiliation and the needless death? Who will be saddled with the myth of a war that might have been won if not for the "stab in the back"? The war which has poisoned America and split it into hostile camps, which has embittered the military and maligned armed-forces leadership, will be blamed on the Jew, who, again, has so many names prominent in opposition to the war. Long after they forget the names of [George] McGovern and [Eugene] McCarthy they will remember [Jerry] Rubin and [Abbie] Hoffman.

— Rabbi Meir Kahane, founder of the Jewish Defense League, *The Story of the Jewish Defense League* (1975)

Your generals are bamboozling you. The notion that all they need is 200,000 more troops is absurd. We have already poured billions of dollars into that swamp and are getting our brains beat out.

— Eppie Lederer, advice columnist also known as Ann Landers, private letter (as Eppie Lederer) written to General William Westmoreland, the U.S. commander in chief in Vietnam, after her visit to Vietnam in 1967, quoted in *Eppie: The Story of Ann Landers* (1982)

So the majority of people in America, while formidably patriotic, were also undecided and tended to shift in their opinion like the weather. Yet the Hawks never seemed to be concerned. They held every power securely but one, a dependable consensus of public opinion.

> —Norman Mailer, author, *The Armies of the Night* (1968)

Certainly any war was a bad war which required an inability to reason as the price of retaining one's patriotism.

> —Norman Mailer, *The Armies of the Night* (1968)

It was true then and I still believe it now. We had been making good—although slow—progress in the Vietnam War, and there's no reason to believe we could not have continued along the same track . . . Tet, after all, was an enemy military failure.

> —Walt W. Rostow, special assistant for national security affairs in the Johnson administration who was the architect of U.S. policy in Vietnam, recalling his infamous prediction made six weeks before the Communists launched their 1968 Tet Offensive that took U.S. and South Vietnamese forces by surprise—Rostow then predicted that he saw a "light at the end of the tunnel," quoted in *Newsday*, February 2, 1998

No question that it was the central fact of journalism for—really, for ten years, or at least eight of those ten years of the big war, from '65 to '75. . . . There's no question that the reporting that I did in Vietnam affected the perception of my bosses at CBS because it was one of those stories where you were on the air every night, sometimes seven days a week. You were covering the most dramatic kind of human tragedy.

> —Morley Safer, *60 Minutes* correspondent who opened the CBS News Saigon bureau in 1965, *Booknotes* interview with Brian Lamb, C-SPAN, May 6, 1990

I remember at the end of Rosh Hashanah looking out on six hundred Jewish faces as I was conducting the Rosh Hashanah service. . . . I was thinking, What in the world are we all doing here? Six hundred Jews in this poor torn land. But the idea of six hundred Jews wanting to be together, coming from all over, flying in by helicopter, going down quite dangerous roads, to get to High Holiday services in Saigon . . .

> —Major General Robert Bailey Solomon, U.S. Army, Fort Jackson, S.C., quoted in *Jewish Times* by Howard Simons (1988)

It is immoral that the United States government will recognize objections only if expressed as unqualified opposition to all wars.

—Rabbi Aaron Soloveitchik, dean of the Hebrew Theological College of Skokie, Ill., who called for an amendment to the draft to allow for selective conscientious objection because he considered U.S. participation in Vietnam "immoral," speaking at a national convention of Yavneh, the orthodox Jewish students association, 1968, quoted in *The Challenge of Shalom*, edited by Murray Polner and Judith Goodman (1994)

The proof of the matter is that we are hated there—and the roots of this hatred are so difficult for millions of goodwilled Americans to understand that further blind goodwill can only make matters worse.

—Theodore White, "Putting Down, For Good, The White Man's Burden," *New York*, May 12, 1975

The episode in Vietnam can be allowed to become unmitigated disaster or it can be reduced to a tragedy that we must mourn but can live with, depending on what we have learned.

—Theodore White, journalist, "Putting Down, For Good, The White Man's Burden," *New York*, May 12, 1975

❖ VIOLENCE ❖

The socialization of most Jewish girls didn't emphasize fighting back. . . .Why shouldn't we learn how to shoot? What are we going to do—call the Anti-Defamation League to come and protect us?

—Pauline Bart, sociologist, commenting on studies revealing that when they are attacked, Jewish women are more likely than women of other ethnic and religious groups to have the assault end in rape, rather than "rape avoidance," quoted in "Jewish Women Get Raped," *Lilith*, Summer 1986

Throughout my career in the racket world, the element of force and violence was something that was expected of you. You didn't ask any questions when you were told to do something, you just did it. But whenever you're asked to do something against somebody, it was always somebody in the racket world who had it in for you. And that guy would do it to you just as fast as you would do it to him.

—Mickey Cohen, Jewish mobster, quoted in *But—He Was Good to His Mother* by Robert A. Rockaway (1993)

I don't know what makes people violent. Some experts say television. I'm sure it does. But I know that the Nazis didn't watch a lot of TV and something tells me the Serbs weren't watching a lot of the *A-Team* during the 70s.

> —Al Franken, comedian and writer, *Rush Limbaugh Is a Big Fat Idiot and Other Observations* (1996)

The story of Cain and Abel is a story of violence, of the old against the new. Cain was the shepherd, the semi-nomad, who feared the emergence of the more sedentary farmer, Abel. Rather than embrace the new he sought to kill the embodiment of the new. We are forever afraid of the future.

> —Rabbi Samuel Z. Glaser, rabbi emeritus of the Elmont Jewish Center on Long Island and professor of psychology, excerpt from sermon, 1996

Every Jew a .22.

> —Rabbi Meir Kahane, founder of the Jewish Defense League, *The Story of the Jewish Defense League* (1971)

For me, when I see something violent happening on the screen, I react against it; I think this is most people's reaction. If there is violence on the screen that can make people act violently in their lives, it's the sterilized Hollywood conception of violence. It's the Western where the bad guy aggravates you so much for ninety minutes that finally, when the good guy gets rid of him in a tidy way, you feel relieved and happy. So what develops in young minds is that when somebody is bad enough, you can get rid of him—and without a mess.

> —Roman Polanski, film director and husband of actress Sharon Tate, who was murdered by Charles Manson and his followers, interview with Larry Dubois in *Playboy*, December 1971

❖ WATERGATE ❖

(see also Politics, Government, and Leaders)

Suddenly I felt awed by the implications of what we were uncovering. There was no precedent, no frame of reference—journalistic or presidential. "The President is going to be impeached," I said to Woodward. He looked at me, shaken, and said, "My God, you're right. And we can never use that word to anybody at this newspaper. Somebody will think we have an agenda."

> —Carl Bernstein, journalist who, with his partner Bob Woodward, uncovered the 1972–1974 Watergate scandal as a reporter for *The Washington Post,* "Remembrances," *Newsweek,* May 2, 1994 (at the time of Nixon's death)

I really do think our Constitution has met the test of time. When Mr. Nixon left power, the only person with a gun was a policeman directing traffic.

> —Albert P. Blaustein, law professor with an expertise in drafting constitutions for nations in transition, interview with Linda Greenhouse of *The New York Times,* September 14, 1983

The Washington press corps thinks Julie Nixon Eisenhower is the only member of the Nixon administration who has any credibility—as one journalist put it, this is not to say that anyone believes what she is saying but simply that people believe she believes in what she is saying.

> —Nora Ephron, author, screenwriter, and director, "The Littlest Nixon," *Esquire,* December 1973

We all do the same thing once in a while; I'd hate to have my business meetings recorded.

> —Max M. Fisher, business executive and philanthropist, responding to a story

in *The New York Times* that claimed that deleted portions of the White House tapes revealed that Nixon referred to members of the Securities and Exchange Commission and some attorneys attached to the Watergate prosecutor's staff as "those Jew boys," 1974, quoted in *Quiet Diplomat: A Biography of Max M. Fisher* by Peter Golden (1992)

The question is not really, Who was it [Deep Throat]? It's more, What was going on? Because if you open that door, you open the Tomb of Tutankhamen—you get into the riches of history and you get a startling education in the spooky business and murderous nature of contemporary politics.

　　—Leonard Garment, former counsel to President Nixon quoted in *Capital Style*, November 1997

I know these people. The abiding characteristic of this administration is that it lies. . . . But he'll get no cheap shots from me; either I get him hard, with facts, solid information, evidence, the truth, or I don't touch him.

　　—Seymour Hersh, journalist, speaking to Bob Woodward and Carl Bernstein of *The Washington Post* at a dinner, April 8, 1973, quoted in *All the President's Men* by Carl Bernstein and Bob Woodward, 1974

To have striven so hard, to have molded a public personality out of such an amorphous identity, to have sustained that superhuman effort only to end with every weakness disclosed and every error compounding the downfall—that was a fate of biblical proportions. Evidently the Deity would not tolerate the presumption that all can be manipulated; an object lesson of the limits of human presumption was necessary.

　　—Henry A. Kissinger, former secretary of state and national security advisor to President Richard Nixon, reflecting on Nixon's 1974 resignation, *Years of Upheaval* (1982)

It sometimes occurred to me—and I was married during that period—and I kept thinking, "Boy, if I had to say to my wife, 'I'm sorry, honey, it's two o'clock in the morning, I know, but I've got to go off and see this source and I can't tell you. . . .'" Do you think if you'd both been married, history would have turned out differently?

　　—Ted Koppel, questioning guests Bob Woodward and Carl Bernstein on June 17, 1982, *Nightline: History in the Making and the Making of Television* by Ted Koppel and Kyle Gibson (1996)

It is imperative that Richard Nixon be allowed to live out his years in tranquility. It is imperative that his talents, his genius, his obsession for peace be allowed to work for this nation.

—Rabbi Baruch Korff, defender and confidant of President Nixon during the Watergate scandal, at a dinner to honor the former president at Knotts Berry Farm, October 21, 1975, quoted in obituary for Rabbi Korff, *Los Angeles Times*, July 28, 1995

I'm proud to say that Richard Nixon was known as a crook in our kitchen some twenty-odd years before this dawned on the majority of Americans as a real possibility.

—Philip Roth, novelist interviewed by Italian critic Walter Mauro, *Reading Myself and Others* by Philip Roth (1975)

My tax returns were audited, but were, happily, in order. Otherwise, I dined out a lot on this new form of notoriety, my lecture fees went up and I seemed to suffer only from the envy of colleagues who didn't make the list.

—Daniel Schorr, senior news analyst for NPR who was a CBS correspondent when he made Nixon's notorious "Enemies List," quoted in "Lives Well Lived: Richard Nixon, the Best of Enemies," *The New York Times*, January 1, 1995

In retrospect, I gather that the lists represented less-than-wholehearted exertions by staff trying to satisfy the insistent demands of the self-besieged Nixon. He left the White House in 1974, saying that when you hate others "you destroy yourself." He may have finally discovered his greatest enemy and it was himself.

—Daniel Schorr, quoted in "Lives Well Lived: Richard Nixon, the Best of Enemies," *The New York Times*, January 1, 1995

❖ WOMEN AND JUDAISM ❖

(see also Feminism, Jewish Observance)

It was therefore determined at the outset that this could not be treated solely as a feminist issue. From that point of view, there was plainly very little to discuss. The complexity of the issue at hand stemmed from the fact that, although there is general agreement concerning the questions which characterize general feminist debates, there is still a wide range of other considerations of which account must be taken. Those considerations include some peculiar to the rabbinate, to Jewish practice in general, and to Conservative Judaism in particular. It was about these special considerations that discussion and debate evolved.

—From the Final Report of the Commission for the Study of the Ordination of Women as Rabbis, Rabbinical Assembly (conservative), 1979

Your hair becomes very potent when you cover it. I went over to my friend's house once and for the first time I saw her with her hair uncovered. It was like seeing her naked. It was shocking and beautiful.

> —Francine, a twenty-eight-year-old ba'alat teshuvah (returnee to Judaism), quoted by Andrea Gurwitt in "The Seduction of Certainty: Losing Feminist Daughters to Orthodoxy," *On the Issues*, Winter 1996

We cannot continue to play in the playpen by the rules of the patriarch. They were not crafted to include us.

> —Bella Abzug, former U.S. Congresswoman (D-N.Y.), keynote address at the Empowerment of Jewish Women conference in Jerusalem, 1988, quoted in *Lilith*, Spring 1989

Women will never be validated as complete Jews—moral initiators independent of their fathers, brothers, husbands and brothers-in-law—by proofs from a tradition . . . that women's holiness is purely contextual, depending on whether they are in correct formal status vis-à-vis some man.

> —Rachel Adler, a psychotherapist who has written extensively on Jewish women's religious issues, from a paper originally delivered at a conference at the Brandeis-Bardin Institute June 1983, *Moment*, 1983

Being a Jewish woman is very much like being Alice at the Hatter's tea party. We did not participate in making the rules, nor were we there at the beginning of the party. At best, a jumble of crockery is being shoved aside to clear a place for us. At worst, we are only tantalized with the tea and bread-and-butter, while being confused, shamed and reproached for our ignorance.

> —Rachel Adler, from a paper originally delivered at a conference at the Brandeis-Bardin Institute June 1983, *Moment*, 1983

When I was Orthodox, I thought that God's Torah was as complete as God: inerrant, invulnerable, invariable truth. I thought that I, the erring, bleeding, mutable creature, had to bend myself to this truth. Whatever I was or saw that did not fit had to be cut off, had to be blocked out. The eye—or the I—was alone at fault. I tried to make a theology to uphold this truth, and as hard as I tried to make it truthful, it unfolded itself to me as a theology of lies.

> —Rachel Adler, theologian and social ethicist, "In Your Blood: Live Re-visions of a Theology of Purity," *Tikkun*, January/February 1993

I have read carefully the responsum of the five talmudists at Yeshiva University, forbidding prayer services by women. I wish to state unequivocally that the so-called T'shuva [responsa] has nothing to do with Halacha [Jewish law]. People will have to realize that knowledge and understanding are not identical. One may know a lot and understand very little. . . . There may be a great deal of Orthodoxy around. Unfortunately, there is only very little halachic Judaism.

> —Rabbi Eliezer Berkovits, scholar and author, reacting to the responsum which declared that separate women's prayers are prohibited by Jewish law, from a September 1985 letter to the editor of the *Jerusalem Post*, quoted in *Lilith*, Summer 1986

When a woman becomes infuriated she goes from one extreme to the other; she is difficult to calm and is overbearing. . . . The average woman can be tempestuous. We find that, when vexed and infuriated, she may not hesitate to betray a confidence or make a false accusation. Sometimes she cannot control her temper or her loquaciousness.

> —Rabbi Menachem M. Brayer, psychiatrist and author, *The Jewish Woman in Rabbinic Literature: A Psychosocial Perspective* (1986)

Feminism means the transformation of all society so that its organizing principle is not power and domination but rather the female values that are at the core of Judaism. What, after all, is Isaiah's vision of a world where "the wolf and the lamb will dwell together" but a metaphor for a nonhierarchical society where relationships between nations, among individuals, and between humans and the natural world are based on respect and compassion, on cooperation and nonviolence, and on the interdependence of all Creation in the web of life?

> —Aviva Cantor, cofounder of *Lilith* and journalist, *Jewish Women, Jewish Men: The Legacy of Patriarchy in Jewish Life* (1995)

In Jerusalem, men throw stones at women who don't have their arms covered. Palestinian boys who throw stones at Israeli soldiers are shot with bullets, rubber-coated or not. Stone throwing at women by Orthodox men is considered trivial, not real assault. Somehow, it's their right. Well, what isn't?

> —Andrea Dworkin, "Israel: Whose Country Is It Anyway?" *Ms.*, September/ October 1990

To deny people's full humanity is to remove them from divinity, and if we lessen the divine image of anyone, we diminish it in all of us. If we say a deaf-mute cannot testify, what are we saying about that person? If we say a woman cannot testify, what do we say about her? If a woman is anchored to someone (who has not given her a divorce), have we subordinated her humanity to his?

—Tikva Frymer-Kensky, professor of biblical studies, "Toward a Liberal Theory of Halakha," *Tikkun*, July/August 1995

A woman at the Wall is like a pig at the Wall.

—Rabbi Yehuda Getz, chief rabbi of the Western Wall in Jerusalem, after
violent demonstrations at the Kotel [Western Wall], December 1988, when
Rivka Haut, an orthodox Jewish woman from Borough Park, N.Y., organized
the first women's Rosh Chodesh [celebrating the New Moon and new
month] Torah reading at the Western Wall, with a Torah scroll and tallitot
[prayer shawls], with seventy women assembled in the women's section,
quoted in "Backs to the Wall" by Kelly Hartog, *JUF News*, April 1997

There is much we can learn from the woman's movement in terms of our
own growth as Jews. There is much that feminism can gain from the perspective
of traditional Jewish values.

—Blu Greenberg, activist, teacher, and author, "Judaism and Feminism," *The
Jewish Woman: New Perspectives*, edited by Elizabeth Koltun (1976)

Two things I know for sure. My questioning will never lead me to abandon
tradition. I am part of a chain that is too strong to break, and though it needs
no protection from me, a child of the tradition, I want to protect it with the
fierceness of a mother protecting her young. But I also know that I never can
yield the new value of women's equality, even though it may conflict with
Jewish tradition. To do so would be to affirm the principle of a hierarchy of
male and female, and this I no longer believe to be an axiom of Judaism.

—Blu Greenberg, *On Women and Judaism* (1981)

I think it will happen within the next two decades, perhaps during my
lifetime. Most likely it will happen in stages.

—Blu Greenberg, commenting on the possibility of ordination of women as
Orthodox rabbis, quoted in *The Jewish Week*, May 26, 1989

Sometimes we are in the outer circle, with our beloved children by our
sides . . . sometimes we are in the inner circle, with men standing behind us.
Wherever we stand, the covenant and the partnership with God is ours too.

—Blu Greenberg, chairman of the First International Conference on Feminism and Orthodoxy, New York City, February 16–17, 1997, commenting
on women's role in Judaism

Where there is a rabbinic will, there is a halachic way.

—Blu Greenberg, commenting on women's role in Judaism, quoted in *Jewish
Telegraphic Agency*, February 20, 1997

Being a feminist Jew might be a contradiction in a male-defined Judaism, but if the feminist is the central actor in the creation of her Judaism, there is no conflict.

—Rabbi Julie Greenberg, activist, "Seeking a Feminist Judaism" in *The Tribe of Dina: A Jewish Woman's Anthology*, edited by Melanie Kaye Kantrowitz and Irena Klepfisz (1986)

If women really want to be "freed" and "unchained" from the religious and moral restrictions which traditional Judaism has halachically [by Jewish law] imposed upon them . . . they must realistically recognize the effect this will have upon modern Orthodox men, who will consequently become even more brazen, demanding still greater liberties in their social lives. So I ask, why exaggerate the need for more feminine freedom in the Jewish religion?

—Rabbi Abraham B. Hecht, president of the Rabbinical Alliance of America, quoted in the *Detroit Jewish News*, July 4, 1997

The crisis has not been brought on by feminism, but feminism clearly discloses the morbid condition of Judaism that has continued untreated throughout the modern period.

—Susannah Heschel, professor of Jewish studies and author, "No Doors, No Guards: From Jewish Feminism to a New Judaism," *Menorah*, March 1983

In an age when the alienation of young Jews from Judaism is a major concern for the Jewish community, we can hardly afford to ignore one half of young Jews. Thus, the challenge of feminism, if answered, can only strengthen Judaism.

—Paula E. Hyman, professor of modern Jewish history, "The Other Half: Women in the Jewish Tradition" in *The Jewish Woman: New Perspectives*, edited by Elizabeth Koltun (1976)

Jewish men constructed a Jewish identity that devalued women, the Other within the Jewish community.

—Paula E. Hyman, *Gender and Assimilation in Modern Jewish History: The Roles and Representation of Women* (1995)

It seems to me at times that the voice of prophecy today speaks more in women's voices than in men's. Feminist criticism opens us to another dimension, a different reading of our history. . . . The survival of Judaism, as well as the survival of humanity, requires the end of sexism.

—Sheldon R. Isenberg, professor of religion and author, "The End of Patriarchy in Jewish Conversation" in *Events and Movements in Modern Judaism*, edited by Raphael Patai and Emanuel Goldsmith (1995)

What does it mean to be a woman in a tradition that teaches its men to rejoice in not being a woman? What does it mean to have self-abnegation built into the very principles of your religion?

> —Erica Jong, novelist and poet, *Fear of Fifty* (1994)

If the seating is segregated according to the Orthodox tradition, the male guest of honor would be seated on the host's right and the female guest of honor at the hostess's right. At such dinners a woman is usually accorded precedence at the women's tables in accordance with her husband's rank.

> —Helen Latner, advice columnist, *The Book of Modern Jewish Etiquette* (1981)

In the past, the primary concern of Jewish education has been the Jewish boy.... His Jewish sister had to be content with a few private lessons at home and with rudimentary instruction in the religious duties of Jewish wifehood and motherhood. The inevitable result was generation upon generation of righteous women, but not of learned women.

> —Rabbi Joseph H. Lookstein, rabbi of Kehilath Jeshurun, lecturer, and founder of the Ramaz School in New York City, "A New Deal for the Forgotten Jewish Woman," *OU*, April–May 1938, quoted in *New York's Jewish Jews: The Orthodox Community in the Interwar Years* by Jenna Weissman Joselit (1990)

It made me cry. Having someone stand on the other side of the mechitza [partition dividing the men's and women's sections] with such hatred twisting in his face just because I was praying.

> —Erika Meitner, graduate student in Israel on a fellowship from Dartmouth College who is a member of Women of the Wall, recalling an experience at the Western Wall with a women's prayer group, quoted in *Lifestyles*, New Year 1998

Even though I don't like women's separate services, I recommend that rabbis should not be hasty in forbidding them.... I do not like them because I want to be where the women in my family pray and, after the service, I want to share reactions with them to all that was said and done. But if there are devout and committed women to whom such services are meaningful, then by all means, they should not be made to feel that their innovation is blameworthy.... Some of the most cherished halachic rules and institutions of today began as innovations upon which one rabbi or another must have frowned when they were first projected.

> —Rabbi Emanuel Rackman, chancellor of Bar Ilan University, author, and

columnist, commenting on women's separate prayer groups, *Los Angeles Messenger*, January 1986, quoted in *Lilith*, Summer 1986

The halacha [Jewish law] needs the woman's touch and her input.
— Rabbi Emanuel Rackman, *The Jewish Week*, January 3, 1997

Peace won't come with facile solutions. It will come when women take their rightful place as students and as experts in Jewish law. It will come when the law is questioned with respect and with the profound knowledge which enables our generation to continue the glorious pages in the responsa literature of our people. It will come when the interpreters of the law have the strength and the courage to say what they believe is right and to decide in accordance with what they believe is right.
— Rabbi Shlomo Riskin, founder of yeshiva in Efrat, Israel, and founding rabbi of Lincoln Square Synagogue in New York City, speaking at the First International Conference on Women and Judaism, held in Jerusalem, 1987

It seems as if my foremothers bulldozed roads on which I can now just stroll. While I am not disappointed that I missed out on certain struggles and oppressions, I think the lack of turmoil for me as a Jewish woman has made it harder to define myself as a Jewish feminist. . . . By no means do I think our struggles are over, just that our struggles are harder to define.
— Elana Rosenfeld Berkowitz, ninth grade student in New York City, "At Age Fourteen" in *Lifecycles 1*, edited by Rabbi Debra Orenstein (1994)

The biggest problem Jewish women face is the built-in ambivalence of wanting to restructure a sexist, oppressive culture and yet at the same time feeling bound to this culture as it is presently constituted by ties too strong to break.
— Susan Weidman Schneider, editor of *Lilith* and author, *Jewish and Female: Choices and Changes in Our Lives Today* (1984)

The women's movement has been powerfully served by Jewish women's energy, and women's strength and self-awareness have changed Jewish life in so many ways that a return to men-only Judaism is out of the question to us now.
— Susan Weidman Schneider, *Jewish and Female: Choices and Changes in Our Lives Today* (1984)

Judaism is not just about Jews and feminism is not only about women.
— T. Drorah Setel, scholar and activist, *Tikkun*, Fall 1986

We have taken action in the area of women's role in the synagogue and in the ritual life of Judaism, because we felt that it was ethically imperative for us to do.

— Rabbi Seymour Siegel, professor of theology, "Theology for Today," *Conservative Judaism*, Summer 1974

I am so sorry you were ejected from the Kotel. However, when you are in Rome, you must do like the Romans.

— Ezer Weizman, Israeli president, speaking to a visiting Hadassah delegation, "Whose Wall Is It?" *Boston Jewish Advocate*, July 26, 1996

It was one thing to consider the abstract possibility that women's role in Judaism was not inherently oppressive, another to live in a culture that made me feel oppressed.

— Ellen Willis, writer, *Beginning to See the Light: Pieces of a Decade* (1981)

God didn't listen to women. . . . Women could get into Heaven because they were wives and daughters of men. Women had no brains for study of God's Torah, but they could be the servants of men who studied the Torah. Only if they cooked for the men, and washed for the men, and didn't nag or curse the men out of their homes; only if they let the men study the Torah in peace, then, maybe, they could push themselves into Heaven with the men, to wait on them there.

— Anzia Yezierska, *The Bread Givers* (voice of the character Sara Smolinsky) (1925)

❖ WORLD WAR I ❖

You must remember that this was in 1911, 1912, 1913. One had high hopes that by the steady progress of free inquiry you could remake the world. It never dawned on anybody that a war like the great World War in 1914 was still possible—you know, "We've gotten beyond that. This is the age of reason."

— Felix Frankfurter, U.S. Supreme Court justice, quoted in *Felix Frankfurter Reminisces*, recorded in talks with Dr. Harlan B. Phillips (1960)

I am not one who is a believer in "Peace at any price." Such a policy is a manifestation of cowardice and of lack of conviction. But neither do I belong to the war party which values fighting for its own sake. The only principle that determines me is the outcome of the struggle, and the good or evil which may result from it for the development of Judaism.

> —Israel Friedlander, scholar and activist, from an unpublished section of a letter to Louis Brandeis, June 20, 1915, quoted in *Practical Dreamer: Israel Friedlander and the Shaping of American Judaism* by Baila Round Shargel (1985)

In the American forces the Jewish soldier ranked with the best; he was an American soldier, and there is no higher praise than that.

> —Rabbi Lee J. Levenger, executive director of the Young Men's Hebrew Association (YMHA) in New York City, formerly First Lieutenant Chaplain, United States Army, *A Jewish Chaplain in France* (1921)

Once, in a different generation that knew firsthand of doughboys and loss, it was well-known what armistice was reached in the 11th hour of the 11th day of the 11th month. Time marches on as young men once marched, wars and old victories become distant, Armistice Day has become Veterans' Day, and Veterans' Day is on the way to becoming an obscure bank holiday, a faded icon in the national attic gathering dust alongside Flag Day or Decoration Day. Few line the sidewalks for the annual parade; fewer mourn other than loved ones.

> —Jonathan Mark, journalist, attending the memorial ceremony at the Soldiers' and Sailors' Memorial Plot in White Plains with Sandy Stogel, quartermaster of Jewish War Veterans Post 191, *The Jewish Week*, November 15, 1996

There is not a man here who is not looking healthier than when he arrived, and this despite the difficulty many of our boys experienced in habituating themselves to goyish food.

> —Maurice Samuel, essayist and novelist, "Soldiering at Yaphank: A Letter from a Zionist Soldier," *Maccabaean*, November 1917, quoted in *Western Jewry and the Zionist Project 1914–1933* by Michael Berkowitz (1997)

[Sholem Aleichem] did not foresee the events that were to come out of the First World War; but unlike so many others in those days, he did not believe that the war would soon be over and all would be well again. He felt in his bones, as some do the forthcoming weather, that a period of woe and evil was opening up for mankind. In time, he recovered enough composure to renew his writing, and some rays of hope broke through the darkness in the sky; but he was never his carefree, jolly self again.

> —Marie Waife-Goldberg, *My Father, Sholem Aleichem* (1968)

Europe was a heap of swords piled as delicately as jackstraws; one could not be pulled out without moving the others.

> —Barbara W. Tuchman, historian, *The Guns of August* (1962)

What glorious men they seem, unheroic in their own sight alone.

> —Rabbi Stephen S. Wise, writing from London upon observing wounded soldiers, 1918, quoted in *Rabbi and Minister: The Friendship of Stephen S. Wise and John Haynes Holmes* by Carl Hermann Voss (1964)

❖ WORLD WAR II ❖

They'd ask, "You know what is done with Jews here?" . . . At Stalag 17 they took pictures of us and shaved our heads. On my POW card they put a big red "J" for Jude. Later I asked our American chaplain, "Father Kane, I'm very anxious. I know what happened to Jews in Germany after Kristallnacht. What should I expect?" He said, "It all depends on how the war goes. If you were a Gentile and you escaped and were caught, you would be brought back. But if you escaped, nobody would ever hear from you again."

> —Daniel S. Abeles, radio operator and gunner on a B-17 who was shot down over Germany and incarcerated in Stalag 17-B in Krems, Austria, 1944, quoted in *We Were Each Other's Prisoners: An Oral History of World War II American and German Prisoners of War* by Lewis H. Carlson (1997)

In less than six years Germany laid waste the moral structure of Western society . . .

> —Hannah Arendt, German-born philosopher and social critic who was forced to flee Germany in 1933 (she moved to Paris and, in 1941, to the United States), "Germany 1950," *Commentary*, October 1950

Amid the ruins, Germans mail each other picture postcards still showing the cathedrals and market places, the public buildings and bridges that no longer exist. And the indifference with which they walk through the rubble has its exact counterpart in the absence of mourning for the dead, or in the apathy with which they react, or fail to react, to the fate of the refugees in their midst. . . . This . . . is only the most conspicuous outward symptom of a deep-rooted, stubborn, and at times vicious refusal to face and come to terms with what really happened.

> —Hannah Arendt, "Germany 1950," *Commentary*, October 1950

Colonel Cannon spoke to us . . . in Plymouth, England, and explained to us that we were going to be the first forces in the Second Front in Europe, and that two out of three of us aren't expected to come back, and if anybody's got butterflies in the belly, to ask for a transfer now, because it's going to be that kind of an operation.

> —Harold Baumgarten, soldier born in New York City, drafted into the U.S. Army June 26, 1943, quoted in *The 116th at Omaha Beach, Voices of D-Day,* edited by Ronald J. Drez (1994)

At the wall, I met a fellow from Company B, from my boat team named Dominick Surrow, a boy from Georgia, about my age, a rugged fellow, who looked at my [wounded] face and said, "Stay here, I'm going to get help." He got killed. . . . I watched him being washed around by the incoming water, and I saw the bodies of my buddies who had tried in vain to clear the beach. It looked like the beach was littered with the refuse of a wrecked ship that were the dead bodies of what was the proud, tough, and the well-trained combat infantrymen of the 1st Battalion of the 116th infantry.

> —Harold Baumgarten, quoted in *The 116th at Omaha Beach, Voices of D-Day,* edited by Ronald J. Drez (1994)

I had never experienced the sense of purpose or morale that I did in the airborne. Being Jewish, I experienced minor anti-Semitic slurs from one individual but in the paratroops we were all in the same boat.

> —Eli Bernheim, Jr., paratroops officer with the 11th Airborne who volunteered to serve in the U.S. Army on Dec. 8, 1941, and remained in the army, also doing a combat tour in Korea and stateside duty during the Vietnam War (he retired as a colonel), quoted in *Crisis in the Pacific: The Battles for the Philippines Island by the Men Who Fought Them: An Oral History* by Gerald Astor (1996)

If the Battle of Britain was England's finest hour, Normandy was ours.

> —Don Feder, journalist, "Omaha Beach: Our Finest Hour," *Boston Herald,* June 6, 1994

Normandy had its ghosts too. Every man who ever fought for his home-land—from the Minuteman to the Grand Army of the Republic, to the Dough-boys of the Rainbow Division—slogged through the icy surf and struggled up the beaches shoulder to shoulder with their spiritual descendants.

> —Don Feder, "Omaha Beach: Our Finest Hour," *Boston Herald,* June 6, 1994

In a real sense, these people too, were drafted by their country; they were uprooted from their homes and substantially deprived of an opportunity to lead a normal life. They are casualties of war.

> —Abe Fortas, Undersecretary of the Interior, speaking after President Roose-velt lifted the executive order excluding Japanese-Americans from the West

Coast in December 1944, asserting the evacuees' right to return to the West
Coast, quoted in *Abe Fortas: A Biography* by Laura Kalman (1990)

I was taken to a schoolroom in the center, probably for children of kindergarten age. As I entered the room as the representative of the Department of the Interior, the children, who were all neatly dressed and scrubbed . . . rose to their feet and sang "America the Beautiful." I am sure you will realize how profoundly affecting this was.

> —Abe Fortas, Washington, D.C., attorney, recalling his tour of the camps in which Japanese-American citizens were interred as the result of an executive order, quoted in *Abe Fortas: A Biography* by Laura Kalman (1990)

In San Diego, when we were being assigned to ships, I said, "What the hell is the *Oglala?*" This young kid says, "It's an old minelayer. An old tub. I got the battleship *Arizona.*" He's still on it.

> —Lee Goldfarb, retiree in East Hanover, N.J., who was a radioman on the minelayer *Oglala* when the attack on Pearl Harbor began, quoted in *Time,* December 2, 1991, on the 50th anniversary of the attack.

It is necessary to have sat in a dim room listening to that incomparable voice at moments when a Nazi victory seemed entirely possible, to understand that Churchill's speeches were not ornamental, but, literally, an essential contribution to the war. Nothing else and no one else could surely buoy up flagging hopes or restore confidence—in Britain and in oneself.

> —Henry Grunwald, editor of *Time,* quoted in *People I Have Known, Loved or Admired* by Leo Rosten (1970)

When people used to ask, "Where were you on Pearl Harbor Day?" I always knew. It was a Sunday and the Giants were playing at home. . . . At about 2:00 P.M., it was announced over the loudspeaker that Pearl Harbor had been bombed by the Japanese. . . . After the announcement, the game resumed. It became just one more time out. After all, sports history was not to be interrupted by real history. Al Blozis who ate up the enemy defenses that day was dead two years later in the South Pacific.

> —Irving Louis Horowitz, author and professor of sociology and political science, *Daydreams and Nightmares: Reflections of a Harlem Childhood* (1990)

Even the most peaceful of men can feel exultation on the threshold of a just war.

> —Jacob K. Javits, U.S. Senator (R-N.Y.), *Javits: The Autobiography of a Public Man,* written with Rafael Steinberg (1981)

None of the guards ever showed any compassion. We were simply ver-
dammte Juden—nothing else. We should have been treated as soldiers. . . . We
were so smelly and foul that I once slept for two nights with a guy before I
realized he was dead.

> —Sanford "Sandy" Lubinsky, soldier captured by the Germans during the
> Battle of the Bulge, Winter 1945, quoted in *We Were Each Other's Pris-
> oners: An Oral History of World War II American and German Prisoners
> of War* by Lewis H. Carlson (1997) (In violation of the 1929 Geneva Con-
> vention, the German commander of Stalag 9-B at Bad Orb singled out
> Lubinsky and approximately eighty other Jewish POWs and sent them to
> the slave labor camp at Berga—he weighed eighty pounds when he was
> liberated.)

I had wonderful treatment from everyone. They did not know I was Jewish.
I had planned very carefully ahead of time. I had three sets of dog tags. When-
ever I flew over northern Germany, I was a Protestant. If we were flying over
France, I was a Catholic. Otherwise, I wore my regular tags.

> —Matthew Radnossky, soldier who was shot down while flying a B-17 bomber
> and saved by Catholic nuns who provided him medical treatment in their
> hospital, 1944, quoted in *We Were Each Other's Prisoners: An Oral History
> of World War II American and German Prisoners of War* by Lewis H.
> Carlson (1997)

I am afraid that my mind is going to get rusty in the army. There is little
opportunity for original thinking. Even the ink I use in my pen has to be
"regulation" stuff.

> —Captain Hyman Samuelson, Jewish officer in charge of African-American
> troops in New Guinea during World War II, diary entry September 29, 1941,
> Fort Bragg, N.C., quoted in *Love, War, and the 96th Engineers (Colored)*,
> edited by Samuelson and Gwendolyn Midlo Hall (1995)

They saw the celebration in his castle as an act of God.

> —Rabbi Joseph Shubow, army chaplain whose troops had just crossed the
> Rhine into Germany and decided to use the nearby castle of Joseph Goeb-
> bels as a place to have a seder in 1945, quoted in *Jewish Telegraphic Agency,*
> April 14, 1995

In a radio address delivered March 3, the Montana [Senator Wheeler]
said, "Now we find these same international bankers with their friends the royal
refugees and with the Sassoons of the Orient and with the Rothschilds and
Warburgs of Europe in another theme song. . . . "Our investments in India,
Africa and Europe must be preserved. Save democracy!". . . It is becoming

increasingly difficult to believe that the resemblance of such remarks to the ranting of Father Coughlin is wholly coincidental.

> —I. F. Stone, journalist, from his weekly column in *The Nation*, March 15, 1941, regarding the debate over the passage of the Lend-Lease bill, *The War Years: A Nonconformist History of Our Times 1939–1945* (1990)

This is really world war, and in my humble opinion it was unavoidable and is better fought now when we still have allies left.

> —I. F. Stone, from his weekly column in *The Nation*, December 13, 1941, after the attack on Pearl Harbor, *The War Years: A Nonconformist History of Our Times 1939–1945* (1990)

There was little excitement in the capital and—significant item—bond sales actually fell off. J.Edgar Hoover called for alertness on the home front, and the War Department asked Congress to establish sixty-nine new national cemeteries.

> —I. F. Stone, from his weekly column in *The Nation*, June 17, 1944, commenting on reactions to D-Day, *The War Years: A Nonconformist History of Our Times 1939–1945* (1990)

❖ WRITING ❖

(see also Books, Language, Literature, Poetry)

And while his grateful readers laughed
Forgetting troubles of their own,
Midst their applause—God only knows—
He wept in secret and alone.

> —Epitaph for Sholem Aleichem in *Ethical Wills: A Modern Jewish Treasury* by Jack Riemer and Nathaniel Stampfer (1986)

One hopes that the lessons of all our centuries of travel, of searching for safe haven, is that they are part of the essential human business of being an expatriate. And one often hopes that to be a Jewish writer is to understand that most of the time, it's the same for everyone, no matter what their port of entry or final destination.

> —Jon Robin Baitz, playwright, quoted in *Fruitful and Multiplying*, edited by Ellen Schiff (1996)

There is no such thing as writer's block when you're a lawyer. If you have something to write, you sit down and write it. The test of the ultimate validity of what you thought about is whether you can write it down. If you can't, something is the matter. If it's in law, something is wrong with the argument. In fiction, something is wrong with the feeling.

> —Louis Begley, lawyer and novelist, quoted in "Inventing a Life, Then Living It" by Esther B. Fein, *The New York Times*, April 14, 1993

You're dunked and soaked in crises. First thing in the morning, before you've had your coffee you turn on the radio and you begin to fill up, to inflate, with warnings, disasters, crises . . . terrorist attacks . . .

> —Saul Bellow, Nobel Prize–winning author, responding to the question of whether it is possible for writers living in Israel to avoid politics, interview wiht Bob Cromie on *Book Beat*, WTTW, Chicago, 1976

The business of the writer as witness is to pass all the things he sees and knows through his own soul.

> —Saul Bellow, 1980 interview, quoted in *Words Still Count With Me* by Herb Mitgang (1995)

I don't choose my subjects. They tend to choose me.

> —Michael Chabon, novelist, speaking at forum "Has American Jewish Fiction a Second Life?" at The New York Public Library, May 19, 1994

People are getting more out of my books than I put into them.

> —Kinky Friedman, singer and writer, quoted in *Newsday*, May 26, 1996

How do I explain that I write plays, that I speak in the voices of other people because I don't know my own; that I write in the second person because I don't know the first; that I have been writing plays most of my adult life waiting to become both an adult and a playwright, and that it takes me so many years to write anything that I am forced to refer to myself during these periods as a playwrote?

> —Herb Gardner, playwright, quoted in program of *Conversations With My Father*, 1991

What you're trying to be as a writer is an enchanter. It has to enchant me— and I know when it's not enchanting.

> —Rebecca Goldstein, novelist, quoted in *Publishers Weekly*, October 23, 1995

In a sense every writer is an ethnic writer, including people like Shakespeare. Shakespeare was trying to write great epics in English. You do drag your childhood behind you and everybody has to grapple with that. Henry James is a perfect example. I think if you're going to feel conflicted about it, you're in good company.

— Allegra Goodman, novelist, speaking at a forum, "A New Chapter in Jewish Fiction," sponsored by *The Jewish Week* in New York City, June 9, 1997

Every writer in a way is a Jew. Even if he is a Chinese or a Japanese or an Indian, there is something so Jewish in the belief that the world is something that you have to decode, to decipher, to understand it and then, to create your system of rules and regulations in order to survive in that.

— David Grossman, Israeli novelist, speaking in the film *A Jew Is Not One Thing,* produced for The Jewish Museum's core exhibition, 1993

When I write fiction I take a part of my life and create a whole other creature around it.

— Laura Z. Hobson, author, 1983, quoted in *Lilith,* Summer 1986

All the stories that have ever been told are the stories of families — from Adam and Eve onward.

— Erica Jong, *Inventing Memory* (1997)

In fact, fiction writers are prickly, obsessed people, selfish and narrow, if you will: They worry about getting from one end of the sentence to the other. And then about how to begin the one that comes next. Certainly there are issues I worry about as a Jew and as a citizen; yet, they may or may not make their way into my fiction. And when they do, often it's only afterward that I recognize it.

— Joanna Kaplan, novelist, quoted in "Making Our Way Back to the Mother Ship," *Forward,* November 1, 1995

There are experiences so extreme that, after living them, one can do nothing with them but put them into words.

— Alfred Kazin, author and literary critic, from his introduction to *The Commentary Reader: Two Decades of Articles and Stories* (1967)

I noticed that the parking lot of the synagogue looked like a good place to hide a body. So I just sat down and started typing.

— Harry Kemelman, mystery novelist, quoted in "Sunday the Writer" by Michele Slung, *The Washington Post,* February 25, 1996

Not writing is more of a psychological problem than a writing problem. All the time I'm not writing I feel like a criminal. Actually, I suppose that's probably an outmoded phrase, because I don't think criminals feel like criminals any-more. I feel like criminals used to feel when they felt guilty about being crim-inals, when they regretted their crimes. It's horrible to feel felonious every second of the day. Especially when it goes on for years. It's much more relaxing actually to work.

> —Fran Lebowitz, essayist, *The Paris Review*, reprinted in *Harper's*, November 1993

My own feeling of Jewishness coincides with my feelings of being a writer. It gives me a certain solidity in who I am as well as a freedom to be critical of our culture.

> —Alan Lelchuk, novelist and professor, quoted in *Growing Up Jewish in America: An Oral History* by Myrna Katz Frommer and Harvey Frommer (1995)

Only the very best and worst novelists can write as if they are invisible.

> —Norman Mailer, author, *Of a Fire on the Moon* (1969)

I am a novelist, and my occupation does require me to try to enter people's minds.

> —Norman Mailer, quoted in *New York*, October 16, 1995

Telling tales is a way of putting together what life means. It's a way of dipping your fingertips into experience, or dipping your fingertips and coming up with some substance—some mysterious writing on the tips of your experi-ence that say this is what you've done and this is what it's all about.

> —Bernard Malamud, novelist and short story writer, during a question-and-answer session following a reading at the University of Tennessee, 1980s, in *Talking Horse: Bernard Malamud on Life and Work*, edited by Alan Cheuse and Nicholas Delbanco (1996)

I don't regret the years I put into my work. Perhaps I regret the fact that I was not two men, one who could live a full life apart from writing; and one who lived in art, exploring all he had to experience and know how to make his work right; yet not regretting that he had put his life into the art of perfecting the work.

> —Bernard Malamud, "Long Life, Short Work," talk at Bennington College, October 13, 1984, in *Talking Horse: Bernard Malamud on Life and Work*, edited by Alan Cheuse and Nicholas Delbanco (1996)

I don't see myself as a Jewish playwright but rather as a playwright who is Jew-ish. I bristle when ethnicity is used as an adjective. It diminishes the work and seems to suggest that writing what one knows is tantamount to cheating. If one writes about his people honestly and unflinchingly, he is writing about all people. I try to tell the truth.

> —Donald Margulies, playwright, quoted in *Fruiful and Multiplying*, edited by Ellen Schiff (1996)

I think I gave up the Jews as literary material because I was afraid that even an innocent literary allusion to the individual wrongdoing of an individual Jew would be inflamed by the atmosphere, ignited by the hatred I suddenly was aware of, and my love would be twisted into a weapon of persecution against Jews. No good writer can approach material in that atmosphere.... There is hardly a story or play I could write about which would not have to contain justifications for behavior that in any other people need not be justified.

> —Arthur Miller, playwright, from a 1947 speech quoted in "American Jewish Writers and Their Judaism" by Harold U. Ribalow, reprinted in *Jews in the Modern World, Volume 2*, edited by Jacob Fried (1962)

In the twenty years I bore and reared my children, usually had to work on a paid job as well, the simplest circumstances for creation did not exist. Nevertheless writing, the hope of it, was "the air I breathed, so long as I shall breathe at all." In that hope, there was conscious storing, snatched reading, beginnings of writing, and always "the secret rootlets of reconaissance."

> —Tillie Olsen, author, *Silences* (1978)

There is no news to report from Auschwitz. There is merely the compulsion to write something about it, a compulsion that grows out of a restless feeling that to have visited Auschwitz and then turned away without having said or written anything would be a most grievous act of discourtesy to those who died here.

> —A. M. Rosenthal, Warsaw bureau chief for *The New York Times*, "There Is No News From Auschwitz," *The New York Times Magazine*, August 31, 1958

My feeling has always been that I owe my fellow beings, my fellow sufferers; I owe them a helping hand. I owe them a helping hand in whatever form I can extend it. While I'm alive I feel an obligation to exercise the long-dormant (or repressed) talent I have—in my case, writing. To me it's an exercise in decency and humanity.

> —Henry Roth, novelist, foreword to *Holding On: Dreamers, Visionaries, Eccentrics and Other American Heroes* by David Isay, photographs by Harvey Wang (1995)

Anybody who enters a writer's life intimately knows that we play for keeps. . . . Really, I should have a big sign that says, BEWARE, VICIOUS WRITER.

> —Philip Roth, novelist, reflecting on the violation of intimacies of family and friends in his work, upon publication of *Deception*, quoted in *Mirabella*, May/June 1997

I turn sentences around. I write a sentence, then I turn it around. Then I look at it, then I turn it around and look at it again. Then I have lunch. Then I come back and write another sentence. Then, I have tea and I turn the new sentence around. Then I read the two sentences over and turn them both around. Then I lie down on my stomach and think. Then I get up and throw them out and start from the beginning.

> —Philip Roth, novelist, *The Ghost Writer* (voice of the character I. L. Lonoff) (1979)

I think I do find writing inseparable from my work. But it's not a double life. Chekhov once said that "literature is my mistress, medicine my lawful-wedded wife." But I don't have a feeling, as it were, of a wife and mistress, but of a single occupation in which the medicine and the writing are fused. And this involves listening and attending to patients and thinking about them and working with them and perhaps writing about them.

> —Oliver Sacks, author and neurologist, "Street Neurologist with a Sense of Wonder," interview in *The Lancet*, October 11, 1997

It is harder to put your foot in your mouth when you have a pen in your hand.

> —William Safire, columnist, speaking at Syracuse University, May 13, 1978, quoted in *Lend Me Your Ears: Great Speeches in History*, edited by Safire (1992)

Most of all, my thanks to Avital, who, after all those years of life as the wife of a prisoner, had to endure another two years as the wife of an author.

> —Natan Sharansky, former refusenik, acknowledgments in *Fear No Evil* (1988)

Someday I hope to have the kind of life where I'll have nothing to think about but writing. Where I won't have to scribble my poems in the subway on the back of the delicatessen bill, where if I file the darn thing under bills I'm out a poem and if I file under poetry the delicatessen man has me in a tight place.

> —Viola Brothers Shore, author, *Saturday Evening Post*, 1920, cited in *Jewish Women in America: An Historical Encyclopedia*, edited by Paula E. Hyman and Deborah Dash Moore (1997)

I see humor in even the grimmest of situations. And I think it's possible to write a play so moving it can tear you apart and still have humor in it.

—Neil Simon, playwright, interview with Lawrence Linderman in *Playboy,* February 1979

I write in Yiddish with a leaky pen on lined paper.

—Isaac Bashevis Singer, Nobel Prize–winning Yiddish writer, 1985, quoted in *Words Still Count With Me* by Herb Mitgang (1995)

If you're a doctor, you get sick people; if you're a lawyer, you get cases; if you're a writer, the Almighty sends you stories, sometimes too many.

—Isaac Bashevis Singer, 1985, quoted in *Words Still Count with Me* by Herb Mitgang (1995)

No writer can resurrect what the wicked have destroyed.

—Isaac Bashevis Singer, *Meshugah* (1995)

Writers don't write American-Jewish fiction. They write stories and novels.

—Ted Solotaroff, editor and writer, speaking at forum "Has American Jewish Fiction a Second Life?" at The New York Public Library, May 19, 1994

My search for words begins at that juncture between divine loneliness and human loneliness captured in the notion that we are created in the image and likeness of God. It begins where the struggle of God to express Himself corresponds to my struggle to express myself through the mysterious source of human expression, the imagination.

—Rabbi Ira Stone, author and rabbi of Beth Zion/Beth Israel Synagogue in Philadelphia, *Seeking the Path to Life: Theological Meditations on God and the Nature of People, Love, Life and Death* (1992)

Writers are what they write, also what they fail to write.

—Diana Trilling, essayist and critic, preface, *The Beginning of the Journey: The Marriage of Diana and Lionel Trilling* (1993)

All American Jewish novelists are college professors, and they all write about Jewish college professors, who are writing novels about Jewish college professors. It is a strictly literary convention of the genre, like the fourteen lines of sonnet form.

—Herman Wouk, writer, *Inside, Outside* (voice of I. David Goodkind) (1985)

❖ Yiddish ❖

The elasticity of the Yiddish language should have been tested in this adaptation.

> —Review of Yiddish version of *Uncle Tom's Cabin* at the Thalia Theater in New York, *The American Hebrew*, May 24, 1901 (The song "Down on the Swanee River" was sung in English.)

Yiddish is the only language without a navy.

> —Alexander Erlich, professor of economics and grandson of the historian Simon Dubnow, speaking to graduates of YIVO/Weinreich Yiddish program, during Israel's Lebanon war, 1982

What is a Yiddish poet? A Yiddish poet is someone who reads Auden but Auden doesn't read him.

> —Jacob Glatstein, Yiddish poet, quoted by Steven J. Zipperstein in "Home Again?" *Judaism*, Fall 1995

In this language, you say "beauty" and mean "spirituality"; you say "kindness" and mean "holiness." Few languages can be spoken so simply and so directly; there are but few languages which lend themselves with such difficulty to falseness.

> —Rabbi Abraham Joshua Heschel, author, activist, and theologian, *The Earth Is the Lord's* (1949)

Yiddish was the language that sprang first to a Jew's lips, a language crackling with cleverness and turmoil, ironic to its bones; yet decades of struggle were

required before the learned, somewhat modernized Jews could be convinced—
some never would be—what this mere zhargon, this street tongue, this dishev-
eled creature wearing the apron of the Jewish week, this harum-scarum of a
language recklessly mixing up bits of German, Hebrew, Russian, Polish, Pro-
vencal, English and God alone know what, could become the vehicle of literature through which Jewish life would regain its bearing.

—Irving Howe, author, editor, and professor, *World of Our Fathers* (1976)

In its years of decline, Yiddish culture was more than ever an international
culture, a fraternity of survivors across the globe.

—Irving Howe, *World of Our Fathers* (1976)

Yiddish wasn't just words, you see, it was an attitude. It was sweet and sour.
It was a shrug and a kiss. It was humility and defiance all in one.

—Erica Jong, author, *Inventing Memory* (1997)

I can imagine a time when Jews will regret that they behaved so frivolously
and condescendingly to the Yiddish word. It will be a time when Yiddish will
have "disappeared." Once "disappeared," it will have become old, dead—and
interesting. The Jews of that time will grow nostalgic—the English-speaking
ones—for the tones of the language generations and generations of Jews had
spoken. They will grow nostalgic for the wounds born in the Middle Ages and
strengthened on the Slavic steppes, sounds of Jewish intimacy and loneliness,
sorrows and jokes, sounds saturated with the heart's blood of a people.

—Abraham Koralnik, author, *Without Mazl* (1940)

It is common sense that we cannot throw away an entire literature, that we
cannot discard a millennium of our history, that we cannot forget or purposely
ignore where we have come from and still expect to know who we are and
where we may yet go from here.

—Aaron Lansky, founder and president of the National Yiddish Book Center,
speaking at the dedication of the Center's new building in Amherst, Mass.,
June 15, 1997

Yiddish came to have the same effect on many American Jews that kryp-
tonite had on Superman—it was a piece of the place they came from and
therefore the one thing they could not abide.

—Jonathan Rosen, associate editor of *Forward*, "A Dead Language: Yiddish
Lives," *The New York Times Magazine*, July 7, 1996

Because Yiddish culture in Europe was essentially destroyed, learning Yiddish in America has a surreal aspect, like planning a trip to a country that doesn't exist. The culture of the country can be anything you want—gay, feminist, secular, religious—and no one can tell you that you don't belong.

> —Jonathan Rosen, "A Dead Language: Yiddish Lives," *The New York Times Magazine*, July 7, 1996

The shtetl, or Jewish market town of eastern Europe, is arguably the greatest single invention of Yiddish literature. What the Western is to American popular culture, the shtetl novella is to the Yiddish imagination. Its symbolic landscape is etched into the Yiddish psyche. Main Street is dominated by the marketplace and is occupied solely by Jews. Instead of the saloon, there is the besmedresh (the house of study); instead of the church, the shul[synagogue]. . . . With this symbolic map firmly in place, the variations on the theme of the small town in a dangerous world were almost inexhaustible.

> —David Roskies, author and professor of Yiddish literature, "Yiddish Literature" in *The Schocken Guide to Jewish Books* edited by Barry W. Holtz (1992)

Yiddish culture is a ghost, the sentimentality to recall it is now inspiring the more it disappears. It is like the Socialist party and the men who built it— gone. It is like my relatives, evaporating into the vacuum that New York has become.

> —Harry Roskolenko, author "America the Thief," in *The Immigrant Experience: The Anguish of Becoming American*, edited by Thomas C. Wheeler (1971)

I think it a tongue that never takes its tongue out of its cheek.

> —Leo Rosten, author, *The Joys of Yiddish* (1968)

Yiddish is the Robin Hood of languages. It steals from the linguistically rich to give to the fledging poor.

> —Leo Rosten, *The Joys of Yiddish* (1968)

It is time to make clear that, through his language, the Yiddish writer is bound to the past. His boundaries are, spatially, the borders of Poland, Russia and Rumania, and, temporally, the date of his departure for America. Here he must, in a literary sense, dine on leftovers; only food prepared in the old world can nourish him in the new.

> —Isaac Bashevis Singer, Nobel Prize–winning Yiddish writer, "Problems of Yiddish Prose in America," 1943, published in English in *Prooftexts*, 1989

I like to write ghost stories and nothing fits a ghost better than a dying language. The deader the language the more alive the ghost. Ghosts love Yiddish, and as far as I know, they all speak it . . . I am sure that millions of Yiddish-speaking corpses will rise from their graves one day, and their first question will be: "Is there any new book in Yiddish to read?"

—Isaac Bashevis Singer, 1961 interview, quoted in *Newsweek*, October 15, 1978

One can find in the Yiddish tongue . . . expressions of pious joy, lust for life, longing for the Messiah, patience, and deep appreciation of human individuality. There is a quiet humor in Yiddish and a gratitude for every day of life, every crumb of success, each encounter of love.

—Isaac Bashevis Singer, Nobel Prize Lecture in Stockholm, 1978

The high honor bestowed upon me by the Swedish academy is also a recognition of the Yiddish language—a language of exile, without a land, without frontiers, not supported by any government, a language which possesses no words for weapons, ammunition, military exercises, war tactics; a language that was despised by both gentiles and emancipated Jews.

—Isaac Bashevis Singer, Nobel Prize Lecture, Stockholm, 1978

❖ ZIONISM ❖

(see also Diaspora, Israel)

WE HEREBY PROCLAIM the establishment of the Jewish State in Palestine, to be called Medinath Yisrael (The State of Israel). . . . With trust in the Rock of Israel, we set our hand to this Declaration, at this Session of the Provisional State Council, on the soil of the Homeland, in the city of Tel-Aviv, on this Sabbath eve, the fifth of Iyar, 5708, the fourteenth of May, 1948.

> —State of Israel Proclamation of Independence, May 14, 1948

Our call goes out to the Jewish people all over the world to rally to our side in the task of immigration and development, and to stand by us in the great struggle for the fulfillment of the dream of generations for the redemption of Israel.

> —State of Israel Proclamation of Independence, May 14, 1948

This is the source of the dream, not Herzl. The siddur [prayer book] contains the dreams of the Jewish people.

> —Rabbi David Algaze of Forest Hills, N.Y., speaking at an International Zionist Convention, quoted in *The Jewish Voice*, May 1996

The people are profoundly happy. And I am filled with foreboding. I feel like the bereaved among the rejoicing.

> —David Ben-Gurion, entry in his diary on the night that he announced the establishment of the State of Israel, May 14, 1948, quoted in *The Boston Jewish Advocate*, May 10, 1996

Zionism, as mirrored in the State of Israel, has proven the point that Jews are in fact just human. Israel has displayed a full range of human achievement and weakness and of decency and its absence common to all nations. Comparatively speaking, one can make the case that Israel had behaved better, given the circumstances.

> —Leon Botstein, president of Bard College, "Zionism at 100: A Symposium," *The New Republic*, September 8 & 15, 1997

We took this man to [Chaim] Weizmann and his head spun with awe and respect at this great honor. We explained to him, "Eddie, you have to say one thing to the President: See Weizmann. Don't get involved with arguments. Concentrate on one thing: 'fair play demands that you listen . . .' "

> —Abba Eban, member of Jewish Agency delegation to the United Nations, recalling President Harry Truman's refusal to meet with Jewish leaders about Palestine affairs at the time when there was great concern over perceived erosion in U.S. support for the U.N. resolution for partition of Palestine into two states, Jewish and Arab, quoted in *Pillar of Fire: A Rebirth of Israel—A Visual History* by Yigal Lossin, translated by Zvi Ofer, edited by Carol Halberstadt (1983) (Truman's old trusted friend and former business partner, Missouri haberdasher Eddie Jacobson, was summoned to save the situation; with Jacobson's intervention, Truman agreed to see Weizmann if he was brought into the White House through the side door.)

I need not tell you that the phrase "that Palestine be established as a Jewish National Home" was a phrase of purposeful ambiguity and gave rise to a good deal of subsequent discussion. Did it mean that there should be a home for Jews in Palestine, or was Palestine to be the national home? Events have largely answered the question as events usually answer the lawyer's ambiguity—that is . . . events pour meaning into the words and give them one vitality rather than another.

> —Felix Frankfurter, U.S. Supreme Court justice, recalling the announcement of the Balfour Declaration, quoted in *Felix Frankfurter Reminisces*, recorded in talks with Dr. Harlan B. Phillips (1960)

For one thousand and eight hundred years we were a people without a state. Now we are in danger of being a state without a people.

> —Rabbi Abraham Joshua Heschel, author, activist, and theologian, speaking at the 1972 Zionist Congress, quoted in "The Jewish State and the Jewish People" by Yosef Gorny, *Jewish Political Studies Review*, Fall 1990

Zionism must be pluralistic. For example, to ask Reform Jews to do Zionism as if Reform were secondary is like asking Jews in Denver or New York to discuss American constitutional law as if their Jewishness is irrelevant to first amendment rights, or asking women to forget they are women while they go about being Jewish.

> —Rabbi Lawrence A. Hoffman, author and professor of liturgy, "Reform Re-
> ligious Zionism," *Sh'ma*, September 30, 1994

One of the greatest cultural duties of the Jewish people is the attempt to enter the promised land, not by means of conquest as Joshua, but through peaceful and cultural means, through hard work, sacrifices, love and with a decision not to do anything which cannot be justified before the world conscience.

> —Rabbi Judah L. Magnes, communal leader and first president of the Hebrew
> University of Jerusalem, opening speech of the Hebrew University academic
> year, 1929–30

I've been a Zionist all my life; but there's learning about baseball, and then there's going to a game.

> —Jeremy Newberger, eighteen-year-old American Jewish student who chose
> to forego freshman year at an American university for a year in Israel,
> "Ticket to a Jewish Future," *Hadassah*, August/September 1992

We can all agree, without difficulty, that what Zionism means is that it is good for the Jewish people to return to the Land of Israel and it is bad for that people to be scattered among the nations. But from that point on—we disagree. I have stated many times that Zionism is not a first name but a surname, a family name, and this family is divided, feuding over the question of a "master plan" for the enterprise: How shall we live here? Shall we aspire to rebuild the kingdom of David and Solomon? Shall we construct a Marxist paradise here? A Western society, a social-democratic welfare state? Or shall we create a model of the petite bourgeoisie diluted with a little Yiddishkeit? Within the Zionist family there are some members who should be happy to be rid of me, and there are some whose familial relation to me causes me some discomfort. But the pluralism is a fact.

> —Amos Oz, novelist and essayist, *In the Land of Israel* (1983)

In the second decade of the 20th century, Zionists like Louis D. Brandeis added a further twist. . . . Zion became a utopian extension of the American dream, a Jewish refuge where freedom, liberty and social justice would reign supreme, an "outpost of democracy" that American Jews could legitimately, proudly and patriotically champion. . . . The Zion of the American Jewish imag-ination, in short, became something of a fantasy-land: a seductive heaven-on-earth where enemies were vanquished, guilt assuaged, hopes realized, and deeply-felt longings satisfied.

—Jonathan D. Sarna, professor of American Jewish history, "The Israel of American Jews," *Sh'ma*, September 30, 1994

I am an American pure and simple and cannot possibly belong to two nations. I feel that Zionism is a purely theoretical and sentimental proposition and as a practicable one has no future.

—Jacob Henry Schiff, banker and philanthropist, from a 1904 letter to Rabbi Stephen S. Wise, quoted in *The Jewish People in America, Volume III* by Gerald Sorin (1992)

It is quite evident that there is a serious break coming between those who wish to force a formation of a distinct Hebraic element in the United States, as distinct from those of us who desire to be American in attachment, thought and action and Jew because of our religion as well as cultural attainments of our people. I am quite convinced of it that the American people will not willingly permit the formation of a large separate Hebraic group with national aspirations, and that, if not we, our posterity are to become sufferers in consequence.

—Jacob Henry Schiff, 1916, quoted in *American Jewish Year Book 1921–1922*

[Satmar accepts the mitzvah of settling the land of Israel.] But this has nothing to do with establishing a state, which is clearly looked upon as taking God out of the equation. If the Zionists had made no claim to ending galus [exile], but had said that establishing the state was simply a practical good for the Jewish people, much of the Satmar opposition might have disappeared. But the Zionists still do not say this.

—Rabbi Meir Schiller, a high school teacher and soccer coach at a yeshiva for boys, explaining the Satmar [a Hasidic sect] position to religious-Zionist students, quoted in *The Jewish Voice*, May 1996

The Zionists were not afraid to take historical responsibility upon themselves, and therein lies their greatness.

—Gershom Scholem, professor of mysticism, 1970, quoted in "The Jewish State and the Jewish People" by Yosef Gorny, *Jewish Political Studies Review*, Fall 1990

There is a time to be an ideologue and a time to put ideology aside. That time has come. Zionist ideology created a state, and in many ways, is now tearing it apart. . . . Ideologues consider opposition to be heresy rather than simply bad judgment and do not easily compromise; yet compromise is essential to political life in a free society.

—Rabbi Daniel Jeremy Silver, professor of religion and rabbi of The Temple in Cleveland, "The Time for Ideology Is Over," *Judaism*, Fall 1983

I am not in favor of a Jewish state in Palestine. But it would be foolish, and it would be completely to misunderstand how history and human beings work, to disparage Zionism. Only a passionate, narrow, and mystical national faith made it possible for Jews to colonize areas the goats despised.

> —I. F. Stone, journalist, from his weekly column in *The Nation*, December 8, 1945, *The War Years: A Nonconformist History of Our Times 1939–1945* (1990)

I have been to Palestine several times and expect to go there again soon. If you are a good Zionist and you haven't got the fare, I'll take you. But the war must stop soon; otherwise I'll not have the money.

> —Nathan Straus, philanthropist, speaking at a Zionist Council of Greater New York rally, May 1917, quoted in *American Jewish Chronicle*, May 11, 1917

I accept the view of Jewish history which holds that we have a mission, a purpose, and that's why we survived. We have certainly been an extraordinary people. But for Jews to be emancipated, part of what is required is for this extraordinary people to have won, among other rights, the right to be ordinary.

> —Marie Syrkin, author and professor, quoted in "Marie Syrkin and Trude Weiss-Rosmarin: A Moment Interview," *Moment*, September 1983

I don't mind if Jews have a very exigent standard for themselves. But I resent it profoundly when Mr. Arafat offers me that standard, or some character in the government of the Soviet Union or some equally unsavory regime.

> —Marie Syrkin, quoted in "Marie Syrkin and Trude Weiss-Rosmarin: A Moment Interview," *Moment*, September, 1983

As a Zionist, despite the stormy history of Israel, I am still convinced that the establishment of the Jewish state in a "small notch"—to use Lord Balfour's phrase—of the vast territories liberated from the Ottoman Empire was an act of absolute, not relative, historic justice.... Nevertheless, I appreciate the intensity of the Arab hostility, however ill-motivated it may appear to me, and the reality of the Arab presence on the West Bank and Gaza.

> —Marie Syrkin, *Tikkun*, Fall 1986

The assertion of vital national interests within the Jewish state is no violation of the liberal conscience.

> —Marie Syrkin, *Tikkun*, Fall 1986

And because of our many sins, now too, this abomination is being done in Israel—that there are those who think and say that there were miracles and wonders performed as if it were by God, just like the miracles accompanying the Exodus from Egypt, and they do not see that these things only increase the impure strength of the Zionists, who are a thousand times worse than the Golden Calf, inasmuch as the Golden Calf did not constitute complete heresy and Zionism does.

> —Rabbi Yoel Teitelbaum, Satmar leader, *Kuntres Al Hageulah V'al Ha-Temurah*, On Redemption and Transformation, translated by Pinchas Peli, quoted in *Judaism: An Anthology of the Key Spiritual Writings of the Jewish Tradition, 3rd edition*, edited and interpreted by Rabbi Arthur Hertzberg (1991)

Israel is seen as a development in the continuing state of Diaspora, a positive development, perhaps, but not one of extraordinary theological importance . . . Of course settling the land is a mitzvah, but so is kashruth [Jewish dietary laws] and observing the Sabbath. Settling the land is not more important than any other mitzvah.

> —Rabbi Mordechai Tendler of New Hempstead, N.Y., representing the "classical yeshiva movement," speaking to religious Zionist students, quoted in *The Jewish Voice*, May 1996

The image of the religious Zionist must no longer be the simplistic one of a tefillin-wearing soldier on a tank or a gun-rattling settler. Instead, the religious Zionist must be seen as a sensitive person living in modern society while grappling with issues of education, the ethics of public life, Jewish continuity, God.

> —Rabbi Daniel Tropper, director of the Gesher Foundation, "When the Vision Collapses," *Jerusalem Report*, December 30, 1993

The Jewish attachment to Jerusalem is the natural connection of a national tie as unbreakable as the bond which links parents and children.

> —Dr. Trude Weiss-Rosmarin, author, editor of the *Jewish Spectator*, and lecturer, *Jerusalem* (1950)

There is no such thing as a spotless state, and there is innocent blood on Israeli hands; but historically and philosophically, this nationalism has been a critical nationalism. It defends itself and it denounces itself. It will not be panicked out of its aspiration to justice.

> —Leon Wieseltier, literary editor, "Washington Diarist," *The New Republic*, September 8 & 15, 1997

We are not beggars gathered together to plead, but sons and daughters of a great people, assembled . . . to make solemn protest against a wrong that is and against a greater wrong that threatens the Jewish Homeland in Palestine. Britain cannot afford to violate her pledge to the Jewish people. No nation is great enough to be free to do wrong.

> —Rabbi Stephen S. Wise, Jewish leader and activist, speaking at the Seventeenth Zionist Congress in Basel, Switzerland, 1930, protesting policies of the British Mandate in Palestine, quoted in *Rabbi and Minister: The Friendship of Stephen S. Wise and John Haynes Holmes* by Carl Hermann Voss (1964)

When you see the flag of Israel, for people like me and my generation, we remember when it wasn't there; we tend to romanticize its creation. Young people are less sentimental.

> —Abba Eban, former foreign minister and Israeli ambassador to the United Nations, quoted in *USA Today*, May 24, 1996

INDEX